Business and Society

A Strategic Approach to Corporate Citizenship

D1303735

Debbie Thorne McAlister
Southwest Texas State University

O. C. Ferrell
Colorado State University

Linda Ferrell
University of Northern Colorado

Houghton Mifflin Company

Boston   New York

This book is dedicated to

Mark, Rebecca, and Reed McAlister
— DEBBIE THORNE McALISTER

Kathlene Ferrell
— O. C. FERRELL

Norlan and Phyllis Nafziger
— LINDA FERRELL

Executive Editor: *George T. Hoffman*
Senior Development Editor: *Susan M. Kahn*
Production/Design Coordinator: *Lisa Jelly Smith*
Senior Manufacturing Coordinator: *Marie Barnes*
Marketing Manager: *Steven Mikels*

Cover Illustration: © *Otto Steininger/The Stock Illustration Source*

Photo Credits: p. 6, Courtesy of Philip Morris; p. 11, Courtesy of Honda Corporation; p. 26, AFP/Corbis; p. 38, Jean Claude Ernst/Wide World Photos; p. 47, Gregory Foster; p. 51, Reuters New Media Inc./Corbis; p. 69, Courtesy of Senesco; p. 78, © 2001 Archer Daniels Midland Company; p. 87, Corbis; p. 106, Reuters New Media Inc./Corbis; p. 117, Reuters New Media Inc./Corbis; p. 137, American Arbitration Association; p. 149, Kristine Larsen; p. 183, Courtesy of The Vanguard Group; p. 189, AFP/Corbis; p. 204, Brian Smale; p. 209, AFP/Corbis; p. 220, Anat Givon/AP/Wide World Photos; p. 243, AP Photo; p. 252, Richard Pasley/Stock Boston; p. 263, Courtesy of JC Penney; p. 280 Myrleen Ferguson/PhotoEdit; p. 284, Courtesy of the Nature Conservancy. Photo by Ron Semrod; p. 287, Courtesy of the World Wildlife Fund; p. 289, Reuters New Media Inc./Corbis; p. 295, Black/Toby Photograph; p. 318, Radhika Chalasani/SIPA; p. 343, Courtesy of Council for Biotechnology Information; p. 374, Jeff Greenberg/PhotoEdit; p. 377, Hulton/Archive/by Getty Images; p. 379, Cindy Charles.

Printed in the U.S.A.

Library of Congress Control Number: 2001131558

ISBN: 0-618-07216-0

123456789-KPA-06 05 04 03 02

Business and Society

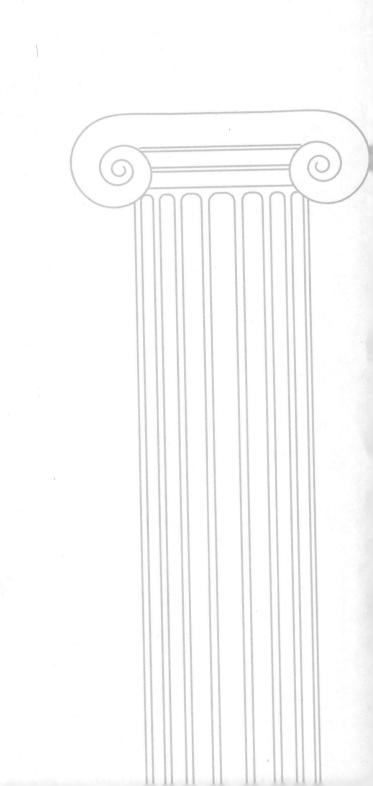

Contents

CHAPTER 3
Strategic Management of Stakeholder Relationships   62

CHAPTER 4
Legal, Regulatory, and Political Issues   97

CHAPTER 5
Business Ethics   *130*

CHAPTER 6
Corporate Governance

CHAPTER 7
Consumer and Community Relations

CHAPTER 8
Employee Relations *240*

CHAPTER 9
Environmental Issues *277*

CHAPTER 10
Technology Issues
315

CHAPTER 11
Strategic Philanthropy
356

CHAPTER 12
The Corporate Citizenship Audit   *386*

CASES   *421*

APPENDIX
The VanCity Social Report 1998/99   *505*

Preface

Social responsibility. Corporate accountability. Social accounting. Business ethics. Compliance. Reputation management. Corporate citizenship. These are terms you may have heard used, or even used yourself, to describe the array of rights, responsibilities, and roles of business organizations. You may have participated in philosophical discussions of whether business owes society anything more than profits. You may have also bought a particular T-shirt or cup of coffee and appreciated that a share of the profits supported a favorite charity. Although there is no universal agreement on the responsibilities, stakeholders, and programs that are required, expected, and desired of business, all businesspeople make decisions and take actions related to corporate citizenship.

Philosophy of This Text

Business and Society: A Strategic Approach to Corporate Citizenship introduces a new strategic corporate citizenship framework for courses that address the role of business in society. Corporate citizenship is concerned with issues related to values and responsibilities, as well as the rights of members of society. We view corporate citizenship as the extent to which a business adopts a strategic focus for fulfilling the economic, legal, ethical, and philanthropic social responsibilities expected by all its stakeholders.

The compact format of this book provides twelve chapters on the topics that professors view as essential in a course on business and society. We have developed manageable teaching materials flexible enough to incorporate current areas of interest. We provide a complete teaching and learning package that includes traditional resources for effectively using the book, diverse cases, behavioral simulations, an example of a corporate citizenship audit, experiential exercises, videos, and student and instructor web sites.

The relationship between business and society is inherently controversial and complex, yet the intersection of its components, such as workplace ethics, the natural environment, government institutions, business objectives, personal values, community needs, and technology, is felt in every organization. For this reason, we developed this text to effectively assist decision making and inspire the application of corporate citizenship principles to a variety of situations and organizations. In sum, we demonstrate and help the instructor prove that corporate citizenship is a theoretically grounded, yet highly actionable, and practical, field of interest.

A Relevant and Engaging Approach

Our book provides cutting-edge knowledge, based on research, best practices, and the latest developments in corporate citizenship. Reviewers inform us that our book takes a fresh look at real-world issues in an engaging, readable way that connects students to reality. We integrate emerging developments in the field of information technology as well as environmental and social issues throughout the text. We balance our coverage by avoiding overemphasis of some topics and providing enough depth on key content areas so students receive the background they need in order to learn more about the relevant topics. For example, the internal environment within organizations changed significantly as a result of the terrorist attacks on the World Trade Center and the Pentagon. We now know that people within organizations are more concerned about values, trust, and helping others, key concepts discussed in Chapter 2. These events shocked millions of Americans into reevaluating their lives and their roles as responsible citizens. This book was written to incorporate both the subtle and obvious long-term ramifications of these and other recent events on corporate citizenship.

Immediately after the terrorist attacks, many corporations and businesspeople mobilized to assist in relief efforts or spent weeks and months trying to return the workplace to some sense of normalcy. Crisis management, a key section in Chapter 3, was fully tested on a scale not known before. Disaster recovery programs are now a part of most large organizations. Corporate and individual donations to community causes, which we discuss in Chapter 7, were collected at astounding rates. Our understanding of the concept of "community" has greatly expanded. The world community has a greater awareness of how advances in communication and transportation have created a seamless connection to people everywhere. The role of employees, discussed in Chapter 8, has been changed not only due to disasters, but also due to issues related to information technology and a changing economy. The weakening economy, along with repercussions in the travel industry and other sectors, left many people without jobs and left others unsure of the delicate relationship between business and society. The importance of values and appreciation of a corporate culture that supports employees is more important today. In Chapter 10 we discuss how the same power of technology that enhances our lives can also be used in questionable or damaging ways. Corporate reputations, whether generally positive or negative, are determined by the corporation's reaction to crisis and the degree to which the organizational environment is based on integrity.

A business and society course provides the necessary grounding for discussing the interactions, effects, and changes to corporate citizenship that we experience every day as new events occur. For this reason our goal is to make *Business and Society: A Strategic Approach to Corporate Citizenship* as interesting, timely, thought provoking, and useful as possible. To accomplish this goal, we incorporate historical, current, and emerging concepts and theories, draw on current news and corporate events from around the world, take an active and experiential learning perspective, and encourage our readers to contemplate their understanding of corporate citizenship and the challenges and opportunities it poses for executives, communities, employees, governments, consumers, and other constituents.

▶ *Content and Organization*

Professors who teach business and society courses come from diverse backgrounds, including law, management, marketing, philosophy, and many others. Such diversity affords great opportunities to the field of business and society and showcases the central role that corporate citizenship has, and will continue to take, within various academic, professional, work, and community circles. Because of the widespread interest and multiplicity of stakeholders, the philosophy and practice of corporate citizenship is both exciting and debatable; it is in a constant state of development—just like all important business concepts and practices.

The term *corporate citizenship* came into widespread use during the 1990s, but many other terms, like those mentioned at the beginning of the preface, are also often used. In Chapter 1, "Corporate Citizenship Framework," we define corporate citizenship as the adoption by a business of a strategic focus for fulfilling the economic, legal, ethical, and philanthropic social responsibilities expected of it by its stakeholders. Corporate citizenship must be fully valued and championed by top managers and granted the same planning time, priority, and management attention as any company initiative. Our framework of corporate citizenship begins with the corporate citizenship philosophy, includes the four types of social responsibility, involves many types of stakeholders, and ultimately results in both short- and long-term performance gains. We take a strategic orientation to corporate citizenship, so students develop knowledge, skills, and attitudes for understanding how organizations achieve many benefits through corporate citizenship.

Chapter 2, "Organizational Benefits of Strategic Corporate Citizenship," offers evidence that resources invested in corporate citizenship and social responsibility programs contribute to improved corporate reputation and financial performance. We explore the central role of trust in maintaining positive relationships with stakeholders, particularly employees, customers, and shareholders. By fostering a high level of trust in stakeholder relationships, companies receive a variety of benefits including lower operating costs and long-term relationships. Misconduct can harm a firm's reputation, sales, and stock price, but addressing stakeholder concerns through a strategic citizenship program can improve a firm's bottom line.

To gain the benefits of corporate citizenship, effective and mutually beneficial relationships must be developed with customers, employees, investors, competitors, government, the community, and others who have a stake in the company. Chapter 3, "Strategic Management of Stakeholder Relationships," examines the types and attributes of stakeholders, how stakeholders become influential, and the processes for integrating and managing their influence on a firm. The impact of corporate reputation and crisis situations on stakeholder relationships is also examined in detail.

Chapter 4, "Legal, Regulatory, and Political Issues," explores the complex relationship between business and government. Every business must be aware of and abide by the laws and regulations that dictate required business conduct. This chapter also examines how business can participate in the public policy process to influence government. A strategic approach for legal compliance and citizenship, based on the Federal Sentencing Guidelines for Organizations, is also provided. Chapter 5, "Business Ethics," is devoted to exploring the role of ethics in business decision making. Business ethics relates to responsibilities and expectations that exist beyond legally prescribed levels. We examine the factors that influence ethical decision making and consider how companies can apply this understanding to improve ethical conduct.

Because both daily and strategic decisions affect a variety of stakeholders, companies must maintain a governance structure for ensuring proper control and responsibility for their actions. Chapter 6, "Corporate Governance," examines the rights of shareholders, the accountability of top management for corporate actions, executive compensation, and strategic-level processes for ensuring that economic, legal, ethical and philanthropic responsibilities are satisfied. Corporate governance is an emerging subfield and important process for business and society, which, until this point, has not received the same level of emphasis as issues such as the environment and human rights.

Chapter 7, "Consumer and Community Relations," and Chapter 8, "Employee Relations," explore relationships with important stakeholders, including consumers, the community, and employees. These constituencies, although different by definition, have similar expectations of the economic, legal, ethical, and philanthropic responsibilities that must be addressed by business. Chapter 9, "Environmental Issues," explores some of the significant environmental issues business and society face today, including air pollution, global warming, water pollution and water quantity, land pollution, waste management, deforestation, urban sprawl, biodiversity, and genetically modified foods. This chapter also considers the impact of government environmental policy and regulation, and examines how some companies are going beyond these laws to address environmental issues and act in an environmentally responsible manner.

Thanks to the Internet and other technological advances, communication is faster than ever before, information can be found about just about anything, and people are living longer, healthier lives. Chapter 10, "Technology Issues" provides cutting-edge information on the unique issues that arise as a result of enhanced technology in the workplace and business environment, including its effects on privacy, intellectual property, and health. The strategic direction for technology depends on government and business's ability to plan, implement, and audit the influence of technology on society. Chapter 11, "Strategic Philanthropy," examines companies' synergistic use of organizational core competencies and resources to address key stakeholders' interests and to achieve both organizational and social benefits. While traditional benevolent philanthropy involves donating a percentage of sales to social causes, a strategic approach aligns employees and organizational resources and expertise with the needs and concerns of stakeholders. Strategic philanthropy involves both financial and nonfinancial contributions (employee time, goods and services, technology and equipment, as well as facilities) to stakeholders, but it also benefits the company.

Regardless of an organization's particular situation, without reliable measurements of the achievement of citizenship objectives, a company has no concrete way to verify their importance, link them to organizational performance, justify expenditures, or adequately address stakeholder concerns. Chapter 12, "The Corporate Citizenship Audit," describes an auditing procedure that can be used to measure and improve the corporate citizenship effort. This chapter takes a complete strategic perspective on corporate citizenship, including stakeholder relations, legal and ethical issues, and philanthropy. This audit is important for demonstrating commitment and ensuring the continuous improvement of the corporate citizenship effort. An example of a company's corporate citizenship or social audit is included in the book's appendix. Since many instructors use the audit as a class project or organizing mechanism for the course, the appendix serves as an important addition to the chapter materials.

▶ *Special Features*

Business and Society: A Strategic Approach to Corporate Citizenship has a highly visible practical orientation. This text provides a variety of features to aid students in understanding the relevance and seeing the real-world application of key concepts, in identifying key points and recalling important ideas, and in applying their knowledge to realistic situations. The purpose of all these tools is to take students through a complete strategic planning and implementation perspective on business and society concerns by incorporating an active and team-based learning perspective.

Examples from companies and circumstances all over the world are found throughout the text. Every chapter opens with a vignette and includes numerous boxed and in-text examples that shed more light on how corporate citizenship works in today's business. Chapter opening objectives, a chapter summary, a list of boldfaced key terms, and discussion questions at the end of the chapter help direct students' attention to key points.

Experiential exercises at the end of each chapter help students apply corporate citizenship concepts and ideas to business practice. Most of the exercises involve research on the activities, programs, and philosophies that companies and organization are using to implement corporate citizenship today. These exercises are designed for higher-level learning and require students to apply, analyze, synthesize, and evaluate knowledge, concepts, practices, and possibilities for corporate citizenship. At the same time, the instructor can generate rich and complex discussions from student responses to the exercises. For example, the experiential exercise for Chapter 1 asks students to poll people regarding their beliefs about corporate citizenship. This exercise sets the stage for a discussion on the broad and potentially conflicted context in which stakeholders, business objectives, and responsibilities converge. The experiential exercise for Chapter 10 requires students to visit web sites targeted at children. In visiting the site, students take on the perspective of a child and then assess the site for any persuasion, potentially worrisome content, privacy issues, and guidelines of the Children's Online Privacy Protection Act. The exercise for Chapter 10 requires knowledge of government policy, strong analytical skills, and the ability to verify information and recognize subjectivity.

So that students learn more about specific practices, problems, and opportunities in corporate citizenship, ten cases are provided at the end of this book. The cases comprise a comprehensive collection for examining corporate citizenship in a multidimensional way. The recent citizenship travails and successes of high profile companies, like Coca-Cola, Home Depot, and Jack in the Box, allow students to consider the effects of stakeholders and responsibility expectations on larger and well-known businesses. Cases on the Texas A&M University Bonfire collapse and Henry Lyons and the National Baptist Convention demonstrate how citizenship is interpreted and implemented in the nonbusiness sector. Cases on smaller organizations, including DoubleClick, New Belgium Brewing, and Wainwright Bank, exemplify the many forms of corporate citizenship that shape today's business environment. Finally, cases on Ethics Officer Association and the Coalition for Environmentally Responsible Economies (CERES) give students more information on the role of associations and interest groups in corporate citizenship.

In addition to many examples, end-of-chapter exercises, and the cases, several behavioral simulation role-play exercises are provided in the *Instructor's Resource Manual*. Behavioral simulations are built around a fictitious yet plausible scenario or case, support higher-level learning objectives, require group decision-making skills, and can be used in classes of any size. Implementation of the simulations can be customized to the time frame, course objectives, student population, and other unique characteristics of a course. These exercises are aligned with trends in higher education toward teamwork, active learning, and student experiences in handling real-world business issues. For example, the Soy-DRI exercise places students in a crisis situation that requires an immediate response and consideration of changes over the long term. The simulations (1) give students the opportunity to practice making decisions that have consequences for corporate citizenship, (2) utilize a team-based approach, (3) recreate the pressures, power, information flows, and other factors that affect decision making in the workplace, and (4) incorporate a debriefing and feedback period for maximum learning and linkages to course objectives. We developed the behavioral simulations to enhance more traditional learning tools and to complement the array of resources provided to users of this text. Few textbooks offer this level of teaching support and proprietary learning devices.

A Complete Supplements Package

The comprehensive *Instructor's Resource Manual with Test Bank* includes chapter outlines, answers to the discussion questions at the end of each chapter, comments on the experiential exercises at the end of each chapter, comments on each case, a sample syllabus, and a test bank. The test bank provides multiple-choice and essay questions for each chapter and includes a mix of descriptive and application questions. HMTesting, a computerized version of the Test Bank, is also available. The behavioral simulation role-play exercises are included in the manual, along with specific suggestions for using and implementing the simulations in class.

The *Student Web Site* includes links to a variety of web sites related to corporate citizenship as well as links to organizations mentioned in the text. The student site also includes practice test questions and decision-making scenarios.

The password-protected *Instructor Web Site* includes PowerPoint slides that can be downloaded and edited or used as-is to aid in lecture presentations. The instructor site also includes files from the *Instructor's Resource Manual,* which can be downloaded and customized to fit any instructor's specific needs.

Finally, several *Videos* are available for instructors wishing to bring real-world examples into the classroom. A video guide presents overviews and questions for discussion and suggested uses for the videos.

Acknowledgments

A number of individuals provided reviews and suggestions that helped improve the text and related materials. We sincerely appreciate their time, expertise, and interest in the project.

Frank Barber, *Cuyahoga Community College*
Wendy S. Becker, *State University of New York at Albany*
Lehman Benson, *University of Arizona*
Sandra Christensen, *Eastern Washington University*
Anne C. Cowden, *California State University Sacramento*
Peggy Cunningham, *Queens University*
Dawn Elm, *University of St. Thomas*
Andrew Forman, *Hofstra University*
John Fraedrich, *Southern Illinois University—Carbondale*
Virginia Gerde, *University of New Mexico*
Kathleen A. Getz, *American University*
Neil Herndon, *Hofstra University*
Kenneth Hoffman, *Emporia State University*
Susan Key, *University of Alabama at Birmingham*
Terry Loe, *Baylor University*

Isabelle Maignan, *University of Nijmegen*
Linda Manzanares, *University of Northern Colorado*
Alan N. Miller, *University of Nevada, Las Vegas*
Jan Morgan, *Colorado State University*
David W. Murphy, *Madisonville Community College*
Larry Overlan, *Stonehill College*
Kurt H. Parkum, *Penn State Harrisburg*
Mark Puclik, *University of Illinois at Springfield*
Diane Scott, *Wichita State University*
Gary Sokolow, *College of the Redwoods*
Marta Szabo White, *Georgia State University*

We wish to acknowledge the many people that played an important role in the development of this book. Gwyneth Walters and Barbara Gilmer, educational consultants with whom we have worked for many years, were pivotal to the project. Gwyn showed her usual dedication to excellence in many ways. Barbara provided great support and organizational oversight throughout the project. Kelly Haws prepared several components of the *Instructor's Resource Manual*. Nikole Haiar, Kevin Sample, Dana Schubert, Timothy Sellnow, Robyn Smith, Tracy Suter, Jane Swoboda, Robert Ulmer, and Maureen Wilson wrote timely and thought-provoking cases. Lisa Jefferson, Jacob Pearson, Robin Boaz, and Kathryn Cuddy assisted with the teaching notes. Finally, we express much appreciation to our colleagues and the administration at Colorado State University, Mississippi State University, Southwest Texas State University, and the University of Northern Colorado.

Debbie Thorne McAlister
O. C. Ferrell
Linda Ferrell

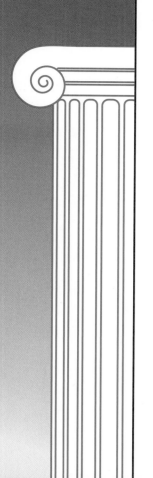

Corporate Citizenship Framework

1

▶ Corporate Citizenship Defined

▶ Development of Corporate Citizenship

▶ Framework for Studying Corporate Citizenship

To define the concept of *corporate citizenship*

To trace the development of corporate citizenship

To examine the global nature of corporate citizenship

To discuss our framework for understanding corporate citizenship

L ike many organizations, Cummins Engine Company of Columbus, Indiana, has faced a number of challenges over the past several decades. Cummins is currently the world leader in the design and manufacture of diesel engines, and its customers include a variety of industrial companies, including the automotive industry. Cummins was founded in 1919, and it was Columbus's largest employer for many years. In the tradition of the era in which it was founded, Cummins provided many benefits to the community, as befits a good corporate citizen, as well as providing job opportunities and economic growth. For example, its top executives provided the funding for architectural designs for public buildings in the city of Columbus. Thanks to that largess, the American Institute of Architects ranks Columbus sixth in the United States for outstanding and innovative architecture, trailing only Los Angeles, San Francisco, Boston, Chicago, and New York.

Throughout its first sixty years of business, Cummins Engine also performed well for its shareholders. The company enjoyed increased profits for forty-three consecutive years, until 1979. Cummins suffered during the 1980s, however, and it had to fend off the threat of hostile takeovers from several overseas companies. Its stock price plummeted, and stock owners demanded short-run profits at the expense of the company's' long-term goals. The founding family repelled one takeover attempt with a large infusion of capital. Expanding the firm's shareholder-rights program thwarted another attempt. Despite its financial woes, Cummins remained focused on research and development, managed to produce a more environmentally friendly diesel engine, and even engaged in limited charitable giving. These actions were consistent with the personality and beliefs of Henry Schacht, Cummins's CEO for more than twenty years, who believed that the company should not focus solely on profit, but rather should develop a balanced set of values that would take into account the needs of the community and the broader economic sector.

Although Schacht's beliefs provided a strong foundation, Cummins Engine did not always achieve its social and economic goals. In 1983, for example, for the first time ever, the company was forced to lay off some of its employees. Later in the decade, the company closed plants and laid off even more people. To reverse these trends, Schacht adopted a new business plan that included cooperation with unions, former employees, and other firms to spur economic development. Negotiations with unions, for example, made it possible for Cummins to rehire former employees and ultimately to reopen a Columbus plant that had been shuttered in 1987. Although the plant offered lower wages and fewer benefits than Cummins's plants in other locations, its reopening was the culmination of an eleven-year labor negotiation that helped the company reduce costs and boost productivity, allowing Cummins to become a formidable competitor once again. Expansion into Japan, India, and China soon followed.

Throughout this difficult period, Cummins still managed to donate to charities and participate in civic activities. The company partnered with Arvin Industries, another leading Columbus employer, to fund an economic development program that attracted several firms to the city, resulting in three thousand to four thousand new jobs. Cummins also recently announced plans to build a child development center in Columbus for its employees' children. This is Cummins's third such facility; the others are located in Iowa and Brazil. In discussing this latest employee benefit, Tim Solso, the current CEO, noted that in addition to satisfying shareholders, Cummins also considered its obligations to employees and the community. By the end of the twentieth century, Cummins was back on track financially, with sales topping $6.6 billion, up 6 percent from the prior year. Cummins's drive to build positive relationships with its employees, its customers, and the community led *Business Ethics* to rank the firm sixty-second on the magazine's list of the 100 Best Corporate Citizens.[1]

Businesses today face increasingly complex, and often competing, motives and incentives in their decision making. In a recent *Business Week*/Harris Poll survey of the general population, 95 percent of respondents agreed with the following statement: "U.S. corporations should have more than one purpose. They also owe something to their workers and the communities in which they operate, and they should sometimes sacrifice some profit for the sake of making things better for their workers and communities."[2] In an era of intense global competition and increasing media scrutiny, consumer activism, and government regulation, all types of organizations need to become adept at fulfilling these expectations. Like Cummins Engine Company, many companies are trying, with varying results, to meet the many economic, legal, ethical, and philanthropic responsibilities they now face. Satisfying the responsibilities of corporate citizenship is a never-ending process of continuous improvement that requires leadership from top management, buy-in from employees, and good relationships across the community, industry, market, and government. Companies must properly plan, allocate, and use their resources in order to satisfy the demands placed on them by investors, employees, customers, business partners, the government, the community, and others.

In this chapter, we examine the concept of corporate citizenship and how it relates to today's complex business environment. First, we define corporate citizenship and consider its relevance to the type of business, strategic focus, social responsibility, and stakeholder orientation. Next, we consider the development of corporate citizenship, including its changing nature in our increasingly global economy. Finally, we introduce the framework for studying corporate citizenship used by this text, which includes such elements as organizational benefits; strategic management for stakeholder relations; legal, regulatory, and political issues; business ethics; corporate governance; consumer and community relations; employee relations; environmental issues; technology issues; strategic philanthropy; and the strategic corporate citizenship audit.

Corporate Citizenship Defined

Business ethics. Social responsibility. Corporate volunteerism. Compliance. Reputation management. These are phrases you may have heard used, or even used yourself, to describe the various rights, roles, and responsibilities of business organizations. You may have pondered what these terms actually mean for business practice and decision making. You may also have wondered what expectations of business these phrases describe. In this chapter, we clarify some of the confusion that exists in the terminology that people use every day when they talk about corporate responsibilities. To this end, we begin by defining corporate citizenship.

In common parlance, the term *citizenship* is concerned with issues of residency, loyalty, privileges, and responsibilities. In many societies, citizenship accords certain rights, such as due process in a court of law, freedom of speech and movement, opportunity, privacy, property ownership, voting privileges, and other rights that you may take for granted. However, citizenship also requires that we look beyond self-interest and recognize that we belong to a larger group that expects our responsible participation. Thus, if any group, society, or institution is to function, there must be a delicate interplay between rights (i.e., what people expect to get) and responsibilities (i.e., what people are expected to contribute) for the common good. The old adage "no man is an island" describes both the idea of citizenship and the relational nature of society.

Just as individuals enjoy the benefits of citizenship, so do corporations. Although corporations are not human beings, they act and behave purposefully. Moreover, the law grants them all the benefits—and the responsibilities—of citizenship. Although the term *corporate citizenship* came into widespread use in the business world during the 1990s, there remains some confusion over the term's exact meaning. Table 1.1 lists some of the different ways in which people commonly use the term to describe business responsibilities. Many of these characterizations have elements in common, such as focusing on the achievement of both corporate and social goals and recognizing the broad groups to which business has an obligation. Only the seventh characterization, which describes corporate citizenship as an oxymoron, is distinctly different from the others. This view of corporate citizenship asserts that business has just one purpose, satisfying its investors or stockholders, and that any other considerations are outside its scope. Although this view still exists today,[3] it has lost some credence as more and more companies have assumed the citizenship orientation. Based on the first six characterizations, we define **corporate citizenship** as the adoption by a business of a strategic focus for fulfilling the economic, legal, ethical, and philanthropic social responsibilities expected of it by

TABLE 1.1

Seven Characterizations of Corporate Citizenship

Characterization	Description
1. Synonymous with social responsibility	Citizenship encompasses the economic, legal, ethical, and discretionary expectations that society has of business
2. License to operate	Citizenship is a condition for doing business, and as with customer requirements, a firm should find the most efficient way to meet requirements from the government and other external groups
3. Long-term business investment	Like research and development, corporate citizenship is designed to improve the business environment for future progress
4. Vehicle for achieving goals and reputation	Companies that focus on citizenship activities will have stronger customer loyalty, more committed employees, better government relations, and, ultimately, stronger reputations
5. Activity to avoid exposure and risk	Citizenship activities help companies avoid being singled out or exposed to unnecessary outsider intrusion
6. Economic and constructive	Companies should reinforce the economic foundation and viability of the communities in which they operate
7. Oxymoron	Companies are not citizens; they are designed to increase shareholder wealth

Note: These are not distinct characterizations, so there is some natural overlap in some of the definitions.
Sources: Barbara W. Altman, "Transformed Corporate Community Relations: A Management Tool for Achieving Corporate Citizenship," *Business and Society Review,* March 22, 1999, p. 43; Melissa A. Berman, "New Ideas, Big Ideas, Fake Ideas," *Across the Board* 36 (January 1999): 28–32; Archie Carroll, "A Three-Dimensional Conceptual Model of Corporate Social Performance," *Academy of Management Review* 4 (1979): 497–505; Kim Davenport, "Corporate Citizenship: A Stakeholder Approach for Defining Corporate Social Performance and Identifying Measures for Assessing It," *Business and Society* 39 (June 2000): 210–219.

its stakeholders. This definition encompasses a wide range of objectives and activities, including both historical views of business and perceptions that have emerged in the last decade. Let's take a closer look at the parts of this definition.

Corporate Citizenship Applies to All Types of Businesses

Although we use the term *corporate citizenship* throughout this text, it is important to recognize that all types of businesses—small and large, sole proprietorships and partnerships as well as corporations—implement citizenship initiatives to further their relationships with their customers, their employees, and the community at large. For example, RunTex, a store in Austin, Texas, that sells athletic shoes, donates used shoes (which customers have traded in for discounts on new shoes) to

Philip Morris understands the importance of corporate citizenship, and it supports numerous social causes such as Chicago's Community Kitchens program.

the community's poor and homeless. The company also cosponsors walk/run events that generate funds for local and national social causes. Thus, the ideas advanced in this book are equally relevant and applicable across a broad spectrum of business firms.

Although the citizenship efforts of large corporations usually receive the most attention in the media, the activities of small businesses may have a greater impact on local communities.[4] Owners of small businesses often serve as community leaders, provide goods and services for customers in smaller markets that larger corporations are not interested in serving, create jobs, and donate resources to local community causes. Medium-sized businesses and their employees have similar roles and functions on both a local and a regional level. Although larger firms produce a large portion of the gross national output of the United States, companies with less than 100 employees account for nearly one-half of total employment.[5] Thus, it is vital that all businesses consider the relationships and social responsibilities that our definition of corporate citizenship suggests.

Corporate Citizenship Adopts a Strategic Focus

Corporate citizenship is not just an academic term. As we have defined it, citizenship involves action and measurement, or the "extent" to which a firm embraces the philosophy of corporate citizenship and then follows through with the implementation of citizenship initiatives. Our definition of corporate citizenship requires a formal commitment, or way of communicating the company's corporate citizenship philosophy. For example, Herman Miller, a multinational provider of office, residential, and health care furniture and services, has crafted a statement that it calls the Blueprint for Corporate Community (shown in Figure 1.1). This statement declares Herman Miller's philosophy and the way it will fulfill its responsibilities to its customers, its shareholders, its employees, the community, and the natural environment. Because this statement takes into account all of Herman Miller's constituents and applies directly to all of the company's operations, products, markets, and business relationships, it demonstrates the company's strategic focus on corporate citizenship. Other companies that embrace corporate citizenship have incorporated similar elements into their strategic communications, including mission and vision statements, annual reports, and web sites.

In addition to a company's verbal and written commitment to corporate citizenship, our definition requires action and results. To implement its citizenship philosophy, Herman Miller has developed and implemented several corporatewide strategic initiatives, including research on improving work furniture and environments, innovation in the area of ergonomically correct products, progressive employee development opportunities, and an environmental stewardship program. These efforts have earned the company many accolades, such as being named the "Most Admired" furniture manufacturer in America by *Fortune* magazine, and a place on numerous prestigious lists, including *Fortune* magazine's "100 Best Companies to Work for in America," *Forbes* magazine's "Platinum List" of America's 400 best-managed large companies, *Business Ethics* magazine's "100 Best Corporate Citizens," and *Industry Week* magazine's "100 Best-Managed Manufacturers" in the world.[6] As this example demonstrates, effective corporate citizenship requires both words and action.

If any such initiative is to have strategic importance, it must be fully valued and championed by top management. Executives must believe in and support the integration of constituent interests and economic, legal, ethical, and philanthropic

FIGURE 1.1

Herman Miller,
Inc.'s, Blueprint
for Corporate
Community

Herman Miller, Inc., is more than just a legal entity. It combines the talents, hopes, and dreams of thousands of people. At its best, it is a high-performance, values-driven community of people tied together by a common purpose. Herman Miller has always stood apart from the crowd because of what we believed, and we have always believed that what we stand for matters. Our strategies will change as the needs of our business change. Our core values will not. We build our business on them. How well we live up to these values will determine whether we are to be trusted by others.

What We Believe in:

- **Making a meaningful contribution to our customers**
- **Cultivating community, participation, and people development**
- **Creating economic value for shareholders and employee-owners**
- **Responding to change through design and innovation**
- **Living with integrity and respecting the environment**

— *A Different Kind of Company* —

Source: "Blueprint for Corporate Community," Herman Miller, Inc., www.hermanmiller.com/CDA/ category/aboutus/0,1243,c13,00.html, (accessed) October 18, 2001. Courtesy of Herman Miller, Inc.

responsibilities into every corporate decision. For example, company objectives for brand awareness and loyalty can be developed and measured from both a marketing and a citizenship standpoint, because researchers have documented a relationship between consumers' perceptions of a firm's citizenship level and their intentions to purchase that company's brands.[7] Likewise, engineers can integrate consumers' desire for reduced environmental impact into product designs, and marketers can ensure that a brand's advertising campaign incorporates this product benefit. Finally, consumers' desire for an environmentally sound product may stimulate a stronger company interest in assuming environmental leadership in all aspects of its operations. Home Depot, for example, responded to demands by consumers and environmentalists for environmentally friendly wood products by launching a new initiative that gives preference to wood products certified as having been harvested responsibly over those taken from endangered forests.[8] With this action, the company, which has long touted its environmental principles, has chosen to take a leadership role in the campaign for environmental responsibility in the home-improvement industry. Although corporate citizenship depends on collaboration and coordination across many parts of the business and among its constituencies, it also produces effects throughout these same groups.

Because of the need for coordination, large companies that are committed to corporate citizenship often create specific positions or departments to spearhead the various components of its citizenship program. For example, Target, the national retailer, uses a decentralized approach to manage employee volunteerism. Each Target store has a "good neighbor captain" who coordinates employees' efforts with a local charity or cause. The captain ensures that his or her store implements the corporation's citizenship objective on volunteerism in ways that will be of most benefit to the local area.[9] The Sara Lee Corporation, whose brands include Bryan Meats, L'Eggs, Coach, Kiwi, and Champion, has established an office of public responsibility to oversee its citizenship efforts.[10] Smaller firms may give an executive, perhaps in human resources or corporate communications, the additional task of overseeing corporate citizenship. In either case, this department or executive should ensure that formal corporate citizenship initiatives are aligned with the company's corporate culture, integrated with companywide goals and plans, fully communicated within and outside the company, and measured to determine their effectiveness and strategic impact. In sum, corporate citizenship must be given the same planning time, priority, and management attention as is given to any other company initiative, such as continuous improvement, cost management, investor relations, research and development, human resources, or marketing research.

Corporate Citizenship Fulfills Social Responsibility

Another element of our definition of corporate citizenship involves society's expectations of corporate responsibility. Many people believe that businesses should accept and abide by four types of responsibility—economic, legal, ethical, and philanthropic—which are collectively known as **corporate social responsibility** (see Figure 1.2). To varying degrees, the four types are required, expected, and/or desired by society.[11]

At the lowest level of the pyramid, businesses have a responsibility to be economically viable so that they can provide a return on investment for their owners, create jobs for the community, and contribute goods and services to the economy. The economy is influenced by the ways in which organizations relate to their stockholders, their customers, their employees, their suppliers, their competitors, the community, and even the natural environment. For example, in nations with corrupt businesses and industries, the negative effects often pervade the entire society. Transparency International, a German organization dedicated to curbing national and international corruption, has conducted research on the effects of business and government corruption on a country's economic growth and prospects. The organization reports that corruption reduces economic growth, inhibits foreign investment, and often channels investment and funds into "pet projects" that may create little benefit other than high returns to the corrupt decision makers.[12] Thus, although business and society may be theoretically

FIGURE 1.2

Pyramid of Corporate
Social Responsibility

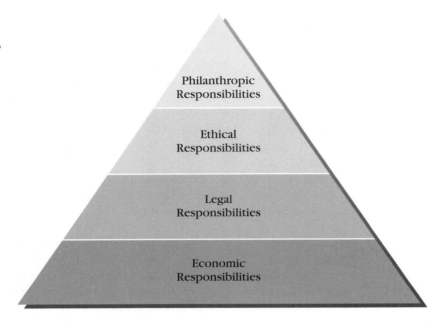

Reprinted with permission from *Business Horizons,* 34 (Jul.–Aug. 1991): 42. Archie B. Carroll, "The Pyramid of
Corporate Social Responsibility: Toward the Moral Management of Organizational Stakeholders." Copyright © 1991
by the Board of Trustees of Indiana State University, Kelley School of Business.

distinct, business has the opportunity to have a real economic impact on many
people.

At the next level of the pyramid, companies are required to obey laws and regulations that specify what is responsible business conduct. Society enforces its
expectations regarding the behavior of businesses through the legal system. If a
business chooses to behave in a way that customers, special-interest groups, or
other businesses perceive as irresponsible, these groups may ask their elected representatives to draft legislation to regulate the firm's behavior, or they may sue the
firm in a court of law in an effort to force it to "play by the rules." For example,
many businesses have complained that Microsoft Corporation effectively had a
monopoly in the computer operating system and Web browser markets and that
the company acted illegally to maintain this dominance. Their complaints were
validated in 2000 when U.S. District Judge Thomas Penfield Jackson ruled in a federal lawsuit that Microsoft had indeed used anticompetitive tactics to maintain its
Windows monopoly in operating-system software and to attempt to dominate the
Web browser market by illegally bundling its Internet Explorer Web browser into

its Windows operating system. Microsoft, which vehemently denied the charges, appealed that decision. The election of George W. Bush and a court of appeal's ruling to overturn Jackson's decision shifted the focus to settlement talks, away from an earlier suggestion to break up the company.[13]

Beyond the economic and legal dimensions of social responsibility, companies must decide what they consider to be just, fair, and right—the realm of business ethics. Business ethics refers to the principles and standards that guide behavior in the world of business. These principles are determined and

Honda understands its ethical responsibilities and has developed efficient and environmentally friendly gasoline-electric hybrid automobiles.

It's an environmental movement all by itself.

How many cars does it take to change the world? Just one, perhaps. Introducing the all-new Honda Insight. It's America's first gasoline-electric hybrid automobile.

Nothing short of an engineering breakthrough, the Insight achieves a terrific 68 miles per gallon on the highway, 61 miles per gallon in the city, and an astounding 700-mile range on one tank of fuel.* How? By combining an efficient three-cylinder gasoline engine with an electric motor powered by nickel-metal hydride batteries that never need to be plugged in. Then add a world-class aerodynamic design, and an extremely lightweight body, and you have the ultra-low-emission† Insight.

It's the culmination of years of research and development into lighter, cleaner, more efficient automobiles. In other words, technology with a conscience. Then again, what else would you expect from a car powered by Honda?

HONDA
The power of dreams.

*Mileage figures based on EPA estimates. Actual mileage may vary. Range based on EPA highway mileage. †California Air Resources Board ULEV-certified for California and some Northeastern states. LEV-certified in rest of country. © 2000 American Honda Motor Co., Inc. honda.com

expected by the public, government regulators, special-interest groups, consumers, industry, and individual organizations. The most basic of these principles have been codified into laws and regulations to require that companies conduct themselves in ways that conform to society's expectations. Many firms and industries have chosen to go beyond these basic laws in an effort to act responsibly. The Direct Selling Association (DSA), for example, has established a code of ethics that applies to all individual and company members of the association. Because direct selling, such as door-to-door selling, involves personal contact with consumers, there are many ethical issues that can arise. For this reason, the DSA code directs the association's members to go beyond legal standards of conduct in areas such as product representation, appropriate ways of contacting consumers, and warranties and guarantees. In addition, the DSA actively works with government agencies and consumer groups to ensure that ethical standards are pervasive in the direct selling industry. The World Federation of Direct Selling Associations (WFDSA) also maintains a code of conduct that provides guidance for direct sellers around the world, in countries as diverse as Argentina, Canada, Finland, Korea, and Poland.[14]

At the top of the pyramid are philanthropic activities, which promote human welfare and goodwill. By making voluntary donations of money, time, and other resources, companies can contribute to their communities and society and improve the quality of life. For example, Hitachi, Ltd., of Tokyo, Japan, established the Hitachi Foundation, a nonprofit philanthropic organization that invests in increasing the well-being of underserved people and communities. With assets of $38 million, the foundation is considered a pioneer of global corporate citizenship.[15] Although Hitachi is not required to support the community, similar corporate actions are increasingly desired and expected by people around the world.

When the pyramid of social responsibility was first introduced, many people assumed that there was a natural progression from economic to philanthropic responsibilities, meaning that a firm had to be economically viable before it could properly consider the other three elements. Today, the pyramid is viewed in a more holistic fashion, with all four responsibilities being seen as related and integrated into a comprehensive citizenship approach, and this is the view we will use in this book.[16] In fact, companies demonstrate varying degrees of good citizenship at different points in time, as illustrated by the Cummins vignette. Figure 1.3 depicts the corporate citizenship continuum. Companies' fulfillment of their economic, legal, ethical, and philanthropic responsibilities can range from minimal to strategic citizenship. Minimal citizenship is demonstrated by firms that focus only on those responsibilities required by laws and contracts. Strategic citizenship is realized when a company has integrated a range of expectations, desires, and constituencies into its strategic direction and planning processes.[17] In this book, we will give many ex-

FIGURE 1.3	
Corporate Citizenship Continuum	

Minimal

Strategic

Economic and legal considerations focusing on contractual stakeholders

Economic, legal, ethical, and philanthropic considerations focusing on all stakeholders

Based on ideas presented in Malcolm McIntosh, Deborah Leipziger, Keith Jones, and Gill Coleman, *Corporate Citizenship: Successful Strategies for Responsible Companies* (London: Financial Times Management, 2000).

amples of firms that are at different places along this continuum to show how the pursuit of corporate citizenship is never-ending. For example, Coca-Cola, the world's largest beverage firm, dropped out of the top ten in *Fortune* magazine's annual list of "America's Most Admired Companies" in 2000 and out of the top one hundred in *Business Ethics* magazine's annual list of "100 Best Corporate Citizens" in 2001. For a company that had spent years on both lists, this was disappointing, but perhaps it was not unexpected, as the company was planning to eliminate six thousand jobs, was facing a racial discrimination lawsuit, was still recovering from a product contamination scare in Europe, and was trying to salvage its relationships with its bottlers.[18]

Corporate Citizenship Requires a Stakeholder Orientation

The final element of our definition involves those to whom an organization is responsible, including customers, employees, investors and shareholders, suppliers, governments, communities, and many others. These constituents have a stake in, or claim on, some aspect of a company's products, operations, markets, industry, and outcomes, and thus are known as **stakeholders.** We explore the roles and expectations of stakeholders in Chapter 3. Companies that consider the diverse perspectives of these constituents in their daily operations and strategic planning are said to have a stakeholder orientation, meaning that they are focused on stakeholders' concerns. Adopting this orientation is part of the corporate citizenship philosophy, which implies that business is fundamentally connected to other parts of society and must take responsibility for its effects in those areas.[19]

R. E. Freeman, one of the earliest writers on stakeholder theory, maintains that business and society are "interpenetrating systems," in that each both affects and is affected by the other.[20] For example, the British home-improvement and garden retailer B&Q has developed a formal process for securing stakeholder input on a variety of issues, including child labor, fair wages, environmental impact, and equal opportunity. To develop a vision and key objectives in these areas, B&Q conferred with suppliers, store managers, employees, customers, and government representatives. Based on these consultations, the retailer now recognizes and measures its progress on all four levels of corporate social responsibility.[21] B&Q strengthened its efforts in the 1990s, a period in which corporate citizenship and the requisite social responsibilities and stakeholder orientation became more popular and more generally accepted within the corporate community. Many events have led to this era of increasing accountability and responsibility.

Development of Corporate Citizenship

In 1959, Harvard economist Edward Mason asserted that business corporations are "the most important economic institutions."[22] His declaration implied that companies probably affect the community and society as much, or perhaps more, in social terms as in monetary, or financial, terms. For example, most businesses use advertising to convey messages that have an economic impact but also have a social meaning. As an extreme example, when Benetton decided to use convicted felons who had been given death sentences in an advertising campaign, many people were outraged. The Italian clothier had a history of using cutting-edge advertising to comment on social ideas and problems, but some people felt that this campaign went too far. Benetton's original goal was to open up a dialog on the controversial issue of the death penalty, but criticism of the campaign was rampant, and Sears dropped its contract with Benetton as a result.[23]

Although most companies do not go to the extremes that Benetton does, companies do influence many aspects of our lives, from the workplace to the natural environment. This influence has led many people to conclude that companies' actions should be designed to benefit employees, customers, business partners, and the community as well as shareholders. "Good corporate citizenship" has become a benchmark for corporations today.[24] However, these citizenship responsibilities and expectations have evolved over time. For example, the first corporations in the United States were granted charters by various state governments because they were needed to serve an important function in society, such as transportation, insurance, water, or banking services. In addition to serving as a "license to operate," these charters specified the internal structure of these firms, allowing their actions to be more closely monitored.[25] During this period, corporate charters were often granted for a limited period of time because many people, including legislators, feared the power that corporations could potentially wield. It was not until the mid-1800s that profit and responsibility to stockholders became a major corporate goal.[26]

▶ Development of Corporate Citizenship in the United States

After World War II, as many large U.S. firms came to dominate the global economy, their actions inspired imitation in other nations. The definitive external characteristic of these firms was their economic dominance. Internally, they were marked by the virtually unlimited autonomy afforded to their top managers. This total discretion meant that the top managers of these firms had the luxury of not having to answer much for their actions.[27] In the current business mind-set, such total autonomy would be viewed as a hindrance to good citizenship because there is no effective system of checks and balances. In Chapter 6, we elaborate on corporate governance, the process of control and accountability in organizations that is necessary for corporate citizenship.

In the 1950s, the 130 or so largest companies in the United States provided more than half of the country's manufacturing output. The top 500 firms accounted for almost two-thirds of the country's nonagricultural economic activity.[28] U.S. productivity and technological advancements also dramatically outpaced those of global competitors, such as Japan and Western Europe. For example, the level of production in the United States was twice as high as that in Europe and quadruple that in Japan. The level of research and development carried out by U.S. corporations was also well ahead of that of overseas firms. For these reasons, the United States was perceived as setting a global standard for other nations to emulate.

The power of these large American corporations was largely mirrored by the autonomy of their top managers.[29] This autonomy could be characterized as "largely unchecked," as most such managers had the authority to make whatever decisions they thought necessary. Because of the relative lack of global competition and shareholder input during the 1950s and 1960s, there were few formal governance procedures to restrain management's actions. However, this laxity permitted management to focus not just on profit margins, but also on a wide variety of discretionary activities, including charitable giving. Thus, it is interesting to note that although top managers' actions were rarely questioned or scrutinized, these managers did use their company's resources to address broader concerns than self-interest. Although the general public was sometimes suspicious of the power held by top managers in large corporations, it also recognized the gains it received from these corporations, such as better products, more choices, good employee salaries, and other such benefits. During this period, many corporations put money into their communities. Although these firms had high executive pay, organizational inefficiencies, high overhead costs, and various other problems, they were quick to share their gains. Employees in the lower echelons of these large corporations received substantially higher wages and better benefits than the national average. This practice has continued into the present; for example, what major automobile manufacturers pay their workers is 50 percent above the national average and 40 percent above the manufacturing national average.[30]

During the 1950s and 1960s, these companies also provided other benefits that are often overlooked. Their contributions to charities, the arts, culture, and other community activities were often quite generous. They spent considerable sums of money on research that was more beneficial to the industry or to society than to the companies' own profitability. For example, the lack of competition meant that companies had the profits to invest in higher-quality products for consumer and industrial use. Although the government passed laws that required companies to take actions to protect the natural environment, make products safer, and promote equity and diversity in the workplace, many companies voluntarily adopted responsible practices and did not constantly fight government regulations and taxes. These corporations once provided many of the services that are now provided by the government in the United States. For example, during this period, the U.S. government spent less than the government of any other industrialized nation on such things as pensions, health benefits, and social insurance, as these were provided by companies rather than by the government.[31] In the 1960s and 1970s, however, the business landscape changed.

Economic turmoil during the 1970s and 1980s almost eliminated the old corporations. Venerable firms that had dominated the economy in the 1950s and 1960s became extinct or ineffective as a result of bankruptcies, takeovers, or other threats, including high energy prices and an influx of foreign competitors. The stability experienced by the American firms of mid-century dissolved. During the 1960s and 1970s, the *Fortune* 500 had a relatively low turnover of about 4 percent. By 1990, however, one-third of the companies in the *Fortune* 500 of 1980 had disappeared, primarily as a result of takeovers and bankruptcies. The threats and instability led companies to protect themselves from business cycles by becoming more focused on their core competencies and reducing their product diversity. To combat takeovers, many companies adopted flatter organizational hierarchies. Flatter organizations meant workforce reduction, but also entailed increasing empowerment of lower-level employees.

Thus, the 1980s and 1990s brought a new focus on profitability and economies of scale. Efficiency and productivity became the primary objectives of business. This fostered a wave of downsizing and restructuring that left some people and communities without financial security. Before 1970, large corporations employed about one of every five Americans, but by the 1990s, they employed only one in ten. The familial relationship between employee and employer disappeared, and along with it went employee loyalty and company promises of lifetime employment. Companies slashed their payrolls to reduce costs, and employees changed jobs more often. Workforce reductions and "job hopping" were almost unheard of in the 1960s, but had become commonplace two decades later. These trends made temporary employment and contract work the fastest-growing forms of employment throughout the 1990s.[32]

Along with these changes, top managers were stripped of their former freedom. Competition heated up, and both consumers and stockholders grew more demanding. The increased competition led business managers to worry more and more about the bottom line and about protecting the company. Escalating use of the Internet provided unprecedented access to information about corporate decisions and conduct and fostered communication among once unconnected groups, furthering consumer awareness and shareholder activism. Consumer demands put more pressure on companies and their employees. The education and activism of stockholders had top management fearing for their jobs. Throughout the last two decades of the twentieth century, legislators and regulators initiated more and more regulatory requirements every year. These factors resulted in difficult trade-offs for management.

The benefits of the corporations of old were largely forgotten in the 1980s, but concern for corporate responsibilities was renewed in the 1990s. Partly as a result of business scandals and Wall Street excesses in the 1980s, many industries and companies decided to pursue and expect more responsible and respectable business practices. Many of these practices focused on creating value for stakeholders through more effective processes and decreased the narrow and sole emphasis on corporate profitability. At the same time, consumers and employees became less interested in making money for its own sake and turned toward intrinsic rewards and a more holistic approach to life and work.[33] This has resulted in increased interest in the development of human and intellectual capital; the installation of corporate ethics programs; the development of programs to promote employee volunteerism in the community, strategic philanthropy efforts, and trust in the workplace; and the initiation of a more open dialog between companies and their stakeholders.

Mark Lilla, a professor of politics, notes that our current perceptions of business and society represent the confluence of the ideas of two decades, the 1960s and 1980s. From the 1960s, we gained a stronger interest in social issues and in how all parts of society can help prevent these issues from arising and resolve them when they do. The economic upheaval and excess of the 1980s alerted many people to the influence that companies have on society when the desire to make money profoundly dominates their activities.[34] In the 1990s and beyond, the balance between the global market economy and an interest in social justice and cohesion best characterizes the intent and need for corporate citizenship. This is evident on a global scale as special-interest groups, companies, human rights activists, and governments strive to balance worldwide economic growth and spending with social, environmental, technological, and cultural issues.

▶ *Global Nature of Corporate Citizenship*

Although many forces have shaped the debate on corporate citizenship, the increasing globalization of business has made it an international concern. For example, as people around the world celebrated the year 2000, there was also a growing backlash against big business, particularly multinational corporations. A wide variety of protests were held around the globe, but their common theme was criticism of the increasing power and scope of business. Questions of human rights, corruption, environmental protection, fair wages, safe working conditions, and the income gap between rich and poor were posed. Most of these protesters believe that global business involves exploitation of the working poor, destruction of the planet, and a rise in inequality.[35] Ruy Teixeira, a pollster from the Century Foundation, says, "There's a widespread sense of unfairness and distrust today, where people think companies are not quite playing by the rules."[36] Even *Business Week* weighed in with a cover story entitled, "Too Much Corporate Power?"[37] Advocates of the global economy counter these allegations by pointing to increases in overall economic growth, new jobs, new products, and other positive effects of global business. Although these differences of opinion provide fodder for debate and discussion, the global economy probably, in the words of author John Dalla Costa, "holds much greater potential than its critics think, and much more disruption than its advocates admit. By definition, a global economy is as big as it can get. This means that the scale of both the opportunity and the consequences are at an apex."[38] Thus, companies around the world are increasingly implementing programs and practices that strive to achieve a balance between economic responsibilities and other social responsibilities. For example, Japanese toilet manufacturer Toto Ltd. has created an office and management structure for its corporate citizenship effort. Toto's manager of social and culture promotion recently commented on his firm's corporate citizenship philosophy, saying, "Toto believes it owes a lot to society. As a good citizen, we need to reciprocate and support the local society."[39]

In most developed countries, corporate citizenship involves economic, legal, ethical, and philanthropic responsibilities to a variety of stakeholders. However, a key question for implementing corporate citizenship on a global scale is, "Who decides on these responsibilities?" Many executives and managers face the challenge of doing business in diverse countries while attempting to maintain their employers' corporate culture and satisfy their expectations. Some companies have adopted an approach in which broad corporate standards can be adapted at a local level. For example, a corporate goal of demonstrating environmental leadership could be met in a number of different ways, depending on local conditions and needs. The Compaq Computer Corporation implements its goal of environmental responsibility in different ways depending on the needs in various regions of the world. In North America, Compaq has focused on recycling and reducing waste.

In Latin America, corporate resources have been devoted to wastewater treatment and cleanup of contaminated soil. Efforts in the firm's Asia Pacific division have included the distribution of "green kits" to educate managers, employees, and other stakeholders about Compaq's commitment to environmental leadership.[40]

Global corporate citizenship also involves the confluence of government, business, trade associations, and other groups. For example, countries that belong to the Asia-Pacific Economic Cooperation (APEC) are responsible for half the world's annual production and trade volume. As APEC works to reduce trade barriers and tariffs, it has also developed meaningful projects in the areas of sustainable development, clean technologies, workplace safety, management of human resources, and the health of the marine environment. This powerful trade group has demonstrated that economic, social, and ethical concerns can be tackled simultaneously.[41] Like APEC, other trade groups are also exploring ways to enhance economic productivity within the context of legal, ethical, and philanthropic responsibilities.

In sum, progressive global businesses recognize the "shared bottom line" that results from the partnership among business, communities, government, customers, and the natural environment. In the Millennium Poll, a survey of more than 25,000 citizens in 23 countries, 66 percent of the respondents indicated that they want companies to go beyond their traditional role of making a profit, paying taxes, and providing jobs. More than half the respondents said that they believe their national government and companies should focus more on social and environmental goals than on economic goals in the first decade of the new millennium.[42] This survey reiterates our philosophy that business is now accountable to a variety of stakeholders and has a number of responsibilities. In companies around the world, there is also recognition of the relationship between strategic corporate citizenship and business performance, as we will see in Chapter 2. Thus, our concept of corporate citizenship is applicable to businesses around the world, although adaptations of implementation and other details on the local level are definitely required.

Framework for Studying Corporate Citizenship

The framework we have developed for this text is designed to help you understand how businesses fulfill their citizenship responsibilities. Figure 1.4 illustrates the concept that corporate citizenship is a process. It begins with the corporate citizenship philosophy, includes the four levels of social responsibilities, involves many types of stakeholders, and ultimately results in both short- and long-term performance benefits. As we discussed earlier, corporate citizenship must have the support of top management—both in words and in deeds—before it can become an organizational reality. For example, in 2000, the Ford Motor Company released its inaugural corporate citizenship report, entitled "Connecting with Society." This

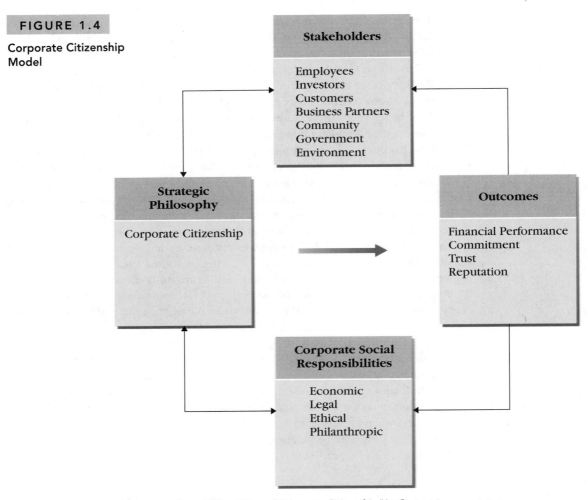

Source: Adapted from Charles J. Fombrun, "Three Pillars of Corporate Citizenship," in *Corporate Global Citizenship,* Noel M. Tichy, Andrew R. McGill, and Lynda St. Clair, eds. (San Francisco: The New Lexington Press, 1997), pp. 27–42.

report was partly commissioned by William Clay Ford, Jr., the company's chairman of the board, who is recognized as an advocate for environmental and social initiatives. The chairman's leadership in this area was a primary driver of this citizenship report, which included the admission that sport utility vehicles (SUVs) have poor fuel efficiency and emit high levels of air pollutants.[43] Once the corporate citizenship philosophy is accepted, the four aspects of corporate social responsibility are defined and implemented through programs that incorporate stake-

FIGURE 1.5

An Overview of This Book

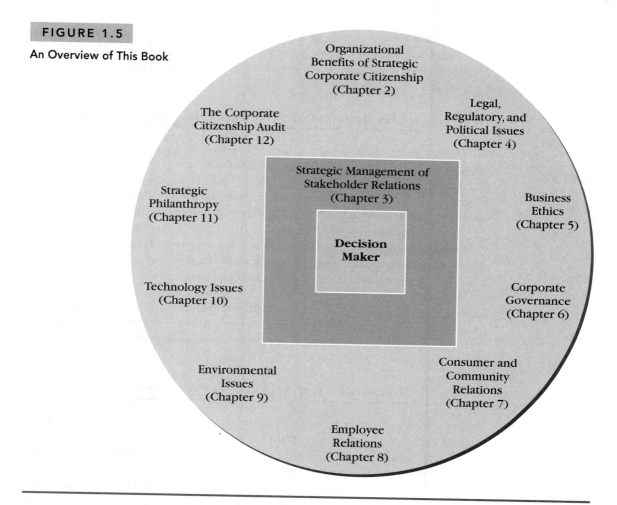

FIGURE 1.5

An Overview of This Book

holder input and feedback. For example, in response to William Clay Ford's corporate citizenship philosophy, criticism from environmental groups, and the recognition that SUVs are harmful to the environment, Ford announced plans to address the issue. However, the company is aware of the potential costs associated with addressing this issue. As Ford will discover, when corporate citizenship programs are put into action, they have both immediate and delayed outcomes.

Figure 1.5 depicts how the chapters of this book fit into our framework. This framework begins with a look at the benefits of citizenship initiatives and the importance of working with stakeholders to achieve corporate citizenship objectives. The framework also includes an examination of the influence on business decisions and actions of the legal, regulatory, and political environment; business ethics; and corporate governance. The remaining chapters of the book explore the responsibilities associated with specific stakeholders and issues that confront business decision makers today.

▶ *Organizational Benefits of Strategic Corporate Citizenship*

In Chapter 2, we offer evidence that the resources invested in corporate citizenship and social responsibility programs contribute to an improved corporate reputation and improved financial performance. This chapter also explores the importance of trust in maintaining positive relationships with stakeholders, particularly employees, customers, and shareholders. For example, the American Society for Training and Development has found that there is a positive relationship between a company's ability to attract and retain employees and its sales, profits, and stock price. This research suggests that a workplace atmosphere that encourages coworkers to respect and support one another also helps to enhance employee satisfaction.[44] By fostering a high level of trust in stakeholder relationships, companies receive a variety of benefits, including lower operating costs and improved long-term relationships. Misconduct can harm a firm's reputation, sales, and stock price, but addressing stakeholder concerns through a strategic citizenship program can improve a firm's bottom line.

▶ *Strategic Management of Stakeholder Relationships*

Corporate citizenship is grounded in effective and mutually beneficial relationships with customers, employees, investors, competitors, government, the community, and others who have a stake in the company. Increasingly, companies are recognizing that these constituents both affect and are affected by their actions. For this reason, many companies attempt to address the concerns of stakeholder groups, recognizing that failure to do so can have serious long-term consequences. For example, the Connecticut Better Business Bureau revoked the membership of Priceline.com after the Internet company failed to address complaints related to misrepresentation of products, billing problems, and refunds.[45] Chapter 3 examines the types of stakeholders and their attributes, how stakeholders become influential, and the processes for integrating and managing stakeholders' influence on a firm. The impact of corporate reputation and crisis situations on stakeholder relationships is also examined in detail.

▶ *Legal, Regulatory, and Political Issues*

In Chapter 4, we explore the complex relationship between business and government. Every business must be aware of and abide by the laws and regulations that dictate acceptable business conduct. This chapter also examines how business can influence government by participating in the public policy process. A strategic approach for legal compliance and citizenship is also provided.

Business Ethics

A recent survey by the Joseph and Edna Josephson Institute of Ethics found that 92 percent of the high school students surveyed had lied to their parents, and that 78 percent had lied to a teacher. More than one in four students indicated that they would lie to get a job.[46] Because individual values are a component of organizational conduct, these findings raise concerns about the ethics of future business leaders. Chapter 5 is devoted to exploring the role of ethics in business decision making. This chapter explores business responsibilities that go beyond the conduct that is legally prescribed. We also examine the factors that influence ethical decision making and consider how companies can apply this understanding to increase their ethical conduct.

Corporate Governance

Because both daily and strategic decisions affect a variety of stakeholders, companies must maintain a governance structure to ensure proper control of their actions and assign responsibility for those actions. In Chapter 6, we define corporate governance and discuss its role in achieving strategic corporate citizenship. Key governance issues addressed include the rights of shareholders, the accountability of top management for corporate actions, executive compensation, and strategic-level processes for ensuring that economic, legal, ethical, and philanthropic responsibilities are satisfied.

Consumer and Community Relations

Chapter 7 explores companies' relationships with two important stakeholders: consumers and the community. These constituencies, although different by definition, have similar expectations concerning the economic, legal, ethical, and philanthropic responsibilities of business that companies must address. Chapter 7 therefore considers the obligations that companies have toward their customers, including health and safety issues, honesty in marketing, and consumer rights. The chapter also examines the larger community by exploring issues that have a profound impact on the communities in which businesses operate. For example, many communities fear that they will lose their unique character when large national chain retailers such as Starbucks, Wal-Mart, and Home Depot move to town, especially when the presence of these firms contributes to the failure of long-time local businesses. These fears have prompted passionate neighborhood and community activism that in some cases has resulted in ordinances that restrict the types and sizes of new businesses.[47]

Movie Industry Agrees to Stop Marketing R-Rated Movies to Children

A recent report by the Federal Trade Commission (FTC) on violence in the media concluded that entertainment companies routinely target children under seventeen years of age when they market movies, music, and video games intended for adults. Among other things, the report indicated that 80 percent of R-rated movies were targeted at children under seventeen and that 50 percent of the thirteen- to sixteen-year-olds taking part in the study were allowed into R-rated movies. The report recommended that entertainment companies should not target children in their advertising, that enforcement of ratings should be strengthened at the retail level, and that more information about ratings should be made available to parents.

In a hearing before the Senate Commerce Committee, Jack Valenti, president and CEO of the Motion Picture Association of America (MPAA), admitted that the movie industry had made mistakes and agreed that targeting "very young children" with advertising for R-rated films is inappropriate. However, Valenti also attempted to rebut a number of allegations made by the FTC report. For example, although the FTC blasted advertising of R-rated movies during certain television programs that it claimed are most popular among children under seventeen, Valenti countered that, with one exception, the percentage of

children watching the programs named is actually "quite small." Since the eighteen-and-over audience for these shows ranged from 79 percent to 63 percent of the total audience, they could not be considered children's shows and therefore were appropriate places for advertising R-rated movies. The MPAA president also defended the industry's effect on children by citing FBI statistics that showed a decrease in crime over the previous seven years—a 10 percent decrease in the last year alone—and also indicated that juvenile crime had declined by 28 percent over the previous five years. Valenti argued that creative works involve subjective judgments, and that what one person sees as reasonable may be viewed as unacceptable by another. Finally, Valenti reminded the senators that a movie's R rating does not mean that it is "for adults only," but rather that children viewing it must be accompanied by a parent or adult guardian. The movie rating system arms parents with a cautionary warning to help them to make their decisions about what movies their children should view. Parents have access to ratings advice in magazines, in newspapers, on television, and through a number of web sites (such as filmratings.com and MPAA.org). Valenti pointed out that monitoring of parental reaction to the thirty-two-year-old movie rating system indicates that 81 percent of parents with children

▶ Employee Relations

In today's business environment, most organizations want to build long-term relationships with a variety of stakeholders, but particularly with employees, the focus of Chapter 8. Employees today want fair treatment, excellent compensation and benefits, and assistance in balancing work and family obligations. Raytheon has developed a computer program called SilentRunner that can detect patterns

under thirteen find the moving rating system "very useful" or "fairly useful."

After defending the industry, Valenti pledged that it would nonetheless examine its advertising and research practices and work with the National Association of Theater Owners to enforce ratings more effectively in order to honor its obligations to parents. The industry association launched a twelve-point plan to limit the marketing of adult-oriented films to children. Among other things, the plan calls for movie studios to ask theaters not to show advertisements for R-rated films during G-rated movies and not to include children younger than seventeen in focus groups for R-rated movies without a parent present. A number of film studios signed on to the plan, including Walt Disney Company, Dreamworks SKG, Metro-Goldwyn-Mayer, Paramount, Sony, Twentieth Century Fox, Universal, and Warner Bros. Although executives from these firms pledged to stop marketing inappropriate movies to children, they affirmed that preventing children from viewing R-rated films is ultimately the parents' responsibility.

Some film studios have chosen to go beyond the industry plan to address their responsibilities. News Corporation, for instance, says that its Twentieth Century Fox film studio will ask theater operators not to show advertisements for R-rated films during G- or PG-rated movies. Fox Network, also owned by News Corporation, will not accept advertisements for R-rated films in "family programming or shows in which 35 per-cent or more of the audience is under age 17." Peter Chernin, News Corporation's president, says, "All of us in the media industry have a fundamental responsibility to help parents cope with the many entertainment choices facing their children."

However, even these initiatives do not go far enough for some lawmakers, who demand that movie executives commit to stop marketing violent films to children. Some legislators have called for movie companies not to advertise R-rated films during TV shows that are popular with children or during the "family hour" (from 8:00 to 9:00 P.M.). If the industry does not make significant improvements in regulating itself on these issues, the ire of parents and senators may bring about regulation of the marketing of movies.

Sources:

"Hollywood Execs Admit Bad Judgment," Associated Press, September 27, 2000, via Netscape, http://dailynews.netscape.com/mynsnews/story.tmpl?table=n&cat=50800&id=200009271209; John King, "Federal Report Finds Entertainment Industry Aims Marketing at Children," CNN, September 11, 2000, www.cnn.com/2000/US/09/11/entertain.report/; "Lights, Camera, Action: Hollywood Must Rewrite Marketing Script," *Columbus Dispatch*, October 3, 2000, p. 6A, via http://web.lexis-nexis.com/universe/; "Under Fire from Lawmakers, Movie Makers Present Plan," CNN.com, September 27, 2000, via Netscape, http://dailynews.netscape.com/dailynews/cnnnews.tmpl?story=hollywood.violence0927.html; Jack Valenti, "Report on Violence in the Media and Children," *FDCH Congressional Testimony*, September 13, 2000, via http://ehostvgw15.epnet.com/ehost1.asp?key=204.179.122.140_8000_633481665&site= ehost&return=y.

of data activity that may reflect employee fraud, insider trading, espionage, or other unauthorized activity.[48] Critics, however, question whether the use of such software contributes to an environment of trust and commitment. Research has shown that committed and satisfied employees are more productive, serve customers better, and are less likely to leave their employers. These benefits are important to successful business performance, but organizations must be proactive in their human resources programs if they are to receive them.

▶ *Environmental Issues*

In Chapter 9, we explore some of the significant environmental issues that business and society face today, including air pollution, global warming, water pollution and water quantity, land pollution, waste management, deforestation, urban sprawl, biodiversity, and genetically modified foods. For example, consumers around the world have expressed fears about the safety of food products that contain genetically modified crops. Although current research suggests that these products pose no threat to health or to the environment, the debate surrounding their use has grown increasingly bitter. Many companies are beginning to rethink their use of these crops in response to consumer concerns. Among these is J. R. Simplot Co., which has asked its farmers to stop growing genetically modified potatoes that may be used in the French fries it supplies to McDonald's.[49] Chapter 9 also considers the impact of government environmental policy and regulation, and examines how some companies are going beyond these laws to address environmental issues and act in an environmentally responsible manner.

▶ *Technology Issues*

Thanks to the Internet and other technological advances, we can communicate faster than ever before, find information about just about anything, and live longer, healthier lives. However, not all of the changes that occur as a result of

During a "New Biotechnology Food and Crops" conference, activists in Thailand protested against genetically modified produce and grains.

new technologies are positive. For example, because shopping via the Internet does not require a signature to verify transactions, credit-card fraud online is now more than three and a half times greater than credit-card fraud through mail-order catalogs and almost nine times higher than for traditional storefront retailers.[50] In Chapter 10, we examine the unique issues that arise as a result of enhanced technology in the workplace and business environment, including the effects of new technology on privacy, intellectual property, and health. The strategic direction for technology depends on government, as well as on business's ability to plan implement the use of new technology and to audit the influence of that technology on society.

▶ *Strategic Philanthropy*

Chapter 11 examines strategic philanthropy, the synergistic use of organizational core competencies and resources to address key stakeholders' interests and to achieve both organizational and social benefits. Whereas traditional benevolent philanthropy involves donating a percentage of sales to social causes, a strategic approach aligns employees and organizational resources and expertise with the needs and concerns of stakeholders. Strategic philanthropy involves both financial and nonfinancial contributions (employee time, goods and services, technology and equipment, and facilities) to stakeholders, but it also benefits the company.

▶ *The Corporate Citizenship Audit*

Without reliable measurements of the achievement of citizenship objectives, a company has no concrete way to verify the importance of these objectives, link them to organizational performance, justify expenditures on them to stockholders and investors, or address any stakeholder concerns involving them. Chapter 12 describes an auditing procedure that can be used to measure and improve the corporate citizenship effort. This chapter takes you through a complete strategic perspective on corporate citizenship, including stakeholder relations, legal and ethical issues, and philanthropy. This audit is important for demonstrating commitment and ensuring the continuous improvement of the corporate citizenship effort.

We hope this framework provides you with a way of understanding the range of concepts, ideas, and practices that are involved in an effective corporate citizenship initiative. So that you can learn more about the practices of specific companies, a number of cases are provided at the end of the book. In addition, every chapter includes an opening vignette and other examples that shed more light on how corporate citizenship works in today's businesses. As you will soon see, the concept of corporate citizenship is both exciting and controversial; it is in a constant state of development—just like all important business concepts and practices. For that reason, we encourage you to draw on current news events and your own experiences to understand corporate citizenship and the challenges and opportunities it poses for your career and the business world.

Summary

The term *corporate citizenship* came into widespread use during the 1990s, but there remains some confusion over the term's exact meaning. This text defines corporate citizenship as the adoption by a business of a strategic focus for fulfilling the economic, legal, ethical, and philanthropic social responsibilities expected of it by its stakeholders.

All types of businesses can implement citizenship initiatives to further their relationships with their customers, their employees, and the community at large. Although the efforts of large corporations usually receive the most attention, the actions of small businesses may have a greater impact on local communities.

The definition of corporate citizenship involves the extent to which a firm embraces the corporate citizenship philosophy and follows through with the implementation of citizenship initiatives. Corporate citizenship must be fully valued and championed by top managers and given the same planning time, priority, and management attention as is given to any other company initiative.

Many people believe that businesses should accept and abide by four types of responsibility—economic, legal, ethical, and philanthropic—which are collectively known as corporate social responsibility. Companies have a responsibility to be economically viable so that they can provide a return on investment for their owners, create jobs for the community, and contribute goods and services to the economy. They are also expected to obey laws and regulations that specify what is responsible business conduct. Business ethics refers to the principles and standards that guide behavior in the world of business. Philanthropic activities promote human welfare or goodwill. These responsibilities can be viewed holistically, with all four being related and integrated into a comprehensive citizenship approach. Corporate citizenship can also be expressed as a continuum.

Because customers, employees, investors and shareholders, suppliers, governments, communities, and others have a stake in or claim on some aspect of a company's products, operations, markets, industry, and outcomes, they are known as stakeholders. Adopting a stakeholder orientation is part of the corporate citizenship philosophy.

The influence of business has led many people to conclude that corporations should benefit their employees, their customers, their business partners, and the community, as well as their shareholders. However, these citizenship responsibilities and expectations have evolved over time. After World War II, many large U.S. firms dominated the global economy. Their power was largely mirrored by the autonomy of their top managers. Because of the relative lack of global competition and stockholder input during the 1950s and 1960s, there were few formal governance procedures to restrain management's actions. The stability experienced by mid-century firms dissolved in the economic turmoil of the 1970s and 1980s, leading companies to focus more on their core competencies and reduce their product diversity. The 1980s and 1990s brought a new focus on efficiency and productivity, which fostered a wave of downsizing and restructuring. Concern for corporate responsibilities was renewed in the 1990s. In the 1990s and beyond, the balance between the global market economy and an interest in social justice and cohesion best characterizes the intent and need for corporate citizenship.

The increasing globalization of business has made corporate citizenship an international concern. In most developed countries, corporate citizenship involves economic, legal, ethical, and philanthropic responsibilities to a variety of stakeholders. Global corporate citizenship also involves the confluence of government, business, trade associations, and other groups. Progressive global businesses recognize the "shared bottom line" that results from the partnership among business, communities, government, customers, and the natural environment.

The process of corporate citizenship begins with the corporate citizenship philosophy, includes the four levels of social responsibilities, involves many types of stakeholders, and ultimately results in both short- and long-term performance benefits. Once the corporate citizenship philosophy is accepted, the four aspects of corporate social responsibility are defined and implemented through programs that incorporate stakeholder input and feedback.

KEY TERMS

corporate citizenship

corporate social responsibility

stakeholders

DISCUSSION QUESTIONS

1. Define corporate citizenship. How does this view of the role of business differ from your previous perceptions? How is it consistent with your attitudes and beliefs about business?

2. If a company is named to one of the lists of the best corporate citizens, what positive effects can it potentially reap? What are the possible costs or negative outcomes that may be associated with being named to one of these lists?

3. What historical trends have affected the social responsibilities of business? In light of current trends and issues, what changes in these responsibilities and expectations do you predict over the next five years?

4. Based on the corporate citizenship model presented in Figure 1.4, describe the philosophy, social responsibilities, and stakeholders that make up a company's approach to corporate citizenship. What are the short- and long-term outcomes of this effort?

5. Consider the role that various business disciplines, including marketing, finance, account-

ing, and human resources, have in corporate citizenship. What specific views and philosophies do these different disciplines bring to the implementation of corporate citizenship?

EXPERIENTIAL EXERCISE

To understand the various perceptions of corporate citizenship that may exist, find three people to answer the following questions: (1) What is corporate citizenship? and (2) To whom are organizations responsible? Record their responses and note any similarities and differences. What do their responses teach you about perceptions of corporate citizenship?

NOTES

1. Cummins Engine Company, www.cummins.com/na/pages/en/whoweare/cumminshistory.cfm, accessed October 20, 2001; Kevin Kelly, "A CEO Who Kept His Eyes on the Horizon," *Business Week,* August 1, 1994, p. 32; Boris Ladwig, "Cummins Plans Child Care Center," *(Columbus, Indiana) Republic,* www.therepublic.com, accessed March 8, 2000; "The 100 Corporate Citizens," *Business Ethics* 14 (March/April 2000): 12–17; Lois Therrien, "Mr. Rust Belt," *Business Week,* October 17, 1988, pp. 72–77; Marina v. N. Whitman, *New World, New Rules* (Boston: Harvard Business School Press, 1999), pp. 112–115.

2. "How Business Rates: By the Numbers," *Business Week,* September 11, 2000, pp. 148–149.

3. Clive Crook, "Why Good Corporate Citizens Are a Public Menace," *National Journal,* April 24, 1999, p. 1087.

4. Nancy J. Miller and Terry L. Besser, "The Importance of Community Values in Small Business Strategy Formation: Evidence from Rural Iowa," *Journal of Small Business Management* 38 (January 2000): 68–85.

5. Paul Willax, "Small Businesses Contribute in a Large Way to Economy," *Business First-Louisville,* February 18, 2000, p. 13.

6. "Awards and Recognition," Herman Miller Inc., www.hermanmiller.com/CDA/award/0,1239,c21,00.html, (accessed) October 18, 2001.

7. "The 1997 Cone/Roper Cause-Related Marketing Trends Report," *Business Ethics* 11 (March/April 1997): 14–16; Ronald Alsop, "Corporate Reputations Are Earned with Trust, Reliability, Study Shows," *Wall Street Journal,* September 23, 1999, http://interactive.wsj.com; Dale Kurschner, "5 Ways Ethical Busine$$ Creates Fatter Profit$," *Business Ethics* 10 (March/April 1996): 21.

8. Jim Carlton, "Against the Grain: How Home Depot and Activists Joined to Cut Logging Abuse," *Wall Street Journal,* September 26, 2000, p. A1.

9. "Setting the Bar: New Benchmarking Study Gives CR Something to Reach For," *Corporate Community Relations Letter* 14 (January 1999): 1.

10. Ann E. Tenbrunsel, Zoe I. Barsness, and Paul M. Hirsch, "Sara Lee Corporation and Corporate Citizenship: Unity in Diversity," in *Corporate Global Citizenship,* ed. Noel M. Tichy, Andrew R. McGill, and Lynda St. Clair (San Francisco: The New Lexington Press, 1997), pp. 197–213.

11. Barbara W. Altman, "Transformed Corporate Community Relations: A Management Tool for Achieving Corporate Citizenship," *Business and Society Review,* March 22, 1999, p. 43; Archie Carroll, "The Four Faces of Corporate Citizenship," *Business and Society Review,* January 1, 1998, p. 1; Diane Swanson and Brian E. Niehoff, "Business Citizenship Outside and Inside Organizations," in *Perspectives on Corporate Citizenship,* ed. Jörg Andriof and Malcolm McIntosh (Sheffield, United Kingdom: Greenleaf Publishing, 2001), pp. 104–116.

12. "Facts and Figures on Corruption," Transparency International, www.transparency.org/contact/media_faq.html, accessed October 20, 2001.

13. "Judge Rules that Microsoft Violated U.S. Antitrust Laws," *Wall Street Journal,* April 3, 2000, http://interactive.wsj.com; Steven Levy, "Look, Ma, No Breaks," *Newsweek,* September 17, 2001, pp. 52–54.

14. "Code of Ethics," Direct Selling Association, www.dsa.org/code.stm, accessed October 18, 2001; "World Codes of Conduct for Direct Selling," World Federation of Direct Selling Associations, www.wfdsa.org/world_codes/code.asp, accessed October 18, 2001; Thomas R. Wotruba, *Teaching Notes to Accompany Ethics and Success in Business* (Washington, D.C.: Direct Selling Education Foundation, 1999).

15. The Hitachi Foundation, www.hitachi.org/, accessed October 18, 2001.

16. Altman, "Transformed Corporate Community Relations," p. 43; Carroll, "The Four Faces of Corporate Citizenship," p. 1.

17. Malcolm McIntosh, Deborah Leipziger, Keith Jones, and Gill Coleman, *Corporate Citizenship: Successful Strategies for Responsible Companies* (London: Financial Times Management, 2000).

18. Betsy Morris and Patricia Sellers, "What Really Happened at Coke," *Fortune,* January 10, 2000; "America's Most Admired Companies," *Fortune,* February 21, 2000, p. 108; "The 100 Best Corporate Citizens for 2001," www.business-ethics.com./100best.htm, (accessed) October 20, 2001.

19. Geoff Mulgan, *Connexity: How to Live in a Connected World* (Boston: Harvard Business School Press, 1997); Ann Svendsen, *The Stakeholder Strategy: Profiting from Collaborative Business Relationships* (San Francisco: Berrett-Koehler Publishers, Inc., 1998).

20. R. E. Freeman, *Strategic Management: A Stakeholder Approach* (Boston: Pitman, 1984).

21. Ken Green, Barbara Morton, and Steve New, "Green Purchasing and Supply Policies: Do They Improve Companies' Environmental Performance?" *Supply Chain Management* 3 (February 1998); B&Q web site, www.dig.com, (accessed) October 20, 2001.

22. Edward S. Mason, "Introduction," in *The Corporation in Modern Society,* ed. Edward S. Mason (Cambridge, Mass.: Harvard University Press, 1959), pp. 1-24.

23. Michael McCarthy and Lorrie Grant, "Sears Drops Benetton After Controversial Death Row Ads," *USA Today,* February 18, 2000, www.usatoday.com.

24. Isabelle Maignan and O. C. Ferrell, "Measuring Corporate Citizenship in Two Countries: The Case of the United States and France," *Journal of Business Ethics* 23 (February 2000): 283; Robert J. Samuelson, "R.I.P.: The Good Corporation," *Newsweek,* July 5, 1993, p. 41.

25. Charles W. Wootton and Christie L. Roszkowski, "Legal Aspects of Corporate Governance in Early American Railroads," *Business and Economic History* 28 (Winter 1999): 325-326.

26. Ralph Estes, *Tyranny of the Bottom Line* (San Francisco: Berrett-Koehler, 1996); David Finn, *The Corporate Oligarch* (New York: Simon & Schuster, 1969).

27. Whitman, *New World, New Rules.*

28. Edward S. Mason, "Introduction," in *The Corporation in Modern Society,* ed. Edward S. Mason (Cambridge, Mass.: Harvard University Press, 1959), pp. 1-24.

29. Carl Kaysen, "The Corporation: How Much Power? What Scope?" in *The Corporation in Modern Society,* ed. Edward S. Mason (Cambridge, Mass.: Harvard University Press, 1959), pp. 85-105.

30. Whitman, *New World, New Rules.*

31. Ibid.

32. David M. Gordon, *Fat and Mean: The Corporate Squeeze of Working Americans and the Myth of Managerial "Downsizing"* (New York: Free Press, 1996).

33. Richard Leider, *The Power of Purpose: Creating Meaning in Your Life and Work* (San Francisco: Barrett-Koehler, 1997).

34. Mark Lilla, "The Big Extract: Does Anyone Remember '68?" *Guardian Editor* (London), August 29, 1998, p. 12; Mark Lilla, "Still Living With '68," *New York Times Magazine,* August 16, 1998, p. 34; Michael Willmott and Paul Flatters, "Corporate Citizenship: The New Challenge for Business," *Consumer Policy Review* 9 (November/December 1999): 230.

35. Martin Wolf, "Comment and Analysis: The Big Lie of Global Inequality," *Financial Times,* February 9, 2000, p. 25.

36. Aaron Bernstein, "Too Much Corporate Power?" *Business Week,* September 11, 2000, pp. 144-158.

37. Ibid., p. 145.

38. John Dalla Costa, *The Ethical Imperative: Why Moral Leadership Is Good Business* (Reading, Mass.: Addison-Wesley, 1998).

39. William H. Miller, "Citizenship: A Competitive Asset," *Industry Week,* August 17, 1998, pp. 104-108.

40. Lynda St. Clair, "Compaq Computer Corporation: Maximizing Environmental Conscientiousness Around the Globe," in *Corporate Global Citizenship,* ed. Noel M. Tichy, Andrew R. McGill, and Lynda St. Clair (San Francisco: The New Lexington Press, 1997), pp. 230-244.

41. Richard Feinberg, "Two Leading Lights of Humane Globalisation," *Singapore Straits Times,* February 21, 2000, p. 50.

42. "The Millennium Poll on Corporate Social Responsibility," Environics International Ltd., September 1999, www.environics.net/eil/millennium/.

43. Carol Stavraka, "Ford Admits SUVs Harm Environment; Looks for Ways to Improve Record," *ResponsibilityInc*, May 17, 2000, www.responsibilityinc.com/.

44. Sue Shellenbarger, "Companies Are Finding Real Payoffs in Aiding Employee Satisfaction," *Wall Street Journal*, October 11, 2000, p. B1.

45. Jennifer Rewick, "Connecticut Attorney General Launches Probe of Priceline.com After Complaints," *Wall Street Journal*, October 2, 2000, p. E16.

46. "Study Finds Lying, Cheating in Teens," CNN, October 19, 2000, www.cnn.com/2000/fyi/real.life/10/18/cheating.teens.ap/.

47. Bernstein, "Too Much Corporate Power?"

48. Glenn R. Simpson, "Raytheon Offers Office Software for Snooping," *Wall Street Journal*, June 14, 2000, p. B1.

49. Bernstein, "Too Much Corporate Power?" p. 153.

50. Julia Angwin, "Credit-Card Scams: The Devil E-stores," *Wall Street Journal*, September 19, 2000, p. B1, B4.

Organizational Benefits of Strategic Corporate Citizenship

2

▶ Trust as an Integral Part of Corporate Citizenship

▶ Relationship of Corporate Citizenship to Performance

OBJECTIVES

To provide evidence that corporate citizenship supports business performance

To demonstrate that corporate citizenship improves customer satisfaction

To show that corporate citizenship encourages employee commitment

To indicate that corporate citizenship contributes to investor loyalty

To discuss the relationship of social institutions that support trust to a nation's economic well-being

Like many companies trying to absorb a new acquisition, Holt Companies experienced a major case of corporate indigestion in the late 1980s. At the same time, Holt, which owns Caterpillar dealerships that sell and service both new and used heavy equipment, was contending with economic declines in the construction and petroleum industries—major markets for its products. The growing pains from the acquisition, coupled with a flagging economy, resulted in poor employee morale and "hip-shot" decision making, and the company's bottom line languished. Chief Executive Officer Peter Holt, the great-grandson of Benjamin Holt, the inventor of the first Caterpillar tractor, felt the company needed to find a new approach to jump-start the business. Holt's quest ultimately resulted in a Values-Based Leadership program that has generated significant results for the company.

Holt's Values-Based Leadership initiative strives to link employees, customers, shareholders, and other stakeholders so that the actions of one stakeholder group directly benefit the others. Holt adapted the process from Michael O'Connor and Kenneth Blanchard's Management by Values program, which defines success in relation to managing by a set of ethical values. Holt's program generates benefits for all stakeholders through "working and managing by a chosen set of ethical business values, constantly assessing progress with respect to that set of values, and committing to make changes needed to stay on track with that set of values." The core values, chosen with input from all organizational employees, include:

Ethics: Doing the right thing
Success: Consistently achieving targeted goals
Excellence: Continuously getting better
Commitment: Being here to stay
Dynamic: Pursuing strategic opportunities

In the years since Holt implemented this values-based approach, the company's gross profits have increased by 100 percent and its sales by 600 percent. Although the firm's employee base has grown from 300 to nearly 1,000, companywide turnover has declined from 20 percent to 5 percent. The program has also reduced employee concerns by half. The positive results from the Values-Based Leadership program spurred the company to establish Holt Consulting Services, a separate firm that offers services ranging from assessment and planning process integration training to facilitation and support services to a variety of industries. Companies that Holt Consulting Services has worked with include Foley, Inc., Spring PCS, San Antonio Spurs, and the San Antonio Water System. As Larry Axline, CEO of the consulting service, says, "It's one thing to proclaim that you've got a set of corporate values, but it's another thing to walk them, to make them come to life."[1]

Like Holt Companies, other organizations today are being challenged by a complex and dynamic business environment. The proliferation of international trade agreements is extending the reach of businesses into the farthest corners of the globe. Technological advances, along with the explosive growth of the Internet, have brought tremendous changes to the way companies do business and armed stakeholders—customers, employees, investors, business partners, and the public—with more information than they've ever had before. These changes have dramatically accelerated the pace of business and created a new breed of stakeholder who is increasingly savvy, well informed, and more demanding than ever. On average, U.S. companies lose half their customers within five years, half their employees within four years, and half their investors in less than one year.[2] Such disloyalty can damage corporate performance because the costs of rebuilding these stakeholder relationships far exceed the costs of maintaining existing relationships.[3] In this dynamic business environment, it is more vital than ever for a company to build positive relationships with its important stakeholders.

The importance of corporate citizenship initiatives in enhancing stakeholder relationships has been debated from many different perspectives. Much of this deliberation has focused on whether citizenship and social responsibility efforts are directly related to financial performance.[4] Many business managers view such programs as costly activities that provide rewards only to society at the expense of the bottom line. Another view holds that some costs of corporate citizenship cannot be recovered through improved performance. Although it is true that some aspects of social responsibility and corporate citizenship may not accrue directly to the bottom line, we believe that organizations benefit indirectly over the long run from these activities. Moreover, ample research and anecdotal evidence demonstrate that there are many rewards for those companies that implement such programs. Some of these rewards include increased efficiency in daily operations, greater employee commitment, higher product quality, improved decision making, increased customer loyalty, and improved financial performance. In short, companies that establish a reputation for trust, fairness, and integrity develop a valuable resource that fosters success, which then translates to greater financial performance.

This chapter provides evidence that resources invested in social responsibility and corporate citizenship programs contribute to improved reputation and financial performance. First, we examine the role of trust in improving stakeholder relationships. We then consider how corporate citizenship initiatives affect specific groups of stakeholders, namely customers, employees, and investors. Finally, we offer evidence that business conduct affects a nation's economic well-being.

Trust as an Integral Part of Corporate Citizenship

Trust is the glue that holds organizations together and allows them to focus on efficiency, productivity, and profits. According to Stephen R. Covey, author of *The 7 Habits of Highly Effective People,* "trust lies at the very core of effective human interactions. Compelling trust is the highest form of human motivation. It brings out the very best in people, but it takes time and patience, and it doesn't preclude the necessity to train and develop people so their competency can rise to that level of trust."[5] Consequently, Covey encourages managers to examine not only traditional indicators of corporate success such as profits and earnings per share, but also the impact of trust on the bottom line. He contends that when trust is low, organizations decay and relationships deteriorate, resulting in politics, infighting, and general inefficiency. Employee commitment to the organization declines, product quality suffers, employee turnover skyrockets, and customers turn to more trustworthy competitors. To provide support for his views, Covey commissioned the America Speaks survey of 600 adults, which reported that 88 percent of respondents believe that teamwork is necessary to accomplish anything in business. The survey also revealed that in the workplace, people feel that they can be trusted more than they can trust others. Using manipulation and short-run tactics to motivate other people to accomplish the company's goals will not work over time. Thus, Covey argues that without trust, there is no foundation for permanent success.[6]

Intel recognizes the importance of values that support relationships with customers, employees, and stockholders. (Reprinted with permission from Intel Corporation.)

For the sake of both productivity and teamwork, it is essential that everyone within an organization share a sense of trust. The influence of greater levels of trust is strongest in relationships within departments or work groups, but trust is also a significant factor in relationships among departments throughout a firm. In a trusting work environment, employees can reasonably expect to be treated with respect and consideration by both their peers and their superiors. They are also more willing to rely and act on the decisions and actions of their coworkers. Thus, trusting relationships between managers and their subordinates contribute to greater decision-making efficiencies. Research by the Ethics Resource Center indicates that trust also contributes to employee satisfaction. The study reported that 93 percent of surveyed employees who say that trust is frequently evident in their organizations report satisfaction with their employers (Figure 2.1).[7]

From employees' perspectives, one way to strengthen trust is through stock ownership plans (ESOPs), which provide the opportunity both to contribute to and gain from organizational success. Such programs confer not only ownership but also opportunities for employees to participate in management planning, which fosters an environment that many organizations believe increases profits. One of the best examples of employee ownership and participation in the workplace can be found at Cisco Systems, Inc., a leading provider of computer networking equipment. All of Cisco's employees participate in its ESOP, and they believe in open

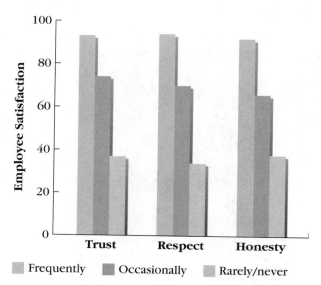

FIGURE 2.1

The Relationship of Values Applied in the Workplace to Employee Satisfaction
At least 92 percent of employees who see trust, respect, and honesty applied frequently in their organizations say they are satisfied with their organizations. However, satisfaction declines among employees who see these values applied only occasionally or rarely.

Source: Reprinted by permission from Ethics Resource Center. *The Ethics Resource Center's 2000 National Business Ethics Survey: How Employees Perceive Ethics at Work* (Washington, D.C.: Ethics Resource Center, 2000), p. 85.

communication, with decision making occurring at even the lowest levels. Employees work as a team in an environment that forges trust and contributes to greater interaction with customers. The company has one of the lowest employee turnover rates in the industry, and each employee contributes $650,000 in revenue to the company per year, compared to an industry average of around $300,000 per employee.[8] Other "employee-owned" companies include Publix Super Markets, United Airlines, and Ferrellgas. After Ferrellgas implemented an ESOP, employee turnover declined by 20 percent in one year.[9]

Trust is a two-way street in an organization. Employees give, and the company gives in return. Consider the actions of FedEx employees when rival United Parcel Service employees went on strike in the late 1990s. Employees at FedEx quickly found themselves overworked and overloaded with packages, but they put in extra hours and effort to satisfy customers with no additional incentive. After the UPS strike ended, FedEx thanked its employees for their extra effort with a $20 million bonus, or 10 percent of their pay, including overtime, over that three-week period. FedEx also has a profit-sharing plan, grievance procedures, and a no-layoff policy.[10] Maintaining trust requires a continuous process of communication and cooperation.

Trust between employer and employee ensures company survival and success over time. Marriott, for example, works to strengthen its employees' trust in the organization through employee-centered programs. It has established a twenty-four-hour hot line for employees who are having family or personal problems. In Atlanta, Marriott offers a child-care center for children of low-income hotel workers.

Coca-Cola Company tests product samples after a product contamination scare in Europe. The company responds quickly to protect quality and public health.

Marriott is also one of the few successful companies in the hospitality industry that does not operate a casino.[11] Maintaining success while choosing not to engage in a more controversial segment of the industry requires hard work and trust among all stakeholders.

Trust is also essential for a company to maintain positive long-term relationships with customers. A study by Cone/Roper reported that three out of four consumers say they avoid or refuse to buy from certain businesses. Poor service was the number one reason cited for refusing to buy, but business conduct was the second reason that consumers gave for avoiding specific companies.[12] After the *Exxon Valdez* oil spill, certain groups and individual citizens aggressively boycotted Exxon because of its response to the environmental disaster. Likewise, many consumers stopped buying Chicken of the Sea and competing tuna products when those companies initially refused to require that their tuna suppliers adopt dolphin-friendly fishing practices.

Consumers have also been known to avoid products from companies that they perceive do not treat their employees fairly. Among the firms that have experienced negative publicity are those that subcontract through foreign manufacturers, or "sweatshops," that abuse or underpay their workforce. J. C. Penney, for example, was accused by the National Labor Committee (NLC) of selling Arizona jeans for $14.99 a pair, when the workers manufacturing them earned only 11 cents a pair. The NLC also charged that for every $12 garment sewn for Victoria's Secret, the worker earned just 3 cents. Wal-Mart, Kmart, and Nike have also been singled out by this watchdog group for outsourcing production to countries with low wages in order to boost profitability.[13] In some cases, new industry codes of conduct have been established to help companies identify and address such issues. For example, the American Apparel Manufacturers Association (AAMA) has endorsed the principles and certification program of Worldwide Responsible Apparel Production (WRAP), a nonprofit organization that is dedicated to promoting and certifying "lawful, human, and ethical manufacturing throughout the world." Companies that endorse the principles are expected to allow independent monitoring to ensure that their contractors are complying with the principles (Figure 2.2).[14]

Relationship of Corporate Citizenship to Performance

Support for a positive relationship between responsible corporate conduct and business performance comes from many diverse sources. Figure 2.3 illustrates this relationship.

Investors, employees, and customers are major stakeholders for firms that want to develop loyalty and competitive advantages. Creating mutually beneficial exchange relationships with customers requires all these parties to work together to understand each other's needs and to develop trust. The challenge is to identify

FIGURE 2.2 The Worldwide Responsible Apparel Production (WRAP) Principles

Worldwide Responsible Apparel Production is an independent, non-profit corporation to the promotion and certification of lawful and ethical manufacturing throughout the world.

About **WRAP**
WRAP Principles
Board and Staff
Endorsements
Certification
Monitors
News
FAQs

Apply Online
Downloads

Worldwide Responsible Apparel Production

Lawence M. Doherty
Executive Director

P.O. Box 10673
Arlington, VA 22210

Tel. 703-524-8209 or
1-877-524-WRAP

Fax 703-522-0486

Email:
lmdoherty@
wrapapparel.org

[HOME]

WRAP Principles *Spanish Version*

The Worldwide Responsible Apparel Production Principles are minimum standards for production facilities participating in the Worldwide Responsible Apparel Production Certification Program. The Program's objective is to demonstrate the apparel industry's commitment to socially responsible business practices and to assure that sewn products are produced under lawful, humane and ethical conditions. Participating companies voluntarily agree that their production and that of their contractors will be certified by an independent monitor as complying with these standards.

- **Laws and Workplace Regulations** Apparel manufacturers will comply with laws and regulations in all locaations where they conduct business.

- **Forced Labor** Apparel manufacturers will not use involuntary or forced labor — indentured, bonded, or otherwise.

- **Child Labor** Apparel manufacturers will not hire any employee under the age of 14, or under the age interfering with compulsory schooling, or under the minimum age established by law, whichever is greater.

- **Harassment or Abuse** Apparel manufacturers will provide a work environment free of harassment, abuse or corporal punishment in any form.

- **Compensation and Benefits** Apparel manufacturers will pay at least the minimum total compensation required by local law, including all mandated wages, allowances and benefits.

- **Hours of Work** Hours worked each day, and days worked each week, shall not exceed the legal limitations of the countries in which apparel is produced. Apparel manufacturers will provide at least one day off in every seven-day period, except as required to meet urgent business needs.

- **Discrimination** Apparel manufacturers will employ, pay, promote, and terminate workers on the basis of their ability to do the job, rather than on the basis of personal characteristics or beliefs.

- **Health and Safety** Apparel manufacturers will provide a safe and healthy work environment. Where residential housing is provided for workers, apparel manufacturers will provide safe and healthy housing.

- **Freedom of Associaton** Apparel manufacturers will recognize and respect the right of employees to exercise their lawful rights of free association, including joining or not joining any association.

- **Environment** Apparel manufacturers will comply with environmental rules, regulations and standards applicable to their operations, and will observe environmentally conscious practices in all locations where they operate.

- **Customs Compliance** Apparel manufacturers will comply with applicable customs law and, in particular, will establish and maintain programs to comply with customs laws regarding illegal transshipment of apparel products.

- **Drug Interdiction** Apparel manufacturers will cooperate with local, national and foreign customs and drug enforcement agencies to guard against illegal shipments of drugs.

Source: "WRAP Principles," Worldwide Responsible Apparel Production, www.wrapapparel.org/ infosite2/index.htm, accessed October 18, 2001. Reprinted with permission from WRAP—Worldwide Responsible Apparel Production.

FIGURE 2.3

The Role of Corporate Citizenship in Performance

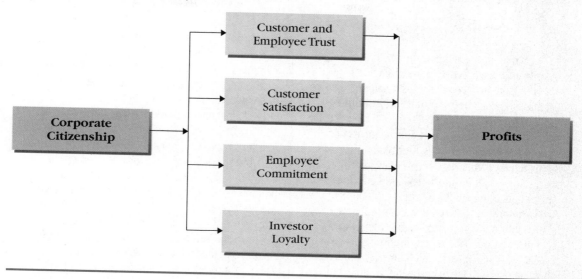

what the company can do to satisfy customers and thereby continually increase their trust and confidence in the firm. Employees spend most of their waking hours preparing for work, being at work, or commuting to and from work. Building strong relationships with employees requires not only providing jobs but also helping them to achieve their own personal objectives and desires for a high quality of life. Investors who are satisfied with a firm's conduct and performance are less likely to sell their stock for short-term gains, so forging positive relationships with investors is important to a firm's long-term capital stability.

▶ *Corporate Citizenship Improves Customer Satisfaction*

The prevailing business philosophy about customer relationships is that a company should strive to market products that satisfy customers' needs through a coordinated effort that also allows the company to achieve its own objectives. It is well accepted that customer satisfaction is one of the most important factors for business success. Although companies must continue to develop and adapt products to keep pace with consumers' changing desires, it is also crucial to develop long-term relationships with customers. Long-term relationships built on mutual respect and cooperation facilitate the repeat purchases that are essential for success. By focusing on customer satisfaction, a business can continually strengthen

Today's Blue-Light Special: Customer Service

While there are many dimensions of corporate citizenship, customer satisfaction is necessary for long-term relationships. Customer service seems to be declining in almost every industry, and horror stories about bad customer service are relayed around office coolers and Internet chat rooms. As companies strive for greater increases in productivity, they are increasingly focusing their efforts on their most profitable customers and encouraging the rest of their customers to utilize less-costly means of interaction, such as automatic teller machines, automated voice-mail systems, and web sites. Even discount stores such as Wal-Mart and Kmart, which have long focused on value over service, have been the subject of mounting criticism over declining service levels. Says one discount store patron, "When you're looking for help, you can't find anyone in certain areas. You have to walk the store or go all the way to the service desk." This situation lowers customer satisfaction and destroys trust and loyalty.

Kmart's chairman and CEO, Charles C. Conaway, hopes to exploit this malaise over service quality to craft a new customer-service-focused strategy for the venerable retail chain. The chain's investors desperately hope his plan works: Despite a $1.1 billion investment in an earlier turnaround attempt, the chain's operating income continues to fall, down 24 percent in 2000 to $986 million. Conaway believes the retailer's woes stem from poor inventory management, inattention to customers, and a marketing strategy that failed to clearly differentiate Kmart from rivals Wal-Mart and Target. Despite these problems, Kmart has a number of strong private-label brands such as Route 66 casual clothing, Jaclyn Smith and Kathy Ireland clothing, Sesame Street children's clothing, and the chain's star brand, Martha Stewart, who sold $1 billion worth of merchandise through Kmart last year.

To capitalize on the strength of these brands, Conaway had to tackle the structural and cultural

its customers' trust in the company, and as their confidence grows, this in turn increases the firm's understanding of their requirements. The most successful companies provide mechanisms for customer feedback (e.g., toll-free telephone numbers and web sites with e-mail feedback) that encourage interaction and provide opportunities to engage in cooperative problem solving. It has often been said that happy customers will come back, but a disgruntled customer will tell ten or more people about his or her dissatisfaction with a company and discourage friends from doing business with that company.

Customers of service-oriented businesses are especially vulnerable when companies fail to respect their rights. Service fairness is a customer's perception of the degree of justice in a firm's behavior. When information about added service costs is omitted or when a guarantee is not honored, customers react negatively to the perceived injustice. Their response—complaining or refusing to deal with the

problems that have troubled Kmart for years. He began by adding some new faces to the management team, closing 72 lackluster stores, and earmarking $2 billion for new technology to address the chain's inefficient, outdated inventory management system. Because the old system didn't adequately tip merchandise planners as to what was selling, too many items languished on clearance racks while customers fumed over shelves that were empty of products they actually wanted. Worse, store clerks were spending just 22 percent of their time interacting with customers because they were stuck in the back room doing paperwork. Conaway hopes new technology, such as Web-enabled registers and scanners, will speed checkout times by 40 percent and facilitate inventory management, freeing up clerks to spend more time with customers. To encourage feedback from customers, store receipts now include a toll-free number on the back so that customers can rate their shopping experience or share complaints. As a part of its Blue Light Always program, Kmart has also lowered the prices on nearly 45 percent of its stores' merchandise.

Conaway has also tinkered with Kmart's merchandise mix, focusing more heavily on women with children. To satisfy this target market, stores will stock more home furnishings and children's toys and clothing. The company also restored its old "blue-light specials" to announce temporary discounts on designated merchandise. Kmart's web site, BlueLight.com, was also revamped. The new web site now offers "hundreds of thousands" of items, which has helped propel Kmart beyond Wal-Mart, at least in terms of drawing in customers online. Only time will tell whether the rest of Conaway's changes in customer focus will improve Kmart's customer satisfaction. Improved customer satisfaction should be a contribution to both corporate citizenship and the bottom line. ■

Sources:
Diane Brady, "Why Service Stinks," *Business Week*, October 23, 2000, pp. 118–128; Joann Muller, with Diane Brady, "A Kmart Special: Better Service," *Business Week*, September 4, 2000, pp. 80–82; Greg Sandoval, "Kmart Flashes BlueLight at Customers," CINet, October 11, 2000, www.cnet.com; "Kmart Turnaround Effort Remains on Track," *Drug Store News*, September 10, 2001, www.findarticles.com/cf_o/m3374/12_23/78269204/print.jhtml.

business again—may be motivated by the need to punish and the desire to limit a future injustice.[15] Millions of customers have experienced being overcharged by retail computer scanners that have not been programmed with the correct "sale" price. If a customer is overcharged for an item that has a highly visible sale price displayed, a feeling of injustice arises and may provoke an angry, verbal response. Repeated instances of overpricing or other service problems can lead to unhappy customers and a bad reputation for the company.

Some technological advances have raised troubling questions with regard to customer service. Because companies can apply computer technology to collect vast amounts of data about their customers, they now have the power to make customer-service decisions on the basis of each customer's contribution to profits. Increasingly, companies are using this information to rank individual customers and reserve stellar levels of service for those who generate the most profit. The remaining customers may see reduced customer service. At Charles Schwab, for example, customers with at least $100,000 in assets never wait longer than 15 seconds before their calls to the company are answered; other customers may wait 10 minutes or more to reach the company. Likewise, some banks have begun imposing extra fees on credit card holders who do not accrue a minimum level of annual interest charges because the costs to provide service to these customers exceeds the revenues they bring in. Although most consumers may view such treatment as unfair, companies defend the practice by saying they can no longer afford to treat every customer like a king or queen in today's competitive business environment.[16]

One of the fundamental responsibilities of a business is promoting the greatest good for its stakeholders, including customers. In a national survey by Cone/Roper, 52 percent of business executives strongly agreed with that view. Frank Walker, president of the Walker Group, stated in the survey that "being bad is extremely costly." Because consumers respond positively to socially concerned businesses, being good can be extremely profitable. Executives overwhelmingly agreed that being compassionate and responsible is absolutely essential.[17] Figure 2.4 shows that the stronger the perception that an organization is ethical, the greater is the customer loyalty that it commands. Remember that ethics is one of the four social responsibilities in our definition of corporate citizenship.

In a Cone/Roper national survey of consumer attitudes, 70 percent of consumers indicated they would be likely to switch to brands associated with a good cause, if price and quality were equal. These results indicate that con-

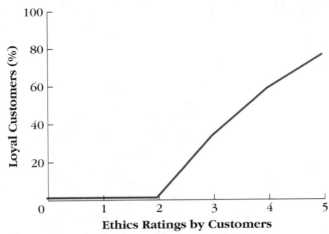

FIGURE 2.4

The Relationship Between Customer Loyalty and Perceptions of Ethics

Source: Walker Information ©1998.

sumers take for granted that they can buy high-quality products at low prices; therefore, companies need to stand out as doing something—something that demonstrates their commitment to society.[18] In another study, this one by Harris Interactive Inc. and the Reputation Institute, one-quarter of the respondents indicated that they had boycotted a firm's products or lobbied others to do so when they did not agree with its policies or activities.[19] Another way of looking at these results is that irresponsible behavior could trigger disloyalty and refusals to buy, whereas good citizenship initiatives could draw customers to a company's products.

Many companies have developed citizenship programs to support their communities and benefit their customers. Home Depot, for example, is committed to community development and at-risk youth programs (Figure 2.5). Suzanne Apple, Home Depot's vice president for community affairs and environmental programs, says that these programs are "as much a part of our strategy as growing our business,

Home Depot's Community Involvement

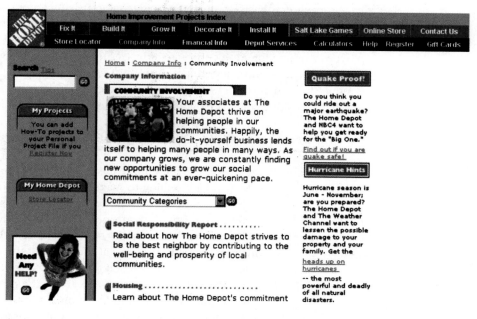

Reprinted by permission from The Home Depot Headquarters, Homer TLC. "Community Involvement," Home Depot, www.homedepot.com, accessed November 2, 2001.

as the products we select and carry" and notes that Home Depot's support for community development offers a "critical competitive advantage."[20] Many other companies have supported causes in which their customers have a strong interest. Northwest Airlines provides support for St. Jude Children's Hospital in Memphis, Tennessee. Timberland encourages every employee to give forty paid hours per year to volunteer activities and contributes $5 million annually to a program called Urban Peace Corp. that is active in eight U.S. cities. Avon has a well-publicized breast cancer awareness campaign, as well as a worldwide fund for women's health. A spokesperson for Avon says these programs "help develop bonds between customers and sales representatives and give customers another reason to choose Avon."[21]

The experiences of many companies indicate that there is a strong relationship between corporate citizenship and customer satisfaction. Customers are likely to favor companies they perceive as having a positive reputation for being concerned about consumers and society. Responsible companies that are dedicated to treating customers fairly, working to improve product quality, and making customer information accessible are more likely to have a competitive advantage and to be profitable. The bottom line is that the costs associated with citizenship efforts may be balanced by improved customer loyalty.

A strong emphasis on corporate citizenship usually focuses on the core value of placing customers' interests first.[22] However, putting customers first does not mean ignoring the interests of employees, investors, and other stakeholders. Employees working for good corporate citizens support and contribute to understanding the demands and concerns of customers. Research indicates that responsible conduct toward customers results in a strong competitive position for a company that has a positive effect on financial performance and product innovation.[23]

▸ *Corporate Citizenship Encourages Employee Commitment*

Employee commitment stems from employees who believe their future is tied to that of the organization and are willing to make personal sacrifices for the organization.[24] Hershey Foods is an example of a business that draws substantial benefits from its long-lasting commitment to corporate citizenship. Every year, Hershey employees receive a booklet entitled *Key Corporate Policies,* which describes the values—fairness, integrity, honesty, respect—at the heart of the company's way of doing business. Employees are asked to signal their acceptance of these principles by signing the booklet. Workers are also made aware of the procedures available to report any concerns about proper conduct or policies in the workplace. These efforts help employees understand the importance of developing and maintaining respectful relationships with both colleagues and customers. Because they support the idea that customers should receive full value for their money, employees are also committed to delivering the highest quality standards possible. One CEO

SAS Institute, a leading software manufacturer, enjoys very high employee retention rates because of generous benefits to employees, including a high-quality on-site daycare facility subsidized by the company.

stated "as long as you take the 'high road' at Hershey, the company will stand behind you regardless of the outcome, but if you choose to take the 'low road,' you're on your own and will suffer the consequences." Hershey continues to be the most profitable company in the confectionery market, and it has outperformed the stock market over the last ten years.[25]

The more a company is dedicated to taking care of its employees, the greater is the likelihood that the employees will take care of the organization. The experience of Starbucks Coffee supports the idea that fair treatment of employees improves productivity and profitability. Starbucks was one of the first importers of agricultural products to develop a code of conduct to protect the workers who harvest coffee beans in countries such as Costa Rica. The company offers excellent health benefits and an employee stock ownership plan (termed "Bean Stock") for all of its workers, even though most of them are part time.[26] Although this policy makes employee benefits at Starbucks much more extensive and expensive than those of its competitors, employees appear to appreciate the company's care and respect. Its annual employee turnover rate is 55 percent, compared to an industry norm of 400 percent, whereas sales and profits have risen 50 percent a year for six consecutive years.[27] Starbucks recognizes its commitment to employees in its mission statement, which says that "we should treat each other with respect and dignity." The company has also made it clear to shareholders that the employees must be taken care of and that the company must find ways to build value for its employees.[28]

TABLE 2.1

Countries Ranked by Employee Loyalty

Top Thirty-Two Countries		
1. Colombia	12. Germany	23. Czech Republic
2. Republic of Korea	13. South Africa	24. Malaysia
3. Cyprus	14. Bolivia	25. Australia
4. Puerto Rico	15. Philippines	26. Japan
5. Saudi Arabia	16. Canada	27. United Kingdom
6. Mexico	17. China	28. Greece
7. United States	18. Finland	29. Indonesia
8. Brazil	19. Italy	30. Chile
9. France	20. Taiwan	31. Hong Kong
10. India	21. Spain	32. Singapore
11. Egypt	22. Thailand	

Reprinted by permission from Walker Information. "Global Workforce Study Highlights Alarming Trends in Workplace Commitment and Ethics," Walker Information, press release, September 18, 2000, http://walkerinfo.com/news/9_18_00_gerr.cfm.

When companies fail to provide value for their employees, loyalty and commitment suffer. A recent survey by Walker Information Global Network found low levels of employee loyalty and commitment worldwide. The study, which surveyed thousands of employees in thirty-two countries, found that only one in three workers is "truly loyal" to the organization for which he or she works. Table 2.1 ranks countries according to levels of employee loyalty. The researchers also found a connection between an employee's loyalty and his or her job performance. Marc Drizin, a Walker Information vice president, says, "Our research shows that employers everywhere need to focus on building relationships with their workers so that these employees can feel truly loyal to their organization and believe they are a valued part of the enterprise."[29] Figure 2.6 shows that an organization's ethical standards are a factor in employees' level of commitment to the organization.

Among the issues that may affect employees' perceptions of an organization's citizenship are providing a safe working environment, paying competitive salaries, and fulfilling all contractual obligations toward employees. Social programs that

FIGURE 2.6
The Importance of Ethics in Employee Commitment

"My organization's concern for ethics and doing the right thing is an important reason that I continue to work here."

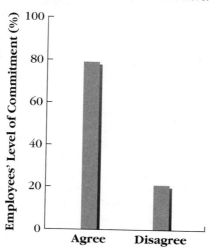

Reprinted with permission from Ethics Resource Center. *The Ethics Resource Center's 2000 National Business Ethics Survey: How Employees Perceive Ethics at Work* (Washington, D.C.: Ethics Resource Center, 2000), p. 67.

may improve this perception include work-family programs, stock ownership plans, and community service. Patagonia, a manufacturer of outdoor clothing and equipment, maintains two on-site child-care centers, donates 1 percent of sales or 10 percent of profits—whichever is greater—to environmental groups, and fills more than half of its top jobs with women.[30] Employees spend much of their waking hours at work; thus, an organization's commitment to goodwill and respect of its employees usually results in increased employee loyalty and support of the company's objectives. A survey by the Wilson Learning Corporation found that 80 percent of employees were inactive—"just doing their job but unwilling to expend their energy."[31] Almost everyone who has worked in an organization has seen people who do the minimum to get by each day or who have no commitment to what the organization is trying to accomplish because they don't feel they are treated fairly.

Employees who do not feel they are being treated fairly may respond in other ways as well. In a survey sponsored by the Ethics Officer Association, 48 percent of respondents indicated that they had misbehaved at work. The number one breach of ethics cited by respondents was compromising quality with respect to customers. It is interesting to note that in this same survey, three-fourths of the respondents said they believed they could be more responsible if they felt freer to bring misconduct issues to the attention of their supervisor and others in their company.[32] When employees perceive that there is an improvement in the standards of their organization, they become more committed to the achievement of high-quality standards in daily operations.[33] These findings suggest that employees who work in companies that promote corporate citizenship are likely to believe that they have to treat all of their business partners respectfully, regardless of whether they operate inside or outside the organization. As a result, it becomes essential for them to provide the best possible value to all customers and stakeholders.[34]

Because employee commitment to quality has a positive effect on a firm's competitive position, an emphasis on corporate citizenship has a positive effect on its bottom line. The quality of customer service affects customer satisfaction, thus improvement in the quality of service will have a direct impact on a company's image, as well as on its ability to attract new customers.[35] A study conducted by the Center for Corporate Community Relations at Boston College found that 84 percent of the employees at Polaroid and Gillette believe that a company's image in the community is important. Employees who believe that their company has a strong community involvement feel more loyal to their employers and more positive about themselves.[36]

▶ *Corporate Citizenship Contributes to Investor Loyalty*

Investors look at a corporation's bottom line for profits or the potential for increased stock prices. To be successful, relationships with stockholders and other investors must rest on dependability, trust, and commitment. The chief executive of the Co-operative Bank in the United Kingdom noted, after a 21 percent increase in pretax profits, that the bank's ethical and environmental standards enhanced customer loyalty and, consequently, profitability.[37] But investors also look for potential cracks or flaws in a company's performance. Legal problems and negative publicity can significantly affect the success of any organization. When the Securities and Exchange Commission investigated Sunbeam for improprieties in accounting procedures, the company's stock plummeted to almost worthless from a high of $54. The negative publicity associated with the alleged misconduct had an enormous impact on investors' confidence in Sunbeam—a previously trusted and respected American brand.[38]

Many shareholders are also concerned about the ethics, social responsibility, and reputation of companies in which they invest. Investors have even been known to avoid buying the stock of firms they view as irresponsible. For example, fifteen mutual fund managers recently announced a boycott of Mitsubishi stock after the Japanese firm refused to cancel a plan to build a salt factory on a Mexican lagoon that is also a major breeding site for gray whales.[39] Many socially responsible mutual funds and asset management firms are available to help concerned investors purchase stock in responsible companies. These investors

Jeff Bezos, CEO of Amazon.com communicates with investors by introducing the company's new web site in Japan.

recognize that corporate responsibility and citizenship are the foundation for efficiency, productivity, and profits. On the other hand, investors know that fines or negative publicity can decrease a company's stock price, customer loyalty, and long-term viability. Consequently, many chief executives spend a great deal of time communicating with investors about their firms' reputations and financial performance and trying to attract them to their stock.

The issue of drawing and retaining investors is a critical one for CEOs, as roughly 50 percent of investors sell their stock in companies within one year, and the average household replaces 80 percent of its common stock portfolio each year.[40] This focus on short-term gains subjects corporate managers to tremendous pressure to boost short-term earnings, often at the expense of long-term strategic plans. The resulting pressure for short-term gains deprives corporations of stable capital and forces decision makers into a "quarterly" mentality. Conversely, those shareholders willing to hold onto their investments are more willing to sacrifice short-term gains for long-term income. Attracting these long-term investors shields companies from the vagaries of the stock market and gives them flexibility and stability in long-term strategic planning.[41] Thus, gaining investors' trust and confidence is vital for sustaining a firm's financial stability.

▶ ## The Bottom Line: Corporate Citizenship and Profits

Corporate citizenship is positively associated with return on investment, return on assets, and sales growth.[42] A company cannot be a good corporate citizen and nurture and develop an ethical organizational culture unless it has achieved financial performance in terms of profits. Businesses with greater resources—regardless of their staff size—have the ability to promote their corporate citizenship along with serving their customers, valuing their employees, and establishing trust with the public.

Many studies have identified a positive relationship between corporate citizenship and financial performance.[43] For example, a survey of the five hundred largest public corporations in the United States found that those that commit to responsible behavior and emphasize compliance with codes of conduct show better financial performance.[44] A managerial focus on stakeholder interests can affect financial performance, although the relationships between stakeholders and financial performance vary and are very complex.[45] A meta-analysis of twenty-five years of research identified thirty-three studies (63 percent) demonstrating a positive relationship between corporate social performance and corporate financial performance, five studies (about 10 percent) indicating a negative relationship, and fourteen studies (27 percent) yielding an inconclusive result or no relationship.[46] Such results provide evidence that corporate concern for responsible conduct and citizenship is becoming a part of strategic planning in obtaining the outcome of higher profitability.[47] Rather than being just a government-required compliance program, citizenship is becoming a strategic management issue in the effort to achieve competitive advantage.

On the other hand, companies that have been convicted of misconduct experience significantly lower returns on assets and lower returns on sales than firms that have not been convicted of a crime. Research suggests that the negative effect on return on sales does not appear until the third year following a conviction, and multiple convictions are more harmful than a single conviction.[48] There are numerous examples of companies that have experienced significant declines in financial performance after their failure to act responsibly toward various stakeholders was publicized. Columbia/HCA, for example, saw its earnings and stock price plummet after it was accused of systematically overcharging the government for Medicare services. Many employees and customers also complained that Columbia/HCA failed to take their interests into account in day-to-day operations. Employees were forced to do jobs beyond their abilities, and customers (patients) were charged for services they did not need or were transferred to competitive hospitals if there was a question about their ability to pay. Once Columbia/HCA's misconduct was publicized, its reputation was diminished within a few months.[49] Cendant saw its stock price plunge 46 percent in one day after accounting irregularities were uncovered; the company later settled a shareholder lawsuit for $2.8 billion over the improprieties.[50] Sears suffered losses as a result of problems with its automotive division selling unneeded parts in its repair shops.[51] Texaco lost business as a result of racial insensitivity by some of its employees. Beechnut struggled after selling juice that was labeled as 100 percent pure but actually contained only the chemical equivalent of apple juice.[52] Every day it seems that the business newspapers and magazines bring more examples of the negative consequences of misconduct.

As you have progressed through this chapter, it should be clear that business misconduct can damage a company's reputation. Sunbeam's accounting problems, Columbia/HCA's overbilling to the Medicare program, and the environmentally damaging oil spill from the wreck of the *Exxon Valdez* illustrate how quickly a reputation can deteriorate. Indeed, anger and resentment toward Exxon linger more than a decade after the *Exxon Valdez* oil spill, and some consumers still refuse to patronize the company because of its handling of the disaster.[53] On the other hand, culturally based citizenship initiatives have provided an organizational infrastructure for improving employee commitment and teamwork, customer loyalty, and economic productivity at many companies, including Ben & Jerry's, Texas Instruments, and Procter & Gamble. A company's reputation has a major effect on its relationships with customers, employees, suppliers, and investors. Levi Strauss, for example, has a strong emphasis on ethics, which led the clothing manufacturer to drop about 5 percent of its subcontractors and mandate improvements for others in response to its concerns about subcontractors' treatment of employees. As Levi's CEO explained, "Over the years, we've found that decisions which emphasize cost to the exclusion of all other factors don't serve a company's and its shareholders' long-term interests."[54]

A study conducted by Harris Interactive Inc. and the Reputation Institute confirms the importance of a reputation based on trust. This nationwide survey established a ranking of the most reputable companies by calculating each firm's "reputation quotient," which was determined by survey respondents' ratings on 20 attributes, including emotional appeal, vision, leadership, workplace environment, social responsibility, and financial performance. Table 2.2 lists the companies with the highest reputation quotients. According to Charles Fombrun, executive director of Reputation Institute, "Reputation is much more than an abstract concept; it's a corporate asset that is a magnet to attract customers, employees and investors."[55]

Viewed from a stock growth perspective, a company's reputation enhances its value in the marketplace, as an examination of *Fortune* magazine's annual list of the most admired companies clearly indicates. An investment of $1,000 ten years ago in each of the ten most admired companies identified by *Fortune* (Table 2.3) would have resulted in a return of nearly three times as much as an investment of $10,000 in the Standard & Poor's 500 stock index.[56] Note that a majority of the "most admired" companies in Table 2.3 also appear on the list of companies with high reputation quotients in Table 2.2. Although some of these firms may have experienced legal and ethical issues (e.g., a U.S. district judge ruled that Microsoft violated antitrust laws to maintain its monopoly in operating-systems software and to dominate the market for Web browsing software[57]), their overall reputation, based on the *Fortune* criteria, was superior to all other companies in the *Fortune* 1000 list of the largest corporations. Some of the specific criteria used in *Fortune*'s evaluation included overall reputation, quality of management, quality of products, innovativeness, and responsibility to the community/environment. Given the

TABLE 2.2

Most Admired Companies in the United States

Top Thirty Companies		
1. Johnson & Johnson	11. Daimler-Chrysler	21. Xerox
2. Maytag	12. GE	22. Boeing
3. Sony	13. FedEx	23. Amazon.com
4. Home Depot	14. Wal-Mart	24. McDonald's
5. Intel	15. Cisco Systems	25. Dell
6. Anheuser-Busch	16. Coca-Cola	26. Southwest Airlines
7. IBM	17. GM	27. Yahoo!
8. Disney	18. Honda	28. Merck
9. Microsoft	19. Toyota	29. Nike
10. Procter & Gamble	20. Hewlett-Packard	30. Ben & Jerry's

Source: "America's Most Admired Companies," *Fortune,* February 19, 2001. Copyright© 2001 by *Fortune.* Reprinted with permission.

Fortune criteria, it is probably impossible to rank high on the list without a strong commitment to social responsibility and corporate citizenship.[58]

The Hay Group, a worldwide management consulting firm, conducted a benchmark study of the ten most admired companies in an attempt to determine what makes these companies great. According to Dr. Bruce N. Pfau, an expert in culture assessment and vice president of Hay, the company "found the corporate cultures of the highest performing global companies dramatically differed from the norm." A detailed analysis of their corporate cultures revealed that the most admired companies emphasized teamwork, had a strong customer focus, valued fair treatment of employees, and rewarded superior performance, as well as innovation.[59]

What is it worth to a company's reputation, employees' pride, and shareholders' confidence to see their company listed on the cover of *Fortune* as one of the most admired companies? Southwest Airlines, Microsoft, Merck, and Hewlett-Packard have all found themselves in this enviable position. Merck's corporate culture is reflected in its credo, which puts patients before profits. Employees take pride in their company's actions, which have included the development of a low-cost anti-AIDS drug and the donation of medicine to prevent river blindness in developing

TABLE 2.3

America's Most Admired Companies Through the Years

1990	1995	2000
1. Merck	1. Rubbermaid	1. General Electric
2. Philip Morris	2. Microsoft	2. Cisco Systems
3. Rubbermaid	3. Coca-Cola	3. Wal-Mart
4. Procter & Gamble	4. Motorola	4. Southwest Airlines
5. 3M	5. Home Depot	5. Microsoft
6. PepsiCo (tie)	6. Intel	6. Home Depot
Wal-Mart	7. Procter & Gamble	7. Berkshire Hathaway
8. Coca-Cola	8. 3M	8. Charles Schwab
9. Anheuser-Busch	9. United Parcel Service	9. Intel
10. DuPont	10. Hewlett-Packard	10. Dell Computer

Sources: Christy Eidson and Melissa Master, "Who Makes the Call?" *Across the Board,* 37 (March 2000): 16+; Rahul Jacob, "Corporate Reputations," *Fortune,* March 6, 1995, pp. 54–60; "America's Most Admired Companies," *Fortune,* (accessed) October 16, 2001.

countries.[60] Research shows that organizations that are perceived as responsible often have a strong and loyal customer base, as well as a strong employee base, because of trust and mutual dependency in the relationship.[61] A study conducted for Sears found that satisfied employees lead to satisfied customers, which leads to satisfied investors.[62] Customers tend to prefer to buy from companies with a reputation for integrity, especially if the price is comparable to competitors' prices. When employees perceive that their organization has high ethical standards, they are more likely to be committed and satisfied in their work. Suppliers usually want long-term partnerships with companies they serve so that through cooperation, inefficiencies, costs, and risks can be eliminated to satisfy customers.

Economic Performance at the National Level

An often-asked question is whether business conduct has any bearing on a nation's overall economic performance. Many economists have wondered why some market-based economies are productive and provide a high standard of living for their citizens, whereas other market-based economies lack the kinds of social institutions that foster productivity and economic growth.[63] Perhaps a society's economic problems can be explained by a lack of corporate citizenship. As the glue that holds organizations and relationships together, trust stems from principles of morality and serves as an important "lubricant of the social system."[64] Many descriptions of market economies fail to take into account the role of such institutions as family, education, and social systems in explaining standards of living and economic success. Perhaps some countries do a better job of developing adequate standards of living and Gross Domestic Product (GDP) ratings than others because of the social structure of their economic relationships.

Social institutions, particularly those that promote trust, are important for the economic well-being of a society.[65] Society has become economically successful over time "because of the underlying institutional framework persistently reinforcing incentives for organizations to engage in productive activity."[66] In some developing countries, opportunities for political and economic development have been stifled by activities that promote monopolies, graft, and corruption and by restrictions on opportunities to advance individual, as well as collective, well-being. Author L. E. Harrison offers four fundamental factors that promote economic well-being: "(1) the degree of identification with others in a society—the radius of trust, or the sense of community; (2) the rigor of the ethical system; (3) the way authority is exercised within the society; and (4) attitudes about work, innovation, saving, and profit."[67]

Trust is the extent to which individuals identify with, or have a sense of community with, others in society. The smallest radius of trust is a society in which people trust only themselves. At the next level are those in which family members and other kin may be trusted. From a societal perspective, economic productivity will decline if day-to-day business activities require maximum use of mechanisms and procedures used to control dishonesty. Countries with strong trust-based institutions foster a productivity-enhancing environment because they have ethical systems in place that reduce transaction costs and make competitive processes more efficient and effective. In market-based systems where there is a great degree of trust, such as Japan, Great Britain, Canada, the United States, and Sweden, highly successful enterprises can develop through a spirit of cooperation and the ease in conducting business.[68]

Superior financial performance at the firm level within a society is measured as profits, earnings per share, return on investment, and capital appreciation. Businesses must achieve a certain level of financial performance in order to survive and reinvest in the various institutions in society that provide support. On the other hand, at the institutional or societal level, a key factor distinguishing societies with high standards of living is trust-promoting institutions. The challenge is to articulate the process by which institutions that support business ethics can contribute to firm-level superior financial performance.[69]

A comparison of countries with high levels of corruption and underdeveloped social institutions with countries that have low levels of corruption reveals differences in the economic well-being of the country's citizens. According to Transparency International's Corruption Perceptions Index, countries such as Nigeria and Bangladesh rank high on corruption, whereas countries such as Denmark and Finland rank low.[70] The differences in these countries' economic well-being and stability offer evidence that the social institutions that support ethics and responsibility play a vital role in economic development. Conducting business in an ethical and responsible manner generates trust and leads to relationships that promote productivity and innovativeness.

There is much evidence that developing effective citizenship programs in business not only helps prevent misconduct, but also leads to economic advantage. Although citizenship in an organization is important from a social and individual perspective, economic prospects are also a factor. One of the problems in gaining support for citizenship initiatives in organizations is the assumption that expenditures for such programs result only in costs and do not provide any return to the organization. In this chapter, we have presented evidence that investing in an infrastructure to promote corporate citizenship within an organization will help provide a foundation for all of the important business activities that are required for success. Citizenship alone will not create financial performance, but it will help establish a corporate culture that serves all stakeholders.

Summary

Trust bonds organizations and allows them to focus on efficiency, productivity, and profits. To find favor with the public, customers, employees, and investors, a company must earn their trust. Trust is essential for maintaining positive long-term relationships with both employees and customers. Creating mutually beneficial relationships with customers, employees, and investors requires all parties to work together to understand each other's needs and to develop trust.

A focus on customer satisfaction helps companies build long-term relationships. Successful businesses give consumers the opportunity for feedback. Service fairness—the customer's perception of the degree of justice in a firm's behavior—is a key element in long-term business success. The stronger the perception that an organization is ethical, the greater is the customer loyalty that it commands. Satisfied customers will return, but dissatisfied ones will continue to damage the firm's reputation through word of mouth. Customers are likely to favor companies they perceive as having a positive reputation for being concerned about consumers and society.

Employee commitment starts with employees who are loyal to a future with their employers and are willing to make personal sacrifices for the organization.

When companies fail to provide value for their employees, loyalty and commitment suffer. A safe work environment, competitive salaries, fulfillment of contractual obligations, work-family programs, stock ownership, and community service all contribute to developing employee commitment to the organization. When employees perceive an improvement in the standards of their organization, they become more committed to the achievement of high-quality standards in daily operations.

To be successful, relationships with stockholders and other investors must rest on dependability, trust, and commitment. Legal problems and negative publicity can significantly affect the success of any organization. Many investors are concerned about the ethics, social responsibility, and reputation of companies in which they invest. Gaining investors' trust and confidence is vital for sustaining a firm's financial stability.

Research has identified a positive relationship between corporate citizenship and financial performance. Misconduct can damage a firm's reputation. A company's reputation has a major effect on its relationships with customers, employees, suppliers, and investors. Research indicates that the most admired companies emphasize teamwork, have a strong customer focus, value fair treatment of employees, and reward superior performance. There is increasing evidence that developing an effective compliance program not only helps prevent misconduct, but also leads to economic productivity. Societies that promote trust have a more secure economic situation. Indeed, trust-promoting institutions are a key factor distinguishing societies with a high standard of living.

DISCUSSION QUESTIONS

1. If stakeholder relationships are important in developing organizational performance, is it possible that this focus on key stakeholders will undermine other members of society?

2. Why does trust play such a key role in building stakeholder relationships?

3. If corporate citizenship improves customer satisfaction, how does this contribute to society?

4. How does employee commitment translate into organizational performance and corporate citizenship?

5. How does corporate citizenship contribute to long-run investor loyalty? Why is investor loyalty so important to a company's long-term stability?

6. What evidence is there that corporate citizenship and integrity improve financial performance? Are there situations in which corporate citizenship could negatively affect this performance?

7. What evidence is available to support the theory that social institutions that promote ethics, trust, legal compliance, and other components of corporate citizenship are important for the economic well-being of a society?

8. How would you respond to the statement that this chapter presents only the positive side of the argument that corporate citizenship results in improved organizational performance?

EXPERIENTIAL EXERCISE

Evaluate *Fortune* magazine's annual list of the most admired companies, found in Table 2.3. These companies as a group have superior financial performance compared to other firms. Go to each company's web site (linked on our text web site) and try to assess its management commitment to the welfare of stakeholders. If any of the companies have experienced legal or ethical misconduct, explain how this may affect specific stakeholders. Rank the companies based on the information available and your opinion on their fulfillment of corporate citizenship.

NOTES

1. Holt Texas, www.holttexas.com/, accessed November 3, 2000; Kimberly Phelan, "Holt Consulting Gets Companies Running on Walking Their Talk," *Construction Equipment Distribution*, 64 (March 1998), www.aednet.org/ced/mar98/holtconsulting. htm; http://www.holtconsulting.com, accessed October 19, 2001.

2. Stephen R. Covey, "Is Your Company's Bottom Line Taking a Hit?" *PRNewswire*, June 4, 1998, www.prnewswire.com.

3. Frederick Reichheld, *The Loyalty Effect* (Cambridge, Mass.: Harvard Business School, 1996).

4. Jeffrey S. Harrison and R. Edward Freeman, "Stakeholders, Social Responsibility, and Performance: Empirical Evidence and Theoretical Perspectives," *Academy of Management Journal*, 42 (October 1999): 479.

5. Covey, "Is Your Company's Bottom Line Taking a Hit?"

6. Ibid.

7. Ethics Resource Center, *The Ethics Resource Center's 2000 National Business Ethics Survey: How Employees Perceive Ethics at Work* (Washington D.C.: Ethics Resource Center, 2000), p. 85.

8. Dale Kurschner, "5 Ways Ethical Busine$$ Creates Fatter Profit$," *Business Ethics*, 10 (March/April 1996): 21.

9. Jacquelyn Yates and Marjorie Kelly, "The Employee Ownership 100," *Business Ethics*, 14 (September/October 2000), www.business-ethics.com/current.htm.

10. Robert Levering and Milton Moskowitz, "The 100 Best Companies to Work for in America," *Fortune*, January 12, 1998, p. 86.

11. Ibid., p. 87.

12. "The 1997 Cone/Roper Cause-Related Marketing Trends Report," *Business Ethics*, 11 (March/April 1997): 14-16.

13. "NLC Names Corporate Names in Sweatshop Report," *Business Ethics*, 12 (January/February 1998): 9.

14. "Industry Social Responsibility Statement," American Apparel Manufacturers Association, www.americanapparel.org/AAMA_Social_Responsibility.html, accessed October 18, 2001; "WRAP Principles," Worldwide Responsible Apparel Production, www.wrapapparel.org, accessed October 18, 2001.

15. Kathleen Seiders and Leonard Barry, "Service Fairness: What It Is and Why It Matters," *Academy of Management Executive*, 12 (May 1998): 9.

16. Diane Brady, "Why Service Stinks," *Business Week*, October 23, 2000, pp. 118-128.

17. "The 1997 Cone/Roper Cause-Related Marketing Trends Report," pp. 14-16.

18. Ibid.

19. Ronald Alsop, "Corporate Reputations Are Earned with Trust, Reliability, Study Shows," *Wall Street Journal*, September 23, 1999, http://interactive.wsj.com.

20. "The 1997 Cone/Roper Cause-Related Marketing Trends Report," p. 14.

21. Ibid.

22. Terry W. Loe, "The Role of Ethical Climate in Developing Trust, Market Orientation and Commitment to Quality," unpublished dissertation, University of Memphis, 1996.

23. O. C. Ferrell, Isabelle Maignan, and Terry W. Loe, "The Relationship Between Corporate Citizenship and Competitive Advantage," Groningen University, The Netherlands, working paper, 2002.

24. Bernard J. Jaworski and Ajay K. Kohli, "Market Orientation: Antecedents and Consequences," *Journal of Marketing,* 57 (July 1993): 10.

25. "Hershey Foods Philosophy and Values," Hershey Foods Corporation Videotape, 1990.

26. Howard Schultz and Dori Jones Yang, *Pour Your Heart Into It,* as excerpted in "Starbucks: Making Values Pay," *Fortune,* September 29, 1997, p. 261.

27. Craig Smith, "Corporate Citizens and Their Critics," *New York Times,* September 8, 1996, p. 11.

28. O. C. Ferrell, John Fraedrich, and Linda Ferrell, *Business Ethics: Ethical Decision Making and Cases,* 5th ed. (Boston: Houghton Mifflin Company, 2002), p. 249.

29. "Global Workforce Study Highlights Alarming Trends in Workplace Commitment and Ethics," Walker Information, press release, September 18, 2000, http://walkerinfo.com/news/9_18_00_gerr.cfm.

30. Levering and Moskowitz, "The 100 Best Companies," p. 86.

31. Marjorie Kelly, "Was 1996 the Year Without Employees?" *Business Ethics,* 11 (March/April 1997): 5.

32. "Ethics in the News," *Managing Ethics,* 5 (August 1997): 3.

33. Loe, "The Role of Ethical Climate in Developing Trust."

34. Ferrell, Maignan, and Loe, "The Relationship Between Corporate Citizenship and Competitive Advantage."

35. Michael D. Hartline and O. C. Ferrell, "The Management of Customer-Contact Service Employees: An Empirical Investigation," *Journal of Marketing,* 60 (October 1996): 52-70.

36. "Does It Pay to Be Ethical?" *Business Ethics,* 11 (March/April 1997): 15.

37. Margaret Doyle, "Ethics Pays—Says Co-op Bank Chief," *[Detroit] Daily Telegraph,* April 19, 1998.

38. John A. Byrne "Chainsaw," *Business Week,* October 18, 1999, pp. 128-149.

39. "Mutual Funds to Boycott Mitsubishi over Proposed Mexican Salt Plant," CNN, October 25, 1999, www.cnn.com.

40. David Rynecki, "Here Are 8 Easy Ways to Lose Your Shirt in Stocks," *USA Today,* June 26, 1998, p. 3B.

41. Ronni L. Tapia, "Investor Loyalty Makes a 'Whale of Difference,'" *Philippine Daily Inquirer,* April 26, 1999, www.inquirer.net/issues/apr99/apr26/features/fea_4.htm.

42. Isabelle Maignan, O. C. Ferrell, and G. Thomas Hult, "Corporate Citizenship: Antecedents and Business Benefits," *Journal of the Academy of Marketing Science,* 24, no. 4 (1999): 455-469.

43. S. B. Graves and S. A. Waddock, "Institutional Owners and Corporate Social Performance: Maybe Not So Myopic After All," *Proceedings of the International Association for Business and Society,* San Diego, 1993; Ronald M. Roman, Sefa Hayibor, and Bradley R. Agle, "The Relationship Between Social and Financial Performance," *Business and Society,* 38 (March 1999); S. Waddock and S. Graves, "The Corporate Social Performance–Financial Performance Link," *Strategic Management Journal,* 18 (1997): 303-319.

44. Chris C. Verschoor, "A Study of the Link Between a Corporation's Financial Performance and Its Commitment to Ethics," *JBE* (October 1998): 1509.

45. Shawn L. Berman, Andrew C. Wicks, Suresh Kotha, and Thomas M. Jones, "Does Stakeholder Orientation Matter? The Relationship between Stakeholder Management Models and Firm Financial Performance," *Academy of Management Journal,* 42 (October 1999): 502-503.

46. Roman, Hayibor, and Agle, "The Relationship Between Social and Financial Performance."

47. Verschoor, "A Study of the Link Between a Corporation's Financial Performance and Its Commitment to Ethics."

48. Melissa A. Baucus and David A. Baucus, "Paying the Payer: An Empirical Examination of Longer Term Financial Consequences of Illegal Corporate Behavior," *Academy of Management Journal,* 40 (1997): 129-151.

49. Kurt Eichenwald and N. R. Kleinfeld, "At Columbia/HCA, Scandal Hurts," *[Memphis] Commercial Appeal,* December 21, 1997, pp. C1, C3.

50. Amy Barrett, "Henry Silverman's Long Road Back," *Business Week,* February 28, 2000, pp. 126-136.

51. Julia Flynn, "Did Sears Take Other Customers for a Ride?" *Business Week,* August 3, 1992, pp. 24-25; Harriet Johnson Brackey, "Auto Repair Rip-offs Bane of Consumer," *USA Today,* July 15, 1992.

52. Chris Welles, "What Led Beech-Nut Down the Road to Disgrace?" *Business Week,* February 22, 1988, pp. 124-128.

53. Alsop, "Corporate Reputations Are Earned with Trust."

54. John S. McClenahen, "Good Enough?" *Industry Week,* February 20, 1995, p. 58.

55. Alsop, "Corporate Reputations Are Earned with Trust."

56. Jeremy Kahn, "The World's Most Admired Companies," *Fortune,* October 26, 1998, pp. 207–226.

57. "Judge Rules that Microsoft Violated U.S. Antitrust Laws," *Wall Street Journal Interactive Edition,* April 3, 2000, http://interactive.wsj.com.

58. Thomas A. Stewart, "Why Leadership Matters," *Fortune,* March 25, 1999, p. 2.

59. *PR Newswire,* October 9, 1998, www.prnewswire.com.

60. Levering and Moskowitz, "The 100 Best Companies," pp. 84–95.

61. Loe, "The Role of Ethical Climate in Developing Trust."

62. Susan Gaines, "Continuing to Make Sears a Compelling Place to Work, Shop and Invest," *Business Ethics,* 11 (November/December 1997): 10–11.

63. D. C. North, *Institutions: Institutional Change, and Economic Performance* (Cambridge: Cambridge University Press, 1990).

64. K. J. Arrow, *The Limits of Organization* (New York: W. W. Norton, 1974), pp. 23, 26.

65. Shelby D. Hunt, "Resource-Advantage Theory and the Wealth of Nations: Developing the Socio-Economic Research Tradition," *Journal of Socio-Economics,* 26 (1997).

66. North, *Institutions,* p. 9.

67. L. E. Harrison, *Who Prospers? How Cultural Values Shape Economic and Political Success* (New York: Basic Books, 1992), p. 16.

68. Hunt, "Resource-Advantage Theory and the Wealth of Nations."

69. Ibid., pp. 351–352.

70. "New Index Highlights Worldwide Corruption Crisis," Transparency International, press release, June 27, 2001, www.transparency.org/documents/cpi/2001/cpi2001.html.

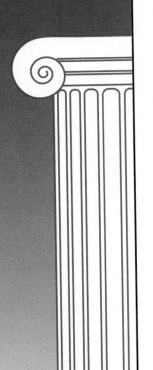

Strategic Management of Stakeholder Relationships

3

- ▶ Stakeholders Defined
- ▶ Stakeholder Identification and Importance
- ▶ Performance with Stakeholders
- ▶ Development of Stakeholder Relationships
- ▶ Link Between Stakeholder Relationships and Corporate Citizenship

Several countries, including Australia, Panama, India, Jamaica, and New Zealand, require foreign airlines to spray their airplanes with insecticides to protect plants, animals, and people from various insects that could be carried on flights arriving from other countries. While Australia, Jamaica, and New Zealand require planes to be sprayed after the passengers disembark, some countries, including India and Madagascar, require planes to be sprayed while passengers are still on board. Government policy and law require the spraying to prevent the spread of disease and other harmful elements to the country, land, and agriculture.

There are two different methods of spraying the insecticides. Aerosol cans are used when passengers are on board, whereas a blanketing technique is used when the plane is empty. With the second technique, workers come on board the plane wearing protective gear and blanket the empty aircraft cabin with pesticides that leave a residue for nearly two months. The pesticides contain permethrin and phenothrin, which are synthetic versions of a natural insecticide commonly found in chrysanthemums. The United States Environmental Protection Agency (EPA) classifies permethrin as a "moderately to practically nontoxic pesticide" that can cause eye or skin irritation. The EPA, however, no longer allows the use of these pesticides on aircraft in the United States.

Both passengers and airline crew have felt the effects of the insecticides. Sharon Dorazio is one passenger who, on a United Airlines' flight to the United States from Sydney, Australia, experienced stomach pain and burning eyes. Her two grandsons also suffered burning skin, itchy eyes, and loss of appetite. On the same flight, several other passengers reported feeling ill. Crew on the flight surmised that residue from the pesticides was causing the symptoms, which ranged from dizziness to rashes to breathing problems. Along with her husband, Ms. Dorazio filed a lawsuit against United Airlines, one of many lawsuits filed recently over the use of pesticides on airplanes. The Dorazios claim that United was not only evasive but also provided misinformation on the possible effects of the spraying.

In an article published in *USA Today*, two flight attendants reported they are no longer able to work because of their exposure to the pesticides.[1] After being a flight attendant for six years, Diana Brown-Dodson is using an oxygen tank most of the day and suffering from loss of short-term memory and concentration. Six doctors have diagnosed the problem as being caused by exposure to pesticides. Ms. Brown-Dodson estimates that she was exposed to pesticides approximately 150 times while working as a flight attendant. The Air Line Pilots Association is considering a campaign against using these pesticides on the planes. The California Department of Health is also examining approximately 100 cases of illnesses reportedly caused by pesticides on United flights. The United States State Department has asked the government of India to stop spraying while passengers are on board unless it is absolutely necessary.

While many groups are protesting the use of pesticides, government officials in countries requiring the insecticides on foreign planes stand by the practice. Officials maintain that the pesticides are not harmful and point out that the World Health Organization also considers the pesticides safe. One Australian spokesperson noted, "You've got more safety and health problems walking out into your garden than with what is sprayed on planes."

Although the governmental agencies probably considered many factors in developing the pesticide spraying policy, they seem to have either underestimated or failed to consider other groups of people who have an interest or stake in the use of insecticides. As this example illustrates, most organizations have a number of constituents who in turn, have other stakeholders to consider. In this case, United Airlines and other carriers are facing the complex task of balancing governmental, customer, and employee concerns. These stakeholders are increasingly expressing concerns and opinions that have an effect on an airline's time, operations, and products. Today, many organizations are learning to anticipate such issues and to address them in their plans and actions long before they become the subject of media stories or negative attention.

In this chapter, we examine the concept of stakeholders and explore why these groups are important for today's business. First, we define stakeholders and examine primary, secondary, and global stakeholders. Next we consider the impact of corporate reputation and crisis situations on stakeholder relationships. Finally, we examine the development of stakeholder relationships and the link between stakeholder relationships and corporate citizenship.

Stakeholders Defined

In Chapter 1, we defined stakeholders as those people and groups to whom an organization is responsible—including customers, investors and shareholders, employees, suppliers, governments, communities, and many others—who have a "stake" or claim in some aspect of a company's products, operations, markets, industry, or outcomes. These groups not only are influenced by businesses, but they also have the ability to affect businesses. The relationship between organizations and their stakeholders is therefore a two-way street. Table 3.1 reviews the evolving definition of stakeholders. The definition from 1963, for example, indicates that organizations are dependent on external influences for existence. The definition written in 1988 focuses on the effects that companies have on others. Our definition of corporate citizenship and stakeholders take these views, and others, into account.

The historical assumption that the foremost objective of business is profit maximization led to the belief that business is accountable primarily to investors and

TABLE 3.1

Historical Perspectives on Stakeholders

	Characterization of Stakeholders
1963	"Those groups without whose support the organization would cease to exist"
1971	"Driven by their own interests and goals are participants in a firm, and thus depending on it and whom for its sake the firm is depending"
1983	"Can affect the achievement of an organization's objectives or who is affected by the achievement of an organization's objectives"
1988	"Benefit from or are harmed by, and whose rights are violated or respected by, corporate actions"
1991	"Have an interest in the actions of an organization and . . . the ability to influence it"
1994	"Interact with and give meaning and definition to the corporation"
1995	"Have, or claim, ownership, rights, or interests in a corporation and its activities"

Source: Ronald K. Mitchell, Bradley R. Agle, and Donna J. Wood, "Toward a Theory of Stakeholder Identification and Salience: Defining the Principle of Who and What Really Counts," *Academy of Management Review,* 22 (October 1997): 853–886.

others involved in the market and economic aspects of an organization. Because stockholders and other investors provide the financial foundation for business and expect something in return, managers and executives naturally strive to maintain positive relationships with them. Customers, who provide a revenue stream, are also viewed as primary constituents by all types of organizations. Employees, too, are fundamental to the operations of any firm, although stories of downsizing, long work hours, and incompetent management raise questions about some organizations' treatment of employees.[2] Finally, suppliers and other business partners have a clear role in any business enterprise, as they provide goods and services (e.g., raw materials, component parts, distribution systems, advertising campaigns, and legal advice) that are necessary for an organization to function effectively and efficiently. Thus, investors, customers, employees, and suppliers are directly tied to a company's market prospects and success. In the late 1940s, the president of Johnson & Johnson developed a list of the company's "strictly business" stakeholders, which included customers, employees, managers, and shareholders. A few years later, Robert Wood, who captained Sears, Roebuck, & Co. after the Second World War, discussed profit as a by-product of satisfying the needs and expectations of various parties, including customers, employees, investors, and the community.[3]

In the latter half of the twentieth century, perceptions of business accountability evolved toward an expanded model of the role and responsibilities of business in society. The expansion included questions about the normative role of business: "What is the appropriate role for business to play in society?" and "Should profit be the sole objective of business?"[4] Theodore Levitt, a renowned business professor, once wrote that although profits are required for business just like eating is required for living, profit is not the purpose of business any more than eating is the purpose of life.[5] Norman Bowie, a well-published philosopher, extended Levitt's sentiment by noting that a sole focus on profit can create an unfavorable paradox that causes a firm to fail to achieve its objective. Bowie contends that when a business also cares about the well-being of other constituencies, it earns trust and cooperation that ultimately reduce costs and increase productivity.[6] These perspectives take into account both market and nonmarket constituencies that may interact with a business.[7] Market constituencies are those that are directly involved and affected by the business purpose, including investors, employees, customers, and other business partners. Nonmarket groups include the general community, media, government, special-interest groups, and others that are not always directly tied to issues of profitability and performance.

Two contrasting models illustrate the relationship between a business and its various stakeholders, as shown in Figures 3.1 and 3.2.[8] The **input-output model,** depicted in Figure 3.1, is based on the traditional profit-maximization approach to business, in which investors, employees, and suppliers provide inputs for a company to transform into outputs that benefit customers. In this model, the customer receives most of the value of the input-output process because investors, suppli-

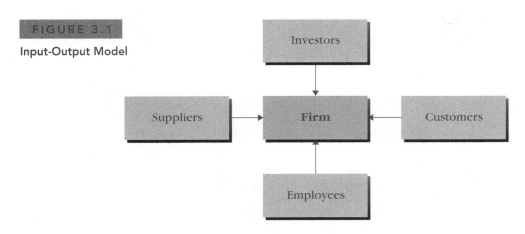

FIGURE 3.1

Input-Output Model

Investors

Suppliers → **Firm** ← Customers

Employees

Source: Thomas Donaldson and Lee E. Preston, "The Stakeholder Theory of the Corporation: Concepts, Evidence and Implications," *Academy of Management Review,* 29 (January 1995): 65–91. Republished with permission of the Academy of Management. Permission conveyed through Copyright Clearance Center.

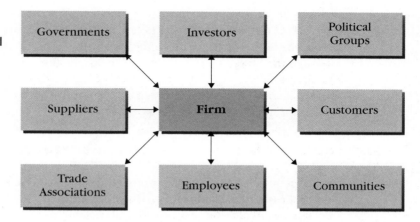

FIGURE 3.2

The Stakeholder Model

Source: Thomas Donaldson and Lee E. Preston, "The Stakeholder Theory of the Corporation: Concepts, Evidence and Implications," *Academy of Management Review,* 29 (January 1995): 65–91. Republished with permission of the Academy of Management. Permission conveyed through Copyright Clearance Center.

ers, and employees are compensated at a level that is normal or market competitive. The arrows in Figure 3.1 indicate a one-way relationship between the firm and these four constituents. It is important to note that in our definition of corporate citizenship, these groups are not really considered true stakeholders by the organization because there is no two-way directionality in the model.

At first glance, the input-output model may seem consistent with marketing strategies and advertising slogans that proclaim the "customer is always right." In reality, however, companies that focus on customer satisfaction are usually equally attuned to the integral role of employees, investors, and suppliers in the process of attracting and retaining customers. Indeed, consultant Frederick F. Reichheld argues in his book, *The Loyalty Effect,* that employee commitment and importance to an organization are necessary precursors to customer satisfaction.[9] Thus, a firm must invest in employee training, retention, compensation, and other relationship factors before it can properly satisfy its customers. At Sears, the national retailer, employee satisfaction has been shown to account for 60 to 80 percent of customer satisfaction.[10] Because the input-output model does not account for two-way relationships between the firm and its investors, suppliers, and employees, it assumes a relatively mechanistic, simplistic, and nonstakeholder view of business.

Figure 3.2 represents a more current conceptualization of business that is better aligned with our definition of corporate citizenship. In the **stakeholder model,** there are two-way relationships between the firm and a host of stakeholders. In addition to the fundamental inputs of investors, employees, and suppliers, this approach recognizes other stakeholders and explicitly acknowledges the two-way dialog and effects that exist between a firm's internal and external environment. As our definition of corporate citizenship suggests, it is vital that all businesses consider a range of stakeholder relationships and social responsibilities. Although the model seems to give relatively equal weight to all stakeholders, resource and time constraints mean that some type of hierarchy or prioritizing is warranted. In the next section, we discuss the process of identifying the importance and salience of stakeholders to an organization.

Stakeholder Identification and Importance

The input-output and stakeholder models provide generic representations of business processes and relationships. However, in order to achieve strategic citizenship, it is essential to understand specific stakeholders and their unique interests, claims, and relationships with an organization. In this section, we classify stakeholders as either primary or secondary, based on their significance to a particular organization. We also consider the complexity of global stakeholders, because more and more firms have interactions and interests beyond domestic borders. Finally, we examine the attributes that determine the type of influence stakeholders can wield in their relationships with organizations.

▶ Primary and Secondary Stakeholders

Walker Information, a research firm that specializes in stakeholder measurement and management, conducted a survey of 1,027 executives in global corporations to ascertain stakeholder importance to their firms. Survey respondents evaluated the importance of customers, financial analysts, government, community, shareholders, suppliers, and employees. Not surprisingly, customers, employees, and shareholders ranked highest (Figure 3.3). Because such groups are fundamental to a company's operations and survival, they are considered **primary stakeholders.** Without these groups, a company would not be able to continue its fundamental operations. There is a high degree of interdependence among these groups, and any dissatisfaction or other serious disruption may threaten the very existence of the firm. Thus, shareholders and investors, employees, customers, and suppliers, as well as public stakeholders, such as government and the community, are primary stakeholders.[11] Balancing the needs and perspectives of primary stakeholders is a strategic imperative, as one group's dissatisfaction or withdrawal from the relationship can cause significant ramifications throughout the entire business. In the late 1990s, 185,000 union workers walked off their jobs at United Parcel Service (UPS) and staged the biggest labor strike of the decade. The strike lasted 18 days, cost UPS nearly $775 million in lost revenue, created a wave of media reports, and caused a crisis of customer confidence in UPS.[12]

Senesco promotes its advancement to primary stakeholders including customers and investors. The Company has found a way to double the shelf life of food crops.

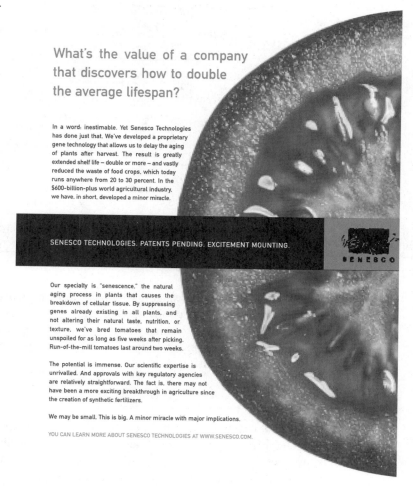

What's the value of a company that discovers how to double the average lifespan?

In a word: inestimable. Yet Senesco Technologies has done just that. We've developed a proprietary gene technology that allows us to delay the aging of plants after harvest. The result is greatly extended shelf life – double or more – and vastly reduced the waste of food crops, which today runs anywhere from 20 to 30 percent. In the $600-billion-plus world agricultural industry, we have, in short, developed a minor miracle.

SENESCO TECHNOLOGIES. PATENTS PENDING. EXCITEMENT MOUNTING.

SENESCO

Our specialty is "senescence," the natural aging process in plants that causes the breakdown of cellular tissue. By suppressing genes already existing in all plants, and not altering their natural taste, nutrition, or texture, we've bred tomatoes that remain unspoiled for as long as five weeks after picking. Run-of-the-mill tomatoes last around two weeks.

The potential is immense. Our scientific expertise is unrivalled. And approvals with key regulatory agencies are relatively straightforward. The fact is, there may not have been a more exciting breakthrough in agriculture since the creation of synthetic fertilizers.

We may be small. This is big. A minor miracle with major implications.

YOU CAN LEARN MORE ABOUT SENESCO TECHNOLOGIES AT WWW.SENESCO.COM.

Secondary stakeholders, although they influence and/or are affected by the company, are neither engaged in economic exchanges with the firm nor fundamental to its daily survival. Media and special-interest groups are usually considered secondary stakeholders. These groups, however, can have a dramatic influence on a firm.[13] For example, after the *Exxon Valdez* spilled 11 million gallons of oil into Alaskan waters—destroying wildlife and ruining the local fishing industry for years—environmental groups encouraged Exxon customers to cut up their credit cards and send them back to the company to protest its handling of the disaster. Nearly twenty thousand Exxon customers did so, demonstrating the

Ranking of Stakeholder
Importance

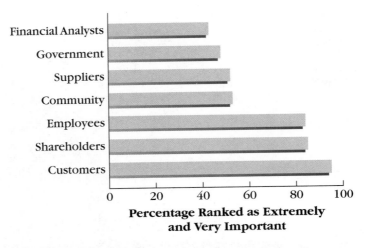

Percentage Ranked as Extremely
and Very Important

Source: Walker Information, *Stakeholder Management Around the World* (Indianapolis, IN: Walker
Information Global Network, 1999). Reprinted by permission of Walker Information.

pressure that secondary stakeholders can put on a business.[14] In differentiating
between primary and secondary stakeholders, it is important for managers to understand that although primary groups may present more day-to-day concerns,
secondary groups cannot be ignored or consistently given less consideration in
the corporate citizenship process.

Stakeholders Around the World

Stakeholder management has become a worldwide phenomenon on two levels.
First, large, progressive companies in most economically developed nations have
embraced the stakeholder model. Second, as more firms conduct business overseas, they encounter the complexity of stakeholder issues and relationships in tandem with other business operations and decisions. This section briefly explores
both concerns.

   In the Walker Information survey, 63 percent of the executives from around
the world recognized the term *stakeholder* as it relates to business organizations
(Figure 3.4). Executives in South Africa, Canada, and the United States had the
highest recognition levels, with Europe, Asia, the Middle East, and Latin America
following. The study concluded that South Africa is the most "stakeholder savvy,"
as company executives there are more aware of the term, take stakeholders into
account for business planning, and link stakeholder measures and issues to other
business outcomes.[15]

   Although general awareness of stakeholders appears to be relatively high
around the world, the importance of stakeholders varies from country to country.

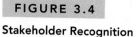

FIGURE 3.4

Stakeholder Recognition Around the World

Latin America
Middle East
Asia
Europe
United States
Canada
South Africa

0   20   40   60   80   100

Percentage Familiar with Term Stakeholder

Source: Walker Information, *Stakeholder Management Around the World* (Indianapolis, IN: Walker Information Global Network, 1999). Reprinted by permission of Walker Information.

In the United States, Canada, and South Africa, employee and customer interests are considered to be nearly equal in importance. Government stakeholders receive greater attention in the Middle East and Latin America than in other parts of the world. In Japan, cultural and legal traditions mean that companies are tightly connected to a number of interrelated stakeholders, including customers, financial institutions, and suppliers. The law in Great Britain obliges British firms to include the interests of employees in strategic plans and decision making. Finally, publicly traded firms in Germany must have employees on second-tier boards of directors.[16]

International business transactions and investments have always entailed more risk and complexity than domestic activities. Although global economic conditions create incentives for market entry and expansion strategies, the environmental and stakeholder factors affecting these strategies must be fully considered. For example, a business expanding into another country will encounter unfamiliar laws, different consumer values, and other issues that create confusion and require adjustments in business philosophy and practice. Although businesses are cognizant of the economic opportunities available through international efforts, fewer firms may have invested resources to fully integrate stakeholder concerns into the business planning process. Other companies may become mired in the age-old dilemma of deciding between local values and customs and those of their country of origin.[17]

Although decision makers bring experience and knowledge to the development and implementation of an international business strategy, there are always gaps in information that can lead to lapses in judgment, unintended consequences, and strategic errors. The decision to enter and remain in a region of the world can promote environmental uncertainty and instability, naturally leading managers to seek guidance on analysis and planning activities. This expertise may derive from sources either within or outside the organization, such as industry and country reports, trade show conversations, governmental repositories, company history, and primary research studies.[18] Thus, understanding the attributes of various global stakeholders may require a more thorough and formal information search than what is conducted with domestic stakeholders.

Despite this complexity, global stakeholders may be granted less attention because of the geographic and often cultural distance between them and a company. However, managers must ensure that they are given due consideration. As some companies have learned, global constituents can have a dramatic influence on business. Monsanto, a manufacturer of pharmaceutical and agricultural products, experienced a flood of criticism in Europe after a British researcher claimed laboratory rats' growth was stunted after they ate the company's genetically modified potatoes. Although the research was later deemed misleading, it brought widespread attention to Monsanto's bioengineering research and genetically modified crops. The protests eventually crossed the Atlantic, where many stakeholders, including the United States federal government, called for tighter regulations on genetically altered crops and foods. At one point in the fray, a Wall Street analyst valued Monsanto's $5-billion-a-year agricultural business unit at less than zero dollars.[19]

Perhaps the most compelling case for building relationships with nondomestic stakeholders occurred in Bhopal, India. In 1984, a gas leak at a pesticide plant owned by Union Carbide killed 3,800 people and injured many more. The Bhopal leak is still considered one of the worst industrial tragedies in global history. Officials at Union Carbide may have thought the Bhopal accident was finally behind them when the company paid the Indian government $470 million to settle a civil lawsuit in 1989. In late 1999, however, victims of the contamination filed a class action suit against Union Carbide and Warren Anderson, who was chairman of the board when the accident occurred. The suit, which claimed "depraved indifference to human life," was filed just as the company was finalizing merger plans with Dow Chemical. Anderson, who has retired to Florida, is not well known in the United States but still garners negative attention and notoriety in India. Every year since the disaster his likeness has been burned in effigy, and graffiti in the city government building still calls for his execution. To some observers, this long-standing reaction seems extreme because Anderson flew to Bhopal immediately after the accident to take moral responsibility for it. At the time, this was an unusual step for such a high-ranking officer to take. However, a recent study found that groundwater surrounding the factory site is still contaminated. More than 15 years after the leak, environmental and human rights groups continue to call for action against Union Carbide and Anderson, including proper restitution to victims and their families.[20]

As the Bhopal example illustrates, a successful stakeholder is not only meaningful to the focal organization but its claims must also pass scrutiny by the larger community, society, or relevant group. However, there may be stakeholders with the desire and means to influence a firm who have claims that are not legitimate or who use tactics that are not reasonable. For example, animal rights activists have thrown blood and paint on customers walking into department stores that sell furs. Although this type of activism clearly exerts power, its unreasonable and harmful tactics lessen the stores' willingness to create a dialog on the issues. The stakeholder process is negated because the stakeholder's attributes and tactics are not amenable to an effective and communicative relationship.

▶ *Stakeholder Attributes*[21]

Traditionally, companies have had an easier time understanding the issues stakeholders raise than their attributes and the tactics they use to affect organizational decision making. It is therefore necessary to understand both the content (specific issues) and process (actions, tactics) of each stakeholder relationship. In the preceding example, the animal rights activists used an unreasonable process to communicate the content of their beliefs. Although they are controversial, animal rights issues do have solid support from a number of citizens. One mechanism for understanding stakeholders and their potential salience to a firm involves assessing three stakeholder attributes, including power, legitimacy, and urgency.[22] This assessment provides one analytical tool to help managers uncover the motivations and needs of stakeholders and how they relate to the company and its interests. In addition, stakeholder actions may also sensitize the firm to issues and viewpoints not previously considered.

Power, legitimacy, and urgency are not constant, meaning stakeholder attributes can change over time and context. For example, there was a very strong "Buy American" sentiment in the United States in the 1980s, a time when Japanese manufacturers were making steady market share gains. Today, there is less consumer activism or retailer strategy on activism toward this nationalistic buying criterion.[23] Thus, although these stakeholders may still have a legitimate claim about buying from U.S. firms, they are neither using their power nor creating a sense of urgency regarding this issue today. It seems that nationalism, as it relates to retail purchasing, is no longer a key buying criteria. The U.S. economy was so strong throughout the 1990s that products from other countries were not seen as threatening.

Power   A stakeholder has **power** to the extent that it can gain access to coercive, utilitarian, or symbolic means to impose or communicate its views to an organization.[24] *Coercive power* involves the use of physical force, violence, or some type of restraint. *Utilitarian power* involves financial or material control, such as boycotts that affect a company's bottom line. Finally, *symbolic power* relies on the use of symbols that connote social acceptance, prestige, or some other attribute. Symbolism contained in letter writing campaigns, advertising messages, and web sites can be used to generate awareness and enthusiasm for more responsible business actions. In fact, the Internet has conferred tremendous power on stakeholder groups in recent years. A number of "hate sites" have been placed on the Internet by disgruntled stakeholders, especially customers and former employees, to share concerns about certain corporate behaviors. Richard B. Freeman, a Harvard labor economist, says, "With the Internet, information flows instantly, so even if we don't have more people concerned about companies, those who are can do more about it."[25] Symbolic power is the least threatening of the three types.

Utilitarian measures, including boycotts and lawsuits, are also fairly prevalent, although they often come about after symbolic strategies fail to yield the desired response. For example, the U.S. government, an important stakeholder for most firms, recently banned the importation of goods made by children under the age of fifteen through indentured or forced labor.[26] This action came about after the media and activist groups exposed widespread abuses in the apparel industry. This law carries financial—utilitarian—repercussions for firms that purchase products manufactured under unacceptable labor conditions.

Finally, some stakeholders use coercive power to communicate their message. During a rally to protest McDonald's as a symbol of global capitalism, worker exploitation, and environmental insensitivity, a handful of protesters stormed a McDonald's restaurant in London, eventually tearing down the hamburger chain's famous "golden arches." A company spokesperson said that although the company abhors violence and destruction, it plans to reopen the damaged restaurant and start a dialog with activists to counter false allegations and accusations. The spokesperson emphasized the local, not global, nature of McDonald's in the United Kingdom, where the company employs 70,000 people and does business with more than 6,000 suppliers.[27]

Legitimacy   The second stakeholder attribute is **legitimacy,** which is the perception or belief that a stakeholder's actions are proper, desirable, or appropriate within a given context.[28] This definition suggests that stakeholder actions are considered legitimate when claims are judged to be reasonable by other stakeholders and by society in general. Legitimacy is gained through the stakeholder's ability and willingness to explore the issue from a variety of perspectives and then to communicate in an effective and respectful manner on the desire for change. Thus, extremist views are less likely to be considered legitimate because these groups often use covert and inflammatory measures that overshadow the issues and create animosity. For example, extreme groups have destroyed property, threatened customers, and committed other acts of violence that ultimately discredit their legitimacy.[29] McDonald's remained open to stakeholder dialog after the London restaurant was destroyed, although other companies might have shunned further communication with the protesters, citing their irrational and dangerous behavior. Although an issue may be legitimate, such as environmental sensitivity, it is difficult for the claim to be evaluated independent of the way the stakeholder group communicates on it.

Urgency   Stakeholders exercise greater pressures on managers and organizations when they stress the **urgency** of their claims. Urgency is based on two characteristics: time sensitivity and the importance of the claim to the stakeholder. Time sensitivity usually heightens the stakeholder's effort and may compress an organization's ability to research and react to a claim. For example, protesters in Thailand formed a human chain around a hotel hosting the Asian Development Bank's annual meeting in 2000. The protest was aimed at increasing the bank's efforts to revitalize the regional economy and create more economic equity for the working poor. The protest was timed to occur during the bank's annual meeting, when officials would be developing new policies. Although bank officials did not formally meet with the protesters, the Asian Development Bank committed monies and projects to reduce poverty and other socioeconomic ills.[30]

In another example, labor and human rights are widely recognized as critical issues because they are fundamental to the well-being of people around the world. These rights have become a focal point for college student associations that have relentlessly criticized Nike, the world's leading shoe company, for its failure to improve the working conditions of suppliers and in not making information available to interested stakeholders. Student interest in these issues prompted several universities, including the University of Michigan, the University of Oregon, and Brown University, to join the Worker's Rights Consortium (WRC), an antisweatshop organization. The consortium has been critical of the corporate-sponsored Fair Labor Association's (FLA) efforts on behalf of worker rights. Nike, a member of the FLA, decided to pull millions of dollars of contributions and contracts from these schools because of their affiliation with WRC. Nike's director of college sports marketing indicated that Nike prefers university partners with similar goals and aspirations.[31]

In this case, students, who represent a major stakeholder of universities, were able to make their claims known and actionable by at least three universities. Because of the students' pressure, one of Nike's key stakeholders and customers, the universities, decided to support workers' rights by joining a powerful interest group, the WRC. Because the WRC has voiced criticism of Nike and other manufacturers, Nike felt the association between the interest group and its university customers was not aligned with its own interests and objectives.[32] Overall, stakeholders are considered more important to an organization when their issues are legitimate, their claims are urgent, and they can make use of their power on the organization. These attributes assist the firm and employees in determining the relative importance of specific stakeholders and making resource allocations for developing and managing the stakeholder relationship.

The Changing Nature of Student Activism

College campuses have long been hotbeds of political activism. Although campus protests no longer grab headlines the way the sit-ins and demonstrations of the 1960s did, college students are continuing the tradition of activism to express their views on today's issues and to bring about change. Student activism today seems to occur primarily through organized, civilized campus groups that discuss issues and strive to broaden their reach. These student protesters have diverse interests, ranging from freedom for Tibet to saving the rain forests. These groups represent virtually every social, cultural, and political interest, and their actions tend to focus on promoting awareness rather than advocating violence.

On campus, tolerance and acceptance of others seem more prevalent than the animosity that characterized the protests of the 1960s. Most colleges are comprised of professors and students with vastly different viewpoints. Although some students are opposed to the status quo, they generally accept that people are different as long as they do not oppress others. This greater acceptance of beliefs and views leads to less conflict. Although most students take the same classes that their grandparents and parents took, they can and do hold different views.

Increased education and the advent of the Internet have led to more informed protest efforts. Campus groups are more sophisticated and tactical than in years past. For example, United Students Against Sweatshops (USAS), with more than 1,000 student members from 100 universities, has employed a campaign of pickets, rallies, and sit-ins to pressure garment manufacturers to close down sweatshops that make their products. Combined with the endeavors of the government and business associations, this activism is actually making a dent in the $70 billion apparel industry's sweatshops. Moreover, the group's efforts prompted Nike, a leading manufacturer of college apparel, to release audits of the 600 plants worldwide that manufacture its shoes and apparel—warts and all.

Student protests are also far less violent than in previous years. The results of violent protests usually have a less-significant impact than effective use of politics, the media, and the Internet. Violence would not have helped the USAS to achieve such results, and indeed, it might have harmed the students' efforts to draw attention to the sweatshop workers' plight.

Performance with Stakeholders

Managing stakeholder relationships effectively requires careful attention to a firm's reputation and the effective handling of crisis situations. Motorola, a large telecommunications company, was not aware that one of its European distributors sold Motorola semiconductor chips to a manufacturer of landmine component parts. When Motorola, the recipient of numerous citizenship accolades, learned of the situation, it investigated, stopped selling to the distributor, and created better oversight for its distribution channels. In the process, Motorola was mindful of potential effects on its reputation with stakeholders.[33]

Although protests in recent years have been subject to less violence, there have been a few exceptions. The protests of the World Trade Organization (WTO) meeting in Seattle in January 2000, which included many students, resulted in $20 million worth of damage when the protest turned violent. A common belief shared by these protesters is that the WTO, International Monetary Fund, and World Bank promote a corrupt capitalist system throughout the world, especially in developing nations. The protesters hold big business responsible for much of the corruption. The protests held in Washington, D.C., in April 2000 were much more peaceful. For example, some protest groups used music and dance to communicate their opinions in nonviolent ways.

Another reason for changes in student activism is that times are more peaceful and stronger economically than in the 1960s and early 1970s. These trends mean different issues to protest and call for different means of protesting. Even finding support for causes has changed. The Internet has become a major gathering and launching ground for activism and Internet-savvy students. Through technology, students from around the world can protest together just as effectively as a group from the same hometown.

Although the twentieth century saw some of the most successful protests and activism of any time, such protests were declining by the end of the century. New technologies and media presence have facilitated student activism by allowing a smaller number to protest less violently and just as effectively as that of the past. Is it that students are protesting less, or are they just protesting better?

The Ten Most Activist College Campuses

1. Yale University
2. Pitzer College
3. Pennsylvania State University
4. Harvard University
5. Howard University
6. University of Michigan
7. Florida A & M University
8. Oberlin College
9. University of California at Los Angeles
10. University of Wisconsin, Madison

Sources:
John Balz, "Fight for Your Rights to Protest," *U. Magazine*, February 2000, pp. 14–16; Jack Brown, "Giving It the Old College Outcry," *Mother Jones*, 26 (September/October 2001): 20–21; Charlotte Houghteling, "Sweat and Tears," *Harvard International Review*, 21 (Fall 1999): 10–13; Andy Humm, "The Activists Who Shaped a Century," *Social Policy*, 30 (Winter 1999): 2; Louise Lee and Aaron Bernstein, "Who Says Student Protests Don't Matter?" *Business Week*, June 12, 2000, pp. 94–96; Tracy Moran, "Protesters and Police, Good Work!" *USA Today*, April 17, 2000, www.usatoday.com/; "Protesters March, Dance and Sing to Own Beat," *USA Today*, April 17, 2000, www.usatoday.com/; Murray Weidenbaum, "Myth of Decline and Fall of US Colleges," *Christian Science Monitor*, May 20, 1999, p. 11.

▶ Reputation Management

As our model of corporate citizenship suggests, there are short- and long-term outcomes associated with positive stakeholder relationships. One of the most significant of these is a positive reputation. Because a corporate reputation has the power to attract or repel customers, it can be either an asset or a liability.[34] Reputations take a long time to build or change, and it is far more important to monitor reputation than many companies believe. And, whereas a strong reputation may take years to build, it can be destroyed seemingly overnight if a company does not handle crisis situations to the satisfaction of the various stakeholders involved. For example, Bridgestone/Firestone, Inc., a subsidiary of Japan's Bridgestone Corporation, saw its corporate reputation nose-dive as a result of negative publicity surrounding the safety of some of its most popular tires. After the U.S. National Highway Traffic Safety Administration received more than 750 complaints and reports of 62 deaths linked to Firestone ATX and Wilderness AT tires, several retailers, including Sears, stopped selling the firm's tires. Bridgestone/Firestone recalled and offered to replace 6.5 million tires, but questions about the firm's handling of the recall—for example, not having enough replacement tires on hand to satisfy customers concerned about their safety—further eroded its reputation with consumers.[35] Once it is sullied, a reputation can take years to rebuild. Exxon still faces ill will and resentment over its handling of the *Exxon Valdez* oil spill more than a decade ago.[36]

Reputation management is the process of building and sustaining a company's good name and generating positive feedback from stakeholders.[37] Various trends may affect how companies manage their reputations. These trends include market factors, such as increased consumer knowledge and community access to information, and workplace factors, including technological advances, closer vendor relationships, and more inquisitive employees. These factors make companies more cautious about their actions because increased scrutiny in this area requires more attention from management. A company needs to understand these factors and how to properly address them in order to achieve a strong reputation. These factors have also helped companies recognize a link between corporate reputation

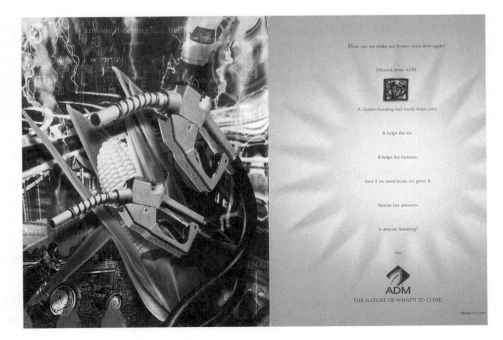

Archer-Daniels-Midland enhances its reputation by promoting its commitment to produce cleaner burning fuel made from corn.

TABLE 3.2

Reputation Measures

Reputation List	Conducted by	Groups Surveyed	Primary Purpose
100 Best Companies to Work for in America	Robert Lebering & Milton Moskowitz and Hewitt Associates	*Fortune* companies' employees and top managers	Publication
America's Most Admired Companies	*Fortune* magazine and Clark Martire & Bartolomeo	Company officers, directors, and analysts of *Fortune* 500 companies	Publication
Corporate Branding Index	Corporate Branding LLC	Vice president-level executives and above in the top 20 percent of U.S. businesses	Customized for clients
Corporate Reputation Index	Delahaye Medialink	Print and broadcast media	Sold as syndicated research
Maximizing Corporate Reputation	Burston-Marsteller	CEOs, executives, board members, financial community, government officials, business media, and consumers	Customized for clients
Reputation Quotient	Reputation Institute and Harris Interactive	General public	Customized for clients
World's Most Respected Companies	Pricewaterhouse Coopers	CEOs from 75 countries	Publication

Sources: Christy Eidson and Melissa Master, "Who Makes the Call?" *Across the Board,* 27 (March 2000): 16+; Klein, "Measure What Matters," *Communication World,* 16 (October/November 1999): 32+; Prema Nakra, "Corporate Reputation Management: 'CRM' with a Strategic Twist," *Public Relations Quarterly,* 45 (Summer 2000): 35+.

and competitive advantage. If these trends are dealt with wisely, a firm can position itself positively in stakeholders' minds, and thus create a competitive advantage.[38]

The importance of corporate reputation has created a need for accurate reputation measures. As indicated in Table 3.2, business publications, research firms, consultants, and public relations agencies have established a foothold in the new field of reputation management through research and lists of "the most reputable" firms. However, some questions have arisen as to who can best determine corporate reputation. For example, some measures survey only chief executives, whereas others also elicit perceptions from the general public. Although executives may be biased toward a firm's financial performance, the general public may lack experience or data on which to evaluate a company's reputation. Due to the

FIGURE 3.5

Reputation Management Process

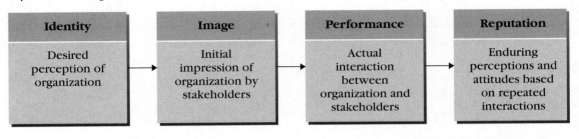

Identity	Image	Performance	Reputation
Desired perception of organization	Initial impression of organization by stakeholders	Actual interaction between organization and stakeholders	Enduring perceptions and attitudes based on repeated interactions

proliferation of methodologies that confuse and weaken the credibility of reputation measures, the Council of Public Relations Firms is considering the development of a standard measure. Regardless of how it is measured, reputation is the result of a process involving an organization and various constituents.[39]

The process of reputation management involves four components that work together: organizational identity, image, performance, and ultimately, reputation (see Figure 3.5).[40] Organizational identity refers to how an organization wants to be viewed by its stakeholders, whereas organizational image is how stakeholders interpret the various aspects of a company in order to form an overall impression of it. Organizational performance involves the actual interaction between the company and its stakeholders. The interaction of organizational image and performance result in organizational reputation, the collective view of all stakeholders after their image of the firm is shaped through interactions with the company.

In order to build and manage a good reputation, these four areas must be aligned. Companies must manage identity and culture by pinpointing those standards and responsibilities that will allow them to achieve their objectives, work with stakeholders effectively, and continuously monitor and change for effectiveness.[41] Ford Motor Company, for example, has embraced quality as a core value and highlighted this value in advertising to foster an identity associated with quality. Companies must also manage their image by communicating their identity to all stakeholders. This will help align the company's identity with stakeholders' image of the company and thus make it easier to live up to stakeholders' expectations. Because Ford was identified with the slogan "Quality is job #1," consumers and other stakeholders had a positive image of Ford and its automobiles. Performance must be managed by ensuring that organizational operations are consistent with the image that the company has built up in stakeholders' minds. At Ford, this effort involved consumers' actual use and evaluation of cars, their quality, and other performance indicators. Finally, stakeholders will reassess their views of the company based on how the company has actually performed. This results in the enduring and collective attitudes that stakeholders have toward the company. For these reasons, Ford took dramatic steps to protect its reputation (and shield itself from liability lawsuits) after Bridgestone/Firestone recalled millions of truck tires due to concerns about their safety. Because these tires were installed as factory equipment on many Ford trucks and sport utility vehicles, including the best-selling Explorer, Ford executives feared growing publicity surrounding the crisis would affect the firm's sales and reputation for quality and safety. Ford began running advertisements reassuring customers that it would replace recalled tires on Ford vehicles, even suspending production at several plants in order to free up 70,000 replacement tires. The company also pressured Bridgestone/Firestone to resolve the crisis as quickly as possible.[42] Thus, all these elements must be continually implemented in order to ensure that the company's reputation is being maximized through community relations. However, most firms will, at one time or another, experience crisis situations that threaten or harm this reputation. How a company reacts, responds, and learns from the situation is indicative of its commitment and implementation of corporate citizenship.

▶ *Crisis Management* [43]

Organizational crises are far-reaching events that can have dramatic effects on both the organization and its stakeholders. Along with the industrialization of society, companies and their products have become ever more complex and therefore more susceptible to crisis. As a result, disasters—like the gas leak in Bhopal—and crisis situations—like Firestone's tire safety issue and product contamination issues at Johnson & Johnson, Coca-Cola, and Jack in the Box—are increasingly common events from which few organizations are exempt. Of course, most crises are not purposeful—meaning there was no intent to cause damage. When an explosion at a Ford Motor manufacturing plant in Michigan killed six people and injured fourteen others, Bill Ford, the new chairman of the board, rushed to the site, consoled families, visited the triage center, and spoke to reporters. The media commended his actions.[44] However, a subsequent investigation uncovered significant safety and health violations that eventually resulted in a monetary sanction against Ford, the largest ever levied under Michigan's Occupational Safety and Health Act. Later, Ford would agree to a $7 million settlement as well as programmatic changes and training in the safety and health areas.[45]

It is critical for companies to manage crises effectively because research suggests that these events are a leading cause of organizational mortality. What follows are some key issues to consider in **crisis management,** the process of handling a high-impact event characterized by ambiguity and the need for swift action. In most cases, the crisis situation will not be handled in a completely effective or

ineffective manner. Thus, a crisis usually leads to both success and failure outcomes for a business and its stakeholders.[46]

Organizational crises are characterized by a threat to a company's high-priority
goals, surprise to its membership, and stakeholder demands for a short response
time. The nature of crises requires a firm's leadership to communicate in an often
stressful, emotional, uncertain, and demanding context. Crises are very difficult on
a company's stakeholders as well. For this reason, the firm's stakeholders, especially its employees, shareholders, customers, government regulators, the media,
competitors, and creditors, will closely scrutinize communication after a crisis.
Hence, crises have widespread implications not only for the organization but also
for each group affected by the crisis.

To better understand how crises develop and move toward resolution, some
researchers use a medical analogy to better understand these events. Using the
analogy, the organization proceeds through chronological recovery stages much
like a patient recovers from an illness. The prodromal stage is a precrisis period
during which warning signs may exist. Next is the acute stage, in which the actual
crisis occurs. During the third, or chronic, stage, the business is required to sufficiently explain its actions in order to move to the final stage, crisis resolution. Figure 3.6 illustrates these stages. Although the stages are conceptually distinct, some
crises happen so quickly and without warning that the organization may move
from the prodromal to acute stage within minutes. Many organizations faced this
situation after terrorists hijacked airplanes and crashed into the World Trade Center and the Pentagon on September 11, 2001.

One of the fundamental difficulties that a company faces is how to communicate effectively to stakeholders during and after a disaster. Once crisis strikes, the
firm's stakeholders need a quick response in the wake of the duress and confusion. They need information about how the company plans to resolve the crisis, as
well as what each constituent can do to mitigate its own negative effects. If a company is slow to respond, stakeholders may feel as though the company does not

FIGURE 3.6

Crisis Management Process

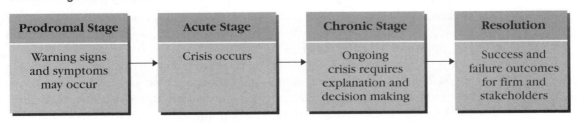

care about their needs or is not remorseful about the crisis. Furthermore, a delayed response may in fact increase the suffering of particular stakeholder groups. For instance, some stakeholders may take on considerable debt due to medical expenses as a result of the crisis. Therefore, rapid response to stakeholders is central to any crisis resolution strategy so that these groups can plan their recovery.

Ironically, crisis events are often so chaotic that a company's leadership may not be certain of the cause of the situation before the media and other relevant groups demand a statement. Thus, it is not surprising for organizations to begin their crisis response with some degree of ambiguity in their statements. In fact, some crisis theorists advise companies to avoid too much detail in their initial response due to the embarrassment that results from changing positions later in the crisis when more information is available. Still, stakeholder groups want and, as a matter of safety in some cases, need access to whatever information the firm can share. Although tensions between the public's needs and the organization's fear of litigation can hamper an organization's willingness to communicate, the demand for information in such situations is unyielding.

Not only should the firm's leadership make a public statement quickly, but it is also necessary for the organization to communicate about specific issues to stakeholder groups. First, leadership should express concern and/or remorse for the event. Second, the organization should delineate guidelines regarding how it intends to address the crisis so that stakeholders can be confident that the situation will not escalate or recur. Finally, the company should provide explicit criteria to stakeholders regarding how each group will be compensated for any negative effects they experience as a result of the crisis. Many companies, however, overlook these three essential conditions of crisis management. More often, they focus on minimizing harm to the organization's image, denying responsibility for the crisis, and shifting blame away from the organization and toward other stakeholder groups. Although this may be an appropriate strategy when the firm is not actually responsible, too often companies choose this course of action under the stress of the crisis without expressing sufficient concern for their stakeholders.

The varying communication needs and levels of concern of stakeholders during and after a crisis often hamper effective communication. The firm's leadership should try to communicate as much accurate information to these groups as possible to minimize their uncertainty. When a firm fails to do so, its credibility, legitimacy, and reputation in the eyes of stakeholders often suffer. Adding to the complexity of communication challenges, the needs of various stakeholder groups may conflict. For instance, the needs of customers who become ill as a result of a contaminated product and their desire to have medical bills paid may be at odds with the company's ability to bolster its stock price to satisfy shareholders. Some stakeholders will obviously have more opportunities than others to voice their concerns after a crisis. Victims and the general public rarely have an opportunity to meet with the organization's leadership after a crisis. Conversely, the organization's stockholders and employees will likely have a greater opportunity to express their views about the crisis and therefore may have their ideas accepted by management. Some researchers suggest that, due to this ability to communicate directly with leadership, internal stakeholder needs often take precedence over those of external stakeholders. Organizations have a responsibility to manage the competing interests of stakeholders to ensure that all stakeholder groups are treated fairly in the aftermath of a crisis. Responsible companies try to balance the needs of their stakeholders rather than favoring some groups over others. Organizations that fail to accomplish this communication function risk alienating stakeholder groups and intensifying the negative media attention toward the company. For many reasons, including effective crisis management, organizations need to understand and pursue solid and mutually beneficial relationships with stakeholders.

Development of Stakeholder Relationships

Relationships of any type, whether they involve family, friends, coworkers, or companies, are founded on principles of trust, commitment, and communication. They also are associated with a certain degree of time, interaction, and shared expectations. For instance, we do not normally speak of "having a relationship" with someone we have just met. We even differentiate between casual acquaintances, work colleagues, and close friends.

In business, the concept of relationships has gained much acceptance. Instead of just pursuing one-time transactions, companies are now searching for ways to develop long-term and collaborative relationships with their customers and business partners.[47] Throughout the 1990s, many companies focused on relationships with suppliers, buyers, employees, and others directly involved in economic exchange. These relationships involve investments of several types. Some investments are tangible, such as buildings, equipment, new tools, and other elements dedicated to a particular relationship. For example, Hormel Foods recently implemented an Internet-based procurement system. Through this system, Hormel's suppliers can view the firm's production schedules and revise their own business operations accordingly.[48] Other investments are less tangible, such as the time, effort, trust, and commitment required to develop a relationship. Although Hormel's suppliers will need the electronic infrastructure and employee knowledge to use the new procurement process, these suppliers must also trust that their relationship with Hormel is solid and will be worth these investments. For example, some suppliers may have concerns that their investment in Hormel's system may not be transferable to other business opportunities and partnerships. They may also have concerns about information privacy.

Whereas tangible investments are often customized for a specific business relationship, intangible efforts have a more lucid and permeable quality. Although corporate citizenship involves tangible activities and other communication signals, the key to good stakeholder relationships resides in trust, communication quality, and mutual respect. As a company strives to develop a dialog and solid relationship with one stakeholder, investments and lessons learned through the process should add value to other stakeholder relationships. These efforts result in **social capital,** an asset that resides in relationships and is characterized by mutual goals and trust.[49] Like financial and intellectual capital, social capital facilitates and smooths internal and external transactions and processes. For example, social capital among companies in the chemical industry led to the development of Responsible Care, a progressive and voluntary program of environmental, health, and safety (EHS) standards in 1988. Several high-profile accidents, like the one in Bhopal, India, had eroded chemical companies' social capital with their communities, the government, and other stakeholder groups. The Chemical Manufacturers Association implemented the program to promote stronger EHS performance and to "improve the legislative, regulatory, market, and public interest climate for the industry." Thus, Responsible Care was aimed at advancing internal company operations as well as various stakeholder relationships.[50] Unlike financial and intellectual capital, however, social capital is not tangible or the obvious property of one organization. In this same regard, corporate citizenship is not compartmentalized or reserved for a few issues or stakeholders, but should have the companywide strategic focus discussed in Chapter 1. This section and Table 3.3 discuss best practices for developing mutually beneficial stakeholder relationships.[51]

The first step in developing stakeholder relationships involves acknowledging and actively monitoring the concerns of all legitimate stakeholders. Thus, a company must have a process for identifying and ordering the myriad of claims and stakes on its business and, as appropriate, taking these interests into account in decision making, operations, and strategy. Although no company is obligated to act on every claim, all claims should be evaluated before a firm decides to ignore or pass judgment on them. In order to make accurate assumptions about stakeholders, managers need to listen to and openly communicate with stakeholders about their respective concerns and contributions. Getting to know stakeholders smoothes the communication process and eventually leads to more consistency in values and expectations between a company and a particular stakeholder.[52]

Based on an accurate understanding of interests and claims, a firm should adopt processes and modes of behavior that are sensitive to the concerns and capabilities of each stakeholder. For example, although America Online (AOL) tracks and maintains records regarding the movements of subscribers throughout its system, it has chosen not to sell this data to third parties. Like many subscriber-based companies, AOL does sell subscriber names and addresses to other firms (a practice it discloses in its online privacy policy), but the firm's executives felt that going beyond this level would be inappropriate because of consumer concerns about privacy.[53] As discussed earlier, not all stakeholders are equal. For example, there are regulations

TABLE 3.3

Best Practices for Developing Stakeholder Relationships

Step	Practice
1.	Acknowledge and actively monitor the concerns of all legitimate stakeholders.
2.	As appropriate, take stakeholder interests in account in decision making, operations, and strategy.
3.	Listen to and openly communicate with stakeholders about their respective concerns and contributions and about any risks they assume because of involvement with the company.
4.	Adopt processes and modes of behavior that are sensitive to the concerns and capabilities of each stakeholder.
5.	Work cooperatively with other entities, both public and private, to insure that risks and harms arising from corporate activities are minimized and, where they cannot be avoided, appropriately compensated.
6.	Avoid activities that might jeopardize inalienable human rights (e.g., the right to life) or give rise to risks that, if clearly understood, would be patently unacceptable to relevant stakeholders.
7.	Acknowledge and openly address the potential conflicts between the company and its social responsibilities and stakeholder interests.
8.	Invest in education, training, and information that improve understanding and relationships with stakeholders.
9.	Periodically assess relationships with stakeholders and use the results for improving the corporate citizenship effort.

Sources: Adapted from "Principles of Stakeholder Management," Clarkson Centre for Business Ethics, http://mgmt.utoronto.ca/~stake/Principles.htm, (accessed) October 21, 2001; Malcolm McIntosh, Deborah Leipziger, Keith Jones, and Gill Coleman, *Corporate Citizenship: Successful Strategies for Responsible Companies* (London: Financial Times Management, 2000).

and legal requirements that govern some aspects of stakeholder relationships, such as holding shareholder meetings and disclosing financial outcomes. Business communications, such as advertising, press releases, and web sites, have the potential to reach many stakeholder groups, whereas formal proceedings may be the modus operandi for dealing with government officials. Regardless of the contact method, information should be communicated consistently across all stakeholders. This is especially salient when a company is facing a complex or crisis situation.

After the safety concerns with product tampering, Tylenol redesigned its products (producing caplets, tablets, and gelcaps instead of capsules) and triple safety sealed its packaging—(1) glued flaps on the outer box, (2) a tight plastic neck seal, and (3) a strong inner foil seal over the mouth of the bottle.

Another key aspect of strong relationships is the willingness to acknowledge and openly address potential conflicts. This is very important because it is likely that some degree of negotiation and conciliation will be needed to align the company with stakeholder interests. Sometimes, the firm will need to find balance among competing stakeholder concerns and claims. A classic conflict arises between investors' needs for a return on their investment and other stakeholders' expectations. Investors may believe that closing an underperforming manufacturing plant is in the company's best financial interest. At the same time, however, the plant's employees may worry that such a closure will jeopardize their own financial stability, whereas members of the community may fear that it will threaten the community's economic health. Thus, the company will need to understand potential ramifications of the plant closure on other stakeholders, such as eliminating employee jobs, creating economic effects within the community, needing fewer suppliers, asking customers to find a new product provider, or answering to the media. In another type of potential conflict, managers and other decision makers must balance their personal and professional needs with those of their employer. Because they also belong to one primary stakeholder of the firm, responsible managers and executives ensure that their decisions and actions are transparent and subject to scrutiny in the best interest of all stakeholders. This special situation raises questions of corporate governance, which is discussed in Chapter 6.

Investments in education, training, and information will improve employees' understanding of and relationships with specific stakeholders. For example, several companies in the United Kingdom have invested in deaf awareness training for employees. Barclays Bank trained its managers and cashiers to better serve hearing-impaired customers. Sainsbury's, a supermarket chain, offered courses in sign language to its employees.[54] Employee training related to stakeholder needs and concerns has the dual benefit of improving relationships with stakeholders while enhancing employee skills and knowledge.

Finally, a company's relationships with stakeholders need to be periodically assessed. Informal methods can be used on an ongoing basis to gauge current relationship strengths and opportunities for improvement. Conversations between salespeople and customers and between purchasing agents and suppliers can serve as informal contact methods. Many companies currently use more formal methods, such as exit interviews, open-door policies, and confidential and toll-free telephone hot lines to get feedback from a primary stakeholder—employees. Questionnaires, focus groups, web sites, and other research tools can be used to gain feedback from customers, members of the local community, suppliers and business partners, investors, and other stakeholders. Royal Dutch/Shell, the global petroleum company, produces an annual report detailing its commitment to corporate citizenship. The report, which is available in printed form and on the firm's web site, employs a "Tell Shell" feedback mechanism for generating questions, criticisms, and other inquiries from its constituents. The report also discloses results of the Shell People Survey, which gathers opinions from employees on a range of issues, including the company's commitment to ethical values and environmental standards. Finally, the report includes an independent evaluation and verification of the company's claims.[55] As the Shell example demonstrates, the results of both formal and informal assessment should be made available to internal and external stakeholders for improving the corporate citizenship effort and stakeholder relationships. By sharing feedback, both positive and critical, a company is engaging in the two-way dialog that characterizes the stakeholder model discussed earlier in this chapter.

Link Between Stakeholder Relationships and Corporate Citizenship

You may be wondering what motivations companies have for pursuing stakeholder relationships. As Table 3.3 indicates, a great deal of time, effort, and commitment goes into the process of developing mutual understanding among so many groups. Some companies have been accused of "window dressing," or publicizing their stakeholder efforts without having a true commitment behind it. For example, The Body Shop, which has received much positive attention for its social responsibility efforts, has also been accused of selectively communicating information and hiding less-favorable company issues.[56] As was discussed in Chapter 1, citizenship is relational and involves the views and stakes of a number of groups. Stakeholders are engaged in the relationships that both challenge and support a company's citizenship efforts. Thus, without a solid understanding of stakeholders and their interests, a firm may miss important trends and changes in its environment and not achieve strategic citizenship.

Rather than holding all companies to one standard, our approach to evaluating performance and effectiveness resides in the specific expectations and actual results that develop between each organization and its stakeholders. Max Clarkson, an influential contributor to our understanding of stakeholders, sums up this view:

> Performance is what counts. Performance can be measured and evaluated. Whether a corporation and its management are motivated by enlightened self-interest, common sense or high standards of ethical behavior cannot be determined by empirical methodologies available today. These are not questions that can be answered by economists, sociologists, psychologists, or any other kind of social scientist. They are interesting questions, but they are not relevant when it comes to evaluating a company's performance in managing its relationships with its stakeholder groups.[57]

Although critics and some researchers may seek answers and evidence as to the motivations of business for corporate citizenship, we are interested in what companies are actually doing that is positive, negative, or neutral for their stakeholders and their interests. The Reactive-Defensive-Accommodative-Proactive Scale (Table 3.4) provides a method for assessing a company's strategy and performance with each stakeholder. This scale is based on a continuum of strategy options and performance outcomes with respect to stakeholders.[58] This evaluation can take place as stakeholder issues arise or are identified. Therefore, it is possible for

TABLE 3.4

The Reactive-Defensive-Accommodative-Proactive Scale

Rating	Strategy	Performance
Reactive	Deny responsibility	Doing less than required
Defensive	Admit responsibility, but fight it	Doing the least that is required
Accommodative	Accept responsibility	Doing all that is required
Proactive	Anticipate responsibility	Doing more than is required

Source: Max B. E. Clarkson, "A Stakeholder Framework for Analyzing and Evaluating Corporate Social Performance," *Academy of Management Review,* 20 (January 1995): 92–117.

one company to be rated at several different levels because of varying performance and transitions over time. For example, a poorly handled crisis situation may
provide feedback for continuous improvement that creates more satisfactory performance in the future. Or, a company may demonstrate a proactive stance toward
employees, yet be defensive with consumer activists.

The reactive approach involves denying responsibility and doing less than is
required. This approach can be characterized by "fighting it all the way."[59] A firm
that fails to invest in safety and health measures for employees is denying its responsibilities. An organization with a defensive strategy acknowledges reluctantly
and partially the responsibility issues that may be raised by its stakeholders. A firm
in this category fulfills basic legal obligations and demonstrates the minimal citizenship discussed in Chapter 1. With an accommodative strategy, a company attempts to satisfy stakeholder demands by doing all that is required and may be
seen as progressive because it is obviously open to this expanded model of business relationships.[60] Today, many organizations are giving money and other
resources to community organizations as a way of demonstrating corporate citizenship. Finally, the proactive approach not only accepts, but also anticipates,
stakeholder interests. In this case, a company sincerely aligns legitimate stakeholder views with its responsibilities and will do more than is required to meet
them.[61] Hoechst, a German life sciences company, has gradually assumed the
proactive orientation with communities in which it operates. The initiation of a
community discussion group led to information sharing and trust building and
helped transform Hoechst into a society-driven company.[62]

The Reactive-Defensive-Accommodative-Proactive Scale is useful because it
evaluates real practice and allows an organization to see its strengths and weaknesses within each stakeholder relationship. Results from this stakeholder assessment should be included in the **corporate citizenship audit,** which assesses and
reports a firm's performance in adopting a strategic focus for fulfilling the economic, legal, ethical, and philanthropic social responsibilities expected of it by its
stakeholders. Chapter 12 takes an extensive look at the corporate citizenship audit. Because stakeholders are so important to the concept of corporate citizenship, as well as to business success, Chapters 4–10 are devoted to exploring
significant stakeholder relationships and issues.

Summary

Stakeholders refer to those people and groups who have a "stake" in some aspect
of a company's products, operations, markets, industry, and outcomes. The relationship between organizations and their stakeholders is a two-way street.

The historical assumption that the key objective of business is profit maximization led to the belief that business is accountable primarily to investors and

others involved in the market and economic aspects of the organization. In the latter half of the twentieth century, perceptions of business accountability evolved to include both market constituencies that are directly involved and affected by the business purpose (e.g., investors, employees, customers, and other business partners) and nonmarket constituencies that are not always directly tied to issues of profitability and performance (e.g., the general community, media, government, special-interest groups).

In the input-output model of stakeholder relationships, investors, employees, and suppliers provide inputs for a company to transform into outputs that benefit customers. This approach assumes a relatively mechanistic, simplistic, and non-stakeholder view of business. The stakeholder model assumes a two-way relationship between the firm and a host of stakeholders. This approach recognizes additional stakeholders and acknowledges the two-way dialog and effects that exist with a firm's internal and external environment.

Primary stakeholders are fundamental to a company's operations and survival and include shareholders and investors, employees, customers, suppliers, and public stakeholders, such as government and the community. Secondary stakeholders influence and/or are affected by the company but are neither engaged in transactions with the firm nor essential for its survival.

As more firms conduct business overseas, they encounter the complexity of stakeholder issues and relationships in tandem with other business operations and decisions. Although general awareness of the concept of stakeholders is relatively high around the world, the importance of stakeholders varies from country to country.

A stakeholder has power to the extent that it can gain access to coercive, utilitarian, or symbolic means to impose or communicate its views to the organization. Such power may be coercive, utilitarian, or symbolic. Legitimacy is the perception or belief that a stakeholder's actions are proper, desirable, or appropriate within a given context. Stakeholders exercise greater pressures on managers and organizations when they stress the urgency of their claims. These attributes can change over time and context.

Reputation management is the process of building and sustaining a company's good name and generating positive feedback from stakeholders. The process of reputation management involves the interaction of organizational identity (how the firm wants to be viewed), organizational image (how stakeholders initially perceive the firm), organizational performance (actual interaction between the company and stakeholders), and organizational reputation (the collective view of stakeholders after interactions with the company). Stakeholders will reassess their views of the company based on how the company has actually performed.

Crisis management is the process of handling a high-impact event characterized by ambiguity and the need for swift action. Some researchers describe an organization's progress through a prodromal, or precrisis, stage to the acute stage, chronic stage, and finally, crisis resolution. Stakeholders need a quick response with information about how the company plans to resolve the crisis, as well as what they can do to mitigate negative effects. It is also necessary to communicate specific issues to stakeholder groups, including remorse for the event, guidelines as to how the organization is going to address the crisis, and criteria regarding how stakeholder groups will be compensated for negative effects.

Companies are searching for ways to develop long-term, collaborative relationships with their customers and business partners. These relationships involve both tangible and intangible investments. Investments and lessons learned through the process of developing a dialog and relationship with one stakeholder should add value to other stakeholder relationships. These efforts result in social capital, an asset that resides in relationships and is characterized by mutual goals and trust.

The first step in developing stakeholder relationships is to acknowledge and actively monitor the concerns of all legitimate stakeholders. A firm should adopt processes and modes of behavior that are sensitive to the concerns and capabilities of each stakeholder. Information should be communicated consistently across all stakeholders. A firm should be willing to acknowledge and openly address potential conflicts. Investments in education, training, and information will improve employees' understanding of and relationships with stakeholders. Relationships with stakeholders need to be periodically assessed through both formal and informal means. Sharing feedback with stakeholders helps establish the two-way dialog that characterizes the stakeholder model.

The Reactive-Defensive-Accommodative-Proactive Scale provides a method for assessing a company's strategy and performance with one stakeholder. The reactive approach involves denying responsibility and doing less than is required. The defensive approach acknowledges only reluctantly and partially the responsibility issues that may be raised by the firm's stakeholders. The accommodative strategy attempts to satisfy stakeholder demands. The proactive approach accepts and anticipates stakeholder interests. Results from this stakeholder assessment should be included in the corporate citizenship audit, which assesses and reports a firm's performance in fulfilling the economic, legal, ethical, and philanthropic social responsibilities expected of it by its stakeholders.

input-output model

stakeholder model

primary stakeholders

secondary stakeholders

power

legitimacy

urgency

reputation management

crisis management

social capital

corporate citizenship audit

DISCUSSION QUESTIONS

1. Define *stakeholder* in your own terms. Compare your definition with the various conceptualizations presented in this chapter, including the historical perspectives in Table 3.1.

2. What is the difference between primary and secondary stakeholders? Why is it important for companies to make this distinction?

3. How do legitimacy, urgency, and power attributes positively and negatively affect a stakeholder's ability to develop relationships with organizations?

4. What is reputation management? Explain why companies are concerned about their reputation and its effects on stakeholders. What are the four elements of reputation management? Why is it important to manage these elements?

5. Define crisis management. What should a company facing a crisis do to satisfy its stakeholders and protect its reputation?

6. Describe the process of developing stakeholder relationships. What parts of the process seem most important? What parts seem most difficult?

7. What are the differences between the reactive, defensive, accommodative, and proactive approaches to stakeholder relationships? Using Table 3.4, assess Ford's response to the Firestone tire recall situation. Is this scale a good assessment tool for companies pursuing strategic corporate citizenship? Why or why not?

EXPERIENTIAL EXERCISE

Choose two companies in different industries and visit their respective web sites. Peruse these sites for information that is directed at three company stakeholders—employees, customers, and the media. For example, a company that places its annual reports online may be appealing primarily to the interests of investors. Make a list of the types of information that are on the site and indicate how the information might be used and perceived by these three stakeholder groups. What differences and similarities did you find between the two companies?

NOTES

1. "Class Action Over Plane Insect Spray," *The Daily Telegraph (Sydney)*, August 24, 2001, p. 22; "Pesticide Policy for International Flights Defended," *The Dominion (Wellington)*, May 17, 2001, p. 13; Chris Woodyard, "Fliers Fume Over Planes Treated with Pesticides," *USA Today*, September 10, 2001, pp. A11, A13.

2. Joanne B. Ciulla, *The Working Life: The Promise and Betrayal of Modern Work* (New York: Times Books, 2000).

3. Lee E. Preston, "Stakeholder Management and Corporate Performance," *Journal of Behavioral Economics*, 19, no. 4 (1990): 361–375.

4. American Productivity & Quality Center, *Community Relations: Unleashing the Power of Corporate Citizenship* (Houston, TX: American Productivity & Quality Center, 1998); Thomas Donaldson and Lee E. Preston, "The Stakeholder Theory of the Corporation: Concepts, Evidence and Implications," *Academy of Management Review,* 29 (January 1995): 65–91; Jaan Elias and J. Gregory Dees, "The Normative

Foundations of Business," Harvard Business School Publishing, June 10, 1997.

5. Theodore Levitt, *The Marketing Imagination* (New York: The Free Press, 1983).

6. Norman Bowie, "Empowering People as an End for Business," in *People in Corporations: Ethical Responsibilities and Corporate Effectiveness,* ed. Georges Enderle, Brenda Almond, and Antonio Argandona (Dordrecht, The Netherlands: Kluwer Academic Press, 1990), pp. 105-112.

7. Chris Marsden, "The New Corporate Citizenship of Big Business: Part of the Solution to Sustainability?" *Business and Society Review,* 105 (Spring 2000): 9-25.

8. Donaldson and Preston, "The Stakeholder Theory of the Corporation."

9. Frederick F. Reichheld, *The Loyalty Effect: The Hidden Force Behind Growth, Profits, and Lasting Value* (Boston: Harvard Business School Press, 1996).

10. Randy Brooks, "Why Loyal Employees and Customers Improve the Bottom Line," *Journal for Quality and Participation,* 23 (March/April 2000): 40-44.

11. Max B. E. Clarkson, "A Stakeholder Framework for Analyzing and Evaluating Corporate Social Performance," *Academy of Management Review,* 20 (January 1995): 92-117.

12. Kate Miller, "Issues Management: The Link Between Organization Reality and Public Perception," *Public Relations Quarterly,* 44 (Summer 1999): 5-11.

13. Clarkson, "A Stakeholder Framework for Analyzing and Evaluating Corporate Social Performance."

14. O. C. Ferrell, John Fraedrich, and Gwyneth Vaughn, "The Wreck of the Exxon Valdez," in *Business Ethics: Ethical Decision Making and Cases,* 5th ed., edited by O. C. Ferrell, John Fraedrich, and Linda Ferrell (Boston: Houghton Mifflin, 2002), pp. 331-339; Tony Freemantle, "Exxon's Quagmire: Billion-Dollar Battle over Cleanup Costs Looms," *The Houston Chronicle,* September 3, 1995, p. 1.

15. Walker Information, *Stakeholder Management Around the World* (Indianapolis, IN: Walker Information Global Network, 1999).

16. Donaldson and Preston, "The Stakeholder Theory of the Corporation"; Walker Information, *Stakeholder Management Around the World.*

17. Thomas Donaldson and Thomas W. Dunfee, *Ties That Bind: A Social Contracts Approach to Business Ethics* (Boston: Harvard Business School Press, 1999).

18. Debbie Thorne LeClair, "Marketing Planning and the Policy Environment in the European Union," *International Marketing Review,* 17, no. 3 (2000): 189-211.

19. Carol Stavraka, "FDA Proposes New Biotech Rules," ResponsibilityInc.com, May 3, 2000, www.responsibilityinc.com/News/fdarules.html; David Stipp, "Is Monsanto's Biotech Worth Less Than a Hill of Beans?" *Fortune,* February 21, 2000, pp. 157-160.

20. Devin Leonard, "Bhopal Ghosts (Still) Haunt Union Carbide," *Fortune,* April 3, 2000, pp. 45-46.

21. This section is adapted from Isabelle Maignan and Debbie Thorne McAlister, "Socially Responsible Organizational Buying: Can Stakeholders Dictate Purchasing Policies?" The University of Nijmegen, working paper, 2001.

22. Ronald K. Mitchell, Bradley R. Agle, and Donna J. Wood, "Toward a Theory of Stakeholder Identification and Salience: Defining the Principle of Who and What Really Counts," *Academy of Management Review,* 22 (October 1997): 853-886.

23. Dana Frank, *Buy American: The Untold Story of Economic Nationalism* (Boston: Beacon, 1999).

24. Amitai Etzioni, *Modern Organizations* (Upper Saddle River, NJ: Prentice Hall, 1964).

25. Aaron Bernstein, "Too Much Corporate Power?" *Business Week,* September 11, 2000, pp. 144-158.

26. Treasury Advisory Committee on International Child Labor Enforcement, "Notices," *Federal Register,* March 6, 2000, 65 FR 11831.

27. Andrew Ward, "McDonald's Eager for Talks with Critics," *[London] Financial Times,* May 3, 2000, p. 3.

28. Mark C. Suchman, "Managing Legitimacy: Strategic and Institutional Approaches," *Academy of Management Review,* 20 (July 1995): 571-610.

29. Brad Knickerbock, "Activists Step Up War to 'Liberate' Nature," *Christian Science Monitor,* January 20, 1999, p. 4.

30. Joshua Kurlantzick, "Protestors Form Human Chain Outside ADB Meeting," *Agence France Presse,* May 8, 2000, via LEXIS®-NEXIS® Academic Universe.

31. Bennett Daviss, "Profits from Principles," *Futurist,* 33 (March 1999): 28-33; Carol Stavraka, "Could Nike's College Pull-Out Hurt Its Bottom Line?" ResponsibiliyInc.com, April 28, 2000, www.responsibilityinc.com/News/nikemoney.html.

32. Thomas Friedman, "Nike Boss Knight Is Right," *Denver Post,* June 21, 2000, p. B11.

33. James E. Post and Shawn L. Berman, "Global Corporate Citizenship in a Dot.com World," in *Perspectives on Corporate Citizenship*, ed. Jörg Andriof and Malcolm McIntosh (Sheffield, United Kingdom: Greenleaf Publishing, 2001): 66–82.

34. Ronald Alsop, "Corporate Reputations Are Earned with Trust, Reliability, Study Shows," *Wall Street Journal*, September 23, 1999, http://interactive.wsj.com.

35. Timothy Aeppel, "Bridgestone/Firestone Set to Replace 6.5 Million Tires," *Wall Street Journal*, August 10, 2000, http://interactive.wsj.com; Robert L. Simison, Norihiko Shirouzu, Timothy Aeppel, and Todd Zaun, "Logistics of Tire Recall, Investigation Cause Increasing Corporate Clashes," *Wall Street Journal*, August 28, 2000, http://interactive.wsj.com.

36. Alsop, "Corporate Reputations Are Earned with Trust, Reliability, Study Shows."

37. Jim Kartalia, "Technology Safeguards for a Good Corporate Reputation," *Information Executive*, 3 (September 1999): 4; Prema Nakra, "Corporate Reputation Management: 'CRM' with a Strategic Twist?" *Public Relations Quarterly*, 45 (Summer 2000): 35–42.

38. Allen M. Weiss, Erin Anderson, and Deborah J. MacInnis, "Reputation Management as a Motivation for Sales Structure Decisions," *Journal of Marketing*, 63 (October 1999): 74–89.

39. Christy Eidson and Melissa Master, "Who Makes the Call?" *Across the Board*, 37 (March 2000): 16+.

40. Alison Rankin Frost, "Brand vs. Reputation," *Communication World*, 16 (February/March 1999): 22–25.

41. Glen Peters, *Waltzing with the Raptors: A Practical Roadmap to Protecting Your Company's Reputation* (New York: John Wiley & Sons, Inc, 1999).

42. Aeppel, "Bridgestone/Firestone Set to Replace 6.5 Million Tires"; Simison, Shirouzu, Aeppel, and Zaun, "Logistics of Tire Recall, Investigation Cause Increasing Corporate Clashes."

43. Much of this section is adapted from Robert R. Ulmer and Timothy L. Sellnow, "Consistent Questions of Ambiguity in Organizational Crisis Communication: Jack in the Box as a Case Study," *Journal of Business Ethics*, 25 (May 2000): 143–155; Robert R. Ulmer and Timothy L. Sellnow, "Strategic Ambiguity and the Ethic of Significant Choices in the Tobacco Industry's Crisis Communication," *Communication Studies*, 48, no. 3 (1997): 215–233; Timothy L. Sellnow and Robert R. Ulmer, "Ambiguous Argument as Advocacy in Organizational Crisis Communication," *Argumentation and Advocacy*, 31, no. 3 (1995): 138–150.

44. Betsy Morris, "This Ford Is Different: Idealist on Board," *Fortune*, April 3, 2000, pp. 123–136.

45. Todd Nighswonger, "Rouge Settlement Sparks Safety Initiative at Ford," *Occupational Hazards*, 61 (October 1999): 101–104.

46. Christine M. Pearson and Judith A. Clair, "Reframing Crisis Management," *Academy of Management Review*, 23 (January 1998): 59–76.

47. Michael John Harker, "Relationship Marketing Defined?" *Marketing Intelligence and Planning*, 17 (January 1999): 13–20; Robert M. Morgan and Shelby D. Hunt, "The Commitment-Trust Theory of Relationship Marketing," *Journal of Marketing*, 58 (July 1994): 20–38.

48. "Hormel Plans Ahead with Oracle Internet Procurement," *Fortune*, May 1, 2000, p. S12.

49. James Coleman, "Social Capital in the Creation of Human Capital," *American Journal of Sociology*, 94 (1988): S95–S120; Carrie R. Leana and Harry J. Van Buren III, "Organizational Social Capital and Employment Practices," *Academy of Management Review*, 24 (July 1999): 538–555.

50. Chemical Manufacturers Association, *Improving Responsible Care Implementation, Enhancing Performance and Credibility* (Washington, D.C.: Chemical Manufacturers Association, 1993); Jennifer Howard, Jennifer Nash, and John Ehrenfeld, "Standard or Smokescreen? Implementation of a Voluntary Environmental Code," *California Management Review*, 42 (Winter 2000): 63–82.

51. Clarkson Centre for Business Ethics, *Principles of Stakeholder Management* (Toronto: Clarkson Centre for Business Ethics, 1999), http://mgmt.utoronto.ca/~stake/Principles.htm; Malcolm McIntosh, Deborah Leipziger, Keith Jones, and Gill Coleman, *Corporate Citizenship: Successful Strategies for Responsible Companies* (London: Financial Times Management, 2000).

52. E. Scholes and D. Clutterbuck, "Communication with Stakeholders: An Integrated Approach," *Long Range Planning*, 31, no. 2 (1998): 227–238.

53. Nick Wingfield and Glenn R. Simpson, "With So Much Subscriber Information, AOL Walks a Cautious Line on Privacy," *Wall Street Journal*, March 15, 2000, http://interactive.wsj.com.

54. McIntosh, Leipziger, Jones, and Coleman, *Corporate Citizenship*, p. 139.

55. Royal Dutch/Shell, *People, Plant & Profits—The Shell Report* (London: Royal Dutch/Shell, 2001);

Royal Dutch/Shell Group, *The Shell Report 1999. People, Planet and Profits—An Act of Commitment* (London: Royal Dutch/Shell, 1999); Royal Dutch/Shell, *Shell Report 2000: How Do We Stand?* (London: Royal Dutch/ Shell, 2000); all available at www.shell.com.

56. Jon Entine, "The Body Shop: Truth & Consequences," *Drug & Cosmetics Industry,* 156 (February 1995): 54.

57. Clarkson, "A Stakeholder Framework for Analyzing and Evaluating Corporate social Performance," p. 105.

58. Ibid., p. 109.

59. Ibid.

60. Ibid.

61. Ibid.

62. Jörg Andriof, "Managing Social Risk through Stakeholder Partnership Building," unpublished dissertation, Warwick Business School, 2000; Jörg Andriof, "Patterns of Stakeholder Partnership Building," in *Perspectives on Corporate Citizenship*, ed. Jörg Andriof and Malcolm McIntosh (Sheffield, United Kingdom: Greenleaf Publishing, 2001): 215–238.

Legal, Regulatory, and Political Issues

4

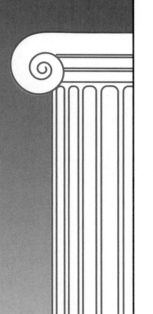

◗ Government's Influence on Business

◗ Business's Influence on Government

◗ A Strategic Approach for Legal Compliance and Organizational Citizenship

OBJECTIVES

To understand the rationale for government regulation of business

To examine key legislation that structures the legal environment for business

To analyze the role of regulatory agencies in the enforcement of public policy

To compare the costs and benefits of regulation

To examine how business participates in and influences public policy

To explore the impact of the Federal Sentencing Guidelines for Organizations

McCormick & Company markets seasonings, flavorings, and other specialty food products to consumers, food-service companies, and industrial food processors. The company's brands include McCormick, Schilling, Fifth Seasons, Spice Classics, Select Seasons, Mojave, Spice Trend, Royal Trading, Crescent, La Cochina De McCormick, and Old Bay. Although it is the world's largest manufacturer of seasonings and spices, with annual sales of about $2 billion, the company recently settled charges that it violated federal antitrust laws by engaging in illegal price discrimination in the sale of its products.

According to the United States Federal Trade Commission (FTC), McCormick charged some retailers a significantly higher net price for its products than it did other competing retailers over a significant period of time. The FTC contended that the price differential resulted from McCormick's practice of offering some retailers cumulative discounts off the list prices of its products. These discounts, known in the trade as "deal rates," occurred in a variety of forms, including up-front cash payments, cash rebates, free goods, off-invoice discounts, performance funds, and other financial rewards. During this time, McCormick faced competition from only one other national firm, Burns Philip Food Inc., as well as a few much smaller independent regional or local firms. The FTC accused McCormick of exploiting its strong market position to provide discounts to those supermarket customers that cooperated with the company's requirement that they allocate a large majority—as much as 90 percent—of their seasoning shelf space to McCormick's products. Other customers had few, if any, alternative sources from which to obtain comparable products at prices and terms equivalent to those that McCormick provided to favored customers. The bottom line was that some customers got discounts, while others paid full price.

The FTC maintained that these discounts violated the Robinson-Patman Act, which bars sellers from charging competing buyers different prices for goods of "like grade and quality," when "the effect of such discrimination may be substantially to lessen competition or tend to create a monopoly in any line of commerce." McCormick settled the charges and agreed not to sell any of its products to any purchaser at a net price higher than it charges the purchaser's competitors, except as permitted under the Robinson-Patman Act. The settlement agreement does permit McCormick to sell products to competing customers at different prices in order to match an equally low price offered by its own competitors, a defense known as "meeting competition," which is permissible under the Robinson-Patman Act. Under the terms of the agreement, however, McCormick must document each instance in which it wishes to "meet competition" and maintain full records on all information on which it bases its use of the defense for five years. Thus, the FTC will be able to ensure that McCormick complies with the settlement agreement and with the law.[1]

The government has the power through laws and regulations to structure how businesses and individuals achieve their goals. The purpose of regulating firms, even the world's largest spice company, is to create a fair competitive environment for businesses, consumers, and society. All stakeholders need to demonstrate a commitment to corporate citizenship through compliance with relevant laws and proactive consideration of social needs. Indeed, a recent study of 900 senior managers found that law ranks as one of the most important business subjects in terms of its effect on organizational practices and activities.[2] Thus, compliance with the law is an important foundation of corporate citizenship.

This chapter explores the complex relationship between business and government. First we discuss some of the laws that structure the environment for regulation of business. Major legislation relating to competition and regulatory agencies is reviewed to provide an overview of the regulatory environment. Next we consider how businesses can participate in the public policy process through lobbying, political contributions, and political action committees. Finally, we offer a framework for a strategic approach to managing the legal and regulatory environment.

Government's Influence on Business

The government has a profound influence on business. In most western countries, there is a history of elected representatives working through democratic institutions to provide the structure for regulation of business conduct. For example, one of the differences that has long characterized the two major parties of the U.S. political system involves the government's role with respect to business. In general terms, the Republican Party favors less federal regulation of business whereas the Democratic Party is more open to these initiatives.[3] Third-party and independent candidates more often focus on specific business issues or proclaim their distance from the two major political parties. However, the power and freedom of big business have resulted in conflicts among private businesses, government, private interest groups, and even individuals.

In the United States, the role that society delegates to government is to provide laws that are logically deduced from the Constitution and the Bill of Rights and to enforce these laws through the judicial system. Individuals and businesses, therefore, live under a rule of law that protects society and supports an acceptable quality of life. Hopefully, by controlling the limitation of force by some parties, the overall welfare and freedom of all participants in the social system will be protected.

The provision of a court system to settle disputes and punish criminals, both organizational and individual, provides for justice and order in society. For example, Columbia/HCA, the world's largest hospital chain, was fined $745 million for defrauding Medicare through overbilling for home health-care and laboratory services. In addition, the executives who were in charge when the violations occurred were convicted of fraud, fined, and sentenced to prison, although they have appealed their convictions.[4] This example illustrates how the judicial system can punish businesses that fail to comply with laws and regulatory requirements.

The legal system is not always accepted in some countries as a legitimate way of doing business. A survey of Russian executives indicated that tax evasion methods, as well as other varieties of illegal corporate behavior, are presented in corporate training. Executives believe that business could not be successful in a completely legal way under Russia's existing conditions. Illegal activities are viewed as socially acceptable.[5]

The existence of businesses, however, is based on laws permitting their creation, organization, and dissolution of operations. From a social perspective, it is significant that a corporation has the same legal status as a "person" that can sue, be sued, and be held liable for debts. Laws may protect managers and stockholders from being personally liable for a company's debts, but individuals as well as organizations are still responsible for their conduct. Because corporations have a perpetual life, larger companies like Exxon, General Motors, and Sony take on an organizational culture, including corporate citizenship values, that extends beyond a specific time period or management team.

Most companies are owned by individual proprietors or operated as partnerships. However, large incorporated firms like Columbia/HCA often receive the most attention because of their size, visibility, and impact on so many aspects of the economy and society. In a pluralistic society, many diverse stakeholder groups (business, labor, consumers, environmentalists, privacy advocates, and so on) attempt to influence the public officials who legislate, interpret laws, and regulate business. The public interest is served though open participation and debate that result in effective public policy. Because no system of government is perfect, legal and regulatory systems are constantly evolving and changing in response to social institutions, including the business environment. For example, increasing use of the Internet for information and business has created a need for legislation and regulations to protect the owners of creative materials from unauthorized use and consumers from fraud and invasions of privacy. The line between acceptable and illegal activity on the Internet is increasingly difficult to discern and is often determined by judges and juries. Companies that adopt a strategic approach to the legal and regulatory system develop proactive organizational values and compliance programs that identify areas of risks and include formal communication, training, and continuous improvement of responses to the legal and regulatory environment.

In this section, we take a closer look at why and how the government affects businesses through laws and regulation, the costs and benefits of regulation, and how regulation may affect companies doing business in foreign countries.

▶ The Rationale for Regulation

Although the United States was established as a capitalist system in which "the invisible hand of competition" would regulate the economy, this system has not always worked effectively or in the best interest of consumers, business, or society as a whole. Since the days of Adam Smith, the federal and state governments have stepped in to enact legislation and create regulations to address particular issues and restrict the behavior of business in accordance with society's wishes. Many of these issues used to justify business regulation can be categorized as economic or social.

Economic and Competitive Reasons for Regulation   A great number of regulations have been passed by legislatures over the last century in an effort "to level the playing field" on which businesses operate. When the United States became an independent nation in the eighteenth century, the business environment consisted of many small farms, manufacturers, and cottage industries operating on a primarily local scale. With the increasing industrialization of the United States after the Civil War, "captains of industry" like John D. Rockefeller (oil), Andrew Carnegie (railroads and steel), Andrew Mellon (aluminum), and J. P. Morgan (banking) began to consolidate their business holdings into large national trusts. **Trusts** are organizations generally established to gain control of a product market or industry by eliminating competition. Such organizations are often considered detrimental because, without serious competition, they can potentially charge higher prices and provide lower-quality products to consumers. Thus, as these firms grew in size and power, public distrust of them likewise grew because of often-legitimate concerns about unfair competition. This suspicion and the public's desire to require these increasingly powerful companies to act responsibly spurred the first antitrust legislation. If trusts are successful in eliminating competition, a monopoly can result.

A **monopoly** occurs when just one business provides a good or service in a given market. Utility companies that supply electricity, natural gas, water, or cable television are examples of monopolies. The government tolerates these monopolies because the cost of supplying the good or providing the service is so great that few companies would be willing to invest in new markets without some protection from competition. Monopolies may also be allowed by patent laws that grant a developer of new technology a period of time (usually seventeen years) during which no other firm can use the same technology without the patent holder's consent. SmithKline Beecham, the maker of the antidepressant Paxil, recently challenged the production of a generic version of the drug because its patent had not expired.[6] These relatively short-term monopolies are permitted in order to encourage businesses to engage in riskier research and development by allowing them time to recoup their research, development, and production expenses and to earn a reasonable profit.

Because trusts and monopolies lack serious competition, there are concerns that they may either exploit their market dominance to restrict their output and raise prices or lower quality in order to gain greater profits. This concern is the primary rationalization for their regulation by the government. Public utilities, for example, are regulated by state public utility commissions and, where they involve interstate commerce, are subject to federal regulation as well. In recent years, some of these industries have been "deregulated" with the idea that greater competition will police the behavior of individual firms.

Related to the issue of regulation of trusts and monopolies is society's desire to restrict destructive or unfair competition. What is considered to be unfair varies with the standard practice of the industry, the impact of specific conduct, and the individual case. When one company dominates a particular industry, it may engage in destructive competition or employ anticompetitive tactics. For example, it may slash prices in an effort to drive competitors out of the market, and then later raise prices. It may conspire with other competitors to set or "fix" prices so that each firm can ensure a certain level of profit. Other examples of unfair competitive trade practices are stealing trade secrets or obtaining other confidential information from a competitor's employees, trademark and copyright infringement, false advertising, and deceptive selling methods such as "bait and switch" and false representation of products. For example, Oracle, which markets database software, was convicted of wrongfully firing an executive who had questioned whether an employee's access to a rival firm's computer systems was appropriate.[7] The jury's finding in the case suggests that such conduct is indeed viewed as anticompetitive.

Antitrust regulations also allow the government to punish firms that engage in anticompetitive practices. For example, the U.S. Department of Justice fined Archer-Daniels-Midland Company (ADM) $100 million after it pleaded guilty to two counts of fixing the price of citric acid (used in soft drinks, processed foods, detergents, textiles, and chemicals) and lysine (used for poultry and hog feed) in the United States. Related lawsuits brought by Canadian and European Union (EU) authorities resulted in fines of $16 million (Canada) and $45 million (EU) for the company.[8] We will take a closer look at specific antitrust regulations later in this chapter.

Social Reasons for Regulation   Regulation may also occur when imperfections in the market result in undesirable consequences for society. Many manufacturing processes, for example, create air, water, or land pollution. Such consequences create "costs" in the form of contamination of natural resources, illness, and so on that neither the manufacturer nor the consumer "pays" for directly. Because few companies are willing to shoulder these costs voluntarily, regulation is necessary to ensure that all firms within an industry do their part to minimize these costs and to pay their fair share. Likewise, regulations have proven necessary to protect natural (e.g., forests, fishing grounds, and other habitats) and social resources (e.g., historical and architecturally or archaeologically significant structures). We will take a closer look at some of these environmental protection regulations and related issues in Chapter 9.

Other regulations have come about in response to social demands for equality in the workplace, especially after the 1960s. Such laws and regulations require that companies ignore race, ethnicity, gender, religion, and disabilities in favor of qualifications that more accurately reflect an individual's capacity for performing a particular job. Likewise, deaths and injuries because of employer negligence resulted in regulations designed to ensure that people can enjoy a safe working environment. Lockheed was fined $1 million, the largest fine ever assessed against a contractor by the Energy Department, for violating such workplace safety regulations at a nuclear weapons plant in Oak Ridge, Tennessee.[9] We will take a closer look at laws and regulations related to the workplace in Chapter 8.

Still other regulations have resulted from special-interest group crusades for safer products. For example, Ralph Nader's *Unsafe at Any Speed,* published in 1965, criticized the automobile industry as a whole, and General Motors specifically, for putting profit and style ahead of lives and safety. Nader's consumer-protection organization, popularly known as Nader's Raiders, successfully campaigned for legislation that required automobile makers to provide safety belts, padded dashboards, stronger door latches, head restraints, shatterproof windshields, and collapsible steering columns in automobiles. As we will see in Chapter 7, consumer activists also helped secure passage of several other consumer protection laws, such as the Wholesome Meat Act of 1967, the Clean Water Act of 1972, and the Toxic Substance Act of 1976.

Issues arising from the increasing use of the Internet have led to demands for new laws protecting consumers and business. As we shall see in Chapter 10, the technology associated with the Internet has generated a number of issues related to privacy, fraud, and copyrights. For instance, creators of copyrighted works such as movies, books, and music are calling for new laws and regulations to safeguard their ownership of these works. In response to these concerns, Congress enacted the Digital Millennium Copyright Act in 1998, which extended existing copyright laws to better protect "digital" recordings of music, movies, and the like.[10] Concerns about the collection and use of personal information, especially regarding children, resulted in the passage of the Children's Online Privacy Protection Act of 2000; further legislation addressing social concerns about privacy is likely. Consumers are also worried about becoming victims of online fraud. Complaints about fraud in online auctions have risen dramatically, with online credit card fraud twelve times as great as in traditional retail environments. With online auctions generating an estimated $6.1 billion per year, consumers and businesses alike are exploring options, including regulation, to protect the security of online transactions.[11]

Laws and Regulations

As a result of business abuses and social demands for reform, the federal government began to pass legislation to regulate business conduct in the late nineteenth century. In this section, we will look at a few of the most significant of these laws. Table 4.1 summarizes many more laws that affect business operations.

TABLE 4.1

Major Federal Legislation

Act (Date Enacted)	Purpose
Sherman Antitrust Act (1890)	Prohibits contracts, combinations, or conspiracies to restrain trade; establishes as a misdemeanor monopolizing or attempting to monopolize
Clayton Act (1914)	Prohibits specific practices such as price discrimination, exclusive dealer arrangements, and stock acquisitions in which the effect may notably lessen competition or tend to create a monopoly
Federal Trade Commission Act (1914)	Created the Federal Trade Commission; also gives the FTC investigatory powers to be used in preventing unfair methods of competition
Robinson-Patman Act (1936)	Prohibits price discrimination that lessens competition among wholesalers or retailers; prohibits producers from giving disproportionate services of facilities to large buyers
Wheeler-Lea Act (1938)	Prohibits unfair and deceptive acts and practices regardless of whether competition is injured; places advertising of foods and drugs under the jurisdiction of the FTC
Lanham Act (1946)	Provides protections and regulation of brand names, brand marks, trade names, and trademarks
Celler-Kefauver Act (1950)	Prohibits any corporation engaged in commerce from acquiring the whole or any part of the stock or other share of the capital assets of another corporation when the effect substantially lessens competition or tends to create a monopoly
Fair Packaging and Labeling Act (1966)	Makes illegal the unfair or deceptive packaging or labeling of consumer products
Magnuson-Moss Warranty (FTC) Act (1975)	Provides for minimum disclosure standards for written consumer product warranties; defines minimum consent standards for written warranties; allows the FTC to prescribe interpretive rules in policy statements regarding unfair or deceptive practices
Consumer Goods Pricing Act (1975)	Prohibits the use of price maintenance agreements among manufacturers and resellers in interstate commerce
Antitrust Improvements Act (1976)	Requires large corporations to inform federal regulators of prospective mergers or acquisitions so that they can be studied for any possible violations of the law

(continued)

TABLE 4.1 *(continued)*

Major Federal Legislation

Act (Date Enacted)	Purpose
Trade Mark Counterfeiting Act (1988)	Provides civil and criminal penalties against those who deal in counterfeit consumer goods or any counterfeit goods that can threaten health or safety
Trademark Law Revision Act (1988)	Amends the Lanham Act to allow brands not yet introduced to be protected through registration with the Patent and Trademark Office
Nutrition Labeling and Education Act (1990)	Prohibits exaggerated health claims and requires all processed foods to contain labels with nutritional information
Telephone Consumer Protection Act (1991)	Establishes procedures to avoid unwanted telephone solicitations; prohibits marketers from using automated telephone dialing system or an artificial or prerecorded voice to certain telephone lines
Federal Trademark Dilution Act (1995)	Provides trademark owners the right to protect trademarks and requires relinquishment of names that match or parallel existing trademarks
Digital Millennium Copyright Act (1998)	Refined copyright laws to protect digital versions of copyrighted materials, including music and movies
Children's Online Privacy Act (2000)	Regulates the collection of personally identifiable information (name, address, e-mail address, hobbies, interests, or information collected through cookies) online from children under age 13

Sherman Antitrust Act   The Sherman Antitrust Act, passed in 1890, is the principal tool employed by the federal government to prevent businesses from restraining trade and monopolizing markets. Congress passed the law, almost unanimously, in response to public demands to curtail the growing power and abuses of trusts in the late nineteenth century. The law outlaws "every contract, combination in the form of trust or otherwise, or conspiracy, in restraint of trade or commerce."[12] It also makes violations of the law a felony crime, punishable by fines of up to $10 million for corporate violators and $350,000 and/or three years in prison for individual offenders.[13]

The Sherman Antitrust Act applies to all firms operating in interstate commerce as well as to U.S. firms engaged in foreign commerce. The law has been used to break up some of the United States' most powerful companies, including

Microsoft Chief Operating Officer Bob Herbold and CEO Bill Gates speak to the media about the federal antitrust trial.

the Standard Oil Company (1911), an American Tobacco Company (1911), and AT&T (1984), and there was an attempt to break up Microsoft. In the Microsoft case, a U.S. district court judge ruled that the software giant inhibited competition by using unlawful tactics to protect its Windows monopoly in computer operating systems and by illegally expanding its dominance into the market for Internet Web-browsing software. In ordering that the company be split into two independent firms, Judge Thomas Penfield Jackson said that Microsoft had placed "an oppressive thumb on the scale of competitive fortune" by targeting competitors that threatened its Windows software monopoly. However, the ruling to break up Microsoft was appealed and the order by Judge Jackson was overturned. The Supreme Court refused to hear an appeal by Microsoft that other aspects of its conviction should be overturned.[14] The Sherman Act remains the primary source of antitrust law in the United States, although it has been supplemented by several amendments and additional legislation.

Clayton Antitrust Act   Because the provisions of the Sherman Antitrust Act were rather vague, the courts have not always interpreted the law as its creators intended. To rectify this situation, Congress enacted the Clayton Antitrust Act in 1914 to limit mergers and acquisitions that have the potential to stifle competition.[15] The Clayton Act also specifically prohibits price discrimination, tying agreements (when a supplier furnishes a product to a buyer with the stipulation that the buyer must purchase other products as well), exclusive agreements (when a supplier forbids an intermediary to carry products of competing manufacturers), and the acquisition of stock in another corporation where the effect may be to substantially lessen competition or tend to create a monopoly. In addition, the Clayton Act prohibits members of one company's board of directors from holding seats on the boards of competing corporations. The law also exempts farm corporations and labor organizations from antitrust laws.

Federal Trade Commission Act   In the same year the Clayton Act was passed, Congress also enacted the Federal Trade Commission Act to further strengthen the antitrust provisions of the Sherman Act. Unlike the Clayton Act, which prohibits specific practices, the Federal Trade Commission Act more broadly prohibits unfair methods of competition. More significantly, this law also created the Federal Trade Commission (FTC) to protect consumers and businesses from unfair competition. Of all the federal regulatory agencies, the FTC has the greatest influence on business activities.

When the FTC receives a complaint about a business or finds reason to believe that a company is engaging in illegal conduct, it issues a formal complaint stating that the firm is in violation of the law. If the company continues the unlawful practice, the FTC can issue a cease-and-desist order, which requires the offender to stop the specified behavior. Although a firm can appeal to the federal courts to have the order rescinded, the FTC can seek civil penalties in court, up to a maximum penalty of $10,000 a day for each infraction, if a cease-and-desist order is ignored. For example, the commission filed a formal complaint against Enforma Natural Products for deceptive advertising of its weight-loss products. Among the company's claims for the Enforma System, which was promoted through 30-minute infomercials and a web site, was that "you can eat what you want and never, ever, ever have to diet again." The FTC's complaint charged that such claims were false and could not be substantiated. To settle the charges, Enforma agreed not to make deceptive claims and to pay the FTC $10 million in reparation.[16] The commission can also require businesses to air corrective advertising to counter previous ads the commission considers misleading. In addition, the FTC helps to resolve disputes and makes rulings on business decisions, especially in emerging areas such as Internet privacy. For example, the commission approved a settlement that would permit the bankrupt Internet retailer Toysmart.com to sell its customer list as long as the buyer of the list agrees to abide by Toysmart's privacy guarantees.[17] Thus, in this case, the FTC helped to reinforce corporate guarantees of consumer privacy on the Internet.

Enforcement of the Laws   Because violations of the Sherman Antitrust Act are felony crimes, the Antitrust Division of the U.S. Department of Justice enforces it. The FTC enforces antitrust regulations of a civil, rather than criminal, nature. There are many additional federal regulatory agencies (Table 4.2) that oversee the enforcement of other laws and regulations. Most states also have regulatory agencies that make and enforce laws for individuals and businesses. In recent years, cooperation among state attorneys general and regulatory agencies and the federal government has increased, particularly in efforts related to control of drugs, organized crime, and pollution. Such cooperation among state attorneys general and the FTC resulted in a $34 million settlement with Nine West Group, one of the nation's

TABLE 4.2

Federal Regulatory Agencies

Agency (Date Established)	Major Areas of Responsibility
Food and Drug Administration (1906)	Enforces laws and regulations to prevent distribution of adulterated or misbranded foods, drugs, medical devices, cosmetics, veterinary products, and potentially hazardous consumer products
Federal Reserve Board (1913)	Regulates banking institutions; protects the credit rights of consumers; maintains the stability of the financial system; conducts the nation's monetary policy; and serves as the nation's Central Bank
Federal Trade Commission (1914)	Enforces laws and guidelines regarding business practices; takes action to stop false and deceptive advertising and labeling
Federal Communications Commission (1934)	Regulates communication by wire, radio, and television in interstate and foreign commerce
Securities and Exchange Commission (1934)	Regulates the offering and trading of securities, including stocks and bonds
National Labor Relations Board (1935)	Enforces the National Labor Relations Act; investigates and rectifies unfair labor practices by employers and unions
Equal Employment Opportunity Commission (1970)	Promotes equal opportunity in employment through administrative and judicial enforcement of civil rights laws and through education and technical assistance
Environmental Protection Agency (1970)	Develops and enforces environmental protection standards and conducts research into the adverse effects of pollution
Occupational Safety and Health Administration (1971)	Enforces the Occupational Safety and Health Act and other workplace health and safety laws and regulations; makes surprise inspections of facilities to ensure safe workplaces
Consumer Product Safety Commission (1972)	Ensures compliance with the Consumer Product Safety Act; protects the public from unreasonable risk of injury from any consumer product not covered by other regulatory agencies

largest manufacturers of women's shoes, on price-fixing charges. Authorities said that Nine West violated federal and state antitrust laws by making agreements with retailers to fix the prices of its shoes and to limit sales promotion periods in order to maintain the prices of its shoes and restrict competition among retailers who sold Nine West brands. In addition to the $34 million payment, the settlement requires that Nine West not fix dealer prices, not pressure dealers to adopt any resale price, not threaten to limit supplies to dealers that adopt their own resale prices, and must satisfy record keeping provisions so the FTC can continue to monitor compliance.[18]

In addition to enforcement by state and federal authorities, lawsuits by private citizens, competitors, and special-interest groups are also used to enforce legal and regulatory policy. Through private civil actions, an individual or organization can file a lawsuit related to issues such as antitrust, price fixing, or unfair advertising. For example, the largest antitrust settlement to date occurred when several corporations brought a lawsuit against six of the world's largest manufacturers of vitamins. The suit accused the manufacturers, which account for 80 percent of the bulk sales of many popular vitamins, of colluding to fix prices with wholesale customers (large food and drug companies) over a nine-year period. The vitamin companies agreed to settle the case for $1.1 billion. Prior to this settlement, three of the manufacturers (F. Hoffman La Roche, BASF, and Rhone-Poulene) had been assessed a $750 million criminal fine for price fixing and market allocation.[19] An organization can also ask for assistance from a federal agency to address a concern. For example, American Express gained the assistance of the Department of Justice's Antitrust Division in accusing Visa and MasterCard of antitrust violations.[20]

▶ Global Regulation

A company that engages in commerce beyond its own country's borders must contend with the potentially complex relationship among the laws of its own nation, international laws, and the laws of the nation in which it will be trading, as well as various trade restrictions imposed on international trade. International business activities are affected to varying degrees by each nation's laws, regulatory agencies, courts, political environment, and special-interest groups. Some countries have established import barriers, including tariffs, quotas, minimum price levels, and port-of-entry taxes that affect the importation of products. France, for example, banned the importation of some cuts of beef and all livestock feed containing meat in order to curtail the spread of "mad cow" disease in that country.[21] Additionally, other laws may govern product quality and safety, distribution methods, and sales and advertising practices.

Although there is considerable variation and focus among different nations' laws, many countries have antitrust laws that are quite similar to those in the

United States. Indeed, the Sherman Act has been copied throughout the world as the basis for regulating fair competition. German authorities, for example, accused Wal-Mart of exploiting its size to sell basic food items, such as milk, sugar, and flour, below cost on a regular basis, in violation of German antitrust laws. Authorities feared the practice would harm small and medium-size businesses that could not match the retail giant's lower prices.[22] Antitrust issues, such as price fixing and market allocation, have become a major area of international cooperation in the regulation of business.[23]

The North American Free Trade Agreement (NAFTA), which eliminates virtually all tariffs on goods produced and traded between the United States, Canada, and Mexico, makes it easier for businesses of each country to make investments in the other countries. The agreement also provides some coordination of legal standards governing business transactions among the three countries. NAFTA promotes cooperation among various regulatory agencies to encourage effective law enforcement in the free trade area.[24] Within the framework of NAFTA, the United States and Canada have developed many joint, cooperative agreements to enforce their respective antitrust laws. The agreement provides for cooperation in investigations, including requests for information and the opportunity to visit the territory of the other nation in the course of conducting investigations.[25]

The European Union (EU) was established in 1958 to promote free trade among its members and now includes 15 European nations, with more expected to join in the next few years. To facilitate trade among its members, the EU is working to standardize business laws and trade barriers, to eliminate customs checks among its members, and to create a standard currency (the *euro*) for use by all members. Moreover, the Commission of the European Communities has entered into an agreement with the United States, similar to NAFTA, regarding joint antitrust laws.[26] Another collaborative law enforcement effort, this one between the 41-nation Council of Europe and the United States, is the crafting of a treaty covering computer crimes.[27]

▶ Costs and Benefits of Regulation

Costs of Regulation   Regulation results in numerous costs for businesses, consumers, and society at large. Although many experts have attempted to quantify these costs, it is actually quite difficult to find an accurate measurement tool. To generate such measurements, economists often classify regulations as economic (applicable to specific industries or businesses) or social (broad regulations pertaining to health, safety, and the environment). One yardstick for the direct costs of regulation is the administrative spending patterns of federal regulatory agencies. In the United States, these expenditures have increased steadily over the years, culminating with a projected budget of $19.8 billion for federal regulatory spending in the year 2001, the highest level ever projected for the budgets of the fifty-four regulatory agencies (Figure 4.1).[28] Another way to measure the direct cost of regulation is to look at the staffing levels of federal regulatory agencies,

FIGURE 4.1

Federal Regulatory Spending Activity, 1960–2000 (Fiscal Years, Billions of Dollars)

■ Social regulation   ■ Economic regulation

Source: Melinda Warren, "Federal Regulatory Spending Reaches a New Height: An Analysis of the Budget of the U.S. Government for the Year 2001" (St. Louis: Center for the Study of American Business, June 2000), p. 3. Reprinted by permission from the Weidenbaum Center on the Economy, Government, and Public Policy at Washington University.

which are shown in Figure 4.2. The expenditures and staffing of state and local regulatory agencies also generate direct costs to society.

Still another way to approach the measurement of the costs of regulation is to consider the burden that businesses incur in complying with regulations. Various federal regulations, for example, may require companies to make changes to their manufacturing processes or facilities (e.g., smokestack "scrubbers" to clean air, wheelchair ramps to make facilities accessible to disabled customers and employees). Companies also must keep records to document their compliance and to obtain permits to implement plans that fall under the scope of specific regulatory agencies. Economist Thomas Hopkins believes that the cost of complying with federal regulations amounts to over $700 billion per year.[29] Again, state regulatory agencies often add additional costs to this burden. Regulated firms may also spend large amounts of money and other resources to prevent additional legislation and to appear to be responsible. Philip Morris USA, for example, is spending $100 million a year to reduce underage smoking.[30]

Of course, businesses generally pass these regulatory costs on to their consumers in the form of higher prices, a cost that some label a "hidden tax" of government. Additionally, some businesses contend that the financial and time costs

FIGURE 4.2

Federal Regulatory
Staffing Levels,
1970–2000
(Full-Time Equivalent Personnel)

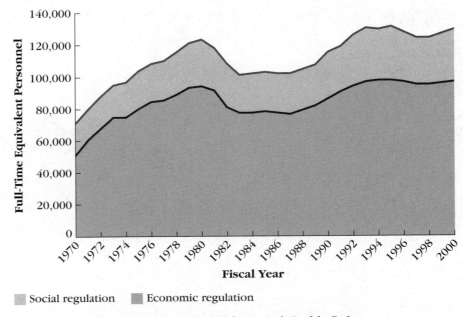

Source: Melinda Warren, "Federal Regulatory Spending Reaches a New Height: An Analysis of the Budget of the U.S. Government for the Year 2001" (St. Louis: Center for the Study of American Business, June 2000), p. 5. Reprinted by permission from the Weidenbaum Center on the Economy, Government, and Public Policy at Washington University.

of complying with regulations stifle their ability to develop new products and make investments in facilities and equipment. Moreover, society must pay for the cost of staffing and operating regulatory agencies, and these costs may be reflected in federal income taxes.

Benefits of Regulation   Despite business complaints about the costs of regulation, it provides many benefits to business, consumers, and society as a whole. Among these benefits are greater equality in the workplace, safer workplaces, resources for disadvantaged members of society, safer products, more information about and greater choices among products, cleaner air and water, and the preservation of wildlife habitats to ensure that future generations can enjoy their beauty and diversity.

Antitrust laws and regulations strengthen competition by preventing monopolies. When markets are free and open to all, businesses must compete for consumers' dollars, and many try to differentiate their offerings by cutting prices or raising their quality. Companies that fail to respond to consumer desires or that employ inefficient processes are often forced out of the marketplace by savvier firms. Truly competitive markets also spur companies to invest in researching and developing product innovations as well as new, more-efficient methods of production. These innovations benefit consumers through lower prices and improved goods and services.[31] For example, companies such as Apple, IBM, and Dell Computer continue to engineer smaller, faster, and more-powerful computers that help individuals and businesses to be more productive.

Regulatory Reform   Many businesses and individuals believe that the costs of regulation outweigh its benefits. They often argue that removing regulation will allow Adam Smith's "invisible hand of competition" to more effectively and efficiently dictate business conduct. Some people desire complete **deregulation,** or removal of all regulatory authority. Proponents of deregulation believe that less governmental intervention allows business markets to work more effectively. For example, many businesses want their industries deregulated in order to decrease their costs of doing business. Many industries have been deregulated to a certain extent in recent years, including trucking, airlines, telecommunications (long-distance telephone and cable television), and, more recently, electric utilities. For example, the Federal Communications Commission (FCC) is diminishing its role in monitoring telephone equipment.[32] In many cases, this deregulation has resulted in lower prices for consumers as well as in greater product choice, particularly in the long-distance telephone industry. However, critics of deregulation point to higher prices and poor service and product quality that have plagued some deregulated industries. The year 2000 was considered one of the worst ever for air travel because of the prevalence of flight delays, high prices, and other issues. The September 11, 2001, airline terrorist attacks also pointed to problems of security in a deregulated environment. Thus, there is still considerable debate on the relative merits and costs of regulation.[33]

Self-Regulation   Many companies attempt to regulate themselves in an effort to demonstrate corporate citizenship and to preclude further regulation by federal or state government. In addition to complying with all relevant laws and regulations, many firms chose to join trade associations that have self-regulatory programs. Although such programs are not a direct outgrowth of laws, many were established to stop or delay the development of laws and regulations that would restrict the associations' business practices. Some trade associations establish codes of conduct by which their members must abide or risk rebuke or expulsion from the association.[34]

Perhaps the best-known self-regulatory association is the Better Business Bureau (BBB), a local organization supported by local member businesses. More than 140 local bureaus help resolve problems between consumers and businesses. Each bureau also works to champion good business practices within a community, although it usually does not have strong tools for enforcing its business conduct rules. When a company violates what the BBB believes to be good business practices, the bureau warns consumers through local newspapers or broadcast media.[35] If the offending organization is a member if the BBB, it may be expelled from the local bureau. For example, the membership of Priceline.com was revoked by a

The BBB*Online* Web site provides consumers and businesses with information about privacy and reliability, a code of online business practices, and information about how to file a complaint. (Reprinted with permission from BBBOnLine, Inc.)

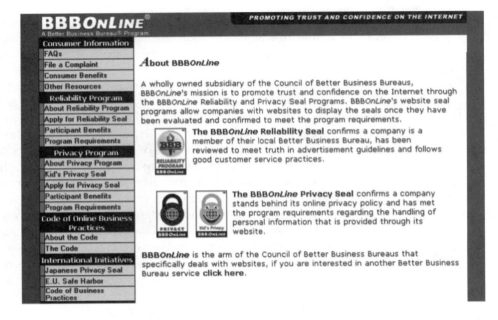

Connecticut Better Business Bureau after the online retailer failed to address numerous complaints related to misrepresentation of products, failure to provide promised refunds, and failure to correct billing problems.[36] The BBB has also developed a web site, BBBOnline, to help consumers identify web sites that collect personal information in an ethical manner. BBB members that use the site agree to binding arbitration with regard to online privacy issues.[37]

Self-regulatory programs like the Better Business Bureau have a number of advantages over government regulation. Establishment and implementation of such programs are usually less costly, and their guidelines or codes of conduct are generally more practical and realistic. Furthermore, effective self-regulatory programs reduce the need to expand government bureaucracy. However, self-regulation also has several limitations. Nonmember firms are under no obligation to abide by a trade association's industry guidelines or codes. Moreover, most associations lack the tools or authority to enforce their guidelines. Finally, these guidelines are often less strict than the regulations established by government agencies.[38]

Business's Influence on Government

Although the government has a profound effect on business activities, especially through its regulatory actions, business has an equal influence on government, and that influence has grown in recent years. Managing this relationship with government officials while navigating the dynamic world of politics is a major challenge for firms both large and small. In our pluralistic society, many participants are involved in the political process, and the economic stakes are high. Because government is a stakeholder of business (and vice versa), businesses and government can work together as both legitimately participate in the political process. For example, the Digital Signature Act of 2000 was initiated by Internet businesses to improve efficiency and avoid the inconvenience and cost of written signatures. In promoting greater use of electronic signatures to authenticate transactions online, many businesses and consumers hope the bill will help reduce the incidence of fraud in E-commerce.[39]

Obviously, many people believe that business participation should not be allowed because of its size, resources, and vested interests. Business participation can be either positive or negative for society's interest depending not only on the outcome, but also on the perspective of various stakeholders. Before we look at specific tactics businesses use to influence government policy, it is useful to briefly examine the current political environment to understand how business influence has grown.

The Contemporary Political Environment

Beginning in the 1960s, a significant "antiestablishment" public, increasingly hostile to business, mounted protests to effect reform. Their increasingly vocal efforts spurred a fifteen-year wave of legislation and regulation to address a number of issues of the day, including product safety, employment discrimination, human rights, energy shortages, environmental degradation, and scandals related to bribery and payoffs. During the Republican-dominated 1980s, the pendulum swung back in favor of business. During the 1990s, economic prosperity driven by technological advances encouraged both the Republican and Democratic Parties to encourage self-regulation of business while protecting competition and the natural environment. With the election of President George W. Bush in 2000, the balance may shift again. Critics have charged that Bush was too soft on business and environmental regulation as governor of Texas and fear that this trend will continue, although after the terrorist attacks of September 11, 2001, national security emerged as the most important issue, and the emphasis on environmental regulation diminished. Such changes in the political environment over the last forty years shaped the political environment in which businesses operate and created new avenues for businesses to participate in the political process. Among the most significant factors shaping the political environment were changes in Congress and the rise of special-interest groups.

Changes in Congress   Among the calls for social reform in the 1960s were pressures for changes within the legislative process of the U.S. Congress itself. Bowing to this pressure, Congress enacted an amendment to the Legislative Reorganization

Act in 1970, which effectively ushered in a new era of change for the political process. This legislation significantly revamped the procedures of congressional committees, most notably stripping committee chairpersons of much of their power, equalizing committee and chair assignments, and requiring committees to record and publish all roll-call votes taken in committee. By opening up the committee process to public scrutiny and reducing the power of senior members and committee leaders, the act reduced the level of secrecy surrounding the legislative process and effectively brought an end to an era of autonomous committee chairmen and senior members.[40]

Another significant change occurred in 1974 when Congress amended the Federal Election Campaign Act to limit contributions from individuals, political parties, and special-interest groups organized to get specific candidates elected or policies enacted.[41] Around the same time, many states began to shift their electoral process from the traditional party caucus to primary elections, further eroding the influence of the party in the political process. These changes ultimately had the effect of reducing the importance of political parties by decreasing members' dependence on their parties. Many candidates for elected offices began to turn to special-interest groups to raise enough funds to mount serious campaigns.

Rise of Special-Interest Groups   The success of activists' efforts in the 1960s and 70s spawned the rise of special-interest groups. The movements to promote African-American and women's rights and to protest the Vietnam War and environmental degradation of the day evolved into well-organized special-interest groups working to educate the public about significant social issues and to crusade for legislation and regulation of business conduct they deemed irresponsible. These progressive groups were soon joined on Capitol Hill by more conservative groups working to further their agendas on issues such as business deregulation, restriction of abortion and gun control, and promotion of prayer in schools. Businesses joined in by forming industry and trade associations. These increasingly powerful special-interest groups now focused on getting candidates elected who could further their own political agendas. Common Cause, for example, is a nonprofit, nonpartisan organization working to fight corrupt government and special interests backed by large sums of money. Since 1970, Common Cause has campaigned for greater openness and accountability in government. Some of its self-proclaimed "victories" include reform of presidential campaign finances, tax systems, congressional ethics, open meeting standards, and disclosure requirements for lobbyists.[42]

▶ *Corporate Approaches to Influencing Government*

Although some businesses view regulatory and legal forces as beyond their control and simply react to conditions arising from those forces, other firms actively seek to influence the political process in order to achieve their goals. In some cases, companies publicly protest the actions of legislative bodies. More often, companies work for the election of political candidates who regard them positively. Lobbying, political action committees, and campaign contributions are some of the tools businesses employ to influence the political process.

Lobbying   Among the most powerful tactics business can employ to participate in public policy decisions is direct representation through full-time staff that communicate with elected officials. **Lobbying** is the process of working to persuade public and/or government officials to favor a particular position in decision making. Organizations may lobby officials either directly or by combining their efforts with other organizations.

Many companies concerned about the threat of legislation or regulation that may negatively affect their operations employ lobbyists to communicate their concerns to officials on their behalf. Microsoft, for example, established a Washington office with a staff of 14 lobbyists and spent $4.6 million to persuade federal officials that breaking up the company for antitrust violations would harm the computer industry and U.S. economy.[43] They were successful in preventing the breakup of the company but not successful in having all antitrust violations overturned. Likewise, DaimlerChrysler, in collaboration with the United Auto Workers (UAW) union, lobbied to oppose new restrictions on fuel-inefficient cars. One event in the effort was a reception held at an automotive museum in honor of several U.S. Representatives, including House Minority Leader Dick Gephardt.[44]

Companies may attempt to influence the legislative or regulatory process more indirectly through trade associations and umbrella organizations that represent collective business interests of many firms. Virtually every industry has one or more trade associations that represent the interests of their members to federal officials and provide public education and other services for their members. Examples of such trade associations include the National Association of Home Builders, the

The tobacco industry is a strong lobbyist of the government. In spite of these efforts, Philip Morris Tobacco Company was ordered to pay $3 billion to a single cancer patient. Here, the patient's attorney holds a press conference after the order was announced.

Tobacco Institute, the American Booksellers Association, and the Pet Food Institute. Additionally, there are often state trade associations, such as the Hawaii Coffee Association and the Michigan Beer and Wine Wholesalers Association, that work on state- and regional-level issues. Umbrella organizations such as the National Federation of Independent Businesses and the U.S. Chamber of Commerce also help to promote business interests to government officials. For example, the U.S. Chamber of Commerce recently opposed a proposal that would prohibit the government from contracting with companies that have poor records for ethical and legal compliance. The proposal would disqualify prospective contractors with histories of substantial noncompliance in the areas of employment, environmental, and antitrust laws. Because the federal government spends more than $170 billion annually on contracts for goods and services and those contracts directly or indirectly provide jobs for about 23 million workers, the members of the national organization fought to protect their ability to secure lucrative federal contracts.[45] Examples like this illustrate how the U.S. Chamber of Commerce takes positions on many political, regulatory, and economic questions. With more than 200,000 member companies, its goal is to promote its members' views of the ideal free-enterprise marketplace.

Political Action Committees   Companies can also influence the political process through political action committees. **Political action committees (PACs)** are organizations that solicit donations from individuals and then contribute these funds to candidates running for political office. Companies are barred by federal law from donating directly to candidates for federal offices or to political action committees, and individuals are limited to relatively small donations. However, companies can organize PACS to which their executives, employees, and stockholders can make significant donations as individuals. PACs operate independently of business and are usually incorporated. Labor unions and other special-interest groups, such as teachers and medical doctors, can also establish PACs to promote their goals.

The Federal Election Committee has established rules to restrict PAC donations to $5,000 per candidate for each election. However, many PACs exploit loopholes in these regulations by donating so-called "soft money" to political parties that do not support a specific candidate for federal office. Under current rules, these contributors can make unlimited donations to political parties for general activities. Microsoft, for example, contributed $1 million to help underwrite both the Republican and Democratic Party conventions in 2000. In addition, the company gave $522,150 in soft money to the Republican Party and $341,250 to the Democratic Party. The Bill and Melinda Gates Foundation contributed another $10 million to the U.S. Capitol Visitors Center. All of this largesse occurred while the Justice Department was passing judgment on Microsoft for antitrust violations.[46] Table 4.3 lists examples of contributions to political parties from different industries.

Campaign Contributions   Although federal laws restrict direct corporate contributions to electoral campaigns, corporate money may be channeled into candidates'

TABLE 4.3

Selected Industry PAC Contributions to Federal Candidates, 1999–2000

Industry	To Democrats	To Republicans
Printing and publishing	$ 97,122	$ 550,359
TV/movies/music	$1,446,754	$1,917,790
Telephone utilities	$2,214,864	$3,613,726
Telecom services & equipment	$ 809,037	$1,265,418
Electronics manufacturing & services	$ 98,383	$ 295,149
Computer equipment & services	$ 941,372	$1,472,716
Defense aerospace	$ 889,404	$1,581,221
Defense electronics	$ 545,597	$1,159,394
Crop production	$1,569,019	$1,699,771
Tobacco	$ 624,400	$1,753,123
Dairy	$ 548,040	$ 788,644
Food processing & sales	$ 461,654	$2,423,687
Forestry & forest products	$ 355,274	$1,734,571

Sources: "Communications/Electronics: PAC Contributions to Federal Candidates, 1999–2000," The Center for Responsive Politics, October 1, 2001, www.opensecrets.org/pacs/sectors.asp?txt= BOI&cycle=2000; "Defense: PAC Contributions to Federal Candidates, 1999–2000," The Center for Responsive Politics, October 1, 2001, www.opensecrets.org/pacs/sectors.asp?txt=DOI&cycle=2000; "Agribusiness: PAC Contributions to Federal Candidates, 1999–2000," The Center for Responsive Politics, October 1, 2001, www.opensecrets.org/pacs/sectors.asp?txt=AOI&cycle=2000.

campaign coffers as corporate executives' or stockholders' personal contributions. Such donations can violate the spirit of corporate campaign laws. A sizable contribution to a candidate may carry with it an implied understanding that the elected official will perform some favor, such as voting in accordance with the contributor's desires on a particular law. Occasionally, some businesses find it so important to ensure favorable treatment that they make illegal corporate contributions to campaign funds.

Although laws limit corporate contributions to specific candidates, it is acceptable for businesses and other organizations to make donations to political parties. Table 4.4 lists selected organizations and their contributions to political parties. Note that labor unions typically donate to the Democratic Party, whereas the National Rifle Association contributes only to the Republican Party. Some companies, including SBC Communications (parent company of Southwestern Bell) and Citigroup, choose to give to both major political parties.

TABLE 4.4

Contributions from Selected Organizations in the 1999–2000 Election Cycle

Organization	Total Contribution	To Democrats	To Republicans
AT&T	$3,452,540	$1,251,734	$2,200,806
Service Employees International Union	$2,380,650	$2,350,250	$ 30,400
Communication Workers of America	$2,100,000	$2,199,000	—
Microsoft	$1,881,006	$ 799,292	$1,081,714
Philip Morris	$1,777,627	$ 256,641	$1,520,986
SBC Communications	$1,426,068	$ 718,650	$ 707,418
Enron Corp.	$1,384,915	$ 359,565	$1,025,350
United Food & Commercial Workers Union	$1,376,250	$1,376,250	—
Citigroup	$1,337,140	$ 651,556	$ 685,584
National Rifle Association	$1,305,515	—	$1,305,515

Source: "Top Soft Money Donors: 2000 Election Cycle," The Center for Responsive Politics, November 1, 2000, Reprinted by permission from The Center for Responsive Politics. www.opensecrets.org/parties/cgi-win/softtop_2000.exe?txtCycle=2000&txtSort=amnt.

A Strategic Approach for Legal Compliance and Organizational Citizenship

Thus far, we have seen that although legal and regulatory forces have a strong influence on business operations, businesses can affect these forces through the political process. In addition, good corporate citizens strive to comply with society's wishes for responsible conduct through legal and ethical behavior. Indeed, the most effective way for businesses to manage the legal and regulatory environment is to establish values and policies that communicate and reward appropriate conduct. Most employees will try to comply with an organization's leadership and directions for responsible conduct. Therefore, top management must develop and implement a highly visible strategy for effective compliance. This means that top managers must take responsibility and be accountable for assessing legal risks and developing corporate programs that promote acceptable conduct.

More and more companies are establishing organizational compliance programs to ensure that they operate legally and responsibly as well as to generate a competitive advantage based on a reputation for responsible citizenship. There are also strong legal incentives to establish such programs. The United States Sentencing Commission established the **Federal Sentencing Guidelines for Organizations (FSGO)** in 1991 not only to streamline the sentencing and punishment for organizational crimes, but also to hold companies, as well as their employees, responsible for misconduct. Previously, the law punished only those employees responsible for an offense, not the company. Under the FSGO, if a court determines that a company's organizational culture rewarded or otherwise created opportunities that encouraged wrongdoing, the firm may be subject to stiff penalties in the event that one of its employees breaks the law. The guidelines apply to all felonies and Class A misdemeanors committed by employees in association with their work. Table 4.5 shows the percentage of organizations receiving fines and/or ordered to make restitution for crimes sentenced in 2000. Of the 151 organizations sentenced under the guidelines, 86 percent were fined,

TABLE 4.5

A Sample of Sentenced Organizations Fined or Ordered to Make Restitution Under FSGO in 2000

Organizational Offense	Number of Organizations Sentenced	Sentenced to Make Restitution	Fined	Sentenced with Both Fines and Restitution
Antitrust	19	0.0%	84.2%	10.5%
Bribes/gratuities	6	16.6%	66.7%	0.0%
Fraud	102	26.5%	35.3%	27.5%
Import/export violation	23	4.4%	73.9%	17.4%
Money laundering	10	40.0%	0.0%	10.0%
Environmental—water	39	5.1%	66.7%	28.2%
Food and drugs	13	7.7%	69.2%	7.7%

Source: U.S. Sentencing Commission's Sourcebook of Federal Sentencing Statistics, www.ussc.gov/ ANNRPT/2000/table 51.pdf., accessed October 22, 2001.

Campaign Finance Reform

Although the current process for financing primary and general presidential election campaigns in the United States has been effective, concerns about large private contributions and special-interest group money have led to renewed calls for reforming the system. Prior to the 1970s, companies financed presidential campaigns despite a direct ban on corporate contributions passed by Congress in 1907. After several scandals associated with campaign finance (e.g., Watergate), Congress passed the Federal Election Campaign Act (FECA) in 1974 to set limits on contributions from individuals, political parties, and political action committees (PACs). Under this law, an individual may contribute no more than $1,000 per election to a federal candidate, no more than $2,000 per year to a political party, and no more than a total of $25,000 to all candidates and parties. PACs are restricted to contributions of $5,000 per candidate per election and $15,000 per year in total donations to national party committees.

Since 1976, major party presidential candidates have received partial public funding for primary campaigns and 100 percent public funding for general election campaigns. Political party conventions also receive public funds. In order to receive these funds, eligible candidates must reach a threshold of $100,000 in individual contributions of $250 or less, and $5,000 of these contributions must be raised from each of at least 20 states. Candidates must also agree to adhere to strict spending limits and state spending caps and to restrict their use of personal funds. To be eligible for public funds for general elections, party nominees must agree not to raise private contributions from individuals, PACs, or party committees, although private contributions may be accepted to meet a campaign's legal and accounting expenses. Moreover, party nominees may not spend any more public funds they receive.

However, this system of financing elections has not always worked as expected. Although federal election laws prohibit corporations and labor unions from directly influencing national elections, the Federal Election Commission ruled in 1978 that "soft-money" contributions—from any source and in any amount—could be made to the national political parties for grassroots campaign activities even when those activities also benefit federal candidates. As a result of this ruling, political parties raised about $45 million in unregulated soft money during the 1988 campaign, which increased to $83 million in 1992, and $262 million in 1996. This amount was expected to reach a half billion dollars for the 2000 election campaign.

These huge sums of money and questions surrounding their effect on public policy made campaign finance reform a major issue during the 2000 presidential election. Two presidential

ordered to make restitution, or both, and the average fine and/or restitution amounted to more than $9 million.[47]

The assumption underlying the FSGO is that good corporate citizens maintain compliance systems and internal governance controls that deter misconduct by their employees. Thus, the guidelines focus on crime prevention and detection by

candidates, John McCain (Republican Party) and Ralph Nader (Green Party), zeroed in on the influence of big business contributions on the U.S. political system. Although McCain did not win the election, as a U.S. senator from Arizona, he proposed legislation that would ban soft-money contributions. Other candidates have proposed legislation that would allow for complete public funding of elections in order to reduce the need for contributions from individuals and businesses. Many Americans support such legislation out of fear that the current campaign finance system bends government policy makers toward the interests of big businesses at the expense of society and democracy. According to a poll by *Business Week* and Harris Poll, 74 percent of surveyed Americans say they think big business has too much power to influence government policy, politicians, and policy makers.

Campaign-finance reform efforts have sprung up all over the United States in an attempt to minimize the influence of moneyed interests over legislative outcomes. This movement has already achieved reform measures based on the public funding of political campaigns in several states. Maine, Arizona, Massachusetts, and Vermont have set up voluntary systems of public financing for state campaigns that prescribe spending limits and reject private contributions. Thirty-four states have placed limits on the size of contributions in state races.

Several organizations are working to achieve similar results on both the state and national level. Common Cause, a nonprofit, nonpartisan organization working to combat corruption, began fighting soft money in 1984, when it sued the Fed for failing to investigate how soft money was being raised and spent in order to curtail violations of the 1907 and 1947 federal laws. Consequently, the Fed issued new regulations requiring the national political parties to disclose soft-money contributions and expenses. In Colorado, a coalition that included Common Cause, the American Association for Retired Persons (AARP), and the League of Women Voters, won a cap on the size of contributions to gubernatorial and state-senate candidates even lower than a standard set by the Supreme Court in the 1970s. The Alliance for Democracy has called for a complete ban on private contributions along with full public financing of federal elections. Whether these efforts will result in any reform of the national political process remains to be seen, and business leaders will almost certainly fight reform efforts in order to retain the ear, if not the votes, of elected officials. ∎

Sources:

Aaron Bernstein, "Too Much Corporate Power?" *Business Week*, September 11, 2000, pp. 144–158; "A Brief History of the System," Common Cause, 2000, http://commoncause.org/pressroom/president_history. html; "The Emergence of Soft Money," Common Cause, 2000, http://commoncause.org/pressroom/president_soft.html; "How Business Rates: By the Numbers," *Business Week*, September 11, 2000, pp. 148–149; "How It Works," Common Cause, 2000, http://commoncause. org/pressroom/president_how.html; "Party Conventions," Common Cause, 2000, http://commoncause.org/pressroom/president_ conventions.html; Abby Scher, "Cleaning up Politics, Clearing out Big Money," *Dollar & Sense*, July/August 2000, p. 24.

mitigating penalties for those firms that have implemented such compliance programs in the event that one of their employees commits a crime. To avoid or limit fines and other penalties as a result of wrongdoing by an employee, the employer must be able to demonstrate that it has implemented a reasonable program for deterring and preventing unlawful behavior.

The United States Sentencing Commission has delineated seven steps that companies must implement to demonstrate the existence of an effective compliance effort and thereby avoid penalties in the event of an employee's wrongdoing. These steps, which are listed in Table 4.6, are based on the commission's determination to emphasize compliance programs and to provide guidance for both organizations and courts regarding program effectiveness. The steps are not "a superficial checklist requiring little analysis or thought."[48] Rather, they help companies understand what is required of a compliance program that is capable of reducing employees' opportunity to engage in misconduct.

To develop an effective compliance program, an organization should first develop a code of conduct that communicates the standards it expects of its employees and identifies key risk areas for the firm. Next, oversight of the program should be assigned to high-ranking personnel in the organization (such as an ethics officer, a vice president of human resources, or a general counsel) who are known to abide by the legal and ethical standards of the industry. Authority should never be delegated to anyone with a known propensity to engage in misconduct. An effective compliance program also requires a meaningful communications system, often in the form of ethics training, to disseminate the company's standards and procedures. This system should provide for mechanisms, such as anonymous toll-free hot lines or company ombudsmen, through which employees can report wrongdoing without fear of retaliation. Monitoring and auditing systems designed to detect misconduct are also crucial ingredients for an effective compliance program. If a company does detect criminal behavior or other wrongdoing by an employee, the firm must take immediate, appropriate, and fair disciplinary action towards all individu-

TABLE 4.6

Seven Steps to Legal Compliance

1. Establish codes of conduct.

2. Appoint or hire high-level compliance manager (ethics officer).

3. Take care in delegating authority (background checks on employees).

4. Institute a training program and communication system (ethics training).

5. Monitor and audit for misconduct (reporting mechanisms).

6. Enforce and discipline (management implementation of policy).

7. Revise program as needed (feedback and action).

Source: U.S. Sentencing Commission, *Federal Sentencing Guidelines for Organizations,* 2001.

als both directly and indirectly responsible for the offense. Finally, if a company discovers that a crime has occurred, it must take steps to prevent similar offenses in the future. This usually involves modifications to the compliance program, additional employee training, and communications about specific types of conduct. The government expects continuous improvement and refinement of these seven steps for compliance programs.[49]

A strong compliance program acts as a buffer to keep employees from committing crimes and to protect a company's reputation should wrongdoing occur despite its best efforts. If a firm can demonstrate that is has truly made an effort to communicate to employees about their legal and ethical responsibilities, the public's response to any wrongdoing may be reduced along with any corporate punishment the courts mete for the offense. It is important to point out, however, that executives who focus on strict legal compliance may be missing part of the picture when it comes to corporate citizenship. An effective compliance program must feature ethics and values as the driving force, as we shall see in the next chapter.

Summary

In a pluralistic society, many diverse stakeholder groups attempt to influence the public officials who legislate, interpret laws, and regulate business. Companies that adopt a strategic approach to the legal and regulatory system develop proactive organizational values and compliance programs that identify areas of risks and include formal communication, training, and continuous improvement of responses to the legal and regulatory environment.

Economic reasons for regulation often relate to efforts to level the playing field on which businesses operate. These efforts include regulating trusts, which are generally established to gain control of a product market or industry by eliminating competition, and eliminating monopolies, which occur when just one business provides a good or service in a given market. Another rationale for regulation is society's desire to restrict destructive or unfair competition. Social reasons for regulation address imperfections in the market that result in undesirable consequences, and protect natural and social resources. Other regulations are created in response to social demands for safety and equality in the workplace, safer products, and privacy issues.

The Sherman Antitrust Act is the principal tool used to prevent businesses from restraining trade and monopolizing markets. The Clayton Antitrust Act limits mergers and acquisitions that could stifle competition and prohibits specific activities that could substantially lessen competition or tend to create a monopoly. The Federal Trade Commission Act prohibits unfair methods of competition and created the Federal Trade Commission (FTC). Legal and regulatory policy is also enforced through lawsuits by private citizens, competitors, and special-interest groups.

A company that engages in commerce beyond its own country must contend with the complex relationship among the laws of its own nation, international laws, and the laws of the nation in which it will be trading. There is considerable variation and focus among different nations' laws, but many countries' antitrust laws are quite similar to those in the United States.

Regulation creates numerous costs for businesses, consumers, and society at large. Some measures of these costs include administrative spending patterns, staffing levels of federal regulatory agencies, and the costs businesses incur in complying with regulations. The cost of regulation is also passed on to consumers in the form of higher prices and may stifle product innovation and investments in new facilities and equipment. Regulation also provides many benefits, including greater equality in the workplace, safer workplaces, resources for disadvantaged members of society, safer products, more information about and greater choices among products, cleaner air and water, and the preservation of wildlife habitats. Antitrust laws and regulations strengthen competition and spur companies to invest in research and development. Many businesses and individuals believe that the costs of regulation outweigh its benefits. Some people desire complete deregulation, or removal of regulatory authority.

Because government is a stakeholder of business (and vice versa), businesses and government can work together as both legitimately participate in the political process. Business participation can be a positive or negative force in society's interest, depending not only on the outcome, but also on the perspective of various stakeholders.

Changes over the last forty years have shaped the political environment in which businesses operate. Among the most significant of these changes were amendments to the Legislative Reorganization Act and the Federal Election Campaign Act, which had the effect of reducing the importance of the political parties. Many candidates for elected offices turned to increasingly powerful special-interest groups to raise funds to campaign for elected offices.

Some organizations view regulatory and legal forces as beyond their control and simply react to conditions arising from those forces; other firms seek to influence the political process in order to achieve their goals. One way they can do so is through lobbying, the process of working to persuade public and/or government officials to favor a particular position in decision making. Companies can also influence the political process through political action committees, which are organizations that solicit donations from individuals and then contribute these funds to candidates running for political office. Corporate funds may also be channeled into candidates' campaign coffers as corporate executives' or stockholders' personal contributions, although such donations can violate the spirit of corporate campaign laws. Although laws limit corporate contributions to specific candidates, it is acceptable for businesses and other organizations to make donations to political parties.

More companies are establishing organizational compliance programs to ensure that they operate legally and responsibly as well as to generate a competitive advantage based on a reputation for good citizenship. Under the Federal Sentencing Guidelines for Organizations (FSGO), a company that wants to avoid or limit fines and other penalties as a result of an employee's crime must be able to demonstrate that it has implemented a reasonable program for deterring and preventing misconduct. To implement an effective compliance program, an organization should develop a code of conduct that communicates expected standards, assign oversight of the program to high-ranking personnel who abide by legal and ethical standards, communicate standards through training and other mechanisms, monitor and audit to detect wrongdoing, punish individuals responsible for misconduct, and take steps to continuously improve the program. A strong compliance program acts as a buffer to keep employees from committing crimes and to protect a company's reputation should wrongdoing occur despite its best efforts.

KEY TERMS

trust

monopoly

deregulation

lobbying

political action committee (PAC)

Federal Sentencing Guidelines for Organizations (FSGO)

DISCUSSION QUESTIONS

1. Discuss the existence of both cooperation and conflict between government and businesses concerning the regulation of business.

2. What is the rationale for government to regulate the activities of businesses? How is our economic and social existence shaped by government regulations?

3. What was the historical background that encouraged the government to enact legislation such as the Sherman Antitrust Act and the Clayton Act? Do these same conditions exist today?

4. What is the role and function of the Federal Trade Commission in the regulation of business? How does the FTC engage in proactive activities to avoid government regulation?

5. How do global regulations influence U.S. businesses operating internationally? What are the major obstacles to global regulation?

6. Compare the costs and benefits of regulation. In your opinion, do the benefits outweigh the costs? What are the advantages and disadvantages of deregulation?

7. Name three tools that businesses can employ to influence government and public policy. Evaluate the strengths and weaknesses of each of these approaches.

8. How do political action committees influence society, and what is their appropriate role in a democratic society?

9. Why should an organization evaluate and possibly implement the Federal Sentencing

Guidelines for Organizations (FSGO) as a strategic approach for legal compliance?

10. What are the seven steps for developing an effective ethical compliance program under the FSGO? What is the appropriate role of top management in developing effective compliance programs?

EXPERIENTIAL EXERCISE

Visit the web site of the Federal Trade Commission (FTC) (**http://www.ftc.gov/**). What is the FTC's current mission? What are the primary areas for which the FTC is responsible? Review the last two months of press releases from the FTC. Based on these releases, what appear to be major issues of concern at this time?

NOTES

1. "Commission Actions: May 2000," Federal Trade Commission, May 2, 2000, www.ftc.gov/opa/2000/fyi0024.html; "Company Briefing Books," *Wall Street Journal,* http://interactive.wsj.com/, accessed June 15, 2000; "World's Largest Manufacturer of Spice and Seasoning Products Agrees to Settle Price Discrimination Charges," Federal Trade Commission, March 8, 2000, www.ftc.gov/opa/2000/03/mccormick.htm.

2. George J. Siedel, "Six Forces and the Legal Environment of Business," *American Business Law Journal,* 37 (Summer 2000): 717–742.

3. Paul Starr, "Liberalism after Clinton," *The American Prospect,* August 28, 2000; Amy Borrus and Paula Dwyer, "Surprise: Bush Is Emerging as a Fighter for Privacy on the Net," *Business Week,* June 5, 2000, p. 63.

4. Julie Appleby, "Columbia Agrees to $745 Million Penalty," *USA Today,* May 19, 2000, p. B1.

5. G. Meirovich and A. Reichel, "Illegal But Ethical: An Inquiry into the Roots of Illegal Corporate Behavior in Russia," *Business Ethics: A European Review,* 9 (July 2000): 126–135.

6. Claudia N. Ginanni, "Generic Drug Manufacturers Are Unhappy with SmithKline Beecham's Paxil Patents," *The Legal Intelligencer,* March 21, 2000, p. 1.

7. Don Clark, "Oracle Loses Wrongful-Termination Suit Involving Trade Secrets of Rival SAP," *Wall Street Journal,* August 18, 2000, p. B6.

8. Scott Kilman, "EU Fines Archer-Daniels, Asian Firms for Rigging the Price of Lysine Additive," *Wall Street Journal,* June 8, 2000, http://interactive.wsj.com/; Randall Palmer, "Canada Fines Food Giant Archer Daniels for Price Fixing," *America Online Newswire,* May 27, 1998.

9. John Fialka, "Lockheed Faces Record Fine for Safety Violations," *Wall Street Journal,* August 29, 2000, p. A8.

10. Lee Gomes, "Ruling in Copyright Case Favors Film Industry," *Wall Street Journal,* August 18, 2000, p. B6.

11. Jim Carlton and Pui-Wing Tam, "Online Auctioneers Face Growing Fraud Problem," *Wall Street Journal,* May 12, 2000, p. B2; Michael Pastore, "Online Fraud: How Bad Is It?" http://cyberatlas.internet.com/markets/retailing/article/0,,6061_464841,00.html, accessed October 20, 2001.

12. "The Sherman Antitrust Act," The Antitrust Case Browser, www.antitrustcases.com/statutes/sherman.html, accessed October 21, 2001.

13. Ibid.

14. Andrew J. Glass, "Judge Splits Microsoft," *Austin American-Statesman,* June 8, 2000, www.austin360.com/statesman/; Jennifer Jones, "Government Drops Breakup Bid," *InfoWorld,* September 10, 2001, http://www.findartices.com, accessed October 20, 2001.

15. Department of Justice, "Antitrust Enforcement and the Consumer," pamphlet (Washington D.C.: U.S. Department of Justice), www.usdoj.gov/atr/public/div_stats/1638.htm, accessed October 21, 2001.

16. "Marketers of 'The Enforma System' Settle FTC Charges of Deceptive Advertising for Their Weight Loss Product," Federal Trade Commission, April 26, 2000, www.ftc.gov/opa/2000/04/enforma.htm.

17. "FTC Approves Pact Allowing Toysmart's Customer-List Sale," *Wall Street Journal,* July 24, 2000, p. A28.

18. "Nine West Settles State and Federal Price Fixing Charges," Federal Trade Commission, Mar. 6, 2000, www.ftc.gov/opa/2000/03/ninewest.htm.

19. "Price Fixing Suit Settled," ABCNews.com, September 7, 1999, www.abcnews.go.com/sections/business/dailyNews/vitamins_settle990907.html.

20. Albert A. Foer and Robert H. Lande, "The Evolution of United States Antitrust Law: The Past, Present & (Possible) Future," *American Antitrust Institute,* October 20, 1999, www.antitrustinstitute.org/recent/64.pdf.

21. "France Bans Beef on Bone," CNN, November 11, 2000, www.cnn.com.

22. Ernest Beck, "Stores Told to Lift Prices in Germany," *Wall Street Journal,* September 11, 2000, p. A27.

23. Brandon Mitchener, "Global Antitrust Process May Get Simpler," *Wall Street Journal,* October 27, 2000, p. A17; Debbie Thorne LeClair, O. C. Ferrell, and Linda Ferrell, "Federal Sentencing Guidelines for Organizations: Legal, Ethical, and Public Policy Issues for International Marketing," *Journal of Public Policy and Marketing,* 16 (Spring 1997): 30.

24. O. C. Ferrell, Thomas N. Ingram, and Raymond W. LaForge, "Initiating Structure for Legal and Ethical Decisions in a Global Sales Organization," *Industrial Marketing Management,* 29 (November 2000): 555–564

25. LeClair, Ferrell, and Ferrell, "Federal Sentencing Guidelines for Organizations," p. 31.

26. Ibid

27. Ted Bridis, "Computer-Crime Treaty," *Wall Street Journal,* October 26, 2000, p. B8.

28. Melinda Warren, *Federal Regulatory Spending Reaches a New Height: An Analysis of the Budget of the U.S. Government for the Year 2001* (St. Louis: Center for the Study of American Business, June 2000), accessible at http://csab.wustl.edu/CSAB%20pubs-pdf%20files/RBR/RBR%2023.pdf.

29. Ibid.

30. Philip Morris USA, "Kids and Tobacco," advertisement, *Newsweek,* August 28, 2000.

31. Department of Justice, "Antitrust Enforcement and the Consumer."

32. Mark Wigfield, "FCC to Diminish Role in Monitoring Phone Equipment," *Wall Street Journal,* May 15, 2000, p. B12.

33. Robert Kuttner, "The Airlines: Less Regulation Won't Fly," *Business Week,* August 7, 2000, p. 24.

34. William M. Pride and O. C. Ferrell, *Marketing: Concepts and Strategies,* 12th ed. (Boston: Houghton Mifflin, 2003), pp. 54–55.

35. Ibid.

36. Jennifer Rewick, "Connecticut Attorney General Launches Probe of Priceline.com After Complaints," *Wall Street Journal,* October 2, 2000, p. B16.

37. Pride and Ferrell, *Marketing: Concepts and Strategies,* pp. 54–55.

38. Ibid.

39. Mark Wigfield, "'Digital Signature' Bill Is Cleared by Congress," *Wall Street Journal,* June 19, 2000, p. B12.

40. Joint Committee on the Organization of Congress, "Historical Overview," *Organization of the Congress,* December 1993, www.house.gov/rules/jcoc2c.htm#b; Joint Committee on the Organization of Congress, "Reorganization in the Modern Congress," *Organization of the Congress,* December 1993, www.house.gov/rules/jcoc2o.htm; Marc A. Triebwasser, "Congressional Leadership and Reform: The Trends Toward Centralization and Decentralization," *American Politics,* www.polisci.ccsu.edu/trieb/Cong-9.html, accessed October 21, 2001.

41. "The FEC and the Federal Campaign Finance Law," Federal Election Commission, www.fec.gov/pages/fecfeca.htm, (accessed) October 21, 2001.

42. "About Common Cause," Common Cause, www.commoncause.org/about/fact.htm, accessed October 21, 2001.

43. Don Corney, Amy Borrus, and Jay Greene, "Microsoft's All Out Counterattack," *Business Week,* May 15, 2000, pp. 103–106.

44. "Driving Mr. Gephardt," *Newsweek,* August 21, 2000, p. 48.

45. John Scorza, "Business Group Vows to Fight New Government Contracting Rule," www.lycos.com/business/cch/news.html, (accessed) May 3, 2000.

46. Corney, Borrus, and Greene, "Microsoft's All Out Counterattack."

47. U.S. Sentencing Commission, "Mean and Median Fine or Restitution Imposed on Sentenced Organizations by Primary Offense and Applicability of Chapter Eight Fine Guidelines," *1999 Sourcebook of Federal Sentencing Statistics,* www.ussc.gov/ANNRPT/1999/table 52.pdf.

48. Win Swenson, "The Organizational Guidelines Carrot and Stick Philosophy and Their Focus on Effective Compliance," in *Corporate Crime in America: Strengthening the Good Citizen Corporation* (Washington D.C.: United States Sentencing Commission, 1993), p. 17.

49. *United States Code Service* (Lawyers Addition), 18 U.S.S.C. Appendix, Sentencing Guidelines for the United States Courts (Rochester, N.Y.: Lawyers Cooperative Publishing, 1995), § 8A.1.

Business Ethics

5

- ▶ The Nature of Business Ethics

- ▶ Foundations of Business Ethics

- ▶ Understanding the Ethical Decision-Making Process

- ▶ Organizational Approaches to Improving Ethical Behavior

- ▶ Strategic Implementation of Business Ethics

To define and describe the importance of business ethics

To discuss the individual factors that influence ethical or unethical decisions

To explore the effect of organizational relationships on ethical decision making

To evaluate the role of opportunity in ethical or unethical decisions

To examine how organizations can improve ethical decisions in business

Like many automakers around the world, Mitsubishi Motors, Japan's number four automaker, faces intense competition in markets both at home in Japan and abroad. The company was losing hundreds of millions of dollars in the early 2000s with decreasing sales, whereas rival Toyota Motor and Honda Motor were experiencing increased sales. Mitsubishi's poor performance led it to make alliances with Volvo and DaimlerChrysler, the latter acquiring a 34 percent stake in the Japanese firm. However, the bad news for Mitsubishi worsened into a scandal after a twenty-year practice of hiding consumer complaints came to light.

Mitsubishi admitted that for more than twenty years, it had systematically covered up customer complaints about tens of thousands of defective automobiles. During this period, when customers brought their cars in for repairs, Mitsubishi employees fixed the defects but pigeonholed the complaints in a file known as "H," for a Japanese word for *conceal* or *defer*. When rumors of the secret file began to circulate in the summer of 2000, company president Katsuhiko Kawasoe at first denied the allegations. Soon after, Transportation Ministry officials, acting on an anonymous tip, found the complaints in a company locker room during an inspection.

By not reporting customer complaints about defects to the government, as required by both Japanese and U.S. law, Mitsubishi headed off the threat of expensive recalls and negative publicity. Although none of the defects resulted in any serious or fatal accidents, Japan's Transportation Ministry made charges. In the United States, the National Highway Traffic Safety Administration investigated to determine the extent of violations of U.S. law.

After the secret files came to light, Mitsubishi admitted to hiding complaints and agreed to recall a total of 620,000 vehicles, including 50,000 that had been exported to the United States, to repair faulty fuel tanks, fuel tank caps, clutches, crankshafts, and brakes. The recalls are expected to cost the company about $69 million. The practice of concealing evidence of defects that could precipitate a recall is not so unusual in Japan. In Japanese culture, product recalls are judged an enormous humiliation, especially for Japan's acclaimed automotive manufacturers.

After the scandal was publicized, Mitsubishi President Katsuhiko Kawasoe apologized to the Minister of Transportation, Hajime Morita, with a deep bow, as well as to Mitsubishi vehicle owners. Kawasoe also promised that the company would punish those directly responsible. "The whole state of affairs is, in a word, the result of a lack of respect for rules and regulations on the part of the company officers and employees involved," he said. Moreover, Kawasoe, along with other top Mitsubishi executives, agreed to take a salary cut to acknowledge his accountability in the cover-up, although he continued to deny knowledge of it. Kawasoe added, "My job is to work to regain the public's trust in this company."[1]

As illustrated by the Mitsubishi scandal, business ethics relates to questions about whether various stakeholders consider specific business practices acceptable. The U.S. Labor Department, for example, required Texaco to pay $3 million to 186 female employees after the agency determined that the women had been paid less than their male counterparts.[2] The Minnesota attorney general sued U.S. Bank for allegedly releasing customers' private information—including social security numbers, account numbers and balances, and credit card numbers—to a telemarketing company.[3] Regardless of the legality of the actions of these companies, others have judged the conduct as unacceptable.

By its very nature, the field of business ethics is controversial, and no universally accepted approach has emerged for resolving its questions. Nonetheless, most businesses are establishing initiatives that include the development and implementation of ethics and legal compliance programs designed to deter conduct that some stakeholders might consider objectionable. Unisys, for example, provides ethics training for 34,000 employees working in 100 countries worldwide. It reaches about 90 percent of them annually through videos, an internal web site, newsletters, and other ethics training.[4] This training helps Unisys communicate its values and policies to ensure that employees understand what the company expects of them, as well as what will happen if they violate the company's policies or the law.

The definition of corporate citizenship that appears in Chapter 1 incorporates society's expectations of corporate social responsibility, which includes four levels of concern: economic, legal, ethical, and philanthropic. Because ethics is becoming an increasingly important issue in business today, this chapter is devoted to exploring its role in business decision making. First, we define business ethics and examine its importance from an organizational perspective. We then look at the individual, organizational, and opportunity factors that influence ethical decision making in the workplace. Finally, we look at some of the approaches businesses can use to improve ethical behavior in the workplace.

The Nature of Business Ethics

To support business decisions that are both agreeable and beneficial to society, it is necessary to examine business ethics and its application in the workplace. The term *ethics* relates to choices and judgments about acceptable standards of conduct that guide the behavior of individuals and groups. These standards require both organizations and individuals to accept responsibility for their actions and to comply with established value systems. As Figure 5.1 indicates, most employees perceive that the values of honesty, respect, and trust are applied frequently in the workplace. Without a shared view of what values and conduct are appropriate and

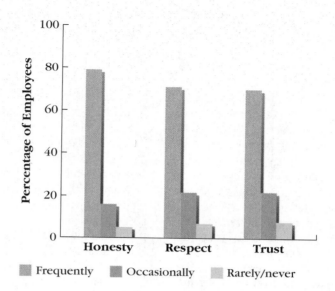

FIGURE 5.1

Values Applied in the Workplace

At least 70 percent of employees say that trust, respect, and honesty are applied frequently in their organizations.

Source: Ethics Resource Center, *The Ethics Resource Center's 2000 National Business Ethics Survey: How Employees Perceive Ethics at Work* (Washington D.C.: Ethics Resource Center, 2000), p. 55. Reprinted by permission from Ethics Resource Center.

acceptable, companies may fail to balance their desires for profits against the wishes and needs of society. Maintaining this balance often demands compromises or trade-offs. For example, the controversy surrounding the promotion of cigarettes to children and teenagers has put pressure on tobacco manufacturers to stop advertising in magazines in which 15 percent or more of the readers are teenagers. In response, leading companies such as Philip Morris have pledged to pull ads from magazines with substantial numbers of young readers, including *Rolling Stone* and *Sports Illustrated*.[5] This example illustrates the legal and social pressures to act appropriately in order to protect children from the dangers of smoking. Society has developed rules—both legal and implied—to guide companies in their efforts to earn profits through means that do not bring harm to individuals or to society at large.

Business ethics comprises the principles and standards that guide the behavior of individuals and groups in the world of business. Managers, employees, consumers, industry associations, government regulators, business partners, and special-interest groups all contribute to these conventions, and they may change over time. As we saw in Chapter 4, the most basic of these standards have been codified as laws and regulations to encourage companies to conform to society's expectations of business conduct. Public concerns about increasing pollution and

Mattel Doesn't Play Around When It Comes to Ethics

Mattel, Inc., the world's largest marketer of children's toys, has 31,000 employees working out of facilities and offices in 36 nations. The company sells $5.5 billion worth of Barbie and American Girl dolls, Cabbage Patch Kids, Hot Wheels and Matchbox cars, Tyco Toys, and board games such as Scrabble in 155 countries around the world. Because of its global reach and the nature of its primary customer, children, Mattel faces a number of ethical issues. To ensure that these issues do not create problems for the El Segundo, California-based company, it has developed a comprehensive ethics program that focuses on protecting children's rights and setting international workplace and business practice standards.

Because Mattel's products are designed primarily for children, the company has an ethical responsibility to be sensitive to social concerns about children's rights, such as privacy. The company has gone to great lengths to inform children—and their parents—about its philosophy regarding the collection of information from its web sites. Each of the company's product web sites includes a statement about Mattel's online privacy policy. This policy specifies that the company does not collect and use any personal information unless it is volunteered, and only from children older than 13. Parental consent is required to collect personal information from children under the age of 13. The policy explains how the company uses the information it collects, so that users can make an educated decision as to whether they wish to reveal such information. Mattel's policy also urges children to consult their parents about any questions they may have about using the company's web sites. The policy stresses that parents should monitor their children's time online and urge them not to provide personal information on Mattel's or any other company's web site without their parent's permission. Finally, the policy emphasizes that Mattel abides by the Children's Online Privacy Protection Act of 1998 as well as the guidelines of the Children's Advertising Review Unit (CARU) of the Council of Better Business Bureaus.

As a multinational company that operates facilities and contracts with companies around the world, Mattel has established international workplace and business practice standards. To minimize the potential for problems associated with doing business in so many different countries, each with its own laws and cultural expectations, Mattel has established a code of conduct called "Global Manufacturing Principles." These principles reflect Mattel's responsibility to conduct

declining habitat, for example, led to the passage of the Clean Air Act and other regulations designed to require businesses to be more environmentally responsible.

However, it is vital to recognize that business ethics goes beyond legal issues. Ethical business decisions foster trust in business relationships, and, as we discussed in Chapter 2, trust is a key factor in improving productivity and achieving success in most organizations. When companies deviate from the prevailing standards of industry and society, the result is customer dissatisfaction, lack of trust,

manufacturing responsibly and to respect the cultural, ethical, and philosophical differences of the many countries in which Mattel operates.

The Global Manufacturing Principles address issues such as wages and working hours at Mattel, child labor, forced labor, discrimination, freedom of association, and working conditions. For example, the code states that facilities that produce toys for Mattel will not employ anyone under the age of 16 or the local legal age limit (whichever is higher). The code emphasizes, "Mattel creates products for children around the world—not jobs." The code specifies that Mattel will not use or permit any manufacturer or supplier to use forced or prison labor of any kind. The code also indicates Mattel's preference for business partners who share its commitment to ethical standards.

To ensure that its principles are followed, Mattel audits all facilities that manufacture products with the Mattel name. The company completed its first full audit of each of its manufacturing sites as well as the facilities of its primary contractors in 1997. Although these audits did not uncover any problems with child labor or forced labor (an issue that has plagued Nike and other consumer product companies), several contractors were found to be in violation of Mattel's principles. These companies were ordered to bring their operations into compliance or risk losing Mattel's substantial business.

Mattel's ethics policies and principles benefit both the people who manufacture its products as well as its customers, who can purchase Mattel products with the confidence that they have been manufactured in an environment that emphasizes safety, respect for individual rights, and respect for the environment. Although the company certainly benefits from these principles, they also indicate its willingness to consider many stakeholders' interests in its business philosophy. The establishment and enforcement of ethical standards signal employees, partners, customers, and other stakeholders that Mattel doesn't play around when it comes to responsible business conduct. ■

Sources:
"Briefing Books," *Wall Street Journal Interactive*, http://interactive. wsj.com/, accessed November 27, 2000; Adam Bryant, "Mattel CEO Jill Barad and a Toyshop that Doesn't Forget to Play," *New York Times*, October 11, 1998; Ronald Grover, "Mattel: A Great Deal of Re-Assembly Required," *Business Week*, April 17, 2000; James Heckman, "Legislation," *Marketing News*, December 7, 1998, pp. 1–16; "Mattel, Inc., Launches Global Code of Conduct Intended to Improve Workplace, Workers' Standard of Living," Canada Newswire, November 21, 1997; "Mattel, Inc. Online Privacy Policy," Mattel, www.Mattel.com/common/ policy.html, accessed November 27, 2000; Marla Matzer, "Deals on Hot Wheels," *Los Angeles Times*, July 22, 1998; "Responsibility: Global Manufacturing Principles," Mattel, www.Mattel.com/corporate/ company/responsibility/index.asp?section=gmp, accessed November 27, 2000; Patricia Sellers, "The 50 Most Powerful Women in American Business," *Fortune*, October 12, 1998; "Toymaker Mattel Bans Child Labor," *Denver Post*, November 21, 1998.

and lawsuits. Indeed, 78 percent of consumers say they avoid certain businesses or products because of negative perceptions about them.[6] One such business may be MCI Worldcom, which faces accusations that it charged unknowing and trusting customers the highest rate possible—$2.49 plus 38 cents a minute—for long-distance services. A class-action lawsuit accused MCI of "arbitrarily" instituting the $2.49 surcharge, a practice the suit labeled "rate slamming." As part of an agreement proposed to settle the suit, MCI agreed to apply the surcharge more appropriately.[7] The lawsuit suggests that most customers would prefer that companies such as MCI Worldcom strive to create long-term loyalty through fair pricing, not manipulation and deception.

Some businesspeople choose to behave ethically because of enlightened self-interest, or the expectation that "ethics pays." They believe that if they do not act responsibly and as good citizens, the public and customers will strike back with legal action and demands for restrictive regulations. The airline industry, for example, adopted a voluntary "fair treatment of passengers" program in the face of mounting criticism from consumers and the threat of legislation that would have mandated an airline passenger bill of rights. Among the airlines' promises are to provide current information about flight delays and cancellations, increase their financial liability for lost baggage, make reasonable efforts to provide necessities (e.g., food, water, toilets) to passengers who are stuck in planes on the ground for extended periods, and respond to customer complaints within sixty days.[8] The airline industry took a voluntary approach to increase customer trust, reduce passenger complaints, and, of course, to lessen the probability of further industry regulation. After the terrorist attacks of September 11, 2001, in which highjacked airliners were used as weapons of destruction, passengers became more concerned about security than comfort and the quality of service. Airlines moved more toward a survival approach and tried to maintain passenger confidence in their services. Improved communication and understanding should result in more ethical treatment of passengers.

Foundations of Business Ethics

Because individuals and groups within a company may not have all embraced the same set of values, there is always the possibility of ethical conflict. Most ethical issues in an organizational context are addressed openly whenever a policy, code, or rule is questioned. Even then it may be hard to distinguish between the ethical issue and the legal means used to resolve it. Because it is difficult to draw a boundary between legal and ethical issues, all questionable issues need an organizational mechanism for resolution.

The legal ramifications of some issues and situations may be obvious, but questionable decisions and actions more often result in disputes that must be resolved through some type of negotiation or even litigation. For example, a number of franchisees of The Body Shop filed lawsuits against the cosmetics firm alleging fraud, fraudulent inducement, inequitable treatment, and retaliatory practices. The British firm settled lawsuits with franchisees in Canada, Singapore, Norway, France, and Israel, in some cases, by buying out franchisees. The lawsuits have involved millions of dollars and years of court proceedings.[9] When ethical disputes wind up in court, the costs and distractions associated with litigation can be crippling to a business. In addition to the compensatory or nominal damages actually incurred, punitive

damages may be imposed on a company that is judged to have acted improperly in order to punish the firm and to send an intimidating message to others. The legal system, therefore, provides a formal venue for businesspeople to resolve ethical disputes as well as legal ones; in fact, many of the examples we cite in this chapter had to be resolved through the courts. To avoid the costs of litigation, companies should develop systems to monitor complaints, suggestions, and other feedback from stakeholders. In many cases, issues can be negotiated or resolved without legal intervention. Strategic citizenship entails systems for listening to, understanding, and effectively managing stakeholder concerns.[10]

A high level of personal morality may not be sufficient to prevent an individual from violating the law in an organizational context in which even experienced attorneys debate the exact meaning of the law. Because it is impossible to train all the members of an organization as lawyers, the identification of ethical issues and implementation of standards of conduct that incorporate both legal and ethical concerns are the best approach to preventing crime and avoiding civil litigation. Codifying ethical standards into meaningful policies that spell out what is and is not acceptable gives businesspeople an opportunity to reduce the probability of behavior that could create legal problems. Without proper ethical training and guidance, it is impossible for the average business manager to understand the exact boundaries for illegal behavior in the areas of price fixing, fraud, export/import violations, copyright violations, and so on. MP3.com, for example, has struggled to determine what constitutes ethical and legal behavior in its business of making music available to consumers while addressing the interests and rights of music companies. MP3.com recently agreed to pay $53.4 million to Universal Music Group and secured a licensing agreement to permit use of the record company's music. Licensing agreements with major music labels such as Warner Music Group, EMI, and Sony Music Entertainment have minimized concerns over copyright violations by the online music service.[11] A corporate focus on ethics helps to create a buffer zone on issues that could potentially trigger serious legal complications for the company.

Although the values of honesty, respect, and trust are often assumed to be self-evident and universally accepted, business decisions involve complex and detailed discussions in which correctness may not be so clear cut. Both employees and managers need experience within their specific industry to understand how to operate in gray areas or to handle close calls in evolving areas, such as Internet privacy. For example, how much personal information should be stored on customers who visit a firm's web site without their permission? Selling or renting mailing lists is prohibited in Europe under the European Union Directive on Data Protection—consumers' data cannot be used without their permission.[12] In the United States, companies have more freedom to decide how to collect and use customers' personal data. Advancing technology raises new questions every day. For example, Sprint Corporation, which provides wireless telephone services, has come under fire for plans to put global-positioning-system (GPS) technology into its cell phones to help pinpoint the location of users making 911 emergency calls. Privacy advocates, however, fear that the technology could be misused to trace customers.[13]

Many people who have limited business experience suddenly find themselves required to make decisions about product quality, advertising, pricing, sales techniques, hiring practices, privacy, and pollution control. The personal values they learned through nonwork socialization from family, religion, and school may not provide specific guidelines for these complex business decisions. In other words, a person's experiences and decisions at home, in school, and in the community may be quite different from the experiences and the decisions he or she has to make at work. Moreover, the interests and values of individual employees may differ from those of the company in which they work, from industry standards, and from society in general. When personal values are inconsistent with the configuration of values held by the group, ethical conflict may ensue. It is important that a shared vision of acceptable behavior develop from an organizational perspective to cultivate consistent and reliable relationships with all concerned stakeholders. A shared vision of ethics that is part of an organization's culture can be questioned, analyzed, and modified as new issues develop. However, business ethics should relate to work environment decisions and should not control or influence personal ethical issues.

Understanding the Ethical Decision-Making Process

To grasp the significance of ethics in business decision making, it is important to understand how ethical decisions are made within the context of an organization. Understanding the ethical decision-making process can help individuals and businesses design strategies to deter misconduct. Our descriptive approach to understanding ethical decision making does not prescribe what to do but, rather, provides a framework for managing ethical behavior in the workplace. Figure 5.2 depicts this framework, which shows how individual factors, organizational relationships, and opportunity interact to determine ethical decisions in business.

▶ Individual Factors

Individuals make ethical choices based on their own concepts of right or wrong, and they act accordingly in their daily lives. For example, studies of high school

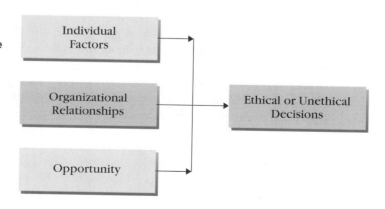

FIGURE 5.2

Factors That Influence the Ethical Decision-Making Process

students suggest that individual ethics are reaching a new low. In a study by the Josephson Institute of Ethics, seven out of ten students admitted to cheating on a test at least once in the last year, and 92 percent to lying to their parents in the last year. One out of six students confessed to showing up for class drunk in the past year.[14] Significant factors that affect the ethical decision-making process include an individual's personal moral philosophy, stage of moral development, motivation, and other personal factors such as gender, age, and experience.

Moral Philosophy[15]   Many people have justified difficult decisions by citing the Golden Rule ("Do unto others as you would have them do unto you.") or some other principle. Such principles, or rules, that individuals apply in deciding what is right or wrong are often referred to as **moral philosophies.** These philosophies are learned through socialization by family members, social groups, religion, and formal education. Most moral philosophies can be classified as consequentialism, ethical formalism, or justice.

Consequentialism is a class of moral philosophy that considers a decision right or acceptable if it accomplishes a desired result such as pleasure, knowledge, career growth, the realization of self-interest, or utility. For example, the president and corporate controller of Right Way Inc., a chain of rent-to-own retail stores, were accused of accounting irregularities. Internal investigators believe that "fictitious" entries in the company's financial statements were intended to lower operating expenses in order to artificially increase the firm's earnings.[16] Egoism and utilitarianism are two important consequentialist philosophies that often guide decision making in business.

Egoism is a philosophy that defines right or acceptable conduct in terms of the consequences for the individual. Egoists believe they should make decisions that maximize their own self-interest, which, depending on the individual, may be defined as physical well-being, power, pleasure, fame, a satisfying career, a good family life, wealth, or something else. In a decision-making situation, the egoist will probably choose the alternative that most benefits his or her self-interest. Many people feel that egoists are inherently unethical, that they focus on the short term, and that they will take advantage of any opportunity to exploit consumers or employees. An example of egoism in the business world might be telemarketers who prey on elderly consumers who may be vulnerable because of loneliness or fear of losing their financial independence. Tens of thousands of senior citizens fall victim to telemarketing fraud every year. In Tucson, Arizona, for example, police uncovered a telemarketing scam in which elderly people received calls telling them they had won a lottery or sweepstakes contest. However, the victims were also told that they needed to pay a "tax" in order to receive the contest winnings. In one case, the tax was $10,000.[17]

Utilitarianism is another consequentialist philosophy that is concerned with consequences, but utilitarians seek the greatest good for the greatest number of people. Using a cost-benefit analysis, a utilitarian decision maker calculates the *utility* of the consequences of all possible alternatives and then chooses the one that achieves the greatest utility. For example, the Occupational Safety and Health Administration (OSHA) recently proposed new standards for ensuring health and safety in the workplace. Thus, the federal agency has concluded that the greatest utility and benefits to society and employees will result from greater corporate efforts and leadership on safety and health issues on the job.[18]

In contrast with consequentialism, **ethical formalism** is a class of moral philosophy that focuses on the rights of individuals and on the intentions associated with a particular behavior rather than on its consequences. Ethical formalists regard certain behaviors as inherently right, and their determination of rightness focuses on the individual actor, not society. Thus, these perspectives are sometimes referred to as *nonconsequentialism* and the ethics of *respect for persons.* Consider that a recent survey by the Institute of Ethics, an independent research arm of the American Medical Association, found that some doctors are manipulating insurance reimbursement rules to ensure treatment for their patients. For instance, a doctor might code a patient's illness as a sleep disorder, which is usually covered by insurance, rather than depression, which is not covered by most insurance plans, so that the insurance company would reimburse the patient for prescribed medications. According to the survey, 39 percent of the physicians reported sometimes or often exaggerating to insurance companies, and 10 percent admitted to outright lies.[19] These doctors may be applying ethical formalism in their decision to flout the rules for their patients' benefit. But, the application of formalism in this context could be illegal if it violates the doctor's requirement to report accurately to the insurance company.

Contemporary ethical formalism has been greatly influenced by the German philosopher Immanuel Kant, who developed the so-called categorical imperative: "Act as if the maxim of thy action were to become by thy will a universal law of nature."[20] Unlike utilitarians, ethical formalists contend that there are some things that people should *not* do, even to maximize utility. For example, an ethical formalist would consider it unacceptable for a coal mine to continue to operate if some workers became ill and died of black lung disease. A utilitarian, however, might consider some disease or death an acceptable consequence of a decision that resulted in large-scale employment and economic prosperity.

Justice theory is a class of moral philosophy that relates to evaluations of fairness, or the disposition to deal with perceived injustices of others. Justice demands fair treatment and due reward in accordance with ethical or legal standards. In business, this requires that the rules an individual uses to determine justice be based on the perceived rights of individuals and on the intentions associated with a business interaction. Justice, therefore, is more likely to be based on nonconsequentialist moral philosophies than on consequentialist ones. Justice primarily addresses the issue of what individuals feel they are due based on their rights and performance in the workplace. For example, the U.S. Equal Employment Opportunity Commission exists to help employees who suspect the injustice of discrimination in the workplace.

There are three types of justice that can be used to assess fairness in different situations. *Distributive justice* evaluates the outcomes or results of a business relationship. For example, if an employee feels that she is being paid less than her coworkers for the same work, she has concerns about distributive justice. *Procedural justice* assesses the processes and activities employed to produce an outcome or results. Procedural justice concerns about compensation would relate to the perception that salary and benefit decisions were consistent and fair to all categories of employees. A recent study found that procedural justice is associated with group cohesiveness and helping behaviors.[21] *Interactional justice* evaluates the communication processes used in the business relationship. Being untruthful about the reasons for missing work is an example of an interactional justice issue.[22]

It is important to recognize that there is no one "correct" moral philosophy to apply in resolving ethical and legal issues in the workplace. It is also important to acknowledge that each philosophy presents an ideal perspective and that most people seem to adapt a number of moral philosophies as they interpret the context of different decision-making situations.[23] Moreover, research suggests that individuals may apply different moral philosophies in different decision situations.[24] Each philosophy could result in a different decision in a situation requiring an ethical judgment. And, depending on the situation, people may even change their value structure or moral philosophy when making decisions.[25]

Stage of Moral Development[26]   One reason that different people make different decisions when confronted with similar ethical situations may be because they are in different stages of moral development. Psychologist Lawrence Kohlberg proposed that people progress through stages in their development of moral reasoning or, as he called it, cognitive moral development.[27] He believes that people progress through the following six stages:

1. *The stage of punishment and obedience.* An individual in this stage of development defines right as literal obedience to rules and authority and responds to rules in terms of the physical power of those who determine such rules. Individuals in this stage do not associate right and wrong with any higher-order or moral philosophy, but instead with a person who has power. For example, a plant supervisor may choose to go along with a superior's order to release untreated wastewater into a nearby stream, even though she knows that would be illegal, because she fears the superior's power to fire her if she does not comply.

2. *The stage of individual instrumental purpose and exchange.* A person in this stage defines right as that which serves his or her own needs. In this

stage, people evaluate behavior on the basis of its fairness to themselves rather than solely on the basis of specific rules or authority figures. For example, a corporate buyer may choose to accept an expensive gift from a salesperson despite the presence of a company rule prohibiting the acceptance of gifts because the gift is something he needs or wants. This stage is sometimes labeled the stage of reciprocity, because from a practical standpoint, ethical decisions are based on "you-scratch-my-back-and-I'll-scratch-yours" agreements instead of on principles such as loyalty or justice.

3. *The stage of mutual interpersonal expectation, relationships, and conformity.* An individual in this stage emphasizes others over himself or herself. Although these individuals still derive motivation from obedience to rules, they also consider the well-being of others. For example, a production manager might choose to obey an order from upper management to speed up an assembly line because she believes this action will generate more profit for the company and thereby preserve her employees' jobs.

4. *The stage of social justice and conscience maintenance.* A person in this stage determines what is right by considering duty to society, as well as to other specific people. Duty, respect for authority, and maintaining social order become fundamental goals in decision making. For example, Jeffrey Wigand, a former executive at Brown & Williamson Tobacco Corporation, believed that the company was hiding from the public the truth that cigarettes are addictive and dangerous. He chose to "blow the whistle" by testifying against his former employer after he was fired.[28] Wigand's story was later dramatized in the movie, *The Insider.*

5. *The stage of prior rights, social contract, or utility.* In this stage, an individual is concerned with upholding the basic rights, values, and legal contracts of society. Such individuals feel a sense of obligation or "social contract" to other groups and recognize that legal and moral points of view may conflict in some instances. To minimize conflict, persons in this stage base decisions on a rational calculation of overall utilities. For example, a business owner may choose to establish an organizational compliance program because it will serve as a buffer to prevent legal problems and to protect the company's good name.

6. *The stage of universal ethical principles.* A person in this stage believes that right is determined by universal ethical principles that everyone should follow. Such individuals believe that there are inalienable rights that are universal in nature and consequence. Justice and equality are examples of such universal rights. Thus, a businessperson in this stage may be more concerned with social ethical issues and rely less on the company for direction in situations with an ethical component.[29] For example, a marketing manager may

argue for the termination of a toy that has resulted in injury and death because she believes the product threatens the universal value of right to life.

Because there is some spillover effect among these stages, cognitive moral development can be viewed as more of a continuum.

Kohlberg's theory suggests that people may change their moral beliefs and behavior as they gain education and experience in resolving conflicts, which helps accelerate their progress along the moral development continuum. A survey by the Ethics Resource Center provides some confirmation that this occurs. Nearly half (49 percent) of 4,000 individuals surveyed believed that their business ethics had improved over the course of their careers. One-third (34 percent) thought their business ethics had improved because of their personal ethics. Surprisingly, nearly one in eight (13 percent) believed that their personal ethics had improved because of their business ethics.[30]

Kohlberg's model also suggests that there are universal values by which people in the highest level of moral development abide. These rights are considered valid not because of a particular society's laws or customs, but because they rest on the premise of universality. Many organizations and researchers have attempted to identify a set of global or universal ethical standards that every individual should follow, regardless of where they live or work. One result of these efforts is the Caux Round Table Business Principles of Ethics, developed in collaboration with business leaders in Europe, Japan, and the United States (Table 5.1). These principles encourage decisions that further fairness and respect for others in promoting free trade, environmental and cultural integrity, and the prevention of corruption in global business,.[31]

Motivation   Another significant factor in the ethical decision-making process is an individual's motivation. Psychologist David McClelland identified three different social needs that may motivate an individual in an ethical decision-making situation—achievement, affiliation, and power.[32]

The *need for achievement* refers to an individual's preference for goals that are well defined and moderately challenging, include employee participation, and provide for feedback. People with a high need for achievement tend to be motivated, show great initiative, and work hard to accomplish common shared goals. McClelland's theory suggests that if employees are given role models that have high ethical standards, they will then emulate these values. At Home Depot, for example, community service is viewed as an important part of corporate citizenship. Therefore, volunteering to build a playground would show initiative toward Home Depot's shared goals.

The *need for affiliation* relates to an individual's inclination to work with others in the organization rather than alone. Individuals with a high need for affiliation

TABLE 5.1

The Caux Round Table Business Principles of Ethics

GENERAL PRINCIPLES	
Principle 1: The responsibilities of businesses: beyond shareholders toward stakeholders	The value of a business to society is the wealth and employment it creates and the marketable products and services it provides to consumers at a reasonable price commensurate with quality. To create such value, a business must maintain its own economic health and viability, but survival is not a sufficient goal. Businesses have a role to play in improving the lives of all their customers, employees, and shareholders by sharing with them the wealth they have created. Suppliers and competitors as well should expect businesses to honor their obligations in a spirit of honesty and fairness. As responsible citizens of the local, national, regional, and global communities in which they operate, businesses share a part in shaping the future of those communities.
Principle 2: The economic and social impact of business: toward innovation, justice, and world community	Businesses established in foreign countries to develop, produce, or sell should also contribute to the social advancement of those countries by creating productive employment and helping to raise the purchasing power of their citizens. Businesses also should contribute to human rights, education, welfare, and vitalization of the countries in which they operate. Businesses should contribute to economic and social development not only in the countries in which they operate, but also in the world community at large, through effective and prudent use of resources, free and fair competition, and emphasis on innovation in technology, production methods, marketing, and communications.
Principle 3: Business behavior: beyond the letter of law toward a spirit of trust	While accepting the legitimacy of trade secrets, businesses should recognize that sincerity, candor, truthfulness, the keeping of promises, and transparency contribute not only to their own credibility and stability but also to the smoothness and efficiency of business transactions, particularly on the international level.
Principle 4: Respect for rules	To avoid trade frictions and to promote freer trade, equal conditions for competition, and fair and equitable treatment for all participants, businesses should respect international and domestic rules. In addition, they should recognize that some behavior, although legal, may still have adverse consequences.
Principle 5: Support for multilateral trade	Businesses should support the multilateral trade systems of the GATT/World Trade Organization and similar international agreements. They should cooperate in efforts to promote the progressive and judicious liberalization of trade and to relax those domestic measures that unreasonably hinder global commerce, while giving due respect to national policy objectives.

(continued)

TABLE 5.1 *(continued)*

The Caux Round Table Business Principles of Ethics

GENERAL PRINCIPLES	
Principle 6: Respect for the environment	A business should protect and, where possible, improve the environment, promote sustainable development, and prevent the wasteful use of natural resources.
Principle 7: Avoidance of illicit operations	A business should not participate in or condone bribery, money laundering, or other corrupt practices; indeed, it should seek cooperation with others to eliminate them. It should not trade in arms or other materials used for terrorist activities, drug traffic, or other organized crime.

STAKEHOLDER PRINCIPLES	
Customers	We believe in treating all customers with dignity, irrespective of whether they purchase our products and services directly from us or otherwise acquire them in the market. We therefore have a responsibility to: • Provide our customers with the highest quality products and services consistent with their requirements • Treat our customers fairly in all aspects of our business transactions, including a high level of service and remedies for their dissatisfaction • Make every effort to ensure that the health and safety of our customers, as well as the quality of their environment, will be sustained or enhanced by our products and services • Assure respect for human dignity in products offered, marketing, and advertising; and respect the integrity of the culture of our customers.
Employees	We believe in the dignity of every employee and in taking employee interests seriously. We therefore have a responsibility to: • Provide jobs and compensation that improve workers' living conditions • Provide working conditions that respect each employee's health and dignity • Be honest in communications with employees and open in sharing information, limited only by legal and competitive constraints • Listen to and, where possible, act on employee suggestions, ideas, requests, and complaints • Engage in good faith negotiations when conflict arises. • Avoid discriminatory practices and guarantee equal treatment and opportunity in areas such as gender, age, race, and religion • Promote in the business itself the employment of differently abled people in places of work where they can be genuinely useful • Protect employees from avoidable injury and illness in the workplace • Encourage and assist employees in developing relevant and transferable skills and knowledge • Be sensitive to the serious unemployment problems frequently associated with business decisions, and work with governments, employee groups, other agencies and each other in addressing these dislocations

(continued)

TABLE 5.1 *(continued)*

The Caux Round Table Business Principles of Ethics

STAKEHOLDER PRINCIPLES

Owners /Investors

We believe in honoring the trust our investors place in us. We therefore have a responsibility to:
- Apply professional and diligent management in order to secure a fair and competitive return on our owners' investment
- Disclose relevant information to owners/investors subject to legal requirements and competitive constraints
- Conserve, protect, and increase the owners/investors' assets
- Respect owners/investors' requests, suggestions, complaints, and formal resolutions

Suppliers

Our relationship with suppliers and subcontractors must be based on mutual respect. We therefore have a responsibility to:
- Seek fairness and truthfulness in all our activities, including pricing, licensing, and rights to sell
- Ensure that our business activities are free from coercion and unnecessary litigation
- Foster long-term stability in the supplier relationship in return for value, quality, competitiveness, and reliability
- Share information with suppliers and integrate them into our planning processes
- Pay suppliers on time and in accordance with agreed terms of trade
- Seek, encourage, and prefer suppliers and subcontractors whose employment practices respect human dignity

Competitors

We believe that fair economic competition is one of the basic requirements for increasing the wealth of nations and ultimately for making possible the just distribution of goods and services. We therefore have a responsibility to:
- Foster open markets for trade and investment
- Promote competitive behavior that is socially and environmentally beneficial and demonstrates mutual respect among competitors
- Refrain from either seeking or participating in questionable payments or favors to secure competitive advantages
- Respect both tangible and intellectual property rights
- Refuse to acquire commercial information by dishonest or unethical means, such as industrial espionage

Communities

We believe that as global corporate citizens we can contribute to such forces of reform and human rights as are at work in the communities in which we operate. We therefore have a responsibility in those communities to:
- Respect human rights and democratic institutions and promote them wherever practicable
- Recognize government's legitimate obligation to the society at large and support public policies and practices that promote human development through harmonious relations between business and other segments of society

(continued)

TABLE 5.1 *(continued)*

The Caux Round Table Business Principles of Ethics

STAKEHOLDER PRINCIPLES	
Communities	• Collaborate with those forces in the community dedicated to raising standards of health, education, workplace safety, and economic well-being • Promote and stimulate sustainable development and play a leading role in preserving and enhancing the physical environment and conserving the earth's resources • Support peace, security, diversity, and social integration • Respect the integrity of local cultures • Be a good corporate citizen through charitable donations, educational and cultural contributions, and employee participation in community and civic affairs

Source: "Principles for Business English Translation," Caux Round Table, www.cauxroundtable.org/ ENGLISH.HTM, accessed October 21, 2001. Reprinted by permission from Caux Round Table.

prefer to interact with others, guide others, and learn from those with whom they work. They are, therefore, more effective working in an environment with peers rather than working at home alone. Such employees will be easier to socialize into the core values of the organization compared to those who telecommute from home. Peers and coworkers have been found to have more influence on ethical decision making in an organizational context than any other factor.[33]

The *need for power* refers to an individual's desire to have influence and control over others. Business environments often limit or constrain what people are able to contribute. To exercise power successfully within an organization, an individual must be accepted, assertive, and capable. The greater the need for power, the greater is the probability that an individual or group may engage in questionable or unethical behavior. Although the need for power does not always lead to negative effects, it is important for employees to balance this need with organizational goals and standards. The emergence of team and project-based organizational structures often means that power and control are decentralized. Such structures require a great deal of trust, communication, and relationship building, all key factors in both corporate citizenship and business performance.

> ### *Organizational Relationships*

Although individuals can and do make ethical decisions, they do not operate in a vacuum.[34] Ethical choices in business are most often made jointly in committees and work groups or in conversations with coworkers. Moreover, people learn to settle ethical issues not only from their individual backgrounds, but also from others with whom they associate in the business environment. The outcome of this learning process depends on the strength of each individual's personal values, opportunity for unethical behavior, and exposure to others who behave ethically or unethically. Consequently, the culture of the organization, as well as superiors, peers, and subordinates, can have a significant impact on the ethical decision-making process.

Organizational Culture   **Organizational,** or **corporate, culture** can be defined as a set of values, beliefs, goals, norms, and rituals shared by members or employees of an organization. It answers questions such as, "What is important?" "How do we treat each other?" "How do we do things around here?" Culture may be conveyed formally in employee handbooks, codes of conduct, memos, and ceremonies, but it is also expressed informally through dress codes, extracurricular activities, and anecdotes. A firm's culture gives its members meaning and offers direction as to how to behave and deal with problems within the organization. The corporate culture at American Express, for example, includes numerous anecdotes about employees who have gone beyond the call of duty to help customers out of difficult situations. This strong tradition of customer service might encourage an American Express employee to take extra steps to help a customer who encounters a problem while traveling overseas. On the other hand, an organization's culture may also encourage employees to make decisions that others may judge as unethical. For example, Ford Motor Credit Company, the nation's largest automobile finance firm, was accused in a lawsuit of charging African-American car

Gordon Bethune, Chairman of Continental Airlines is building trust with union members by telling them the truth and promising only what he can deliver. He is trying to build a corporate culture based on trust.

buyers higher interest rates for auto loans than white customers with similar credit histories. The suit, filed by four African Americans who insist they were overcharged, alleges that the company empowers dealers to inflate loan costs to buyers they think will pay higher rates. Ford denied the allegations.[35]

Whereas a firm's overall culture establishes ideals that guide a wide range of behaviors for members of the organization, its **ethical climate** focuses specifically on issues of right and wrong. We think of ethical climate as that part of a corporate culture that relates to an organization's expectations about appropriate conduct. To some extent, ethical climate is the character component of an organization. Corporate policies and codes, the conduct of top managers, the values and moral philosophies of coworkers, and opportunity for misconduct all contribute to a firm's ethical climate. When top managers strive to establish an ethical climate based on responsibility and citizenship, they set the tone for ethical decisions. For example, executives and employees of the New Belgium Brewing Company chose to switch from coal power to wind power when the firm decided to purchase all of its electricity from wind turbines (making it the single largest private customer for wind-generated electric power in Colorado). Although the investment adds 20 to 30 cents to the cost of each barrel of beer the company produces, executives felt that the benefits achieved from reducing emissions of carbon dioxide was worth the cost.[36] In addition, New Belgium gives all of its employees a bicycle after one year on the job, possibly reducing carbon monoxide gases generated from automobiles used for commuting to work. Thus, top management attempted to establish an ethical climate promoting responsible environmental conduct. Ethical climate also determines whether or not an individual perceives an issue as having an ethical component. Recognizing ethical issues and generating alternatives to address them are manifestations of ethical climate.

Significant Others **Significant others** include superiors, peers, and subordinates in the organization who influence the ethical decision-making process. Although people outside the firm, such as family members and friends, also influence decision makers, organizational structure and culture operate through significant others to influence ethical decisions.

Most experts agree that the chief executive officer establishes the ethical tone for the entire firm. Lower-level managers obtain their cues from top managers, and then, in turn, impose some of their personal values on the company. This interaction between corporate culture and executive leadership helps determine the ethical value system of the firm. However, obedience to authority can also explain why many people resolve workplace issues by following the directives of a superior. An employee may feel obligated to carry out the orders of a superior, even if those orders conflict with the employee's values of right and wrong. If that decision is later judged to have been wrong, the employee may justify it by saying, "I was only carrying out orders," or "My boss told me to do it this way."

Coworkers' influence on ethical decision making depends on the person's exposure to unethical behavior in making ethical decisions. The more a person is exposed to unethical activity by others in the organization, the more likely it is that he or she will behave unethically, especially in ethically "gray" areas. Thus, a decision maker who associates with others who act unethically is more likely to behave unethically as well. Within work groups, employees may be subject to the phenomenon of "groupthink," going along with group decisions even when those decisions run counter to their own values. They may rationalize the decision with "safety in numbers" when everyone else appears to back a particular decision. Most businesspeople take their cues or learn from coworkers how to solve problems—including ethical dilemmas.[37] Close friends at work exert the most influence on ethical decisions that relate to roles associated with a particular job.

Superiors and coworkers can create organizational pressure, which plays a key role in creating ethical issues. For example, Mitsubishi employees kept silent for eight years about potential defects in large-screen televisions the firm manufactured between 1987 and 1990. Despite ten major cases of TV sets overheating, six of which caused extensive home fires, employees choose not to disclose the liability until recently, when the firm announced a major recall.[38] Remember from the opening vignette that, in Japan, concealing evidence of defects that could result in a recall is not uncommon in a culture that views product recalls as a source of great humiliation. In such a culture, pressure from superiors and coworkers to remain silent may be enormous.

Nearly all businesspeople face difficult issues where solutions are not obvious or where organizational objectives and personal ethical values may conflict. For example, a salesperson for a web-based retailer may be asked by a superior to lie to a customer over the phone about a late product shipment. In one survey, 47 percent of human resources managers said they had felt pressured by other employees or managers to compromise their firm's standards of business conduct in order to attain business objectives.[39] A study by the Ethics Resource Center found that 60 percent of those surveyed said they had experienced pressure from superiors or coworkers to compromise ethics standards in order to achieve business objectives.[40] Figure 5.3 shows the sources of pressure reported by employees.

> ## *Opportunity*

Together, organizational culture and the influence of coworkers may foster conditions that either hinder or permit misconduct. **Opportunity** is a set of conditions that limit barriers or provide rewards. When these conditions provide rewards—be it financial gain, recognition, promotion, or simply the good feeling from a job well done—the opportunity for unethical conduct may be encouraged—or discouraged. For example, a company policy that fails to specify the

FIGURE 5.3

Sources of Pressure to Compromise Ethics Standards

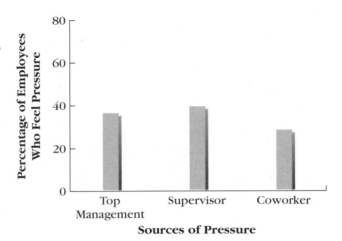

Source: Ethics Resource Center, *The Ethics Resource Center's 2000 National Business Ethics Survey: How Employees Perceive Ethics at Work* (Washington D.C.: Ethics Resource Center, 2000), p. 38. Reprinted by permission from Ethics Resource Center.

punishment for employees who violate the rules provides an opportunity for unethical behavior because it allows individuals to engage in such behavior without fear of consequences. Thus, company policies, processes, and other factors may create opportunities to act unethically. Advancing technology associated with the Internet is challenging companies working to limit opportunities to engage in unethical and illegal behavior. In a survey of online retailers, 83 percent reported that fraud is a problem in online transactions, and 61 percent indicated that they were taking precautions to limit the opportunity to engage in fraud.[41] Individual factors as well as organizational relationships may influence whether an individual becomes opportunistic and takes advantage of situations in an unethical or even illegal manner.

Opportunity usually relates to employees' immediate job context—where they work, with whom they work, and the nature of the work. This context includes the motivational "carrots and sticks," or rewards and punishments, that superiors can use to influence employee behavior. Rewards, or positive reinforcers, include pay raises, bonuses, and public recognition, whereas reprimands, pay penalties, demotions, and even firings act as negative reinforcers. For example, a manager who decides to sell customers' personal data may be confident that such behavior is an easy way to boost revenue because other companies sell customer account information. Even if this activity violates the employee's personal value system, it may be viewed as acceptable within the organization's culture. This manager may be motivated by opportunities to increase company revenue and his or her performance standing within the organization.

If an employee takes advantage of an opportunity to act unethically and is rewarded or suffers no penalty, he or she may repeat such acts as other opportunities arise. For example, about 1,500 coal miners died of black lung disease in 1994, but experts believe that almost no deaths would have occurred if mining companies had obeyed thirty-year-old federal regulations. Miners say that companies routinely falsify air-quality reports and run sample pumps less than the required time or place them in clean air away from working areas.[42] Because monitoring and enforcement of federal regulations was inadequate, the opportunity to falsify reports existed. When company managers got away with the illegal conduct, their behavior was reinforced. Indeed, opportunity to engage in unethical conduct is often a better predictor of unethical activities than personal values.[43]

In addition to rewards and the absence of punishment, other elements in the business environment tend to create opportunities. Professional codes of conduct and ethics-related corporate policies also influence opportunity by prescribing what behaviors are acceptable. The larger the rewards and the milder the punishment for unethical behavior, the greater is the probability that unethical behavior will be practiced.

Organizational Approaches to Improving Ethical Behavior

Understanding the factors that influence how individuals make decisions to resolve ethical issues in the workplace can help companies encourage ethical behavior and discourage undesirable conduct. Fostering ethical decisions within an organization requires eliminating unethical persons and improving the firm's ethical standards. Consider the "bad apple-bad barrel" analogy. Some people are "bad apples" who will always do things in their own self-interest, regardless of organizational goals or accepted standards of conduct. For example, Elliot Lavigne was forced to resign his position as executive vice president of Perry Ellis Men's Division after being indicted on charges of manipulating initial public offerings in the early 1990s. In addition to the criminal and civil charges against Lavigne, the Securities and Exchange Commission is attempting to recover the nearly $7.4 million he made in profits and interest associated with fraudulent stock transactions.[44] Eliminating such bad apples through screening techniques and enforcement of the firm's ethical standards can help improve the firm's behavior. Organizations can also become "bad barrels," not because the individuals within them are bad, but because the pressures to succeed create opportunities that reward unethical decisions. In the case of bad barrels, the organization must redesign its image and culture to conform to industry and social standards of acceptable behavior.[45] Most businesses attempt to improve ethical decision making by establishing and implementing organizational compliance programs, which ensures compliance to the Federal Sentencing Guidelines for Organizations that were discussed in Chapter 4.

▶ *Organizational Compliance Programs*

To be a good corporate citizen and promote legal and ethical conduct, an organization should develop an **organizational compliance program** by establishing, communicating, and monitoring ethical values and legal requirements that characterize its history, culture, industry, and operating environment. Without such programs, along with uniform standards and policies of conduct, it is difficult for employees to determine what behaviors are acceptable within a company. In the absence of such programs and standards, employees will generally make decisions based on their observations of how their peers and superiors behave. A strong compliance program includes a written code of conduct, an ethics officer to oversee the program, and formal ethics training. An investigation into the effectiveness of compliance programs in European biotech companies indicated that many companies lacked the tools (code of ethics, ethics training) that allowed a values approach to operationalize an integrity approach to decision making.[46]

Codes of Conduct   Because people come from diverse business, educational, and family backgrounds, it cannot be assumed that they know how to behave appropriately when they enter a new organization or job. Many companies therefore begin the process of establishing organizational compliance programs by developing **codes of conduct** (also called codes of ethics), which are formal statements that describe what an organization expects of its employees. According to the Ethics Resource Center survey, 79 percent of respondents reported that their firm has written standards of ethical business conduct—such as codes of ethics, policy statements on ethics, or guidelines on proper business conduct—up from 60 percent in 1994.[47] Codes of conduct may address a variety of situations, from internal operations to sales presentations and financial disclosure practices. Figure 5.4 presents Fidelity Investments' code of ethics. Note that Fidelity's code focuses on ensuring that employees do not have a conflict of interest that could create problems for the company's mutual funds.[48]

Codes of conduct will not resolve every ethical issue encountered in daily operations, but they help employees and managers deal with ethical dilemmas by prescribing or limiting specific activities. By communicating to employees both what is expected of them and what punishments they face if they violate the rules, codes of conduct curtail opportunities for unethical behavior and thereby improve ethical decision making. Fidelity's code, for example, specifies that sanctions for violating its code range from cautions and warnings to dismissal and criminal prosecution.[49] Codes of conduct do not have to be so detailed that they take into account every situation, but they should provide guidelines for employees that are capable of achieving organizational ethical objectives in an accepted manner.

Ethics Officers   Organizational compliance programs must also have oversight by high-ranking persons in the organization known to respect legal and ethical standards. This person is often referred to as an **ethics officer.** Ethics officers are usually responsible for

- Meeting with the board of directors, managers, and employees to discuss or provide advice about ethical issues
- Distributing a code of conduct or ethics
- Establishing and maintaining an anonymous, confidential service to answer questions about ethical issues
- Taking action on possible violations of the code
- Reviewing and updating the code of conduct[50]

Many ethics officers employ toll-free telephone "hot lines" to provide advice, anonymously where desired, to employees confronting an ethical issue. Sears, for example, maintains a 24-hour, toll-free "assist line" so that employees can express any concerns they may have at any time to a company representative. The line gives the company the opportunity to listen to and counsel employees, clarify its policies, and receive reports of misconduct. The information obtained from the 15,000 calls the firm receives each year is analyzed and used to target the firm's ethics initiatives to address specific issues that have been raised. For example, after employees expressed fears about the potential for workplace violence, the company incorporated the issue into its training program to reduce the chance of such violence occurring at the venerable retailer.[51] According to the Ethics Resource Center survey, 50 percent of respondents reported that their firm has a designated office, person, or telephone line where they can get advice about ethical issues.[52] Hot lines can also provide a mechanism for employees to report misconduct by others.

Ethics Training   In Chapter 4, we discussed the requirements of the Federal Sentencing Guidelines for Organizations and the seven steps needed to implement an organizational compliance program. The fourth step (refer back to Table 4.6)

FIGURE 5.4

Fidelity Investments' Code of Ethics

— *FIDELITY* —

General Provisions

New employees are briefed on the Code and are given a copy when hired. Within one week of joining the company, they must indicate in writing that they have read the Code and agree to its provisions. After that, we require employees at the beginning of each year to review the Code and acknowledge in writing by January 31 that their personal investing has complied with its requirements.

The following provisions of Fidelity's Code of Ethics apply to all employees.

A. *Personal Transactions:* The Code requires all employees to report their personal securities transactions to Fidelity. This includes activity in any account where an employee has a monetary interest.

B. *Reportable Securities:* The Code applies to the buying and selling of virtually *all securities,* including options and futures on groups of securities or securities indexes. The SEC has exempted from reporting certain securities, including open-end mutual funds, certificates of deposit, and short-term government obligations.

C. *Brokerage Accounts:* All employees must conduct their personal investing through a Fidelity Brokerage account. This practice helps us to achieve compliance with the Code and allows us to more easily monitor personal account activity on an ongoing basis.

D. *Reporting Requirements:* All employees must report their personal transactions to Fidelity. How often depends on whether they are "access" or "non-access" people.

"Access" people are employees with access to Fidelity's investment research, recommendations, or fund transactions. This includes fund managers, research analysts, traders, and senior executives, as well as people in our legal, compliance, and treasurer's departments. "Access" employees must report all personal transactions monthly.

"Non-access" people must report all personal transactions annually.

E. *General Restrictions:* The following restrictions also apply to all of Fidelity's employees. They may not:
- knowingly buy or sell a security just before transactions in the same or equivalent securities (e.g., convertible preferred stocks or bonds) by a Fidelity fund;
- cause or prevent fund activity for personal benefit;
- use knowledge about fund transactions for personal benefit;
- sell short any security, unless the employee already owns the security in his or her personal account. (Selling short involves borrowing securities from a brokerage for return at a future date. The investor sells the stock in the expectation that the security's price will decline by the time he or she has to buy it back.);

(continued)

requires instituting a training program and communication system to communicate and educate about the firm's ethical standards. Such training can educate employees about the firm's policies and expectations, relevant laws and regulations, and general social standards. Training programs can make employees aware of available resources, support systems, and designated personnel who can assist them with ethical and legal advice. Training can also help empower employees to ask tough questions and make ethical decisions. According to the

FIGURE 5.4 *(continued)*

Fidelity Investments' Code of Ethics

> - engage in "excessive" trading in a personal account;
> - participate in initial public offerings, hedge funds, investment clubs, or similar groups;
> - use options or futures to take positions in securities which would not be allowed under the Code;
> - accept gifts of a value greater than $100.
>
> ### Added Provisions for "Access" People
>
> In addition to these general provisions, there are certain requirements that apply only to "access" employees—those with access to information about Fidelity's investment research recommendations and fund transactions.
>
> **F.** *Pre-Clearance of Trades:* Under the Code, "access" employees must get permission from Fidelity before making a personal transaction. We restrict pre-clearance when fund trades are pending.
>
> **G.** *Restricted Securities:* "Access" people cannot buy either securities issued by a broker-dealer or Fidelity closed-end funds for their personal accounts.
>
> ### Added Provisions for Investment Professionals and Senior Executives
>
> Investment professionals and senior executives are subject to the general provisions and provisions for "access" people, as well as to some additional requirements. (One provision applies just to fund managers.)
>
> **H.** *Short-Term Trading:* Investment professionals and senior executives cannot keep profits made from transactions in the same or equivalent securities if the transactions are made within 60 calendar days of each other. If this happens, we give the profits away to a charitable organization.
>
> **I.** *Research Notes:* When a Fidelity analyst issues a research note on a company, investment professionals and senior executives must wait two business days before they can trade in the securities of that company for their personal account.
>
> **J.** *Additional Restrictions for Investment Professionals and Senior Executives:* Furthermore, investment professionals and senior executives:
> - must get approval from Fidelity to serve on a board of directors;
> - must get approval from Fidelity to participate in private placement transactions;
> - must disclose all securities holdings within seven days of joining the company and annually thereafter.
>
> Additionally, investment professionals have an affirmative duty to recommend suitable securities for the benefit of the funds.
>
> **K.** *Additional Restriction for Portfolio Managers:* Portfolio managers may not personally buy or sell a security either seven calendar days before or after their fund buys or sells the same security.

Source: "Corporate Information," Fidelity Investments, www100.fidelity.com/about/world/ethics_code. html, accessed November 20, 2000. Copyright 2001 FMR Corp. All rights reserved. Reprinted by permission.

Ethics Resource Center survey, 55 percent of respondents employed by for-profit organizations reported that their firm provides ethics training, up from 33 percent in 1994.[53] Figure 5.5 indicates that a significant number of employees report that they frequently find such training useful. Many companies are now incorporating ethics training into their employee and management development training efforts.[54]

The Defense Industry Initiative helps defense industry contractors develop organizational compliance programs. (www.dii.org. Reprinted with permission from Defense Industry Initiatives.)

THE DEFENSE INDUSTRY INITIATIVE ON BUSINESS ETHICS AND CONDUCT

DII is a consortium of U.S. defense industry contractors which subscribes to a set of principles for achieving high standards of business ethics and conduct.

ANNUAL REPORTS

The DII Annual Reports include the DII Principles, a list of DII Signatories, the content of the DII Information Clearinghouse, the membership of the DII Steering Committee and Working Group, and a description of DII Signatories' ethics and compliance programs. The 2000 report is now available on this web site and in Word.

ETHICS TRAINING RESOURCES

DII and its signatories offer a wide variety of training tools including manuals for the video tapes *Cases for Ethics Training I* and *Cases for Ethics Training II* as well as an Information Clearinghouse of program materials arranged by signatory.

OTHER SITES OF INTEREST

A list of selected web sites generally related to signatories, business ethics, or government ethics and professional ethics associations.

Implementing Organizational Compliance Programs

A company has to have an effective ethics program to ensure that all employees understand the values of the business and comply with policies and codes of conduct that create the ethical climate of the business. To foster such an ethical climate, open communication and education on ethical issues are crucial. Citizens Bank of Canada, for example, helped communicate its value system by establishing an Ethical Policy that acknowledges the bank's role as steward of the funds it holds and demonstrates its desire to be responsible and conscientious about what it does with those funds.[55] Maintaining an ethical climate requires providing employees with ethics training, clear channels of communication, and support throughout the organization. Unisys, for example, provides extensive annual training on ethics as well as an internal ethics web site and a telephone help line to handle employee questions on ethical issues.[56]

Effective implementation also requires that companies consistently enforce standards and punish those who violate codes of conduct. The company must also revise the compliance program as necessary to diminish the likelihood of future misconduct. To be implemented successfully, a compliance program should be viewed as a part of the overall business strategy implementation.

The accountability and responsibility for the success of organizational compliance programs lie in the hands of top management. If the firm's ethics officers and

FIGURE 5.5

Usefulness of Ethics Training

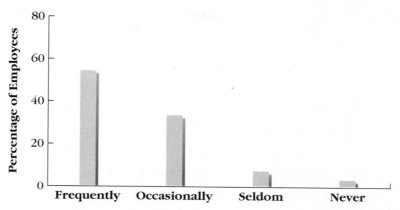

"How often have you found ethics training to be useful in guiding your decisions and conduct at work?"

Source: Ethics Resource Center, *The Ethics Resource Center's 2000 National Business Ethics Survey: How Employees Perceive Ethics at Work* (Washington D.C.: Ethics Resource Center, 2000), p. 38. Reprinted by permission from Ethics Resource Center.

other top executives are not committed to the principles and initiatives of business ethics and corporate citizenship, then the program's effectiveness will be in question. If top managers develop and enforce programs to promote ethical decision making, then they become a force to help individuals make better ethical decisions within the organization.

An effectively implemented organizational ethics program should help reduce the potential for misconduct as well as the possibility for penalties and negative public reaction should misconduct occur despite a firm's best efforts to prevent it. Additionally, promoting ethical and legal conduct can result in higher-quality products. This in turn creates the potential for an ethical advantage with better reputation, sales, market share, and profits, as we saw in Chapter 2. A proactive ethical approach to business should consider at least four fundamental values of interpersonal communication: respect, understanding, caring, and fairness.[57] Table 5.2 shows one recommended method for developing ethical relationships and promoting integrity in business.

Strategic Implementation of Business Ethics

The Ethics Resource Center survey found that employees' satisfaction with their organization is higher when the firm has a comprehensive organizational compliance program including a code of conduct, an ethics officer or advice line, and training.[58] Although all organizations hope to have "good apples," it is impossible

TABLE 5.2

A Method to Create Ethical Relationships in Business

Step	Explanation
1. Listen and learn.	Recognize the problem or decision-making opportunity that confronts your company, team, or unit. Don't argue, criticize, or defend yourself—keep listening and reviewing until you are sure you understand others.
2. Identify the ethical issues.	Examine how coworkers and consumers are affected by the situation or decision at hand. Examine how you feel about the situation and understand the viewpoint of those who are involved in the decision or the consequences of the decision.
3. Create and analyze options.	Try to put aside strong feelings such as anger or the desire for power and prestige and come up with as many alternatives as possible before developing an analysis. Ask everyone involved for ideas about which options offer the best long-term results for you and the company. Which option will increase your self-respect even if, in the long run, things don't work out the way you hope?
4. Identify the best option from your point of view.	Consider it and test it against some established criteria, such as respect, understanding, caring, fairness, honesty, and openness.
5. Explain your decision and resolve any differences that may arise.	This may require neutral arbitration from a trust manager or taking "time out" to reconsider, consult, or exchange written proposals before a decision is reached.

Source: Tom Rusk with D. Patrick Miller, "Doing the Right Thing," *Sky* (Delta Airlines), August 1993, pp. 18-22.

for individual employees to understand and enforce the ethical climate of the organization without widespread communication about values, areas of risk, and appropriate means of ethical decision making.

Creating an ethical climate in an organization requires a commitment through both values and formal programs. First, top managers, employees, and stakeholders must buy into the philosophy that *all* organizations have responsibilities that extend beyond legal and economic obligations. Second, members of the organization must also be willing to share their values about workplace ethics. Top management must express a commitment that can change the way an organization operates. Third, ethical concerns should be incorporated into the strategic planning process. Most organizations are well versed on the economic and legal aspects of social responsibility, but far fewer have explored how core values, employee satisfaction, and consumer satisfaction, as well as contributions to the community, can be aligned with their vision, mission, and strategy. Finally, the firm must develop a mechanism for assessing its progress in making ethical decisions

Hershey Foods emphasizes a high level of ethics in its corporate philosophy. (Reprinted with permission of Hershey Foods Corporation.)

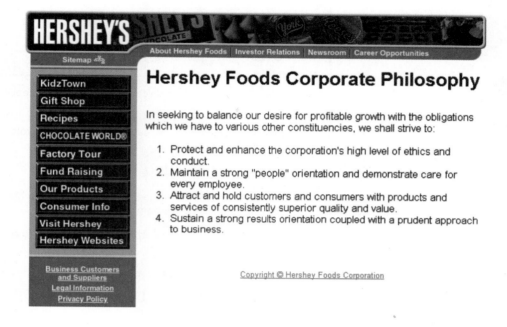

Hershey Foods Corporate Philosophy

In seeking to balance our desire for profitable growth with the obligations which we have to various other constituencies, we shall strive to:

1. Protect and enhance the corporation's high level of ethics and conduct.
2. Maintain a strong "people" orientation and demonstrate care for every employee.
3. Attract and hold customers and consumers with products and services of consistently superior quality and value.
4. Sustain a strong results orientation coupled with a prudent approach to business.

Copyright © Hershey Foods Corporation

that contribute to its efforts to be a good corporate citizen. We recommend a formal audit process and general review of the organizational compliance program that correlates with the annual strategic planning process. The questions listed in Table 5.3 provide the basis for an audit to assess a firm's compliance efforts. These issues can also be implemented into the firm's corporate governance mechanisms to ensure legal and ethical compliance as well as achievement of the organization's corporate goals.

Summary

Business ethics comprises principles and standards that guide individual and work group behavior in the world of business. Stakeholders determine these conventions, and they may change over time. The most basic of these standards have been codified as laws and regulations. Business ethics goes beyond legal issues.

Because individuals and groups within a company may not have embraced the same set of values, ethical conflict may occur. Questionable decisions and actions may result in disputes that must be resolved through some type of negotiation or even litigation. Codifying ethical standards into meaningful policies that spell out what is and is not acceptable gives businesspeople an opportunity to reduce the possibility of behavior that could create legal problems. Business decisions involve

TABLE 5.3

Ethical Compliance Audit

Yes	No	
❏	❏	Do top managers in your organization communicate shared values and beliefs about ethical conduct?
❏	❏	Do top managers in your organization provide leadership and serve as role models for organizational accountability and ethical conduct?
❏	❏	Does your organization have a code of conduct?
❏	❏	Is there an individual or department in your organization that is responsible for developing and implementing an ethical compliance program?
❏	❏	Are there communications and training programs in your organization to create an effective ethical climate to prevent misconduct?
❏	❏	Does your organization have monitoring and auditing systems to consistently enforce ethical compliance policies?
❏	❏	Does your organization have a method for reporting misconduct without fear?
❏	❏	Is there a system to determine ethical issues and risks associated with your industry?
❏	❏	Has your organization developed an ethical compliance program that complies with the requirements of the Federal Sentencing Guidelines for Organizations?
❏	❏	Is there a mechanism for improving the organization's future ethical compliance after problems or issues are discovered and resolved?

complex and detailed discussions in which correctness may not be clear cut. It is important that a shared vision of acceptable behavior develop from an organizational perspective to develop consistent and reliable relationships with all concerned stakeholders.

Understanding the ethical decision-making process can help individuals and businesses design strategies to prevent misconduct. Three of the important components of ethical decision making are individual factors, organizational relationships, and opportunity.

Significant individual factors that affect the ethical decision-making process include personal moral philosophy, stage of moral development, motivation, and other personal factors such as gender, age, and experience. Moral philosophies are the principles or rules that individuals apply in deciding what is right or wrong. Most moral philosophies can be classified as consequentialism, ethical formalism, or justice. Consequentialist philosophies consider a decision to be right or acceptable if it accomplishes a desired result such as pleasure, knowledge, career growth, the realization of self-interest, or utility. Consequentialism may be further classified as egoism and utilitarianism. Ethical formalism focuses on the rights of individuals and on the intentions associated with a particular behavior rather than on its consequences. Justice theory relates to evaluations of fairness, or the disposition to deal with perceived injustices of others. Kohlberg proposed that people progress through six stages in their development of cognitive moral development. McClelland identified three different social needs that may motivate an individual in an ethical decision-making situation—achievement, affiliation, and power.

The culture of the organization, as well as superiors, peers, and subordinates, can have a significant impact on the ethical decision-making process. Organizational, or corporate, culture can be defined as a set of values, beliefs, goals, norms, and rituals shared by members or employees of an organization. Whereas a firm's overall culture establishes ideals that guide a wide range of behaviors for members of the organization, its ethical climate focuses specifically on issues of right and wrong. Significant others include superiors, peers, and subordinates in the organization who influence the ethical decision-making process. Interaction between corporate culture and executive leadership helps determine the ethical value system of the firm, but obedience to authority can also explain why many people resolve workplace issues by following the directives of a superior. The more a person is exposed to unethical activity by others in the organization, the more likely it is that he or she will behave unethically. Superiors and coworkers can create organizational pressure, which plays a key role in creating ethical issues.

Opportunity is a set of conditions that limit barriers or provide rewards. If an individual takes advantage of an opportunity to act unethically and escapes punishment or gains a reward, that person may repeat such acts when circumstances favor them.

Companies can encourage ethical behavior and discourage undesirable conduct by eliminating unethical persons and improving the firm's ethical standards. An organization should develop an organizational compliance program by establishing, communicating, and monitoring ethical values and legal requirements that characterize its history, culture, industry, and operating environment. A strong compliance program includes a written code of conduct, an ethics officer to oversee the program, and formal ethics training. Codes of conduct are formal statements that describe what a company expects of its employees. Ethics officers are usually responsible for developing and implementing a code of conduct, providing a confidential service to answer questions about ethical issues, and providing ethics training. Ethics training educates employees about the firm's policies, expectations, and resources available for ethical and legal advice; laws and regulations; and general social standards.

A company needs an effective ethics program to ensure that all employees understand the firm's values and comply with policies and codes of conduct that create its ethical climate. Effective implementation requires that companies consistently enforce standards and punish those who violate codes of conduct. An effectively implemented program should help reduce the potential for misconduct as well as the possibility for penalties and negative public reaction should misconduct occur despite a firm's best efforts to prevent it. Ethical concerns should be incorporated into the strategic planning process. The firm must develop a mechanism for assessing its progress in making ethical decisions that contribute to its efforts to be a good corporate citizen.

KEY TERMS

business ethics

moral philosophies

consequentialism

egoism

utilitarianism

ethical formalism

justice theory

organizational, or corporate, culture

ethical climate

significant others

opportunity

organizational compliance program

codes of conduct

ethics officer

3. How do moral philosophies influence the individual factor in organizational ethical decision making?

4. How can ethical formalism be used in organizational ethics programs and still respect diversity and the right for individual values?

5. What are the potential benefits of an emphasis on procedural justice?

6. How can knowledge of Kohlberg's stages of moral development be useful in developing an organizational ethics programs?

7. How do organizations create an ethical climate?

8. What is the best approach to improving ethical decisions in business?

9. How can people with different personal values work together to make ethical decisions in an organization?

10. What are the key considerations in developing an organizational compliance program?

DISCUSSION QUESTIONS

1. Why is business ethics a strategic consideration in organizational decisions?

2. How do individual, organizational, and opportunity factors interact to influence ethical or unethical decisions?

EXPERIENTIAL EXERCISE

Visit the web site of the Ethics Officer Association (**http://www.eoa.org**). What is the association's current mission and membership composition? Review the web site to determine the issues and concerns that comprise the EOA's most recent programs, publications, and research. What trends do you find? What topics seem to be most important to ethics officers today?

NOTES

1. Yuri Kageyama, "Mitsubishi Motors Says Massive Defect Cover-ups Were Intentional," *Boston Globe,* August 22, 2000, www.boston.com/; Yuri Kageyama, "Mitsubishi Motors Says Massive Defect Cover-ups Were Intentional," *SF Gate,* August 22, 2000, www.sfgate.com/; "Mitsubishi Cover-up May Bring Charges," *Detroit News,* August 23, 2000, www.detnews.com/2000/autos/0008/23/b03-109584.htm; Miki Tanikawa, with Katy Marquardt, "Mitsubishi Concealed Evidence of Defects," *Austin American-Statesman,* August 23, 2000, http://austin360.com/statesman/.

2. "Company News," *Business Ethics,* 13 (March/April 1999): 7.

3. "Privacy for Sale," *Business Ethics,* 13 (July/August 1999): 8.

4. Andrew Singer, "CEO's Focus on 'Reputation' Buoys Unisys's Ethics Program," *Ethikos,* 13 (November/December 1999): 1–3, 8, 16.

5. Erin White, "Study on Teen Readership of Magazines May Step up Pressure on Tobacco Firms," *Wall Street Journal,* October 31, 2000, p. A8.

6. *Business Ethics,* 9 (January/February 1995): 13.

7. Paul Davidson, "MCI May Pay $100M to Settle," *USA Today,* March 13, 2000, p. B1.

8. Jim Glab, "The Death of the Passenger Bill of Rights," Travel and Leisure.com, September 1999, www.travelandleisure.com.

9. "Sales Slump, Lawsuits Grow at Body Shop," *Business Ethics,* 12 (July/August 1998): 8.

10. Debbie Thorne McAlister and Robert Erffmeyer, "A Content Analysis of Outcomes and Responsibilities for Consumer Complaints to Third Party Organizations," *Journal of Business Research,* 2002.

11. Larry Neumeister, "MP3.com to Pay $53.4 Million Settlement to Universal," *American Online News,* November 14, 2000.

12. "Worth Noting," *Business Ethics,* 13 (January/February 1999): 5.

13. "Sprint Phone-Tracking Chip Raises Privacy Issues, WSJ Reports," *Bloomberg News Service,* November 10, 2000, via America Online.

14. Gisele Durham, "Study Finds Lying, Cheating in Teens," *AOL News,* October 16, 2000.

15. This section was adapted from O. C. Ferrell, John Fraedrich, and Linda Ferrell, *Business Ethics: Ethical Decision Making and Cases,* 5th ed. (Boston: Houghton Mifflin, 2002), pp. 54–68.

16. "Rent-Way Confirms 2 Targets of Probe into Accounting Entries," *Wall Street Journal,* November 1, 2000, p. B2.

17. "Police Warn of Phone Scam," *Inside Tucson Business,* November 11, 1999, p. 3.

18. Lawrence J. H. Schulze, "OSHA's Proposed Ergonomics Standard," *Professional Safety,* 45 (August 2000): 8.

19. Joanne Silberner, "All Things Considered," National Public Radio, April 11, 2000.

20. Immanuel Kant, "Fundamental Principles of the Metaphysics of Morals," in *Problems of Moral Philosophy: An Introduction,* 2nd ed., ed. Paul W. Taylor (Encino, CA: Dickenson, 1972), p. 229.

21. Stefanie E. Naumann and Nathan Bennett, "A Case for Procedural Justice Climate: Development and Test of a Multilevel Model," *Academy of Management Journal,* 43 (October 2000): 881–889.

22. Joel Brockner and P. A. Siegel, "Understanding the Interaction Between Procedural and Distributive Justice: The Role of Trust," in *Trust in Organizations: Frontiers of Theory and Research,* ed. R. M. Kramer and T. R. Tyler (Thousand Oaks, Calif: Sage), pp. 390–413.

23. Ferrell, Fraedrich, and Ferrell, *Business Ethics,* p. 55.

24. John Fraedrich and O. C. Ferrell, "Cognitive Consistency of Marketing Managers in Ethical Situations," *Journal of the Academy of Marketing Science,* 20 (Summer 1992): 245–252.

25. Debbie Thorne LeClair, O. C. Ferrell, and John P. Fraedrich, *Integrity Management: A Guide to Managing Legal and Ethical Issues in the Workplace* (Tampa, Fl.: University of Tampa Press, 1998), p. 37.

26. This section was adapted from Ferrell, Fraedrich, and Ferrell, *Business Ethics,* pp. 106–109 and LeClair, Ferrell, and Fraedrich, *Integrity Management,* pp. 37–39.

27. Lawrence Kohlberg, "Stage and Sequence: The Cognitive Developmental Approach to Socialization," in *Handbook of Socialization Theory and Research,* ed. D. A. Goslin (Chicago: Rand McNally, 1969), pp. 347–480.

28. Suein L. Hwang, "The Executive Who Told Tobacco's Secrets," *Wall Street Journal,* November 28, 1995, pp. B1, B6.

29. Kohlberg, "Stage and Sequence: The Cognitive Developmental Approach to Socialization," pp. 347–480.

30. Rebecca Goodell, *Ethics in American Business: Policies, Programs and Perceptions* (Washington D.C.: Ethics Resource Center, 1994), p. 15.

31. Patricia Carlson and Mark. S. Blodgett, "International Ethics Standards for Business: NAFTA, Caux Principles and Corporate Codes of Ethics," *Review of Business,* 18 (Spring 1997), p. 20+.

32. David McClelland, "The Urge to Achieve," in *The Great Writings in Management and Organizational Behavior,* ed. Louis E. Boone and Donald D. Bowen (New York: McGraw-Hill, 1987), p. 386.

33. O. C. Ferrell and Larry G. Gresham, "A Contingency Framework for Understanding Ethical Decision Making in Marketing," *Journal of Marketing,* 49 (Summer 1985): 87–96.

34. Joseph W. Weiss, *Business Ethics: A Managerial, Stakeholder Approach* (Belmont, Calif.: Wadsworth, 1994), p. 13.

35. "Ford's Finance Unit Is Accused of Charging Higher Rates to Blacks," *Wall Street Journal,* November 2, 2000, p. B20.

36. Peter Asmus, "Goodbye Coal, Hello Wind," *Business Ethics,* 13 (July/August 1999): 10–11.

37. O. C. Ferrell, Larry G. Gresham, and John Fraedrich, "A Synthesis of Ethical Decision Models for Marketing," *Journal of Macromarketing,* 9 (Fall 1989): 58–59.

38. David Oyama, "Mitsubishi Electric Reveals TV Dangers After 8-Year Silence," *Wall Street Journal,* September 13, 2000, p. A21.

39. "Lack of Formal Ethics Program Connected to Workplace Problems; Survey Looks at Why People Sometimes Bend the Rules," *PRNewswire,* February 3, 1998.

40. Ethics Resource Center, *The Ethics Resource Center's 2000 National Business Ethics Survey: How Employees Perceive Ethics at Work* (Washington D.C.: Ethics Resource Center, 2000), p. 38.

41. "Fraud a Growing Problem, Wall Street Journal Reports," *Bloomberg Newswire,* November 3, 2000, via America Online.

42. "Deception: Three Disturbing Case Studies," *Business Ethics,* 13 (July/August 1999): 10.

43. Ferrell, Gresham, and Fraedrich, "A Synthesis of Ethical Decision Models for Marketing," pp. 58–59.

44. John Poirer, "Fashion Exec Indicted on Charges of Manipulating IPOs," *Reuters Newswire,* November 2, 2000, via America Online.

45. Linda K. Trevino and Stuart Youngblood, "Bad Apples in Bad Barrels: A Causal Analysis of Ethical Decision Making Behavior," *Journal of Applied Psychology,* 75, no.4 (1990): 378–385.

46. A. Kleinfeld, "Benchmarking the Moral Decision-Making Strength of European Biotech Companies: A European Research Project," *Business Ethics: A European Review,* 10 (April 2001): 122–139.

47. Ethics Resource Center, *The Ethics Resource Center's 2000 National Business Ethics Survey,* p. 16.

48. "Corporate Information," Fidelity Investments, www100.fidelity.com/about/world/ethics_code.html, accessed November 20, 2000.

49. Ibid.

50. Judith Kamm, "Ethics: Easier Said than Done," Summer 1993, Josephson Institute.

51. Anatomy of an Ethics Office," *Business Ethics,* 13 (September/October & November/December 1999): 14.

52. Ethics Resource Center, p. 22.

53. Ethics Resource Center, p. 18.

54. This section was adapted from LeClair, Ferrell, and Fraedrich, pp. 104–107.

55. "A Bank with Ethics, Without Branches," *Business Ethics,* 13 (July/August 1999): 7.

56. Singer, "CEO's Focus on 'Reputation' Buoys Unisys' Ethics Program," pp. 1–3, 8, and 16.

57. Tom Rusk and D. Patrick Miller, *The Power of Ethical Persuasion: From Conflict to Partnership at Work and in Private Life* (New York: Viking, 1993).

58. Ethics Resource Center, p. 84.

Corporate Governance

6

▶ Corporate Governance Defined

▶ Corporate Governance and Corporate Citizenship

▶ Issues in Corporate Governance Systems

▶ Future of Corporate Governance

OBJECTIVES

Define corporate governance

Describe the history and practice of corporate governance

Examine key issues to consider in designing corporate governance systems

Provide information on the future of corporate governance

Throughout the 1990s, W. R. Grace & Co., a leading supplier of specialty chemical, construction, and container products, faced several legal battles. In addition to Securities and Exchange Commission charges of falsified earnings within one of its divisions, company shareholders brought a $4 million shareholder lawsuit against several former officers and directors of the company. Their lawsuit contended that the officers and directors should not have paid a $20 million severance package to a chief executive officer (CEO) who resigned amid sexual harassment allegations in 1995.

Although no formal charges were ever filed against J. P. Bolduc, the former CEO, five Grace employees accused him of sexual harassment, according to reports in the *New York Times*. Bolduc vehemently denied any misconduct, but resigned in March 1995 under pressure because of the sexual harassment allegations. A month later, a proxy statement filed by Grace indicated that a law firm had told the company's board of directors that grounds existed to find that Bolduc had sexually harassed several employees and other individuals associated with the company.

After his resignation, Grace's board of directors awarded Bolduc a generous severance package, even though his employment contract did not stipulate one. Company shareholders believed that Grace's board members wasted company assets and breached their fiduciary duty in giving Bolduc this benefit and sued to recover shareholder dollars that were part of the severance package. One of Grace's largest shareholders, the California Public Employees' Retirement System (CalPERS), intervened in the lawsuit and eventually was named lead plaintiff. Known as an aggressive institutional investor, CalPERS bolstered the effort because it demanded stronger corporate governance mechanisms, including a sexual harassment policy, than the original lawsuit stipulated.

The lawsuit was finally settled in 1999 and included a recovery of nearly $4 million, to be divided among all company stockholders. The $4 million was paid by the insurer that covers the company's board of directors. In addition, the company agreed to develop a progressive policy against sexual harassment and to appoint more independent, outside directors on the board of directors' auditing, nominating, and compensation committees. In this case, pressure from stockholders forced a large multinational corporation not only to rectify past misjudgments but also to adopt stronger governance mechanisms to ensure future corporate citizenship.[1]

The W. R. Grace shareholder lawsuit spotlights the increasing accountability that accompanies business decisions today, especially those made by high-level personnel in publicly held corporations. Stakeholders are demanding greater transparency in business, meaning that company motives and actions must be clear, open for discussion, and subject to scrutiny. Although some organizations have operated fairly independently in the past, the current increasing focus on the role of business in society has highlighted a need for systems that take into account the needs, goals, and expectations of various stakeholders. To respond to these pressures, businesses must effectively implement policies that provide strategic guidance on appropriate courses of action. This focus is part of corporate governance, the system of checks and balances that ensures that organizations are fulfilling their economic, legal, ethical, and citizenship responsibilities.

Governance procedures and policies are typically discussed in the context of publicly traded firms, especially as they relate to corporations' responsibilities to investors.[2] However, the trend is toward discussing governance within many industry sectors, including nonprofits, small businesses, and family-owned enterprises. We believe governance deserves broader consideration because there is evidence of a link between good governance and strong corporate citizenship. As James McRitchie, editor of *Corporate Governance.Net,* recently noted about corporate governance, "Despite its still relatively low profile, it's where much of the real action is going on when it comes to positively changing corporate behavior."[3] A report issued by the Institute of Chartered Accountants in Great Britain concurs, citing corporate governance and accountability as one of the key drivers of change for business in the twenty-first century.[4]

In this chapter, we define corporate governance and integrate the concept with the other elements of corporate citizenship. Next, we trace the evolution of corporate governance and provide information on the status of corporate governance systems in several countries. We also examine primary issues that should be considered in the development and improvement of corporate governance systems, including the roles of boards of directors, shareholders and investors, internal control and risk management, and executive compensation. Finally, we consider the future of corporate governance and indicate how strong governance is tied to corporate performance and economic growth. Our approach in this chapter is to demonstrate that corporate governance is a fundamental aspect of corporate citizenship.

Corporate Governance Defined

In a general sense, the term *governance* relates to the exercise of control and authority. For example, most institutions, governments, and businesses are organized so that control and authority are clearly delineated. These organizations usually have an owner, president, chief executive officer, or board of directors that serves as the ultimate authority on decisions and actions. A clear delineation of power and accountability helps employees, customers, investors, government authorities, and other stakeholders understand why and how the organization chooses and achieves its goals. Although many companies have adopted decentralized decision making, empowerment, team projects, and less-hierarchical structures, governance remains important as a mechanism for ensuring continued growth, change, and accountability for organizational resources and strategy. Even if a company has adopted a consensus approach for its operations, there has to be authority for delegating tasks, making tough and controversial decisions, and balancing power throughout the organization. Governance also provides oversight to uncover and address mistakes, problems, and risks.

Because this book is concerned with corporate citizenship, this chapter will focus on the governance activities of business organizations. We define **corporate governance** as the formal system of accountability and control for organizational decisions and resources. Accountability relates to how well the content of workplace decisions is aligned with a firm's stated strategic direction. Control involves the process of auditing and improving organizational decisions and actions. The philosophy that a board or firm holds regarding accountability and control directly affects how corporate governance works.

Table 6.1 lists examples of the major categories to consider in corporate governance discussions. As you can see, these issues normally involve strategic-level decisions and actions taken by boards of directors, business owners, executives, and other people with high levels of authority and accountability. Although these groups have often been relatively free from scrutiny in the past, changes in technology, consumer activism, government attention, and other factors have raised questions about such issues as executive pay, risk and control, resource accountability, strategic direction, shareholder rights, and other decisions made for the organization.

From a control perspective, companies want to develop, reinforce, and refine policies in order to achieve consistency across organizational decisions and actions. This consistency may relate to a range of business practices, including product quality, human resources, and selection of vendors and business partners.

TABLE 6.1

Corporate Governance Issues

Issue
• Shareholder rights
• Executive compensation
• Mergers and acquisitions
• Composition and structure of the board of directors
• Auditing and control
• Risk management
• CEO selection and executive succession plans

Accountability for organizational decisions and resources begins with a strategic mission and vision that informs all levels of employees and stakeholders. From this strategic directive, it is possible to account for and assess decisions made on behalf of the organization. Thus, corporate governance is about the process and content of decision making in business organizations.

For example, a common board-level decision that relates to corporate governance concerns is in the area of mergers and acquisitions. When a corporation seeks to merge with or purchase another firm, complex questions must be answered. Among these is whether the action makes sense from a strategic perspective. A number of mergers and acquisitions occurred throughout the 1960s, 1970s, and 1980s that seemed to benefit executives and some shareholders, yet made little sense from a strategic and long-term point of view. Another issue that often emerges is conflict in corporate culture, policies, and operating standards that must be remedied through the merger process.[5] Although top executives may recognize the importance of maintaining traditions from premerger organizations, it is also important to resolve conflicts that may present legal risks, perceptions of inequity, differences in quality standards, or problems in strategic direction.

When Daimler Benz and Chrysler merged in 1998, it was obvious that the integration of the two automakers' operations, policies, standards, and cultures was going to be a long and complex process.[6] The companies not only had distinct histories and corporate cultures, but they were also headquartered on different sides of the Atlantic Ocean. A year into the merger, Thomas T. Stallkamp, president of DaimlerChrysler's North American division and the person charged with handling details of the merger, resigned. Stallkamp, who had been a key executive during Chrysler's financial turnaround in the early 1990s, was widely regarded as the merged automaker's "spiritual leader." In this role, Stallkamp had sought to integrate the two firms in many areas, ranging from trust to organizational values to supplier relationships. However, analysts say that his outspoken manner may have led to conflict with DaimlerChrysler's German cochairman of the board, Jurgen E. Schrempp. When discussing his brief time within the merged company, Stallkamp noted a number of areas in which it was difficult to reach agreement or consensus. For example, because of Daimler Benz's luxury image and status, its employees were accustomed to flying first class, whereas only top officers at Chrysler were allowed to do so under company travel policy. Labor relations, steel specifications, and emission-control policies also created problems. At the time of Stallkamp's resignation, DaimlerChrysler's cochairmen had agreed to put a hold on the integration of the company's three automotive units. Business analysts wondered how long it would take for the merged firm to realize its goal of global integration and the $3 billion in cost savings promised through the deal.[7] Two years later, DaimlerChrysler acquired one-third of the stock of Mitsubishi, and within six months of that purchase, Chairman Schrempp had effectively assumed control of that Japanese automaker. Analysts questioned this move, citing strategic problems and even greater differences between the initial German-American deal and this additional Asian venture.[8]

Corporate Governance and Corporate Citizenship

Although most executives and managers do not deal with issues as complex as mergers on a daily basis, they are concerned with strategic-level decisions and their effects throughout the organization and society. However, there is variability in how individuals, industries, and even nations approach business accountability and control. In order to understand the role of corporate governance in business today, it is also important to consider how it relates to fundamental beliefs about the purpose of business organizations. Some people believe that as long as a company is maximizing shareholder wealth and profitability, it is fulfilling its core responsibility. Although this must be accomplished in accordance with legal and ethical standards, the primary focus is on the economic dimension of corporate citizenship. Thus, this belief places the philanthropic dimension of citizenship beyond the scope of business. Other people, however, take the view that a business is an important member, or citizen, of society and must assume broad responsibilities. This view assumes that business performance is reflexive, meaning it both affects and is influenced by internal and external factors. In this case, performance is often considered from a financial, social, and ethical perspective. From these assumptions, we can derive two major conceptualizations of corporate governance—the shareholder model and the stakeholder model.[9]

The **shareholder model of corporate governance** is founded in classic economic precepts, including the maximization of wealth for investors and owners. For publicly traded firms, corporate governance focuses on developing and improving the formal system of performance accountability between top management and the firms' shareholders.[10] Thus, the shareholder orientation should drive management decisions toward what is in the best interests of investors. Underlying these decisions is a classic agency problem, where ownership (i.e., investors) and control (i.e., managers) are separate. Managers act as agents for investors, whose primary goal is shareholder value. However, investors and managers are distinct parties with unique insights, goals, and values with respect to the business. Managers, for example, may have motivations beyond shareholder value, such as market share, personal compensation, or attachment to particular products and projects. Because of these potential differences, corporate governance mechanisms are needed to ensure an alignment between investor and management interests. Although the shareholder orientation is primarily relevant to publicly held businesses, it also has implications for private firms. The shareholder model has been criticized for its somewhat singular purpose and focus, because there are other ways of "investing" in a business. Suppliers, creditors, customers, employees, business partners, the community, and other groups also invest resources into the success of the firm.[11]

In the **stakeholder model of corporate governance,** the purpose of business is conceived in a broader fashion. Although a company has a responsibility for economic success and viability, it must also answer to other parties, including employees, suppliers, government agencies, communities, and groups with which it interacts. This model presumes a collaborative and relational approach to business and its constituents. Because management time and resources are limited, a key decision within the stakeholder model is to determine which stakeholders are primary. Once primary groups have been identified, appropriate corporate governance mechanisms are implemented to promote the development of long-term relationships.[12] As we discussed in Chapter 3, primary stakeholders include stockholders, suppliers, customers, employees, the government, and the community. This approach is characterized by governance systems that consider stakeholder welfare in tandem with corporate needs and interests. Occidental Petroleum Corporation experienced the complexity of the stakeholder model when it began drilling for oil in Colombia. The Colombian government hired Occidental, but the native tribe of U'wa opposed the drilling on religious and historical grounds. The clash of interests has placed Occidental in the difficult position of balancing consumer, investor, government, and other stakeholder concerns.

Although these two approaches seem to represent both ends of a continuum, the reality is that the shareholder model is a more restrictive precursor to the stakeholder orientation. Many businesses have evolved into the stakeholder model as a result of government initiatives, consumer activism, industry activity, and other external forces. Public hospitals, for example, have recently experienced a transition to the more holistic approach to corporate governance. Although public hospitals serve as a "safety net" for local governments' ability to provide health care, some experts object to the influence of government officials on these hospitals' boards of directors and operations. A new model of governance has emerged that calls for fewer government controls, more management autonomy, and extraction from the body politic.[13]

The shareholder model focuses on a primary stakeholder—the investor—whereas the stakeholder model incorporates a broader philosophy toward internal and external constituents. According to The World Bank, a development institution whose goal is to reduce poverty by promoting sustainable economic growth around the world, corporate governance is defined by both internal (i.e., long-term value, efficient operations) and external (i.e., public policy, economic development) factors.[14] We are concerned with the broader conceptualization of corporate governance in this chapter.

In the corporate citizenship model that we propose, governance is the organizing dimension for keeping a firm focused on continuous improvement, accountability, and responses to varying stakeholder interests. Although financial return, or economic viability, is an important measure of success for all firms, the legal dimension of corporate citizenship is also a compulsory consideration. The ethical and philanthropic dimensions, however, are not usually mandated through regulation or contracts. This represents a critical divide in our corporate citizen model and associated governance goals and systems, because there are some critics who challenge the use of organizational resources for concerns beyond financial performance and legalities. This view was recently summarized in an editorial in *National Journal,* a nonpartisan magazine on politics and government: "Corporations are not governments. In the everyday course of their business, they are not accountable to society or to the citizenry at large . . . corporations are bound by the law, and by the rules of what you might call ordinary decency. Beyond this, however, they have no duty to pursue the collective goals of society."[15] This type of philosophy, long associated with the shareholder model of corporate governance, was prevalent throughout the twentieth century, as we shall see in the next section.

History of Corporate Governance

In the United States, a discussion of corporate governance draws on many parallels with the goals and values held by America's founding fathers.[16] As we mentioned earlier in the chapter, governance involves a system of checks and balances, a concept associated with the distribution of power within the executive, judiciary, and legislative branches of the U.S. government. The U.S. Constitution and other documents have a strong focus on accountability, individual rights, and the representation of broad interests in decision making and resource allocation.

In the late 1800s and early 1900s, corporations were headed by such familiar names as Carnegie, DuPont, and Rockefeller. These "captains of industry" had ownership investment and managerial control over their businesses. Thus, there was less reason to talk about corporate governance because the owner of the firm was also the same individual who made strategic decisions about the business. The owner primarily bore the consequences—positive or negative—of decisions made. During the twentieth century, however, an increasing number of public companies and investors brought about a gradual shift in the separation of ownership and control. By the 1930s, corporate ownership was dispersed across a large number of individuals. This raised new questions about control and accountability for organizational resources and decisions.

One of the first known anecdotes that helped shape our current understanding of accountability and control in business occurred in the 1930s. In 1932,

Lewis Gilbert, a stockholder in New York's Consolidated Gas Company, found his questions repeatedly ignored at the firm's annual shareholders' meeting. With his brother, Gilbert pushed for reform, which led the brand-new U.S. Securities and Exchange Commission (SEC) to require corporations to allow shareholder resolutions to be brought to a vote of all stockholders. Because of the Gilbert brothers' activism, the SEC formalized the process by which executives and boards of directors respond to the concerns and questions of investors.[17]

Since the mid-1900s, the approach to corporate governance has involved a legal discussion of principals and agents to the business relationship. Essentially, owners are "principals" who hire "agents," the executives, to run the business. A key goal of businesses is to align the interests of principals and agents so that organizational value and viability are maintained. Achieving this balance has been difficult, as evidenced by these terms coined about business in the media—"junk bonds," "empire building," "golden parachute," and "merger madness." In these cases, the long-term value and competitive stance of organizations were traded for short-term financial gains or rewards. The results of this short-term view included workforce reduction, closed manufacturing plants, struggling communities, and a generally negative perception of corporate leadership. In our philosophy of corporate citizenship, these long-term effects should be considered alongside decisions designed to generate short-run gains in financial performance.

The lack of effective control and accountability mechanisms in years past has prompted much current interest in corporate governance. A Conference Board survey of eighty-two companies in Europe and the United States indicated that boards of directors are playing a greater role in strategy formulation than they did in the early 1990s. In addition, survey results also showed some movement toward corporate governance committees that would allow for greater participation and dialogue between directors and other stakeholders.[18] From these results, it is apparent that boards are assuming greater responsibility for strategic decisions and have decided to implement more effective governance mechanisms. This trend is in progress around the world, with many constituents now calling for more formalization and professionalism in corporate control systems and accountability to stakeholders.

Corporate Governance Around the World

Increased globalization, enhanced electronic communications, economic agreements and zones, and the reduction of trade barriers have created opportunities for firms around the world to conduct business with both consumers and industrial partners. These factors are propelling the need for greater homogenization in corporate governance principles. Standard & Poor's recently launched a new service, Corporate Governance Scores, that analyzes four macro forces that affect the general governance climate of a country, including legal infrastructure, regulation, information infrastructure, and market infrastructure. Based on these factors, a country can be categorized as having strong, moderate, or weak support for effective governance practices at the company level. Institutional investors are very interested in this measure, as it helps determine possible risk.[19] As financial, human, and intellectual capital cross borders, a number of business, social, and cultural concerns arise. In response to this business climate, the Organisation for Economic Co-operation and Development (OECD), a forum for governments to discuss, develop, and enhance economic and social policy, issued a set of principles intended to serve as a global model in corporate governance.[20] After years of discussion and debate among institutional investors, business executives, government representatives, trade unions, and nongovernment organizations, thirty OECD-member governments signaled their agreement with the principles by signing a declaration to integrate them within their countries' economic systems and institutions. The purpose of the OECD Corporate Governance Principles (Table 6.2) is to formulate minimum standards of fairness, transparency, accountability, disclosure, and responsibility for business practice. The principles focus on the board of directors, which

TABLE 6.2

OECD Principles of Corporate Governance

Principle	Explanation
I. The rights of shareholders	The corporate governance framework should protect shareholders' rights.
II. The equitable treatment of shareholders	The corporate governance framework should ensure the equitable treatment of all shareholders, including minority and foreign shareholders. All shareholders should have the opportunity to obtain effective redress for violation of their rights.
III. The role of stakeholders in corporate governance	The corporate governance framework should recognize the rights of stakeholders as established by law and encourage active co-operation between corporations and stakeholders in creating wealth, jobs, and the sustainability of financially sound enterprises.
IV. Disclosure and transparency	The corporate governance framework should ensure that timely and accurate disclosure is made on all material matters regarding the corporation, including the financial situation, performance, ownership, and governance of the company.
V. The responsibilities of the board	The corporate governance framework should ensure the strategic guidance of the company, the effective monitoring of management by the board, and the board's accountability to the company and the shareholders.

Source: "OECD Principles for Corporate Governance," Organisation for Economic Co-operation and Development, www.oecd.org/daf/governance/principles.htm, accessed October 31, 2001.

the OECD says should recognize the impact of governance on the firm's competitiveness. In addition, the OECD charges boards, executives, and corporations with maximizing shareholder value while responding to the demands and expectations of their key stakeholders.

The OECD Corporate Governance Principles cover many specific best practices, including (1) rights of shareholders to vote and influence corporate strategy; (2) greater numbers of skilled, independent members on boards of directors; (3) fewer techniques to protect failing management and strategy; (4) wider use of international accounting standards; and (5) better disclosure of executive pay and remuneration. We will discuss these aspects in the next section of this chapter. Although member governments of the OECD are expected to uphold the governance principles, there is some room for cultural adaptation. Thus, best practices may vary slightly from country to country because of unique factors such as market structure, governmental control, role of banks and lending institutions, labor unions, and other economic, legal, and historical factors. Table 6.3 provides information on the relative

TABLE 6.3

Comparing Corporate Governance Mechanisms Around the World[a]

Mechanism	France	Germany	Japan	United Kingdom	United States
Codes of best practice in governance established by key sectors within the nation	8	0	2	7	9
Prevalence of nonexecutive board members	10	5	1	6	8
Prevalence of independent members on board of directors	3	2	0	3	6
Split chairman and chief executive role	2	10	10	9	1
Effective accounting and control standards	4	6	1	9	10
Executive pay disclosure	3	2	3	10	10
Overall Score[b]	**5.3**	**5.1**	**3.5**	**8.3**	**7.0**

a. Scores are based on a scale of 1–10, where 10 is the best.
b. Overall score is based on ten categories, not all of which are disclosed in this table.
Source: Davis Global Advisors, *Leading Corporate Governance Indicators™ 1999: An International Comparison,* November 1999, Newton, MA. Reprinted by permission from Davis Global Advisors, www.davisglobal.com.

strengths and weaknesses of developed markets with respect to the OECD principles and other established best practices. As you can see, the United Kingdom has made the greatest progress with respect to corporate governance, whereas Japan lags behind other nations on these dimensions. Reasons for the financial crisis that occurred in Southeast Asia in the late 1990s partly involved corporate governance. For example, the government structure of some Asian countries created greater opportunities for corruption and nepotism. In addition, the concentration of business power within a few families and tycoons also reduced the need for competitiveness and transparency. Finally, the crisis brought to light a reliance on American and European capital and the associated necessity for governance mechanisms expected in those regions.[21]

Issues in Corporate Governance Systems

Organizations that strive to develop effective corporate governance systems consider a number of internal and external issues. In this section, we look at four areas that need to be addressed in the design and improvement of governance mechanisms. We begin with boards of directors, which have the ultimate responsibility for ensuring a governance focus. Then, we discuss the role of shareholders and investors, internal control and risk management, and executive compensation within the governance system. These issues affect most organizations, although individual businesses may face unique factors that create additional governance questions. For example, a company operating in several countries will need to resolve issues related to international governance policy.

Boards of Directors

Members of a company's board of directors assume legal responsibility for the firm's resources and decisions, and they appoint its top executive officers. This is also true of a university's board of trustees, and there are similar arrangements in the nonprofit sector. In each of these cases, board members have fiduciary duty, meaning they have assumed a position of trust and confidence that entails certain requisite responsibilities. These responsibilities include acting in the best interests of those they serve. Thus, board membership is not designed as a vehicle for personal financial gain; rather, it provides the intangible benefit of ensuring the success of the organization and the people involved in the fiduciary arrangement.

The traditional approach to directorship assumed that board members managed the corporation's business. Research and practical observation have shown that boards of directors rarely, if ever, perform the management function.[22] Because boards meet only a few times a year, there is no way that time allocation would allow for effective management. In addition, the complexity of organizations requires full attention on a daily basis. Today, boards of directors are concerned primarily with monitoring the decisions made by managers on behalf of the company. This includes choosing top executives, assessing their performance, helping to set strategic direction, and ensuring that control and accountability mechanisms are in place. In sum, board members assume the ultimate authority for organizational effectiveness and subsequent performance.

Just as corporate citizenship objectives require more of employees and executives, boards of directors are also experiencing increasing accountability and disclosure mandates. In the past, board members were often retired company executives or friends of current executives, but the trend today is toward "outside directors," who had little vested interest in the firm before assuming the director role. Directors today are increasingly chosen for their expertise, competence, and ability to bring diverse perspectives to strategic discussions. Outside directors are also thought to bring more independence to the monitoring function because they are not bound by past allegiances, friendships, a current role in the company, or some other issue that may create a conflict of interest.

Board independence has become so desirable that it is one of the criteria, along with board quality, diversity of board members, and corporate performance, that *Chief Executive* magazine uses to assess the quality of corporate boards of directors. Table 6.4 shows the five best and five worst boards, as evaluated by governance experts for *Chief Executive.* Several factors stand out about the best boards of directors. These boards are generally more independent and have greater accountability to shareholders than other corporations. Their directors often own company stock, making them more sympathetic to shareholder

TABLE 6.4

Best and Worst Boards of Directors

Five Best Boards	Five Worst Boards
1. Verizon	1. Lucent
2. Texas Instruments	2. Xerox
3. 3M	3. United Airlines
4. General Motors	4. Dillards
5. The New York Times Co.	5. Veritas Software

Source: Robert W. Lear and Boris Yavitz, "America's Best and Worst Boards," *Chief Executive,* 171 (October 2001): 54–59.

Cendant

Most people view accounting as a routine but necessary business practice, but for Henry R. Silverman, it now has far greater significance than most other business practices. Accounting irregularities almost brought down Silverman's company after it merged with the direct-marketing firm CUC International Inc. to form Cendant in 1997. The accounting improprieties in CUC's books came to light only after the merger occurred, and thus began two years of turmoil for Henry Silverman.

Henry Silverman built his company, HFS, into a giant franchiser of well-known hotel and real-estate brands, including Days Inn, Ramada Inn, Howard Johnson, Century 21, and Coldwell Banker, through strategic acquisitions. Silverman took HFS public in 1992 and was rewarded by a stock increase of 1,836 percent over the next five years. In 1997, he merged HFS with CUC International, which sold memberships in discount buying clubs, to form Cendant. Under the merger

agreement, Silverman became Cendant's CEO, and CUC's chief executive, Walter A. Forbes, became its chairman. The agreement also stipulated that the two men would switch jobs in 2000, at which time Silverman planned to slow down and relax more.

However, in July 1998, Cendant executives discovered accounting irregularities in CUC's books, which, when compounded with errors, had allowed CUC to overstate its earnings by $700 million between 1995 and 1997. When an investigation by Cendant's board of directors audit committee confirmed the improprieties, the company announced that it would have to restate earnings for 1997 and perhaps earlier. Cendant's stock plummeted 46 percent in one day. Forbes and nine of his allies on the company's board of directors soon resigned, although Forbes eventually received a severance package of $35 million and stock options worth about $12.5 million.

In 1999 Cendant sued Ernst & Young, CUC's auditors, for "gross negligence." The company

concerns. Moreover, these directors often encourage innovative practices and take a more active role than directors of other firms. At 3M, for example, all investors receive user-friendly communications regarding the rights and responsibilities of shareholders, along with explanation of basic board processes and rules. Even companies not on the list are starting to use innovative governance techniques. For example, Home Depot's outside directors visit five stores every quarter, giving them a stronger sense of what is going on within the company, as well as the opportunity to address issues before they become problems.[23]

Although insiders represent just 18 percent of members on most boards of directors today, many new "dot-com" high-technology companies fill their boards with insiders who are heavily invested in the firm. In addition to higher percentages of inside directors, these boards are often smaller than those found in large,

also settled a class-action shareholder suit for $2.8 billion. Settling the shareholder suit minimized one of Cendant's greatest threats after the scandal was revealed: If shareholders had been able to convince the judge that the damages were equal to the market decline, then Cendant would have been forced to liquidate. The settlement required Cendant to give a majority of its board seats to independent directors in an attempt to provide greater corporate governance. Before the scandal emerged, Cendant's twenty-eight-member board had included equal representation from CUC and HFS, and some board members had close business ties to one of the firms.

The pain still kept coming, however, for in 2000, *Business Week* ranked Cendant as having one of the worst boards of directors. Although the company's board members were entirely new by that time, some people still wondered, "Where was the board of directors during the CUC accounting scandal?"

Some people see Henry Silverman as a victim, but others think that the whole fiasco is his own fault, that he should have been more thorough in examining CUC before the merger. Some experts have questioned the due diligence process used in the premerger analysis. Regardless of fault, Silverman must now work to rebuild his credibility. Although most analysts believe that Cendant will eventually fully recover, Silverman's own credibility is a different story. Always a Wall Street "darling," Henry Silverman's credibility and stock were built on his "wheeling and dealing." The strategy and tactics that he used to build his empire helped to shatter his credibility. Silverman was consumed with rage over the whole matter, ultimately consulting a psychiatrist for help. Forbes, on the other hand, has gone on with his life, relaxing and staying out of the spotlight. Forbes continues to deny any knowledge of the CUC irregularities, but is still under investigation by the Securities and Exchange Commission as well as the U.S. Attorney in Newark, New Jersey. ■

Sources:
These facts are from Amy Barrett, "Henry Silverman's Long Road Back," *Business Week*, February 28, 2000, pp. 126–136; John A. Byrne, "The Best & Worst Boards," *Business Week*, January 24, 2000, pp. 142–152; Andy Serwer, "Are Investors Ready to Check Back into Cendant?" *Fortune*, January 24, 2000, pp. 183–184.

traditional businesses. Yahoo!, for example, has a board of six, including three company executives. Directors of new high-tech firms are usually brought in to add management and strategic expertise to the business, whereas traditional firms tend to choose board members who understand governance, succession planning, and other oversight roles. Although it may be too early to draw broad conclusions as to the effectiveness of these smaller, insider boards in the high-tech industry, legal expert Charles M. Elson notes, "It's really not until something goes wrong that people focus on (governance)."[24]

Regardless of the size and type of business for which boards are responsible, a system of governance is needed to ensure effective control and accountability. As a corporation grows, matures, enters international markets, and takes other strategic directions, it is likely that the board of directors will evolve and change to meet its new demands. Sir Adrian Cadbury, president of the Centre for Board Effectiveness in the United Kingdom and an architect of corporate governance changes in Europe, has predicted several trends that will affect boards in the future:

- Boards will be responsible for developing company purpose statements that cover a range of aims and stakeholder concerns.

- Annual reports and other documents will include more nonfinancial information.

- Boards will be required to define their role and implement self-assessment processes better.

- Selection of board members will become increasingly formalized, with less emphasis on personal networks and word of mouth.

- Boards will need to work more effectively as teams.

- Serving on boards will require more time and commitment than in the past.[25]

These trends are consistent with our previous discussion of corporate citizenship. In all facets of organizational life, greater demands are being placed on business decisions and people. Many of these expectations emanate from those who provide substantial resources in the organization, namely shareholders and other investors.

▶ *Shareholders and Investors*

Because they have allocated scarce resources to the organization, shareholders and investors expect to grow and reap rewards from their investments. This type of financial exchange represents a formal contractual arrangement and provides the capital necessary to fund all types of organizational initiatives, such as new product development and facilities construction. A shareholder is concerned with his or her ownership investment in publicly traded firms, whereas an investor is a more general term for any individual or organization that provides capital to another firm. Investments may include financial, human, and intellectual capital.

Shareholders, particularly large institutional ones, have become more active in articulating their positions with respect to company strategy and executive decision making. For example, Maurice Coman, a member of the Sierra Club and a stockholder in DuPont, helped support a Sierra Club-sponsored shareholder resolution urging the company to halt construction of a titanium dioxide mine in Georgia. Although the resolution failed, it received 3.4 percent of the vote, representing more than 51 million shares of DuPont stock.[26] One of the most celebrated acts of shareholder activism occurred when the Episcopal Church, a member of the Interfaith Center on Corporate Responsibility, filed a resolution in 1971 calling on General Motors to withdraw from South Africa because of that nation's policy of apartheid. Apartheid was an official policy of racial segregation

Vanguard offers social funds
for investors concerned with
corporate governance.

practiced in South Africa, involving political, legal, and economic discrimination
against nonwhites. Many organizations and individuals supported the Episcopal
Church's condemnation of South Africa's policy and urged other companies to
suspend doing business there until racial equality was restored.[27] Examples like
these, along with CalPERS' pressure on W. R. Grace, illustrate that although shareholders and investors want their resources used efficiently and effectively, they are
increasingly willing to take a stand to encourage companies to change for reasons
beyond financial return.

Many investors assume the stakeholder model to corporate governance, which carries into a strategy of social investing, "the integration of social and ethical criteria into the investment decision-making process."[28] Nearly three-quarters of American investors take social responsibility issues into account when choosing investment opportunities. Twelve percent indicate they are willing to take a lower rate of return if the company is a strong performer in the corporate citizenship area.[29] Although social investing has received strong media attention over the last few years, the Quakers, a religious group, applied social investment criteria in the seventeenth century when they refused to invest, patronize, or partner with any business involved in the slave trade or military concerns.[30] Investors today use similar screening criteria in determining where to place their funds and resources. Table 6.5 provides an example of the screening criteria used to exclude or include

TABLE 6.5

Performance Criteria in the Calvert Social Investment Fund

Performance Areas	Sample Criteria
1. Environment	• Maintain at least an average record in industry • Develop products or processes that reduce or minimize environmental impact • Implement innovative pollution prevention programs
2. Workplace issues	• Actively hire and promote minorities/women • Provide safe and healthy workplace • Provide work–family programs
3. Product safety and impact	• No major manufacturers of alcohol or tobacco or business in gambling establishments • Produce or market products that enhance health or quality of life • Respond promptly to product problems
4. International operations and human rights	• Have adopted specific human rights standards to to govern international operations • Use more stringent environmental and workplace standards than required by local law
5. Weapons contracting	• Avoids companies that have weapons contracts exceeding 10 percent of gross annual sales
6. Indigenous peoples' rights	• Respect land, sovereignty, and natural resource rights of indigenous communities • Contribute to community-drive development and environmental management plans

Source: "Social and Environmental Criteria for Group Funds," Calvert Group, www.calvertgroup.com/sri_647.html, accessed October 29, 2001.

companies in the Calvert Social Investment Fund. Several other mutual funds and investors have similar standards.

By the late 1990s, social investment outlays totaled more than $2 trillion in the United States.[31] Not only do these social investments help individuals and institutions meet their corporate citizenship goals, but they also provide strong financial returns. The Domini Social Equity Fund, for example, won an award from *Business Ethics* magazine for its 1998 return of 32.99 percent, a rate that outpaced the Standard & Poor's 500 index return of 28.58 percent for the same year.[32] This type of evidence is consistent with our discussion of the link between corporate citizenship and organizational performance in Chapter 2.

Shareholder activism and social investing are especially prevalent in the United States and United Kingdom, two countries that score relatively high on the corporate governance index listed in Table 6.3. Several other European countries are also experiencing increasing rates of activism and social investing. Although most activism and investing take place on an organizational level through mutual funds and other institutional arrangements, some individual investors have affected company strategy and policy. Robert Monks, a leading corporate governance activist, once described Warren Buffett, the legendary investor from Omaha, Nebraska, as "epitomizing the kind of monitoring shareholder whose involvement enhances the value of the whole enterprise. Mr. Buffett personally salvaged the rogue Salomon Brothers [now Salomon Smith Barney] from the bankrupting implications of its illegal activities."[33] Although few investors have Buffett's financial clout and respect, he serves as a role model by paying attention to the control and accountability mechanisms of the companies in which he invests.

Colleges and universities are also becoming active in social investing. For example, most colleges have endowment funds, or monies that are invested for the long-term future of the university. Because of these investments, stakeholders of higher education institutions are drawing attention to corporate citizenship issues. Harvard University, with an estimated endowment of nearly $13 billion, solicits input from the university community when deciding how to vote in a socially responsible manner on shareholder resolutions. A committee of faculty, students, and alumni advises the endowment fund's governing board, which ultimately votes on the resolutions. In 1999, the governing board voted with the advisory group's recommendation in 50 of 80 cases. In the remaining 30 votes, the board abstained in 26 votes and went against the advisory group in only four cases.[34]

The newly formed Student Alliance to Reform Corporations (STARC) has student contacts at 120 colleges and universities who are dedicated to implementing socially responsible investment policies.[35] Such student pressure has led colleges to sell stocks that are deemed counter to socially responsible investment goals. For example, the University of Wisconsin and the University of Minnesota divested shares of corporations with operations that support the military regime in Burma.

Stanford, Tufts, Haverford, and the University of Washington no longer invest in tobacco companies. STARC campaigns are committed to the following principles for investor responsibility at universities and colleges:

- Challenge corporate conduct that harms humans, animals, and the environment.

- Disclose to the university community all actions affecting corporate conduct that the institution takes as an investor or shareholder, including votes on shareholder resolutions.

- Empower a democratically selected committee to review the social implications of institutional investment decisions and policy.

- Commit to following the recommendations of this investor responsibility advisory committee in order to fulfill the institution's aim of advancing the public interest.

- Adopt guidelines for investment and shareholder activity that support responsible corporate conduct promoting human rights, indigenous rights, equity and diversity, animal rights, environmental quality, labor rights, and the production of safe and beneficial products; guidelines should also include requirements for corporate disclosure of records of corporate performance in these areas.[36]

Internal Control and Risk Management

Controls are fundamental to effective operations, as they allow for comparisons between the actual performance and the planned performance and goals of the organization. Controls are used to safeguard corporate assets and resources, protect the reliability of organizational information, and ensure compliance with regulations, laws, and contracts. The area of internal control covers a wide range of company decisions and actions, not just the accuracy of financial statements and accounting records. Controls also foster understanding when discrepancies exist between corporate expectations and stakeholder interests and issues.

Internal controls effectively limit employee or management opportunism, or the use of corporate assets for individualistic or nonstrategic purposes. Controls also ensure the board of directors has access to timely and quality information that can be used to determine strategic options and effectiveness. For these reasons, the board of directors should have ultimate oversight for the integrity of the internal control system.[37] Although board members do not develop or administer the control system, they are responsible for ensuring that an effective system exists. The need for internal controls is rarely disputed, and it does represent a set of tasks and resource commitment that requires high-level attention.

Although most large corporations have designed internal controls, smaller companies and nonprofit organizations are less likely to have invested in a complete system. For example, a small computer shop in Columbus, Ohio, lost thousands of dollars due to embezzlement by the accounts receivable clerk. Because of the clerk's position and role in the company, she was able to post credit card payments due her employer to her own account and then later withdraw the income. Although she faces felony theft charges, her previous employer admitted feeling ashamed and did not want his business associated with a story on employee theft.[38] Such crime is common in small businesses because they often lack effective internal controls. Simple, yet proven, control mechanisms that can be used in all types of organizations are listed in Table 6.6. These techniques are not costly, but they conform to best practices in the prevention of ethical and legal problems that threaten the efficacy of governance mechanisms.

Another element of control is the ability to anticipate and remedy organizational risks. A strong internal control system should alert decision makers to possible problems, or risks, that may threaten business operations, including worker safety, company solvency, vendor relationships, proprietary information, the environment, or stakeholders. The term *risk management* is normally used in a narrow sense to indicate responsibilities associated with insurance, liability, financial decisions, and related issues. Kraft General Foods, for example, has a risk management policy for understanding how prices of commodities, such as coffee, sugar, wheat, and cocoa, will affect its relationships throughout the supply chain.[39]

Risk is always present within organizations, so executives must develop processes for remedying or managing its effects. There are at least three ways to consider how risk poses either a potentially negative or positive concern for

TABLE 6.6

Internal Control Mechanisms for Small Businesses and Nonprofits

Control Mechanism
• Develop and disseminate a code of conduct that explicitly addresses ethical and legal issues in the workplace.
• Segregate job functions to reduce the opportunity for opportunism (i.e., the person reconciling bank statements is not making deposits or paying invoices).
• Screen employment applicants thoroughly, especially those who would assume much responsibility if hired.
• Require all employees to take at least one week of vacation on an annual basis.
• Limit access to valuable inventory and financial records.
• Ask questions about confusing financial statements and other records.

Sources: "Protecting Against Employee Fraud," *Business First—Western New York,* June 14, 1999, p. 31; Kathy Hoke," Eyes Wide Open," *Business First—Columbus,* August 27, 1999, pp. 27–28.

organizations.[40] First, risk can be categorized as a hazard. In this view, risk management is focused on minimizing negative situations, such as fraud, injury, or financial loss. Second, risk may be considered an uncertainty that needs to be hedged through quantitative plans and models. This type of risk is best associated with the term *risk management,* which is used in financial and business literature. Third, risk also creates opportunity for innovation and entrepreneurship. Just as management can be criticized for taking too much risk, it can also be subject to concerns about the lack of risk taking. All three types of risk are implicitly covered by our definition of corporate governance, because there are risks for both control (i.e., preventing fraud, ensuring accuracy of financial statements) and accountability (i.e., innovation to develop new products and markets). For example, the Internet and electronic commerce capabilities have introduced new risks of all types for organizations. Privacy, as we discuss in Chapter 10, is a major concern for many stakeholders and has created the need for policies and certification procedures. A board of directors may ensure that the company has established privacy policies that are not only effective but can also be properly monitored and improved as new technology risks and opportunities emerge in the business environment.[41]

▶ *Executive Compensation*

How executives are compensated for their leadership, organizational service, and performance has become a controversial topic. Indeed, 73 percent of respondents in a recent *Business Week*/Harris poll indicated they believe that top officers of large U.S. companies receive too much compensation, whereas only 21 percent reported executive compensation was "just about the right amount."[42] Many people believe that no executive is worth millions of dollars in annual salary and stock options, even if he or she has brought great financial returns to investors. Their concerns often center on the relationship between the highest-paid executives and median employee wages in the company. If this ratio is perceived as too large, then critics believe that either rank-and-file employees are not being compensated fairly or high executive salaries represent an improper use of company resources. According to a recent report by United for a Fair Economy, the average executive now earns 419 times the average blue-collar worker's salary. Because of this enormous difference, the business press is now usually careful to support high levels of executive compensation only when they are directly linked to strong company performance. Although the issue of executive compensation has received much attention in the media of late, some business owners have long recognized its potential ill effects. In the early twentieth century, for example, capitalist J. P. Morgan implemented a policy that limited the pay

Former GE Chairman and CEO Jack Welch, shown here with current Chairman Jeffrey Immelt, was one of the highest paid CEOs in the world.

of top managers in businesses he owned to no more than 20 times the pay of any other employee.[43]

Other people argue that because executives assume so much risk on behalf of the company, they deserve the rewards that follow from strong company performance. In addition, many executives' personal and professional lives meld to the point that they are "on call" twenty-four hours a day. Because not everyone has the skill, experience, and desire to become an executive and assume so much pressure and responsibility, market forces dictate a high level of compensation. When the pool of qualified individuals is limited, many corporate board members feel that offering a large compensation package is the only way to attract and retain a top executive to ensure their firm is not left without strong leadership. In an era where top executives are increasingly willing to "jump ship" to other firms, especially in the high-tech field, that offer higher pay, potentially lucrative stock options, bonuses, and other benefits, such thinking is not without merit.[44] The average salary, benefits, and options package for chief executives of major corporations in the United States in 1998 was more than $5 million.[45] Table 6.7 lists the median total compensation of chief executives in fourteen different U.S. industries.

John Lauer, CEO of Cleveland-based Oglebay Norton, decided to modify his own compensation package after he completed a doctoral dissertation on executive compensation. His research suggested that most top managers are overcompensated, with their pay having very little to do with company performance. In another

TABLE 6.7

Total Median Compensation of Chief Executive Officers (including salary, bonus, value of other long-term incentives)

Industry	Median Compensation
Energy	$2,448,000
Utilities	$2,133,000
Computer Services	$1,885,000
Communications	$1,808,000
Financial Services	$1,803,000
Telecommunications	$1,788,000
Manufacturing	$1,705,000
Retail Trade	$1,594,000
Transportation	$1,509,000
Diversified Service	$1,425,000
Construction	$1,390,000
Commercial Banking	$1,197,000
Insurance	$1,193,000
Wholesale Trade	$1,054,000

Source: "Compensation of Outside Directors and CEOs Rise," The Conference Board, Inc., press release, November 27, 2000, www.conferenceboard.org/whoweare/frames.cfm?main= about.cfm.

situation, when AMR Corp., the corporate parent of American Airlines, was experiencing financial difficulties, CEO Robert Crandall asked the company's board of directors not to grant him a bonus or stock options. Because he was asking airline employees to take pay cuts at the time, he felt he could not justify being treated differently than the rest of the workforce. Moreover, he did not want to create more tension within the organization at a time when spirits were already low.[46]

These examples show that executive compensation is a difficult issue. However, it is an important one for boards of directors and other stakeholders to consider because it receives much media attention, sparks shareholder concerns, and is hotly debated in corporate governance discussions. One area for board members to consider is the extent to which executive compensation is linked to company performance. Plans that base compensation on the achievement of several performance goals, including profits and revenues, are intended to align the interests of owners with management. Other governance concerns include the disclosure of executive compensation, industry standards for remuneration, the ability to attract top talent, and incentives for superior performance.[47]

Future of Corporate Governance

As the issues discussed in the previous section demonstrate, corporate governance is primarily focused on strategic-level concerns for accountability and control. Although many discussions of corporate governance still revolve around responsibility in investor-owned companies, good governance is fundamental to effective performance in all types of organizations. As you have gleaned from history and government classes, a system of checks and balances is important for ensuring a focus on multiple perspectives and constituencies; proper distribution of resources, power, and decision authority; and the responsibility for making changes and setting direction.

In order to pursue corporate citizenship successfully, organizations must consider issues of control and accountability. As we learned earlier, the concept of corporate governance is in transition from the shareholder model to one that considers broader stakeholder concerns and inputs to financial performance. Although not all companies have made the transition from a shareholder to stakeholder orientation, a number of market and environmental forces, such as the OECD and shareholder activism, have created pressures in this direction. This evolution is consistent with our view of corporate citizenship. Although some critics deride this expanded focus, a number of external and internal forces are driving business toward the stakeholder orientation and formalization of governance mechanisms. One concern centers around the cost of governance. For example, the cost of meeting regulations for safety, health, labor standards, employee benefits, and civil rights is estimated at $91.9 million for all companies operating in the United States.[48]

Most businesspeople and academicians agree that the benefits of a strong approach to corporate governance outweigh its costs. However, the positive return on governance goes beyond organizational performance to benefit the industrial competitiveness of entire nations. For example, corrupt organizations often fail to develop competitiveness on a global scale and can leave behind financial ruin, thus negating the overall economic growth of the entire region or nation. At the same time, corrupt governments usually have difficulty sustaining and supporting the types of organizations that can succeed in global markets. Thus, a lack of good governance can lead to insular and selfish motives because there is no effective system of checks and balances. In today's interactive and interdependent business environment, most organizations are learning the benefits of a more cooperative approach to commerce. It is possible for a company to retain its competitive nature while seeking a "win-win" solution for all parties to the exchange.[49] Further, as nations with large economies embrace governance principles, it becomes even more difficult for nations and organizations that do not abide by the principles to compete in these lucrative and rich markets. There is a contagion effect toward corporate governance among members of the global economy, much like peer pressure influences the actions and decisions of individuals.

Because governance is concerned with the decisions made by boards of directors and executives, it has the potential for far-reaching positive—and negative—effects. A recent study by the Organization for Economic Co-operation and Development found that stronger financial performance is the result of several governance factors and practices, including (1) large institutional shareholders that are active monitors of company decisions and boards, (2) owner-controlled firms, (3) fewer mergers, especially between firms with disparate corporate values and business lines, and (4) shareholders' decisions on executive remuneration, not boards of directors.[50] The authors of the study note that these practices may not hold true for strong performance in all countries and economic systems. However, they also point out that a consensus view is emerging, with fewer differences among OECD countries than exist among all other nations. Similarities in organizational-level accountability and control should lead to smoother operations between different companies and countries, thereby bolstering competitiveness on many levels.

The future of corporate governance is directly linked to the future of corporate citizenship. Because governance is the control and accountability process for achieving citizenship, it is important to consider who should be involved in the future. First and most obviously, business leaders and managers will need to embrace governance as an essential part of effective performance. Some of the elements of corporate governance, particularly executive pay and shareholder rights, are likely to stir debate for many years. However, business leaders must recognize the forces that have brought governance to the forefront as a precondition of management responsibility. Thus, they may need to accept the "creative tension" that exists between managers, owners, and other primary stakeholders as the preferable route to mutual success.[51]

Second, governments have a key role to play in corporate governance. National competitiveness depends on the strength of various institutions, with primacy on the effective performance of business and capital markets. Strong corporate governance is essential to this performance, and thus, governments will need to be actively engaged in affording both protection and accountability for corporate power and decisions. The Asian economic crisis discussed earlier has already prompted governments to consider tighter governance procedures. Finally, other stakeholders may become more willing to use governance mechanisms to influence corporate strategy or decision making. Investors, whether shareholders, employees, or business partners, have a stake in decisions and should be willing to take steps to align various interests for long-term benefits. Like CalPERS, there are many institutional investors willing to exert great influence on underperforming companies.

Governance is one area in the business literature that has not received the same level of attention as other issues, such as environmental impact, diversity, and sexual harassment. In the future, however, corporate governance will emerge as the operational centerpiece to the corporate citizenship effort. Governance holds people at the highest organizational levels accountable and responsible to a broad and diverse set of stakeholders. Although top managers and boards of directors have always assumed responsibility, their actions are now subject to greater transparency. The future will require that business leaders have a different set of skills and attitudes, including the ability to balance multiple interests, handle ambiguity, manage complex systems and networks, create trust among stakeholders, and improve processes so leadership is pervasive throughout the organization.[52] As Robert Monks, the activist money manager and leader on corporate governance issues, recently wrote, effective corporate governance requires understanding that the "indispensable link between the corporate constituents is the creation of a credible structure (with incentives and disincentives) that enables people with overlapping but not entirely congruent interests to have a sufficient level of confidence in each other and the viability of the enterprise as a whole."[53] We will take a closer look at some of these constituents and their concerns in the next few chapters.

Summary

To respond to stakeholder pressures to answer for organizational decisions and policies, organizations must effectively implement policies that provide strategic guidance on appropriate courses of action. Such policies are often known as corporate governance, the formal system of accountability and control for organizational decisions and resources. Accountability relates to how well the content of workplace decisions is aligned with the firm's stated strategic direction, whereas control involves the process of auditing and improving organizational decisions and actions.

There are two major conceptualizations of corporate governance. The shareholder model of corporate governance focuses on developing and improving the formal system of performance accountability between top management and the firms' shareholders. The stakeholder model of corporate governance views the purpose of business in a broader fashion, in which the organization not only has a responsibility for economic success and viability but also must answer to other stakeholders. The shareholder model focuses on a primary stakeholder—the investor—whereas the shareholder model incorporates a broader philosophy toward internal and external constituents.

In the late 1800s and early 1900s, corporate governance was not a major issue because company owners made strategic decisions about their businesses. By the

1930s, ownership was dispersed across many individuals, raising questions about control and accountability. In response to shareholder activism, the Securities and Exchange Commission (SEC) required corporations to allow shareholder resolutions to be brought to a vote of all shareholders. Since the mid-1900s, the approach to corporate governance has involved a legal discussion of principals (owners) and agents (managers) to the business relationship. The lack of effective control and accountability mechanisms in years past has prompted a current trend toward boards of directors playing a greater role in strategy formulation than they did in the early 1990s. The Organisation for Economic Co-operation and Development (OECD) has issued a set of principles to formulate minimum standards of fairness, transparency, accountability, disclosure, and responsibility for business practice.

Members of a company's board of directors assume legal responsibility and fiduciary duty for organizational resources and decisions. Boards today are concerned primarily with monitoring the decisions made by managers on behalf of the company. The trend today is toward boards composed of outside directors who have little vested interest in the firm.

Shareholders have become more active in articulating their positions with respect to company strategy and executive decision making. Many investors assume the stakeholder model to corporate governance, which carries into a strategy of integrating social and ethical criteria into the investment decision-making process. Although most activism and investing take place on an organizational level through mutual funds and other institutional arrangements, some individual investors have affected company strategy and policy.

Another significant governance issue is internal control and risk management. Controls allow for comparisons between actual performance and the planned performance and goals of the organization and are used to safeguard corporate assets and resources, protect the reliability of organizational information, and ensure compliance with regulations, laws, and contracts. Controls foster understanding when discrepancies exist between corporate expectations and stakeholder interests and issues. A strong internal control system should alert decision makers to possible problems or risks that may threaten business operations. Risk can be categorized (1) as a hazard, in which case risk management focuses on minimizing negative situations, such as fraud, injury, or financial loss; (2) as an uncertainty that needs to be hedged through quantitative plans and models; or (3) as an opportunity for innovation and entrepreneurship.

How executives are compensated for their leadership, service, and performance is another governance issue. Many people believe the ratio between the highest-paid executives and median employee wages in the company should be reasonable. Others argue that because executives assume so much risk on behalf of the organization, they deserve the rewards that follow from strong company performance. One area for board members to consider is the extent to which executive compensation is linked to company performance.

Most businesspeople and academicians agree that the benefits of a strong approach to corporate governance outweigh its costs. Because governance is concerned with the decisions taken by boards of directors and executives, it has the potential for far-reaching positive, and negative, effects. The future of corporate governance is directly linked to the future of corporate citizenship. Business leaders and managers will need to embrace governance as an essential part of effective performance. Governments also have a role to play in corporate governance. National competitiveness depends on the strength of various institutions, with primacy on the effective performance of business and capital markets. Other stakeholders may become more willing to use governance mechanisms to affect corporate strategy or decision making.

KEY TERMS

corporate governance

shareholder model of corporate governance

stakeholder model of corporate governance

DISCUSSION QUESTIONS

1. What is corporate governance? Why is corporate governance an important concern for companies that are pursuing the corporate citizenship approach? How does it improve or change the nature of executive and managerial decision making?

2. Compare and contrast the shareholder and stakeholder models of corporate governance. Which one seems to predominate today? What implications does this have for businesses in today's complex environment?

3. How have laws and economic circumstances contributed to the growing trend toward increasing corporate governance? Why are accountability and control so important in the twenty-first century?

4. What is the role of the board of directors in corporate governance? What responsibilities does the board have?

5. What role do shareholders and other investors play in corporate governance? How can investors effect change?

6. Why are internal control and risk management important in corporate governance? Describe three approaches organizations may take to managing risk.

7. Why is the issue of executive compensation controversial? Are today's corporate executives worth the compensation packages they receive?

8. As corporate governance becomes a more important aspect of corporate citizenship, what new skills and characteristics will managers and executives need? Consider how pressures for governance require managers and executives to relate and interact with stakeholders in new ways.

EXPERIENTIAL EXERCISE

Visit the web site of the Organisation for Economic Co-operation and Development (**http://www.oecd.org**). Examine the origins of the organization and its unique role in the global economy. After visiting the site, answer the following questions:

1. What are the primary reasons that OECD exists?

2. How would you describe OECD's current areas of concern and focus?

3. What role do you think OECD will play in the future with respect to corporate governance and related issues?

NOTES

1. Mark Anderson, "W. R. Grace Settles Shareholder Suit Led by CalPERS," *Sacramento Business Journal,* October 29, 1999, p. 12; "CalPERS Settles Lawsuit with W. R. Grace & Co.," CalPERS, press release, October 13, 1999, www.calpers-governance.org/news/1999/1013a.asp.

2. Rafael LaPorta and Florencio Lopez-de-Silanes, "Investor Protection and Corporate Governance," *Journal of Financial Economics,* 58 (October/November 2000): 3-38.

3. James McRitchie, "Ending the Wall Street Walk: Why Corporate Governance Now?" Corporate Governance, www.corpgov.net/forums/commentary/ending.html, accessed October 31, 2001.

4. "The 2020 Vision Project," *Institute of Chartered Accountants in England & Wales,* www.icaew.co.uk/, accessed October 29, 2001.

5. "Let's Call the Whole Thing Off . . . ," *Directors & Boards,* 1999 Special Report Issue, p. 4.

6. Keith Bradsher, "A Struggle over Culture and Turf at Auto Giant," *New York Times,* September 25, 1999, p. C1.

7. Joann Muller, "Lessons from a Casualty of the Culture Wars," *Business Week,* November 29, 1999, p. 198; Joann Muller, Kathleen Kerwin, and Jack Ewing, "Man with a Plan," *Business Week,* October 4, 1999, p. 34; Christine Tierney, Matt Karnitschnig, and Joann Muller, "Defiant Daimler," *Business Week,* August 7, 2000, pp. 90-94.

8. Christine Tierney and Ken Belson, "Mitsubishi: Conquest or Quicksand for Daimler?" *Business Week,* September 25, 2000, p. 62.

9. Maria Maher and Thomas Anderson, *Corporate Governance: Effects on Firm Performance and Economic Growth* (Paris: Organisation for Economic Co-operation and Development, 1999).

10. A. Demb and F. F. Neubauer, *The Corporate Board: Confronting the Paradoxes* (Oxford: Oxford University Press, 1992).

11. Maher and Anderson, *Corporate Governance.*

12. Organisation for Economic Co-operation and Development, *The OECD Principles of Corporate Governance* (Paris: Organisation for Economic Co-operation and Development, 1999).

13. Edward A. Stolzenberg, "Governance Change for Public Hospitals," *Journal of Healthcare Management,* 45 (September/October 2000): 347-350.

14. The World Bank Group, *Corporate Governance: As Issue of Global Concern* (Washington, DC: The World Bank, 1999), available at www.worldbank.org/html/fpd/privatesector/cd/introduction.htm.

15. Clive Crook, "Why Good Corporate Citizens Are a Public Menace," *National Journal,* April 24, 1999, p. 1087.

16. Robert A. G. Monks, *Corporate Governance in the Twenty-First Century: A Preliminary Outline* (Portland, Maine: LENS, Inc, 1996), available at www.lens-library.com/info/cg21.html.

17. McRitchie, "Ending the Wall Street Walk."

18. Ronald E. Berenbeim, *The Corporate Board: A Growing Role in Strategic Assessment* (New York: The Conference Board, 1996).

19. "Measuring Corporate Governance Standards," *Asiamoney,* 11 (December 2000/January 2001): 94-95.

20. Barbara Crutchfield George, Kathleen A. Lacey, and Jotta Birmele, "The 1998 OECD Convention," *American Business Law Journal,* 37 (Spring 2000): 485-525; Ira Millstein, "Corporate Governance: The Role of Market Forces," *The OECD Observer* (Summer 2000): 27-28; "What Is OECD," Organisation for Economic Co-operation and Development, www.oecd.org/about/general/index.htm, accessed December 1, 2000.

21. "Asian Capitalism: The End of Tycoons," *The Economist,* April 29, 2000, pp. 67-69; "The Importance of Corporate Governance," *Asiamoney,* 10 (December 1999/January2000): 92-94.

22. Melvin A. Eisenberg, "Corporate Governance: The Board of Directors and Internal Control," *Cordoza Law Review,* 19 (September/November 1997): 237.

23. John A. Byrne, "The Best & Worst Boards," *Business Week,* January 24, 2000, pp. 142-152; Robert W. Lear and Boris Yavitz, "America's Best and Worst Boards," *Chief Executive* 171 (October 2001): 54-59.

24. Jennifer Reingold, "Dot.Com Boards Are Flouting the Rules," *Business Week,* December 20, 1999, pp. 130-134.

25. Adrian Cadbury,"What Are the Trends in Corporate Governance? How Will They Impact Your Company?" *Long Range Planning,* 32 (January 1999): 12–19.

26. John Byrne Barry,"Taking It to DuPont," *The Planet,* 5 (July/August 1998), www.sierraclub.org/plant/199806/dupont.html.

27. "Understanding the Shareholder Resolution and Proxy Voting Process," Calvert Group, www.calvertgroup.com/investor/ind-sri-resolutions.html, accessed December 1, 2000.

28. Peter D. Kinder, Steven D. Lyndenberg, and Amy L. Domini, *The Social Investment Almanac* (New York: Henry Holt and Co., 1992).

29. "Companies Fail Social Investors, Most Investors Value Corporate Responsibility, Few Are Satisfied," *Investor Relations Business,* August 6, 2001, pp. 1, 13.

30. R. Bruce Hutton, Louis D'Antonio, and Tommi Johnsen,"Socially Responsible Investing: Growing Issues and New Opportunities," *Business and Society,* 37 (September 1998): 281–305.

31. Barry B. Burr,"Social Investing Tops $2 Trillion," *Pensions & Investments,* November 15, 1999, p. 8.

32. Christine Williamson,"Social Investing Funds Beat Benchmarks," *Pensions & Investments,* March 9, 1999, p. 8.

33. Robert A. G. Monks,"What Will Be the Impact of Active Shareholders? A Practical Recipe for Constructive Change," *Long Range Planning,* 32 (January 1999): 20–27.

34. "An Institutional Investor Models Democratic Governance," *Business Ethics,* 13 (September/October and November/December 1999): 29.

35. "Worth Noting: At Random," *Business Ethics,* 13 (September/October and November/December 1999): 5.

36. "Proposal for Socially Responsible Investments by Colleges and Universities," Student Alliance to Reform Corporations, www.corpreform.org/SRI.html, accessed October 29, 2001. Reprinted with permission from the STARC Alliance.

37. Eisenberg,"Corporate Governance."

38. Kathy Hoke,"Eyes Wide Open," *Business First—Columbus,* August 27, 1999, pp. 27–28.

39. Ray A. Goldberg,"Kraft General Foods: Risk Management Philosophy," (Boston, MA: Harvard Business School Press, 1994).

40. Jim Billington,"A Few Things Every Manager Ought to Know about Risk," *Harvard Management Update,* March 1997, pp. 10–11; Lee Puschaver and Robert G. Eccles,"In Pursuit of the Upside: The New Opportunity in Risk Management," *PW Review,* December 1996.

41. Scott Alexander,"Achieving Enterprisewide Privacy Compliance," *Insurance & Technology,* 25 (November 2000): 53; M. Joseph Sirgy and Chenting Su,"The Ethics of Consumer Sovereignty in an Age of High Tech," *Journal of Business Ethics,* 28 (November 2000): 1–14.

42. "How Business Rates: By the Numbers," in Aaron Bernstein,"Too Much Corporate Power?" *Business Week,* September 11, 2000, pp. 148–149.

43. Sarah Anderson, John Cavanagh, Ralph Estes, Chuck Collins, and Chris Hartman, *A Decade of Executive Excess: The 1990s Sixth Annual Executive Compensation Survey* (Boston, MA: United for a Fair Economy, 1999).

44. Louis Lavelle,"CEO Pay, The More Things Change …," *Business Week,* October 16, 2000, pp. 106–108.

45. Jeremy Kahn,"A CEO Cuts His Own Pay," *Fortune,* October 26, 1998, pp. 56–58.

46. Crystal Graef,"If Kodak Employees Have to Bite the Bullet, Why Not the CEO?" *South Florida Business Journal,* December 12, 1997, p. 23.

47. Stephen M. Davis,"Global Governance: How Nations Compare," *Corporate Board,* 20 (September/October 1999): 5–9.

48. "Cost of Workplace Regulation," *USA Today,* October 24, 2001, p. 1B.

49. Adam M. Brandenburger and Barry J. Nalebuff, *Co-opetition: 1. A Revolutionary Mindset That Redefines Competition and Cooperation; 2. The Game Theory Strategy That's Changing the Game of Business* (New York: Doubleday, 1997).

50. Maher and Andersson, *Corporate Governance.*

51. Monks, *Corporate Governance in the Twenty-First Century.*

52. "Three Skills for Today's Leaders," *Harvard Management Update,* 4 (November 1999): 11.

53. Monks, *Corporate Governance in the Twenty-First Century.*

Consumer and Community Relations

◗ Consumer Stakeholders

◗ Responsibilities to Consumers

◗ Community Stakeholders

◗ Responsibilities to the Community

◗ Strategic Implementation of Responsibilities to Consumers and the Community

To describe customers as stakeholders

To investigate consumer protection laws

To examine six consumer rights

To describe the community as a stakeholder

To discuss the community relations function

To describe a neighbor of choice

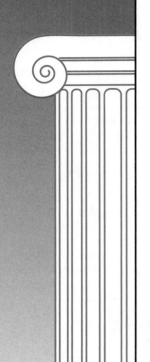

Wal-Mart, one of the world's largest retailers, has its share of both supporters and critics. Satisfied customers appreciate the width of the chain's merchandise mix, commitment to low prices, and the friendly "hello" from greeters at the front of each store. To honor employees and connect with everyday people, Wal-Mart features employees and their children in its advertising. Other supporters respect the retailer's commitment to the community, environment, and American-made products. For example, the company awards nearly $11 million annually to outstanding high school seniors and teachers. Award recipients are chosen by employees in each community where Wal-Mart operates.

The $167 billion-a-year retail chain boasts a unique corporate culture based on an intense competitive drive and a strong focus on frugality. Whereas other companies take managers to resorts for annual training and conventions, Wal-Mart opts for meetings in hot locales like Dallas in the summer and chilly ones like Kansas City in the winter. The company's headquarters are notoriously spartan, which reduces spending and reminds vendors that they are expected to offer the best possible prices. Although some manufacturers lament Wal-Mart's power within the supply chain, they also relish the tremendous exposure that comes from a relationship with the retailer. Wal-Mart has made substantial investments in technology, including e-commerce and programs for collaborating with suppliers in the forecasting and merchandising process.

At the other end of the spectrum, however, some people believe Wal-Mart's presence has contributed to the demise of locally owned pharmacies and variety stores in many small towns. The chain's buying power ensures lower prices and wider product variety for consumers but also makes it difficult for smaller retailers to compete. Other consumers and community leaders worry about traffic congestion and urban sprawl that accompany new retail sites. For example, the city council of Alpharetta, Georgia, rejected a zoning change that would have allowed the development of a new Wal-Mart superstore after traffic experts estimated that an additional 14,000 cars would travel the road to the proposed store. Although the developer had agreed to land and road improvements, most council members and many Alpharetta citizens were opposed to the sprawling superstore. Several cities and counties have instituted statutes to limit the allowable square footage of such superstores unless local voters approve otherwise.

Some Wal-Mart critics have taken their discontent with the retailer to the Internet and to the courts. One disgruntled customer developed a web site as a forum for sharing complaints about the retail chain. The site, http://www.walmartsucks.com, includes sections for rating local stores, updates on legal action against Wal-Mart, and customer and employee complaints. Another web site, http://www.walmartsurvivor.com, details court rulings against Wal-Mart and lists attorneys who have been successful in opposing the retail giant. Moreover, judges have sanctioned the retailer more than 100 times for abuses in the litigation process, including failing to produce relevant documents and delays in the process. Wal-Mart has responded that because it has approximately 10,000 cases pending at a time, the sanctions represent less than 1 percent of its entire caseload. Nonetheless, in one case, the firm's legal counsel apologized to a judge for delays and pledged that the retailer would engage "in a searching reevaluation of the litigation processes which have led the parties to this courtroom on this day."[1]

This vignette illustrates that even well-known organizations with strong profitability, operations expertise, and other core competencies may experience problems satisfying some stakeholder groups. From a corporate citizenship perspective, the key challenge is how an organization responds, reconciles differences, strives for better relationships, achieves mutual understanding, and finds solutions for problems. In this chapter, therefore, we explore relationships with two important stakeholders—consumers and the community. Although these constituencies are different by definition, they often have similar expectations of the economic, legal, ethical, and philanthropic responsibilities that must be addressed by business.

Consumer Stakeholders

Throughout the 1980s and much of the 1990s, "green marketing," the promotion of more environmentally friendly products, became a much-discussed strategy in the package goods industry. Both Energizer and Rayovac, for example, marketed environmentally friendly batteries. Today, those products have disappeared from most store shelves, replaced by the alkaline batteries needed to run electronic devices that have become so common for both children and adults. Around the same time, Procter & Gamble (P&G), the venerable manufacturer of soap, paper goods, and other household products, feared that increasing environmental consciousness among consumers would lead to a resurgence in the use of cloth diapers, which would have a negative effect on its disposable diaper business. P&G launched a marketing campaign touting the benefits of disposables, including the fact that their use does not require hot water for laundering or fuel for diaper service trucks. P&G also initiated a pilot project for composting disposable diapers. Today, the debate over cloth versus disposables has largely faded, and the P&G marketing campaign and composting sites have disappeared.

The dawn of the twenty-first century brought many new products, including disposable tableware, food containers that can be used repeatedly or thrown away, and electrostatic mops with cloths that are disposed of after one use. Although these product introductions suggest a decline in environmental consciousness among consumers, other initiatives counter this assumption. Whole Foods Markets, a grocery chain that specializes in organic and environmentally friendly items, has seen its sales grow fivefold in ten years.[2] Indeed, environmental initiatives have become a global phenomenon. One goal of the annual "Buy Nothing Day," sponsored by consumer associations in fifteen countries, is to encourage consumers to consider the environmental consequences of their buying habits. The event's organizers remind consumers that the richest 20 percent of people consume 80 percent of the world's resources.[3]

Although the future of green marketing can be debated, the real test of its effectiveness lies in the expectations, attitudes, and buying patterns of consumers. The preceding examples illustrate that there is no true consensus around issues such as environmental responsibility, and companies therefore face complex decisions about how to respond to them. This is true for all types of social responsibilities, including the ones we explore in this chapter. In this section, we examine the economic, legal, ethical, and philanthropic responsibilities that businesses have to **consumers,** those individuals who purchase, use, and dispose of products for personal and household use.

Responsibilities to Consumers

Consumers International, a London-based nonprofit federation of more than 260 consumer organizations in 120 countries, is dedicated to protecting and promoting consumers' interests and implementing campaigns and research programs to aid governments, businesses, and nonprofit groups in decision making.[4] For example, the federation sponsors an annual World Consumer Rights Day to further solidarity among the global consumer movement by promoting consumer rights, demanding the protection of these rights, and protesting abuses and injustices. Each observance has a particular theme—a pressing issue that is likely to affect a majority of consumers around the world. Recent issues include genetically modified foods, the natural environment, and food safety.[5] The association's efforts led to the development of the Consumer Charter for Global Business, which offers guidance on a variety of business practices, including product standards, advertising, guarantees, consumer complaint procedures, and competitive tactics. At a minimum, the charter asks companies to consider their economic relationship with consumers through all stages of the production, distribution, and marketing process; to obey all relevant laws; and to establish clear ethical standards for business practice.[6] The charter therefore covers three of the four responsibilities we have used to define corporate citizenship throughout this book.

▶ *Economic Issues*

As we saw in Chapter 3, consumers are primary stakeholders because their awareness, purchase, use, and repurchase of products are vital to a company's existence. Fundamentally, therefore, consumers and businesses are connected by an economic relationship. This relationship begins with an exchange, usually of a good or service for money, which often leads to deeper attachments or affiliation. An advertising campaign slogan, "You are what you drive," typifies the close relationship that some consumers develop with the products they purchase. Other consumers may choose to shun particular brands or opt for the environmentally sensitive products described earlier. In all of these cases, however, consumers expect the products they purchase to perform as guaranteed by their sellers. Thus, a firm's economic responsibilities include following through on promises made in the exchange process. Although this responsibility seems basic today, business practices have not always been directed in this way. In the early part of the 1900s, the caveat "Let the buyer beware" typified the power that business—not consumers—wielded in most exchange relationships.[7]

Fulfillment of economic responsibilities depends on interactions with the consumer. However, there are situations where the consumer does not act as a fair participant in the exchange.[8] **Consumer fraud** involves intentional deception to derive an unfair economic advantage over an organization. Examples of fraudulent activities include shoplifting, collusion or duplicity, and guile. Collusion typically involves an employee who assists the consumer in fraud. For example, a cashier may not ring up all merchandise or give an unwarranted discount. Duplicity may involve a consumer staging an accident in a grocery store and then seeking damages against the store for its lack of attention to safety. A consumer may purchase, wear, and then return an item of clothing for a full refund. In other situations, the consumer may ask for a refund by claiming a defect that either is nonexistent or was caused by consumer misuse.[9] Although some of these acts warrant legal prosecution, they can be very difficult to prove, and many companies are reluctant to accuse patrons of a crime when there is no way of verifying it. Businesses that operate with the "customer is always right" philosophy have found that some consumers will take advantage of this promise and have therefore modified return policies to curb unfair use. Because of the vague nature of some types of consumer fraud, its full financial toll has been difficult to tally. However, rough estimates indicate that shoplifting alone costs U.S. businesses more than $30 billion per year.[10] Shoplifting represents about one-third of all inventory shrinkage experienced by retail companies. Retailers of toys, convenience items, alcohol, and hobby-related products experience higher than average shrinkage rates.[11]

Most consumers, of course, do not engage in such activities. However, there are cases where buyers and sellers disagree on whether or how well companies have satisfied their economic responsibilities. Thus, a consumer may believe that a product is not worth the price paid for one reason or another, perhaps because he or she believes the product's benefits have been exaggerated by the seller. For example, although some marketers claim that their creams, pills, special massages, and other techniques can reduce or even eliminate cellulite, most medical experts and dermatologists believe that only exercise and weight loss can reduce the appearance of this undesirable condition. Most of the products for reducing cellulite remain on the market, but many consumers have returned these products and complained about the lack of results.[12] If consumers believe that a firm has not fulfilled its basic economic responsibilities, they may ask for a refund, tell others about their bad experience, discontinue their patronage, contact a consumer agency, and even seek legal redress. The Internet has created new opportunities for consumers to express dissatisfaction with companies, including the Wal-Mart "hate" web sites discussed earlier. To protect consumers and provide businesses with guidance, a number of laws and regulations have been enacted to ensure that economic responsibility is met in accordance with institutionalized standards.

▶ Legal Issues

As we discussed in Chapter 4, legal issues with respect to consumers in the United States primarily fall under the domain of the Federal Trade Commission (FTC), which enforces federal antitrust and consumer protection laws. Within this agency, the Bureau of Consumer Protection works to protect consumers against unfair, deceptive, and fraudulent practices.[13] For example, consumer complaints about problems receiving merchandise ordered online prompted the FTC to launch "Project TooLate.com" to investigate whether Internet retailers had violated the Mail and Telephone Order Rule during the 1999 holiday season. Seven online retailers eventually settled with the FTC over charges that they did not provide consumers with adequate notice of shipping delays or promised specific delivery dates that they knew were impossible to meet. The companies, which included CDnow, Macy's, The Original Honey Baked Ham Company, and Toys 'R' Us, agreed to modify their procedures and paid civil fines totaling $1.5 million.[14] In this case, the companies' inability to honor the economic exchange agreement resulted in legal action on behalf of consumers. The lessons learned in the 1999 holiday shopping season prompted online retailers to intensify their focus on customer service and associated expectations, and many chose to modify procedures and resources accordingly.[15]

In addition to the FTC, several other federal agencies regulate specific goods, services, or business practices to protect consumers. The Food and Drug Administration, for example, enforces laws and regulations enacted to prevent distribution of adulterated or misbranded foods, drugs, medical devices, cosmetics, veterinary products, and potentially hazardous consumer products. The Consumer Product Safety Commission enforces laws and regulations designed to protect the public from unreasonable risk of injury from consumer products. Many states also have regulatory agencies that enforce laws and regulations regarding business practices within their states. Most federal agencies and states also have consumer affairs or information offices to help consumers. For example, the Federal Communications Commission's Consumer Information Bureau educates consumers on issues related to cable service, telecommunications, and other areas under the FCC's domain.[16] In Iowa, the Attorney General's Consumer Protection Division publishes brochures to assist consumers in complaining effectively, buying a new or used car, recognizing scams, and avoiding identity theft.[17]

In this section, we focus on U.S. laws related to exchanges and relationships with consumers. Table 7.1 summarizes some of the laws that are likely to affect a wide range of companies and consumers. State and local laws can be more stringent than federal statutes, so it is important that businesses fully investigate the laws applicable to all markets in which they operate. In Texas, for example, the Deceptive Trade Practices Act prohibits a business from selling anything to a consumer that he or she does not need or cannot afford.[18]

Health and Safety   One of the first consumer protection laws in the United States came about in response to public outrage over a novel. In *The Jungle*, Upton Sinclair

Lawyer Richard Scruggs from Mississippi led the charge in a $240 billion settlement of health-related claims with the tobacco industry.

TABLE 7.1

Major Consumer Laws

Act (Date Enacted)	Purpose
Pure Food and Drugs Act (1906)	Established the Food and Drug Administration; outlaws the adulteration or mislabeling of food and drug products sold in interstate commerce
Cigarette Labeling and Advertising Act (1965)	Requires manufacturers to add to package labels warnings about the possible health hazards associated with smoking cigarettes
Fair Packaging and Labeling Act (1966)	Outlaws unfair or deceptive packaging or labeling of consumer products
Truth in Lending Act (1968)	Requires creditors to disclose in writing all finance charges and related aspects of credit transactions
Child Protection and Toy Safety Act (1969)	Requires childproof devices and special labeling
Fair Credit Reporting Act (1970)	Promotes accuracy, fairness, and privacy of credit information; gives consumers the right to see their personal credit reports and to dispute any inaccurate information therein
Consumer Product Safety Act (1972)	Established the Consumer Product Safety Commission to regulate potentially hazardous consumer products
Odometer Act (1972)	Provides protections for consumers against odometer fraud in used-car sales
Equal Credit Opportunity Act (1974)	Outlaws denial of credit on the basis of race, color, religion, national origin, sex, marital status, age, or receipt of public assistance, and requires creditors to provide applicants, on request, with the reasons for credit denial
Magnuson-Moss Warranty (FTC) Act (1975)	Establishes rules for consumer product warranties, including minimum content and disclosure standards; allows the FTC to prescribe interpretive rules in policy statements regarding unfair or deceptive practices
Consumer Goods Pricing Act (1975)	Prohibits the use of price maintenance agreements among manufacturers and resellers in interstate commerce
Fair Debt Collection Practices Act (1977)	Prohibits third-party debt collectors from engaging in deceptive or abusive conduct when collecting consumer debts incurred for personal, family, or household purposes

(continued)

TABLE 7.1 *(continued)*

Major Consumer Laws

Act (Date Enacted)	Purpose
Toy Safety Act (1984)	Authorizes the Consumer Product Safety Commission to recall products intended for use by children when they present substantial risk of injury
Nutrition Labeling and Education Act (1990)	Prohibits exaggerated health claims and requires all processed foods to contain standardized labels with nutritional information
Telephone Consumer Protection Act (1991)	Establishes procedures to avoid unwanted telephone solicitations; prohibits marketers from using automated telephone dialing systems or an artificial or prerecorded voice to certain telephone lines
Home Ownership and Equity Protection Act (1994)	Requires home equity lenders to disclose to borrowers in writing the payment amounts, the consequences of default, and the borrowers' right to cancel the loan within a certain time period
Telemarketing and Consumer Fraud and Abuse Prevention Act (1994)	Authorized the FTC to establish regulations for telemarketing, including prohibiting deceptive, coercive, or privacy-invading telemarketing practices; restricting the time during which unsolicited telephone calls may be made to consumers; and requiring telemarketers to disclose the nature of the call at the beginning of an unsolicited sales call

Sources: "Statutes Relating to Consumer Protection Mission," Federal Trade Commission, www.ftc.gov/ogc/stat3.htm, accessed October 31, 2001; O. C. Ferrell, John Fraedrich, and Linda Ferrell, *Business Ethics: Ethical Decision Making and Cases* (Boston: Houghton Mifflin, 2000), p. 75; Roger L. Miller and Gaylord A. Jentz, *Business Law Today* (Cincinnati: West Legal Studies in Business, 2000).

exposed atrocities, including unsanitary conditions and inhuman labor practices, by the meatpacking industry in turn-of-the-century Chicago. Appalled by the unwholesome practices described in the book, the public demanded reform. Congress responded by passing the Pure Food and Drug Act in 1906, just six months after *The Jungle* was widely published.[19] In addition to prohibiting the adulteration and mislabeling of food and drug products, the new law also established one of the nation's first federal regulatory agencies, the Food and Drug Administration.

Since the passage of the Pure Food and Drug Act, public health and safety have been major targets of federal and state regulation. For example, the Consumer Product Safety Act established the Consumer Product Safety Commission (CPSC), whereas the Flammable Fabrics Act set standards for the flammability of clothing, children's sleepwear, carpets and rugs, and mattresses. Recently, the

Standard Mattress Co. paid $60,000 to settle charges that it violated the Flammable Fabrics Act by making and selling futons that failed to meet flammability standards. Despite its agreement with the CPSC, the company denies that it violated any consumer product safety laws.[20] Other laws attempt to protect children from harm, including the Child Protection and Toy Safety Act and the Children's Online Privacy Protection Act.

Credit and Ownership   Abuses and inequities associated with loans and credit have resulted in the passage of laws designed to protect consumers' rights and public interests. The most significant of these laws prohibit discrimination in the extension of credit, require creditors to disclose all finance charges and related aspects of credit transactions, give consumers the right to dispute and correct inaccurate information on their credit reports, and regulate the activities of debt collectors. For example, the Home Ownership and Equity Protection Act requires home equity lenders to disclose, in writing, the borrower's rights, payment amounts, and the consequences of defaulting on the loan. Together, the U.S. Department of Justice and the Department of Housing and Urban Development enforce laws that ensure equal access to sale and rental housing. Every April, the government sponsors "Fair Housing Month" to educate property owners, agents, and consumers on rights with respect to housing.[21]

Marketing, Advertising, and Packaging   Legal issues in marketing often relate to sales and advertising communications and information about product content and safety. Abuses in promotion can range from exaggerated claims, concealed facts, and deception to outright lying. Such misleading information creates ethical issues because the communicated messages do not include all the information consumers need to make sound purchasing decisions. For example, Publishers Clearing House recently settled charges brought by 23 states and the District of Columbia that it used deceptive sweepstakes promotions in order to get consumers to buy magazines. The settlement required the company to pay $18 million to the states to give refunds to customers, especially the elderly, who bought magazines under the belief that such purchases would boost their chances of winning the oft-touted million-dollar sweepstakes. Although Publishers Clearing House did not admit to any wrongdoing, it agreed to stop using the phrase, "You are a winner," unless adequately balanced with statements specifying the conditions necessary to win, and to clearly indicate the odds of winning in sweepstakes promotions. In the same year, United States Sales Corporation and Time Inc. agreed to similar settlements over allegations of deceptive sweepstakes promotions with 48 states and the District of Columbia.[22]

Although a certain amount of exaggeration and hyperbole is tolerated, deceptive claims or claims that cannot be substantiated are likely to invite legal action from the FTC. For example, the FTC asked SmartScience Laboratories Inc. to stop making claims that its JointFlex skin cream eliminates significant joint pain because the claims are unsubstantiated. The company agreed not to make any further claims about the product's efficacy without reliable scientific evidence to substantiate such claims.[23]

Since the Federal Trade Commission Act of 1914 outlawed all deceptive and unfair trade practices, additional legislation has further delineated what activities are permissible and which are illegal. For example, the Telemarketing and Consumer Fraud and Abuse Prevention Act requires telemarketers to disclose the nature of the call at the beginning of an unsolicited sales call and restricts the times during which such calls may be made to consumers.

Another legal issue in marketing has to do with the promotion of products that involve health or safety issues. Numerous laws regulate the promotion of alcohol and tobacco products, including the Public Health Cigarette Smoking Act (1970) and the Cigarette Labeling and Advertising Act (1965). The Eighteenth Amendment to the U.S. Constitution prohibited the manufacture and sale of alcoholic beverages in 1919; the prohibition was repealed in 1933 by the Twenty-first Amendment. However, this amendment gave to the states the power to regulate the transportation of alcoholic beverages across state lines. Today, each state has unique regulations, some of which require the use of wholesalers and retailers to limit direct sales of alcoholic beverages to final consumers in other states. In this case, a law aimed at protecting consumers by promoting temperance in alcohol consumption now affects wine sellers' ability to implement e-commerce and subsequent interstate sales.[24]

Sales and Warranties   Another area of law that affects business relationships with consumers has to do with warranties. Many consumers consider the warranty behind a product when making a purchase decision, especially for expensive durable goods such as automobiles and appliances. One of the most significant laws affecting warranties is the Magnuson-Moss Warranty (FTC) Act, which established rules for consumer product warranties, including minimum content and standards for disclosure. All fifty states have enacted "lemon laws" to ensure that automobile sales are accompanied by appropriate warranties and remedies for defects that impair the safety, use, or value of the vehicle.[25]

Product Liability   One area of law that has a profound effect on business and its relations with consumers is **product liability,** which refers to a business's legal responsibility for the performance of its products. This responsibility, which has evolved through both legislation and court interpretations (common law), may include a legal obligation to provide financial compensation to a consumer who has been harmed by a defective product. To receive compensation, a consumer who files suit must prove that the product was defective, that the defect caused an injury, and that the defect made the product unreasonably dangerous. For example, in a landmark class-action lawsuit, a Florida jury awarded nearly $13 million in compensatory damages to three Florida smokers and $145 billion in punitive damages to all Florida smokers who have developed health problems because of smoking. The jury determined that five leading tobacco companies—Philip Morris, R. J. Reynolds, Brown & Williamson, Lorillard, and the Liggett Group—had sold a dangerous product that caused illness and death, and that the industry had concealed information, made false or misleading statements, and conspired to misrepresent information about the effects of smoking. The tobacco industry has appealed the verdict, the largest ever punitive damage awarded in a product liability lawsuit in the United States, saying that it will bankrupt the five firms.[26] Under the concept of *strict liability,* an injured consumer can apply this legal responsibility to any firm in the supply chain of a defective product, including contractors, suppliers of component parts, wholesalers, and retailers.

Because the law holds businesses liable for their products' performance, many companies choose to recall potentially harmful products, although such recalls may be required by legal or regulatory authorities as well. Warner-Lambert, for example, was asked by the Food and Drug Administration to recall Rezulin, a diabetes drug, after thirty-five cases of liver damage occurred in patients using the drug during its first year on the market.[27]

Product liability lawsuits have increased dramatically in recent years, and many suits have resulted in huge damage awards to injured consumers or their families. In a much-publicized case, a jury awarded a McDonald's customer $2.9 million after she was scalded when she spilled hot McDonald's coffee in her lap. Although that award was eventually reduced on appeal, McDonald's and other fast-food restaurants now display warning signs that their coffee is hot in order to eliminate both further injury and liability. Because of multimillion-dollar judgments like that against McDonald's, companies sometimes pass on the costs of damage awards to their customers in the form of higher prices. Most companies have taken steps to minimize their liability, and some firms—such as pharmaceutical firms making serum for the

Ford Motor Company president and CEO Jacques Nasser announced a recall of 13 million Firestone Wilderness AT tires to reduce product liability claims.

Are Tobacco Companies More Responsible?

In 1998 the five largest tobacco manufacturers in the United States reached a landmark $246 billion settlement with the attorneys general of forty-six states. The master settlement agreement (MSA) required the companies to give billions of dollars to the state governments every year to help relieve the burden that smoking-related illnesses put on state health-care systems and to fund campaigns designed to discourage smoking, especially among children. Under the settlement, the companies agreed to stop using cartoon characters, like R. J. Reynolds' Joe Camel. The MSA also bars companies from a number of traditional promotion strategies, such as using billboards or direct-mail advertising or passing out samples at shopping malls to tout their products. To help pay for the costs of the settlement, the companies were forced to raise prices by 44 percent over the next two years. Thus, the settlement was designed to force the tobacco firms to bear more of the costs of illnesses caused by their product and to make them act more responsibly.

To comply with the agreement, the cigarette marketers were forced to make radical changes to their marketing strategies. As agreed, all firms contributed to the funding of the Washington-based antismoking group, American Legacy Foundation. The companies also shifted some of their promotion budgets to image campaigns. Philip Morris, for example, ran commercials explaining the provisions of the MSA, whereas R. J. Reynolds Tobacco launched the "Right Decisions, Right Now" program, which creates and distributes antismoking educational materials to teachers. Brown & Williamson and other companies contributed funds to support the "We Card" program for retailers. Although some critics questioned the companies' enthusiasm for such programs, Nick Brookes, chairman and CEO of Brown & Williamson, summed up their position: "The viability of every industry, whether it sells soap or software, depends ultimately on its ability to win and sustain public support, given if not wholeheartedly, at least grudgingly."

The tobacco companies didn't stop advertising cigarettes, but they restricted their advertising to comply with the agreement. However, even limiting advertisements to magazines and newspapers has proven problematic. After a Massachusetts Public Health study reported finding cigarette ads in magazines with large numbers

DPT (diphtheria-pertussis-tetanus) vaccine and manufacturers of small planes—have stopped making products or withdrawn completely from problematic markets because of the high risk of expensive liability lawsuits.[28] Although some states have limited damage awards and federal reforms are likely within the next few years, the issue of product liability reform remains politically controversial.[29]

International Issues   Concerns about protecting consumers' legal rights are not limited to the United States. Most developed nations have laws and offices devoted to this goal. In the European Union (EU), the Health and Consumer Protection Directorate General oversees efforts to increase consumer confidence in the uniof young readers, Philip Morris announced that it would suspend advertising in publications with 15 percent or higher youth readership.

The tobacco companies are now concentrating their marketing efforts on those areas where adult smokers are readily found. Representatives of Brown & Williamson, for example, seek out smokers on the streets (because smoking is prohibited inside most buildings), offering them coffee and free samples to enjoy on their smoke breaks. Tobacco company representatives are also passing out free samples to patrons of bars, but only after observing them smoking and checking their IDs. Philip Morris has also focused on bars with "Party at the Ranch" and "Racing School" sweepstakes to promote its Marlboro brand. Point-of-sale promotions in convenience stores have become crucial because these retailers represent the last large public spaces available to larger cigarette ads. However, Mike Pfeil, vice president of communications and public affairs at Philip Morris, insists that his company has not shifted billboard spending to retail point-of-sale, saying that Philip Morris' strategy is to "lower the profile of cigarette ads in stores because that's what the public expects of a tobacco company."

Some tobacco firms are investing in research in an attempt to make a "safer" cigarette. Star Scientific, for example, is test marketing a cigarette with a charcoal filter and tobacco cured to reduce nitrosamine, a carcinogen. Philip Morris began test-marketing the Accord, a low-smoke cigarette inserted in a battery-powered lighter, before the MSA. In 2000, R. J. Reynolds began marketing the Eclipse, which produces fewer toxins because it heats the tobacco instead of burning it.

The tobacco companies' efforts under the MSA have had a noticeable effect on teen smoking. A University of Michigan study found that the proportion of teen smokers has been gradually declining from its 1996 peak. However, the settlement does not seem to have affected total cigarette sales. R. J. Reynolds' 1999 net sales rose 32 percent over the prior year, and domestic revenues for Philip Morris's tobacco division were up 28 percent from the prior year. Although corporate executives point to declining teen smoking rates as evidence of their responsibility, many antismoking activists believe that the responsible thing to do is to stop selling a product that causes illness and death. ■

Sources:
Steve Jarvis, "They're Not Quitting," *Marketing News,* November 20, 2000, pp. 1, 9; Marianne Lavelle, "Big Tobacco Rises from the Ashes," *U.S. News & World Report,* November 13, 2000, p. 50; Nancy Shute, "Building a Better Butt," *U.S. News & World Report,* September 18, 2000, pp. 66+.

fied market. Its initiatives center on health, safety, economic, and public-health interests. One recently passed EU directive establishes minimum levels of consumer protection in member states. For example, EU consumers now have a legal guarantee of two years on all consumer goods. If they find a defective product, they may choose repair or replacement or, in special circumstances, ask for a price reduction or rescind the contract altogether.[30] Table 7.2 outlines legal expectations in the EU relative to consumer transactions and relationships.

In Japan, unlike the United States, product liability lawsuits are much less common. In the early 1990s, Chikara Minami filed one of the first such lawsuits against Japanese automaker Mitsubishi. Minami's suit alleged a defect in the Mitsubishi

TABLE 7.2

Legal Requirements and Marketing Strategy in the European Union

Legislative Category	Information for Businesses
Advertising	Directive 84/450/EEC defines misleading advertising to include any form of advertising that deceives or is likely to deceive and is also likely to affect economic behavior
	Directive on misleading advertising amended to include comparative advertising in 1997
	Comparative advertising is permitted if it is not misleading, compares products designed to meet the same need or purpose, does not create any confusion between the advertiser and competitor, and does not denigrate the competition
	Member States have the option of using legal action and/or other administrative bodies to resolve complaints
Product	Product sold in one Member State eligible for sale in other states
	Many directives on safety measures and other requirements in specific product categories
	Companies liable for any damage caused by products even if there is no proof of negligence or fault
	Metric-only labels probably not required until 2009
Distance selling	Directive 97/7/EC affects businesses' exclusive use of mail, telephone, and/or electronic means for consumer contracts
	Consumers have seven-day "cooling off" period
	Communication by fax and automated dialing/calling machine illegal without prior consent
Data collection and privacy	Directive 95/46/EC ensures individuals' right of access to personal data and right to rectify inaccurate data
	Data on health, sexual life, ethnic or racial origin, political persuasion, religious beliefs, and trade union membership can be collected only with explicit consent of the individual (except in rare cases)
	Data can be transferred to a non-EU country only if they will be adequately protected in that country
Electronic commerce	Covers all forms of consumer and business-to-business electronic communications, including free services, online newspapers, online databases, advertising, entertainment services, and online shopping malls
	Online contracts will be permitted
	Companies must provide easily accessible contract information on each web site
Economic and Monetary Union	Began January 1999, with full conversion January 2002
	Requires investment and commitment of retailers

(continued)

TABLE 7.2 *(continued)*

Legal Requirements and Marketing Strategy in the European Union

Legislative Category	Information for Businesses
Economic and Monetary Union	Reduces foreign-exchange risk
	Lowers cross-border transaction costs
	Eases access to formerly "foreign" customers
	Enhances access to financial capital
Competition policy	Policy is the result of Articles 37 and 85 to 94 of the Treaty on the European Union, with implementation through Regulation 17/62
	Covers antitrust and monopoly activity, merger regulation, and policy toward Member State aid to industry and organizations
	Companies should assess policy with respect to joint ventures, mergers and takeovers, public subsidies, distribution agreements, and other marketing strategy

Source: Debbie Thorne LeClair, "Marketing Planning and the Policy Environment in the European Union," *International Marketing Review,* 17 no. 3 (2000): 200. ©McB University Press, 2000. Reprinted with permission.

Pajero. Although the court sided with the automaker in that case, ten years later Mitsubishi was accused of deliberately covering up consumer complaints. Despite this revelation and an enhanced product liability law in 1995, consumer rights are often subverted in order to preserve the power and structure of big business in Japan.[31] China's consumer rights movement is also relatively new and resulted from economic policy changes away from isolationism and central planning. The China Consumers' Association was established in 1984 and has helped create consumer expectations and company responses that are starting to resemble those found in Western economies.[32]

As we have discussed in this section, there are many laws that influence business practices with respect to consumers all over the world. Every year, new laws are enacted and existing rules are modified in response to the changing business environment. For example, the EU recently implemented new standards for labeling beef products after the "mad cow disease" scare of tainted beef.[33] Although companies must monitor and obey all laws and regulations, they also have to keep abreast of the ethical obligations and standards that exist in the marketplace.

▶ *Ethical Issues*

In 1962, President John F. Kennedy proclaimed a Consumer Bill of Rights that includes the rights to choose, to safety, to be informed, and to be heard. Kennedy also established the Consumer Advisory Council to integrate consumer concerns into government regulations and processes. These four rights established a philosophical basis on which state and local consumer protection rules were later developed.[34] Around the same time, Ralph Nader's investigations of auto safety and his publication of *Unsafe at Any Speed* in 1965 alerted citizens to the dangers of a common consumer product. Nader's activism and Kennedy's speech provided support for **consumerism,** the movement to protect consumers from an imbalance of power with business and to maximize consumer welfare in the marketplace.[35] When Nader ran for the U.S. presidency in 2000, his platform included many of the same concerns about consumers and business that were being discussed thirty-five years earlier.[36] As we pointed out earlier, the consumer movement is a global phenomenon, including the World Consumer Rights Day celebrated every year.

Over the last four decades, consumerism has affected public policy through a variety of mechanisms. Early efforts were aimed primarily at advocating for legislation and regulation, whereas more recent efforts have shifted to education and protection programs directed at consumers.[37] The Consumers Union (CU), for example, works with regional and federal legislators and international groups to protect consumer interests, sponsors conferences and research projects, and tests consumer products, with the results published in the organization's *Consumer Reports* magazine. A recent issue of the magazine detailed business practices that CU deems unfair to consumers, including predatory lending, the poor value of some life insurance products, and advertisements aimed at vulnerable people, like children.[38] The Internet has also created new vehicles for consumer education and protection. Visitors to www.consumerworld.org find product reviews, retailer rankings, updates on legal matters, ways to track used car histories, travel discounts, and many other types of services. Thus, consumer groups and information services have shifted the balance of power between consumer and business because consumers are able to compare prices, read independent rankings, communicate with other buyers, and, in general, have greater knowledge about products, companies, and competitors.[39] Despite the opportunities to exert more power, some researchers question whether most consumers actually take the time and energy to do so. For example, although the Internet provides a great deal of information and choices, access to the Internet partly depends on education level and income. In addition, the volume of information available online may actually make it more difficult to analyze and assimilate.

All U.S. presidents since Kennedy have confirmed the four basic consumer rights and added new ones in response to changing business conditions. President William J. Clinton, for example, appointed a commission to study the changing health-care environment and its implications for consumer rights. The result was the proposal of a *Patient's Bill of Rights and Responsibilities* to ensure rights to confidentiality of patient information, to participate in health-care decisions, to access to emergency services, and other issues. By 2000, committees in the U.S. House and Senate were considering legislation on the Patient's Bill of Rights and Responsibilities.[40] During the same period, a Financial Consumer's Bill of Rights Act was proposed in the U.S. House of Representatives to curb high bank fees, automated teller machine surcharges, and other practices that have angered consumers.[41]

Although consumer rights were first formalized through a presidential speech and subsequent affirmations, they have not yet reached the legal domain of social responsibility. Some specific elements of these rights have been mandated through law, but the relatively broad nature of the rights means they must be interpreted and implemented on a company-by-company basis. Table 7.3 lists six consumer rights that have become part of the ethical expectations of business. Although these rights are not necessarily provided by all organizations, our corporate citizenship philosophy requires attention and implementation of them.

Right to Choose   The right to choose implies that, to the extent possible, consumers have the opportunity to select from a variety of products at competitive prices. This right is based on the philosophy of competitive nature of markets, which should lead to high-quality products at reasonable prices. Antitrust activities that reduce competition may jeopardize this right. This right has been called into question with respect to the safety of some parts of the U.S. Domino's Pizza, for example, was accused of discriminating against African-American customers through a delivery policy that seemed to be based on a neighborhood's racial composition rather than the legitimate threat of danger to drivers delivering in those neighborhoods. In effect, consumers in these neighborhoods were denied access

TABLE 7.3

Basic Consumer Rights

Right	General Issues
To choose	Access to a variety of products at competitive and reasonable prices
To safety	Protection of health, safety, and financial well-being in the marketplace
To be informed	Opportunity to have accurate and adequate information on which to base decisions and protection from misleading or deceptive information
To be heard	Consideration given to consumer interests in government processes
To redress	Opportunity to express dissatisfaction and to have the complaint resolved effectively
To privacy	Protection of consumer information and its use

Source: Adapted from: E. Thomas Garman, *Consumer Economic Issues in America* (Houston, Tex: Dame Publications, 1997).

to pizza delivery service. Although no lawsuit was filed, Domino's worked with the U.S. Justice Department to revise the delivery policy to narrowly define delivery limitations on the basis of real safety threats and to reevaluate the status of excluded areas on a yearly basis.[42]

Right to Safety   The right to safety means that businesses have an obligation not to knowingly market a product that could harm consumers. Some consumer advocates believe that this right means that the manufacture and sale of firearms should be outlawed in the United States. Although organizations like the National Rifle Association have vehemently opposed this view, questions about gun safety, especially around children, have prompted a number of state laws to regulate the manufacture and sale of guns. For example, Massachusetts recently required that all guns sold in that state meet stringent standards and carry internal identification numbers. Maryland requires that all guns be equipped with trigger locks.[43]

The right to choose also implies that all products should be safe for their intended use, include instructions for proper and safe use, and have been sufficiently tested to ensure reliability. Companies must take great care in designing warning messages about products with potentially dangerous or unsafe effects. These messages should take into account consumers' ability to understand and respond to the information. Warnings should be relevant and meaningful to every potential user of the product. Some warnings use symbols or pictures to communicate. For example, cleaning products often have the poison symbol on the label so children will not assume the liquid is a beverage.[44] Companies that fail to honor the right to safety risk expensive product liability lawsuits.

Right to Be Informed   Consumers also have the right to be informed. Any information, whether written or verbal, should be accurate, adequate, and free of deception so that consumers can make a sound decision. This general assertion has also led to specific legislation, such as the Nutrition Labeling and Education Act of 1990, which requires certain nutrition facts on food labels and limits the use of terms such as *low fat*. This right can be associated with safety issues if consumers do not have sufficient information to purchase or use a product effectively. For example, when a Dutch tourist and his wife rented a car from Alamo Rent-A-Car in Tampa, Florida, they were not explicitly told to avoid an area in Miami where tourists had recently been attacked. When they stopped to ask for directions in the high-crime area, the couple was robbed and the wife killed. Alamo failed to warn them of the danger and did not provide a safety brochure, which is common practice in most car rental companies. A jury ultimately awarded $5.2 million to the Dutch tourist in a wrongful death civil suit. Legal experts asserted that it may not be reasonable to expect companies to warn consumers of all possible dangers or to somehow prohibit them from going to such places.[45]

In an age of rapid technological advances and globalization, the degree of complexity in product marketing is another concern related to consumers' right to information. This complexity may relate to the ways in which product features and benefits are discussed in advertising, how effective salespeople are in answering consumer questions, the expertise needed to operate or use the product, and ease of returning or exchanging the product. To help consumers make decisions based on adequate and timely information, some organizations sponsor consumer education programs. For example, pharmaceutical companies and health maintenance organizations sponsor free seminars, health screenings, web sites, and other programs to educate consumers about their health and treatment options. This type of education is often required for consumers with less access to other sources, including the indigent, less educated, or elderly.[46] In Russia, consumer advocacy organizations have established a telephone hot line to educate consumers about their rights and to advise them when they encounter poor-quality products marketed as leading consumer brands. According to hot line director Yelena Poluektova, "Although there has been a law on consumer rights since 1992 it turns out very many people have no knowledge of their rights."[47]

Right to Be Heard   The right to be heard relates to opportunities for consumers to communicate or voice their concerns in the public policy process. This also implies that governments have the responsibility to listen and take consumer issues into account. One mechanism for fulfilling this responsibility is through the FTC and state consumer affairs offices. Another vehicle includes congressional hearings held to educate elected officials about specific issues of concern to consumers. At the same time, consumers are expected to be full participants in the process, meaning they must be informed and willing to take action against wrongs in the marketplace.

Right to Seek Redress   In addition to the rights described by Kennedy, consumers also have the right to express dissatisfaction and seek restitution from a business when a good or service does not meet their expectations. However, consumers need to be educated in the process for seeking redress and to recognize that the first course of action in such cases should be with the seller. At the same time, companies need to have explicit and formal processes for dealing with customer dissatisfaction. Although some product problems lead to third-party intervention or the legal system, the majority of issues should be resolvable between the consumer and business. One third party that consumers may consult in such cases is the Better Business Bureau (BBB), which promotes self-regulation of business. In order to gain and maintain membership, a firm must agree to abide by the ethical standards established by the BBB. This organization collects complaints on businesses and makes this information, along with other reports, available for consumer decision making. The BBB also operates the Dispute Resolution Division to assist in out-of-court settlements between consumers and businesses. For example, this division has a program, BBB Auto Line, to handle disputes between consumers and twenty-five automobile manufacturers.[48] This self-regulatory approach not only provides differentiation in the market, but can also stave off new laws and regulations.

Right to Privacy   The advent of new information technology and the Internet have prompted increasing concerns about consumer privacy. This right relates to consumers' awareness of how personal data are collected and used, and it places a burden on firms to protect this information. How information is used can create concerns for consumers. For example, Wells Fargo & Co. operates an online search mechanism for potential home buyers that is licensed from Homefair.com. The tool's "Community Calculator" uses zip codes from the consumer's current address to recommend neighborhoods for future consideration. The Association of Community Organizations for Reform Now opposes the search mechanism, saying it steers minorities to other minority neighborhoods, whereas consumers with zip codes from predominantly white neighborhoods are steered away from minority neighborhoods.[49] Although some e-commerce firms have joined together to develop privacy standards for the Internet, a report by the FTC indicates that only 20 percent of web sites currently meet its criteria for fair information practices, including notice, choice, access, and security.[50] We will take a closer look at the debate surrounding privacy rights in Chapter 10.

A firm's ability to address these consumer rights can serve as a competitive advantage. In the highly competitive market for air travel, for example, many airlines have developed a strong focus on customer service and satisfaction. Together with the Air Transport Association, several airlines launched the Airline Customer Service Commitment to demonstrate an industry focus on alleviating passenger frustrations and complaints. Delta Airlines established the Delta Customer Commitment, a twelve-point plan that details the airline's practices before, during, and after a customer flight (Figure 7.1).[51]

When consumers believe a firm is operating outside ethical or legal standards, they may be motivated to take some type of action. As we discussed earlier, there are a number of strategies consumers can employ to communicate their dissatisfaction, such as complaining or discontinuing the exchange relationship. Some consumers have accessed www.conscientiousconsuming.com, a web site that collects and disseminates articles from "citizen journalists," who advocate action on a particular consuming or purchasing situation. Among other things, the site has been used to inform people about the vast product holdings of tobacco firms beyond cigarettes, including watches, food, sporting goods, clothing, leather goods, and other nontobacco products.[52] Stakeholders may use the three types of power—symbolic, utilitarian, and coercive—that were discussed in Chapter 3 to create organizational awareness on an important issue. For example, some Chinese

FIGURE 7.1

Delta Customer Commitment (12-Point Plan)

Before You Fly

1. Delta will offer on our telephone reservations system the lowest fare for which the customer is eligible for the date, flight, and class of service requested.

2. Delta will give customers time to compare our fares with those of other airlines. We will hold reservations without payment until midnight one day after the reservation is made.

3. Delta will issue refunds for eligible tickets within seven business days for domestic credit card purchases and 20 business days for purchases made by cash or check.

4. Delta will inform customers, upon your request by telephone, if the flight on which they are ticketed is overbooked. We also will provide information at airports about our policies and procedures for handling situations when all ticketed customers cannot be accommodated on a flight.

5. Delta will provide customers timely and complete information about policies and procedures that affect your travel.

6. Delta will ensure that our domestic codeshare partners commit to providing comparable consumer plans and policies. Our partners are regional airlines that connect small- and medium-sized markets with Delta's network.

At the Airport

7. Delta will provide customers with information about our policies and procedures for accommodating disabled and special-needs customers, and unaccompanied minors.

8. Delta will provide full and timely information on the status of delayed and canceled flights.

9. Delta will provide full and timely information regarding the status of a flight if there is an extreme delay after customers have boarded or after the plane has landed, and we will provide for customers' essential needs while onboard.

After Landing

10. Delta will strive to return customers' misplaced baggage within 24 hours, and will attempt to contact owners of unclaimed baggage when a name or address or telephone number are available.

11. Delta supports a proposal of the U.S. Department of Transportation to increase the per-passenger domestic baggage liability limitation from $1,250 to $2,500.

12. Delta will respond to written customer complaints within 30 days.

Source: "12-Point Plan: Airline Customer Service Commitment," *Sky,* June 2000, p. 183 (also available at www.delta-air.com/care/service_plan/index.jsp). Courtesy of Delta Airlines.

McDonald's faced a boycott in Hong Kong because a Chinese manufacturer allegedly used child labor in its factory to make Happy Meal toys.

consumers feel that Japanese people believe they are racially superior to the Chinese. This sentiment stems from Japan's occupation of China in the 1940s. More recently, Toshiba has been accused of racism for not compensating Chinese users of potentially faulty Toshiba laptop computers. Although the Japanese firm offered a remedy for laptop owners in the United States, it did not do so in Japan or China. This perceived slight, along with feelings of nationalism, have prompted Chinese consumers to dismiss Toshiba and other Japanese manufacturers. Chinese retailers have pulled Japanese products off their shelves as well.[53] These consumers are engaging in another form of consumer action, a **boycott,** by abstaining from using, purchasing, or dealing with an organization. The World Jewish Congress encouraged its members to boycott the insurance company Transamerica after its parent company, Aegon NV, refused to join the International Commission on Holocaust Era Insurance Claims. The commission was established to resolve insurance claims that resulted from the Holocaust and World War II.[54]

▶ *Philanthropic Issues*

Although relationships with consumers are fundamentally grounded in economic exchanges, the previous sections demonstrate that additional levels of expectations exist. As we discussed in Chapter 2, a national survey by Cone/Roper reported that 70 percent of consumers would be likely to switch to brands associated with a good cause, as long as price and quality were equal. These results suggest that today's consumers take it for granted that they can obtain high-quality products at

Wal-Mart provides many philanthropic programs to support the community. (From www.walmartfoundation.org.)

reasonable prices, so businesses need to do something to differentiate themselves from the competition.[55] More firms are therefore investigating ways to link their philanthropic efforts with consumer interests. Eastman Kodak, for example, has funded environmental literacy programs of the World Wildlife Fund. These programs not only link between the company's possible effects and its interest in the natural environment, but also provide a service to its customers and other stakeholders.[56]

From a strategic perspective, a firm's ability to link consumer interests to philanthropy should lead to stronger economic relationships. As we shall see in Chapter 11, philanthropic responsibilities to consumers usually entail broader benefits, including those that affect the community. For example, large pharmaceutical and health insurance firms provide financial support to the Foundation for Accountability (FACCT), a nonprofit organization that assists health-care consumers in making better decisions. FACCT initiated an online system for patients to evaluate their physician on several quality indicators.[57]

Community Stakeholders

Whereas customers of all types, including consumers, are considered key constituents in the input-output and stakeholder models presented in Chapter 3, the community does not always receive the same level of acceptance as other stakeholders. One reason for this may be that *community* can be an amorphous concept, making it difficult to define and delineate.[58] Some people even wonder how a company determines who is in the community. Is a community determined by city or county boundaries? What if the firm operates in multiple locations? Or is a community prescribed by the interactions a firm has with various constituents who do not fit neatly into other stakeholder categories? The definition and scope of community seemed to expand in the aftermath of the September 11, 2001, terrorist attack on the World Trade Center and the Pentagon. People and organizations from around the world rallied to provide financial and emotional support to those affected by the tragedy. For a small restaurant in a large city, the owner may define the community as the immediate neighborhood where most of his or her patrons live. The restaurant may demonstrate corporate citizenship by hiring people from the neighborhood, participating in the neighborhood crime watch program, donating food to the elementary school's annual parent-teacher meetings, or sponsoring a neighborhood Little League team. For example, Merlino's Steak House in North Conway, New Hampshire, sponsors an annual golf tournament that benefits the Center for Hope, an organization that provides transportation for local individuals with disabilities.[59] For a corporation with facilities in North and South America, Europe, and Africa, the community may be viewed as virtually the entire world. To focus its corporate citizenship efforts, the multinational corporation might employ a community relations officer in each facility who reports to and coordinates with the company's head office.

Under our corporate citizenship philosophy, the term *community* should be viewed from a global perspective, beyond the immediate town, city, or state where a business is located. Thus, we define **community** as those members of society who are aware, concerned, or in some way affected by the operations and output of the organization. With information technology, high-speed travel, and the emergence of global business interests, the community as a constituency can be quite geographically, culturally, and attitudinally diverse. Issues that could become important include pollution of the environment, land use, economic advantages to the region, and discrimination within the community, as well as exploitation of workers or consumers.

From a positive perspective, an organization can significantly improve the quality of life through employment opportunities, economic development, and financial contributions for educational, health, the arts, and recreational activities. Through such efforts, a firm may become a **neighbor of choice,** an organization that builds and sustains trust with the community.[60] To become a neighbor of choice, a company should strive for positive and sustainable relationships with key individuals, groups, and organizations; demonstrate sensitivity to community concerns and issues; and design and implement programs that improve the quality of community life while promoting the company's long-term business strategies and goals.[61] For example, Julian Claudio Nabozny, who owns a McDonald's franchise in Phoenix, Arizona, has made his restaurant a surrogate "community center," which serves as a gathering place for neighborhood activities and celebrations, such as Thanksgiving dinners, mammogram screenings, and opportunities to raise money for local schools and to learn about immigration laws. For his efforts, Nabozny received the Cornerstone Humanitarian Award from the National Restaurant Association.[62]

Similar to other areas of life, the relationship between a business and the community should be symbiotic. A business may support educational opportunities in the community because the owners feel it is the right thing to do, but it also helps develop the human resources and consumer skills necessary to operate the business. Customers and employees are also community members who benefit from contributions supporting recreational activities, environmental initiatives, safety, and education. Many firms rely on universities and community colleges to provide support for ongoing education of their employees. Sykes Enterprises, for example, often locates its customer call and support centers in towns where the local community college is willing to develop courses that educate employees in the skills and aptitude needed to effectively operate a call center.

In order to build and support these initiatives, companies may invest in **community relations,** the organizational function dedicated to building and maintaining relationships and trust with the community. In the past, most businesses have not viewed community relations as strategically important or associated them with the firm's ultimate performance. Although the community relations department interacted with the community and often doled out large sums of money to charities, it essentially served as a "buffer" between the organization and its immediate community. Today, community relations activities have achieved greater prominence and responsibility within most companies, especially due to the rise of stakeholder power and global business interests. The function has gained strategic importance through linkage to overall business goals, professionalizing its staff and their knowledge of business and community issues, assessing its performance in quantitative and qualitative terms, and recognizing the breadth of stakeholders to which the organization is accountable.[63] For example, as director of community relations for Universal Studios Florida, Jan Stratton has been instrumental in the firm's community projects, including the Universal Studios Escape Foundation, which raises funds for four-year college scholarships, the Universal Studios Employee Volunteer Program, the Children's Advocacy Center at the Howard Phillips Center for Children and Families, and the company's internal United Way campaign.[64] Community relations also assist in short-term and crisis situations, such as the product liability situations discussed earlier in the chapter.[65]

In a survey of more than 250 top executives, the majority of whose firms employed less than 500 people, nearly 45 percent indicated that they manage formal community programs and allocate resources to these initiatives. According to the survey results, the top five social responsibilities that companies have include supporting environmental issues, demonstrating ethical behavior in business operations, earning profits, employing local residents, and paying taxes. The top five issues with the greatest impact on business include education, job training and development, health care, crime, and substance abuse.[66]

In a diverse society, however, there is no general agreement as to what constitutes the ideal model of responsibility to the community. Businesses that provide diverse products to serve market-driven economies are likely to experience conflicts among stakeholders as to what constitutes a real commitment to the community. Therefore, the community relations function should cooperate with various internal and external constituents to develop community mission statements and assess opportunities and develop priorities for the types of contributions it will make to the community. Table 7.4 provides several examples of company missions with respect

TABLE 7.4

Community Mission Statements

Organization	Community Mission
Portland Trail Blazers	Encourages employees to volunteer in health, education, and sports programs for youngsters living in communities near the Rose Garden Arena, the team's home.
Johnson Controls, Inc.	Focuses on community projects aligned with the company's mission of delivering quality indoor environments. For example, the company recently secured most of the funding to install heating, air conditioning, fire protection, security, and lighting controls in a new school in Milwaukee, Wisconsin, where the firm is headquartered.
Colgate-Palmolive Company	Sponsors an oral health education program that has reached 5 million children, and recruits volunteers to provide dental health services to children with Medicaid or no insurance.
LensCrafters	Created the "Give the Gift of Sight" program that has helped more than 1.3 million underprivileged people in the United States and in fifteen developing countries. Employees work with the Lions Club International to collect and distribute glasses around the world.

Sources: "Five Corporations Honored by Points of Light Foundation for Commitment to Community Service," Points of Light Foundation, press release, October 20, 1999, www.pointsoflight.org/awards/corporateawards/Corp%20Awards.htm; "Progress Report," America's Promise, www.americaspromise.org/OurPartners/ViewCommitments.cfm, accessed December 6, 2000; "Give the Gift of Sight," LensCrafters, www.lenscrafters.com/helping_1.html, accessed December 6, 2000; Gret Mazurkiewicz, "HVAC Manufacturers Show Their Good Samaritan Side," *Air Conditioning, Heating & Refrigeration News,* February 7, 2000, p. 122.

to community involvement. As you can see, these missions are specific to the needs of the people and areas in which the companies operate and are usually aligned with the competencies of the organizations involved and their employees.

Community mission statements are likely to change as needs are met and new issues emerge. For example, when Delphi Automotive opened a manufacturing site in Mexico, it worked with the Mexican government to help build subsidized housing for Delphi employees. The project helped more than 2,000 employees find better housing and was recently extended to serve nonemployees through a partnership with Habitat for Humanity.[67] This effort addressed a basic need in life, and now that it has been largely met, Delphi may consider investments in other community areas, such as education or health care. Thus, as stakeholder needs and concerns change, the organization will need to adapt its community relations efforts. In order to determine key areas that require support and to refine the mission statement, a company should periodically conduct a community needs assessment like the one presented in Table 7.5.[68]

TABLE 7.5

Community Needs Assessment Please check yes or no for each of the following areas that may need support from business to improve quality of life in this community:

Yes	No	Community Issues
❏	❏	Parks
❏	❏	Recreational facilities
❏	❏	Air quality
❏	❏	Pollution control
❏	❏	Water quality
❏	❏	Arts and cultural activities
❏	❏	Police and law enforcement
❏	❏	Drug enforcement
❏	❏	Gang control
❏	❏	Domestic violence
❏	❏	Child abuse
❏	❏	Traffic and safety
❏	❏	Fire department
❏	❏	Open spaces and planned use
❏	❏	Education
❏	❏	Affordable housing
❏	❏	Economic development
❏	❏	City planning for growth
❏	❏	Zoning
❏	❏	Beautification and landscaping
❏	❏	Health care and medical services
❏	❏	Volunteerism

Responsibilities to the Community

It is important for a company to view community stakeholders in a trusting manner, recognizing the potential mutual benefit to each party. In a networked world, much about a company can be learned with a few clicks of a mouse button. Activists and disgruntled individuals have used web sites to publicize the questionable activities of some companies. McDonald's Corporation, like Wal-Mart, has been the target of numerous "hate" web sites that broadcast concerns about the company's products, pricing strategies, and marketing to children. Because of the visibility of business activities and the desire for strategic corporate citizenship, successful companies strive to build long-term mutually beneficial relationships with relevant communities. Achieving these relationships may involve some trial and error. Table 7.6 illustrates some of the common mistakes that organizations make in planning for and implementing community responsibilities. In contrast, Eli Lily Pharmaceuticals, headquartered in Indianapolis, Indiana, is a strong supporter of the Indianapolis Symphony Orchestra. In return, the Symphony stages private concerts for Eli Lily employees. Dell Computer has a similar relationship with the Round Rock Express, a minor league (Texas League) baseball team. A community focus can be integrated with concerns for employees and consumers. Chapter 2 provided evidence that satisfied customers and employees are correlated with improved organizational performance.

Economic Issues

From an economic perspective, business is absolutely vital to a community. Companies play a major role in community economic development by bringing jobs to the community and allowing employees to support themselves and their families. These companies also buy supplies, raw materials, utilities, advertising services, and other goods and services from area firms, which in turn produce more economic effects. In communities with few employers, an organization that expands in or moves to the area can reduce some of the burden on community services and other subsidized support. Even in large cities with many employers, some companies choose to address social problems that tax the community. In California, for example, a coalition of insurance companies has invested more than $40 million in affordable housing projects throughout the state. By increasing the capital available for low-income housing, the coalition aims to help satisfy the state's escalating demand for affordable housing.[69] In countries with developing economies, a business or industry can also provide many benefits. A new company brings not only jobs, but also new technology, related businesses, improvements to infrastructure, and other positive factors. Conversely, the "McDonaldization" of developing countries is a common criticism regarding the effects of U.S. businesses on other parts of the world. For example, although

TABLE 7.6

Ten Common Myths and Mistakes About Community Relations

WE WON'T NEED CONSENT OR SUPPORT FROM OUR LOCAL GOVERNMENT OFFICIALS OR LOCAL COMMUNITY.

Many organizations have learned the importance of community relations the hard way when they have tried to clean up sites; get permits; and site, expand and operate facilities. It is difficult to put a dollar value on community relations until negative relations threaten or jeopardize a company's goals or operations. Organizations often do not allocate sufficient resources to community relations until it is too late. Unresolved conflicts which result from inadequate communication or poor relations can result in ugly and expensive ramifications for companies including injunctions from localities, permit denials, delays in projects, negative press, cease and desist orders, law suits, new legislation, etc. Community relations is much more rewarding and well received than crisis management.

WE WILL BE STIRRING UP TROUBLE IF WE TALK TO THE COMMUNITY.

Many project managers are afraid to talk with the community because they are afraid that they will make things worse by stirring up issues that might not already exist. It generally works the opposite. In fact, they are usually flattered and disarmed (and maybe a tad suspicious) when organizations care enough to talk with them. If you have never initiated dialogue before, you can expect the first few times to be contentious as negative comments, complaints and fears are expressed. But if you are committed to establishing and maintaining good relations, you have the opportunity to turn those negative comments into positive, or at least neutral and balanced, ones. That is, if your organization's plans are solid. Proactive community relations efforts are very rewarding and can actually make your job much easier in the future. You can even establish yourself as a leader in the community.

WE CAN IMPROVE RELATIONS WITH ONE-WAY COMMUNICATIONS EFFORTS (WITHOUT INTERACTION WITH INTERESTED PARTIES).

If your company or facility is experiencing negative press or strained relations with the community, controlled one-way communication is not the answer. Human nature causes us to want to play it close to the chest. Productive (and perhaps facilitated) interaction is necessary to allow both parties to work through and resolve the issues. Many conflicts are caused by a lack of information, misinformation, different interpretations, stereotypes, repetitive negative behavior, a perception of different interests. Many of these conflicts can only be resolved through improved, effective communication and joint problem solving which can only occur through interaction and dialogue.

THE COMMUNITY CANNOT ADD ANYTHING MEANINGFUL TO THIS PROCESS BECAUSE IT IS TOO TECHNICALLY COMPLEX.

I am consistently amazed at the level of contribution communities have made to a number of very complex projects that we have been involved with. When given the opportunity and sufficient time to review technical information, it is amazing how much local residents can grasp and contribute to projects. Local involvement and buy-in on engineering projects may even reduce the liability of technical decisions in the future.

COMMUNITY LEADERS WILL REQUEST THE MOST UNREASONABLE OR COSTLY SOLUTIONS.

We usually approach issues based on the way we define them. As a community relations firm, we often find that the way our clients define community relations issues and the way the community defines them is quite

(continued)

TABLE 7.6 *(continued)*

Ten Common Myths and Mistakes About Community Relations

COMMUNITY LEADERS WILL REQUEST THE MOST UNREASONABLE OR COSTLY SOLUTIONS.

different. We can't truly know how people will react until we talk with them. We often find that community leaders are sympathetic to companies and facilities in terms of the cost associated with regulatory compliances and environmental cleanup and are much more practical (e.g., when it comes to cleanup levels, etc.) than one might imagine.

WE SHOULDN'T TALK TO THE COMMUNITY UNTIL WE HAVE ALL THE ANSWERS.

Actually, you gain more credibility by being open enough to allow the community to be involved throughout the process. There is a comfort in knowing all the layers, steps, models, assumptions, and coordination that organizations are undertaking to develop and implement cleanup and other engineering projects. The more the community knows about this effort the more credible the information will be.

CONSULTING WITH ELECTED OFFICIALS IS ENOUGH COMMUNITY RELATIONS.

The old-fashioned public affairs approach focused on covering your bases with the media and with elected officials. The truth is that elected officials and the media usually tend to their constituents when issues stir up. Your efforts are better spent on improving relations with the local community. This is not to suggest that you shouldn't have relations with the local media and elected officials, but be careful of relying too heavily (or exclusively) on them when an issue escalates.

IF OUR RELATIONS ARE CURRENTLY STRAINED, WE WILL MAKE RELATIONS WORSE BY COMMUNICATING WITH THE COMMUNITY NOW.

The first step is to find out why relations are strained (which may require an independent reliable source to uncover). If your intentions are sound and mutually beneficial in some way, how can communication make relations worse? How can relationships get better if you don't communicate?

IT WILL BE EASIER TO IMPLEMENT OUR PROJECT WITHOUT COMMUNITY RELATIONS.

Reactive communication efforts resulting from unexpected community concern or media interest always seems to cause more upheaval, require more time and money, and is more disruptive to my clients than planned communication efforts.

WE NEED TO DO A BETTER JOB COMMUNICATING THE TECHNICAL ISSUES.

Don't underestimate the value of the trust and credibility factors that are less technically based: caring and empathy, commitment, openness and honesty. Messages that communicate these are much more powerful in relations building than technical knowledge.

Source: "10 Common Myths About Community Relations," Chaloux Environmental Communications, Inc., www.ce-com.com/10commonmyths.htm, accessed October 23, 2001. ©2000 Chaloux Environmental Communications, Inc. All Rights Reserved.

Coca-Cola has been criticized for selling sugared water and exploiting consumers in less-developed countries, the firm's market expansion strategy often involves developing a network of distributors that improves both employment and entrepreneurship opportunities in a given area.[70]

Interactions with suppliers and other vendors also stimulate the economy. Some companies are even dedicated to finding local or regional business partners in an effort to enhance their economic responsibility. For example, the Vision-Land Theme Park, located near Birmingham, Alabama, relies on local vendors for all of its food products and services. The theme park's food service equipment and restaurant design was contracted to a Birmingham company, and park guests enjoy hot dogs manufactured by Bryan, a food marketer with a Southern heritage.[71] Furthermore, there is often a contagion effect when one business moves into an area: By virtue of its prestige or business relationships, such a move can signal to other firms that the area is a viable and attractive place for others to locate. In the United States, there are parts of the country that are highly concentrated with automotive manufacturing, financial services, and technology. Local chambers of commerce and economic development organizations often entice new firms to a region because of the positive reputation and economic contagion it brings. Finally, business contributions to local health, education, and recreation projects not only benefit local residents and employees, but also may bring additional revenue into the community from tourism and other businesses that appreciate the region's quality of life. John Deere, for example, sponsors the John Deere Classic golf tournament and contributed to the Quad Cities Graduate Studies Center and the John Deere Commons Project, a multiuse development on the Illinois river front.[72]

Just as a business brings positive economic effects by expanding in or relocating to an area, it can also cause financial repercussions when it exits a particular market or geographic location. Thus, workforce reduction, or downsizing—a topic that we will revisit in Chapter 8—is a key issue with respect to economic responsibility. The impact of layoffs due to plant closings and corporate restructuring often extends well beyond the financial well-being of affected employees. Laid-off employees typically limit their spending to basic necessities while they look for new employment, and many may ultimately leave the area altogether. Even employees who retain their jobs in such a downsizing may suffer from poor morale, distrust, guilt, and continued anxiety over their own job security, further stifling spending in a community. Although the current economy with its ultralow unemployment rates has absorbed most employees laid off or "downsized" in the last few years, some areas of the country are still smarting from past waves of restructuring.

Because companies have such a profound impact on the economic viability of the communities in which they operate, firms that value corporate citizenship consider both the short- and long-term effects of changes in their workforce on the community. Today, many companies that must reduce their workforce—regardless of the reasons why—strive to give both employees and the community advance notice and offer placement services to help the community absorb those employees who lose their jobs. For example, when Service Merchandise Co. closed 150 stores and laid off more than 10,000 employees, the company offered those employees placement services that included coaching on interviewing and résumé writing and lists of other job opportunities available in the area.[73] Other companies may choose to offer extra compensation commensurate with an employee's length of employment that gives laid-off employees a financial cushion while they find new work.

Legal Issues

In order to do business, a company must be granted a "license to operate." For many firms, a series of legal and regulatory matters must be resolved before the first employee is hired or the first customer served. If you open a restaurant, for example, most states require a business license and sales tax number. These documents require basic information, such as business type, ownership structure, owner information, number of expected employees, and other data.

On a fundamental level, society has the ability to dictate what types of organizations are allowed to operate. In exchange for the license to operate, organizations are expected to uphold all legal obligations and standards. We have discussed many of these laws throughout this book, although individual cities, counties, and municipalities will have additional laws and regulations that firms must obey. For example, the city of Baltimore, Maryland, enacted an ordinance that requires companies with municipal contracts to pay their employees a "living wage" to keep them above the area's poverty level. Today, fifty cities and counties, including Los Angeles, Chicago, Detroit, and San Francisco, have passed similar laws. Critics of these ordinances believe living wages, because they exceed the federal minimum wage, harm communities through job losses and other negative effects. However, recent studies comparing cities with and without living-wage laws found no significant differences in job losses, tax rates, and corporate defections. The conclusion: Living wages actually do more good than harm to both businesses and the community.[74]

Other communities have concerns about whether and how businesses "fit" into existing communities, especially those threatened by urban sprawl and small towns working to preserve a traditional way of life. As mentioned in the chapter-opening Wal-Mart vignette, some states, cities, and counties have enacted legislation that limits the square footage of stores in an effort to deter "big-box stores," such as Wal-Mart and Home Depot, unless local voters approve otherwise. In most cases, these communities have called for such legislation to combat the noise and traffic congestion that may be associated with such stores, to protect neighborhoods, and to preserve the viability of local small businesses.[75] Thus, although living wages and store location may be ethical issues for business, some local governments have chosen to move them into the legal realm.

▶ *Ethical Issues*

As more companies view themselves as corporate citizens of the community, they will contemplate their role and the impact of their decisions on communities from an ethical perspective. Consider Clyde Oatis, who is renovating an abandoned rice mill in Houston's Fifth Ward to house a business that he hopes will address both environmental and economic issues in the low-income neighborhood. Oatis's U.S. Custom Feed will process food waste once destined for landfills into nutritious food pellets customized for the needs of different species of animals. The company will also employ and pay a living wage to workers in an area that desperately needs the jobs. Says Oatis, "You've got to have some social responsibility . . . I think I should do my part."[76]

Business leaders are increasingly recognizing the significance of the role their firms play in the community and the need for their leadership in tackling community problems. One executive who has taken the lead in addressing a community's issues is Ross Garber, cofounder of Vignette, the world's largest e-business software firm. Vignette's rise to prominence in the software industry parallels the dramatic growth of its hometown, Austin, Texas, which now experiences problems more typical of larger cities, including traffic congestion, long commute times, diminished air quality, loss of affordable housing, and the loss of long-time local traditions. Recognizing the high-tech industry's contribution to these problems, Garber helped found Get Around Austin (GAA), an organization working to promote light rail as one tool for addressing the city's traffic woes. Garber applied personal funds, well-placed contacts, and high-tech marketing savvy to attack the problem and educate Austinites about the role a rail-based mass-transit system can play in solving transportation issues.[77] Although a referendum on the light-rail issue was narrowly defeated, Garber's leadership role helped the community to examine the issues and work to find solutions. Vignette also provided a $1 million grant to help sustain live music in the city that bills itself as "the live music capital of the world."

These examples demonstrate that the ethical dimension of community responsibility can be multifaceted. This dimension and related programs are not legally mandated, but emanate from the particular corporate citizenship philosophy of a company and its top managers. For example, most cities have not yet mandated a living wage, so Clyde Oatis's actions in Houston are based on an ethical obligation that he feels to employees and the community. There are many ways that a company can demonstrate its ethical commitment to the community. We examine many of these issues, such as effects on the natural environment. A common extension of "doing the right thing" ethically is for companies to begin to allocate funds and other resources to assist community groups and others in need.

▶ ### *Philanthropic Issues*

The community relations function has always been associated with philanthropy, as one of the main historical roles of community relations was to provide gifts, grants, and other resources to worthy causes. Today, that thinking has shifted. Although businesses have the potential to help solve social issues, the success of a business can be enhanced from the publicity generated by and through stakeholder acceptance of community activities. For example, Colorado-based New Belgium Brewing Company donates $1 for every barrel of beer brewed the prior year to charities within the markets it serves. The brewery tries to divide the funds among states in proportion to interests and needs, considering environmental, social, drug and alcohol awareness, and cultural issues. Donation decisions are made by the firm's philanthropy committee, which is a volunteer group of diverse employees and one or two of the owners; employees are encouraged to bring philanthropy suggestions to the committee.[78] However, New Belgium belongs to an industry that some members of society believe contributes to social problems. Thus, regardless of the positive contributions such a firm makes to the community, some members will always have a negative view of the business.

One of the most significant ways that organizations are exercising their philanthropic responsibilities is through volunteer programs. **Volunteerism,** the donation of employee time by companies in support of social causes, has been increasing among companies of all sizes. The number of companies who are now members of volunteer councils has increased from 600 in the mid-1980s to more than 1,500. Benefits of volunteering accrue to both the individual, in terms of greater motivation, enjoyment, and satisfaction, and to the organization through employee retention and productivity increases.[79] Communities benefit from the application of new skills and initiative toward problems, better relations with corporate citizens, a greater supply of volunteers, assistance to stretch limited resources, and social and economic regeneration.[80]

In the mid-1990s, Americans spent nearly 15.7 million hours supporting formal volunteer activities. At Toyota, for example, the Volunteers in Place (VIP) program offers incentives to encourage employees to volunteer at least thirty hours per year. The top volunteers win recognition and additional cash contributions to the charity of their choice. A spokesperson for Toyota Motor Manufacturing states, "... employee morale, productivity, and turnover have all improved since the VIP program was implemented four years ago."[81] IBM contributes $1,500 to the charity of any employee who donates more than 100 hours of volunteer time to a community school each year.[82]

There are several considerations in deciding how to structure a volunteer program. Attention must be paid to employee values and beliefs; therefore, political or religious organizations should be supported on the basis of individual employee initiative and interest. Warner Brothers, the motion picture company, allows its employees to select from a menu outlining volunteer opportunities. It is sometimes less controversial for an organization to support federations of groups, such as the United Way, or less-controversial causes such as health and human welfare. One very successful program for Time Warner Communications is "Time to Read," which pairs tutors with children throughout the company's 300 sites.[83] Another issue is what to do when some employees do not wish to volunteer. If the company is not paying for the employees' time to volunteer, and volunteering is not a condition of employment or an aspect of the job description, it may be difficult to convince a certain percentage of the workforce to participate. If the organization is paying for one day a month, for example, to allow the employee exposure to volunteerism, then individual compliance is usually expected.

Strategic Implementation of Responsibilities to Consumers and the Community

As this chapter has demonstrated, corporate citizenship entails many responsibilities to many stakeholders—including consumers and the community—and many firms are finding creative ways to meet these responsibilities. Although consumers are commonly recognized as key stakeholders, the inclusion of community views and beliefs into corporate planning is a more recent and progressive phenomena. Just as in other aspects of corporate citizenship, these relationships must be managed, nurtured, and continuously assessed. Resources devoted to this effort may include programs for educating and listening to consumers, surveys to discover strengths and weaknesses in stakeholder relationships, hiring consumer affairs professionals, the development of a community relations office, and other initiatives.

The utility industry represents an interesting case study in its resource investments and relationship with both consumers and the community. There is much public interest in issues related to utility prices, environmental impact, plant closures, plant location, and more. In the late 1980s and early 1990s, larger utilities held "town hall" meetings and other sessions to obtain stakeholder views and feedback. This approach, along with sophisticated and directed programs, is making a comeback. Kansas City Power & Light (KCPL), for example, held an open house that attracted more than 1,000 people. Employees of KCPL served as baby sitters while parents learned more about electric and magnetic fields and other emerging topics. The open house not only addressed the information needs of customers, but also provided for their family needs by utilizing employee time and talent.[84] KCPL understands the importance of integrating all stakeholders in its corporate citizenship effort, including employees, as we will discover in the next chapter.

Summary

Companies face complex decisions about how to respond to the expectations, attitudes, and buying patterns of consumers, those individuals who purchase, use, and dispose of products for personal and household use. Consumers are primary stakeholders because their awareness, purchase, use, and repurchase of products are vital to a company's existence.

Consumers and businesses are fundamentally connected by an economic relationship. Economic responsibilities include following through on promises made in the exchange process. Consumer fraud involves intentional deception to derive an unfair economic advantage over an organization. If consumers believe that a firm has not fulfilled its economic responsibility, they may ask for a refund, tell others about the bad experience, discontinue their patronage, contact a consumer agency, or seek legal redress.

In the U.S., legal issues with respect to consumers fall under the jurisdiction of the Federal Trade Commission (FTC), which enforces federal antitrust and consumer protection laws. Other federal and state regulatory agencies regulate specific goods, services, or business practices. Among the issues that may that have been addressed through specific state or federal laws and regulations are consumer health and safety, credit and ownership, marketing and advertising, sales and warranties, and product liability. Product liability refers to a business's legal responsibility for the performance of its products. Concerns about protecting consumers' legal rights are not limited to the United States.

Ethical issues related to consumers include the rights enumerated by President John F. Kennedy. Consumerism refers to the movement to protect consumers from an imbalance of power with business and to maximize consumer welfare in the marketplace. Some specific elements of consumer rights have been mandated by law, but the relatively broad nature of the rights means they must be interpreted and implemented on a company-by-company basis. Consumer rights have evolved to include the right to choose, the right to safety, the right to be informed, the right to be heard, the right to seek redress, and the right to privacy. When consumers believe a firm is operating outside ethical or legal standards, they may be motivated to take action, including boycotting-abstaining from using, purchasing, or dealing with an organization.

More firms are investigating ways to link their philanthropic efforts with consumer interests. From a strategic perspective, a firm's ability to link consumer interests to philanthropy should lead stronger economic relationships.

The community—those members of society who are aware, concerned, or in some way affected by the operations and output of the organization—does not always receive the same level of acceptance as other stakeholder groups. Community relations is the organizational function dedicated to building and maintaining relationships and trust with the community. In order to determine the key areas that require support and to refine the mission statement, a company should periodically conduct a community needs assessment.

Companies play a major role in community economic development by bringing jobs to the community, interacting with other businesses, and making contributions to local health, education, and recreation projects that benefit local residents and employees. When a company leaves an area, financial repercussions may be devastating. Because they have such a profound impact on the economic viability of their communities, firms that value corporate citizenship consider both the short- and long-term effects of changes in their workforce on the community.

For many firms, a series of legal and regulatory matters must be resolved before launching a business. On a basic level, society has the ability to dictate what types of organizations are allowed to operate. As more companies view themselves as corporate citizens of the community, they consider their role and the impact of their decisions on communities from an ethical perspective.

The success of a business can be enhanced from the publicity generated by and through stakeholder acceptance of community activities. One way that organizations are exercising their philanthropic responsibilities is through volunteerism, the donation of employee time by companies in support of social causes. In structuring volunteer programs, attention must be paid to employee values and beliefs.

Many companies are finding creative ways to satisfy their citizenship responsibilities to consumers and the community. These relationships must be managed, nurtured, and continuously assessed. Resources devoted to this effort may include programs for educating and listening to consumers, surveys to discover strengths and weaknesses in stakeholder relationships, hiring consumer affairs professionals, the development of a community relations office, and other initiatives.

KEY TERMS

consumers

consumer fraud

product liability

consumerism

boycott

community

neighbor of choice

community relations

volunteerism

DISCUSSION QUESTIONS

1. List and describe the consumer rights that have become social expectations of business. Why have some of these rights been formalized through legislation? Should these rights be considered ethical standards?

2. Review Delta's Twelve-Point Plan for customer service in Figure 7.1. Create a chart to link each of the twelve points to a specific economic, legal, ethical, or philanthropic responsibility that Delta has to its customers.

3. What is the purpose of a boycott? Describe the characteristics of companies and consumers that are likely to be involved in a boycott situation. What circumstances would cause you to consider participating in a boycott?

4. Define community as a business stakeholder. Is it better to define community in a narrow or broad fashion? Explain.

5. Why would an organization want to develop an employee volunteer program? Explain the costs and benefits associated with this type of program. How would a volunteer program affect your interest in a potential employer?

EXPERIENTIAL EXERCISE

Visit the web site of Consumer World (**http://www.consumerworld.org**). What is the purpose of this web site? Examine at least three of the site's different sections. What type of information and resources did you find? How could these sections be improved in terms of their usefulness to consumers? What information could a business derive from this site to improve its corporate citizenship?

NOTES

1. "Best of Century: Award Winner Wal-Mart," *DSN Retailing Today,* May 8, 2000, p. B1; "Neurosis, Arkansas-Style," *Fortune,* April 17, 2000, p. 134; "Wal-Mart Bucks for Education," *Home Textiles Today,* June 5, 2000, p. 11; Mike France and Joann Muller, "A Site for Soreheads," *Business Week,* April 12, 1999, p. 86; Wendy Zellner, "Wal-Mart: Why an Apology Made Sense," *Business Week,* July 3, 2000, pp. 65–66; Wendy Zellner and Aaron Bernstein, "Up Against the Wal-Mart," *Business Week,* March 13, 2000, p. 76.

2. Jack Neff, "It's Not Trendy Being Green," *Advertising Age,* April 10, 2000, pp. 16–18.

3. "A Day When 'Shop Till You Drop' Is a Dirty Phrase," *Houston Chronicle,* November 23, 2000, p. 1C.

4. Consumers International, www.consumersinternational.org/, accessed October 31, 2001.

5. "Campaigns & Issues," Consumers International, www.consumersinternational.org/campaigns/index.html, accessed October 31, 2001.

6. "Consumer Charter for Global Business," Consumers International, www.consumersinternational.org/campaigns/trade/charter_en.html, accessed October 31, 2001.

7. M. Joseph Sirgy and Chenting Su, "The Ethics of Consumer Sovereignty in an Age of High Tech," *Journal of Business Ethics,* 28 (January 2000): 1–14.

8. Lee E. Norrgard and Julia M. Norrgard, *Consumer Fraud: A Reference Handbook* (New York: ABC-Clio, 1998); Ernie Scarbrough, "Ethics in Business Is a 'Two-Way' Street," *Phoenix Business Journal,* September 3, 1999, p. 71.

9. David M. Gardner, Jim Harris, and Junyong Kim, "The Fraudulent Consumer," in *Marketing and Public Policy Conference Proceedings,* ed. Gregory Gundlach, William Wilkie, and Patrick Murphy (Chicago, Ill.: American Marketing Association, 1999), pp. 48–54.

10. Janine Latus Musick, "Keeping Would-Be Thieves at Bay," *Nation's Business,* 86 (October 1998): 41–43.

11. *2000 National Retail Security Survey,* 9th ed. (Gainesville, Fl.: University of Florida, 2000).

12. Christine Doyle, "How to Beat Cellulite—Part Two: Do Anti-Cellulite Creams, Lotions and Massage Really Work, or Do Women Just Like to Think They Do?" *Ottawa Citizen,* May 23, 2000, p. D8; Kristin Hohenadel and Sasha Emmons, "Smoothing Away Age, Time," *Advertising Age,* September 9, 1996, p. 1; Anne Stein, "Can Anything Conquer Cellulite?" MSNBC, January 18, 2000, www.msnbc.com/news/357076.asp.

13. "Bureau of Consumer Protection," Federal Trade Commission, www.ftc.gov/bcp/bcp.htm, accessed October 31, 2001.

14. "Seven Internet Retailers Settle FTC Charges Over Shipping Delays During 1999 Holiday Season," Federal Trade Commission, July 26, 2000, www.ftc.gov/opa/2000/07/toolate.htm.

15. Chris Tucker, "Welcome to the Cybermall," *Spirit,* November 2000, pp. 66–70, 168–169.

16. "Consumer Information Bureau," Federal Communications Commission, www.fcc.gov/cib/, accessed October 31, 2001.

17. "Consumer Brochures," Iowa Attorney General, www.state.ia.us/government/ag/brochure.htm, accessed October 31, 2001.

18. Roger L. Miller and Gaylord A. Jentz, *Business Law Today* (Cincinnati, OH: West Legal Studies in Business, 2000).

19. Robert B. Downs, "Afterward," in Upton Sinclair, *The Jungle* (New York: New American Library, 1960).

20. "Manufacturers Pay $460,000 in Civil Penalties," *Consumer Product Litigation Reporter,* 11 (June 2000): 15.

21. "Fair Housing 2000: An Interview with Eva M. Plaza," *Journal of Housing and Community Development,* 57 (March/April 2000): 14–21.

22. "Publishers Clearing House Settles with States," CNN, August 22, 2000, www.cnn.com; "Time Inc. Agrees to Refund $4.9 Million over Sweepstakes Mailings," CNN, August 24, 2000, www.cnn.com.

23. "SmartScience Laboratories, Inc. Agrees to Settle FTC Charges of Making Unsubstantiated Health Claims for Skin Cream Product," Federal Trade Commission, August 16, 2000, www.ftc.gov/opa/2000/08/smartscience.htm.

24. Monica Soto, "Federal Laws Have Wine Sellers Over a Barrel," *Seattle Times,* July 18, 2000, p. 5B.

25. Leslie Kane, "What to Do If Your New Car's a Lemon," *Medical Economics,* May 11, 1998, pp. 105–111.

26. "Big Tobacco Defiant," ABCNews, July 15, 2000, http://more.abcnews.go.com/sections/us/dailynews/engleverdict000713.html; "Miami Jury Awards Nearly $13 Million in Tobacco Lawsuit," CNN, April 7, 2000, www.cnn.com.

27. Christine Gorman, "Diabetes Recall," *Time,* April 3, 2000, p. 94.

28. Thomas H. Kister, "General Aviation Revitalization Act: Its Effect on Manufacturers," *Defense Counsel Journal,* 65 (January 1998): 109–115.

29. O. C. Ferrell and Geoffrey Hirt, *Business: A Changing World,* 3rd ed. (Boston: Irwin/McGraw-Hill, 2000), p. 38.

30. Sandra N. Hurd, Peter Shears, and Frances E. Zollers, "Consumer Law," *Journal of Business Law,* May 2000, pp. 262–277.

31. Irene M. Kunii, "Stand Up and Fight," *Business Week,* September 11, 2000, pp. 54–55.

32. Suk-ching Ho, "Executive Insights: Growing Consumer Power in China," *Journal of International Marketing,* 9 (Issue I): 64–84.

33. "Agreement Reached on EU-Wide Beef Labeling Rules," July 18, 2000, and "Final Conclusions on Geographical BSE Risk," EUBusiness, August 1, 2000, www.eubusiness.com/consumer/index.html.

34. Kenneth J. Meier, E. Thomas Garman, and Lael R. Keiser, *Regulation and Consumer Protection: Politics, Bureaucracy and Economics* (Houston, Tx: Dame Publications, 1998).

35. Allan Asher, "Going Global: A New Paradigm for Consumer Protection," *Journal of Consumer Affairs,* 32 (Winter 1998): 183–203; Benet Middleton, "Consumerism: A Pragmatic Ideology," *Consumer Policy Review,* 8 (November/December 1998): 213–217; Audhesh Paswan and Jhinuk Chowdhury, "Consumer Protection Issues and Non-governmental Organizations in a Developing Market," in *Developments in Marketing Science,* ed. Harlan E. Spotts and H. Lee Meadow (Coral Gables, Fl.: Academy of Marketing Science, 2000), pp. 171–176.

36. "On the Left: What Makes Ralph Run," *Business Week,* September 25, 2000, pp. 82, 86.

37. Paul N. Bloom and Stephen A. Greyser, "The Maturing of Consumerism," *Harvard Business Review,* 59 (November/December 1981): 130–139.

38. Consumers Union, www.consumersunion.org/, accessed October 31, 2001; Rhoda H. Karpatkin, "Toward a Fair and Just Marketplace for All Consumers: The Responsibilities of Marketing Professionals," *Journal of Public Policy and Marketing,* 18 (Spring 1999): 118–123.

39. "Empowerment to the Consumer," *Marketing Week,* October 21, 1999, p. 3; Pierre M. Loewe and Mark S. Bonchek, "The Retail Revolution," *Management Review,* 88 (April 1999): 38–44.

40. Advisory Commission on Consumer Protection and Quality in the Health Care Industry, "Consumer Bill of Rights and Responsibilities: Report to the President of the United States," November 1997, www.hcqualitycommission.gov/cborr/; Mary Jane Fisher, "Pressure Mounts for Patient Rights Agreement," *National Underwriter/Life & Health Financial Services,* May 22, 2000, pp. 3-4; Michael Pretzer, "New Mind 'Patient Relations.' Get Ready for 'Consumer Rights'," *Medical Economics,* February 23, 1998, pp. 47–55.

41. "Comprehensive Consumer Rights Bill Addresses Bank Fees, Identity Theft," *Consumer Financial Services Law Report,* May 15, 2000, p. 2.

42. Nichole Christian, "Domino's Reaches Deal on Accusations of Bias," *New York Times,* June 7, 2000, p. A28; T. J. Degroat, "Domino's Revises Delivery Policy," DiversityInc., June 6, 2000, www.diversityinc.com.

43. Marianne Lavelle, "The States Take the Lead on Gun Control," *U.S. News & World Report,* April 17, 2000, pp. 24+.

44. David W. Stewart, Valerie S. Folkes, and Ingrid Martin, "Consumer Response to Warnings and Other Types of Product Hazard Information," in *Handbook of Marketing and Society,* ed. Paul N. Bloom and Gregory T. Gundlach (Thousand Oaks, Calif.: Sage, 2001), pp. 335–371.

45. Stephanie Ernst, "Alamo Rent-A-Car Held Liable for Murder of Dutch Tourist," DiversityInc., May 18, 2000, www.diversityinc.com.

46. A. Ben Oumlil and Alvin J. Williams, "Consumer Education Programs for Mature Consumers," *Journal of Services Marketing,* 14, no. 3 (2000): 232–243.

47. Lyuba Pronina, "Top Firms Team Up to Create Consumer Telephone Hot Line," *Moscow Times,* November 29, 2000.

48. "Dispute Resolution Programs," Better Business Bureau, www.dr.bbb.org/drprograms.cfm/, accessed October 31, 2001.

49. Dee DePass, "Regulators Likely to Scrutinize Wells Fargo Web Site," *Star Tribune,* June 24, 2000, p. 1D; Barbara Frankel, "Wells Fargo Charged With Steering By Race in Online Home Service," DiversityInc., June 23, 2000, www.diversityinc.com.

50. Federal Trade Commission, *Privacy Online: Fair Information Practices in the Electronic Marketplace: A Federal Trade Commission Report to Congress* (Washington, D.C.: FTC, May 2000), also available at www.ftc.gov/reports/privacy2000/privacy2000.pdf.

51. "12-Point Plan: Airline Customer Service Commitment," *Sky,* June 2000, p. 183 (also available at www.delta-air.com/care/service_plan/index.jsp).

52. Conscientious Consuming, www.conscientiousconsuming.com, accessed October 31, 2001.

53. Damien McElroy, "Chinese Shun Toshiba in Anti-Japan Protests," *Sunday Telegraph [London,]* June 4, 2000, p. 27.

54. Andy Altman-Ohr, "World Boycott of Transamerica Launched," *Jewish Bulletin News of Northern California,* January 21, 2000, www.angelfire.com/biz4/consumerama/transam.htm.

55. "The 1997 Cone/Roper Cause-Related Marketing Trends Report," *Business Ethics,* 12 (March/April 1997): 14–16.

56. Edwin R. Stafford and Cathy L. Hartman, "Environmentalist-Business Collaborations: Social Responsibility, Green Alliances, and Beyond," in *Advertising Research: The Internet, Consumer Behavior and Strategy,* ed. George Zinkhan (Chicago, Ill.: American Marketing Association, 2000), pp. 170–192.

57. Ken Terry, "New Patients Will Rate You Online," *Medical Economics,* April 24, 2000, pp. 42–49; Foundation for Accountability, www.facct.org, accessed December 4, 2000.

58. Sandra A. Waddock and Mary-Ellen Boyle, "The Dynamics of Change in Corporate Community Relations," *California Management Review,* 37 (Summer 1995): 125–138.

59. Robin Lee Allen, "Restaurant Neighbor Honorees Break Barriers, Link Communities," *Nation's Restaurant News,* October 9, 2000, p. 146.

60. American Productivity and Quality Center, *Community Relations: Unleashing the Power of Corporate Citizenship* (Houston, TX: American Productivity and Quality Center, 1998); Edmund M. Burke, *Corporate Community Relations: The Principle of the Neighbor of Choice* (Westport, Conn.: Praeger, 1999).

61. Bradley K. Googins, "Why Community Relations Is a Strategic Imperative," *Strategy & Business,* (Third Quarter, 1997): 14-16 (also available at www.strategy-business.com/briefs/97311).

62. Allen, "Restaurant Neighbor Honorees Break Barriers, Link Communities."

63. "Community Involvement," Business for Social Responsibility, www.bsr.org/resourcecenter/, accessed December 4, 2000; Sandra A. Waddock and Mary-Ellen Boyle, "The Dynamics of Change in Corporate Community Relations," *California Management Review,* 37 (Summer 1995): 125-138; Barron Wells and Nelda Spinks, "Communicating with the Community," *Career Development International,* 4, no. 2 (1999): 108-116.

64. Noelle Haner-Dorr, "Women Who Mean Business," *Orlando Business Journal,* March 24, 2000, pp. 37+.

65. Dirk C. Gibson, "The Cyber-Revolution in Product Recall Public Relations," *Public Relations Quarterly,* 45 (Summer 2000): 24-26.

66. Royal Weld, "Great Expectations," *Industry Week,* September 4, 2000, pp. 30–34.

67. "Community Involvement," Business for Social Responsibility.

68. "Why We Develop an Assessment of Community Needs," United Way Community Services, http://comnet.org/local/orgs/semic/whyneed.html, accessed October 31, 2001; "Community Needs Assessment Survey Guide," Utah State University Extension, www.ext.usu.edu/crd/survey/survey.htm, accessed December 5, 2000.

69. Mitchel Benson, "Insurers Test Investments in Housing," *Wall Street Journal Interactive,* August 9, 2000, http://interactive.wsj.com.

70. Thomas A. Klein and Robert W. Nason, "Marketing and Development: Macromarketing Perspectives," in *Handbook of Marketing and Society,* ed. Paul N. Bloom and Gregory T. Gunlach (Thousand Oaks, Calif.: Sage, 2001), pp. 263-297.

71. Tim O'Brien, "VisionLand's Food Vision: Local Suppliers, Low Cost," *Amusement Business,* June 8, 1998, p.13.

72. H. W. Becherer, "A More Cosmopolitan Way of Life: Why Local Economic Development Matters," *Vital Speeches of the Day,* New York, May 15, 2000.

73. Gavin Souter, "Carefully Handling Layoffs Could Head off Lawsuits," *Business Insurance,* May 8, 2000, pp. 3-4.

74. "What's So Bad About a Living Wage?" *Business Week,* September 4, 2000, pp. 68-70.

75. Zellner and Bernstein, "Up Against the Wal-Mart," pp. 76-78.

76. Rebecca Mowbray, "Turning Trash into Profits: An Entrepreneur's Plans to Turn Waste into Animal Feed Take the Community into Consideration," *Houston Chronicle,* August 1, 1999, p. 4D.

77. Helen Thorpe, "Austin, We Have a Problem," *New York Times Magazine,* August 20, 2000, www.nytimes.com/library/magazine/home/20000820mag-austin.html.

78. New Belgium Brewing Company, www.newbelgium.com, accessed October 31, 2001.

79. Diane E. Lewis, "Volunteering Is a Way of Life for Some and at Some Firms, It Is Something That Is Expected," *Minneapolis Star Tribune,* April 26, 1999, p. D8.

80. "What Are the Benefits of an Employee Community Involvement Programme?" National Centre for Volunteering, www.volunteering.org.uk/eitcn1.htm, accessed October 31, 2001.

81. Bill Leonard, "Supporting Volunteerism as Individuals Americans Invest More Hours into Volunteer Activities," *HR Magazine,* June 6, 1998, p. 4.

82. Lewis, "Volunteering Is a Way of Life for Some."

83. Ibid.

84. James L. Creighton, "The Utility as Civic Partner," *Public Utilities Fortnightly,* June 15, 2000, pp. 32-38.

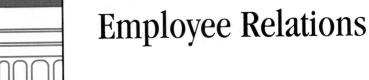

Employee Relations

8

▶ Employee Stakeholders

▶ Responsibilities to Employees

▶ Strategic Implementation of Responsibilities
to Employers

OBJECTIVES

To discuss employees as stakeholders

To examine the economic, legal, ethical, and philanthropic responsibilities
related to employees

To describe an employer of choice and its relationship to corporate
citizenship

For the employees of SAS Institute, a global software maker, the workplace resembles a modern-day utopia. Although the North Carolina company competes with Silicon Valley firms, its workplace bears little resemblance to the fast-paced and demanding atmosphere that often characterizes other high-tech firms. James Goodnight, SAS's founder, believes that dinnertime should be spent with family and friends, not in the office. Most employees leave by 5:00 P.M. or participate in flextime or job-sharing arrangements that allow for work/life balance. Other perks, such as on-site day care and a health center staffed with dentists and physicians, also contribute to the company's high ranking on *Fortune* magazine's annual list of the 100 Best Companies to Work For.

> Beyond these perks, piano melodies entertain employees at lunch, which many of them share with their children. Meals are subsidized, so employees rarely spend more than $3 for lunch. Shiatsu, Swedish, and deep-tissue massages are available on-site, as is a 55,000-square-foot athletic facility supporting yoga, tennis, walking, golf, Frisbee, and a host of other sports.

> Once an employee has finished exercising, gym clothes are laundered and returned the next day. Other time-saving benefits, such as free car washes and a farmer's market on the SAS campus, are available. Ergonomically designed work spaces ensure employees are inspired and physically comfortable in their daily tasks.

Cynics may question the lengthy list of unusual benefits that SAS provides its employees. A key concern is the link between the expenditures for these perks and the private firm's performance. For example, annual employee turnover rate is 4 percent, compared to a 20 percent rate in the computer software industry. In 1999, SAS's sales grew 17 percent, reaching more than $1 billion. Employees earned $16 million in bonuses and $30 million in profit sharing.

Although many firms say they are dedicated to providing work/life balance for their employees, SAS's efforts led one employee to say, "We're spoiled rotten." When Goodnight founded SAS, he vowed to create a work atmosphere in stark contrast to that of his first employer, NASA. He believes that treating people as if they make a difference will foster employee loyalty, performance, and innovation. Like employees, clients and business partners, including Hewlett-Packard, PricewaterhouseCoopers, and Computer Sciences Corporation, experience low-pressure and cooperative tactics that inspire mutual goals and commitment. Thus, the corporate citizenship philosophy that began with Goodnight's vision has a major focus on responsibilities to employees and extends to a variety of stakeholders.[1]

This vignette illustrates the extent to which some firms consider the needs, wants, and characteristics of employees in designing various business processes and practices. Although proponents of both the input–output and stakeholder models presented in Chapter 3 recognize the importance of employees, beliefs about the extent and types of responsibilities that organizations should assume toward employees are likely to vary. For example, the input–output model is more consistent with the economic and legal responsibilities, whereas the stakeholder approach entails a broader perspective. As this chapter will show, a delicate balance of power, responsibility, and accountability resides in the relationships a company develops with its employees.

Because employee stakeholders are so important to the success of any company, this chapter is devoted to the employer–employee relationship. We explore the many issues related to the social responsibilities employers have to their employees, including the employee–employer contract, workforce reduction, wages and benefits, labor unions, health and safety, equal opportunity, sexual harassment, whistle-blowing, diversity, and work/life balance. Along the way, we discuss a number of significant laws that affect companies' human resources programs. Finally, we look at the concept of employer of choice and what it takes to earn that designation.

Employee Stakeholders

Think for a minute about the first job or volunteer position you held. What information were you given about the organization's strategic direction? How were you managed and treated by supervisors? Did you feel empowered to make decisions? How much training did you receive? The answers to these questions may reveal the types of responsibilities that employers have toward employees. If you worked in a restaurant, for example, training should have covered safety, cleanliness, and other health issues that are mandated by law. If you volunteered at a hospital, you may have learned about the ethical and economic considerations in providing health care for the uninsured or poor and the philanthropic efforts used to support the hospital financially. Although such issues may have seemed subtle or even unimportant at the time, they are related to the responsibilities that employees, government, and other stakeholders expect of employing organizations.

Responsibilities to Employees

In her book, *The Working Life: The Promise and Betrayal of Modern Work,* business professor Joanne B. Ciulla writes about the different types of work, the history of work, the value of work to a person's self-concept, the relationship between work and freedom, and, as the title implies, the rewards and pitfalls that exist in the employee–employer relationship. Ciulla contends that two common phrases, "Get a job!" and "Get a life!" are antithetical in today's society, meaning

Southwest Airlines ranks 4th in *Fortune's* annual survey of the best companies to work for. Known for helping to create a fun atmosphere, Herb Kelleher, founder and CEO, is shown here at a company party.

they seem to be diametrically opposed goals or values.[2] For ancient Greeks, work was seen as the gods' way of punishing humans. Centuries later, Benedictine monks, who built farms, church abbeys, and villages, were considered the lowest order of monks because they labored. By the eighteenth century, the Protestant work ethic had emerged to imply that work was a method for discovering and creating a person.[3] Today, psychologists, families, and friends lament how work has become the primary source of many individuals' fulfillment, status, and happiness. Just as in the complicated history of work, the responsibilities, obligations, and expectations between employees and employers are also fraught with challenges and debates. In this section, we review the four levels of corporate social responsibilities as they relate to employees. Although we focus primarily on the responsibilities of employers to employees, we also acknowledge the role that employees have in achieving strategic citizenship.

▶ *Economic*

Perhaps no story in recent memory underscores the economic realm of employment more vividly than the saga of Malden Mills Industries. In 1995, 750,000 square feet of factory and office space at Malden Mills burned to the ground. It was just a few weeks before the winter holidays, and in addition, workers were injured. In an unusual move, CEO Aaron Feurstein paid end-of-year bonuses and employees' full wages and benefits while the buildings were reconstructed. Human resource managers set up a temporary job-training center, collected Christmas gifts for employees' children, and worked with community agencies to support employees and their families.[4] Even after injured employees filed a workers' compensation claim against Malden Mills, Feuerstein said, "The welfare of our employees has always been and continues to be a priority of Malden Mills."[5] When economic factors forced Malden Mills through several employee layoffs in the late 1990s, employees were offered jobs at another plant and received career transition assistance.[6] Essentially, Feuerstein believes in an unwritten contract that considers the economic prospects of both employer and employees.

Employee–Employer Contract   As we discussed in Chapter 1, the recent history of corporate citizenship has brought many changes to bear on stakeholder relationships. One of the more dramatic shifts has been in the "contract" that exists between employee and employer. At the beginning of the twenty-first century, many companies had to learn and accept new rules for recruiting, retaining, and compensating employees. For example, although employers held the position of power for many years, the new century brought record employment rates and the tightest job market in years. Huge salaries, signing bonuses, multiple offers, and flexible, not seniority-based, compensation plans became commonplace throughout the late 1990s and early 2000s.[7]

Regardless of salary, perks, and specific position, a **psychological contract** exists between an employee and his or her employer. This contract is largely unwritten and includes the beliefs, perceptions, expectations, and obligations that comprise an agreement between individuals and their organizations.[8] Details of the contract develop through interactions with managers and coworkers and through perceptions of the corporate culture.[9] This contract, though informal, has a significant influence on the way employees act. When promises and expectations are not met, a psychological contract breach occurs, and employees may become less loyal, inattentive to work, or otherwise dissatisfied with the employment situation.[10] On the other hand, when employers present information in a credible, competent, and trustworthy manner, employees are more likely to be supportive of and committed to the organization.[11] Just as in other stakeholder relationships, expectations in the employment psychological contract are subject to a variety of influences. This section discusses how the contract has evolved over the last 100 years. Table 8.1 profiles six characteristics that have evolved over time in employees' psychological contract with employers.

Until the early 1900s, the relationship between employer and employee was best characterized as a master–servant relationship.[12] In this view, there was a natural imbalance in power that meant employment was viewed as a privilege that

TABLE 8.1

Changes in Employees' Psychological Contract with Employers

Characteristic	Old	New
Attachment to employer	Long-term	Near-term
Readiness to change jobs	Not interested	Not looking, but will listen
Priorities on the job	Company and its goals	Personal life and career
Devotion to employer goals	Follows orders	Usually buys in
Effort on the job	100 percent	110 percent
Motto	Semper fidelis "Always faithful"	Carpe diem "Seize the day"

Source: Jennifer Laabs, "The New Loyalty: Grasp It, Earn It, Keep It," *Workforce,* 77 (November 1998): 34–39.

included few rights and many obligations. Employees were expected to work for the best interests of the organization, even at the expense of personal and family welfare. At this time, most psychologists and management scholars believed that good leadership required aggressive and domineering behavior.[13] Images from Upton Sinclair's novel, *The Jungle,* which we discussed briefly in Chapter 7, characterized the extreme negative effects of this employment contract. Although the 1906 book was fictitious, it chronicled real safety and health issues in Chicago's meatpacking plants that prompted outrage from the nation, including Theodore Roosevelt, then president of the United States. *The Jungle* precipitated changes in industry standards and worker rights.[14]

In the 1920s and 1930s, employees assumed a relationship with employers that was more balanced in terms of power, responsibilities, and obligations. This shift meant that employees and employers were coequals, and in legal terms, employees had many more rights than under the master–servant model.[15] Much of the employment law in the United States was enacted in the 1930s, when legislators passed laws related to child labor, wages, working hours, and labor unions.[16] Throughout the twentieth century, the employee–employer contract evolved along the coequals model, although social critics began to question the influence large companies had on employees.

In the 1950s, political commentator and sociologist C. Wright Mills criticized white-collar work as draining on employees' time, energy, and even personalities. He also believed that those individuals with business power were apt to keep employees happy in an attempt to ward off the development of stronger labor unions and unfavorable government regulations.[17] A few years later, the classic book, *The Organization Man,* was published by William H. Whyte. This book examined the social nature of work, including the inherent conflict between belonging and contributing to a group on the job while maintaining a sense of independence and identity.[18] Organizational researchers and managers in the 1960s began to question authoritarian behavior and consider participatory management styles that assumed employees were motivated and eager to assume responsibility for work. A study by the U.S. Department of Health, Education, and Welfare in the early 1970s confirmed that employees wanted interesting work and a chance to demonstrate their skills. The report also recommended job redesign and managerial approaches that increased participation, freedom, and democracy at work.[19] By the 1980s, a family analogy was being used to describe the workplace. This implied strong attention to employee welfare and prompted the focus on business ethics that we explored in Chapter 5. At the same time, corporate mission statements touted the importance of customers and employees, and *In Search of Excellence,* a best-selling book by distinguished professor Thomas J. Peters and consultant Robert H. Waterman, Jr., profiled companies with strong corporate cultures that inspired employees toward better work, products, and customer satisfaction.[20] The total quality management (TQM) movement increased empowerment and teamwork on the job throughout the 1990s and led the charge toward workplaces simultaneously devoted to employee achievement at work and home.[21]

Although there were many positive initiatives for employees in the 1990s, the confluence of economic progress with demands for global competitiveness convinced many executives of the need for cost cutting. For individuals accustomed to messages about the importance of employees to organizational success, workforce reduction was both unexpected and traumatic. These experiences effectively ended the loyalty and commitment-based contract that employees had developed with employers. A study of Generation X employees showed that their greatest psychological need in the workplace is security, but that they viewed many employers as "terminators."[22]

Workforce Reduction[23] At different points in a company's history, there are likely to be factors that dictate the question, "What can we do to decrease our overall costs?" In a highly competitive business environment, where new companies, customers, and products emerge and disappear every day, there is a continuous push for greater organizational efficiency and effectiveness. This pressure often leads to difficult decisions, including ones that require careful balance and consideration for the short-run survival and long-term vision of the company. This situation can create the need for **workforce reduction,** the process of eliminating employment positions. This process places considerable pressure on top management, causes speculation and tension among employees, and raises public ire about the role of business in society.[24]

There are several strategies that companies can use to reduce overall costs and expenditures. For example, organizations may choose to reduce the number of employees, simplify products and processes, decrease quality and promises in service delivery, or develop some other mechanism for eliminating resources or nonperforming assets. Managers may find it difficult to communicate about cost reductions, as this message carries both emotional and social risk. Employees may wonder, "What value do I bring to the company?" and "Does anyone really care about my years of service?" Customers may inquire, "Can we expect the same level of service and product quality?" Governments and the community may ask, "Is this really necessary? How will it affect our economy?" For all of these questions, company leadership must have a clear answer. This response should be based on a thorough analysis of costs within the organizational system and how any changes are likely to affect business processes and outcomes.

In the last two decades, many firms chose to adopt the strategy that also creates the most anxiety and criticism—the reduction of the workforce. Throughout the 1990s, the numbers were staggering, as Sears eliminated 50,000 jobs, Kodak terminated nearly 17,000 people, and IBM laid off 63,000 employees. These and other layoffs signaled the "end of the old contract" that employees had with employers.[25] This strategy, sometimes called "downsizing" or "rightsizing," usually entails employee layoffs and terminations. In other cases, a company freezes new hiring, hopes for natural workforce attrition, offers incentives for early retirement, or encourages job sharing among existing employees. With a reduction strategy, the reality is that some employees will lose their current positions one way or another. Thus, although workforce reduction may be the strategy chosen to control and reduce costs, it may have profound implications for the welfare of employees, their families, and the economic prospects of a geographic region and other constituents, as well as for the corporation itself.

As with other aspects of business, it is difficult to separate financial considerations for costs from other obligations and expectations that develop between a company and its stakeholders. Depending on a firm's resource base and current financial situation, the psychological contract that exists between an employer and employee is likely to be broken through layoffs, and the social contract between employers, communities, and other groups may also be threatened. Downsizing makes the private relationship between employee and employer a public issue that affects many stakeholders and subsequently draws heavy criticism.[26]

The impact of the workforce reduction process depends on a host of factors, including corporate culture, long-term plans, and creative calculations on both quantitative and qualitative aspects of the workplace. Because few human resource directors and other managers have extensive experience in restructuring the workforce, there are several issues to consider before embarking on the process.[27] First, a comprehensive plan must be developed that takes into account the financial implications and qualitative and emotional toll of the reduction strategy. This plan may include a systematic analysis of workflow so that management understands how tasks are currently completed and how they will be completed after restructuring. Second, the organization should commit to assisting employees who must make a career transition as a result of the reduction process. To make the transition productive for employees, this assistance should begin as soon as management is aware of possible reductions. Through the Worker Adjustment and Retraining Notification Act, employers are required to give at least sixty days' advance notice if a layoff will affect fifty or more workers or more than one-third of the workforce. Offering career assistance is beneficial over the long term, as it demonstrates corporate citizenship.

External factors also play a role in how quickly employees find new work and affect perceptions of a firm's decision to downsize. When the Opryland Hotel in Nashville, Tennessee, laid off 160 employees, other hotels in the area quickly hired them. With the unemployment rate in Nashville below 2.7 percent at the time, the other hotels appreciated the service training and competency of the former Opryland employees.[28] Thus, the Opryland Hotel probably did not suffer the types of reputation problems that other firms may have experienced in less-favorable labor markets. Individuals who are reemployed quickly, whether through company efforts or market circumstances, experience fewer negative economic and emotional repercussions.[29]

Companies must be willing to accept the consequences of terminating employees. Although workforce reduction can improve a firm's financial performance, especially in the short run,[30] there are costs to consider, including the loss of intellectual capital. The years of knowledge, skills, and commitment that employees develop cannot be easily replaced or substituted, and the loss of one employee can cost a firm between $50,000 and $100,000.[31] Skandia Assurance and Financial Services, based in Stockholm, Sweden, is one of a few firms to measure and report its intellectual capital to investors, a move that illuminates an intangible asset for better decision making.[32] Although workforce reduction lowers costs, it often results in lost intellectual capital, strained customer relationships, negative media attention, and other issues that drain company resources. Thus, a long-term understanding of the qualitative and quantitative costs and benefits should guide downsizing decisions.[33]

Although workforce reduction is a corporate decision, it is also important to recognize the potential role of employees in these decisions. Whereas hiring and job growth reached a frantic pace by the late 1990s, a wave of downsizings in the early 1990s meant that most individuals had embraced the reality of having little job security. Instead of becoming cynical or angry, most employees reversed roles and began asking, "What is this company doing for me?" and "Am I getting what I need from my employer?" Employees of all types began taking more responsibility for career growth, demanding balance in work and personal responsibilities, and seeking opportunities in upstart firms and emerging industries, particularly those associated with the Internet and e-commerce. Thus, although workforce reduction has negative effects, it has also shifted the psychological contract and power between employee and employer. The following suggestions examine how individuals can potentially mitigate the onset and effects of downsizing.

First, all employees should understand how their skills and competencies affect business performance. Not recognizing and improving this relationship makes it more difficult to prove their worth to managers faced with workforce reduction decisions. Second, employees should strive for cost-cutting and conservation strategies regardless of the employer's current financial condition. This is a workforce's first line of defense against layoffs—assisting the organization in reducing its costs before drastic measures are necessary. Third, today's work environment requires that most employees fulfill diverse and varying roles. For example, manufacturing managers must understand the whole product development and introduction process, ranging from engineering to marketing and distribution activities. Thus, another way of ensuring worth to the company, and to potential employers, is through an employee's ability to navigate different customer environments and organizational systems. It is now necessary to "cross train," show flexibility, and learn the entire business, even if a company does not offer a formal program for gaining this type of experience and exposure. Although this advice may not prevent workforce reduction, it does empower employees against some of its harmful effects. Through laws and regulations, the government has also created a system for ensuring that employees are treated properly on the job. The next section covers the myriad of laws that all employers and employees should consider in daily and strategic decisions.

▶ Legal

Employment law is a very complex and evolving area. In fact, most large companies employ human resource managers and legal specialists who are trained in the detail and implementation of specific statutes related to employee hiring, compensation, benefits, safety, and other areas. Smaller organizations often send human resource managers to workshops and conferences in order to keep abreast of legal imperatives in the workplace. Table 8.2 lists the major federal laws that cover employer responsibilities with respect to wages, labor unions, benefits, health and safety, equal opportunity, and other areas. Until the early 1900s, employment was primarily governed by the concept of **employment at will,** a common-law doctrine that allows either the employer or employee to terminate the relationship at any time as long as it does not violate an employment contract. Today, many states still use the employment-at-will philosophy, but laws and statutes may limit true discretion in this regard.[34] The following discussion highlights employment laws and their fundamental role as corporate citizenship responsibilities.[35]

Wages and Benefits   After the Great Depression, the U.S. Congress enacted a number of laws to protect employee rights and extend employer responsibilities.

TABLE 8.2

Major Employment Laws

Act (Date Enacted)	Purpose
National Labor Relations Act (1935)	Established the rights of employees to engage in collective bargaining and to strike
Fair Labor Standards Act (1938)	Established minimum wage and overtime pay standards, record keeping, and child labor standards for most private and public employers
Equal Pay Act (1963)	Protects women and men who perform substantially equal work in the same establishment from gender-based wage discrimination
Civil Rights Act, Title VII (1964)	Prohibits employment discrimination on the basis of race, national origin, color, religion, and gender
Age Discrimination in Employment Act (1967)	Protects individuals aged forty or older from age-based discrimination
Occupational Safety and Health Act (1970)	Ensures safe and healthy working conditions for all employees by providing specific standards that employers must meet
Employee Retirement Income Security Act (1974)	Set uniform minimum standards to assure that employee benefit plans are established and maintained in a fair and financially sound manner
Americans with Disabilities Act (1990)	Prohibits discrimination on the basis of physical or mental disability in all employment practices and requires employers to make reasonable accommodation to make facilities accessible to and usable by persons with disabilities
Family and Medical Leave Act (1993)	Requires certain employers to provide up to twelve weeks of unpaid, job-protected leave to eligible employees for certain family and medical reasons

Sources: "Federal Laws Prohibiting Job Discrimination Questions and Answers," Equal Employment Opportunity Commission, www.eeoc.gov/facts/quanda.html, accessed November 1, 2001; Gillian Flynn, "Looking Back on 100 Years of Employment Law," *Workforce,* 78 (November 1999): 74–77; Roger LeRoy Miller and Gaylord A. Jentz, *Business Law Today* (Cincinnati: West Legal Studies in Business, 2000); United States Department of Labor, *Small Business Handbook: Laws, Regulations, and Technical Assistance Services,* 1997, www.dol.gov/dol/asp/public/programs/handbook/contents.htm.

The Fair Labor Standards Act (FLSA) of 1938 prescribed minimum wage and overtime pay, record keeping, and child labor standards for most private and public employers. The minimum wage is set by the federal government and is periodically revised. For example, the minimum wage was raised from $4.45 per hour to $5.15 per hour in September 1997. Most employees who work more than 40 hours per week are entitled to overtime pay in the amount of one and a half times their regular pay. There are exemptions to the overtime pay provisions for four classes of employees: executives, outside salespeople, administrators, and professionals.[36]

The FLSA also affected child labor, including the provision that individuals under the age of fourteen are allowed to do only certain types of work, such as delivering newspapers and working in their parents' businesses. Children under age sixteen are often required to get a work permit, and their work hours are restricted so that they can attend school. Persons between the ages of sixteen and eighteen are not restricted in terms of number of work hours, but cannot be employed in hazardous or dangerous positions. Although passage of the FLSA was necessary to eliminate abusive child labor practices, its restrictions became somewhat problematic during the booming economy of the early 2000s, when unemployment rates were extremely low in the United States. Some business owners may have even considered lobbying for relaxed standards in very restrictive states so that they could hire more teens. In addition, general FLSA restrictions have created problems in implementing job-sharing and flextime arrangements with employees who are paid on an hourly basis.[37]

Two other pieces of legislation relate to employer responsibilities for benefits and job security. The Employee Retirement Income Security Act (ERISA) of 1974 set uniform minimum standards to assure that employee benefit plans are established and maintained in a fair and financially sound manner. ERISA does not require companies to establish retirement pension plans; instead, it developed standards for the administration of plans that management chooses to offer employees. A key provision relates to **vesting,** the legal right to pension plan benefits. In general, contributions an employee makes to the plan are vested immediately, whereas company contributions are vested after five years of employment. ERISA is a very complicated aspect of employer responsibilities because it involves tax law, financial investments, and plan participants and beneficiaries.[38]

The Family and Medical Leave Act (FMLA) of 1993 requires certain employers to provide up to twelve weeks of unpaid, job-protected leave to eligible employees for certain family and medical reasons. However, if the employee is paid in the top 10 percent of the entire workforce, the employer does not have to reinstate him or her in the same or comparable position.[39] Typical reasons for this type of leave include the birth or adoption of a child, personal illness, or the serious health condition of a close relative. The FMLA applies to employers with fifty or more employees, which means that a large number of U.S. employees are not covered by its provisions. In addition, employees must have worked at least one year for the firm and at least twenty-five hours per week during the past year before the FMLA is required.

Labor Unions   In one of the earliest pieces of employment legislation, the National Labor Relations Act (NLRA) of 1935 legitimized the rights of employees to engage in collective bargaining and to strike. This law was originally passed to protect employee rights, but subsequent legislation gave more rights to employers and restricted the power of unions. Before the NLRA, many companies attempted to prohibit their employees from creating or joining labor organizations. Employees who were members of unions were often discriminated against in terms of hiring and retention decisions. This act sought to eliminate the perceived imbalance of power between employers and employees. Through unions, employees gained a collective bargaining mechanism that enabled greater power on several fronts, including wages and safety.[40] For example, after a weeks-long strike against Verizon Communications, members of the Communications Workers of America (CWA) and International Brotherhood of Electrical Workers (IBEW) negotiated a deal that gave workers of the telecommunications firm a 12 percent pay raise (over three years), a cap on overtime hours, and other provisions, including the elimination of the threat of layoffs for the period of the labor contract.[41]

Health and Safety   In 1970, the Occupational Safety and Health Act (OSHA) sought to ensure safe and healthy working conditions for all employees by providing specific standards that employers must meet. This act led to the development

Hardigg Industries, manufacturer of specialized containers, recognizes the need to protect employees through safety equipment such as face shields.

of the Occupational Safety and Health Administration, also known as OSHA, the agency that oversees the regulations intended to make workplaces in the United States the safest in the world. In its more than thirty years of existence, OSHA has made great strides to improve and maintain the health and safety of employees. For example, since the 1970s, the workplace death rate in the United States has been reduced by 50 percent, and the agency's initiatives in cotton dust and lead standards have reduced disease in several industries.[42] OSHA has the authority to enter and make inspections of most employers. Because of its far-reaching power and unwarranted inspections made in the 1970s, the agency's relationship with business has not always been positive. For example, OSHA recently proposed rules to increase employer responsibility for **ergonomics,** the design, arrangement, and use of equipment to maximize productivity and minimize fatigue and physical discomfort. Without proper attention to ergonomics, employees may suffer injuries and long-term health issues as a result of work motion and tasks. Many business and industry associations have opposed the proposal, citing enormous costs and unsubstantiated claims.[43] Despite differences between this federal agency and some companies on a number of regulations, most employers are required to display the poster shown in Figure 8.1 or one required by their state safety and health agency.

An emerging issue in the area of health and safety is the increasing rate of violence in the workplace. According to OSHA, 1.5 million workers are assaulted and nearly 1,000 are murdered in the workplace every year.[44] A recent survey of *Fortune* 1000 companies indicates that workplace violence is the most important security issue they face, costs them $36 billion annually, and results in three deaths daily and thousands of injuries each year.[45] Surveys in the insurance industry show that nearly 25 percent of insurance employees have been threatened, harassed, or attacked in job-related circumstances.[46]

The State of California's Occupational Safety and Health Agency has identified three types of workplace violence: (1) crimes committed by strangers and intruders in the workplace; (2) acts committed by nonemployees, such as customers, patients, students, and clients, who have expected or normal contact with employees; and (3) violence committed by coworkers.[47] Taxi drivers and clerks working late-night shifts at convenience stores are often subject to the first type of violence. Airline attendants are increasingly experiencing the second category of workplace violence when passengers become unruly, drunk, or otherwise violent while in-flight. In 2000, airline employees across the U.S., Australia, and Switzerland staged a campaign to combat "air rage," the uncivil and dangerous acts of passengers that are not only punishable by large fines, but can also threaten the safety of everyone aboard the aircraft. The groups plan to take a proposal to toughen penalties and control of air rage perpetrators to government officials in many countries.[48] The terrorist attacks on the World Trade Center and the Pentagon further highlight workplace risks and violence, including the steps that many organizations are taking to protect employees and other stakeholders.

FIGURE 8.1

Job Safety and Health
Protection Poster

You Have a Right to a Safe and Healthful Workplace.

IT'S THE LAW!

- You have the right to notify your employer or OSHA about workplace hazards. You may ask OSHA to keep your name confidential.
- You have the right to request an OSHA inspection if you believe that there are unsafe and unhealthful conditions in your workplace. You or your representative may participate in the inspection.
- You can file a complaint with OSHA within 30 days of discrimination by your employer for making safety and health complaints or for exercising your rights under the OSH Act.
- You have a right to see OSHA citations issued to your employer. Your employer must post the citations at or near the place of the alleged violation.
- Your employer must correct workplace hazards by the date indicated on the citation and must certify that these hazards have been reduced or eliminated.
- You have the right to copies of your medical records or records of your exposure to toxic and harmful substances or conditions.
- Your employer must post this notice in your workplace.

The *Occupational Safety and Health Act of 1970 (OSH Act)*, P.L. 91-596, assures safe and healthful working conditions for working men and women throughout the Nation. The Occupational Safety and Health Administration, in the U.S. Department of Labor, has the primary responsibility for administering the *OSH Act*. The rights listed here may vary depending on the particular circumstances. To file a complaint, report an emergency, or seek OSHA advice, assistance, or products, call 1-800-321-OSHA or your nearest OSHA office: • Atlanta (404) 562-2300 • Boston (617) 565-9860 • Chicago (312) 353-2220 • Dallas (214) 767-4731 • Denver (303) 844-1600 • Kansas City (816) 426-5861 • New York (212) 337-2378 • Philadelphia (215) 861-4900 • San Francisco (415) 975-4310 • Seattle (206) 553-5930. Teletypewriter (TTY) number is 1-877-889-5627. To file a complaint online or obtain more information on OSHA federal and state programs, visit OSHA's website at **www.osha.gov**. If your workplace is in a state operating under an OSHA-approved plan, your employer must post the required state equivalent of this poster.

1-800-321-OSHA
www.osha.gov

U.S. Department of Labor   • **Occupational Safety and Health Administration** • **OSHA 3165**

☼ U.S. GOVERNMENT PRINTING OFFICE: 2000-467-940

Source: "New OSHA Workplace Poster," Occupational Safety and Health Administration, 2000, http://www.osha.gov/oshpubs/poster.html.

Finally, disagreements and stress in the workplace may escalate into employee-on-employee violence. For example, a Xerox Corporation warehouse employee opened fire during a team meeting at a facility in Honolulu, killing seven coworkers. The employee, Bryan Uyesugi, was eventually convicted of murder and sentenced to life in prison without parole for the shooting, which Xerox officials described as the "worst tragedy" in the company's history. The Hawaii Occupational Safety and Health Division later cited Xerox for failing to enforce workplace-violence policies that might have prevented the deaths.[49] In many of these cases, the perpetrator has been recently reprimanded, dismissed, or received other negative feedback that prompted the violent attack. Although crimes reflect general problems in society, employers have a responsibility to assess risks and provide security, training, and safeguards to protect employees and other stakeholders from such acts.[50] Some companies now purchase insurance policies to cover the costs of workplace violence, including business interruption and medical claims related to injuries.[51]

Equal Opportunity   Title VII of the Civil Rights Act of 1964 prohibits employment discrimination on the basis of race, national origin, color, religion, and gender. This law is fundamental to employees' rights to join and advance in an organization according to merit, not one of the characteristics in the preceding list. For example, employers are not permitted to categorize jobs as just for men or women, unless there is a reason gender is fundamental to the tasks and responsibilities. Additional laws passed in the 1970s, 1980s, and 1990s were also designed to prohibit discrimination related to pregnancy, disabilities, age, and other factors. For example, the Americans with Disabilities Act prohibits companies from discriminating on the basis of physical or mental disability in all employment practices and requires them to make facilities accessible to and usable by persons with disabilities. These legal imperatives require that companies formalize employment practices to ensure that no discrimination is occurring. Thus, managers must be fully aware of the types of practices that constitute discrimination and work to ensure hiring, promotion, annual evaluation, and other procedures are fair and based on merit. The spread of HIV and AIDS has prompted multinational firms with operations in Africa to distribute educational literature and launch prevention programs. Some companies work with internal and external stakeholders and even fund medical facilities that help prevent the disease and treat HIV/AIDS patients. Another component to their initiatives involves education on fair treatment of employees with the disease.[52]

To ensure that they build balanced workforces, many companies have initiated **affirmative action programs,** which involve efforts to recruit, hire, train, and promote qualified individuals from groups that have traditionally been discriminated against on the basis of race, sex, or other characteristics. Such initiatives may be imposed on an employer by federal law; for federal government contractors and subcontractors; as part of a settlement agreement with a state or federal agency; or by court order.[53] For example, Safeway, a chain of supermarkets, established a program to expand opportunities for women in middle- and upper-level management after settling a sex-discrimination lawsuit.[54] However, many companies voluntarily implement affirmative action plans in order to build a more diverse workforce.[55] For example, a Chicago real estate developer launched the Female Employment Initiative, an outreach program designed to create opportunities for women in the construction industry through training programs, counseling and information services, and referral listings to help employers identify available women workers.[56]

Although many people believe that affirmative action requires the use of quotas to govern employment decisions, it is important to note that two decades of Supreme Court rulings have made it clear that affirmative action does *not* permit or require quotas, reverse discrimination, or favorable treatment of unqualified women or minorities. To ensure that affirmative action programs are fair, the Supreme Court has established a number of standards to guide their implementation: (1) there must be a strong reason for developing an affirmative action program; (2) affirmative action programs must apply only to qualified candidates; and (3) affirmative action programs must be limited and temporary and therefore cannot include "rigid and inflexible quotas."[57]

The Equal Employment Opportunity Commission (EEOC) monitors compliance with Title VII, with a mission to "promote equal opportunity in employment through administrative and judicial enforcement of the federal civil rights laws and through education and technical assistance."[58] For example, the EEOC recently won a lawsuit against the Chuck E. Cheese's pizza chain for firing a mentally disabled janitor because of his disability; the jury in the case awarded the victim $13 million in compensatory and punitive damages.[59] A special type of discrimination, sexual harassment, is also prohibited through Title VII.

Sexual Harassment The flood of women into the workplace during the last half of the twentieth century brought new challenges and opportunities for organizations. Although harassment has probably always existed in the workplace, the presence of both genders in roughly equal numbers changed norms of behavior. When men dominated the workplace, it may have been acceptable to have photos of partially nude women or sexually suggestive materials posted on walls or in lockers. Today, such materials could be viewed as illegal if they contribute to a work environment that is intimidating, offensive, or otherwise interferes with an employee's work performance. The U.S. government indicates the nature of this illegal activity:

> Unwelcome sexual advances, requests for sexual favors, and other verbal or physical conduct of a sexual nature constitutes **sexual harassment** when submission to or rejection of this conduct explicitly or implicitly affects an individual's employment, unreasonably interferes with an individual's work performance, or creates an intimidating, hostile or offensive work environment.[60]

Prior to 1986, sexual harassment was not a specific violation of federal law in the United States. In *Meritor Savings Bank v. Vinson,* the U.S. Supreme Court ruled that sexual harassment creates a "hostile environment" that violates Title VII of the Civil Rights Act, even in the absence of economic harm or demand for sexual favors in exchange for promotions, raises, or related work incentives.[61] In other countries, sexual harassment in the workplace is considered an illegal act, although the specific conditions may vary by legal and social culture. In Mexico, the law protects employees only if their jobs are jeopardized on the basis of the exchange of sexual favors or relations. Employees of Mexican public entities, such as government offices, will be fired if found guilty of the offending behavior.[62] In the European Union, sexual harassment legislation focuses on the liability that employers carry when they fail to promote a workplace culture free of harassment and other forms of discrimination.[63]

There are two general categories of sexual harassment: quid pro quo and hostile work environment.[64] **Quid pro quo harassment** is a type of sexual extortion, where there is a proposed or explicit exchange of job benefits for sexual favors. For example, telling an employee, "You will be fired if you do not have sex with me," is a direct form of sexual harassment. Usually, the person making such a statement is in a position of authority over the harassed employee, and thus, the threat of job loss is real. One incident of quid pro quo harassment may create a justifiable legal claim. **Hostile work environment harassment** is less direct than quid pro quo harassment and can involve epithets, slurs, negative stereotyping, intimidating acts, graphic materials that show hostility toward an individual or group, and other types of conduct that affect the employment situation. For example, an e-mail message containing sexually explicit jokes that is broadcast to employees could be viewed as contributing to a hostile work environment. Some hostile work environment harassment is nonsexual, meaning the harassing conduct is based on gender without explicit reference to sexual acts. For example, in *Campbell v. Kansas State University* (1991) the courts found repeated remarks about women "being intellectually inferior to men" to be part of a hostile environment. Unlike quid pro quo cases, one incident may not justify a legal claim. Instead, the courts will examine a range of acts and circumstances to determine if the work environment was intolerable and the victim's job performance was impaired.[65] From a corporate citizenship perspective, a key issue in both types of harassment is the employing organization's knowledge and tolerance for these types of behaviors. A number of court cases have shed more light on the issues that constitute sexual harassment and organizations' responsibility in this regard.

In *Harris v. Forklift Systems* (1993), Teresa Harris claimed that her boss at Forklift Systems made suggestive sexual remarks, asked her to retrieve coins from his pants pocket, and joked that they should go to a motel to "negotiate her raise." Courts at the state level threw out her case because she did not suffer major psychological injury. The U.S. Supreme Court overturned these decisions and ruled that employers can be forced to pay damages even if the worker suffered no proven psychological harm. This case brought about the "reasonable person" standard in evaluating what conduct constitutes sexual harassment. From this case, juries now evaluate the alleged conduct with respect to commonly held beliefs and expectations.[66]

Several global firms have been embroiled in sexual harassment suits. For example, Ford Motor Company settled a class-action lawsuit for $7.75 million in the late 1990s, the fourth-largest sexual harassment settlement in the Equal Employment Opportunity Commission's history, after more than 500 female employees claimed they were groped and sexually harassed at two different Ford plants. The settlement also required that the company spend an additional $10 million on sensitivity training programs.[67] Mitsubishi Motors agreed in 1998 to pay $34 million in a settlement with 350 women who made serious allegations of harassment and brought lawsuits against the company. Their allegations of sexual harassment included the distribution of lewd videos and photos, inappropriate conversations and jokes, and general tolerance by management for these actions and overtones. As part of the settlement, the company also agreed to periodic monitoring by a three-member panel and implementing an effective sexual harassment policy.[68]

Recent U.S. Supreme Court decisions on sexual harassment cases indicate that (1) employers are liable for the acts of supervisors; (2) employers are liable for sexual harassment by supervisors that culminates in a tangible employment action (loss of job, demotion, etc.); (3) employers are liable for a hostile environment created by a supervisor, but may escape liability if they demonstrate that they exercised reasonable care to prevent and promptly correct any sexually harassing behavior and that the plaintiff employee unreasonably failed to take advantage of any preventive or corrective measures offered by the employer; and (4) claims of hostile environment sexual harassment must be severe and pervasive in order to be viewed as actionable by the courts.[69]

Much like the underlying philosophy of the Federal Sentencing Guidelines for Organizations that we discussed in Chapters 4 and 5, these decisions require top managers in organizations to take the detection and prevention of sexual harassment seriously. To this end, many firms have implemented programs on sexual harassment. In order to satisfy current legal standards and set a higher standard for corporate citizenship, employees, supervisors, and other close business partners should be educated on the company's zero-tolerance policy against harassment. Employees must be educated on the policy prohibiting harassment, including the types of behaviors that constitute harassment, how offenders will be punished, and what to do if they experience harassment. Just like an organizational compliance program, employees must be assured of confidentiality and no retaliation for reporting harassment. Training on sexual harassment should be balanced in terms of legal definitions and practical tips and tools. Although employees need to be aware of the legal issues and ramifications, they also may need assistance in learning to recognize and avoid behaviors that may constitute quid pro quo or hostile environment harassment. Finally, employees should be aware that same-sex conduct may also constitute sexual harassment.[70] Table 8.3 lists facts about sexual harassment that should be used in company communication and training on this workplace issue.

Whistle-blowing[71]   An employee who reports individual or corporate wrongdoing to either internal or external sources is considered a **whistle-blower.**[72] Whistle-blowers usually focus on issues or behaviors that need corrective action, although managers and other employees may not appreciate reports that expose company weaknesses, raise embarrassing questions, or otherwise detract from organizational tasks. Although not all whistle-blowing activity leads to an extreme

TABLE 8.3

Sexual Harassment in the Workplace

FACTS

Sexual harassment is a form of sex discrimination that violates Title VII of the Civil Rights Act of 1964.

Unwelcome sexual advances, requests for sexual favors, and other verbal or physical conduct of a sexual nature constitutes sexual harassment when submission to or rejection of this conduct explicitly or implicitly affects an individual's employment, unreasonably interferes with an individual's work performance, or creates an intimidating, hostile, or offensive work environment.

Sexual harassment can occur in a variety of circumstances, including but not limited to the following:
- The victim as well as the harasser may be a woman or a man. The victim does not have to be of the opposite sex.
- The harasser can be the victim's supervisor, an agent of the employer, a supervisor in another area, a coworker, or a nonemployee.
- The victim does not have to be the person harassed but could be anyone affected by the offensive conduct.
- Unlawful sexual harassment may occur without economic injury to or discharge of the victim.
- The harasser's conduct must be unwelcome.

It is helpful for the victim to inform the harasser directly that the conduct is unwelcome and must stop. The victim should use any employer complaint mechanism or grievance system available.

When investigating allegations of sexual harassment, the Equal Employment Opportunity Commission looks at the whole record: the circumstances, such as the nature of the sexual advances, and the context in which the alleged incidents occurred. A determination on the allegations is made from the facts on a case-by-case basis.

Source: "Facts About Sexual Harassment," U.S. Equal Employment Opportunity Commission, www.eeoc.gov/facts/fs-sex.html, accessed November 1, 2001.

reaction, whistle-blowers have been retaliated against, demoted, fired, and even worse as a result of their actions. For example, Jacob F. Horton, senior vice president at Gulf Power, was on his way to talk with company officials about alleged thefts, payoffs, and cover-ups at the utility when he died in a plane crash in 1989. Allegations that his death was related to whistle-blowing still linger.[73]

Partly as a result of business and industry scandals in the 1980s, most large corporations have the formal organizational compliance programs discussed in Chapters 4 and 5, including toll-free hot lines and other anonymous means for employees to ask questions, gain clarification, or report suspicious behavior. These programs are designed to facilitate internal whistle-blowing, as they engender a more ethical organizational culture and provide mechanisms for monitoring and supporting appropriate behavior. Thus, an effective ethics and legal compliance program should provide employees and other stakeholders with opportunities to make possible transgressions known (e.g., ethics hot line, open-door policy, and strong ethical climate).

The federal government and most state governments in the United States have enacted measures to protect whistle-blowers from retaliation. For example, the Whistleblower Protection Act of 1986 protects federal employees from retaliatory behavior. Other legislation actually rewards whistle-blowers for revealing illegal behavior. Under the False Claims Act of 1986, an individual who reports fraud perpetrated against the federal government may receive between 15 and 25 percent of the proceeds if a suit is brought against the perpetrator.

▶ *Ethical*

Laws are imperative for corporate citizenship. The ethical climate of the workplace, however, is more subjective and dependent on top management leadership and corporate culture. In this section, we examine several trends in employment practices that have not fully reached the legal realm. Company initiatives in these areas indicate a corporate philosophy or culture that respects and promotes certain ethical values.

Training and Development   As discussed in Chapter 5, organizational culture and the associated values, beliefs, and norms operate on many levels and affect a number of workplace practices. Some organizations value employees as individuals, not just "cogs in a wheel." Firms with this ethical stance fund initiates to develop employees' skills, knowledge, and other personal characteristics. Although this development is linked to business strategy and aids the employer, it also demonstrates a commitment to the future of the employee and his or her interests. Employees of the Taco Cabana restaurant chain, for example, receive training in Spanish along with cross training of skills needed in various parts of restaurant operations. At each workstation, employees find reminders and instructions in both

English and Spanish to promote greater retention. Employees also rotate through the workstations, which not only reinforces and extends their skill sets, but also reduces boredom and fatigue.[74]

Professionals also appreciate and respect a training and development focus from their employers. For example, the Los Angeles-based law firm of Latham & Watkins launched a series of initiatives, including "Latham & Watkins University" for first- and fourth-year associates. This training program covers legal updates, professional skill development, and information on career management and planning. Other law firms have upgraded their development opportunities, including mentoring programs, sabbaticals, and feedback sessions for commenting on firm policies and procedures.[75] These firms are finding many benefits of employee training and development, including stronger employee recruitment and retention strategies. Indeed, there is a link between investments in employees and the amount of commitment, job satisfaction, and productivity demonstrated by them. Happier employees intend to stay with their employer and better serve fellow coworkers, customers, and other constituents, which has direct bearing on the quality of relationships and financial prospects of a firm. Management training is also critical, as the top reason employees leave a company is because of poor or unskilled managers, not salary, benefits, or other organizational factors.[76]

Employees recognize when a company is diligently investing in programs that not only improve operations but also give them and coworkers increased empowerment and new opportunities to improve knowledge and grow professionally. Through formal training and development classes, workers get a better sense of where they fit and how they contribute to the overall organization. This understanding empowers them to become more responsive, accurate, and confident in workplace decisions. Training also increases accountability and responsibility, a situation most employees prefer to micromanaging or "hand-holding." All these effects contribute to the financial and cultural health of an organization.[77] Thus, a firm can enhance its organizational capacity to fulfill stakeholder expectations.

Training and development activities require resources and the commitment of all managers to be successful. For example, a departmental manager must be supportive of an employee using part of the workday to attend a training session on a new software package. At the same time, the organization must pay for the training, regardless of whether it uses inside or outside trainers and develops in-house materials or purchases them from educational providers. A study by the American Society for Training and Development indicates that, on average, employers in developed countries spend about $627 per employee on training every year. Figure 8.2 graphically depicts training expenditures per employee in six regions of the world. As you can see, Asia lags behind other regions with respect to this type of corporate spending. Despite the differences in training expenditures, the types of training programs and workplace practices in effect in these regions are remarkably similar. Managerial skills, supervisory strategies, information technology skills,

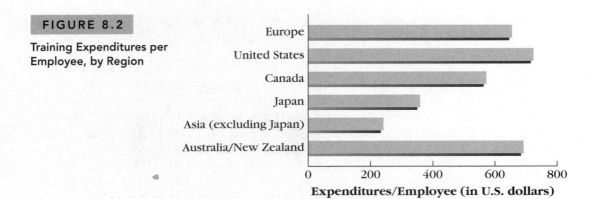

Source: Mark E. Van Buren and Stephen B. King, *ASTD's Annual Accounting of Worldwide Patterns in Employer-Provided Training* (Alexandria, Va.: American Society for Training and Development, 2000), p. 4. © 2000 by the American Society for Training and Development. Reprinted with permission.

occupational safety and compliance, and customer relations are the topic of training programs in all countries.[78] Another area that has received much attention in the United States but less focus in other countries involves the diverse nature of today's workforce.

Diversity Whereas Title VII of the Civil Rights Act grants legal protection to different types of employees, initiatives in **workplace diversity** focus on recruiting and retaining a diverse workforce as a business imperative.[79] With diversity programs, companies assume an ethical obligation to employ and empower individuals, regardless of age, gender, physical and mental ability, and other characteristics. These firms go beyond compliance with EEOC guidelines to develop cultures that not only tolerate, but also embrace, the unique skills and contributions of all types of people. Thus, legal statutes focus on removing discrimination, whereas diversity represents a management approach for harnessing and cultivating employee talent.[80] A study of eight multinational corporations found that these firms linked their diversity mission statement with the corporate strategic plan, implemented plans to recruit and retain a diverse talent pool, supported community programs of diverse cultural groups, and held management accountable for various types of diversity performance.[81]

Many firms embrace employee diversity to deal with customer diversity. Their assumption is that in order to effectively design, market, and support products for different target groups, a company must employ individuals who reflect its customers' characteristics.[82] Organizations and industries with a populationwide customer base may use national demographics for assessing their diversity effort. For example, a study in the newspaper industry found that although racial and ethnic

JCPenney recognizes the importance of partnering with minority- and women-owned businesses.

minorities comprise nearly 30 percent of the U.S. population, less than 12 percent of all news reporters fall into that category. This finding prompted the National Association of Black Journalists to call for greater attention to diversity in the newsroom. Although specific newspapers, like the *Austin American-Statesman* and the *Orange County Register,* have made significant progress in recent years, the entire industry is not yet aligned with demographic trends.[83] After the 2000 United States census data were released, some companies began to reconsider marketing strategy, including the link between employee and customer characteristics. For example, census data revealed sharp growth in the Hispanic population and for some firms, may prompt hiring of Hispanic employees and consultants.[84]

As we discussed in Chapter 2, there are opportunities to link corporate citizenship objectives with business performance, and many firms are learning the benefits of employing individuals with different backgrounds and perspectives. For example, Ernst & Young executives believe diversity brings a competitive advantage to the consulting firm through multiple perspectives.[85] Even small businesses are discovering these advantages. The Wilson Street Grill, an upscale restaurant in Madison, Wisconsin, makes a point of hiring mentally disabled workers. Owners Nancy Christy and Andrea Craig have established a flexible workplace that designs jobs around workers' abilities instead of trying to fit the person into a job description. Their efforts have been richly rewarded with loyal, creative, hard-working employees who stay for years, a rare occurrence in an industry known for its high turnover, as well as the National Restaurant Association's Restaurant Neighbors Award and an Americans with Disabilities Act award.[86] Verizon, a global provider of wireless communication services, is also committed to including people with disabilities into the workplace. Along with other businesses and nonprofit organizations, Verizon helped establish several initiatives to educate businesses on the unique opportunities and challenges with this employment category.[87]

Although workplace diversity reaps benefits for both employees and employers, it also brings challenges that must be addressed. For example, diverse employees may have more difficulty communicating and working with each other. Watlow, an aluminum radiator plant based in Chicago, implemented an English-only policy for business communications in order to smooth communications between English and non-English-speaking employees. After Hispanic workers were allegedly fired for speaking Spanish on the job, the EEOC brought a lawsuit against Watlow. The case was settled for $192,500. Watlow believes its English-only policy is lawful in order to maintain product and service quality. The EEOC disagrees, claiming that such policies are warranted only in safety- and security-sensitive areas.[88] Although differences can breed innovation and creativity, they can also create an atmosphere of distrust or lack of cooperation. Many companies found a way to turn general anger, fear, and confusion over the September 11, 2001, terrorist strikes into an opportunity for discussing diversity and creating stronger bonds between employees of different ethnicities, religions, beliefs, and experiences related to the strikes.

Finally, the diversity message will not be taken seriously unless top management and organizational systems fully support a diverse workforce. After Home Depot settled a sex-discrimination lawsuit, it developed an automated hiring and promotion computer program. Although the Job Preference Program (JPP) was originally intended as insurance against discrimination, the system opens all jobs and applicants to the companywide network, eliminates unqualified applications, and enables managers to learn employee aspirations and skills in a more effective manner. JPP has also brought positive change to the number of female and minority managers within Home Depot.[89] In contrast to this success story, some employees of companies with diversity training programs have viewed such training as intended to blame or change white men only. Other training has focused on the reasons diversity should be important, not the actual changes in attitudes, work styles, expectations, and business processes that are needed for diversity to work.[90]

Work/Life Balance   A recent in-depth study focused on two women and their career and family progression over sixteen years. Both women had great work achievements in their twenties and later decided to marry, have children, and devote more time to family than career. From this study and many others, the authors note the inherent trade-offs between work and family life. They conclude that most working women are typically forced to make tough trade-offs among career goals, child rearing, household management, and economic realities. These are not easy decisions for everyone, thus giving rise to potential stress and conflict at home and work.[91] Just as increasing numbers of women in the workplace have changed norms of behavior at work and prompted attention to sexual harassment, it has also brought challenges in work/life balance. This balance is not just an issue for women, as men also have multiple roles that can create the same types of stress and conflict.[92]

Because employees have roles within and outside the organization, there is increasing corporate focus on the types of support that employees have in balancing these obligations. Deloitte & Touche, an international professional services firm, recently came to grips with issues of work/life balance when it discovered the alarming rate at which women were leaving the firm. In 1991, only four of the fifty employees being considered for partner status were women, despite the company's heavy recruitment of women from business schools throughout the 1980s. A closer examination of the company's turnover rate also illuminated the gender issue, although many executives assumed the women had left to have and raise children. The company convened the Initiative for the Retention and Advancement of Women task force in 1992 and soon uncovered cultural beliefs and practices that needed modification. The task force found that younger employees—both male and female—wanted a balanced life, were willing to forgo some pay for more time with family and less stress, and had similar career goals. Thus, Deloitte & Touche set out to change its culture and operating practices so that all employees were given similar opportunities and to ensure that concerns and issues were open for discussion. A major initiative included reduced travel schedules and flexible work arrangements to benefit both men and women employees of the firm.[93]

Such **work/life programs** assist employees in balancing work responsibilities with personal and family responsibilities. A central feature of these programs is flexibility, so that employees of all types are able to achieve their own definition of balance. For example, a single parent may want child care and consistent work hours, whereas another employee may need assistance in finding elder care or support for a parent with Alzheimer's disease. A working mother may need access to "just in time" care when a child is sick or school is out of session. Employees of all types appreciate flextime arrangements, which allow them to work forty hours per week in a schedule they develop within a range of hours specified by the company. Other employees work some hours at home or in a location more conducive to their personal obligations. Intel, for example, opened several satellite offices in the San Francisco area to minimize the stress some employees experienced as a result of hour-plus-long commutes to and from the company's main office.[94]

More than 65 million Americans suffer from symptoms of stress at work, including headaches, sleeplessness, and other physical ailments. To remedy these concerns, Americans spend more than $370 million per year on stress-reducing products, services, and strategies. Compared to Japanese workers, however, the U.S. figures are moderate. A study by the Japanese Ministry of Health and Welfare found that nearly 60 percent of Japanese employees feel fairly fatigued from work, whereas only 15 to 30 percent of U.S. workers feel the same way. The work ethic in both countries is among the strongest in the world. However, 10,000 Japanese men die every year as a result of job-related stressors, physical problems, and associated psychological ramifications.[95]

There is no generic work/life program. Instead, companies need to consider their employee base and the types of support they are likely to need and appreciate. Successful work/life programs, like that developed by the SAS Institute, are an extension of the diversity philosophy, so that employees are respected as individuals in the process of contributing to company goals. Thus, connecting employees' personal needs, lives, and goals to strategic business issues can be fruitful for both parties. This perspective is in contrast to the "employee goals vs. business goals" trade-off mentality that has been pervasive for decades.[96]

A recent study by jobtrack.com found that nearly 50 percent of all applicants consider work/life balance the most important consideration in identifying potential employers and considering job offers.[97] For this reason, companies have become quite innovative in their approach to work/life balance. Daimler-Chrysler, for example, developed the work/family account, where employees allocate $4,000 for child care, adoption costs, elder care, education costs, or retirement. The allocation will be gradually increased, with a goal of each employee having $8,000 in his or her account by 2003.[98] Cisco Systems opened a $10 million child-care facility at its San Jose, California, headquarters with Internet cameras that enable parents to log on to check on their children even while they are at work.[99] Such efforts are able to accommodate diverse interests and employee needs.

❱ *Philanthropic*

In Chapter 11, we examine the philanthropic efforts of companies and the important role that employees play in the process of selecting and implementing projects that contribute time, resources, and human activity to worthy causes. In corporate citizenship, philanthropic responsibilities are primarily directed outside the organization, so they are not that focused on employees. However, as discussed in Chapter 7, employees benefit from participating in volunteerism and other philanthropic projects. A recent study by the Points of Light Foundation asked corporate executives about the effect of employee volunteerism on organizational competitiveness and success. The surveyed executives reported that this aspect of philanthropy increases employee productivity and builds teamwork skills. In a tight job market, employees may even view philanthropic activity, such as volunteer opportunities, as one criterion in evaluating potential employers. Thus, the benefits of corporate philanthropy in the community reflect back on the organization.[100] McDonald's recently launched a series of web sites intended to serve both employment needs and community relations goals. On a state-by-state basis, the venerable fast-food chain set up sites, such as www.McWisconsin.com and www.McMinnesota.com, to aid both corporate and local franchisees' ability to hire new employees, educate consumers, deliver promotional materials, and reach other business goals.[101]

Strategic Implementation of Responsibilities to Employees

As this chapter has demonstrated, responsibilities toward employees are varied and complex, as legal issues alone require full-time attention from lawyers and human resource specialists. These issues are also emotional, because corporate decisions have ramifications on families and communities, as well as employees. In light of this complexity, many companies have chosen to embrace these obligations to benefit both employee and organizational goals. This philosophy stands in stark contrast to the master–servant model popular more than 100 years ago. Today, companies are using distinctive programs and initiatives to set themselves apart and to become known as employers of choice. Low unemployment levels in the late 1990s, along with diversity, work/life balance, and generational differences, prompted companies to use marketing strategy and business insight normally applied to customer development in the employee recruitment and retention realm. For example, Small Dog Electronics, a small Vermont computer retailer, recently began offering a rather unusual perk in order to satisfy and retain its fourteen employees: dog insurance. The firm, which already allows employees to bring their dogs to work, picks up 80 percent of employees' vet bills, minus a deductible.[102]

Generations at Work

Conflicting views and voices of different generations abound in the workplace, and this is the first time in history that the workforce has been composed of so many generations at one time. Generations have worked together in the past, but these groups were usually divided by organizational stratification. Many workplaces now include members of multiple generations sitting side by side and working shoulder to shoulder. The result may be greater dissension among the age groups than when they were previously stratified by the organizational hierarchy. Because employees serve an important role in the corporate citizenship framework, managers need to be aware of generational differences and their potential effects on teamwork, conflict, and other workplace behaviors.

Veterans, people born between 1922 and 1943, tend to bring stability and loyalty to the workplace. Although veterans are very hard working and detail oriented, they are often uncomfortable with conflict and ambiguity and reluctant to buck the system. The *Baby Boomers,* born generally between 1943 and 1960, are service oriented, are good team players, and want to please. However, they are also known for being self-centered, overly sensitive to feedback, and not naturally budget minded. People born between 1961 and 1980, known as *Generation X,* are adaptable, technologically literate, independent, and not intimidated by authority. However, their liabilities include impatience, cynicism, and inexperience. The latest generation to enter the workforce, the *Nexters,* is technologically savvy. They also bring the assets of collective action, optimism, and tenacity to the workplace. However, they bring the liabilities of inexperience, especially with difficult people issues, and a need for supervision and structure.

Although generational issues existed in the workforce in the 1920s and the 1960s, there are some new twists to today's generations. The older generations no longer have all the money and power. Times of anxiety and uncertainty can aggra-

An **employer of choice** is an organization of any size in any industry that is able to attract, optimize, and retain the best employee talent over the long term.[103] Firms with this distinction value the human component of business, not just financial considerations, ensure that employees are engaged in meaningful work, and stimulate the intellectual curiosity of employees.[104] Thus, becoming an employer of choice is an important manifestation of strategic citizenship. Advertising, web sites, and other company communications often use the term to describe and market the organization to current and potential employees. These messages center on the various practices that companies have implemented to create employee satisfaction. For example, the Employer of Choice Initiatives in the Electronics Sector of Lockheed Martin focus on providing competitive com-

vate differences and generational conflict, and these conflicts need to be handled correctly when they occur. Understanding the different generations and how they see things is a crucial part of handling this conflict. The Generation Xers and the Nexters probably want the same things as the Veterans and Baby Boomers, but they tend to go about achieving them in different ways. This is why it is crucial to understand where different groups are coming from and how they view things. The same goes for the younger generations. They should not ignore the older generations, and they shouldn't expect the older generations to accommodate them. It is a two-way street.

Ron Zemke, Claire Raines, and Bob Filipczak, authors of *Generations at Work: Managing the Clash of Veterans, Boomers, Xers, and Nexters in Your Workplace,* developed the ACORN, five principles that managers can use deal with generational issues. *Accommodating* employee differences entails treating employees as customers and giving them the best service that the company can give. This is crucial in retaining good employees, regardless of their generation, especially in tight job markets. *Creating* workplace choices as

to what and how employees work can allow for change and satisfaction. Casual dress policies, less hierarchy and bureaucracy, and more job switching are all aspects of allowing choices for employees. *Operating* from a sophisticated management style requires that management be direct but tactful. All generations want good leadership that is also thoughtful and can handle big problems. *Respecting* competence and initiative assumes the best from the different generations and responds accordingly. *Nourishing* retention means keeping the best employees. Managers should view the workplace as a magnet for excellence rather than an anvil for hammering out good employees. When combined with aggressive communication efforts, the ACORN principles can help managers mend generational conflicts for the benefit of everyone in the company. ∎

Sources:
Jeffrey B. Cufaude, "Cultivating New Leadership," *Association Management,* 52 (January 2000): 73; Scott Hays, "Generation X and the Art of the Reward," *Workforce,* 78 (November 1999): 45; Jennifer Salopek, "Interview with Rom Zemke," *Training and Development,* 54 (January 2000): 60; and Ron Zemke, Claire Raines, and Bob Filipczak, *Generations at Work: Managing the Clash of Veterans, Boomers, Xers, and Nexters in Your Workplace* (New York: AMACOM, 2000).

pensation and a strong benefits package, maintaining balance between work and personal life, providing training and employee development opportunities, and utilizing other programs to ensure employee pride and a positive company reputation.[105]

Becoming an employer of choice has many benefits, including the enhanced ability to hire and retain the best people. The expectations of such businesses are very high because employee stakeholders have specific criteria in mind when assessing the attractiveness of a particular employer. Although top managers must decide on how the firm will achieve strategic citizenship with employees, Table 8.4 provides general guidance on some of the best practices that are implemented by employers of choice.

TABLE 8.4

Best Practices of Employers of Choice

Practice	Explanation
Foster openness	Give all employees full access to company information.
Foster community	Instill in employees a concern for coworkers and society at large.
Foster creativity	Allow workers to create their own work environments.
Foster loyalty	Train workers extensively, then pay them generously for greater productivity.
Foster responsibility	Put new workers in charge and move them quickly through the ranks.
Foster individuality	Allow workers to do their own thing, no matter how wacky their thing is.
Foster teamwork	Throw out the old management hierarchy and encourage group over individual success.

Source: Mark Mazetti, "Managing, Texas-Style," *Texas Monthly,* 28 (December 2000): 64–78.

 Summary

Throughout history, humans' perception of the concept of work and employment has evolved from necessary evil to source of fulfillment. The relationship between employer and employee involves responsibilities, obligations, and expectations as well as challenges.

On an economic level, many believe there is an unwritten, informal psychological contract that includes the beliefs, perceptions, expectations, and obligations that comprise the agreement between individuals and their employers. This contract has evolved from a primarily master–servant relationship, in which employers held the power, to one in which employees assume a more balanced relationship with employers. Workforce reduction, the process of eliminating employment positions, breaches the psychological contract that exists between an employer and employee and threatens the social contract between employers, communities, and other groups. Although workforce reduction lowers costs, it often results in lost intellectual capital, strained customer relationships, negative media attention, and other issues that drain company resources.

Employment law is a complex and evolving area. In the past, employment was primarily governed by employment at will, a common-law doctrine that allows either the employer or employee to terminate the relationship at any time as long as it does not violate an employment contract. Many laws have been enacted to regulate business conduct with regard to wages and benefits, labor unions, health and safety, equal employment opportunity, sexual harassment, and whistle-blowing. Title VII of the Civil Rights Act, which prohibits employment discrimination on the basis of race, national origin, color, religion, and gender, is fundamental to employees' rights to join and advance in an organization according to merit. Sexual harassment is defined as unwelcome sexual advances, requests for sexual favors, and other verbal or physical conduct of a sexual nature when submission to or rejection of this conduct explicitly or implicitly affects an individual's employment, unreasonably interferes with an individual's work performance, or creates an intimidating, hostile, or offensive work environment. Sexual harassment may take the form of either quid pro quo harassment or hostile work environment harassment. An employee who reports individual or corporate wrongdoing to either internal or external sources is considered a whistle-blower.

Although legal compliance is imperative for corporate citizenship, the ethical climate of the workplace is more subjective and dependent on top management support and corporate culture. Companies with a strong ethical stance fund initiatives to develop employees' skills, knowledge, and other personal characteristics. With diversity programs, companies assume an ethical obligation to employ and empower individuals, regardless of age, gender, physical and mental ability, and other characteristics. Work/life programs assist employees in balancing work responsibilities with personal and family responsibilities.

Employees may play an important role in a firm's philanthropic efforts. Employees benefit from such initiatives through participation in volunteerism and other projects.

In light of the complexity of and emotions involved with responsibilities toward employees, many companies have chosen to embrace these obligations to benefit both employee and organizational goals. An employer of choice is an organization of any size in any industry that is able to attract, optimize, and retain the best employee talent over the long term.

psychological contract

workforce reduction

employment at will

vesting

ergonomics

affirmative action programs

sexual harassment

quid pro quo harassment

hostile work environment harassment

whistle-blower

workplace diversity

work/life programs

employer of choice

DISCUSSION QUESTIONS

1. Review Table 8.1, Changes in Employees' Psychological Contract with Employers. Create additional columns to indicate the positive and negative effects associated with the "old" and "new" contract characteristics. For example, what is positive and negative about the belief that employees should follow orders? What is positive and negative about giving 110 percent effort on the job?

2. What is workforce reduction? How does it affect employees, consumers, and the local community? What steps should a company take to address these effects?

3. What responsibilities do companies have with respect to workplace violence? Using the three categories of violence presented in the chapter, describe the responsibilities and actions that you believe are necessary for an organization to demonstrate corporate citizenship in that area.

4. Describe the differences between workplace diversity and equal employment opportunity. How do these differences affect managerial responsibilities and the development of corporate citizenship programs?

5. Why are organizations developing work/life programs? What trends have contributed to these programs?

6. What is an employer of choice? Describe how a firm could use traditional marketing concepts and strategies to appeal to current and potential employees.

7. Review the seven suggestions (Table 8.4) for becoming an employer of choice. What are some potential drawbacks to each tactic? Rank the seven suggestions in terms of their importance to you.

EXPERIENTIAL EXERCISE

Develop a list of five criteria that describes your "employer of choice." Then visit the web sites of three companies in which you have some employment interest. Peruse each firm's web site to find evidence on how it fulfills your criteria. Based on this evidence, develop a chart to show how well each firm meets your description and criteria of an employer of choice. Finally, provide three recommendations on how these companies can better communicate their commitment to employees and the employer-of-choice criteria.

NOTES

1. Michelle Conlin and Kathy Moore, "Dr. Goodnight's Company Town," *Fortune,* June 19, 2000, pp. 192–202; "About SAS Institute," SAS Institute, www.sas.com/corporate/index.html, accessed December 11, 2000; Karen Govel McDermott, "Walking the Talk at SAS Institute," *Nation's Restaurant News,* 3 (June 2000): 38; Lance Secretan, "Customer Connections," *Industry Week,* May 15, 2000, p. 25.

2. Joanne B. Ciulla, *The Working Life: The Promise and Betrayal of Modern Work* (New York: Times Books, 2000).

3. Ciulla, *The Working Life*; Adriano Tilgher, *Work: What It Has Meant to Men Through the Ages,* trans. Dorothy Canfield Fisher (New York: Harcourt, Brace & World, 1958).

4. These facts are derived from Brenda Paik Sunoo, "Relying on Faith to Rebuild a Business," *Workforce,* 78 (March 1999): 54-59.

5. Karen Sarkis, "Injured Workers File Claim with Malden Mills," *Occupational Hazards,* 62 (February 2000): 16.

6. Sunoo, "Relying on Faith to Rebuild a Business."

7. Michelle Conlin, Peter Coy, Ann Therese Palmer, and Gabrielle Saveri, "The Wild New Workforce," *Business Week,* December 6, 1999, pp. 38-44.

8. Denise M. Rousseau, *Psychological Contracts in Organizations: Understanding Written and Unwritten Agreements* (Thousand Oaks, Calif.: Sage, 1995).

9. William H. Turnley and Daniel C. Feldman, "The Impact of Psychological Contract Violations on Exit, Voice, Loyalty, and Neglect," *Human Relations,* 52 (July 1999): 895-922.

10. Ibid.

11. Kimberly D. Elsbach and Greg Elafson, "How the Packaging of Decision Explanations Affects Perceptions of Trustworthiness," *Academy of Management Journal,* 43 (February 2000): 80-89.

12. Gillian Flynn, "Looking Back on 100 Years of Employment Law," *Workforce,* 78 (November 1999): 74-77.

13. "A Guru Ahead of Her Time," *Nation's Business,* 85 (May 1997): 24.

14. Steve Sayer, "Cleaning Up the Jungle," *Occupational Health & Safety,* 66 (May 1997): 22.

15. Flynn, "Looking Back on 100 Years of Employment Law."

16. "Employee Relations in America," *IRS Employment Review* (March 1997): E7-E12; Roger LeRoy Miller and Gaylord A. Jentz, *Business Law Today* (Cincinnati: West Legal Studies in Business, 2000).

17. C. Wright Mills, *White Collar: The American, Middle Classes* (New York: Oxford University Press, 1951).

18. Ciulla, *The Working Life*; William H. Whyte, *The Organization Man* (New York: Simon & Schuster, 1956).

19. *Work in America: Report of a Special Task Force to the Secretary of Health, Education, and Welfare* (Cambridge, Mass.: MIT Press, 1973).

20. Ciulla, *The Working Life.*

21. Taina Savolainen, "Leadership Strategies for Gaining Business Excellence Through Total Quality Management: A Finnish Case Study," *Total Quality Management,* 11 (March 2000): 211-226.

22. "Younger Employees Want Security," *USA Today,* October 3, 2001, p. 1B.

23. This section is adapted from Debbie Thorne LeClair, "The Ups and Downs of Rightsizing the Workplace," *ABACA Profile,* November-December 1999, p. 25.

24. Priti Pradhan Shah, "Network Destruction: The Structural Implications of Downsizing," *Academy of Management Journal,* 43 (February 2000): 101-112.

25. *New York Times Special Report: The Downsizing of America* (New York: Times Books, 1996); Victor B. Wayhan and Steve Werner, "The Impact of Workforce Reductions on Financial Performance: A Longitudinal Perspective," *Journal of Management,* 26 (2000): 341-363; Jennifer Laabs, "The New Loyalty: Grasp It, Earn It, Keep It," *Workforce,* 77 (November 1998): 34-39.

26. Harry J. Van Buren, III, "The Bindingness of Social and Psychological Contracts: Toward a Theory of Social Responsibility in Downsizing," *Journal of Business Ethics,* 25 (January 2000): 205-219.

27. Steve Beigbeder, "Easing Workforce Reduction," *Risk Management,* 47 (May 2000): 26-30.

28. Robert A. Nozar, "Nashville's Hot Job Market May Absorb Opryland Cuts," *Hotel and Motel Management,* 214 (August 1999): 4, 40.

29. Angelo J. Kinicki, Gregory E. Prussia, and Francis M. McKee-Ryan, "A Panel Study of Coping with Involuntary Job Loss," *Academy of Management Journal,* 43 (February 2000): 90-100.

30. Wayhan and Werner, "The Impact of Workforce Reductions on Financial Performance."

31. Nicholas Stein, "Winning the War to Keep Top Talent," *Fortune,* May 29, 2000, pp. 132-138.

32. Kathleen Melymuka, "Showing the Value of Brainpower," *Computerworld,* March 27, 2000, pp. 58-59.

33. Kyle Dover, "Watch the External Traps," *Management Review,* 88 (January 1999): 54; Susan Reynolds

Fisher and Margaret A. White, "Downsizing in a Learning Organization," *Academy of Management Review,* 25 (January 2000) 244–251.

34. Susan Beck, "What to Do Before You Say 'You're Outta Here,'" *Business Week,* December 8, 1997, p. 6.

35. United States Department of Labor, *Small Business Handbook.* www.dol.gov/asp/programs/handbook, accessed November 1, 2001.

36. Miller and Jentz, *Business Law Today.*

37. Flynn, "Looking Back on 100 Years of Employment Law."

38. Robert J. Nobile, "HR's Top 10 Legal Issues," *HR Focus,* 74 (April 1997): 19–20.

39. Miller and Jentz, *Business Law Today.*

40. Flynn, "Looking Back on 100 Years of Employment Law."

41. Peter Elstrom, "Needed: A New Union for the New Economy," *Business Week,* September 4, 2000, p. 48.

42. *The New OSHA: Reinventing Worker Safety and Health* (Washington, D.C.: Department of Labor, Occupational Safety and Health Administration, 1995), available at www.osha.gov/oshinfo/reinvent/reinvent.html.

43. Judith N. Mottl, "Industry Fights OSHA's Proposed Ergonomic Rule," *Informationweek,* June 19, 2000, p. 122; Daniel R. Miller, "OSHA Goes Too Far with Ergonomics Rules," *National Underwriter,* May 8, 2000, p. 59; John D. Schulz, "Trucking Wants Out," *Traffic World,* May 29, 2000, pp. 21–22.

44. "Workplace Violence," Occupational Safety and Health Administration, July 29, 2000, www.osha-slc.gov/SLTC/workplaceviolence/index.html.

45. Karen Sarkis, "Workplace Violence Top Concern for Employers," *Occupational Hazards,* 62 (June 2000): 23.

46. *Fear and Violence in the Workplace: A Survey Documenting the Experiences of American Workers* (Minneapolis: Northwestern National Life Insurance Company, 1993).

47. *Cal/OSHA Guidelines for Workplace Security* (State of California: 1995), available at www.dir.ca.gov/DOSH/dosh_publications/worksecurity.html.

48. Steve Rubenstein, "Flight Attendants Fight 'Air Rage,'" *San Francisco Chronicle,* July 7, 2000, p. A2; Alan Levin, "'Air Rage' a Threat on Flights," *USA Today,* June 12, 2000, p. 1.

49. "Suspect in Honolulu Shooting Spree Faces First-Degree Murder Charges," CNN, November 3, 1999, www.cnn.com; "Xerox Hawaii Cited Unsafe in Connection with Mass Shooting," CNN, November 7, 2000, www.cnn.com.

50. Richard V. Denenberg and Mark Braverman, *The Violence-Prone Workplace: A New Approach to Dealing with Hostile, Threatening, and Uncivil Behavior* (Ithaca, N.Y.: Cornell University Press, 1999); Bill Merrick, "Make Work a Safe Place," *Credit Union Magazine,* 66 (June 2000): 19.

51. John Leming, "New Product Covers Losses Related to Workplace Violence," *Journal of Commerce,* April 6, 2000, p. 15.

52. Judy Greenwald, "Employers Confront AIDS in Africa," *Business Insurance,* 35 (July 23, 2001): 15.

53. "What Is Affirmative Action," HR Content Library, www.hrnext.com/content/view.cfm?articles_id=2007&subs_id=32, accessed November 1, 2001.

54. "What Affirmative Action Is (And What It Is Not)," National Partnership, www.nationalpartnership.org/workandfamily/workplace/affirmact/aa_whatitis.htm, accessed November 1, 2001.

55. "What Is Affirmative Action."

56. "What Affirmative Action Is (And What It Is Not)."

57. Ibid.

58. *U.S. Equal Employment Opportunity Commission: An Overview* (Washington, D.C.: U.S. Equal Employment Opportunity Commission, 1997), available at www.eeoc.gov/overview.html.

59. "Jury Awards $13 Million in Disability Discrimination Case," Equal Employment Opportunity Commission, press release, November 6, 1999, www.eeoc.gov/press/11-06-99.html.

60. "Facts About Sexual Harassment," U.S. Equal Employment Opportunity Commission, www.eeoc.gov/facts/fs-sex.html, accessed November 1, 2001.

61. Donald J. Petersen and Douglas P. Massengill, "Sexual Harassment Cases Five Years After *Meritor Savings Bank v. Vinson*," *Employee Relations Law Journal,* 18 (Winter 1992–1993): 489–516.

62. Maria E. Conway, "Sexual Harassment Abroad," *Workforce,* 77 (September 1998): 8–9.

63. "EU Bids to Outlaw Sexual Harassment at the Workplace," European Commission, press release, June 7, 2000, www.eubusiness.com/employ/index.html.

64. Robert D. Lee and Paul S. Greenlaw, "The Legal Evolution of Sexual Harassment," *Public Administration Review,* 55 (July 1995): 357-364.

65. Ibid.

66. George D. Mesritz, "Hostile Environment Sexual Harassment Claims: When Once Is Enough," *Employee Relations Law Journal,* 22 (Spring 1997): 79-85; Laura Hoffman Roppe, "*Harris v. Forklift Systems, Inc.*: Victory or Defeat?" *The San Diego Law Review,* 32 (Winter 1996): 321-342.

67. Joann Muller, "Ford: The High Cost of Harassment," *Business Week,* November 15, 1999, pp. 94-96.

68. "Mitsubishi Agrees to $34 Million Sexual Harassment Settlement," *Business Week,* June 15, 1998, pp. 1-3; Samuel Greengard, "Zero Tolerance: Making It Work," *Workforce,* 78 (May 1999): 28-34.

69. Jonathan W. Dion, "Putting Employers on the Defense: The Supreme Court Develops a Consistent Standard Regarding an Employer's Liability for a Supervisor's Hostile Work Environment Sexual Harassment," *Wake Forest Law Review,* 34 (Spring 1999): 199-227; Darlene Orlov and Michael T. Roumell, *What Every Manager Needs to Know About Sexual Harassment* (New York: Amacom, 1999).

70. Richard Korman, David Kohn, Stephen H. Daniels, and Janice I. Dixon, "The Jokes Aren't Very Funny Anymore," *Engineering News Record,* September 7, 1998, p. 26.

71. This section is adapted from Randy Chiu, Richard Tansey, Debbie Thorne, and Michael White, "Is Procedural Justice the Dominant Whistleblowing Motive Among Employees?" submitted to *Journal of Applied Psychology,* June 2000.

72. J. P Near and M. P. Miceli, "Organizational Dissidence: The Case of Whistleblowing," *Journal of Business Ethics,* 4 (January 1985): 1-16.

73. Nancy Klingener, "Case Ends Utility Suit, but Plane Crash Still a Mystery," *Miami Herald,* May 8, 1991, p. B4.

74. Ron Ruggles, "Education, Training Is Beneficial to Employees 'Knowing It All' About Industry," *Nation's Restaurant News,* October 16, 2000, pp. 80, 162.

75. Jill Schachner Chanen, "You Rang, Sir?" *ABA Journal,* 86 (October 2000): 82-84.

76. Jennifer Brown, "Employees Leave Managers, Not Organizations," *Computing Canada,* 27 (April 6, 2001): 25.

77. Betsy Cummings, "Training's Top Five," *Successful Meetings,* 49 (October 2000): 67-73; Adam J. Grossberg, "The Effect of Formal Training on Employment Duration," *Industrial Relations,* 39 (October 2000): 578-599.

78. Mark E. Van Buren and Stephen B. King, *ASTD's Annual Accounting of Worldwide Patterns in Employer-Provided Training* (Alexandria, Va.: American Society for Training and Development, 2000).

79. "Diversity: A 'New' Tool for Retention," *HR Focus,* 77 (June 2000): 1, 14.

80. Vijay Govindarajan and Anil K. Gupta, "Building an Effective Global Business Team," *MIT Sloan Management Review,* 42 (Summer 2001): 63-71; Robin Kramer, "Managing Diversity: Beyond Affirmative Action in Australia," *Women in Management Review,* 13, no. 4 (1998): 133-142.

81. Rose Mary Wentling and Nilda Palma-Rivas, "Current Status of Diversity Initiatives in Selected Multinational Corporations," *Human Resource Development Quarterly,* 11 (Spring 2000): 35-60.

82. Marilyn Loden and Judith B. Rosener, *Workforce America! Managing Employee Diversity as a Vital Resource* (Burr Ridge, Ill.: Irwin/McGraw-Hill, 1991).

83. "Diversity Low Priority Reaps Low Numbers," *Editor & Publisher,* April 17, 2000, p. 16.

84. Ira Teinowitz, "Courting Change," *Advertising Age,* 72 (May 14, 2001): 16-20.

85. Debby Scheinholtz, "Ernst & Young's New Leadership Vows Strong Commitment to Diversity," *DiversityInc.,* July 5, 2000, www.diversityinc.com.

86. Cathy Lynn Crossman, "Wisconsin Restaurant Fills Staff with Workers Once Thought Unemployable," CNN, February 16, 2000, www.cnn.com.

87. "Verizon Takes the Lead in Business Network to Promote Employment of People with Disabilities," press release, November 1, 2000, Corporate Social Responsibility Newswire, CSRwire.com, www.csrwire.com/article.cgi/490.html.

88. Stephanie Ernst, "Fired for Speaking Spanish on the Job," *DiversityInc.,* September 5, 2000, www.diversityinc.com.

89. Cora Daniels, "To Hire a Lumber Expert, Click Here," *Fortune,* April 3, 2000, pp. 267-270.

90. Judy Zhu and Brian Kleiner, "The Failure of Diversity Training," *Nonprofit World,* 18 (May/June 2000): 12-14.

91. Robert D. Winsor and Ellen A. Ensher, "Choices Made in Balancing Work and Family: Following Two Women on a 16-year Journey," *Journal of Management Inquiry,* 9 (June 2000): 218–231.

92. Jeffrey R. Edwards and Nancy P. Rothbard, "Mechanisms Linking Work and Family," *Academy of Management Review,* 25 (January 2000): 178–199.

93. Douglas M. McCracken, "Winning the Talent War for Women: Sometimes It Takes a Revolution," *Harvard Business Review,* 78 (November/December 2000): 159–167.

94. Pui-Wing Tam, "Silicon Valley Belatedly Boots Up Programs to Ease Employees' Lives," *Wall Street Journal Interactive,* August 29, 2000, http://interactive.wsj.com/.

95. Rebecca Segall, "Japanese Killer," *Psychology Today,* 33 (September/October 2000): 10–11.

96. Lotte Bailyn, Joyce K. Fletcher, and Deborah Kolb, "Unexpected Connections: Considering Employees' Personal Lives Can Revitalize Your Business," *Sloan Management Review,* 38 (Summer 1997): 11–20.

97. Michael A. Verespej, "Balancing Act," *Industry Week,* May 15, 2000, pp. 81–85.

98. Debby Scheinholtz, "Work/Life Professionals Discuss Trends for the 21st Century," *DiversityInc.,* March 16, 2000, www.diversityinc.com/.

99. Pui-Wing Tam, "Silicon Valley Belatedly Boots Up Programs to Ease Employees Lives."

100. "Corporate Volunteerism," Points of Light Foundation, www.pointsoflight.org/assistance/assistance_corporate.html, accessed December 11, 2000.

101. Alan J. Liddle, "McD Franchisees Make Online Mc-State-ment to Workers, Communities," *Nation's Restaurant News,* September 18, 2000, pp. 19, 94.

102. "Small Dog Gives Pet Perk," CNNfn, July 10, 2000, www.cnnfn.com.

103. Roger E. Herman and Joyce L. Gioia, *How to Become an Employer of Choice* (Winchester, Va.: Oakhill Press, 2000).

104. Ibid.

105. "Employer of Choice," Electronics Sector, Lockheed Martin, http://electronics.external.lmco.com/elec-sector/choice/index.html, accessed July 7, 2000.

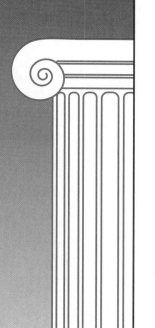

Environment Issues

9

▶ Global Environmental Issues

▶ Environmental Policy and Regulation

▶ Business Response to Environmental Issues

▶ Strategic Implementation of Environmental Responsibility

OBJECTIVES

To define the nature of the natural environment as it relates to corporate citizenship

To explore a variety of environmental issues faced by business and society

To examine the impact of environmental policy and regulations

To discuss a strategic approach to respond to environmental issues

M any companies today face a dilemma: Should they invest resources in creating, supporting, and maintaining organizational initiatives that protect the natural environment? By striving to be one of the most environmentally conscious companies, Herman Miller, Inc. has answered that question with a resounding yes. The ergonomic furniture maker has implemented a comprehensive strategy to protect the environment. Today, Miller's environmental responsibility initiatives encompass every element of its product supply chain, from the acquisition of raw materials through production and design, to the end user who ultimately purchases its furniture.

Herman Miller has committed to designing and manufacturing environmentally friendly furniture that has minimal impact on the environment. The strategy begins with an analysis of the "life cycle" of raw materials and finished goods to identify opportunities to reduce, reuse, and recycle. For example, the company is increasingly replacing its paint and lacquer finishes with a powder coat technology that uses fewer volatile organic compounds (VOCs). Toxic glues used in foam application have been replaced with water-based ones that are less harmful to the environment. The company also chooses woods carefully to ensure that they come from renewable sources. In fact, one of Herman Miller's most famous designs, the Eames lounge chair, is no longer made of rosewood due to diminishing renewable supplies of that wood. Some furniture requires simple assembly to compress space and box requirements, thereby reducing waste. The company also seeks ways to combine outgoing delivery shipments with incoming raw material pickups to move products with the greatest efficiency possible. Miller is also establishing an Internet presence to sell directly to the consumer, eliminating the waste of "double shipping" to stores and then to customers as well as other expenses. The company requires its suppliers to replace single-use packaging materials with packaging that can be reused. It also gives preferential treatment to suppliers that use recycled materials in their products.

Although many companies have become more environmentally responsible by improving their products, Herman Miller has gone a step farther by designing and managing production facilities that function as efficiently as possible, thereby reducing waste and energy use. The buildings employ natural light whenever possible. Awnings have been installed over factory and office windows to reduce cooling costs in the summer, but retract to take advantage of the sun's energy for wintertime heating. Landscaping on the company site incorporates local natural prairies and meadows that require no additional energy for maintenance. Miller's "Energy Center" converts material waste into heat to boil water to generate energy that can be used for manufacturing processes.

Miller's environmental initiatives have not only supported its founder's and managers' own personal beliefs of environmental stewardship and self-actualization, but have also proven effective in reducing costs and building shareholder value. While

Herman Miller has invested in the environment, it has also reduced waste and improved overall operating efficiency. For example, the Energy Plant has reduced landfill and fuel costs by $750,000 a year. In addition, the firm saves $250,000 a year in shipping and packaging materials. Herman Miller has embraced a strategic approach to making the natural environment an important concern in achieving long-run success.[1]

As Herman Miller's efforts illustrate, public and business support for environmental causes has increased since the first Earth Day was held in 1970. Four out of five respondents in a Gallup poll reported that they agree with the goals of the environmental movement, and another 80 percent indicated that they have participated in environmentally conscious activities such as recycling, avoiding products that harm the environment, trying to use less water, and reducing household consumption of energy.[2] Another survey found that 83.5 percent of *Fortune* 500 respondents have a written environmental policy, 74.7 percent recycle, and 69.7 percent have made investments in waste-reduction efforts.[3]

In this chapter, we explore the concept of the natural environment in the context of strategic corporate citizenship in today's complex business environment. First, we define the natural environment and explore some of the significant environmental issues that businesses and society face. Next we consider the impact of government environmental policy and regulation on business and examine how some companies are going beyond the scope of these laws to address environmental issues and act in an environmentally responsible manner. Finally, we highlight a strategic approach to environmental issues, including risk management and strategic audits.

Global Environmental Issues

Most people probably associate the term *environment* with nature, including wildlife, trees, oceans, rivers, mountains, and prairies. Until the twentieth century, people generally thought of the environment solely in terms of how these resources could be harnessed to satisfy their needs for food, shelter, transportation, and recreation. As the earth's population swelled throughout the twentieth century, however, humans began to use more and more of these resources, and, with technological advancements, to do so with ever-greater efficiency. Although these conditions have resulted in a much-improved standard of living, they come with a cost. Plant and animal species, along with wildlife habitats, are disappearing at an accelerated rate; water use has become a critical issue in some parts of the globe; and pollution has rendered some cities to a gloomy haze. How to deal with these issues has become a major concern for business and society in the twenty-first century.

Land pollution presents an on-going challenge to the EPA. This EPA scientist is testing the soil in California for arsenic.

Although the scope of the natural environment is quite broad—including plants, animals, human beings, oceans and other waterways, land, and the atmosphere—in this book, we discuss the term from a strategic business perspective. Thus, we define the **natural environment** as the physical world, including all biological entities, as well as the interaction among nature and individuals, organizations, and business strategies. In recent years, business has played a significant role in adapting, using, and maintaining the quality of the natural environment.

The protection of air, water, land, biodiversity, and renewable natural resources emerged as a major issue in the twentieth century in the face of increasing evidence that pollution, uncontrolled use of natural resources, and population growth were putting increasing pressure on the long-term sustainability of these resources. As the environmental movement sounded the alarm over these issues, governments around the globe responded with environmental protection laws during the 1970s. In recent years, companies have been increasingly incorporating these issues into their overall business strategies. Most of these issues have been the focus of concerned citizens as well as government and corporate efforts. Some nonprofit organizations have stepped forward to provide leadership in gaining the cooperation of diverse groups in responsible environmental activities. For example, the Coalition for Environmentally Responsible Economies (CERES), a coalition of businesses, consumer groups, environmentalists, and other stakeholders, has established a set of goals for environmental performance.

In this section, we examine some of the most significant environmental issues facing business and society today, including air pollution, acid rain, global warming, water pollution and water quantity, land pollution, waste management, deforestation, urban sprawl, biodiversity, and genetically modified foods.

Atmospheric Issues

Among the most far-reaching, and controversial, environmental issues are those that relate to the air we breathe. These include air pollution, acid rain, and global warming.

Air Pollution   Air pollution typically arises from three different origins: stationary sources such as factories and power plants; mobile sources such as cars, trucks, planes, and trains; and natural occurrences such as windblown dust and volcanic eruptions.[4] These sources discharge gases, as well as particulates that can be carried long distances by surface winds or linger on the surface for days if lack of winds or geographic conditions permit. Mexico City, for example, is surrounded by mountains, which trap the emissions from automobiles and industry and leave that city with the poorest air quality in the world. Such conditions can cause respiratory problems (e.g., asthma, bronchitis, allergies) in humans and animals, especially in the elderly and the very young. Some of the chemicals associated with air pollution may contribute to birth defects, cancer, and brain, nerve, and respiratory system damage. Air pollution can also harm plants, animals, and water bodies. Haze caused by air pollution can reduce visibility, interfering with aviation, driving, and recreation.[5]

Acid Rain   In addition to the health risks posed by air pollution, when nitrous oxides and sulfur dioxides emitted from manufacturing facilities react with air and rain, the result is acid rain. This phenomenon has contributed to the deaths of many valuable forests and lakes in North America as well as in Europe. Acid rain can also corrode paint and deteriorate stone, leaving automobiles, buildings, and cultural resources such as architecture and outside art vulnerable unless they are protected from its effects.[6]

Global Warming   When carbon dioxide and other gases collect in the earth's atmosphere, they trap the sun's heat like a greenhouse and prevent the earth's surface from cooling. Without this process, the planet would become too cold to sustain life. However, during the twentieth century, the burning of fossil fuels—gasoline, natural gas, oil, and coal-accelerated dramatically, increasing the concentration of "greenhouse" gases like carbon dioxide and methane in the earth's atmosphere. Chlorofluorocarbons—from refrigerants, coolants, and aerosol cans—also harm the earth's

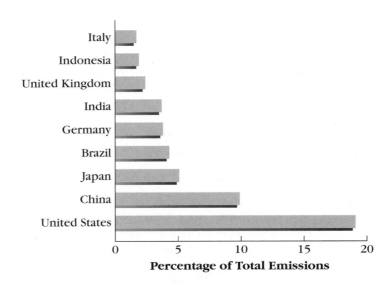

FIGURE 9.1

Leading Emitters of
Greenhouse Gases
(by percentage)

Source: Miles O'Brien, "Causes of Global Warming: Messing with the Thermostat Can Be Devastating," CNN, www.cnn.com/SPECIALS/1997/global.warming/causes/, accessed December 10, 2001.

ozone layer, which filters out the sun's harmful ultraviolet light. The United States produces almost 20 percent of all the greenhouse gases emitted (Figure 9.1).[7]

Many scientists believe that increasing concentrations of greenhouse gases like methane and carbon dioxide in the atmosphere are warming the planet. In fact, accumulations of greenhouse gases have increased dramatically since preindustrial times.[8] The accumulation of these gases does appear to have increased average temperatures by an estimated 1° F over the last century. The year 2000—with many cities breaking records for the longest period without rain since the Dust Bowl of the 1930s and for the highest number of days over 100° F—was the hottest year on record. Although 1° doesn't sound like much change, it is sufficient to increase the rate of polar ice sheet melting, which has already started to occur. Additionally, larger-than-normal icebergs are breaking away from the Antarctic ice shelf and drifting into shipping lanes. If this global warming continues, scientists warn that the planet's polar ice caps will begin to melt, potentially raising the sea level and perhaps flooding some of the world's most populated areas. With less snow and ice cover to reflect the sun's rays, the earth absorbs even more of the sun's heat, accelerating the warming process. Some scientists also think that global warming may alter long-term weather patterns, causing drought in some parts of the world while bringing floods to others.[9]

The theory of global warming has been rather controversial, and some scientists continue to dispute its existence. Critics of global warming argue that apparent temperature increases are part of a natural cycle of temperature variation that the planet has experienced over millions of years. Many companies and organizations have also maligned the theory. Indeed, one of the most aggressive critics has been the Global Climate Coalition, an alliance of electric utilities, coal and oil companies, petrochemical manufacturers, automakers, and related trade associations. The coalition has sponsored scientific research, public speaking tours, and advertising campaigns in an effort to thwart the **Kyoto Protocol,** a treaty proposed among industrialized nations to slow global warming. In the face of mounting evidence in support of global warming, however, many member firms have left the organization in recent years, including BP Amoco, Royal Dutch Shell, Dow Chemical, Ford, DaimlerChrysler, and Texaco.[10] The Kyoto treaty continues to be a controversial and contentious issue in global politics. The United States has balked at signing the treaty, which would require slashing its greenhouse gas emissions to a level of 7 percent below that released in 1990 by 2012, because leaders fear that compliance would jeopardize American businesses and the economy.[11]

▶ *Water Issues*

Water Pollution Water pollution results from the dumping of raw sewage and toxic chemicals into rivers and oceans, from oil and gasoline spills, and from the burial of industrial wastes in the ground where they may filter into underground water supplies. Fertilizers and pesticides used in farming and grounds maintenance also drain into water supplies with each rainfall. When these chemicals reach the oceans, they encourage the growth of algae that use up all the nearby oxygen, thus killing the sea life. According to the Environmental Protection Agency (EPA), more than a third of the nation's rivers, lakes, and coastal waters are not safe for swimming or fishing as a result of contaminated runoff. Lake Chaplain and the Great Lakes, for example, have been polluted by mercury-contaminated rain caused by air pollution from coal-burning power plants, making the waters' fish unsafe to eat.[12] Water pollution problems are especially notable in heavily industrialized areas.

Water pollution can affect drinking water quality, whether a community obtains its water from surface reservoirs (rivers and lakes) or underground aquifers. In central Texas, for example, local citizens concerned about gasoline leaks contaminating drinking water supplies have vehemently protested a project to refit a fifty-year-old pipeline to carry gasoline across the state, directly over one major aquifer. One out of five drinking water systems in the United States is in violation of federal safety standards, and nearly one million Americans get sick every year because of contaminated water, according to a report by the EPA.[13] One source of water contamination may be somewhat surprising. Researchers have found traces of antibiotics and other pharmaceuticals in streams, rivers, and municipal water supplies in the United States and Europe. Scientists worry that the presence of antibiotics in water supplies may

The Nature Con-
servancy works
with businesses
and communities
to protect
our natural
environment.

encourage the development of "superbugs," infection-causing bacteria that are im-
mune to currently available antibiotics.[14]

Mark Van Putton, president of the National Wildlife Foundation, believes that
many states are ignoring federal legislation and regulations that would improve
water quality. Many states have not aggressively enforced federal requirements,
and many sources of pollution—agribusiness, logging, and power plants—often
have strong political power to resist efforts to regulate their operations in ways
that would reduce discharges that contaminate water supplies.[15] Special interests make it even more difficult to regulate water pollution in other parts of the
world. Tougher regulations are needed globally to address pollution from activities such as dumping wastes into the ocean, large animal feeding operations, logging sites, public roads, parking lots, and industrial waste created by production
operations.

Water Quantity   In addition to concerns about the quality of water, some parts of
the globe are increasingly worried about its quantity. There has been a sixfold increase in water use worldwide since 1990, and as a result, one-fifth of the world's
population now has no access to safe drinking water. Since 1960, irrigation has
jumped by 60 percent, with serious consequences for the global water supply. For
example, the Aral Sea, once the fourth-largest inland body of water in the world,

has been depleted to less than half its original size through thirty years of surface water removal for irrigation.[16]

In other areas, growing demand for water by booming populations has outpaced nature's ability to replenish surface and underground water sources—especially during periods of prolonged drought. During the drought of 2000, three Texas towns nearly ran out of water as their reservoirs dried up, and many Texas cities and towns were forced to mandate strict water rationing to conserve limited supplies. Concerns about water quantity have led to intense political and legal wrangling in a number of states. Indeed, Mark Twain (Samuel Clemens) once said, "Whiskey is for drinking, water is for fighting over." In Colorado, for example, an agreement by federal, state, and local officials to protect the longtime water rights of ranchers and farmers while preserving fish, wildlife, habitat, and public recreation finally put an end to decades of "water wars."[17]

▶ *Land Issues*

Land Pollution   Land pollution results from the dumping of residential and industrial wastes, strip mining, and poor forest conservation. Such pollution jeopardizes wildlife habitats, causes erosion, alters watercourses (leading to flooding), poisons groundwater supplies, and can contribute to illnesses in humans and animals. For example, the dumping of toxic industrial wastes into Love Canal, near Niagara Falls, New York, caused residents who moved to the area years later to experience high rates of birth defects and cancer.

Waste Management   Another aspect of the land pollution problem is the issue of how to dispose of waste in an environmentally responsible manner. Consumers contribute an average of 1,500 pounds of garbage per person each year to landfills, and landfill space is declining. By the year 2005, 70 percent of the nation's landfills will be full. Also compounding the waste-disposal problem is the fact that more than 50 percent of all garbage is made out of plastic, which does not decompose. Some communities have passed laws that prohibit the use of plastics such as Styrofoam for this reason.

Deforestation   In Brazil and other South American countries, rain forests are being destroyed—at a rate of one acre per minute—to make way for farms and ranches, at a cost of the extinction of the many plants and animals (including some endangered species) that call the rain forest home. Nearly 60 percent of the world's rain forests have been lost to agricultural or timber interests.[18] Large-scale deforestation also depletes the oxygen supply available to humans and other animals. Deforestation may also contribute to flooding when it destroys erosion-controlling plants. In 1998, for example, floods worsened by deforestation killed 3,600 people and left another 14 million homeless.[19]

Urban Sprawl   One cause of deforestation in the United States is urban sprawl. Author James Howard Kunstler has defined urban sprawl as "a degenerate urban form that is too congested to be efficient, too chaotic to be beautiful, and too dispersed to possess the diversity and vitality of a great city."[20] Urban sprawl began with the post–World War II building boom that transformed the nation from primarily low-density communities designed to accommodate one-car households, bicyclists, and pedestrians to large-scale suburban development at the edges of established towns and cities. Downtowns and inner cities deteriorated as strip and shopping malls, office parks, corporate campuses, and residential developments sprang up on what was once forest, prairie, or farm and ranch land. As the places where people live, work, and shop grew further apart, people began spending more time in automobiles, driving ever-greater distances.[21] According to the Surface Transportation Policy Project (STPP), almost 70 percent of the increase in driving between 1983 and 1990 was due to the effects of sprawl.[22] Urban sprawl has not only consumed wildlife habitat, wetlands, and farmland, but it has also contributed to land, water, and especially air pollution. Table 9.1 lists the U.S. cities most threatened by sprawl.

TABLE 9.1

U.S. Cities Threatened by Urban Sprawl

Large Cities (population one million or more)	Medium Cities (population 500,000 to one million)	Small Cities (population 200,000–500,000)
1. Atlanta, GA	1. Orlando, FL	1. McAllen, TX
2. St. Louis, MO	2. Austin, TX	2. Raleigh, NC
3. Washington, D.C.	3. Las Vegas, NV	3. Pensacola, FL
4. Cincinnati, OH	4. West Palm Beach, FL	4. Daytona Beach, FL
5. Kansas City, MO	5. Akron, OH	5. Little Rock, AR
6. Denver, CO		
7. Seattle, WA		
8. Minneapolis-St. Paul, MN		
9. Ft. Lauderdale, FL		
10. Chicago, IL		

Source: "Thirty Most Sprawl-Threatened Cities," *The Dark Side of the American Dream: The Costs and Consequences of Suburban Sprawl,* Sierra Club, 1998, available at www.sierraclub.org/sprawl/report98/map.html. Reprinted by permission from Sierra Club.

Because of the problems associated with urban sprawl, some communities have taken drastic steps to limit it. Oregon, for example, has established an Urban Growth Boundary around the city of Portland to restrict growth and preserve open space and farm and ranch land around the city. In Texas, the city of Austin implemented a Smart Growth initiative that directs development away from environmentally sensitive areas. A number of Colorado cities, including Boulder and Fort Collins, require as much as 80 percent of new residential housing developments to be devoted to agriculture, wetlands, or open spaces for wildlife.

▶ *Biodiversity*

Deforestation, pollution, development, and urban sprawl have put increasing pressure on wildlife, plants, and their habitats. Many plants and animals have become extinct, and thousands more are threatened. In the Florida Everglades, for example,

The World Wildlife Fund seeks to raise funds to protect habitats and their native wildlife.

GIVE THEM
SHELTER FROM
THE STORM.
1.800.CALL.WWF
www.worldwildlife.org/act

Man's abuse of Earth's natural resources has created a storm that many animals and their habitats have difficulty weathering. Help World Wildlife Fund protect them by ordering a free Action Kit. Together we can help leave our children a living planet. **WWF**

channeling, damming, and diverting water for urban and agricultural uses have dramatically altered the sensitive ecosystem. As a result, 68 percent of the Everglades' native resident species, including the manatee and the panther, are now endangered.[23]

The world's tropical forests, which cover just 7 percent of the earth's land surface, account for more than half of the planet's biological species.[24] The importance of these ecosystems is highlighted by the fact that 25 percent of the world's prescription drugs are extracted from plants primarily growing in tropical rain forests. Seventy percent of the 3,000 plants identified as sources of cancer-fighting drugs come from tropical forests, and scientists suspect that many more tropical plants may have pharmaceutical benefits. However, these forests are being depleted at alarming rates because of commercial logging, mining, and drilling and to make way for roads, farms, and ranches. More than half of the world's tropical forests have disappeared in the last century, and with them, many plant and animal species.[25] The most recent extinction: the Miss Waldron's red colobus monkey, a primate that once frequented the tropical forests of West Africa. With experts predicting that West Africa will lose 70 percent of its remaining forests, scientists fear that many more primates will become extinct during the twenty-first century.[26]

Many ecologists believe that the loss of such species threatens the success of entire ecosystems, which require a diversity of organisms in order to function properly. Recent global research indicates that declining numbers of available plant species result in lower ecosystem productivity, whereas increasing the number of species raises productivity.[27] Because each biological species plays a unique role in its ecosystem, the loss of any one of them may threaten the entire ecosystem. Pollinators, for example, play a significant role in any ecosystem. However, increasing development and widespread use of pesticides have reduced the populations of bees, insects, and bats that help plants reproduce. Among honeybees, the primary pollinators of food-producing plants, populations of domestic honeybees have declined by one-third, whereas many wild honeybees have become virtually extinct in many places around the world. Declines in pollinating species not only threaten the success of their relevant ecosystems, but may also harm long-term global food production because one-third of all food products require pollinators to reproduce.[28]

Despite evidence of the importance of biodiversity in ecosystems, many people argue that human beings are more important than any single plant or animal species. This argument lies at the heart of environmental battles over endangered species habitats throughout the United States and around the globe. In the Pacific Northwest, for example, old-growth forests are prime habitat for the endangered northern spotted owl, but their valuable timber provides jobs for hundreds of families as well as lumber to house a multiplying society. Although statistical evidence suggests that timber-related job losses in the Pacific Northwest are due as much to decades of overcutting of timberlands as to conservation measures to protect the owl,[29] the battle of people's needs versus endangered species' needs continues there and elsewhere around the globe.

▶ *Genetically Modified Foods*

New technologies are also creating environmental issues, especially with regard to manipulating genes in plants and animals. Genetic engineering involves transferring one or more genes from one organism to another to create a new life form that has unique traits. Many of these genetically modified organisms have been developed to provide natural immunity against insects and viruses. Companies like Monsanto and DuPont marketed the idea that genetically modified (GM) corn, soybeans, potatoes, canola oil seeds, and cotton plants are more pest resistant, require fewer chemicals to produce, and have higher yields.[30] Indeed, one of the primary goals of using these GM plants is the reduction in the use of pesticides and other farming practices that harm the environment. Moreover, the resulting increase in crop yields can reduce costs, thereby making potentially more food available for world consumption.

On the other hand, the long-term impact of this genetic tinkering is not known. A study sponsored by the National Academy of Sciences reported that the GM varieties developed so far do not pose allergy problems. However, the report called for further research to determine how to prevent genetically modified crops from killing beneficial and harmless insects, such as the monarch butterfly, and to deter herbicide-resistant genes from spreading into weeds.[31] Health, safety, and environmental concerns have prompted consumers around the world, particularly in Europe and Japan, to boycott products made from genetically modified crops.

Even while a backlash against genetically modified products builds, biotech companies are extending genetic engineering by experimenting with inserting

Greenpeace activists are shown here protesting against genetically modified foods in Hong Kong.

artificial chromosomes into the cells of animals. For example, genetically engineered animal milk can be used as a culture for producing a vast range of drugs. However, many consumers are finding this technology as unpalatable as genetically modified plants. Regulators in Germany and France have already banned its use, and the U.S. Food and Drug Administration will not approve the testing of artificial chromosomes in people as therapies for genetic diseases. As with genetically modified plants, the problem with genetic engineering of animal cells is that the long-run effects cannot currently be predicted. Large numbers of genetically altered animals could upset the balance in relationships among various species with undetermined effects, such as the ability to reproduce or fight diseases and pests.[32] Until further research addresses public concerns about the safety and long-term environmental effects of these technologies, their success in the marketplace is uncertain. We will take a further look at some of the issues associated with the technology of genetically modified foods in Chapter 10.

Environmental Policy and Regulation

The United States, like most other nations, has passed numerous laws and established regulatory agencies to address environmental issues. Most of these efforts have focused on the activities of businesses, government agencies, and other organizations that use natural resources in providing goods and services.

▶ Environmental Protection Agency

The most influential regulatory agency that deals with environmental issues and enforces environmental legislation in the United States is the Environmental Protection Agency (EPA). The EPA's founding in 1970 was the culmination of a decade of growing protests over the deterioration of the natural environment. This movement reached a significant climax with the publication of Rachel Carson's *Silent Spring,* an attack on the indiscriminate use of pesticides, which rallied scientists, activists, and citizens from around the country to crusade to protect the environment from abuses of the time. Twenty million Americans joined together on April 22, 1970, for Earth Day, a nationwide demonstration for environmental reforms. President Richard Nixon responded to these events by establishing the EPA as an independent agency to establish and enforce environmental protection standards, conduct environmental research, provide assistance in fighting pollution, and assist in developing and recommending new policies for environmental protection.[33] The agency is also charged with ensuring that

- All Americans are protected from significant risks to their health and to the environment in which they live and work

- National efforts to manage environmental risk are based on the best scientific information available

- Federal laws protecting human health and the environment are enforced fairly and effectively

- Environmental protection is an integral consideration in U.S. policies concerning natural resources, human health, economic growth, energy, transportation, agriculture, industry, and international trade, and that these factors are considered in establishing environmental policy

- All parts of society have access to accurate information sufficient to participate effectively in managing human health and environmental risks

- Environmental protection contributes to diverse, sustainable, and economically productive communities and ecosystems

- The United State plays a leadership role in working with other nations to protect the environment.[34]

With these charges, the EPA has become one of the most powerful regulatory forces in the United States. For example, the agency recently reached an agreement with Syngenta, the leading manufacturer of diazinon, to phase out home and garden use of the commonly used pesticide and permit only limited commercial use of the product, which belongs to a class of pesticides that have been linked to neurological disorders and other health problems in children. Although diazinon is considered less risky than other organophosphates, Syngenta executives said the company could not justify paying for the research needed to prove the pesticide's safety for consumer use and therefore agreed to the phaseout.[35]

To fulfill its primary mission to protect human health and the natural environment into the next century, the EPA recently established ten long-term strategic goals to define its planning, budgeting, analysis, and accountability processes (Table 9.2). To determine these goals, the agency solicited and evaluated significant stakeholder input on priority areas related to human health and environmental protection activities. Thus, these goals reflect public priorities as voiced by Congress in the form of statutes and regulations designed to achieve clean air and water, proper waste management, and other important concerns.[36]

To achieve these goals and carry out its public mission, the EPA may also file civil charges against companies that violate the law. For example, the EPA, along with the U.S. Department of Justice and the state of Texas, settled two lawsuits against Koch Industries over more than 300 oil spills from the Kansas-based firm's pipelines and facilities in six states. The settlement imposed $30 million in civil penalties—the largest ever in the history of federal environmental law—against Koch and required the firm to hire an independent auditor to oversee repairs on 2,500 miles of pipeline, to improve its maintenance and training programs, and to spend $5 million on environmental projects in Kansas, Oklahoma, and Texas.[37] In comparison, Exxon's settlement with state and federal governments amounted to nearly $6 billion in compensatory and punitive damages after its tanker, the *Exxon Valdez*, ran aground and leaked 11 million gallons of oil into

TABLE 9.2

Goals of the Environmental Protection Agency

Goal	Long-Term Outcome
1	Clean air
2	Clean and safe water
3	Safe food
4	Preventing pollution and reducing risk in communities, homes, workplaces, and ecosystems
5	Better waste management, restoration of contaminated waste sites, and emergency response
6	Reduction of global and cross-border environmental risks
7	Expansion of Americans' right to know about their environment
8	Sound science, improved understanding of environmental risk, and greater innovation to address environmental problems
9	A credible deterrent to pollution and greater compliance with the law
10	Effective management

Source: "Strategic Plan," Office of the Chief Financial Officer, Environmental Protection Agency, www.epa.gov/ocfo/plan/2000strategicplan.pdf, accessed December 10, 2001.

Alaska's Prince William Sound. The company also paid more than $2 billion to clean up damage from the ecological disaster and to reimburse government agencies for their expenses in response to the spill. Although the Exxon oil spill occurred more than a decade ago, the legal, political, and social implications of this event are still evolving.[38]

Environmental Legislation

A significant number of laws have been passed to address both general and specific environmental issues, including public health, threatened species, toxic substances, clean air and water, and natural resources. Table 9.3 summarizes some of the most significant laws related to environmental protection.

Clean Air Act   The Clean Air Act, passed in 1970, is a comprehensive federal law that regulates atmospheric emissions from a variety of sources.[39] Among its most

TABLE 9.3

Major Environmental Laws

Act (Date Enacted)	Purpose
National Environmental Policy Act (1969)	Established national environmental policy, set goals, and provided a means for implementing the policy; promotes efforts to prevent damage to the biosphere and to stimulate human health and welfare, established a Council on Environmental Quality
Occupational Safety and Health Act (1970)	Ensures worker and workplace safety by requiring employers to provide a place of employment free from health and safety hazards
Clean Air Act (1970)	Regulates emissions from area, stationary, and mobile sources; authorized the EPA to establish National Ambient Air Quality Standards (NAAQS) to protect public health and the environment
Federal Insecticide, Fungicide and Rodenticide Act (1972)	Provides for federal control of pesticide distribution, sale, and use; requires users to register when purchasing pesticides
Endangered Species Act (1973)	Established a conservation program for threatened and endangered plants and animals and their habitats; prohibits the import, export, interstate, and foreign commerce or any action that results in a "taking" of a listed species or that adversely affects habitat
Safe Drinking Water Act (1974)	Protects the quality of drinking water in the United States; authorized the EPA to establish water purity standards and required public water systems to comply with health-related standards
Toxic Substances Control Act (1976)	Empowered the EPA to track industrial chemicals currently produced or imported into the United States; authorized the EPA to require reporting or testing of chemicals and to ban the manufacture and import of chemicals that pose an unreasonable risk
Resource Conservation and Recovery Act (1976)	Empowered the EPA to control the generation, transportation, treatment, storage, and disposal of hazardous waste
Clean Water Act (1977)	Authorized the EPA to set effluent standards on an industry basis and to continue to set water quality standards for all contaminants in surface waters; made it unlawful for any person to discharge any pollutant from a point source into navigable waters without a permit

(continued)

TABLE 9.3 *(continued)*

Major Environmental Laws

Act (Date Enacted)	Purpose
Comprehensive Environmental Response, Compensation, and Liability Act (1980)	Established prohibitions and requirements concerning closed and abandoned hazardous waste sites; authorized a tax on the chemical and petroleum industries to establish a "Superfund" to provide for cleanup when no responsible party could be identified
Superfund Amendments and Reauthorization Act (1986)	Amended the Comprehensive Environmental Response, Compensation, and Liability Act to increase the size of the Superfund; required Superfund actions to consider the standards and requirements found in other state and federal environmental laws and regulations; provided new enforcement authorities and tools
Emergency Planning and Community Right-to-Know Act (1986)	Enacted to help local communities protect public health, safety, and the environment from chemical hazards; requires each state to appoint a State Emergency Response Commission (SERC) and to establish Emergency Planning Districts
Oil Pollution Act (1990)	Requires oil storage facilities and vessels to submit plans detailing how they will respond to large spills; requires the development of Area Contingency Plans to prepare and plan for responses to oil spills on a regional scale
Pollution Prevention Act (1990)	Promotes pollution reduction through cost-effective changes in production, operation, and use of raw materials and practices that increase efficiency and conserve natural resources, such as recycling, source reduction, and sustainable agriculture.
Food Quality Protection Act (1996)	Amended the Federal Insecticide, Fungicide, and Rodenticide Act and the Federal Food, Drug, and Cosmetic Act to change the way the EPA regulates pesticides; applies a new safety standard—reasonable certainty of no harm—to all pesticides used on foods

Source: "Major Environmental Laws," Environmental Protection Agency, www.epa.gov/epahome/laws.htm, accessed November 1, 2001.

significant provisions is the requirement that the Environmental Protection Agency establish national air quality standards as well as standards for significant new pollution sources and for all facilities emitting hazardous substances. These maximum pollutant standards, called National Ambient Air Quality Standards (NAAQS), were mandated for every state in order to protect public health and the environment. The states were further directed to develop state implementation plans (SIPs) pertinent to the industries in each state. The law also established deadlines for reducing automobile emission levels—90 percent reductions in hydrocarbon and carbon monoxide levels by 1975 and a 90 percent reduction in nitrogen oxides by 1976. Because many areas of the country failed to meet these deadlines, the Clean Air Act was amended in 1977 to set new dates for attainment of the NAAQS.[40]

The Clean Air Act was revised again as the Clean Air Act Amendments of 1990 to address lingering problems or issues that were not acknowledged in the original law, such as acid rain, ground-level ozone, stratospheric ozone depletion, and air toxins. The amended act also increased the number of regulated pollutants from fewer than 20 to more than 380.[41]

Federal Insecticide, Fungicide, and Rodenticide Act   The primary focus of the Federal Insecticide, Fungicide, and Rodenticide Act of 1972 was to place the distribution, sale, and use of pesticides under federal control. The law granted the EPA the authority to study the consequences of pesticide use and to require all users to register when purchasing pesticides. All pesticides used in the United States must be registered (licensed) with the EPA to assure that they will be properly labeled and

Farmers are increasingly affected by government regulation of herbicides and pesticides.

Royal Caribbean Cleans Up

Miami-based Royal Caribbean Cruise Lines (RCCL) is working to become a more environmentally responsible corporate citizen. One of its board directors is an ex-administrator of the Environmental Protection Agency (EPA), and all of its cruise ships now have environmental officers. It is also building new ships with gas turbines instead of diesel, which will dramatically reduce airborne exhaust. The company has adopted the slogan, "Save the Waves," and its turquoise logo is displayed on every employee's name badge and on every ship. Such environmental consciousness was not always part of RCCL's culture, however.

In the early 1990s, Royal Caribbean dumped thousands of gallons of oily bilge, photo-developing chemicals, and dry-cleaning fluids into Caribbean waters, New York Harbor, Alaska's Inside Passage, and the Port of Miami. Five of its ships had secret pipes in their engine rooms that allowed oily bilge to be discharged directly overboard. These pipes bypassed the ships' expensive onboard Oil Water Separators, pollution-treatment devices that process bilge waste before it can be discharged overboard. There was even video footage of one of the ships leaving an oily wake.

These environmental crimes were exposed in a five-year federal investigation. Royal Caribbean initially fought the investigation with the contention that the U.S. government had no jurisdiction over a Liberian-registered company with ships registered in other countries. However, the company eventually pleaded guilty to twenty-two federal charges. It was fined $27 million, $2 million more than Exxon was fined for the *Valdez* oil spill, and placed on five years of corporate probation. RCCL also agreed to pay Alaska $3.5 million for dumping waste in the state's waters and not to discharge wastewater within three miles of the Alaskan coastline. Most of this money will be used to buy spill-response equipment and related materials. Although no senior corporate officials were charged with any wrongdoing as a result of the investigation, the company quickly replaced several high-level managers. Jack Williams, the company's new president, spent much of his initial time at the

so that, if used according to specifications, will not cause unreasonable harm to the environment. Later amendments to the law also require users to take exams in order to be certified as applicators of pesticides.[42]

Endangered Species Act The Endangered Species Act of 1973 established a program to protect threatened and endangered species as well as the habitats in which they are found.[43] An endangered species is one that is in danger of extinction, whereas a threatened species is one that may become endangered without protection. The U.S. Fish and Wildlife Service of the Department of the Interior maintains the list of endangered and threatened species, which currently includes 632 endangered species (326 are plants) and 190 threatened species (78 are

RCCL helm apologizing to the public for Royal Caribbean's wrongdoing.

Today, Royal Caribbean is actively working to build more environmentally responsible ships. RCCL's newest ship, the *Voyager of the Sea*, is the largest cruise ship ever built, three times the size of the *Titanic* and 75 percent bigger than the rest of Royal Caribbean's ships. It is also one of the most efficient and environmentally friendly ships ever built. The ship can even turn completely around without moving forward or backward. When winds become too gusty, on-deck restaurants are closed down to prevent trash from blowing into the ocean.

In an effort to promote and recognize environmental innovation and improvement throughout the firm, Royal Caribbean is sponsoring internal annual awards. The company presented its first Environmental Ship of the Year award to the *Enchantment of the Seas* on the basis of seven criteria: environmental performance, effectiveness of corrective actions, completion of corrective action to clear audit findings, reports of near incidents, weekly and monthly environmental reports, performance of environmental equipment, and innovative thinking. The first Best Environmental Innovation of the Year Award, de-signed to reward ships and crews that think "outside of the box," went to the *Monarch of the Seas*. These winners were selected by independent external auditors from Haley and Aldrich according to which ship most closely adhered to the company's new Environmental Compliance Plan.

Royal Caribbean Cruise Lines may have needed a wake-up call to become environmentally responsible, but it is now serving as a lesson for other cruise lines. After the problems and penalties RCCL has endured, other cruise lines will hopefully strive to ensure that their practices are legal without waiting to be caught in the act. However, the cruise lines are not the only ones at fault. Federal regulations still allow for certain types of dumping within coastlines and other areas that are potentially harmful to the environment. ■

Sources:
"Alaska's Black Water: Cruise Ship Dumping Sparks Regulators' Interests," ABCNEWS, December 2, 1999, http://abcnews.go.com/sections/travel/DailyNews/cruiseships991202.html; "Cruise Line Pays Alaska $3.5 Million for Dumping Violations," Fox News Online, January 14, 2000, www.foxmarketwire.com/wires/0114/f_ap_0114_65.sml; Charles Fishman, "Fantastic Voyage," *Fast Company*, March 2000, pp. 169–186; Royal Caribbean Cruise Lines, *1998 Environmental Report*, http://206.103.136.193/savethewaves/intro.html/, accessed December 19, 2000.

plants). The Endangered Species Act prohibits any action that results in the harm to or death of a listed species or that adversely affects endangered species habitat. It also makes the import, export, and interstate and foreign commerce of listed species illegal. Protected species may include birds, insects, fish, reptiles, mammals, crustaceans, flowers, grasses, cacti, and trees.[44]

The Endangered Species Act has become one of the most controversial environmental laws passed in the United States. Some environmentalists fear the law may backfire if landowners who find endangered or threatened species on their property fail to notify authorities in order to avoid the expense and hassle of complying with the law; in some cases, threatened or endangered species have been harmed by landowners seeking to avoid the law. Concerns about the restrictions and costs associated with the law are not entirely unfounded. Consider the case of Brandt Child, who purchased 500 acres in Utah with the intention of building a campground and golf course there. However, the U.S. Fish & Wildlife Service ordered Child not to use the land because 200,000 federally protected Kanab ambersnails inhabited three lakes on the premises. The federal government not only refused to compensate Child for his loss of the use of the property, it also threatened to fine him $50,000 per snail if geese that wandered onto the property had eaten any of the snails (the geese were later found to be snail free).[45] Such anecdotes have angered many property rights activists who believe that the Endangered Species Act goes too far in protecting threatened species at the expense of human rights.

Toxic Substances Control Act   Congress passed the Toxic Substances Control Act in 1976 to empower the Environmental Protection Agency with the ability to track the 75,000 industrial chemicals currently produced or imported into the United States. The agency repeatedly screens these chemicals and can require reporting or testing of those that may pose an environmental or human-health hazard. It can also ban the manufacture and import of those chemicals that pose an unreasonable risk. The EPA also has the ability to track the thousands of new chemicals developed by industry each year with either unknown or dangerous characteristics. The EPA then can control these chemicals as necessary to protect human health and the environment.[46]

Clean Water Act   In 1977, Congress amended the Federal Water Pollution Control Act of 1972 as the Clean Water Act. This law granted the EPA the authority to establish effluent standards on an industry basis and continued the earlier law's requirements to set water quality limits for all contaminants in surface waters. The Clean Water Act makes it illegal for anyone to discharge any pollutant from a point source into navigable waters without a permit.[47]

Emergency Planning and Community Right-to-Know Act   The Emergency Planning and Community Right-to-Know Act was enacted in 1986 to help local communities identify and protect public health, safety, and the environment from chemical hazards. To achieve this goal, the law requires that businesses report the locations and quantities of stored chemicals to state and local governments to help them respond to chemical spills and similar emergencies. Additionally, the law mandates that most manufacturers file a **Toxics Release Inventory (TRI)** of all releases of specified chemicals into the air, water, or land, as well as transfers of chemicals for treatment or disposal. TRIs must also be filed with the U.S. EPA, which compiles the reports in a publicly accessible online database. As such, the TRI program serves as a "public report card" of chemical pollution from U.S. manufacturing facilities. It also creates a powerful incentive for manufacturers to reduce their emissions and wastes.[48]

Pollution Prevention Act   The Pollution Prevention Act of 1990 focused industry, government, and public attention on reducing pollution through cost-effective changes in production, operation, and raw materials use. Practices include recycling, source reduction, sustainable agriculture, and other practices that increase efficiency in the use of energy, water, or other natural resources and protect resources through conservation.[49]

Food Quality Protection Act   In 1996, the Food Quality Protection Act amended the Federal Insecticide, Fungicide, and Rodenticide Act and the Federal Food, Drug, and Cosmetic Act to fundamentally change the way the EPA regulates pesticides. The law included a new safety standard—reasonable certainty of no harm—that must be applied to all pesticides used on foods.[50] The legislation establishes a more consistent, science-based regulatory environment and mandates a single, health-based standard for all pesticides in all foods. The law also provides special protections for infants and children, expedites approval of safer pesticides, provides incentives for the development and maintenance of effective crop protection tools for farmers, and requires periodic reevaluation of pesticide registrations and tolerances to ensure that they are up to date and based on good science.[51]

Business Response to Environmental Issues

Partly in response to federal legislation such as the National Environmental Policy Act of 1969 and partly due to stakeholder concerns, businesses are applying creativity, technology, and business resources to respond to environmental issues. In many cases, these firms have not only improved their reputations with interested stakeholders, but have also seen dramatic cost savings by making their operations more efficient. Moreover, many companies, including Walt Disney, Chevron, and Scott Paper, have created a new executive position, Vice President of Environmental Affairs. This position is designed to help these companies achieve their business goals in an environmentally responsible manner. Corporate efforts to respond to environmental issues focus on green marketing, recycling, emissions reductions, and socially responsible buying.

▶ Green Marketing

Green marketing refers to the specific development, pricing, promotion, and distribution of products that do less harm to the environment. General Motors, for example, is developing new "hybrid" pickup trucks and buses that employ electric motors to augment their internal-combustion engines, improving the vehicles' fuel economy without a loss in power. The full-size trucks, for example, will get nearly 15 percent better gas mileage than a conventional pickup.[52] One truly "green" firm is the Parks Company, which donates 5 percent of the gross profit from its catalog sales to U.S. national parks to help bridge their $9 billion budget shortfall. Since the company was founded in 1995, the mailing list for its catalog of parks-related gift items has grown to 60,000, and the firm donated $20,000 in its first 28 months of business. The company also established a grassroots campaign, One for the Parks, to crusade for using 1 percent of the federal budget surplus to help meet the parks' budget needs.[53]

Even some real estate developers are attempting to integrate environmental concerns into new communities to protect the land. One example, in Colorado, is Meadow Ranch. The developer of Meadow Ranch deliberately designed a community that spares wildlife habitat to ensure that new homeowners do not evict the hawks and red foxes that have long roamed the land. Homes in Meadow Ranch sit on land once zoned light industrial, which, had it been developed as such, would have destroyed thirty of the forty wetland acres preserved on the site today. The developers also consulted the Colorado National Plant Society, the Army Corps of Engineers, and the Soil Conservation District to ensure that new landscaping harmonized with the native plants. The firm even prints its brochures on recycled paper.[54]

Many products are certified as "green" by environmental organizations such as Green Seal and carry a special logo identifying them as such. In Europe, companies can voluntarily apply for an Eco-label (Figure 9.2) to indicate that their product is less harmful to the environment than competing products, based on scientifically determined criteria. About 250 products have been awarded an Eco-label.[55] Lumber products at Home Depot and the U.K.-based B&Q may carry a seal from the Forest Stewardship Council to indicate that they were harvested from sustainable forests using environmentally friendly methods.[56] Likewise, most Chiquita bananas are certified through the Better Banana Project as having been grown with more environmental- and labor-friendly practices.[57]

However, a recent study by Consumers International suggests that consumers are being confused and even misled by green marketing claims. Researchers compared claims on products sold in ten countries, including the United States, to labeling guidelines established by the International Standards Organization (ISO), which prohibit vague and misleading claims as well as unverifiable ones such as

FIGURE 9.2

The European Eco-label

Source: "European Union Eco-label Logo," Europa [European Union], www.europa.eu.imp/comm/ environment/ecolabel, accessed December 10, 2001.

"environmentally friendly" and "nonpolluting." The study found that many products' claims are too vague or misleading to meet ISO standards. For example, one brand of flour claimed to be "nonpolluting," and a German compost was described as "earthworm friendly." Among the products with the highest number of misleading or unverifiable claims were laundry detergents, household cleaners, and paints. Anna Fielder, the director of Consumers International, contends that the study shows that although there are many useful claims made about the environmental responsibility of products, there is still a long way to go to ensure that shoppers are adequately informed about the environmental impact of the products they buy.[58]

Although demand for legal and practical solutions to environmental issues is widespread, the environmental movement includes many diverse groups, whose values and goals often conflict. There is growing agreement among environmentalists and businesses, however, that companies should work to protect and preserve the natural environment by implementing a number of goals. First, companies should strive to eliminate the concept of waste. Because pollution and waste usually stem from inefficiency, the issue should not be what to do with waste, but, rather, how to make things more efficiently so that no waste is produced. Second, companies should rethink the concept of a product. Products can be classified as consumables—those that are eaten or biodegradable; durable goods—such as cars, televisions, computers, and refrigerators; and unsalables— including such undesirable byproducts as radioactive materials, heavy metals, and toxins. The design of durable goods should utilize a closed loop system of manufacture, use, and a return to the manufacturing process that allows products and resources to be disassembled and recycled and minimizes the disposal of unsalables. Third, the price of products should reflect their true costs, including the cost of replenishing natural resources that are utilized or damaged during the production process. Finally, businesses should seek ways to make their commitment to the environment profitable.[59]

▶ *Recycling Initiatives*

Many organizations engage in **recycling,** the reprocessing of materials—especially of steel, aluminum, paper, glass, rubber, and some plastics—for reuse (Figure 9.3). Proctor and Gamble, for example, uses recycled materials in some of its packaging and markets refills for some products, which reduces packaging waste. Sonoma County (California) Stable and Livestock markets rubber mats recycled from used tires for use in horse stalls.[60] More than 50 percent of all products sold in stores are packed in 100 percent recycled paperboard. Other markets using 100 percent recycled paperboard include book covers, jigsaw puzzles, board games, greeting cards, and video and CD covers.[61] Starbucks makes coffee grounds available free to those who wish to use them for compost to add nutrition to their

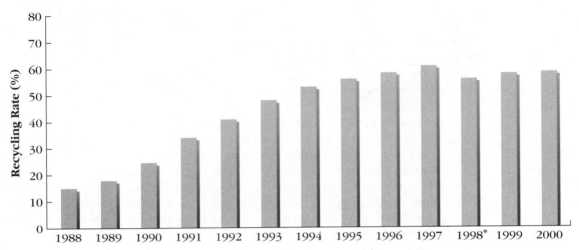

FIGURE 9.3

Recycling Steel Cans

*Drop in 1998 recycling rates can be attributed to U.S. steel industry production cutbacks caused by record increases in unfairly traded foreign steel imports.

Source: "A Few Facts About Steel—North America's #1 Recycled Material," Steel Recycling Institute, www.recycle-steel.org/index2.html, accessed November 1, 2001. Reprinted by permission from the Steel Recycling Institute. www.recycle-steel.org.

gardens. Ben Pachard, Starbucks' Environmental Affairs Manager, says, "Recycling the grounds back into the garden is a better alternative then throwing them away into the trash."[62]

A number of beverage companies have formed an alliance called WasteWise to represent and share industry goals and best practices with respect to recycling and waste management. Anheuser-Busch Companies, for example, reduced its total solid waste by 15 percent, or 19 million pounds, in one year through waste prevention and recycling. Coca-Cola purchases more than $2 billion in recycled content materials in the United States alone. Pepsi-Cola switched to reusable plastic shipping cases and saved $44 million. Coors, by using a lighter-weight bottle, saved more than one million pounds of glass.[63] Table 9.4 shows some of the goals and techniques the beverage industry maintains in managing waste.

Future Solutions, Inc., distributes recycled products ranging from automated teller machine (ATM) supplies and toilet bowl brushes to recycled mousepads and vacuum cleaners from more than 300 manufacturers. Among the firm's clients are the U.S. Department of Energy and the states of Colorado, California, and Arizona. Plans for Future Solutions, Inc. include constructing a new office headquarters out

TABLE 9.4

A Sampling of Beverage Industry Waste Management Initiatives

INITIATIVE
Utilize lightweight plastic and glass bottles
Switch from corrugated shippers to reusable plastic cases
Institute a glove-reuse program in manufacturing facilities
Develop a waste tracking system for syrup production facilities that measures and tracks the amount of waste generated on a per-unit basis
Refurbish, rather than replace, vending equipment
Implement a six-pack ring-recycling program
Collect and bale corrugated shipping containers from the public
Establish a facility to buy back used beverage containers from the public
Increase recycled content in glass bottles
Increase recycled content in corrugated shipping containers

SUPPORT FROM COMPANIES
Among the companies supporting the Beverage Industry "Waste Wise" Initiatives are 7UP/ RC Bottling, Anheuser-Busch Companies, Coors Brewing Companies, Pepsi-Cola Company, The Coca-Cola Company, Poland Spring Natural Spring Water, and Very Fine Products.

Source: "Doing What It Takes to Be Wastewise," Environmental Protection Agency, April 1999, www.epa.gov/epaosrver/non-hvv/reduce/wstewise/about/id, accessed December 10, 2001.

of 100 percent recycled materials that utilizes both energy efficient and water-conserving products.[64]

Companies are finding ways to recycle water to avoid discharging chemicals into rivers and streams and to preserve diminishing water supplies. Daimler-Chrysler, for example, has three manufacturing plants that operate wastewater-recycling facilities. The company's facility in Toluca, Mexico, which manufactures the PT Cruiser, operates a comprehensive recycling system that treats more than 610,000 gallons of wastewater—enough to fill up ten medium-sized baseball stadiums—each day from both manufacturing operations and sanitary operations (restrooms, showers, cafeterias). Because the plant totally recycles all the water used, it draws less from the area's receding aquifer and minimizes the potential for polluted water to reach a nearby river system. Moreover, the system allows Daimler-Chrysler's water quality standards to be stricter than those set by Mexico or the United States.[65]

▶ *Emissions Reduction Initiatives*

To combat air pollution and the threat of global warming, many companies have begun to take steps to reduce the emissions of greenhouse gases from their facilities. Many firms, such as Herman Miller, Inc., which designs and manages production facilities to function as efficiently as possible, are finding new ways to light and heat their buildings and factories to improve efficiency, thereby reducing waste and energy use. Making improvements in energy efficiency can save a company approximately $1 per square foot of office or factory space per year.[66]

Many companies are going beyond the emission reductions called for by the 1997 Kyoto Protocol treaty, which set a goal of reducing greenhouse emissions by signing countries by 7 percent from their 2000 levels. DuPont, for example, is slashing its greenhouse gas emissions to 58 million tons, or 40 percent of their 1991 levels. Royal Dutch/Shell is working to reduce greenhouse gas emissions from its plants to 100 million tons, or 25 percent below 1990 levels, by 2002. (To achieve an equivalent reduction, every car in New England would have to be taken off the road for five years.) [67] Those companies that achieve reductions in excess of that called for by the Kyoto Protocol earn credits that may then be "traded" to other firms that have not yet achieved their targets. Nations may also trade credits earned from reducing emissions to other nations that have yet to do so. Russia, for example, plans to use the revenue from the sale of these credits to fund clean-energy projects.[68]

▶ *Socially Responsible Buying*

Socially responsible buying initiatives are another way that companies are finding to incorporate environmental responsibility into their business strategies. Minette Drumwright has defined socially responsible buying (SRB) as "that which attempts to take into account the public consequences of organisational buying or bring about positive social change through organisational buying behavior."[69] Daimler-Chrysler, for example, requires its plastic parts suppliers to include 20 percent recycled content in 2000 and 30 percent by 2002.

A company that takes a proactive approach to socially responsible buying is likely to (1) be actively involved in the development of SRB principles and practices both within and outside of its own operations, (2) routinely and objectively evaluate its suppliers' achievements with respect to the social responsibilities involved, and (3) communicate its achievements and failures to its primary stakeholders. How companies implement SRB strategies ranges from terminating relations with suppliers who will not abide by the firm's environmental goals to seeking out partners who can supply environmentally friendly parts and supplies to forming industrywide agreements. In the U.K., for example, Co-operative Bank, after discovering that one of its furniture suppliers was unknowingly using endangered tropical hardwoods, introduced the manufacturer to a firm that could supply it with more sustainable resources.[70]

Strategic Implementation of Environmental Responsibility

Businesses have responded to the opportunities and threats created by environmental issues with varying levels of commitment. As Figure 9.4 indicates, a low-commitment business attempts to avoid dealing with environmental issues and hopes that nothing bad will happen or that no one will ever find out about an environmental accident or abuse. Such firms may try to protect themselves against lawsuits. Hooker Chemical, for example, disposed of its chemical wastes in and

FIGURE 9.4

Strategic Approaches to Environmental Issues

Low Commitment	Medium Commitment	High Commitment
Deal only with existing problems	Attempts to comply with environmental laws	Strategic programs to address environmental issues
Limited planning to anticipate issues	Deals with issues that could cause public relations issues	Views environment as an opportunity to advance the business strategy
Failure to consider stakeholder environmental issues	Views environmental issues from a tactical, not a strategic, perspective	Consults with stakeholders about their environmental concerns
Operates without concern for long-term environmental impact	Views environment as more of a threat than an opportunity	Conducts an environmental audit to assess performance issues and adopts international standards

around Love Canal near Niagara Falls, New York, because the area was sparsely populated. When the area was developed years later, new residents were surprised when toxic fumes were detected in some basements. Many families were ultimately forced to abandon their homes. Many people felt that Hooker had failed by not being actively involved in preventing this tragedy. On the other hand, some companies take a high-commitment approach toward natural environment issues. Such firms develop strategic management programs, which view the environment as an opportunity for advancing organizational interests. These companies respond to stakeholder interests, assess risks, and develop a comprehensive environmental strategy. Home Depot, for example, has established a set of environmental principles that include selling responsibly marketed products, eliminating unnecessary packaging, recycling and encouraging the use of products with recycled content, and conserving natural resources by using them wisely. The company also makes contributions to many environmental organizations, including Keep America Beautiful, the Tampa Audubon Society, and the World Wildlife Fund.[71]

▶ *Stakeholder Assessment*

Stakeholder analysis, as discussed in Chapter 3, is an important part of a high-commitment approach to environmental issues. This process requires acknowledging and actively monitoring the environmental concerns of all legitimate stakeholders. Thus, a company must have a process in place for identifying and prioritizing the many claims and stakes on its business and for dealing with trade-offs related to the impact on different stakeholders. Although no company can satisfy every claim, all risk-related claims should be evaluated before a firm decides to take action on or ignore a particular issue. In order to make accurate assumptions about stakeholder interests, managers need to conduct research, assess risks, and communicate with stakeholders about their respective concerns.

As we discussed in Chapter 3, not all stakeholders are equal. There are specific regulations and legal requirements that govern some aspects of stakeholder relationships, such as air and water quality. Additionally, some special-interest groups take extreme positions that, if adopted, would undermine the economic base of many other stakeholders (e.g., fishing rights, logging, hunting). Regardless of the final decision a company makes with regard to particular environmental issues, information should be communicated consistently across all stakeholders. This is especially important when a company faces a crisis or negative publicity about a decision. Another aspect of strong relationships is the willingness to acknowledge and openly address potential conflicts. Some degree of negotiation and conciliation will be necessary to align a company's decisions and strategies with stakeholder interests.

▶ *Risk Analysis*

The next step in a high-commitment response to environmental concerns is assessing risk. Through industry and government research, an organization can usually identify environmental issues that relate to manufacturing, marketing, and consumption and use patterns associated with its products. Through risk analysis, it is possible to assess the environmental risks associated with business decisions. The real difficulty is measuring the costs and benefits of environmental decisions, especially in the eyes of interested stakeholders. Research studies often conflict. For example, a well-respected researcher reported in a leading journal that a certain type of genetically modified corn kills significant numbers of monarch butterflies. However, twenty other studies and the EPA have found that genetically modified corn does not pose a significant risk to the monarch butterfly. In fact, in the year before the study was reported, Monarch Watch found a 30 percent increase in the monarch butterfly population when 40 percent more genetically modified corn was planted.[72]

Debate surrounding environmental issues will force corporate decision makers to weigh the evidence and take some risks in final decisions. The important thing for high-commitment organizations is to continue to evaluate the latest information and to maintain communication with all stakeholders. For example, if the 68 million sport utility vehicles (SUVs) on U.S. roads today were replaced with fuel-efficient electric-powered cars and trucks, there would be a tremendous reduction of greenhouse gas emissions.[73] However, the cooperation and commitment needed to gain the support of government, manufacturers, consumers, and other stakeholders to accomplish this would be next to impossible. Although SUVs may harm the environment, many of their owners believe they provide greater protection in an accident.

The issue of environmental responsibility versus safety in SUVs illustrates that many environmental decisions involve trade-offs for various stakeholders' risks. Through risk management, it is possible to quantify these trade-offs in determining whether to accept or reject environmentally related activities and programs. Usually, the key decision is either investment to reduce the risk of damage or the amount of risk acceptable in stakeholder relationships. A company should assess these relationships on an ongoing basis. Both formal and informal methods are needed to get feedback from stakeholders. For example, the employees of a firm can use formal methods such as exit interviews, an open-door policy, and toll-free telephone hot lines. Conversations between employees could provide informal feedback. But it is ultimately the responsibility of the business to make the best decision possible after processing all available research and information. Then, if it is later discovered that a mistake has been made, change is still possible through open disclosure and thoughtful reasoning. Finally, a high-commitment organization will incorporate new information and insights into the strategic planning process.

▶ The Strategic Environmental Audit

Organizations that are highly committed to environmental responsibility may conduct an audit of their efforts and report the results to all interested stakeholders. Table 9.5 provides a starting point for examining environmental sensitivity. Such organizations may also wish to use globally accepted standards, such as ISO 14000, as benchmarks in a strategic environmental audit. The International Standards Organization developed **ISO 14000** as a comprehensive set of environmental standards that encourage a cleaner, safer, and healthier world. There is currently considerable variation among the environmental laws and regulations of nations and regions, making it difficult for high-commitment organizations to find acceptable solutions on a global scale. The goal of the ISO 14000 standards is thus to promote a common approach to environmental management and to

TABLE 9.5

Strategic Natural Environment Audit

Yes	No	Checklist
❏	❏	Does the organization show a high commitment to a strategic environmental policy?
❏	❏	Do employees know the environmental compliance policies of the organization?
❏	❏	Do suppliers and customers recognize the organization's stand on environmental issues?
❏	❏	Are managers familiar with the environmental strategies of other organizations in the industry?
❏	❏	Has the organization compared its environmental initiatives with those of other firms?
❏	❏	Is the company aware of the best practices in environmental management regardless of industry?
❏	❏	Has the organization developed measurable performance standards for environmental compliance?
❏	❏	Does the firm reconcile the need for consistent responsible values with the needs of various stakeholders?
❏	❏	Do the organization's philanthropic efforts consider environmental issues?
❏	❏	Does the organization comply with all laws and regulations that relate to environmental impact?

help companies attain and measure improvements in environmental performance.[74] Companies that choose to abide by the ISO standards may receive a certificate to indicate their compliance; some companies, including DaimlerChrysler, Ford Motor Co., and General Motors, require their suppliers to be ISO 14000 certified.[75] Other performance benchmarks available for use in environmental audits come from nonprofit organizations such as CERES, which has also developed standards for reporting information about environmental performance to interested stakeholders.

As this chapter has demonstrated, corporate citizenship entails responding to stakeholder concerns about the environment, and many firms are finding creative ways to address environmental challenges. Although many of the companies mentioned in this chapter have chosen to implement strategic environmental initiatives in order to capitalize on opportunities and achieve greater efficiency and cost savings, most also believe that responding to stakeholders' concerns about environmental issues will help improve relationships with a variety of stakeholders and make the world a better place.

Summary

Although the scope of the natural environment is quite broad, we define the term as the physical world, including all biological entities, as well as the interaction among nature and individuals, organizations, and business strategies. In recent years, companies have been increasingly incorporating environmental issues into their business strategies.

Air pollution arises from stationary sources such as factories and power plants; mobile sources such as cars, trucks, planes, and trains; and natural occurrences such as windblown dust and volcanic eruptions. Acid rain results when nitrous oxides and sulfur dioxides emitted from manufacturing facilities react with air and rain. Scientists believe that increasing concentrations of "greenhouse gases" in the atmosphere are warming the planet, although this theory is rather controversial. The Kyoto Protocol is a treaty proposed among industrialized nations to slow global warming.

Water pollution results from the dumping of raw sewage and toxic chemicals into rivers and oceans, from oil and gasoline spills, from the burial of industrial waste in the ground where it may filter into underground water supplies, and from runoff of fertilizers and pesticides used in farming and grounds maintenance. The amount of water available is also a concern and the topic of political disputes.

Land pollution results from the dumping of residential and industrial waste, strip mining, and poor forest conservation. How to dispose of waste in an environmentally responsible manner is another issue. Deforestation to make way for agriculture and development threatens animal and plant species. Urban sprawl, the result of changing human development patterns, consumes wildlife habitat, wetlands, and farmland.

Deforestation, pollution, and urban sprawl threaten wildlife, plants, and their habitats and have caused many species to become extinct or endangered. Genetic engineering involves transferring one or more genes from one organism to another to create a new life form that has unique traits. However, the long-term impact of this technology is not known, and many people fear its use.

The U.S. Environmental Protection Agency (EPA) is an independent regulatory agency that establishes and enforces environmental protection standards, conducts environmental research, provides assistance in fighting pollution, and assists in developing and recommending new policies for environmental protection. The Clean Air Act regulates atmospheric emissions from a variety of sources, whereas the Federal Insecticide, Fungicide, and Rodenticide Act regulates the distribution, sale, and use of pesticides. The Endangered Species Act protects threatened and endangered species as well as the habitats in which they are found. The Toxic Substances Control Act empowered the EPA to track, test, and ban industrial chemicals. The Clean Water Act authorized the EPA to establish effluent standards and to set water quality limits for all contaminants in surface waters. The Emergency Planning and Community Right-to-Know Act required most manufacturers to file Toxics Release Inventories detailing their releases of chemicals into the air, water, and land. The Pollution Prevention Act focused industry, government, and public attention on pollution reduction efforts. The Food Quality Protection Act changed the way the EPA regulates pesticides by applying the same standard to all pesticides used in food products.

Businesses are applying creativity, technology, and business resources to respond to environmental issues. Some firms have created a new executive position, Vice President of Environmental Affairs, to help them achieve their business goals in an environmentally responsible manner. Green marketing refers to the specific development, pricing, promotion, and distribution of products that do less harm to the environment. There is growing agreement among environmentalists and businesses, however, that companies should work to protect and preserve the natural environment by implementing a number of goals to: (1) eliminate the concept of waste, (2) rethink the concept of a product, (3) make the price of products reflect their true costs, and (4) seek ways to make business's commitment to the environment profitable. Many organizations engage in recycling, the reprocessing of materials—especially of steel, aluminum, paper, glass, rubber, and some plastics—for reuse. To combat air pollution and the threat of global warming, many companies are striving for greater efficiency, waste reduction, and the reduction of greenhouse-gas emissions. Socially responsible buying initiatives are another way that companies are finding to incorporate environmental responsibility into their business strategies.

Businesses have responded to the opportunities and threats created by environmental issues with varying levels of commitment. A high-commitment business develops strategic management programs, which view the environment as an opportunity for advancing organizational interests. Stakeholder analysis requires a process for identifying and prioritizing the many claims and stakes on its business and for dealing with trade-offs related to the impact on different stakeholders. Through risk analysis, it is possible to assess the environmental risks and trade-offs associated with business decisions. Organizations that are highly committed to environmental responsibility may conduct an audit of their efforts and report the results to all interested stakeholders. Such organizations may use globally accepted standards, such as ISO 14000, as benchmarks in a strategic environmental audit.

KEY TERMS

natural environment

Kyoto Protocol

Toxics Release Inventory (TRI)

green marketing

recycling

ISO 14000

DISCUSSION QUESTIONS

1. Define the natural environment in the context of corporate citizenship. How does this definition differ from your own definition of the environment?

2. Identify how some of the environmental issues discussed in this chapter are affecting your community. What steps have local businesses taken to address these issues?

3. How serious is the issue of global warming? Discuss the need for global cooperation in addressing this issue.

4. Discuss some of the potential problems associated with attempts to manage biodiversity and endangered species.

5. What is the role of the EPA in U.S. environmental policy? What impact does this agency have on businesses?

6. What federal laws seem to have the greatest impact on business efforts to be environmentally responsible?

7. What role do stakeholders play in a strategic approach to environmental issues? How can businesses satisfy the interests of diverse stakeholders?

8. What is environmental risk analysis? Why is it important for an environmentally conscious company?

9. What is ISO 14000? What is its potential impact on key stakeholders, community, businesses, and global organizations concerned about environmental issues?

10. How can businesses plan and manage for environmental responsibility?

EXPERIENTIAL EXERCISE

Visit the web site of the U.S. EPA (**http://www. epa.gov**/). What topics and issues fall under the authority of the EPA? Peruse the agency's most recent news releases. What themes, issues, regulations, and other areas is the EPA most concerned with today? How can this site be useful to consumers and businesses?

NOTES

1. "Fortune 500, 1999," *Fortune,* www.fortune.com; Herman Miller Furniture, www.hermanmiller.com, accessed December 16, 2000; Info Quotes Fundamentals, NASDAQ/AMEX Online, http://quotes. nasdaq.com/, May 10, 1999; David Woodruff, "Herman Miller: How Green Is My Factory," *Business Week,* September 16, 1991, http://bwarchive/ businessweek.com.

2. "Gallup Poll: Public Supports Environmental Movement, But Not as a Priority," CNN, April 17, 2000, www.cnn.com/.

3. Alan K. Reichert, Marion S. Webb, and Edward G. Thomas, "Corporate Support for Ethical and Environmental Policies: A Financial Management Perspective," *Journal of Business Ethics,* 25 (2000): 53–64.

4. "Air Quality," Office of Air Quality Planning and Standards, Environmental Protection Agency, July 10, 2000, www.epa.gov/oar/oaqps/cleanair.html.

5. "The Plain English Guide to the Clean Air Act," Office of Air Quality Planning and Standards, Environmental Protection Agency, July 18, 2000, www.epa. gov/oar/oaqps/peg_caa/pegcaa01.html#topic1.

6. "Environmental Effects of Acid Rain," Environmental Protection Agency, www.epa.gov/docs/acidrain/ effects/envben.html, accessed December 16, 2000.

7. "Texaco Quits Global Warming Group," CNN, March 1, 2000, www.cnn.com/.

8. www.newscientist.com/hottopics/climate/climate/ faq.jsp, accessed November 1, 2001.

9. "Global Warming FAQ: All You Ever Wanted to Know about Climate Change."

10. "Texaco Quits Global Warming Group."

11. Traci Watson, "Global Warming Good News?" *USA Today,* November 16, 2000, p. 16A.

12. Erin Kelly, "States Foul Out on Clean Water Act," *Coloradoan,* April 6, 2000, p. B1.

13. Ibid.

14. Kathleen Fackelmann, "Teen Discovers Antibiotics in Public Supplies; Scientists Fear 'Superbugs,'" *USA Today,* November 8, 2000, pp. 1D, 2D.

15. Kelly, "States Foul Out on Clean Water Act."

16. Richard J. Labrecque, "Water Management for the 21st Century," essay in special advertising section, *Business Week,* May 3, 1999.

17. Mark H. Hunter, "San Luis Valley Water War Settled," *Denver Post,* March 16, 2000, www.denverpost. com/news/news0316c.htm.

18. Robert Rosenblatt, "Man and Nature: All the Days of the Earth," *Time Earth Day 2000,* 155 (Spring 2000): 12.

19. Eugene Linden, "State of the Planet: Condition Critical," *Time Earth Day 2000,* 155 (Spring 2000): 18.

20. James Howard Kunstler, *The Geography of Nowhere: The Rise and Decline of America's Man-made Landscape* (New York: Simon & Schuster, 1994).

21. Mark Walters, "Current Regulatory Environment and Impediments to the Establishment of a Compact City," directed research project, Southwest Texas University, November 1, 2001.

22. Sierra Club, "Roads and Highways," *Sprawl Costs Us All: How Your Taxes Fuel Suburban Sprawl,* Sierra Club, 2000, www.sierraclub.org/sprawl/report00/ roads.asp

23. Eugene Linden, "State of the Planet: Condition Critical," *Time Earth Day 2000,* 155 (Spring 2000): 24.

24. "Tropical Forest Species Richness," World Resources Institute, www.wri.org/wri/biodiv/b01-koa.html, accessed December 16, 2000.

25. G. T. Miller, "Deforestation and Loss of Diversity," in *Living in the Environment: Principles, Connections and Solutions,* 8th ed. (Belmont, Calif.: Wadsworth Publishing Co., 1994) also available at www.bse.vt. edu/dillaha/green/biodiver.htm.

26. "Monkey's Extinction May Be a Sign," CNN, September 13, 2000, www.cnn.com.

27. Laura Tangley, "Keeping the Delicate Balance of Nature," *U.S. News & World Report,* November 15, 1999, p. 95.

28. "Earth Matters: Pollinator Decline Puts World Food Supply at Risk, Experts Warn," CNN, May 5, 2000, www.cnn.com.

29. "Overcutting Costs More Timber Jobs than Owl, Study Says," *Idaho Statesman,* Feb. 16, 1997, also available at http://bachman.ecology.uga.edu/~dstewart/ecoweb/news001.htm.

30. Paul Magnusson, Ann Therese, and Kerry Capell, "Furor over Frankenfood," *Business Week,* October 18, 1999, pp. 50, 51.

31. "Biotech Food Safe, but More Tests Needed, Study Suggests," *Coloradoan,* April 6, 2000, p. B3.

32. Ellen Licking, "Tinkering with Genes: Time for a National Debate," *Business Week,* November 8, 1999, p. 44.

33. Jack Lewis, "The Birth of the EPA," *EPA Journal,* November 1985, also available at www.epa.gov/history/topics/epa/15c.htm.

34. "EPA's Mission, Goals, and Principles," *EPA Strategic Plan,* Office of the Chief Financial Officer, Environmental Protection Agency, www.epa.gov/ocfo/plan/sec2.pdf, (accessed) March 15, 2000.

35. Peter Eisler, "EPA to Phase out Popular Insecticide Diazinon," *USA Today,* December 5, 2000, p. 1A.

36. "EPA's Mission, Goals, and Principles."

37. John J. Fialka, "Koch Industries' $30 Million Fine Is Biggest-Ever Pollution Penalty," *Wall Street Journal Interactive,* January 14, 2000, http://interactive.wsj.com.

38. O. C. Ferrell, John Fraedrich, and Gwyneth Vaughn, "The Wreck of the Exxon Valdez," in *Business Ethics: Ethical Decision Making and Cases,* ed. O. C. Ferrell, John Fraedrich, and Linda Ferrell, 5th edition (Boston: Houghton Mifflin, 2002), pp. 331–339.

39. "Major Environmental Laws: Clean Air Act," Environmental Protection Agency, www.epa.gov/region5/defs/html/caa.htm, accessed December 16, 2000.

40. Lewis, "The Birth of the EPA"; "Major Environmental Laws: Clean Air Act."

41. "Major Environmental Laws: Clean Air Act."

42. "Major Environmental Laws: Federal Insecticide, Fungicide, and Rodenticide Act," Environmental Protection Agency, www.epa.gov/region5/defs/html/fifra.htm, accessed November 1, 2001.

43. "Major Environmental Laws: Endangered Species Act," Environmental Protection Agency, www.epa. gov/region5/defs/html/esa.htm, accessed, November 1, 2001.

44. Ibid.

45. "How Has the ESA Impacted People," National Endangered Species Act Reform Coalition, www.nesarc.org/stories.htm, accessed November 1, 2001.

46. "Major Environmental Laws: Toxic Substances Control Act," Environmental Protection Agency, www.epa.gov/region5/defs/html/tsca.htm, accessed November 1, 2001.

47. "Major Environmental Laws: Clean Water Act," Environmental Protection Agency, www.epa.gov/region5/defs/html/cwa.htm, accessed November 1, 2001.

48. "What Is the Toxics Release Inventory?" Environmental Protection Agency, www.epa.gov/tri/general.htm, accessed November 1, 2001.

49. "Major Environmental Laws: Pollution Prevention Act," Environmental Protection Agency, www.epa.gov/region5/defs/html/ppa.htm, accessed November 1, 2001.

50. "Food Quality Protection Act (FQPA) of 1996," Office of Pesticide Programs, Environmental Protection Agency, www.epa.gov/opppsps1/fqpa/, accessed November 1, 2001.

51. "The Food Quality Protection Act (FQPA) Background," Office of Pesticide Programs, Environmental Protection Agency, www.epa.gov/opppsps1/fqpa/backgrnd.htm, accessed November 1, 2001.

52. Jeffrey Ball, "GM to Produce Hybrid Trucks, Buses in Scramble to Build 'Green' Vehicles," *Wall Street Journal,* August 3, 2000, p. A4.

53. "Entrepreneurs Bring in Revenue for U.S. Parks," CNN, November 8, 1999, www.cnn.com/; "Supporting Our National Parks," The Parks Company, www.theparksco.com/support/onefortheparks.html, accessed November 1, 2001.

54. Nikki Sameshima, "Natural Born 'Burbs," *Coloradobiz,* 27 (April 2000): 72, 74.

55. "The European Eco-label at a Glance," European Commission booklet; "The Eco-label and Exporting to Europe," *Business America,* November 29, 1993, p. 21.

56. "Saving the Forest for the Trees," *Business Week,* November 20, 2000, pp. 62–63.

57. Jim Carlton, "Chiquita to Take Part in Environmental Program," *Wall Street Journal,* November 16, 2000, p. A3.

58. Jason Hopps, "Study Finds 'Green' Product Labeling Misleading," Reuters Newswire, March 31, 2000, via America Online.

59. Paul Hawken and William McDonough, "Seven Steps to Doing Good Business," *Inc.* November 1993, pp. 79–90.

60. "Tire Recycling Gains Traction with Help from Business," CNN, April 25, 2000, www.cnn.com.

61. "AF and PA Recycling Programs," American Forest and Paper Association, www.afandpa.org/recycling/afandpa_initiatives.html, accessed November 1, 2001.

62. Helen Chung, "Starbucks Serves Up Coffee Grounds for Compost: Great Coffee Is Also Good for the Garden," *Business Wire,* March 20, 2000, www.businesswire.com/cnn/sbux.htm.

63. "Doing What It Takes to Be Wastewise," Environmental Protection Agency, April 1999, www.epa.gov/epaoswer/non-hw/reduce/wstewise/id-bev.htm.

64. Eric Peterson, "The Wal-Mart of Recycling," *Coloradobiz,* 26 (October 1999): 66.

65. "Complete Recycling of Water Will Protect Environment, Resources at Daimler Chrysler Plant in Mexico," *PR Newsletter,* March 29, 2000, via America Online.

66. Sharon Begley, "The Battle for Planet Earth," *Newsweek,* April 24, 2000, pp. 50–53.

67. Ibid.

68. John J. Fialka, "An Environment-Business Global-Warming Link," *Wall Street Journal,* November 22, 2000, p. A2.

69. Minette E. Drumwright, "Socially Responsible Organisational Buying: Environmental Concern as a Noneconomic Buying Criterion," *Journal of Marketing,* 58 (July 1994): 1.

70. Isabelle Maignan and Debbie Thorne McAlister, "Socially Responsible Organizational Buying: Can Stakeholders Dictate Purchasing Policies," Nijmegen University working paper, 2002.

71. "Social Responsibility at Home Depot," in *Marketing: Concepts and Strategies,* ed. William M. Pride and O. C. Ferrell, 2000e (Boston: Houghton Mifflin, 2000), pp. 104–105.

72. "BIO Statement Regarding Purported New Findings on Bt Corn and Monarch Butterflies," The Life Sciences Knowledge Center, August 21, 2000, www.biotechknowledge.com/showlib_us.php3?3854.

73. Begley, "The Battle for Planet Earth."

74. "International Standard ISO 14000," Quality Network, www.quality.co.uk/iso14000.htm, accessed November 1, 2001.

75. "DaimlerChrysler Sets Registration Deadline," ISO 14000 Information Center, October 24, 2000, www.iso14000.com/WhatsNew/News02.htm; "Ford Requires Suppliers to Achieve ISO 14001 Certification," ISO 14000 Information Center, September 23, 1999, www.iso14000.com/WhatsNew/News01.htm.

Technology Issues

10

▶ The Nature of Technology

▶ Technology's Influence on the Economy

▶ Technology's Influence on Society

▶ Strategic Implementation of Responsibility for Technology

OBJECTIVES

To examine the nature and characteristics of technology

To explore the economic impact of technology

To examine technology's influence on society

To provide a framework for strategic management of technology issues

Napster is an online service that allows computer users to share high-quality digital copies (MP3s) of music recordings via the Internet. The San Mateo, California–based company doesn't actually store the recordings on its own computers, but instead provides an index of all the songs available on the computers of members currently logged onto the service. Napster therefore functions as a sort of clearinghouse that members can log onto, search by artist or song title, and identify where MP3s of interest are so that they can download them from another user's computer hard drive. Napster has become one of the most popular sites on the Internet, claiming some 15 million users in little more than a year. Indeed, so many students were downloading songs from Napster, that many universities were forced to block the site from their systems in order to regain bandwidth.

Napster's service has been almost as controversial as it has been popular. Barely a year after its launch, it was sued by the Recording Industry Association of America (RIAA), which represents major recording companies such as Universal Music, BMG, Sony Music, Warner Music Group, and EMI. The RIAA claimed that by allowing users to swap music recordings for free, Napster's service violated copyright laws. The RIAA also sought an injunction to stop the downloading of copyrighted songs owned by its members as well as damages for lost revenue. The RIAA argued that song swapping via Napster and similar firms has cost the music industry more than $300 million in lost sales. A few months after the RIAA lawsuit was filed, Metallica, a heavy metal band, and rap star Dr. Dre filed separate lawsuits accusing Napster of copyright infringement and racketeering. Lars Ulrich, Metallica's drummer, told a Senate committee that Napster users are basically stealing from the band every time they download one of its songs.

Napster initially argued that because it does not directly provide the copyrighted music, the Digital Millennium Copyright Act protects its actions. The firm's attorneys asserted that Napster is merely a conduit because it does not copy music and has no way of knowing whether its members have paid for the recordings they offer for trade. However, Cary Sherman, RIAA's executive vice president and general counsel, says, "Whether or not it is lawful for users to share music one-on-one, it is entirely different for a commercial entity to create a business that induces users to do that." When a U.S. District Court judge rejected Napster's defense, its attorneys changed tactics, arguing that a 1992 law permits music purchasers to copy music for their own use, and that its service merely provides a directory to those legally copied songs. Napster also cited a study by the University of Pennsylvania, which indicated that Napster use actually stimulates sales of music CDs. The company also pointed out that many unknown artists granted permission for their songs to be traded online via Napster.

In July 2000, a federal judge granted the RIAA's request for an injunction and ordered Napster to stop making copyrighted recordings available for download, but that order was stayed a few days later by the 9th Circuit Court of Appeals. In 2001, the appeals court ruled that Napster had knowingly allowed users to download copyrighted material and ordered the firm to halt all downloads of copyrighted recordings. Napster has appealed that ruling. Regardless of the outcome of these legal proceedings, many Internet observers believe that swapping music online will continue, through services such as Gnutella, Scour, and Gigabeat, and that the record industry must learn to adapt to changing technology in order to satisfy music fans.[1]

The technology behind Napster is just one example of the many advances that have enriched our lives in recent decades. Technology brings to mind scientific advances as well as concerns about the impact of technology on society. Although we enjoy the benefits of communicating through the Internet, we are increasingly concerned about protecting our privacy and our intellectual property. Although health and medical research creates new drugs that save lives, cloning and genetically modified foods have become controversial issues to many segments of society. In various ways and to varying degrees, home environments, health care, leisure, and work performance are all influenced by both current technology and advances in technology.

In this chapter, we explore the nature of technology and its positive and negative effects on society. Technology's influence on the economy is very powerful, especially with regard to growth, employment, and working environments. This influence on society includes issues related to the Internet, privacy, intellectual property, health, and the general quality of life. The strategic direction for technology depends on government, as well as on business's ability to plan, implement, and audit the influence of technology on society.

The Nature of Technology

Technology relates to the application of knowledge, including the processes and applications to solve problems, perform tasks, and create new methods to obtain desired outcomes. It includes intellectual knowledge as well as the physical systems devised to achieve business and personal objectives. The evolution of civilization is tied to developments in technology. Through technological advances, humans have moved from a hunter–gatherer existence to a stable agricultural economy to the Industrial Revolution. Today, our economy is based more on information technology and services than on manufacturing. This technology is changing the way we take vacations, have dinner, do homework, track criminals, know where we are, and maintain friendships. Technology has made it possible to go to work or meetings without leaving the house. Our new economy is based on these dynamic technological changes in our society.

▌ *Characteristics of Technology*

Some of the characteristics of technology include the dynamics, reach, and self-sustaining nature of technological progress. The dynamics of technology relate to the constant change that often challenges the structure of social institutions. The automobile, airplane, and personal computer all created major changes and influenced government, the family, social relationships, education, military, and leisure. These changes can come so fast that they require significant adjustments in the political, religious, and economic structures of society. Some societies have difficulty adjusting to this rate of change to the point that they even attempt to legislate against new technologies in order to isolate themselves. Countries such as Iran and China have attempted to isolate their societies from innovations such as the Internet and social trends that result from the application of new technology to products such as music and movies on compact discs and digital video discs. But even China has responded to the new Internet technology by issuing trial online advertising licenses in a country where advertising has not been widely accepted.[2]

The future dynamics of technology are challenging many traditional products, including books. E Ink and Xerox, for example, are developing thin paper and plastic films that can function as screens with digital ink. Users of the technology would still be able to turn the pages as with a traditional book or newspaper, but the pages could be reloaded with a new article or best-seller through wireless transmission. The flat sheet of enhanced paper could even be used to receive a

Computers and information technology are found everywhere including this marketplace in Kampala, Uganda.

movie.[3] The challenges to traditional ways of receiving information are accelerating change in every aspect of life. In many cases, a new technology may become obsolete in a very short period after introduction. Thus, the dynamic characteristic of technology keeps challenging society to adjust.

Reach relates to the broad nature of technology as it moves through society. For instance, every community in both developed and developing countries has been influenced by cellular and wireless telephones. The ability to make a call from almost any location has many positive effects, but negative side effects include increases in traffic accidents and noise pollution as well as fears about potential health risks. Through telecommunications, businesses, families, and governments have been linked from far distances. Satellites allow instant visual and voice electronic connections almost anywhere in the world. These technologies have reduced the need for business travel, as shown in Figure 10.1.

The self-sustaining nature of technology relates to the fact that technology acts as a catalyst to spur even faster development. As new innovations are introduced, they stimulate the need for more technology to facilitate further development. For example, the Internet has created the need for broadband transmission of electrical signals through phone lines (DSL), satellites, and cable. Broadband allows connections to the Internet to be fifty times faster than through a traditional phone modem, allows users to download large files, and creates the opportunity for a rich multimedia experience. As broadband becomes available to more businesses and households, other technologies will have to advance to keep up with the ability to access so much data quickly.[4] In the future, it could be possible to have broadband transmission to computers through electric lines. This means that users could

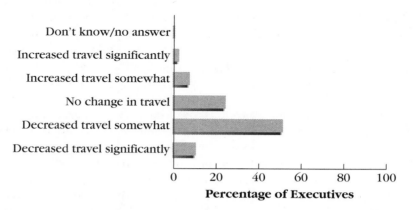

FIGURE 10.1

Technology Decreases the Need for Business Travel
Sixty-three percent of executives surveyed indicated that technology has decreased their business travel.

Source: Darryl Haraison and Marcy E. Mullins, "More Technology, Less Business Travel," *USA Today,* December 6, 2000, p. 1B. Copyright 2000, USA Today. Reprinted with permission.

have a broadband connection anywhere that a computer can be plugged in. The invention of the personal computer resulted in changes in personal financial management related to banking, insurance, taxes, and stock trading. Technology starts a change process that creates new opportunities for new technologies in every industry segment or personal life experience that it touches. At some point, there is even a multiplier effect that causes an even greater demand for more change to improve performance.

▶ *Effects of Technology*

Civilizations must harness and adapt to changes in technology in order to maintain a desired quality of life. The cell phone, for example, has dramatically altered communication patterns, particularly in underdeveloped nations where there are few telephone lines. New innovations can also change entire industries. For example, Swedish researchers have developed microscopic robots, or microrobots, that can be used underwater and within biological fluids. These devices have great potential in biomedical applications because they can operate in blood, urine, or cell-cultured media. They could also be used to assemble goods underwater.[5] Such examples illustrate how technology can provide new methods to accomplish tasks that were once thought impossible. These advancements create new processes, products, and economic progress, and ultimately have profound effects on society.

The global economy is experiencing the greatest acceleration of technological advancement that has ever occurred, propelling increases in productivity, output, corporate profits, and stock prices.[6] Advances in information technology have driven productivity and economic growth over the last ten years. Among the positive contributions of these advances are reductions in the number of worker hours required to generate the nation's output. At the same time, the economic conditions that have accompanied this period of technical innovation have resulted in increased job opportunities. Indeed, the U.S. unemployment rate has fallen to record lows as the pace of technological advancement has accelerated.[7] The traditional work environment has changed in the last ten years because telecommunications (e.g., e-mail, videoconferencing) reduce the need for face-to-face interaction. Through online shopping, the Internet can also reduce the need for trips to a shopping center.

However, there are concerns that dramatic shifts in the acceleration and innovations derived from technology may be spurring imbalances not only in the economy, but also in our social existence. The flow of technology into developing countries can serve as a method to jump-start economic development. On the other hand, a failure to share technology or provide methods to disseminate technology could cause a major divide in the quality of life. Nick Grouf, cofounder and

CEO of PeoplePC, articulates the issue: "It's in the nation's interest to have a technologically savvy and wired citizenry. If that social issue isn't addressed today, we're going to have larger social issues ten years from now." In the United States, the federal government is stepping in with plans to spend $50 million to subsidize computers and Internet access for 300,000 low-income households across the nation. Although this initiative is somewhat controversial, proponents believe it has the potential to raise the standard of living for low-income families much as the Rural Electrification Administration did in the 1930s, after President Franklin Delano Roosevelt established it to extend electrical power and telephone services to remote communities and rural areas.[8] Some companies are also trying to help bridge the technology gap that is developing between those who can afford technology and those who are on the other side of the so-called "digital divide." Gateway, Inc., the second-largest computer manufacturer, in partnership with the Association of Equal Opportunity in Higher Education (NAFEO), is working to provide discounted computers to 118 predominately African-American colleges and universities.[9] Gateway is an example of a corporate attempt to keep the positive effects of the reach of technology available to all segments of society.

There are concerns about the way information technology can improve the quality of life for society. In addition, there are concerns about the negative consequences of the reduction of privacy and the emergence of cybercrime. At some point, abrupt adjustment could occur as changes in our economy or members of society become unhappy about changes in lifestyles or the role of business and government in our lives. Public advocacy organizations are helping by participating in charting the future of our computer networks to integrate these technological innovations into the way we live.[10]

Technology's Influence on the Economy

Technological advancements have had a profound impact on economic growth and employment, but they raise concerns as well.

▶ Economic Growth and Employment

Over the past fifty years, technology has been a major factor in the economic growth in the United States. Investments in educational technologies, increased support for basic government research, and continued commitment to the mission of research and development (R&D) in both the public and private sectors have become major drivers of economic growth. Through deficit reduction, lower interest rates, tax credits, and liberalization of export controls, the government established the economic infrastructure for using technology to drive economic

TABLE 10.1

Industries with the Highest Federal Support for Research and Development

Industry	Payoff
Computers and Communications	Defense-related research and development to provide for communications in the event of war led to what has become the Internet.
Semiconductors	The U.S. semiconductor industry developed as a direct result of federal R&D investments and procurement activities.
Biotechnology	Federally funded discoveries in biology, food science, agriculture, genetics, and drugs on which the private sector has been able to build and expand a world-class industry.
Aerospace	The federal government traditionally has funded the lion's share of aerospace R&D, and this support has made U.S. aerospace companies the world's most advanced.
Environmental Technologies	The federal government provides nearly $2 billion a year in support of R&D related to environmental technologies.
Energy Efficiency	Many of the products sold and installed by this industry are the product of partnerships between the federal government and private industry.
Lasers	Refined though government, industry, and university research, lasers are now one of the most powerful, versatile, and pervasive technologies in our lives.
Magnetic Resonance Imaging	Nuclear physicists and chemists worked out the fundamental technique of using radio beams and magnetic fields to analyze the chemical structure of biomedical and other materials.

Source: Technology and Economic Growth: Producing Real Results for the American People,
The White House, November 8, 1995, www.whitehouse.gov/WH/EOP/OSTP/html/techgrow.html.

development. The expansion of industry-led technology partnerships between corporations, governments, and nonprofit organizations has also been a key component of growth. Table 10.1 shows the industries that have received the highest federal support for research and development.

Investments in research and development are among the highest-return investments a nation can make. A report by the Council of Economic Advisors notes that over the past fifty years, technological innovation has been responsible for half or more of the nation's growth in productivity.[11] For example, the ability to access information in "real time" through the electronic data interface between retailers, wholesalers, and manufacturers has reduced delivery lead times as well as the hours required to produce and deliver products. Likewise, product design times and costs have declined because computer modeling has minimized the need for architectural drafters and some engineers required for building projects. Medical diagnoses have become faster, more thorough, and more accurate, thanks to access to information and records over the Internet, hastening treatment and eliminating unnecessary procedures.[12]

The relationship between businesses and consumers already is being changed by the expanding opportunities for e-commerce, the sharing of business information, maintaining business relationships, and conducting business transactions by means of telecommunications networks.[13] More and more people are turning to the Internet to purchase computers and related peripherals, software, books, music, and even furniture; consumers are increasingly using the Internet to book travel reservations, transact banking business, and trade securities. The forces unleashed by the Internet are particularly important in business-to-business relationships, where the improved quantity, reliability, and timeliness of information have reduced uncertainties. This is the case in companies such as General Motors, IBM, and Procter and Gamble, which are learning to consolidate and rationalize their supply chains using the Internet.[14] Consider the Covisint alliance between Ford, General Motors, DaimlerChrysler, Renault, Nissan, Oracle, and Commerce One, which makes parts from suppliers available through a competitive online auction, reducing months of negotiations into a single day. The goal of the alliance is to reduce the time it takes to bring a new vehicle to market from fifty-four months to eighteen.[15] In many cases, companies are moving toward making most of their purchases online.[16] Business-to-business Internet sales are expected to exceed $1.33 trillion by 2003, with computer and electronics sales contributing nearly $400 billion.[17]

Economic growth means more jobs and improved living standards. Americans hold millions of jobs in industries that have grown as a result of public and private investment in R&D. These include biotechnology, computers, communications, software, aerospace, semiconductors; even retailing, wholesaling, and other commercial institutions have been transformed by technology. Average pay for workers in these high-technology industries is about 60 percent higher than the average wage for all American workers.

Science and technology are powerful drivers of economic growth and improvements in the quality of life in America. Advances in technology have created not only millions of new jobs, but also better health and longer lives, new opportunities, and enrichment of our lives in ways we could not have imagined half a century ago. For example, electrical plugs and outlets are becoming a thing of the past. Because of improved battery technologies and better utilization of radio frequencies (RFs), we are becoming a wireless society. Wireless devices in use today include radios, cell phones, TVs, pagers, and car keys. In the future, most long-distance communication will likely be through fiber optics, and short-distance communication will be wireless.[18] Demand for wireless technology is accelerating, with 50 percent of *Fortune* 1,000 companies expected to commit 15 percent of all network spending to wireless voice and data technology.[19] In the future, refrigerators, medicine cabinets, and even product packaging may contain wireless microdevices that broadcast product characteristics, features, expiration dates, and other information.[20]

▶ *Economic Concerns about the Use of Technology*

Despite the staggering economic growth fostered by technological advancements, there are economic downsides to technology. Small businesses in particular may have difficulty taking advantage of the opportunities surrounding the Internet. Consider the case of Joseph Serna, who thought the Internet could be a powerful tool to attract more customers to his seven-employee print shop in Denver. However, like millions of other small businesspeople and thousands of communities, Serna now fears the new medium will crush his small business instead. Serna's customers want to send art, photos, and layouts to him via e-mail, but his conventional computer modem requires a laborious twenty minutes to send or receive a simple eight-page brochure. A new high-speed Internet connection could slash that time to seconds—if it was available in his area. Phone companies are now offering high-speed service in other, often more upscale, Denver areas, but they have no immediate plans to bring service to Serna's neighborhood. His choice: Pay more than $1,000 a month for a dedicated T-1 phone line or stand by and watch while competitors with greater resources steal his customers. High-speed connections, also known as broadband, are becoming a must-have for businesses of any size.[21]

This example illustrates the effects of technological imbalances on competition by creating classes of high-tech "haves" and "have-nots." Although 90 percent of businesses with more than 500 employees have high-speed Internet connections, just 5 to 7 percent of 21 million smaller businesses have high-speed access. Moreover, 86 percent of high-capacity lines and broadband connections is concentrated in the nation's twenty largest cities. And even in those cities, although phone companies compete fiercely to bring high-speed service to large corporations and wealthy neighborhoods, many other sections of the cities are left behind.[22] Without greater access to the latest technology, especially high-speed Internet services, economic development could suffer in underserved communities, especially poor suburban neighborhoods, inner cities, and rural areas. The ability to purchase other types of technology may affect the nature of competition and the success of various types of businesses.

There are several ways to address these problems that are the inevitable consequences of accelerating change in the technology drivers of the new economy. One way is to examine the outcomes associated with the attempts to use technology. For example, the small town of Glasgow, Kentucky, thanks to the foresight of local leaders, was hard-wired for high-speed Internet access years before the technology was available in many larger urban areas. Community leaders thought the technology would not only benefit citizens, but also lead to a high-tech boom for the town of 14,000. The city exploits the high-speed wiring to control traffic lights, share computerized maps to coordinate utility repairs, and monitor electric meters, and a number of businesses have incorporated Internet access into their business strategies. However, only two-thirds of the community's businesses and a quarter of its residences have signed up for the service, and the high-tech boom has yet to begin. Nonetheless, many other small communities are installing similar high-speed links in preparation for the future.[23] Another way to address negative consequences is to assess problems related to the impact of technology on competition. Restraining competition, domestic or international, to suppress competitive turmoil is a major concern of governments. Allowing anticompetitive practices, price fixing, or other unfair methods of competition would be counterproductive to rising standards of living.[24]

Technology's Influence on Society

Information and telecommunications technology minimizes the borders between countries, businesses, and people and allows people to overcome the physical limitations of time and space. Technological advances also enable people to acquire customized goods and services that cost less and are of higher quality than ever imagined.[25] For example, parents can give their children robotic pets and dolls, which often cost less than $50, that can be programmed to respond to their child's voice.[26] Airline passengers can purchase tickets online and print out boarding passes on their home or office printers so that they can go straight to their plane on arrival at the airport after clearing security.[27] Cartographers and geologists can create custom maps—even in three dimensions—that may help experts manage water supplies, find oil, and pinpoint future earthquakes.[28] In this section, we explore four broad issues related to technology and its impact on society, including the Internet, privacy, intellectual property, and health and biotechnology. Although there are many other pressing issues related to technology, these seem to be the most widely debated at this time. As technology advances, there will probably be more issues by the time you read this book.

The Internet

The Internet, the global information system that links many computer networks together, has profoundly altered the way people communicate, learn, do business, and find entertainment. Although many people believe the Internet began in the early 1990s, its origins can actually be traced to the late 1950s (Table 10.2). Over

TABLE 10.2

History of the Internet

Year	Event	Significance
1836	Telegraph	The telegraph revolutionized human (tele)communications with Morse Code, a series of dots and dashes used to communicate between humans.
1858–1866	Transatlantic Cable	Transatlantic cable allowed direct instantaneous communication across the Atlantic Ocean.
1876	Telephone	The telephone created voice communication, and telephone exchanges provided the backbone of Internet connections today.
1957	USSR launches *Sputnik*	*Sputnik* was the first artificial earth satellite and the start of global communications.
1962–1968	Packet switching networks developed	The Internet relies on packet switching networks, which split data into tiny packets that may take different routes to a destination.
1971	Beginning of the Internet	People communicate over the Internet with a program to send messages across a distributed network.
1973	Global networking becomes a reality	Ethernet outlined—this is how local networks are basically connected today, and gateways define how large networks (maybe of different architecture) can be connected together.
1991	World Wide Web established	User-friendly interface to World Wide Web established with text-based, menu-driven interface to access Internet resources.
1992	Multimedia changes the face of the Internet	The term "surfing the Internet" is coined.
1993	World Wide Web revolution begins	Mosaic, a user-friendly Graphical Front End to the World Wide Web, makes Web more accessible and evolves into Netscape.
1995	Internet service providers advance	Online dial-up systems (CompuServe, America Online, Prodigy) begin to provide Internet access.
2000	Broadband emerges	Provides fast access to multimedia and large text files.
2002	Wireless expands	Devices for wireless linkage to the Internet grow rapidly.

Source: Adapted from "History of the Internet," Internet Valley, www.internetvalley.com/archives/mirrors/davemarsh-timeline-1.htm, accessed November 2, 2001.

the last four decades, the network evolved from a system for government and university researchers into an information and entertainment tool used by millions around the globe. With the development of the World Wide Web, which organizes the information on the Internet into interconnected "pages" of text, graphics, audio, and video, use of the Internet exploded in the early 1990s.

Today, nearly half a billion people around the world tap into the Internet. In the United States alone, about 168 million Americans access the Internet at home or at work. Internet use by consumers in other countries, especially Japan (26.9 million users), the United Kingdom (33 million), Germany (26 million), China (22.5 million), Japan (22 million), and Canada (14 million), is escalating rapidly.[29] To keep up with the growing demand for new e-mail and web site addresses, the Internet Corporation for Assigned Names and Numbers has added seven new domain name suffixes to allow for the creation of millions of new addresses. Now, in addition to .com (for companies), .edu (schools and universities), .gov (government agencies and offices), .mil (military use), .net (networks), and hundreds of country codes, computer users will see addresses followed by .zero (air-transport industry), .biz (businesses), .coop (nonprofit cooperatives), .info (unrestricted), .museum (museums), .name (personal names), and .pro (professionals such as doctors and accountants).[30]

The interactive nature of the Internet has created tremendous opportunities for businesses to forge relationships with consumers and business customers, target markets more precisely, and even reach previously inaccessible markets. The Internet also facilitates supply-chain management, allowing companies to network with manufacturers, wholesalers, retailers, suppliers, and outsource firms to serve customers more efficiently.[31] Despite the growing importance and popularity of the Internet, fraud has become a major issue for businesses and consumers. Because shopping via the Internet does not require a signature to verify transactions, credit-card fraud online is more than three and a half times greater than credit-card fraud through mail-order catalogs and almost nine times greater than for traditional storefront retailers.[32] In a survey of online retailers, 83 percent reported that fraud is a problem in online transactions, and 61 percent indicated that they were taking precautions to limit the opportunity for customers to engage in fraud.[33]

Consumers are also increasingly worried about becoming victims of fraud online. For example, complaints about fraud in online auctions have risen dramatically over the last five years.[34] One online auction site, eBay, has more than 16 million regular customers exchanging $14 million every day. The company received 10,700 fraud complaints in one year. Among the complaints are accusations of "shill bidding," which involves sellers bidding on their own items to heighten interest, and competitive bidding. Another problem is sellers not delivering promised items after receiving the buyers' funds. The formula for fraud is enhanced by anonymity, quick access, low overhead, satellite access, and little regulation.[35] Increasing complaints about online auctions have made them one of the Federal Trade Commission's top ten "dot cons" (Figure 10.2). With online

FIGURE 10.2

The Top Ten "Dot Cons"

Top Ten Dot Cons

Dot Con? Dot Con.

**File a
Complaint Online**

**Con artists have gone high-tech, using new
technology to peddle traditional scams.
Scam artists can be just a click away.**

Consumers	Business	Media	Law Enforcement

Internet Auctions	International Modem Dialing
Internet Access Services	Credit Card Fraud
Web Cramming	Multilevel Marketing Plans and Pyramids
Travel and Vacation	Business Opportunities
Investments	Health Care Products and Services

Source: "Dot Con? Dot Con," Federal Trade Commission, www.ftc.gov/bcp/conline/edcams/dotcon, accessed November 7, 2001.

auctions generating an estimated $6.1 billion, consumers and merchants alike are exploring options, including regulation, to protect the security of online transactions.[36]

▶ *Privacy*

The extraordinary growth of the Internet has generated issues related to privacy. Businesses have long tracked consumers' shopping habits with little controversy. However, observing the contents of a consumer's shopping cart or the process a consumer goes through when choosing a box of cereal generally involves the collection of aggregate data, rather than specific personally identifying data. And, although some consumers' use of credit cards, shopping cards, and coupons involves giving up a certain degree of anonymity in the shopping process, consumers could still choose to remain anonymous by paying cash. Shopping on the Internet, however, allows businesses to track consumers on a far more personal level, from their online purchases to the web sites they favor.[37] Indeed, current technology has made it possible to amass vast quantities of personal information, often without consumers' knowledge. The Internet allows for the collection, sharing, and selling of this information to interested third parties. The web site people-search.com, for example, permits anyone to do asset verification checks and criminal background checks on any individual for a fee of $39 to $125. Another web site, whowhere.com, supplies background information, including property ownership, civil judgments, driver's license, physical description, and summary of assets, on any individual in its database for only $39.95.[38] Privacy has therefore become one of Web users' biggest concerns, with 69 percent of Americans indicating that they are "very concerned" about their ability to keep such sensitive personal information private on the Internet.[39]

On the positive side, today's technology makes it easier for law enforcement agents to catch criminals, for banks to detect fraud, and for consumers to learn about goods and services and to communicate directly with businesses about their needs. Because of the ease of access to personal information, however, unauthorized use of this information may occur.[40] You may be bombarded with unwanted e-mail messages (junk mail, or "spam"), or you may be classified on the basis of your buying behavior. For example, some companies are using information about purchasing behavior to focus their efforts on "good" customers while paying less attention to "average" or "poor" customers. One danger with this tactic is misclassifying customers on the basis of old or inaccurate data.[41]

Information can be collected on the Internet with or without a person's knowledge. Many web sites follow users' tracks through their site by storing a "cookie," or identifying string of text, on their computers. These cookies permit web site operators to track how often a user visits the site, what he or she looks at while there, and in what sequence. Cookies also allow web site visitors to customize services, such as virtual shopping carts, as well as the particular content they see when they log onto a Web page. However, if a web site operator can exploit cookies to link a visitor's interests to a name and address, that information could be sold to advertisers and other parties without the visitor's consent or even knowledge. The potential for misuse has left many consumers rather uncomfortable with this technology.[42] Complaints have also led to investigations and legal action in some cases. Toys "R" Us, for example, was investigated by New Jersey's Division of Consumer Affairs for allegedly sharing with marketing researchers the personal information that the firm collected via cookies about its Internet customers.[43]

Cookies aren't the only way that businesses can track consumers online. Companies such as DoubleClick, Digital Envoy, and Quova are developing technology that can match Internet addresses with geographical locations. This technology involves bouncing homing bits to a browser's computer from multiple locations and then analyzing the data to triangulate the computer's actual location. Quova says that it can provide its customers with a web site visitor's city in a fiftieth of a second with 90 percent accuracy. These companies claim that they are not collecting specific customer names and addresses, only their city of origin so that web site operators can tailor their content—and advertisements—to different users. The

TRUSTe is a non-profit organization devoted to building users' trust and confidence on the Internet. One way it is achieving its goals is through its third-party oversight "seal" program that alleviates users' concerns about online privacy. (www.truste.com. Reprinted with permission from TRUSTe.)

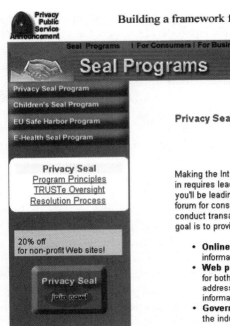

technology also gets around the problem of savvier users who block Web pages from storing cookies on their computers.[44]

A growing number of Internet web sites require visitors to register and provide information about themselves in order to access some or all of their content. How this information will be used is also generating concern. For example, 75 percent of users of health-related web sites worry that the information they supply when they register for access to the site or respond to surveys may be sold to third parties without their permission.[45] Some people are concerned that personal information about their health may be sold to insurance companies that may deny them coverage on the basis of that information. Although many health-oriented and other web sites post privacy policies that specify whether and how they will use any personal information they gather, some consumers still worry that such policies are just "lip service." Amazon.com received complaints through the Federal Trade Commission (FTC) after it modified its privacy policy, which allows it to disclose personal information to third parties and to sell customer information in the event it goes out of business or sells assets.[46] According to the FTC, about two-thirds of commercial web sites post information on their privacy policies. However, about 93 percent of these sites collect at least one type of personally identifying information from visitors, and 57 percent gather some type of demographic information.[47] Moreover, only 20 percent of sites have voluntarily implemented adequate privacy-protection standards.[48] Even the Federal Trade Commission's own web site fails to meet its privacy standards.[49]

Privacy issues related to children are generating even more debate—as well as laws to protect children's interests. Concerns about protecting children's privacy were highlighted by a recent study by the Annenberg Public Policy Center, which reported that two-thirds of children aged ten to seventeen would divulge their favorite online stores in order to receive a free gift, whereas more than half would reveal their parents' favorite stores, and another quarter would disclose details about their parents' activities on the weekend. The study also found that many children would share information about the family car and the amount of their allowance. It should be noted that this survey was conducted before the U.S. Children's Online Privacy Protection Act (COPPA) went into effect in 2000. That law prohibits web sites and Internet providers from seeking personal information from children under age thirteen without parental consent.[50]

Another area of growing concern is "identity theft," which occurs when criminals obtain personal information that allows them to impersonate someone else and use their credit to obtain financial accounts and make purchases. Because of the Internet's relative anonymity and speed, it fosters legal and illegal access to databases containing Social Security numbers, drivers' license numbers, dates of birth, mothers' maiden names, and other information that can be used to establish a credit card or bank account in another person's name in order to make transactions. According to the National Fraud Center, arrests for identity theft fraud have increased to nearly 10,000 a year, with losses from such fraud reaching $745 million. To deter identity theft, the National Fraud Center wants financial institutions to implement new technologies, such as digital certificates, digital signatures, and biometrics—the use of fingerprinting or retina scanning.[51] Rising cases of identity theft and stalking have prompted both the U.S. House of Representatives and Senate to consider legislation that would outlaw the sale of Social Security numbers and prohibit government agencies from disclosing those numbers on public documents.[52]

Some measure of protection for personal privacy is already provided by the U.S. Constitution, as well as Supreme Court rulings and federal laws (Table 10.3). The U.S. Federal Trade Commission (FTC) also regulates and enforces privacy standards and monitors web sites to ensure compliance. A recent study commissioned by the FTC reported that 98 percent of the 100 top web sites collect at least one type of personal information, and 93 percent have posted at least one type of disclosure (privacy policy notice or the site practices).[53] As FTC Chairman Robert Pitofsky told a Senate panel, "Companies say self-regulation will work, but it's becoming clear that companies on the Net are not protecting the privacy of consumers."[54] For example, the FTC accused GeoCities, a popular entertainment web site, of misrepresenting the purposes for which it was harvesting personal information from both children and adults. GeoCities did not disclose the information

TABLE 10.3

Privacy Laws

Act (Date Enacted)	Purpose
Privacy Act (1974)	Requires federal agencies to adopt minimum standards for collecting and processing personal information; limits the disclosure of such records to other public or private parties; requires agencies to make records on individuals available to them on request, subject to certain conditions
Right to Financial Privacy Act (1978)	Protects the rights of financial institution customers to keep their financial records private and free from unjust government investigation
Computer Security Act (1987)	Brought greater confidentiality and integrity to the regulation of information in the public realm by assigning responsibility for standardization of communication protocols, data structures, and interfaces in telecommunications and computer systems to the National Institute of Standards and Technology (NIST), which also announced security and privacy guidelines for federal computer systems
Computer Matching and Privacy Protection Act (1988)	Amended the Privacy Act by adding provisions regulating the use of computer matching, the computerized comparison of individual information for purposes of determining eligibility for federal benefits programs
Video Privacy Protection Act (1988)	Specifies the circumstances under which a business that rents or sells videos can disclose personally identifiable information about a consumer or reveal an individual's video rental or sales records
Telephone Consumer Protection Act (1991)	Regulates the activities of telemarketers by limiting the hours during which they can solicit residential subscribers, outlawing the use of artificial or prerecorded voice messages to residences without prior consent, prohibiting unsolicited advertisements by telephone facsimile machines, and requiring telemarketers to maintain a "do not call list" of any consumers who request not to receive further solicitation
Driver Privacy Protection Act (1993)	Restricts the circumstances under which state departments of motor vehicles may disclose personal information about any individual obtained by the department in connection with a motor vehicle record
Fair Credit Reporting Act (amended in 1997)	Promotes accuracy, fairness, and privacy of information in the files of consumer reporting agencies (e.g., credit bureaus); grants consumers the right to see their personal credit reports, to find out who has requested access to their reports, to dispute any inaccurate information with the consumer reporting agency, and to have inaccurate information corrected or deleted

(continued)

TABLE 10.3 *(continued)*

Privacy Laws

Act (Date Enacted)	Purpose
Children's Online Privacy Protection Act (2000)	Regulates the online collection of personally identifiable information (name, address, e-mail address, hobbies, interests, or information collected through cookies) from children under age thirteen by specifying what a web site operator must include in a privacy policy, when and how to seek consent from a parent, and what responsibilities an operator has to protect children's privacy and safety online

Sources: "Privacy Act of 1974," U.S. Bureau of Reclamation, www.usbr.gov/laws/privacy.html, accessed December 27, 2000; "Right to Financial Privacy Act (RFPA) Summary," Right Data, www.rightdata.com/graphics/info_d.htm, accessed Dec. 27, 2000; "Statement of Customer Rights Under the Right to Financial Privacy Act of 1978," Associated Mortgage Professionals, Inc., http://cyber-mortgage.com/amp_disclosureofprivacy.htm, accessed December 27, 2000; E. Maria Grace, "Privacy vs. Convenience: The Benefits and Drawbacks of Tax System Modernization," *Federal Communications Law Journal,* 47 (December 1994), www.law.indiana.edu/fclj/pubs/v47/no2/grace.html; "A Citizen's Guide on Using the Freedom of Information Act and the Privacy Act of 1974 to Request Records," Tennessee Criminal Law Defense Resources, http://tncrimlaw.com/foia/VII_B.html, accessed December 27, 2000; "Sec. 2710. Wrongful Disclosure of Video Tape Rental or Sale Records," Legal Information Institute, www4.law.cornell.edu/uscode/18/2710.text.html, accessed December 27, 2000; "Summary and Analysis of Rules Implementing the Telephone Consumer Protection Act of 1991," Arent Fox Kintner Plotkin & Kahn, PLLC, www.arentfox.com/publications/alerts/cpa1991/cpa1991.html, accessed December 27, 2000; "Sec. 2721. Prohibition on Release and Use of Certain Personal Information from State Motor Vehicle Records," Legal Information Institute, www4.law.cornell.edu/uscode/18/2721.text.html, accessed December 27, 2000; "A Summary of Your Rights Under the Fair Credit Reporting Act," Federal Trade Commission, www.ftc.gov/bcp/conline/edcams/fcra/summary.htm, accessed December 27, 2000; "How to Comply With the Children's Online Privacy Protection Rule According to the Federal Trade Commission," COPPA, Nov. 1999, http://coppa.org/ftc_how_to.htm.

collected, the purpose, or to whom it would be disclosed. The company settled the charges, agreeing to post an explicit privacy policy detailing what information it collects, for what purpose, to whom it will be disclosed, and how consumers can access and remove the information.[55]

International Initiatives on Privacy Privacy concerns are not limited to the United States. The European Union (EU) has made great strides in protecting the privacy of its citizens. The 1998 European Union Directive on Data Protection specifically requires companies that want to collect personal information to explain how the information will be used and to obtain the individual's permission. Companies must make customer data files available on request, just as U.S. credit reporting firms must grant customers access to their personal credit histories. The law also bars web site operators from selling e-mail addresses and using cookies to track visitors' movements and preferences without first obtaining permission. Because of this legislation, no company may deliver personal information about EU citizens to countries whose privacy laws do not meet EU standards.[56] Some European countries have taken further steps to protect their citizens. Italy, for example, established an Italian Data Protection Commission to enforce its stringent privacy laws. Such agencies highlight the differences in how Europeans and Americans approach the online privacy issue.[57]

In Canada, private industry has taken the lead in creating and developing privacy policies through the Direct Marketing Association of Canada (DMAC). The DMAC's policies resulted in the proposal of legislation to protect personal privacy. The Personal Information Protection and Electronic Documents Act, which went into effect on January 1, 2001, established a right of personal privacy for information collected by Canadian businesses and organizations. The new law instituted rules governing the collection, use, and disclosure of personal information in the private sector. The law also works in conjunction with other legislation that protects personal information collected by federal and/or provincial governments. The Canadian Standards Association (CSA) was also instrumental in bringing about privacy protection guidelines in Canada. The CSA 1996 Model Code for the Protection of Personal Information requires organizations to protect personal information and to allow individuals access to their own personal information, allowing for correction, if necessary.[58]

In Japan, the Ministry of International Trade and Industry established the Electronic Network Consortium (ENC) to resolve issues associated with the Internet. The ENC (which comprises ninety-two corporate members, fifty-one local community organizations, and fifteen special members) has prepared guidelines for protecting personal data gathered by Japanese online service providers. These guidelines require web sites to obtain an individual's consent before collecting personal data or using or transferring such data to a third party. The guidelines also call for organizations to appoint managers who understand the ENC guidelines to oversee the collection and use of personal data and to utilize privacy information management systems such as the Platform for Privacy Protection (P3P).[59] P3P is a set of standards under development by the World Wide Web Consortium that would permit web sites to translate their privacy statements and standards into a uniform format that Web browsing software could access in order to supply users with relevant information about a particular firm's policies. Web site visitors could then decide what information, if any, they are willing to share with web sites.[60]

Protection of citizens' privacy on the Internet is not a major public concern in Russia. Few Russian web sites have privacy policy or disclosure statements explaining how collected information will be used. International companies conducting business in Russia or managing Russian subsidiaries maintain online privacy information for their U.S. customers, but not for Russian customers.[61] Until recently, Russian law gave authorities the right to monitor private e-mail. However, Nail Murzakhanov, the founder of a small Internet service provider in Volgograd, challenged this right when he refused to purchase the equipment that would have permitted Russian security agencies to eavesdrop on his customers' e-mail. Murzakhanov stood firm in his belief that complying with the law would jeopardize his guarantee of privacy to his customers, even after the Ministry of Communications threatened to revoke his license to operate. Eventually, the Ministry of Communications dropped all charges against Murzakhanov's company, setting a precedent for other Internet service providers who wish to protect their customers' privacy.[62]

Privacy Officers and Certification   Businesses are beginning to recognize that the only way to circumvent further government regulation with respect to privacy is to develop systems and policies to protect consumers' interests. In addition to creating and posting policies regarding the gathering and use of personal information, more companies—including American Express, AT&T, Citigroup, and Prudential Insurance—are beginning to hire chief privacy officers (CPOs). These high-level executives are typically given broad powers to establish policies to protect consumer privacy—and their companies from negative publicity and legal scrutiny. According to Michael Lamb, AT&T's privacy officer, "Some companies name a CPO because they have a problem, and some do because they don't have a problem and want to keep doing the right thing." Most CPOs, who are often recruited from universities, report directly to the CEO or chairman of the board.[63]

Several nonprofit organizations have also stepped in to help companies develop privacy policies. Among the best known of these are TRUSTe and the Better Business Bureau Online. TRUSTe is a nonprofit organization devoted to promoting global trust in Internet technology by providing a standardized, third-party oversight program that addresses the privacy concerns of consumers, web site operators, and government regulators. Companies that agree to abide by TRUSTe's privacy standards may display a "trustmark" on their web sites. These firms must disclose their personal information collection and privacy policies in a straightforward privacy statement. TRUSTe is supported by a network of corporate, industry, and nonprofit sponsors including the Electronic Frontier Foundation, CommerceNet, America Online, Compaq, Ernst & Young, Excite, IBM, MatchLogic, Microsoft, Netcom, and Netscape.[64] For example, eBay's web site is TRUSTe-certified, which means that its online privacy practices fulfill TRUSTe's requirements. The online auction company's privacy policy promises that eBay will not share any personal information gathered from customers with any third parties and specifies how it will use the information it obtains. Roughly 500 companies display the trustmark seal of approval from TRUSTe.[65]

The mission of BBBOnLine is to promote trust and confidence in the Internet by promoting ethical business practices. The BBBOnLine program provides verification, monitoring and review, consumer dispute resolution, a compliance seal, enforcement mechanisms, and an educational component. It is managed by the Council of Better Business Bureaus, an organization with considerable experience in conducting self-regulation and dispute-resolution programs, and it employs guidelines and requirements outlined by the Federal Trade Commission and the U.S. Department of Commerce.[66]

❱ *Intellectual Property*

In addition to protecting personal privacy, Internet users and others are concerned about protecting their rights to property they create, including songs, movies, books, and software. Such **intellectual property** consists of the ideas and creative materials developed to solve problems, carry out applications, educate, and entertain others. It is the result or end product of the creative process. Intellectual property is generally protected via patents and copyrights. However, technological advancements are increasingly challenging the ownership of such property. For example, the FTC sued to block Internet retailer Toysmart.com from selling the names, addresses, billing information, family profiles, and buying habits of customers who have visited its web site. The company, which filed for bankruptcy, had posted a privacy policy specifying that it would not share such personal information with third parties and had once been certified by TRUSTe. The FTC's suit may open the door for litigation against other failing Internet companies that attempt to sell their only significant assets—their databases.[67]

Intellectual property losses in the United States total more than $11 billion a year in lost revenue from the illegal copying of computer programs, movies, compact discs, and books. This issue has become a global concern because of disparities in enforcement of laws throughout the world. For example, according to the trade association International Intellectual Property Alliance, more than half of the business software used in Israel is pirated, costing U.S. companies roughly $170 million in one year.[68] The software industry estimates that piracy worldwide costs its companies roughly $12 billion every year.[69] Russia and China are the two worst countries in terms of piracy violations. It is predicted that the trade-related aspects of intellectual property rights disputes will make countries more accountable for adhering to copyright standards.[70]

Microsoft has been particularly aggressive in battling software piracy. The company has initiated legal action against 7,500 Internet listings in thirty-three countries for products it says are pirated. The company's efforts to stamp out piracy have been facilitated by software that searches the Internet for offers to sell counterfeit or illegally copied software.[71] The company is also employing a new "Office Registration Wizard" that authorizes purchasers of its software to load the programs onto only one desktop and one portable computer. If a purchaser attempts to register the software on more than two computers, the program will abort.[72]

U.S. copyright laws protect original works in text form, pictures, movies, computer software, musical multimedia, and audiovisual work. Owners of copyrights have the right to reproduce, derive from, distribute and publicly display, and perform the copyrighted works. Copyright infringement is the unauthorized execution of the rights reserved by a copyright holder. Congress passed the Digital Millennium Copyright Act (DMCA) in 1998 to protect copyrighted materials on the Internet and to limit the liability of online service providers (OSPs). The

DMCA provides a "safe harbor" provision that limits judgments that can be levied against OSPs for copyright infringement by their customers. In order to limit their liability, service providers must pay a nominal fee and comply with the act's reporting requirements.[73] In a lawsuit brought by Ticketmaster against Tickets.com under the DMCA, a judge ruled that Tickets.com could legally place a hypertext link to Ticketmaster on its web site. Although Ticketmaster claimed that the link infringed its copyrights, Tickets.com contended that it placed the Ticketmaster and other similar hotlinks on its web site so that its customers could access those sites to obtain tickets not available through Tickets.com. Because the link automatically directed potential customers to Ticketmaster's actual web site, the court ruled no copyright violation occurred.[74] Table 10.4 provides additional facts about copyrights.

The Internet has created other copyright issues for some organizations that have found that the Web addresses (URLs) of other online firms either match or are very similar to their own trademarks. In some cases, "cybersquatters" have deliberately registered Web addresses that match or relate to other firms' trademarks and then attempted to sell the registration to the trademark owners. A number of companies, including Taco Bell, MTC, and KFC, have paid thousands of dollars to gain

TABLE 10.4

Facts About Copyrights

- A copyright notice is not necessary to protect private and original work created after April 1, 1989.

- Granting work to the public domain relinquishes all of the copyright holder's rights.

- The "fair use" exemption to copyright law allows for commentary, parody, news reporting, as well as research and education without seeking the copyright holder's permission, but giving appropriate acknowledgment.

- Legal defense of a copyright is not necessary for maintaining the copyright—unlike trademarks, which may be damaged if not defended.

- Derivative works, based on another copyrighted work, come under the control of the original copyright holder. A notable exception is parody—making fun of an original work.

- Most copyright litigation is civil versus criminal in nature, but criminal litigation is possible with more than ten copies of an original work and a valuation of over $2,500 (representing a commercial copyright violation).

Source: Brad Templeton, "10 Big Myths About Copyrights Explained," Brad Templeton's Home Page, www.templetons.com/brad/copymyths.html, accessed November, 2, 2001.

control of names that match or parallel company trademarks.[75] The Federal Trademark Dilution Act of 1995 was enacted to help companies resolve this conflict. The law gives trademark owners the right to protect their trademarks, prevents the use of trademark-protected entities by others, and requires cybersquatters to relinquish trademarked names.[76]

The World Intellectual Property Organization (WIPO), an agency of the United Nations, has launched a global attack against cybersquatters who try to hijack Internet addresses. The agency recently implemented a Uniform Dispute Resolution Policy to help resolve Internet trademark conflicts. The procedure has been used to evict cybersquatters using names associated with World Wrestling Federation Entertainment Inc., Nike, and actress Julia Roberts. Until recently, the agency's efforts focused on misleading use of trademarks in domain names, but it plans to expand its reach to address other intellectual property rights such as trade and personal names and geographic regions—including places that have a product associated with them, such as Roquefort (cheese) and Bordeaux (wine). However, it will be more difficult to find a uniform approach to address these areas because, unlike trademarks, there is more diversity in the various national approaches to these areas.[77]

▶ *Health and Biotechnology*

The advance of life-supporting technologies has raised a number of medical and health issues related to technology. **Bioethics** refers to the study of ethical issues in the fields of medical treatment and research, including medicine, nursing, law, philosophy, and theology, though today medical ethics is also recognized as its own discipline.[78] All of these fields have been influenced by rapid changes in technology that require new approaches for solving issues. New genetic technologies promise to give medical ethics an even greater role in social decision making. For example, the Human Genome Project, a fifteen-year, $3 billion federally funded program to decode the entire human genetic map, has already identified a number of genes that may contribute to particular diseases or traits.[79]

Because so many of our resources are spent on health care, the role of the private sector in determining our quality of health care is an important consideration to society. The pharmaceutical industry, for example, has been sharply criticized by politicians, health-care organizations, and consumers because of escalating drug costs. Investigators from federal and state agencies have threatened legal action over allegations that Medicare and Medicaid overpaid for drugs by $1 billion or more a year.[80] In one example, Florida-based Ven-A-Care Inc. was involved as a whistle-blower in a case where Medicare paid $56 in reimbursement for an anticancer drug, leucovorin calcium, for which it paid about $10 for a 50-milligram dose.[81] On the other hand, pharmaceutical companies claim that the development of new lifesaving drugs and tests requires huge expenditures in research and development. Figure 10.3 provides evidence that large amounts of money are spent in this process. The pharmaceutical industry is among the most profitable U.S. industries and spends nearly $14 billion a year in promotion, including drug samples provided to doctors.[82]

Biotechnology Driven by human genome projects, the value of biotech firms is three and a half times greater than it was two years ago.[83] The remarkable feat of mapping the human genome has spurred a rush to cash in on the booming business of genetic research. In fact, genetic research is one of the fastest-growing areas of high technology. Patent applications from biotechnology companies are flooding into the U.S. Patent Office at a rate of 400 a week, and there are some 20,000 applications pending for gene-related discoveries. There are 1,283 biotechnology companies with 153,000 employees and a stock worth of almost $100 billion.[84]

The government and the private sector often partner with academic researchers and nonprofit institutes to develop new technologies in health and biotechnology. Research ranges from mapping the human genetic code, to finding drugs that cure cancer, to genetically modifying food products. Many of these collaborative efforts to improve health involve scientists, funded globally by a variety of sources. For example, British and Brazilian scientists are developing a full genetic map of a cancerous tumor. Their effort involves more than 100 Brazilian scientists and thirty laboratories in Sao Paulo.[85] Boston researchers from the Joslin

FIGURE 10.3

Research and Development Expenditures by Pharmaceutical Companies, in billions of dollars

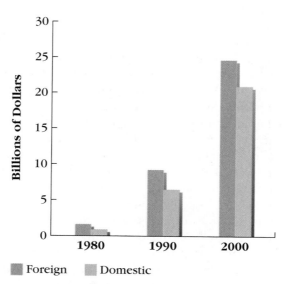

Source: Republished with permission of Dow Jones & Company from *Wall Street Journal*, PhRMAAnnual Survey, 2000, in Shailagh Murray and Lucette Lagnado, "Drug Companies Face Assault on Prices," *Wall Street Journal*, May 11, 2000, p. B1. Permission conveyed through Copyright Clearance Center, Inc.

Diabetes Center and Harvard Medical School created insulin-producing cells from pancreatic cells, which may lead to a source of tissue for transplanting into diabetics.[86] Using cell-engineering techniques, scientists may have found a way to generate unlimited supplies of brain cells for transplanting into Parkinson's disease patients. These examples illustrate technology advances that could result in commercially viable products that save and/or prolong life.

Cloning, the replication of organisms that are genetically identical to their parent, has become a highly controversial topic in biotechnology and bioethics. In 1997, Scottish scientists cloned a sheep named Dolly from a cell of an adult ewe. The following year, scientists in South Korea announced that they had created an embryo from the cells of an adult woman; however, they stopped the embryo's growth at just four cells.[87] In the years since then, researchers have cloned a number of species, including cattle, chickens, and an extinct bucardo (a Spanish mountain goat).[88] Cloning has the potential to revolutionize the treatment of diseases and conditions such as Parkinson's disease and cancer. Cloning technology might also allow doctors to create replacement organs, thereby lengthening human lives. Some scientists believe that cloning could be used to recreate extinct or endangered species in a "last-ditch" conservation effort. The ability to create and modify life processes is often generated through business and government collaborative research; the results of such research may contribute to life-altering products of tomorrow.

Despite the potential of this technology, many people have negative views about cloning. Some contend that it is unethical to "meddle with nature," whereas others believe that cloning is wrong because every time it is used to treat a patient, a cloned human embryo is destroyed, one that might otherwise have been capable of life.[89] Some people argue that cloning of human beings should be banned, and several bills have been introduced in Congress and various state legislatures to do just that. Additionally, nineteen European nations have signed an agreement prohibiting the genetic replication of humans. However, scientists fear that banning human cloning outright could threaten important research, especially in the area of infertility and cancer treatment.[90]

Genetic research holds the promise to revolutionize how many diseases are diagnosed and treated. However, consumer advocates have urged the World Trade Organization (WTO) to place limits on gene patents, which they claim are tantamount to "ownership of life." Patents dealing with human DNA have increased dramatically in the last decade as researchers have identified more genes that play a role in a number of diseases. WTO rules governing patents on intellectual property currently permit patents to be owned for twenty years and allow patent holders to prevent other firms from profiting from a particular technology during that period. But some consumer groups, including Ralph Nader's Public Citizen, fear that these patents have the potential to permit a company to "corner the market" on the diagnosis and treatment of specific diseases for years. These groups worry that such long-term protection could prohibit other companies from developing alternative tests and treatments that might result in improved care at lower prices.[91]

Genetically Modified Foods As many as 800 million people around the world don't have enough to eat. Increasing food production to satisfy growing demand for food without increasing land use will require farmers to achieve significant increases in productivity. Experts believe that genetic modification is one solution to addressing the problem of the world's growing population and shrinking land for growing food.[92] As we discussed in Chapter 9, genetically modified, or transgenic, crops are created when scientists introduce a gene from one organism to another. Scientists believe that genetically engineered crops could raise overall crop production in developing countries as much as 25 percent.[93] According to a report by seven independent academies from both developed and developing nations, in order to combat world hunger, developed nations must boost funding for research into genetically modified crops, and poor farmers must be protected from corporate control of the technology.[94] Table 10.5 lists some examples of genetically modified (GM) foods. Genetic modification has raised numerous health, ethical, and environmental questions. We looked at some of the environmental issues in Chapter 9.

TABLE 10.5

Genetically Modified Foods

Product	Genetic Modification	Purpose
Tomatoes, peas, peppers, tropical fruit, broccoli, raspberries, melons	Controlled ripening	Allows shipping of vine-ripened tomatoes; improves shelf life, quality
Tomatoes, potatoes, corn, lettuce, coffee, cabbage family, apples	Insect resistance	Reduces insecticide use
Peppers, tomatoes, cucumbers	Fungal resistance	Reduces fungicide use
Potatoes, tomatoes, cantaloupe, squash, cucumbers, corn, oilseed rape (canola), soybeans, grapes	Viral resistance	Reduces diseases caused by plant viruses and, because insects carry viruses, reduces use of insecticides
Soybeans, tomatoes, corn, oilseed rape (canola), wheat	Herbicide tolerance	Improves weed control
Corn, sunflowers, soybeans, and other plants	Improved nutrition	Increases amount of essential amino acids, vitamins, or other nutrients in the host plants
Oilseed rape (canola), peanuts	Heat stability	Improves the processing quality, permits new food uses for healthier oils

Source: Food Marketing Institute, The Hale Group/Decision Resources, Inc., Food Processing and BIO/technology magazines, as reported in "Weighing the Future of Biotech Food," MSNBC, www. msnbc.com, accessed July 18, 2000. Courtesy of Food Marketing Institute.

Many people do not realize that some of the foods they eat were made from genetically engineered crops. Consumer groups are increasingly concerned that these foods could be unhealthy and/or harmful to the environment. Concerns about the safety of genetically altered crops have led to a backlash in Europe and, more recently, in the United States and Japan. For example, Campbell Soup, the first firm to license a genetically modified food—the FlavSavr tomato, which was engineered for a longer shelf life—has been the target of a massive letter-writing campaign by consumers worried about the lack of safety testing and labels on foods containing gene-altered crops.[95] Many consumers are boycotting so-called "Frankenfoods," products made from genetically modified materials. Several countries have opposed trade in GM foods through the World Trade Organization, and Japan has asked U.S. corn producers not to include genetically modified corn in animal feed imported to Japan. The European Parliament has called for all GM foods to be labeled.[96]

A number of companies have responded to public concerns about genetically modified food products by limiting or avoiding their use altogether. Major European supermarkets are considering banning GM foods, and Nestlé UK and Unilever have stopped using them in their food products. In the United States, Archer Daniels Midland, the largest buyer of genetically modified crops in the United States, has asked farmers and grain merchants to segregate GM crops from traditionally grown plants. The company may discard a load of grain when tests detect even a tiny amount of altered genes. In fact, large agribusiness purchasers of farm crops are paying less per bushel for genetically altered products.[97] McDonald's and Frito-Lay have asked their suppliers to stop using GM potatoes developed by Monsanto.[98] Gerber and Heinz both announced that they will not permit genetically engineered corn or soybeans in their baby food products.[99] Concerns about genetically modified foods have also affected the supply of some related food products. Frito-Lay, for example, projected that the supply of Cheetos fell by as much as 10 percent as the company tested all cornmeal to detect GM corn.[100]

Ethical questions about the use of some types of genetically modified products have also been raised. For example, Monsanto and other companies are developing so-called "terminator technology" to create plants that are genetically engineered to produce sterile seeds. Dr. Jane Rissler, a scientist with the Union of Concerned Scientists, says, "The fact that terminator technology will work to the disadvantage of the subsistence farmer who depends on harvesting seeds for the next year's crops illustrates the intent of the companies, which is to get the maximum return on their investment." Other plants in development will require spraying with chemicals supplied by the seed companies in order to demonstrate desired traits, such as resistance to certain pests or disease. Farmers say the issue isn't the technology itself, but rather, who controls the technology—in most cases, the multinational seed companies. In response to global concerns about this issue, Monsanto announced that it would halt commercial development of the terminator technology, although it plans to continue researching it.[101]

Biotechnology helps farmers use fewer chemicals and protects crops against certain pests.

Biotechnology is helping him protect the land and preserve his family's heritage.

"I'm raising a better soybean crop that helps me conserve the topsoil, keep my land productive and help this farm support future generations of my family." —Rod Gangwish, farmer

Biotechnology is helping Rod Gangwish to grow a type of soybean that requires less tilling of the soil. That helps him preserve precious topsoil and produce a crop with less impact on the land. Preserving topsoil today means a thriving farm for generations to come.

Biotechnology allows farmers to choose the best combination of ways to help grow their crops. It helps cotton farmers use fewer chemicals to protect their crops against certain pests. And, it's helping provide ways for developing countries to better feed a growing population. And, in the future, it can help farmers grow better quality, more nutritious food.

Biotechnology is also enhancing lives in other ways, helping to create more effective treatments for diseases such as leukemia and diabetes.

Biotechnology is helping create solutions that are improving lives today, and solutions that could improve our world tomorrow. If you're interested in learning more, visit our Web site or call the number below for a free brochure about biotechnology and agriculture.

COUNCIL FOR
BIOTECHNOLOGY
INFORMATION

good ideas are growing

1-800-980-8660
www.whybiotech.com

Defenders of biotechnology say consumer fears about genetically modified foods have not been substantiated by research.[102] A coalition of agribusinesses and food industry groups launched a $50 million campaign in 2000 to persuade consumers that the thousands of tests companies have conducted over the past decade demonstrate that gene-altered foods are no different from conventional ones. In response to public concerns, however, the U.S. Food and Drug Administration is preparing new regulations that would require food producers to consult with its scientists before launching a biotech food.[103]

Cybercrime

The growing popularity of the Internet has created tremendous opportunities for both entertainment and business. However, the complex nature of the medium also creates opportunities for criminals to take advantage of businesses and consumers alike. Every day, it seems, the media report on new viruses or attacks by hackers. Although many of these crimes are relatively harmless, others do billions of dollars in damage, defraud innocent people, and frighten would-be online shoppers away.

The term *hacker* has evolved over the years to mean a person who breaks into a computer system or network to explore, steal, or wreak havoc. Many hackers are simply teenagers looking for a thrill or a chance to test their skills by outwitting a system's security measures. The more secure the system, the more desirable a target it becomes. Hackers often use specialized software, readily available on the Internet, that can enter millions of possible passwords until one is accepted by the system. Once inside a system, they may use other specialized programs to search for sensitive information. Although many hackers simply explore the contents of a computer network and later brag about their exploits to other hackers, others have much more malicious intent. Some hackers deface web sites to express political or personal opinions or to damage the site's reputation. Hackers may sell the information they find, such as customers' credit-card numbers, telephone calling-card numbers, or plans for new products or marketing strategies. For example, hackers stole 300,000 credit-card numbers from CD Universe in 1999. Phone companies lost an estimated $2 billion as a result of hackers stealing calling-card numbers and selling them to organized crime gangs. Other hackers may damage systems by altering or deleting files, unleashing "denial-of-service attacks," mail bombs, or computer viruses.

Denial-of-service attacks inundate a computer system with fake requests for access to Web pages in order to slow its performance. When Yahoo!, CNN, eBay, Amazon.com, and E*Trade were attacked in 2000, hackers used software that sent millions of bogus requests for Web pages, effectively shutting down the systems while they spent all their resources trying to process the requests. Although nothing was stolen from or damaged at these sites, customers were unable to access or make purchases from the companies' web sites for hours. Mail bombs are similar but involve attacks to mail servers.

Hackers may also unleash viruses, which are self-replicating programs. A virus may attach itself to a file, such as an e-mail message or a word-processing macro. Some viruses are rela-

Strategic Implementation of Responsibility for Technology

In order to accrue the maximum benefits from the technologies driving the New Economy, many parties within society have important roles to play. While the media and public continue to debate the issues associated with technology, the government must take steps to provide support for continued technological advancements

tively harmless, leaving behind nothing more than simple "hello" messages. Others may crash the affected computer by using up all its resources, attacking and corrupting critical files, or erasing the hard drive. The Melissa virus, which paralyzed e-mail systems around the world, caused an estimated $80 million in damage. Closely related to viruses are worms (programs that use a system's resources in order to replicate themselves), Trojan horses (programs that appear to be something other than what they are), and logic bombs (programs that are triggered by an event, such as a certain date, to release a virus or damage the system).

In addition to stolen credit cards, credit-card fraud has become a major problem for online retailers. In some cases, criminals use stolen credit-card numbers to order merchandise, the cost of which is then charged to the card owner. Thieves may also use credit cards to order merchandise but then complain to the merchant that never received it when in fact they did, or that they never ordered it (and then keep it). When customers dispute the charges on their statements, most banks delete the charges and then require the merchant to repay the loss. First Data Corporation estimates that 1.25 percent of all Internet transactions are charged back to the merchant because of fraud (in comparison, only 0.33 percent of catalog transactions and 0.14 percent of storefront retail transactions are charged back). For example, Expedia, a travel web site owned by Microsoft, had to write off $4.1 million to cover disputed credit-card charges. Thus, credit-card fraud generates significant losses for online retailers. It also hurts e-commerce in general because it increases customers' fears that they may become victims of such fraud, which may stifle online spending.

To combat cybercrime, companies are spending huge sums to hire security consultants and purchase specialized software to deter or detect unauthorized entry. Even so, cybercrime is detected only about 40 percent of the time. The problem is further compounded by the fact that companies are reluctant to report such crimes, often because it makes both customers and shareholders uncomfortable and damages the companies' reputations. As the Internet grows ever more popular, the threat of losses from cybercrime will only grow. The best way for companies to prevent such crimes is to understand how they occur, eliminate security gaps, and remain vigilant. ■

Sources:
These facts are from Julia Angwin, "Credit-Card Fraud Has Become a Nightmare for E-Merchants," *Wall Street Journal,* September 19, 2000, http://interactive.wsj.com/; David Mandeville, "Hackers, Crackers, and Trojan Horses: A Primer," CNN, March 29, 1999, www.cnn.com/TECH/specials/hackers/primer/; Amy Rogers, "Capitalizing on Cyber Crime," *Computer Reseller News,* February 21, 2000, pp. 3, 10; Ira Sager, Steve Hamm, Neil Gross, John Carey, and Robert D. Hof, "Cyber Crime," *Business Week,* February 21, 2000, pp. 36–42; Ara C. Trembly, "Cyber Crime Means Billions in Losses," *National Underwriter,* June 28, 1999, p. 19.

and establish regulations, as needed, to ensure that the benefits of technology apply to as many people as possible while minimizing any potential for harm, especially to competition, the environment, and human welfare. Various stakeholders, including employees, customers, and special-interest groups, as well as the general public, can influence the use and control of technology through the public policy process. Businesses also have a significant role to play in supporting technology. New technologies are developed, refined, and introduced to the market through the research and development and marketing activities of business. Businesses that aspire to be good corporate citizens must monitor the impact of technology and harness it for the good of all.

The Role of Government

With an economy that is increasingly driven by technology, the government must maintain the basic infrastructure and support for technology in our society. The Defense Department, for example, explores ways that technology can improve the quality of life. The government also serves as a watchdog to ensure that technology benefits society, not criminals. However, as the pace of technology continues to escalate, law enforcement agencies ranging from the FBI to local police forces are struggling to recruit and retain officers and prosecutors who are knowledgeable about the latest technology and the ways criminals can exploit it. The nation currently has only a few hundred high-caliber forensic computer experts, but many of these officers are being lured to technology firms and private security outfits by salaries more than twice their government paychecks. Only a handful of police and sheriffs' departments across the country have enough money to support squads of high-tech investigators, and many top detectives leap to the corporate realm anyway.[104]

In addition to cybercriminals, many commercial users of the Internet are implementing new technologies in ways that our existing legal system could not have conceived of when our laws were framed. Hollywood film studios, for example, are concerned that new technology will allow computer users to copy and trade entire videos on the Internet, much like they now trade music recordings via Napster and other services. Several studios have filed a lawsuit against *2600,* a computer hacker magazine and web site, for distributing software that can bypass video copy protections. The software, Decode Content Scrambling System (DeCSS), enables computer users to compress a full-length DVD movie in order to copy it to any computer disk. The film studios want to use the Digital Millennium Copyright Act to stop *2600* from providing links to what they consider to be illegal software.[105]

Both the Napster and DeCSS lawsuits illustrate a significant difference in opinion in the interpretation of existing laws when exploiting the evolving multimedia potential of the Internet. Although the government's strategy thus far has been not to interfere with the commercial use of technology, disputes and differing interpretations of current laws increasingly bring technology into the domain of the legal system. New laws related to breakthrough technologies that change the nature of competition are constantly being considered. Usually, the issues of privacy, ownership of intellectual property, health and safety, environmental impact, competition, or consumer welfare are the legislative platforms for changing the legal and regulatory system.

▶ ### The Role of Business

Business, like government, is involved in both reactive and proactive attempts to market and make effective use of technology. Reactive concerns relate to issues that have legal and/or ethical implications as well as to productivity, customer welfare, or other stakeholder issues. One example of a reactive response to the consequences of new technologies relates to employee access to and use of the World Wide Web. Many companies, including Compaq, IBM, and NCR, have turned to Internet filtering software like Cyber Patrol, Surfcontrol, Surfwatch, and Websense to block employee access to web sites that their employers deem objectionable or distracting.[106] There is ample evidence that employees are using the Internet to conduct personal business while on company time. Among the most-visited web sites during work hours are Amazon.com, eBay, RealNetworks, and Travelocity—sites unlikely to be work-related for most employees. When the employment site Vault.com surveyed 1,200 employees, it found that 37.1 percent of them admitted to surfing nonwork-related sites constantly during work hours.[107] International Data Corporation estimates that such "cyberloafing" accounts for 30 to 40 percent of lost worker productivity, and Websense, which markets employee-monitoring software, assesses the cost of all this Internet distraction at $54 billion annually.[108]

More companies are reacting to such unauthorized uses of technology by monitoring their employees' behavior online. For example, companies can employ software that records every keystroke an employee makes on his or her computer. Managers may turn to such software to ensure that their employees are doing the work expected of them, instead of sending proprietary information to competitors, taking care of personal business, or randomly surfing web sites, especially pornographic ones.[109] About 40 percent of companies are now using such software, and the International Data Corporation projects that 80 percent of companies will be monitoring online behavior by 2001. The American Management Association reports that three-quarters of major U.S. companies are now monitoring employee communications, including phone calls, e-mail, and Internet connections, and that figure has doubled since 1997.[110] The courts have ruled that because communications occurring on company-provided equipment are not private under current law, such monitoring is legal.[111] However, established high-tech companies like Microsoft and Oracle, and many startups like MP3.com, often choose not to monitor or limit employees' Web usage or e-mail.[112]

Concerns about undesirable employee use of telecommunications equipment represent reactions to changes in information technology that affect the workplace. Even though companies may be legally within their right to monitor and control the use of certain web sites by employees, such control raises strategic issues related to trust and the type of long-run relationships that firms want to have with their employees.

On the other hand, a strategic, proactive approach to technology will consider the impact on corporate citizenship. Proactive management of technology requires developing a plan for utilizing resources to take advantage of competitive opportunities. For example, there is great demand for high-speed Internet connections, including cable modems, DSL, and other broadband connections, because computing speed and power have moved beyond current bandwidth capacity. Many telecommunications firms are racing to install and market the infrastructure for broadband connections to satisfy this demand. In a few years, however, new technologies—probably wireless connections—will more than likely provide even greater connection speeds, and the opportunity for new companies to provide broadband service will vanish.

With competition increasing, companies are spending more time and resources to establish technology-based competitive advantages. The strategic approach to technology requires an overall mission, strategy, and coordination of all functional activities, including a concern for corporate citizenship, to have an effective program. To promote the responsible use of technology, a firm's policies, rules, and standards must be integrated into its corporate culture. Reducing undesirable behavior in this area is a goal that is no different from reducing costs, increasing profits, or improving quality that is aggressively enforced and integrated into the corporate culture to be effective in improving appropriate behavior within the organization.

Top managers must consider the social consequences of technology in the strategic planning process. When all stakeholders are involved in the process, everyone can better understand the need for and requirements of responsible development and use of technology. There will always be conflicts in making the right choices, but through participation in decision making, the best solutions can be found. Individual participants in this process should not abdicate their personal responsibility as concerned members of society. Organizations that are concerned about the consequences of their decisions create an environment for different opinions on important issues. As Richard Purcell, Microsoft's chief privacy officer, says, "... no matter what legislation is enacted, it is the responsibility of the leaders in the online industry to provide and implement technologies that help consumers feel safer and more comfortable online."[113]

▶ Strategic Technology Assessment

In order to calculate the effects of new technologies, companies can employ a procedure known as **technology assessment** to foresee the effects new products and processes will have on their firm's operation, on other business organizations, and on society in general. This assessment is a tool that managers can use to evaluate their firm's performance and to chart strategic courses of action to respond to new technologies. With information obtained through a technology assessment or audit, managers can estimate whether the benefits of adopting a specific technology outweigh costs to the firm and to society at large. The assessment process can also help companies ensure compliance with government regulations related to technology. Remember that one of the four components of citizenship is legal compliance. Because technology is evolving so rapidly, even lawyers are struggling to keep up with the legal implications of these advances. Social institutions, including religion, education, the law, and business, have to respond to changing technology by adapting or developing new approaches to address the evolving issues. A strategic technology assessment or audit can help organizations understand these issues and to develop appropriate and responsible responses to them.

If the assessment process indicates that the company has not been effective at utilizing technologies or is using them in a way that raises questions, changes may be necessary. Companies may need to consider setting higher standards, improving reporting processes, improving communication of standards and training programs, as well as participating in aboveboard discussions with other organizations. If performance has not been satisfactory, management may want to reorganize the way certain kinds of decisions are made. Table 10.6 contains some issues to assess

TABLE 10.6

Strategic Technology Assessment Issues

Yes	No	Checklist
❏	❏	Are top managers in your organization aware of the federal, state, and local laws related to technology decisions?
❏	❏	Does your organization have an effective system for monitoring changes in the federal, state, and local laws related to technology?
❏	❏	Is there an individual, committee, or department in your organization responsible for overseeing governmental technology issues?
❏	❏	Does your organization do checks on technology brought into the organization by employees?
❏	❏	Are there communications and training programs in your organization to create an effective culture to protect employees and organizational interests related to technology?
❏	❏	Does your organization have monitoring and auditing systems to determine the impact of technology on key stakeholders?
❏	❏	Does your organization have a method for reporting concerns about the use or impact of technology?
❏	❏	Is there a system to determine ethical risks and appropriate ethical conduct to deal with technology issues?
❏	❏	Do top managers in your organization understand the ramifications of using technology to employees and customers?
❏	❏	Is there an individual or department in your organization responsible for maintaining compliance standards to protect the organization in the areas of privacy and intellectual property?

for proactive and reactive technology responsibility issues. Some social concerns might relate to a technology's impact on the environment, employee health and working conditions, consumer safety, and community values.

Finally, the organization should focus on the positive aspects of technology to determine how it can be used to improve the work environment, its products, and the general welfare of society. Technology can be used to reduce pollution, encourage recycling, and save energy. Also, information can be made available to customers to help them maximize the benefits of products. Technology has been and will continue to be a major force that can improve society.

Summary

Technology relates to the application of knowledge, including the processes and applications to solve problems, perform tasks, and create new methods to obtain desired outcomes. The dynamics of technology relate to the constant change that requires significant adjustments in the political, religious, and economic structures of society. Reach relates to the far-reaching nature of technology as it moves through society. The self-sustaining nature of technology relates to the fact that technology acts as a catalyst to spur even faster development. Civilizations must harness and adapt to changes in technology in order to maintain a desired quality of life. Although technological advances have improved our quality of life, they have also raised ethical, legal, and social concerns.

Advances in technology have created millions of new jobs, better health and longer lives, new opportunities, and enrichment of lives. Without greater access to the latest technology, however, economic development could suffer in underserved areas. The ability to purchase technology may affect the nature of competition and business success. Information and telecommunications technology minimizes borders, allows people to overcome the physical limitations of time and space, and enables people to acquire customized goods and services that cost less and are of higher quality.

The Internet, a global information system that links many computer networks together, has altered the way people communicate, learn, do business, and find entertainment. The growth of the Internet has generated issues never before encountered and that social institutions, including the legal system, have been slow to address.

Because current technology has made it possible to collect, share, and sell vast quantities of personal information, often without consumers' knowledge, privacy has become a major concern associated with technology. Many web sites follow users' tracks through their site by storing a cookie, or identifying string of text, on the users' computers. What companies do with the information about consumers they collect through cookies and other technologies is generating concern. Privacy issues related to children are generating even more debate and laws to protect children's interests. Identity theft occurs when criminals obtain personal information that allows them to impersonate someone else in order to use their credit to obtain financial accounts and to make purchases. Some measure of protection of personal privacy is provided by the U.S. Constitution, as well as by Supreme Court rulings and federal laws. Europe and other regions of the world are also addressing privacy concerns. In addition to creating and posting policies regarding the gathering and use of personal information, more companies are beginning to hire chief privacy officers.

Intellectual property consists of the ideas and creative materials developed to solve problems, carry out applications, educate, and entertain others. Copyright infringement is the unauthorized execution of the rights reserved by a copyright holder. Technological advancements are challenging the ownership of intellectual property. Other issues relate to "cybersquatters" who deliberately register Web addresses that match or relate to other firms' trademarks and then attempt to sell the registration to the trademark owners.

Bioethics refers to the study of ethical issues in the fields of medical treatment and research, including medicine, nursing, law, philosophy, and theology. Genetic research, including cloning, may revolutionize how diseases are diagnosed and treated. Genetically modified crops are created when scientists introduce a gene from one organism to another. However, these technologies are controversial because some people believe they are immoral, unsafe, and/or harmful to the environment.

To accrue the maximum benefits from the technology driving the New Economy, many parties within society have important roles to play. With an economy that is increasingly driven by technology, the government must maintain the basic infrastructure and support for technology in our society. The government also serves as a watchdog to ensure that technology benefits society, not criminals.

Business is involved in both reactive and proactive attempts to make effective use of technology. Reactive concerns relate to issues that have legal and/or ethical implications as well as to productivity, customer welfare, or other stakeholder issues. Proactive management of technology requires developing a plan for utilizing resources to take advantage of competitive opportunities. The strategic approach to technology requires an overall mission, strategy, and coordination of all functional activities, including a concern for corporate citizenship, to produce an effective program. To calculate the effects of new technologies, companies can employ a procedure known as technology assessment to foresee the effects of new products and processes on their firm's operation, on other business organizations, and on society in general.

technology

intellectual property

bioethics

technology assessment

DISCUSSION QUESTIONS

1. Define technology and describe three characteristics that can be used to assess it.

2. What effect has technology had on the U.S. and global economies? Have these effects been positive or negative?

3. Many people believe that the government should regulate business with respect to privacy online, but companies say self-regulation is more appropriate. Which approach would most benefit consumers? Business?

4. What is intellectual property? How can owners of intellectual property protect their rights?

5. What is bioethics? What are some of the consequences of biomedical research?

6. Should genetically modified foods be labeled? Why or why not?

7. How can a strategic technology assessment help a company?

EXPERIENTIAL EXERCISE

Visit three web sites that are primarily designed for children or that focus on products of interest to children under age thirteen. For example, visit the web sites for new movies, games, action figures, candy, cereal, or beverages. While visiting these sites, put yourself in the role and mind-set of a child. What type of language and persuasion is used? Is there a privacy statement on the site that can be understood by children? Are there any parts of the site that might be offensive or worrisome to parents? Provide a brief evaluation of how well these sites attend to the provisions of the Children's Online Privacy Protection Act.

NOTES

1. "Federal Court Sets October Trial Date for Napster Case," CNN August 29, 2000, www.cnn.com; Lee Gomes, "Judge Orders Napster to Stop Downloads of Copyrighted Music," *Wall Street Journal,* July 27, 2000, http://interactive.wsj.com/; Carolyn Duffy Marsan, "Is Rock and Roll Bad for Your Net?" CNN, February 15, 2000, www.cnn.com; Walter S. Mossberg, "Behind the Lawsuit: Napster Offers Model for Music Distribution," *Wall Street Journal,* May 11, 2000, p. B1; "Napster and Recording Association to Face Off in Court," CNN, July 26, 2000, www.cnn. com; "Napster Defends Its Song Technology," MSNBC, July 3, 2000, www.msnbc.com; "Napster, Inc., Response to Ninth Circuit Court of Appeals Ruling on the U.S. District Court Injunction in A&M, Inc., v. Napster," February 12, 2001, www.napster. com/pressroom/pr/010212.html; "Napster Says It Will Appeal Ruling," CNN, February 12, 2001, www.cnn.com; "Recording Industry and Online Music Services Battle Over Copyright Laws," CNN, May 16, 2000, www.cnn.com.

2. Jason Dean, "China Issues 'Trial' Online Ad Licenses in First Step Toward Regulating Sector," *Wall Street Journal,* June 1, 2000, p. B18.

3. Kevin Kelly, "Will We Still Turn?" *Time,* June 19, 2000.

4. Dana James, "Broadband Horizons," *Marketing News,* March 13, 2000, pp. 1, 9.

5. Alan Boyle, "Microrobots Could Play a Biotech Role," MSNBC, www.msnbc.com, accessed July 10, 2000.

6. Alan Greenspan, Remarks to the Economic Club of New York, January 13, 2000, Federal Reserve Board, www.federalreserve.gov/boarddocs/speeches/2000/200001132.htm.

7. Ibid.

8. Stacey Wells, "Across the Divide," *Business2.com,* December 12, 2000, pp. 186–204.

9. Jordan T. Pine, "Gateway to Help Bridge Technology Gap," DiversityInc.com, April 28, 2000, www. diversityinc.com.

10. "Charting the Future of the Net," MSNBC, July 7, 2000, www.msnbc.com.

11. "Supporting Research and Development to Promote Economic Growth: The Federal Government's Role," The Council of Economic Advisers, October 1995, http://library.whitehouse.gov/WH/EOP/CEA/econ/html/econ-top.html.

12. Greenspan, Remarks to the Economic Club of New York.

13. Vladimir Zwass, "Electronic Commerce: Structures and Issues," *International Journal of Electronic Commerce,* Fall 1995, pp. 3–23.

14. Greenspan, Remarks to the Economic Club of New York.

15. "Covisint Parts Exchange Officially Opens for Business," *Bloomberg Newswire,* December 11, 2000, via AOL.

16. Greenspan, Remarks to the Economic Club of New York.

17. "Hard-Core Internet Sales," *Business Week Online,* March 9, 2000, www.businessweek.com.

18. Nicholas Negroponte, "Will Everything Be Digital?" *Time,* June 19, 2000.

19. "Novell Extends Net Services to the Mobile Internet," Novell, press release, September 11, 2000, www.novell.com/news/press/archive/2000/09/pr00092.html.

20. Negroponte, "Will Everything Be Digital?"

21. David Leiberman, "America's Digital Divide," *USA Today,* October 11, 1999, www.usatoday.com/life/cyber/tech/ctg382.htm.

22. Ibid.

23. Anick Jesdanun, "Wiring Rural America," MSNBC, September 5, 2000, www.msnbc.com.

24. Greenspan, Remarks to the Economic Club of New York.

25. "The Future of Purchasing and Supply: A Five and Ten Year Forecast," iPlanet, www.iplanet.com/center/purchasing_future.html, accessed September 12, 2000.

26. Karen Thomas, "An Early Education in Tech Toys," *USA Today,* December 6, 2000, pp. 1D, 2D.

27. David Field, "Some E-ticket Fliers Can Print Boarding Passes on PC," *USA Today,* December 5, 2000, p. 12B.

28. Glenda Chui, "Technology Brings a Revolution in Cartography," *Silicon Valley News,* September 11, 2000, www.mercurycenter.com/svtech/news/indepth/docs/maps091200.htm.

29. "The World's Online Populations," *CyberAtlas,* November 27, 2000, http://cyberatlas.internet.com/big_picture/geographics/article/0,1323,5911_151151,00.html.

30. Elizabeth Weise, "Web Users to Get More Places to Visit," *USA Today,* December 5, 2000, p. 3D.

31. William M. Pride and O. C. Ferrell, *Marketing: Concepts and Strategies,* 12th ed. (Boston: Houghton Mifflin, 2003), p. 493.

32. Julia Angwin, "Credit-Card Scams: The Devil E-stores," *Wall Street Journal,* September 19, 2000, pp. B1, B4.

33. "Fraud a Growing Problem, Wall Street Journal Reports," *Bloomberg Newswire*, November 3, 2000, via America Online.

34. Jim Carlton and Pui-Wing Tam, "Online Auctioneers Face Growing Fraud Problem," *Wall Street Journal,* May 12, 2000, p. B2.

35. David H. Freedman, "Sleaze Bay," *Forbes ASAP,* November 27, 2000, pp. 134–140.

36. Carlton and Tam, "Online Auctioneers Face Growing Fraud Problem."

37. Eve M. Caudill and Patrick E. Murphy, "Consumer Online Privacy: Legal and Ethical Issues," *Journal of Public Policy & Marketing,* 19 (Spring 2000): 7–12.

38. "Internet Privacy," E-Center for Business Ethics, www.e-businessethics.com/privacy/internet.htm, accessed November 2, 2001.

39. Marcia Stepanek, "The Privacy Penalty on Dot-Coms," *Business Week Online,* June 13, 2000, www.businessweek.com; Lee Walczak, Richard S. Dunham, Howard Gleckman, et al., "The Politics of Prosperity," *Business Week,* August 7, 2000, p. 106.

40. "Privacy Initiatives," Federal Trade Commission, www.ftc.gov/privacy/index.html, accessed November 7, 2001.

41. Edward C. Baig, Marcia Stepanek, and Neil Gross, "Privacy," *Business Week Online,* April 5, 1999, www.businessweek.com.

42. Pride and Ferrell, *Marketing: Concepts and Strategies,* pp. 600–601.

43. "Toys R Us Probed over Web Privacy," Associated Press, December 12, 200, via AOL.

44. Scott Wooley, "We Know Where You Live," *Forbes,* November 13, 2000, p. 332.

45. Nancy Weil, "Report Prompts Investigation of Health-Oriented Web Sites," CNN, April 3, 2000, www.cnn.com.

46. "FTC Gets Complaints About Amazon.com's New Privacy Policy," *Wall Street Journal,* December 5, 2000, p. A10.

47. Edward C. Baig, "Progress in Online Privacy, But Critics Say Not Enough," *Business Week Online,* May 13, 1999, www.businessweek.com.

48. Heather Green, "Commentary: Privacy—Don't Ask Technology to Do the Job," *Business Week Online,* June 26, 2000, www.businessweek.com.

49. "Federal Web Sites Fail FTC Privacy Test," *USA Today,* September 12, 2000, www.usatoday.com.

50. "Survey: Kids Disclose Private Details Online," CNN, May 17, 2000, www.cnn.com.

51. Jack McCarthy, "National Fraud Center: Internet Is Driving Identity Theft," CNN, March 20, 2000, www.cnn.com.

52. Rob O'Dell, "House Panel Approves Bill to Help Halt Identity Theft," *Austin American-Statesman,* July 21, 2000, http://austin360.com/statesman/.

53. "Georgetown Internet Privacy Policy Survey," E-Center for Business Ethics, www.e-businessethics.com/privacy/georgetown.htm, accessed November 1, 2001.

54. Stepanek, "The Privacy Penalty on Dot-Coms."

55. "The Federal Trade Commission," E-Center for Business Ethics, January 18, 2000, www.e-businessethics.com/privacy/ftc.htm; "Internet Site Agrees to Settle FTC Charges of Deceptively Collecting Personal Information in Agency's First Internet Privacy Case," Federal Trade Commission, press release, August 13, 1998, www.ftc.gov/opa/1998/9808/geocitie.htm.

56. "European Union Directive on Privacy," E-Center for Business Ethics, www.e-businessethics.com/privacy.eud.htm, accessed November 1, 2001.

57. Thomas E. Weber, "Views on Protecting Privacy Diverse in U.S. and Europe," *Wall Street Journal Interactive,* June 19, 2000, http://interactive.wsj.com.

58. "Privacy in Canada," E-Center for Business Ethics, www.e-businessethics.com/privacyCA.htm, accessed November 7, 2001. "A Private Sector Privacy Law," Privacy Commissioner of Canada, www.privcom.gc.ca/legislation/02_06_01_e.asp, accessed November 2, 2001.

59. "Privacy in Japan," E-Center for Business Ethics, www.e-businessethics.com/privacyJA.htm, accessed November 2, 2001.

60. Lorrie Cranor, "No Quick Fix for Protecting Online Privacy," *Business Week Online,* March 14, 2000, www.businessweek.com.

61. "Privacy in Russia," E-Center for Business Ethics, www.e-businessethics.com/privacyRU.htm, accessed November 2, 2001.

62. Guy Chazan, "A High-Tech Folk Hero Challenges Russia's Right to Snoop," *Wall Street Journal,* November 27, 2000, p. A28.

63. "Latest Obligatory Corporate Title: Chief Privacy Officer," CNN, July 11, 2000, www.cnn.com.

64. "TRUSTe.com," E-Center for Business Ethics, www.e-businessethics.com/privacy/truste.htm, accessed November 7, 2001.

65. Baig, Stepanek, and Gross, "Privacy."

66. "Better Business Bureau Online," E-Center for Business Ethics, www.e-businessethics.com/privacy/BBBOnline.htm, accessed November 7, 2001.

67. "FTC Sues Toysmart.com Over Customer Data," *USA Today,* July 10, 2000, www.usatoday.com/life/cyber/tech/cti204.htm.

68. David G. McDonough, ". . . But Can the WTO Really Sock It to Software Pirates?" *Business Week Online,* March 9, 1999, www.businessweek.com.

69. Stephen H. Wildstrom, "Can Microsoft Stamp Out Piracy?" *Business Week Online,* October 2, 2000, www.businessweek.com.

70. McDonough, ". . . But Can the WTO Really Sock It to Software Pirates?"

71. Rebecca Buckman, "Microsoft Steps Up Software Piracy War," *Wall Street Journal,* August 2, 2000, p. B6.

72. Wildstrom, "Can Microsoft Stamp Out Piracy?"

73. Rebecca Edelson, Esq., and Adrienne D. Herman, "The Digital Millennium Copyright Act: A Tool to Limit Liability for Copyright Infringement and to Protect and Enforce Copyrights on the Internet," Alschuler, Grossman, Stein, and Kahan LLP, www.agsk.com/print/index.html, accessed December 20, 2000.

74. Elijah Cocks, "Internet Ruling: Hypertext Linking Does Not Violate Copyright," Intellectual Property and Technology Forum, Boston College Law School, April 4, 2000, www.bc.edu/bc_org/avp/law/st_org/iptf/headlines/index.html.

75. William T. Neese and Charles R. McManis, "Summary Brief: Law, Ethics and the Internet: How Recent Federal Trademark Law Prohibits a Remedy against 'Cyber-Squatters,'" *Proceedings from the Society of Marketing Advances,* November 4–7, 1998.

76. Ibid.

77. "Fighting Cybersquatters," MSNBC, July 10, 2000, www.msnbc.com.

78. "Introduction to Bioethics," Bioethics.net, www.med.upenn.edu/bioethic/01/introduction. shtml, accessed December 20, 2000.

79. Ibid.

80. Lucette Lagundo, "Drug Companies Face Assault on Prices," *Wall Street Journal,* May 11, 2000, p. B1.

81. David S. Cloud, "How a Whistle-Blower Spurred Pricing Case Involving Drug Makers," *Wall Street Journal,* May 12, 2000, p. A1.

82. Lagundo, "Drug Companies Face Assault on Prices."

83. Christopher Oster, "Cracking the Code on Biotech Investing," *Wall Street Journal,* June 9, 2000, p. C1.

84. Mike Jensen, "A Modern Goldrush in Genetics," MSNBC, www.msnbc.com, accessed July 18, 2000.

85. "In Brazil, Scientists are Mapping Genes in Cancerous Tumor," *Wall Street Journal,* July 5, 2000, p. B12.

86. "Diabetes Researchers Create Pancreas Cells the Produce Insulin," *Wall Street Journal,* July 5, 2000, p. B12.

87. Ibid.

88. "Cloning Special Report: Raising the Dead," *New Scientist,* www.newscientist.com/nsplus/insight/ clone/raisingthedead.html, accessed December 11, 2000; Andy Coghlan, "Cloning Special Report: Egg Medicine," *New Scientist,* December 6, 2000, www.newscientist.com/nsplus/insight/clone/ eggmedicine.html; "Should Cloning Be Banned?" October 2000, www.reason.com/biclone.html.

89. Andy Coghlan, "Cloning Special Report: Cloning Without Embryos," *New Scientist,* January 29, 2000, via www.newscientist.com/nsplus/insight/cone/ cloningwithoutemb.html.

90. "Should Cloning Be Banned?"

91. Jacqueline Stensen, "Gene Patents Raise Concerns," MSNBC, www.msnbc.com, accessed July 18, 2000.

92. "Weighing the Future of Biotech Food," MSNBC, www.msnbc.com, accessed July 18, 2000.

93. Bill Gates, "Will Frankenfood Feed the World?," *Time,* June 19, 2000.

94. "Weighing the Future of Biotech Food."

95. "Green Groups Target Campbell Soup in GM Food Fight," CNN, July 20, 2000, www.cnn.com.

96. Paul Magnusson, Ann Therese, and Kerry Capell, "Furor over Frankenfood," *Business Week,* October

18, 1999, pp. 50, 51; "Japan Asks That Imports of Corn Be StarLink-Free," *Wall Street Journal,* October 30, 2000, p. A26.

97. Magnusson, Therese, and Capell, "Furor over Frankenfood."

98. "McDonald's to Bar GMO Fries," CNNfn, April 28, 2000, www.cnnfn.com.

99. Magnusson, Therese, and Capell, "Furor over Frankenfood."

100. "Testing Corn Affects Cheetos Supply," Associated Press, December 9, 2000, via AOL.

101. " 'Terminator' Victory a Small Step in Long War," CNN, October 7, 1999, www.cnn.com.

102. Francesca Lyman, "Biotech Battle of Seattle, and Beyond, MSNBC, www.msnbc.com, accessed July 18, 2000.

103. "Green Groups Target Campbell Soup in GM Food Fight."

104. Greg Farrell, "Police Have Few Weapons Against Cyber-Criminals," *USA Today,* December 6, 2000, p. 5B; Edward Iwata and Kevin Johnson, "Computer Crime Outpacing Cybercops," *USA Today,* June 7, 2000, www.usatoday.com/life/cyber/tech/cth404.htm.

105. "Attorneys in Video Hacker Court Case Predict Mass Piracy," CNN, July 18, 2000, www.cnn.com.

106. Julene Snyder, "Should Overworked Employees Be Allowed to Surf the Web on the Job?" CNN, May 11, 2000, www.cnn.com.

107. Ibid.

108. Michelle Conlin, "Workers, Surf at Your Own Risk," *Business Week,* June 12, 2000, pp. 105–106.

109. Michael J. McCarthy, "Keystroke Loggers Save E-mail Rants, Raising Workplace Privacy Concerns," *Wall Street Journal,* March 7, 2000, http://interactive. wsj.com.

110. Conlin, "Workers, Surf at Your Own Risk."

111. McCarthy, "Keystroke Loggers Save E-mail Rants, Raising Workplace Privacy Concerns."

112. Snyder, "Should Overworked Employees Be Allowed to Surf the Web on the Job?"

113. Roberta Fusaro, "Chief Privacy Officer: A Conversation with Richard Purcell," *Harvard Business Review,* 78 (November/December 2000), accessible at www.hbsp.harvard.edu/ideasatwork/purcell_conv. html.

Strategic Philanthropy

11

▶ Strategic Philanthropy Defined

▶ Strategic Philanthropy and Corporate Citizenship

▶ Stakeholders in Strategic Philanthropy

▶ Benefits of Strategic Philanthropy

▶ Implementation of Strategic Philanthropy

OBJECTIVES

Define strategic philanthropy

Describe the history of corporate philanthropy in the United States

Distinguish between strategic philanthropy and cause-related marketing

Provide examples of strategic philanthropy

Identify the benefits of strategic philanthropy

Explain the key factors in implementing strategic philanthropy

When Noah's Bagels began expanding beyond its original Berkeley, California, location in the late 1980s, the company focused not only on opening new retail stores, but also on helping surrounding neighborhoods. Noah's sought to be a positive, dynamic force in its local communities because it "recognizes the importance of giving the community more than just exhilarated taste buds." Thus, the company began to link its philanthropic efforts directly with the core operations and skills required to run the business. For example, Noah's donates bagels and other foods to fight community hunger. The company also gives employees paid time off to work on service projects that benefit surrounding neighborhoods. Store managers can choose a local charity and apply for matching funds from corporate headquarters. Customers are encouraged to comment on the company's bagels, coffee, and community affairs. All of these efforts directly link Noah's philanthropy to issues that positively affect, and reflect, its operations and marketing.

Noah's efforts to be a good corporate citizen have reaped many rewards. The San Francisco Volunteer Council and Hitachi Foundation named Noah's a "Leader for Corporate Commitment to Community" for its concerted efforts to mobilize employees for projects that benefit the economic and social landscape of cities it serves. Noah's has also received recognition from the Association for Retarded Citizens (ARC), the National Association for the Advancement of Colored People (NAACP), and Disability Rights Advocates for its hiring and employment practices and support of community initiatives to improve employment readiness. These rewards not only demonstrate the company's commitment to equal opportunity, but also provide Noah's with excellent personnel and a good reputation. The same motivation, skills, and creativity required to run a successful business are channeled into Noah's philanthropy efforts. Because the company carefully chooses projects and charities that are aligned with its core competencies, Noah's Bagels is taking a strategic approach to corporate philanthropy.[1]

Like Noah's Bagels, more companies are considering how to integrate their philanthropic efforts with their organizational objectives and core competencies. Research by the American Productivity and Quality Center (APQC) indicates that the definition of corporate success is slowly evolving to include four equal and complementary goals: Corporations are seeking to become the (1) supplier and provider of choice, (2) employer of choice, (3) investment of choice, and (4) neighbor of choice. Progressive businesses are investigating ways to tie their corporate objectives to community relations activities, especially through the development of citizen advisory panels, public hearings, meetings with community service organizations, and participation in community events. Such practices are intended to create "corporate equity with communities and stakeholders"[2] These activities are also aligned with our concept of corporate citizenship and strategic philanthropy.

In this chapter, we define strategic philanthropy and integrate this concept with other elements of corporate citizenship. Next, we trace the evolution of corporate philanthropy and distinguish the concept from cause-related marketing. We also provide examples of best practices of addressing stakeholders' interests that meet our definition of strategic philanthropy. Next, we consider the benefits of investing in strategic philanthropy to satisfy both stakeholders and corporate objectives. Finally, we examine the process of implementing strategic philanthropy in business. Our approach in this chapter is to demonstrate how companies can link strategic philanthropy with economic, legal, and ethical concerns for the benefit of all stakeholders.

Strategic Philanthropy Defined

In a general sense, philanthropy involves any acts of benevolence and goodwill, such as making gifts to charities, volunteering for community projects, and taking action to benefit others. For example, your parents may have spent time on nonwork projects that directly benefitted the community or a special population. Perhaps you have participated in similar activities through work, school clubs, or associations. Have you ever served Thanksgiving dinner at a homeless shelter? Have you ever raised money for a neighborhood school? Most religious organizations, educational institutions, and arts programs rely heavily on philanthropic donations from both individuals and organizations. Philanthropy is a major driver of the nonprofit sector of the economy, as these organizations rely on the time, money, and talents of both individuals and organizations to operate and fund their programs. Consider the Sakharov Museum in Moscow. The museum, named for Nobel Peace Prize winner and human rights activist Andrei Sakharov, recently faced a severe financial crisis because Russia lacks a culture of corporate philanthropy and the associated funding of nongovernment museums. The museum's political bent, along with Russian laws prohibiting tax benefits on charitable donations, has caused museum managers to look outside their country for funding.[3]

Figure 11.1 displays the major recipients of the more than $203 billion in philanthropic donations made in 2000. As Figure 11.2 indicates, individuals made 75 percent of these donations, with corporations contributing over 5 percent, or almost $11 billion a year.[4] In addition to their financial resources, companies also contribute goods and services. Apple Computer, for example, was one of the first companies to make major inroads in education with donated and deeply discounted computers after it recognized that student loyalty to a computer system would extend beyond the educational environment. Johnson & Johnson donates medical products to hospitals and similar facilities, which enhances its relationships with a key stakeholder group.[5] Table 11.1 provides additional examples of philanthropic activities.

FIGURE 11.1

Focus of Philanthropic Donations

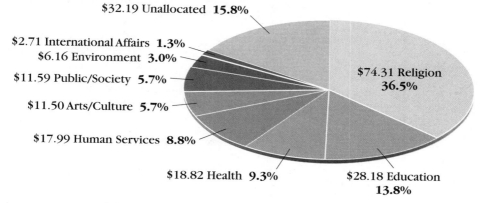

2000 Contributions: $203.45 Billion by Type of Recipient Organization

$32.19 Unallocated **15.8%**

$2.71 International Affairs **1.3%**
$6.16 Environment **3.0%**
$11.59 Public/Society **5.7%**

$11.50 Arts/Culture **5.7%**

$17.99 Human Services **8.8%**

$18.82 Health **9.3%**

$74.31 Religion **36.5%**

$28.18 Education **13.8%**

Source: "2000 Contributions: $203.45 Billion by Type of Recipient Organization," AAFRC Trust for Philanthropy/*Giving USA 2001,* www.aafrc.org/images/graphics/chart2.jpg, accessed November 5, 2001. AAFRC Trust for Philanthropy/Giving USA 2001.

FIGURE 11.2

Sources of Philanthropic Donations

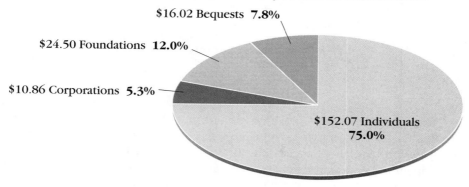

2000 Contributions: $203.45 Billion by Source of Contributions

$16.02 Bequests **7.8%**

$24.50 Foundations **12.0%**

$10.86 Corporations **5.3%**

$152.07 Individuals **75.0%**

Source: "2000 Contributions: $203.45 Billion by Source of Contribution," AAFRC Trust for Philanthropy/*Giving USA 2001,* www.aafrc.org/images/graphics/chart1.jpg, accessed November 5, 2001. AAFRC Trust for Philanthropy/Giving USA 2001.

TABLE 11.1

Examples of Corporate Philanthropy

- After British Petroleum (now BP Amoco) was criticized by Greenpeace for its environmental practices, the company created a $1 billion business and many new jobs in solar power, a renewable and nonpolluting source of energy

- Dayton-Hudson Corporation regularly donates 5 percent of pretax income to charities, whereas employees both select and volunteer in many of these community-based organizations

- Scientists at Bell Laboratories are involved in making recommendations for grants to universities in areas of teaching and research that are of current interest to the company

- Through the company's foundation, executives at AT&T are strongly encouraged to join nonprofit organizations' boards of directors

- Customers of Hanna Andersson, a manufacturer of high-quality children's clothes, can return worn clothing for credit toward their next purchase, with the used clothing donated to needy children

- Kraft Foods donates about half of its corporate giving dollars to hunger relief and school nutrition programs

- Seafirst Bank's partnership with Indian Nations in the state of Washington resulted in education programs for Native Americans in financial management and tribal economic development and helped Seafirst employees to better understand cultural issues related to business relationships and development

- More than 6,000 companies sponsor matching-gift programs, where an employee's personal donation to an educational institution is matched by the employer

Sources: Reynold Levy, *Give and Take: A Candid Account of Corporate Philanthropy* (Boston: Harvard Business School Press, 1999); "Better to Give and To Receive," *Hemispheres* (January 1997); Glen Peters, *Waltzing with the Raptors: A Practical Roadmap to Protecting Your Company's Reputation* (New York: John Wiley and Sons, Inc., 1999); Ann Svendsen, *The Stakeholder Strategy* (San Francisco: Berrett-Koehler, 1998).

Because we are concerned with corporate citizenship, this chapter will focus on the philanthropic activities of businesses. Our concept of corporate philanthropy extends beyond financial contributions and explicitly links company missions, organizational competencies, and various stakeholders. Thus, we define **strategic philanthropy** as the synergistic use of an organization's core competencies and resources to address key stakeholders' interests and to achieve both organizational and social benefits. Strategic philanthropy goes well beyond the traditional benevolent philanthropy of donating a percentage of sales to social causes by involving employees (utilizing their core skills); organizational resources and expertise (equipment, knowledge, and money); and the ability to link employees, customers, suppliers, and social needs with these key assets. Strategic philanthropy involves both financial and nonfinancial contributions to stakeholders (employee time, goods and services, and company technology and equipment, as well as facilities), but it also benefits the company.

John Damonti, president of the Bristol-Myers Squibb Foundation, reflected, "When you align your contributions with your business focus, you then can draw on the greater wealth of the corporation's people, information, and resources."[6] Organizations are best suited to deal with social or stakeholder issues in areas with which they have some experience, knowledge, or expertise. From a business perspective, companies want to reinforce and refine their competencies and to develop synergies between business and philanthropic activities. The process of addressing stakeholder concerns through philanthropy should be strategic to a company's ongoing development and improvement. For example, American Express, a global financial and travel company, contributed funds and know-how to initiate the development of the Academy of Travel and Tourism in Hungary. This project benefitted the Hungarian economy, tested the entrepreneurial spirit and skills of American Express employees, and reinforced the company's understanding of the Hungarian market.[7] Some critics would argue that this was not true philanthropy because American Express received business benefits. Because corporate citizenship includes responsibilities on many levels, effective philanthropy depends on the synergy between stakeholder needs and business competencies and goals. Thus, the fact that each partner to the Academy of Travel and Tourism had different goals and earned unique benefits does not diminish the overall good that resulted from the project. As global competition escalates, companies are increasingly responsible to stakeholders in justifying their philanthropic endeavors. This ultimately requires greater planning and alignment of philanthropic efforts with overall strategic goals.

Strategic Philanthropy and Corporate Citizenship

It is important to place strategic philanthropy in the context of corporate citizenship and organizational responsibilities at the economic, legal, ethical, and philanthropic levels. Most companies understand the need to be economically successful for the benefit of all stakeholders and to comply with the laws required within our society and others in which they do business. Additionally, through the establishment of core values and ethical cultures, most firms are recognizing the many benefits of good ethics. As we saw in Chapter 2, evidence is accumulating that there is a positive relationship between citizenship and performance, especially with regard to customer satisfaction and employee commitment. Strategic citizenship can reduce the cost of business transactions, establish trust among stakeholders, improve teamwork, and preserve the social capital necessary for an infrastructure for doing business.[8]

Many companies consider philanthropy only after they have met their financial, legal, and ethical obligations.[9] As companies strive for good corporate citizenship, their ability to meet each obligation lays the foundation for success on other responsibilities. In addition, there is synergy in corporate efforts directed at the four levels of responsibility. As one of the most voluntary dimensions of corporate citizenship, philanthropy has not always been linked to profits or the ethical components of corporate citizenship. In fact, the traditional approach to philanthropy separates giving from business performance and its impact on all stakeholders. Before the evolution of strategic philanthropy, most corporate gift programs separated the company from the organizations, causes, and individuals that its donations most benefitted.[10]

Research has begun to highlight organizations' formalization of philanthropic activities and their efforts to integrate philanthropic goals with other business strategies and implementation. A Conference Board survey of 463 U.S. companies found that those adopting a more businesslike approach to philanthropy experienced a better image, increased employee loyalty, and improved customer ties.[11] Because philanthropy involves using organizational resources, formal methods should deliver more effective and professional results to the effort. In this case, philanthropy is viewed as an investment from which a company can gain some type of value.[12]

The traditional approach to corporate philanthropy is characterized by donations and related activities that are not purposefully aligned with the strategic goals and resources of the firm. For example, employees may be encouraged to volunteer in the community but receive little direction on where or how to spend their time. Employees of Fuji Bank of Japan, for example, may apply for leaves of absence to take part in volunteer opportunities.[13] After the September 11, 2001, terrorist attacks, companies and employees became quite creative in their philanthropic efforts. One result was "leave-based donation programs," that allow employees to donate the value of accumulated vacation and sick- and personal-leave days to a nonprofit cause. The United States Treasury Department approved the idea and clarified regulations to benefit employees, companies, and nonprofits.[14] Indeed, there are numerous examples of companies supporting community involvement. Although these actions are noble, they are not always considered in tandem with organizational goals and strengths. In other cases, corporate contributions may be made to nonprofit organizations in which top managers have a personal interest. Ben & Jerry's Homemade, for example, traditionally gave 1 percent of its pretax profits to programs supporting peace initiatives because this cause is dear to its founders; it also donated an overall 7.5 percent of pretax profits to support environmental and social causes. Ben & Jerry's has successfully tied "caring capitalism" to its company image and mission to clearly differentiate its products in the marketplace.[15] Finally, many companies will match employees' personal gifts to educational institutions. Although gift-matching programs instill employee pride and assist education, they are rarely linked to company operations and competencies.[16] In the traditional approach to corporate philanthropy, then, companies have good intentions, but there is no true integration with organizational resources and objectives.

In the corporate citizenship model that we propose, philanthropy is only one focal point for a corporate vision that includes both the welfare of the firm and benefits to stakeholders. This requires support from top management, as well as a strategic planning structure that incorporates stakeholder concerns and benefits. Corporate giving, volunteer efforts, and other contributions should be considered and aligned not only with corporate strategy, but also with financial, legal, and ethical obligations. The shift from traditional benevolent philanthropy to strategic philanthropy has come about as companies struggled in the 1980s and 1990s to redefine their missions, alliances, and scope, while becoming increasingly accountable to stakeholders and society.

▶ History of Corporate Philanthropy

Downsizing, mergers, divestitures, growing international competition, consumer activism, and investor demands have led many firms to reassess their business practices and outcomes. As we discussed in previous chapters, organizations are experiencing increasing pressure to demonstrate responsibility at many levels, including financial and social performance. As a result, companies integrating a strategic philanthropy approach now blend both organizational and social needs. Under this approach, neither philanthropy nor business objectives have a dominant role, as both collaborate to benefit and inform the other. This is a relatively recent phenomenon, as most companies are just beginning to realize the benefits of "caring as fiercely as you compete."[17] Table 11.2 traces the evolution of corporate philanthropy in the United States.

Until the middle of the twentieth century, corporate donations were virtually outlawed in the United States. Companies began making contributions when laws were changed in the 1950s. Many firms began to establish separate foundations to make donations in the 1960s. Most large corporations in the United States allocated much less than 5 percent of pretax profits to their foundations. Under this model, the foundations were deliberately kept distinct from business interests and goals. These foundations continue to contribute millions of dollars to the nonprofit and charitable sector of the United States, as demonstrated in Table 11.3.

TABLE 11.2

Evolution of Corporate Philanthropy in the United States

Time Period	General Characteristics
Through 1950s	Federal law prohibits corporate donations
1960s and 1970s	Public begins to believe companies should donate some of their profits to social causes
	Large corporations set up foundations
	Few criteria for choosing philanthropic projects
1970s and 1980s	Stagnant economy slows corporate philanthropy
	Public and government lower expectations of business
	Merger and acquisition strategies leave little room for philanthropic effort and donations
Early 1990s	Pressure to formalize corporate governance and accountability
	Public reacts to "greed" of 1980s by raising expectations of business
	Companies take more active role in community and societal causes
Mid 1990s and Beyond	Expansion of philanthropy model to include time and human resources
	Recognition of relationship between philanthropy and corporate benefits with customers, employees, business partners, and community
	Collaboration between business and other groups to resolve social problems
	Focus on aligning business goals to philanthropic activity through overall corporate vision

Sources: Craig N. Smith, "The New Corporate Philanthropy," *Harvard Business Review,* 72 (May/June 1994); Ann Svendsen, *The Stakeholder Strategy: Profiting from Collaborative Business Relationships* (San Francisco: Berrett-Koehler Publishers, 1998).

During the 1960s, the public began to question the role of business in society, and many individuals called for corporations to give some of their profits back to society. This sentiment continued throughout most of the 1970s. However, corporate philanthropy remained a low priority for many businesses through the 1980s. This era of acquisitions and cost cutting stripped away many of the incentives for philanthropy, although some financially sound and progressive organizations began formalizing their efforts during this time. By the early 1990s, attitudes about

TABLE 11.3

Ten Largest Corporate Foundations by Total Giving

Foundation	Total Grants	As of
1. Ford Motor Company Fund	$97,789,429	December 31, 1999
2. Bank of America Foundation	90,999,532	December 31, 1999
3. SBC Foundation	64,047,020	December 31, 1999
4. Wal-Mart Foundation	62,617,641	January 31, 2000
5. AT&T Foundation	39,626,024	December 31, 1999
6. BP Amoco Foundation	36,944,795	December 31, 1999
7. GE Fund	36,126,991	December 31, 1999
8. Verizon Foundation	35,332,818	December 31, 1999
9. The Chase Manhattan Foundation	35,227,314	December 31, 1999
10. Fannie Mae Foundation	33,926,500	December 31, 1999

Source: "50 Largest Corporate Foundations by Total Giving," The Foundation Center, March 28, 2001, http://fdncenter.org/grantmaker/trends.

the responsibilities of business in society had shifted again.[18] Today, most company leaders understand the benefits of well-managed corporate philanthropy initiatives, even if they have not fully formalized their approach in this area. For example, Cadbury Schweppes, along with other firms in the United Kingdom, donates money to Crisis, a national charity that relieves poverty and homelessness, every holiday season. Instead of sending holiday greeting cards to thousands of customers, vendors, and other business partners, these firms donate their greeting card and postage budget to Crisis.[19]

Strategic philanthropy emerged as a management practice to support corporate citizenship in organizations in the 1980s. AT&T was one of the first organizations to formalize strategic philanthropy when it appointed Reynold Levy to head its foundation to provide leadership in this area. Levy's ideas altered the link between organizational and social needs by tying AT&T's foundation activities to its business goals and objectives and by emphasizing that such activities could advance business interests.[20] Levy, reflecting on his role at AT&T and in the strategic philanthropy movement, noted, "What I soon discovered was that the special value of corporate philanthropy resides in the business perspectives and array of resources it brings to addressing societal needs."[21] Large corporations such as AT&T have been fundamentally responsible for shaping our understanding of strategic philanthropy. Although some companies have advanced toward strategic philanthropy, most firms are still developing their efforts.

Once organizations become interested in philanthropy, they have a number of options for providing contributions and other resources. For instance, sponsorships provide an opportunity to associate a company's name and brands to a particular event. This business activity is normally considered a marketing tactic rather than a philanthropic act, as sponsorships may have little effect on a social cause or issue. Although sponsoring a sports stadium may assist team and venue owners, it is not fully linked to bettering some aspect of society.[22] One common method for tying the business purpose and philanthropy to society and community concerns is through the implementation of cause-related marketing campaigns. BP (British Petroleum) recently launched a pan-European project with the Red Cross, where customers at BP's gas stations across Europe can donate money to the Red Cross. The cause-related marketing effort is part of an overall strategy to reposition BP as a strong corporate citizen.[23]

▶ *Strategic Philanthropy versus Cause-Related Marketing*

The first attempts by organizations to coordinate organizational goals with philanthropic giving emerged with cause-related marketing in the early 1980s. Whereas strategic philanthropy links corporate resources and knowledge to address broader social, customer, employee, and supplier problems and needs, **cause-related marketing** ties an organization's product(s) directly to a social concern. Table 11.4 compares cause-related marketing and strategic philanthropy. With cause-related marketing, a percentage of a product's sales is usually donated to a cause appealing to the relevant target market. The Avon Breast Cancer Crusade, for example, generates proceeds for the breast cancer cause through several fundraising efforts, including the sale of special "pink ribbon" products by Avon independent Sales Representatives nationwide (Figure 11.3 on page 368). Gifts are awarded by the Avon Products Foundation, Inc., a nonprofit 501(c)(3) accredited public charity, to support five vital areas of the breast cancer cause with a focus on medically underserved women, biomedical research, clinical care, financial assistance and support services, educational seminars and advocacy training, and early detection and awareness programs nationwide. Both the cause and Avon Crusade "pink ribbon" products appeal to Avon's primary target market, women. Between 1993 and fall 2001 the Avon Breast Cancer Crusade has generated more than $150 million net in the United States to fund access to care and finding a cure for breast cancer.[24]

American Express was the first company to use cause-related marketing widely, when it began advertising in 1983 that it would give a percentage of credit

TABLE 11.4

Strategic Philanthropy Contrasted with Cause-Related Marketing

	Strategic Philanthropy	**Cause-Related Marketing**
Focus	Organizational	Product or product line
Goals	Improve organizational competency or tie organizational competency to social need or charitable cause	Increase product sales
Time Frame	Ongoing	Traditionally of limited duration
Organizational Members Involved	Potentially all organizational employees	Marketing department and related personnel
Cost	Moderate—requires alignment with organizational strategies and mission	Minimal—alliance development and promotion expenditures

card charges to the Statue of Liberty and Ellis Island Restoration Fund.[25] In a more recent alliance, Regis Hair Salons offered $10 haircuts during its "Clip for the Cure" campaign, which raised more than $200,000 for breast cancer research.[26] As is the case with Avon, American Express, and Regis, companies generally prefer to support causes that are of interest to their target markets. In a single year, organizations paid more than $500 million for the rights to support various social programs, ultimately raising roughly $2.5 billion for these causes.[27] Thus, a key feature of cause-related marketing is the promise of donations to a particular social cause based on customer sales or involvement.[28]

Although cause-related marketing has its roots in the United States, the marketing tool is gaining widespread usage in other parts of the world. A study by Saatchi & Saatchi found that about 40 percent of European senior marketers were aligning their cause-related marketing budgets with brand communication programs. For example, the New Covent Garden Soup Co. recently partnered with a homeless charity in Great Britain. During the Christmas season, portions of sales of New Covent Garden's pea and ham soup were donated to help renovate the charity's kitchens. Tesco, a large European grocery chain, also joined the cause by donating funds based on every soup carton sold in the six-week holiday season.[29] Business in the Community, a nonprofit group in the United Kingdom, sponsors annual

FIGURE 11.3

The Avon Breast Cancer Crusade

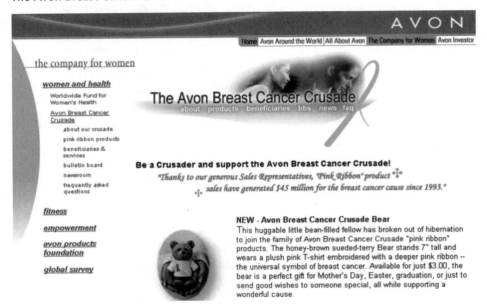

Source: "Avon Breast Cancer Crusade," Avon, www.avoncrusade.com/, accessed January 3, 2001.
Reprinted with permission from Avon. For updated information, see www.avoncrusade.com.

awards for British firms that demonstrate excellence in cause-related marketing. Walkers, a manufacturer of cookies and biscuits, is a recent winner, based on its effort to distribute more than 2.3 million books to schools in the United Kingdom.[30]

Research suggests that cause-related marketing activities have the potential to affect buying patterns. One study found that a vast majority of consumers (86 percent) said that, given equal price and product quality, they would be more likely to buy the product associated with a charitable cause. The study also noted that 70 percent of marketing directors felt that cause-related marketing would increase in importance over the coming years.[31] Through cause-related marketing, companies first become aware that supporting social causes, such as environmental awareness, health and human services, education, and the arts, can support business goals.[32] One of the main weaknesses with cause-related marketing, however, is that 90 percent of consumers cannot link specific philanthropic efforts with companies.[33] Consumers may have difficulty recalling specific philanthropic relationships because cause-related marketing campaigns tend to be of short duration and do not always have a direct correlation to the sponsoring firm's core business. Because strategic philanthropy is more pervasive and relates to company attributes and skills, such alliances should have greater consumer recognition and appreciation.

Stakeholders in Strategic Philanthropy

Although more businesses are moving toward adopting a strategic philanthropy model, others are still focusing only on the needs of individual stakeholders. Although these efforts are important and commendable, companies may not be realizing the full benefits for themselves and their stakeholders. For example, the implementation of cause-related marketing efforts may not reinforce employee skills and competencies. Instead, such campaigns usually focus on generating product sales and donations to a specific cause. Volunteer programs may benefit the community and employee morale, but the value of this service could be greatly enhanced through synergies between current and future job-related aptitude and nonprofit needs.

In this section, we offer examples of organizations that have effectively collaborated with various stakeholders in the pursuit of mutual benefits. Their efforts serve as examples of best practices in implementing and managing strategic philanthropy. Arnold Hiatt, former CEO of Stride Rite Corporation noted, "Look at a well-run company and you will see the needs of its stockholders, its employees, and the community at large being served simultaneously."[34] The following strategic philanthropic efforts demonstrate a dual concern for meeting stakeholder needs while strengthening organizational competencies.

Employees

A key to organizational success is the ability of organizations to attract, socialize, and retain competent and qualified employees. Through strategic philanthropy initiatives, companies have the opportunity to increase employee commitment and motivation. For example, United Airlines Foundation adopted four focus areas for its philanthropic strategy. One of those focus areas is education and careers, with a global emphasis. Using the professional expertise of United Airlines employees, the foundation helped develop the Virtual Trade Mission, a collaboration between the U.S. federal government, labor groups, and private companies to teach high school and middle school students the importance of America's export economy. This educational program, which has been implemented in more than thirty communities around the world, employed multimedia technology to simulate a trade mission. United Airlines employees contributed expertise on world geography, global economic conditions, and cross-cultural communication to the Virtual

Trade Mission. These elements were not only effective for student learning, but also mirror the skills and knowledge necessary for the airline to operate effectively on a daily basis. United Airlines' core competencies include the ability to transfer knowledge and best practices between countries in which it operates.

BE & K, an international construction and engineering firm headquartered in Birmingham, Alabama, has mobilized its retirees for supporting special community service projects. Because these retirees have years of experience in the construction business, they are particularly suited for philanthropic efforts that involve renovation, design, and related skills. For example, one retired employee heads up a YWCA effort to renovate housing for disabled and low-income women.[35] BE & K has also extended its employee safety and drug abuse programs into the philanthropic realm. These programs were originally designed to assist employees, reduce accidents, and help the business perform more effectively. After taking this experience and program to others in the industry and beyond, the company received the FBI Director's Community Leadership Award for outstanding contributions to the community in the prevention of drug abuse.[36]

▶ *Customers*

As industries become increasingly competitive, companies are seeking ways to differentiate themselves in customers' minds. Home Depot, for example, has been progressive in the way it approaches philanthropy. The company has aligned its expertise and resources to address community needs. Its relationship with Habitat for the Humanities gives employees a chance to improve their skills and bring direct knowledge back into the workplace to benefit customers. It also enhances Home Depot's image of expertise as the "do-it-yourself" center. Home Depot also responded to customers' needs when Hurricane Andrew hit the Miami area. Many home building supply and hardware stores were taking advantage of customers by inflating prices on emergency materials, but Home Depot opened its stores 24 hours a day and made materials available at reduced costs to help customers survive the disaster.

Bankers Trust Private Bank, part of German-headquartered Deutsche Bank AG, introduced its "Wealth of Responsibility" program to assist wealthy families in planning for philanthropy. In addition to financial experts, the bank employs consultants and advisors who help families set goals, invest for future wealth, and provide funds to charities and other groups. Thus, BT is providing services that not only benefit wealthy clients but also direct assets into philanthropic directions to benefit society. The program targets clients around the world, with a focus on Europeans who are just beginning to become interested in philanthropy.[37]

GTE, through its philanthropic foundation, distributed more than $30 million nationwide in 1999. Literacy and technology education are two of GTE's greatest concerns. GTE's Family Literacy program funds forty-four technology learning centers nationwide. With an estimated 40 million U.S. citizens classified as illiterate, GTE feels it can influence customers' quality of life with such a broad-based initiative. Employees are also encouraged to volunteer in education-related programs and to take part in initiatives that will strengthen their own literacy and technology use.[38] Target is another firm that contributes significant resources to education, including direct donations of $14 million to schools as well as fund-raising and scholarship programs to assist teachers and students. Through the retailer's Take Charge of Education program, customers using a Target Guest Card can designate a specific school to which Target donates 1 percent of that customer's total purchase. This program is designed to make customers feel that their purchases are benefitting their community while increasing the use of Target Guest Cards.[39] Education is the second largest category of philanthropic donations (behind religion) that appeals to GTE's and Target's broad target markets.

▶ *Business Partners*

More companies are using philanthropic goals and social concerns as a measure of with whom they would like to do business. Companies are increasingly requiring social audits, adoption of industry codes of ethics, and social responsibility on the part of their business partners. The Freeplay Group, based in South Africa, is an example of a company founded on the principle of "making money and making a difference." The company manufactures and markets wind-up radios that were originally intended for use in poor nations where electricity and batteries are scarce. For example, these radios have been used to transmit elementary school lessons in South Africa and election results in Ghana. The radios now sell in many countries at retailers such as Sharper Image, Radio Shack, and Harrod's. Freeplay's investors include the General Electric Pension Trust and Liberty Life, a South African insurance firm. Rotary International and other community organizations are using the radios to implement programs that benefit society and communities. These investors and customers have chosen Freeplay for its solid business plan founded on broader social goals.[40]

BJC Health System is working with other area health-care systems to make health insurance available to St. Louis, Missouri, residents who cannot afford it. BJC manages Care Partners and ConnectCare. Care Partners offers twenty-four-hour emergency care and primary-care facilities to anyone in need, whether they are insured or not. ConnectCare was launched by city officials and community leaders with the same goal of providing health services to all citizens. BJC has won praise for its ability to work with insurers, other systems, and the public in supporting health insurance initiatives with the collective goal of improving people's lives. These collaborative ventures allocate the costs of caring for indigent and uninsured

Venturing into Socially Responsible Investing

The "New Economy," driven by the growth of high-tech industries, made millionaires of many entrepreneurs, stockholders, and even employees. Many of these individuals, who seemed to have secure financial futures, look for opportunities to invest in the well-being of their local communities and neighborhoods. Some of these investors have chosen to apply the concept of venture capital, which once funded many of the companies that made them wealthy, to socially responsible initiatives through charitable organizations. In other words, social venture capitalists donate funds and other resources to nonprofit organizations that support the community and local neighborhoods. Hundreds of such social venture capital funds have sprouted in recent years, particularly on the West Coast, and these now account for as much as 5 percent of the $22 billion in charitable grants made across the country every year.

Social venture capital organizations typically require their donors (or partners, as many organizations refer to them) to contribute $5,000 to $10,000 a year for a minimum of two years and to participate in selecting and overseeing the charitable organizations to which they contribute. Although these organizations apply the concepts of traditional venture capital, they often feel more like neighborhood investment clubs. Partners' funds are pooled and "invested" in local organizations that fit with the social venture capitalists' goals. In addition to money, partners in these organizations may also draw on their talents, contacts, and other resources in order to serve as strategy consultants, media advisors, tech experts, and even headhunters to help targeted nonprofit organizations reach their objectives.

One of the best-known social venture capital organizations is the Social Venture Partners of Seattle (SVP), which was established in 1997 by Paul Brainerd, the founder of Aldus Corp. Within its first two years of offering grants, the partnership awarded thirteen nonprofit organizations a total of about $1 million. SVP has grown rapidly,

patients across the community, a strategy that benefits all hospitals and care providers representing suppliers and business partners' best interests.[41]

Finally, nonprofit organizations are finding innovative ways to raise money and partner with business firms. For example, Social Venture Partners, founded in 1997 by a former software entrepreneur, brings together business professionals with an interest in solving social and community problems. These partners pool their financial and business expertise to assist nonprofit organizations. This model includes high expectations for measurable change and impact in the community. The Austin Social Venture Partners (ASVP) developed from the rapid growth of technology firms in Central Texas. Founders and executives of companies such as Dell Computer Corporation are committed to improving the prospects for nonprofit activity in Austin.[42]

from 30 members to more than 260, about half of whom are current or former Microsoft employees. The organization has also spawned chapters in other communities, including Austin, Texas; Boulder, Colorado; Calgary, Alberta; Denver, Colorado; Kansas City, Kansas; and Phoenix, Arizona. The Kansas City chapter of Social Venture Partners, for example, combines the funds and expertise of its partners to invest in new start-up nonprofit organizations in the area. Partners can designate where their funds go, and each is expected to serve on an administrative committee or volunteer team that assists the nonprofit organizations. The Kansas City group's Nonprofit Growth Fund provides grant money that supports the core business of selected area nonprofits, whereas its Social Venture Capital Fund provides debt and/or equity financing to meet the capital needs of nonprofit organizations.

Another social venture fund from the Peninsula Community Foundation, in San Jose, California, supports The Assets for All Alliance, a program that teaches low-income clients to manage and save money. The program requires clients to save at least $20 a month and to make at least ten deposits a year. The fund matches clients' savings, which can then be applied toward college tuition, small business start-ups, first-home purchases, and retirement. Of the first 207 clients to participate in the program, only six failed to follow through with their savings plans.

Through the investments and assistance of wealthy individuals like Paul Brainerd, social venture capitalists can help nonprofit charities enhance their positive impact on the entire community. Although some nonprofit organizations are uncomfortable with the hands-on approach adopted by social venture capitalists, most charities welcome their experience, contacts, and other resources that can help them achieve their goals more efficiently and effectively. Thus, one entrepreneur calls social venture capitalism the "new philanthropy for the new economy." ∎

Sources:
Alisa Gravitz, "Soul into Money: Four Tools," *Whole Earth,* Spring 1998, p. 177; Carol Tice, "Social Venture Partners Sharpens Mission, Values," *Puget Sound Business Journal,* August 4, 2000, p. 8; David Whitford, "The New Shape of Philanthropy," *Fortune,* June 12, 2000, pp. 315+; S. L. Wykes, "San Jose, Calif.-Area Venture Capital Group Helps Low-Income Become Savers," *San Jose Mercury News,* September 20, 2000.

▶ *Community and Society*

Society expects businesses to be good corporate citizens and to contribute to the well-being of the communities in which they operate. The Coca-Cola Company takes a strategic view of its role in society by linking its company resources and operating practices to stakeholder issues. Although it acknowledges the profusion of problems in today's world, Coca-Cola has chosen to focus its energies and resources on environmental issues where the company has an impact and relevant expertise. Water quality, water conservation, and waste reduction are therefore key considerations in its packaging and operational decisions.[43] Coca-Cola has also contributed funds and expertise around the world to support collaborations that respond to these environmental concerns. These projects involve bottlers, employees, suppliers, regulators, customers, and other corporations interested in building strategies for environmental excellence.

Merck developed a drug to combat "river blindness," a disease afflicting more than eighteen million people worldwide. Merck's expertise as a pharmaceutical laboratory allowed it to develop Mectizan to treat river blindness, and its humanitarian orientation led it to donate the drug to nearly twenty-five million people at risk in thirty-one countries in Africa, Latin America, and the Middle East. A Merck scientist who worked on the project noted, "I've received more mail based on this decision than anything else we've done as a company. Not only was it positive, more important than our shareholders, I thought, was the effect on the people at Merck, . . . about what a fantastic move this was for the company."[44] The benefits of the decision to develop and donate the drug to heavily afflicted areas demonstrates Merck's understanding of strategic philanthropy and the positive effects on society, as well as on employees, investors, and even customers.

LensCrafters has pledged to give one million pairs of glasses to the needy by 2003. Not wanting the firm's motives questioned, CEO Dave Brown has directed employees not to seek publicity. He states, "I do not want anyone thinking the company is doing this for any reason other than it's the right thing to do." Brown also noted that employees could engage in other philanthropy, but that this effort makes more sense because it leverages LensCrafters' eye care provision skills.[45]

McDonald's supports communities through its Ronald McDonald Houses, which give housing to families of children undergoing extended cancer treatments at hospitals far from home.

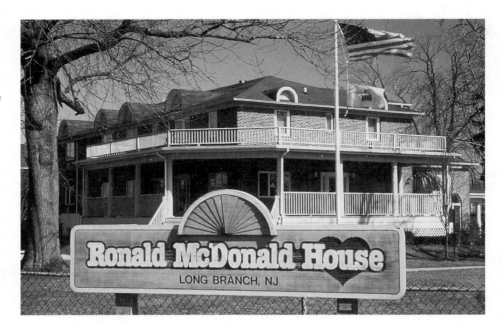

Finally, groups of companies and industry associations are also working to extend the philanthropic efforts of their member companies. For example, the American Apparel Manufacturers Association assists manufacturers in donating surplus apparel to the needy, homeless, and disaster victims. More than $54 million of surplus has been donated to more than 250 charitable organizations in 16 countries.[46] By working with their trade association, apparel manufacturers have been able to benefit from strategic philanthropy.

▶ Natural Environment

As we saw in Chapter 9, environmental causes have become increasingly important to stakeholders in recent years. Environmental abuses have damaged company and industry reputations and resulted in lost sales. 3M is one company that has been very aggressive in implementing environmentally friendly processes and procedures throughout its operations. This commitment extends to employees, as the company provides van transportation to work for employees within a fifteen-mile radius of the corporate office. If a van has only a few riders, each rider pays a minimal monthly fee to help offset some of the costs of the program. If the number of employees using the program increases to a specified level, 3M drops the monthly fee. The vanpooling initiative has minimized pollution levels. Additionally, the company has found that employees participating in the van transport program are less likely to use sick leave and more likely to manage their time well while at work.[47] 3M is able to coordinate its commitment to various stakeholders, including employees, customers, the natural environment, and the community. For this reason, 3M recently ranked second among the top fifty chemical manufacturers and users in the world for environmental performance.[48] The company also scores very highly on *Fortune* magazine's annual "Most Admired Corporations" list.

Benefits of Strategic Philanthropy

To pursue strategic philanthropy successfully, organizations must weigh both the costs and benefits associated with planning and implementing it as a corporate priority. Companies that assume a strategic approach to philanthropy are using an investment model with respect to their charitable acts and donations. In other words, these firms are not just writing checks—they are investing in solutions to stakeholder problems and corporate needs. Such an investment requires the commitment of company time, money, and human talent in order to succeed. Companies often need to hire staff to manage projects, communicate goals and opportunities throughout the firm, develop long-term priorities and programs, handle requests for funds, and represent the firm on other aspects of philanthropy. In addition, philanthropy consumes the time and energy of all types of employees within the organization. Thus, strategic philanthropy involves real corporate costs that must be justified and managed.

Most scholars and practitioners agree that the benefits of strategic philanthropy ultimately outweigh its costs. The positive return on strategic philanthropy is closely aligned with benefits obtained from overall good corporate citizenship, which we examined in Chapter 2. First, in the United States, businesses can declare up to 10 percent of pretax profits as tax-deductible contributions. Most firms do not take full advantage of this benefit, as 10 percent is viewed as a very generous contribution level. In fact, whereas corporate profits increased threefold in the 1990s, charitable contributions rose only 70 percent. In addition, just 25 percent of all U.S. firms claim any charitable tax deductions.[49]

Second, companies with a strategic approach to philanthropy experience rewards in the workplace. Employees involved in volunteer projects and related ventures not only have the opportunity to refine their professional skills, they also develop a stronger sense of loyalty and commitment to their employer. When Target, a division of Dayton-Hudson, surveyed employees involved in volunteerism, 74 percent agreed or strongly agreed that employee morale and commitment to the company were strengthened. In addition, they indicated that the volunteer experience brought new skills to the company and significantly enhanced Target's image in the community.[50] Results such as these lead to improved productivity and commitment, enhanced employee recruitment practices, and reduced employee turnover, each contributing to the overall effectiveness and efficiency of the company.

As a third benefit, companies should experience enhanced customer loyalty as a result of their strategic philanthropy. By choosing projects and causes with links to its core business, a firm can create synergies with its core competencies and customers. For example, Rosie O'Donnell has used her celebrity status and television talk show to establish the For All Kids Foundation to support social and cultural development of disadvantaged children. The foundation has been funded by a number of creative projects, including *Kids Are Punny,* a compilation of riddles, puns, and drawings sent by kids to *The Rosie O'Donnell Show.* Warner Books, the publisher, also agreed to contribute its net profits to the foundation. The book is expected to raise more than $1 million. Warner-Lambert, the manufacturer of Listerine Antiseptic mouthwash, donated $500,000 for kisses ($1,000/kiss) Rosie received from guests on her show. In addition to grants from corporations, the foundation is also funded through celebrity charity auctions on eBay.[51] To the benefit of Warner Brothers studio and production, these creative projects not only support hundreds of children's causes and charities, but also have earned the show critical praise and customer loyalty. Because a majority of Rosie O'Donnell's

Microsoft Chairman Bill Gates understands the importance of strategic philanthropy. Microsoft assists communities in improving education through software donations, and the company benefits from having so many children "trained" on Microsoft programs.

viewers are women with children, her For All Kids Foundation is a natural and strategic vehicle.

Finally, strategic philanthropy should improve a company's overall reputation in the community and ease government and community relations. Research indicates a strong negative relationship between illegal activity and reputation, whereas firms that contribute to charitable causes enjoy enhanced reputations. Moreover, companies that contribute to social causes, especially to problems that arise as a result of their actions, may be able to improve their reputations after committing a crime.[52] If a business is engaged in a strategic approach to contributions, volunteerism, and related activities, a clear purpose is to enhance and benefit the community. By properly implementing and communicating these achievements, the company will "do well by doing good." Essentially, community members and others use cues from a strategic philanthropy initiative, along with other corporate citizenship initiatives, to form a lasting impression—or reputation—of the firm. These benefits, along with others discussed in this section, are consistent with research conducted on European firms. Table 11.5 highlights the perceived benefits of corporate philanthropy to companies located in France, Germany, and the United Kingdom. The table suggests that companies in these countries believe that their charitable activities generally have a positive effect on goodwill, public relations, community relations, employee motivation, and customer loyalty.[53]

TABLE 11.5

Perceived Benefits of Corporate Philanthropy

Potential Benefit	Mean Value[a]		
	UK	France	Germany
Building goodwill	6.1	5.6	5.9
Facilitating public relations	6.1	6.3	6.2
Involving the company in the community	5.9	6.0	5.5
Improving social and economic life and infrastructures	5.7	6.0	6.1
Improving the company's image	5.7	6.4	6.3
Improving the loyalty and motivation of employees	4.9	3.6	4.1
Increasing general public awareness of the firm and/or its products	4.5	5.9	5.1
Encouraging loyalty among existing customers	4.3	3.5	4.0

a. Based on a seven-point scale: 1 = no contribution whatsoever; 7 = vitally important contribution.

Source: Adapted from Roger Bennett, "Corporate Philanthropy in France, Germany, and the UK," *International Marketing Review,* 15 (June 1998): 469. © MCB University Press, 2000. Reprinted with permission.

Implementation of Strategic Philanthropy

Realizing the benefits of strategic philanthropy depends on the integration of corporate competencies, business stakeholders, and corporate citizenship objectives to be fully effective. However, effectively implementing a strategic philanthropy approach is not simple and requires organizational resources and strategic attention. In this section, we examine some of the key factors associated with implementing strategic philanthropy.

Although some organizations and leaders see beyond economic concerns, other firms are far less progressive and collaborative in nature. To the extent that corporate leaders and others advocate for strategic philanthropy, planning and evaluation practices must be developed just as with any other business process. Almost all effective actions taken by a company are well-thought-out business plans. However, although most large organizations have solid plans for philanthropy and other community involvement, these activities typically do not receive the same attention that other business forays garner. A study by the American Productivity and Quality Center found that organizations are not yet taking a systematic or comprehensive approach in evaluating the impact of philanthropy on the business and other stakeholders.[54]

▶ *Top Management Support*

The implementation of strategic philanthropy is impossible without the endorsement and support of the chief executive officer and other members of top management. Although most executives care about their communities and social

Gymboree CEO Gary White supports children's causes through his volunteer work for the March of Dimes and Kids in Distressed Situations (K.I.D.S.).

issues, there may be debate or confusion over how their firms should meet stakeholder concerns and corporate citizenship responsibilities. When Al Dunlap became CEO of Sunbeam, for example, he eliminated the company's annual giving program of $1 million. He was very clear that he felt that Sunbeam's primary responsibility was to shareholders, noting that the company was giving to society by making money for shareholders.[55] In contrast, Robert Allen, chairman of the board for AT&T, noted that although some corporations are solely motivated by financial returns, he is confident that "the men and women who guide AT&T firmly believe that our business has the responsibility to contribute to the long-term well-being of the society. . . ."[56]

Top managers often have unique concerns with respect to strategic philanthropy. For example, chief executive officers may worry about having to defend the company's commitment to charity. Some investors may see these contributions as damaging to their portfolios. A related concern involves the resources required to manage a philanthropy effort. Top managers must be well versed in the performance benefits of corporate citizenship that we discussed in Chapter 2. Additionally, some executives may believe that less philanthropic-minded competitors have a profit advantage. If these competitors have any advantage at all, it is probably just a short-term situation. The tax benefits and other gains that philanthropy provides should prevail over the long run.[57] In today's environment, there are many positive incentives and reasons that strategic philanthropy and corporate citizenship make good business sense.

▸ Planning and Evaluating Strategic Philanthropy

As in any initiative, strategic philanthropy must prove its relevance and importance. In order for philanthropy and other stakeholder collaborations to be fully diffused and accepted within the business community, a performance benefit must be evident. In addition, philanthropy should be treated as a corporate program that deserves the same professionalism and resources as other strategic initiatives. Thus, the process for planning and evaluating strategic philanthropy are quite important to its success.

To make the best decisions when dealing with stakeholder concern and issues, there should be a defensible, workable strategy that insures that every donation is wisely spent. Author Curt Weeden, CEO of the Contributions Academy, has developed a multistep process for ensuring effective planning and implementation of strategic philanthropy.

1. **Research**   If a company has too little or inaccurate information, it will suffer when making philanthropic decisions. Research should cover the internal organization and programs, organizations, sponsorship options, and events that might intersect with the interests and competencies of the corporation.

2. **Organize and design** The information collected by research should be classified into relevant categories. For example, funding opportunities can be categorized according the level of need and alignment with organizational competencies. The process of organizing and designing is probably the most crucial step in which management should be thoroughly involved.

3. **Engage** This step consists of engaging management early on so as to ease the approval process in the future. Top managers need to be co-owners of the corporate philanthropy plan. They will have interest in seeing the plan receive authorization, and they will enrich the program by sharing their ideas and thoughts.

4. **Spend** Deciding what resources and dollars should be spent where is a very important task. A skilled manager who has spent some time with the philanthropy program should preferably handle this. If the previous steps were handled appropriately, this step should go rather smoothly.[58]

Evaluating corporate philanthropy should begin with a clear understanding of how these efforts are linked to the company's vision, mission, and resources. As our definition suggests, philanthropy can only be "strategic" if it is fully aligned with the values, core competencies, and long-term plans of an organization. Thus, the development of philanthropic programs should be part of the strategic planning process.

Assuming that key stakeholders have been identified, organizations need to conduct research to understand stakeholder expectations and their willingness to collaborate for mutual benefit. Although many companies have invested time and resources to understand the needs of employees, customers, and investors, fewer have examined other stakeholders or the potential for aligning stakeholders and company resources for philanthropic reasons. Philanthropic efforts should be evaluated for their effects on and benefits to various groups.

Methods used to evaluate strategic philanthropy should include an assessment of how these initiatives are communicated to stakeholders. Vancouver City Savings and Credit Union of Canada (VanCity) initiated the process of increasing its social accountability to its various stakeholders when its executives and board of directors recognized that VanCity's level of disclosure, not necessarily its social responsibility, was below many other financial institutions in Canada. By increasing its disclosure and reporting, VanCity improved awareness of its commitment to social responsibility and ultimately refined its corporate strategy to meet other stakeholder concerns.[59] We elaborate on VanCity's approach in Chapter 12. Such reporting mechanisms not only improve stakeholder knowledge but also lead to improvements and refinements. Although critics may deride organizations for communicating their philanthropic efforts, the strategic philanthropy model is dependent on feedback and learning to create greater value for the organization and its stakeholders, as we shall see in the next chapter.

Summary

Generally, philanthropy involves any acts of benevolence and goodwill. Strategic philanthropy is defined as the synergistic use of organizational core competencies and resources to address key stakeholders' interests and to achieve both organizational and social benefits. Strategic philanthropy involves both financial and nonfinancial contributions to stakeholders, but it also benefits the company. As such, strategic philanthropy is part of a broader philosophy that recognizes how participation in corporate citizenship can help an organization improve its overall performance. Research suggests that those companies that adopt a more businesslike approach to philanthropy will experience a better image, increased employee loyalty, and improved customer ties.

Corporate giving, volunteer efforts, and other philanthropic activities should be considered and aligned with corporate strategy and financial, legal, and ethical obligations. The concept of strategic philanthropy has evolved since the middle of the twentieth century, when contributions were prohibited by law, to emerge as a management practice to support corporate citizenship in the 1990s. Whereas strategic philanthropy links corporate resources and knowledge to address broader social, customer, employee, and supplier problems and needs, cause-related marketing ties an organization's product(s) directly to a social concern. By linking products with charities and social causes, organizations acknowledged the opportunity to align philanthropy to economic goals, and to acknowledge stakeholder interests in organizational benevolence.

Many organizations have skillfully used their resources and core competencies to address the needs of employees, customers, business partners, the community and society, and the natural environment. In order to pursue strategic philanthropy successfully, organizations must weigh the costs and benefits associated with planning and implementing it as a corporate priority. The benefits of strategic philanthropy are closely aligned with benefits obtained from overall corporate citizenship. Businesses that engage in strategic philanthropy often gain a tax advantage. Research suggests that they may also enjoy improved productivity, employee commitment and morale, and reduced turnover and experience greater customer loyalty and satisfaction. Research indicates that corporate citizenship has a positive influence on financial performance. In the future, many companies will devote more resources to understand how strategic philanthropy can be developed and integrated to support their core competencies.

The implementation of strategic philanthropy is impossible without the support of top management. To integrate strategic philanthropy into the organization successfully, the efforts must fit with the company's mission, values, and resources. Organizations must also understand stakeholder expectations and propensity to support such activities for mutual benefit. This process relies on the feedback of stakeholders in improving and learning how to better integrate the strategic philanthropy objectives with other organizational goals. Finally, companies will need to evaluate philanthropic efforts and assess how these results should be communicated to stakeholders.

KEY TERMS

strategic philanthropy

cause-related marketing

DISCUSSION QUESTIONS

1. What are some of the issues you might include in a defense of strategic philanthropy to company stockholders?

2. Describe your personal experiences with philanthropy. In what types of activities have you participated? What companies that you do business with have a philanthropic focus? How did this focus influence your decision to buy from that company?

3. How have changes in the business environment contributed to the growing trend of strategic philanthropy?

4. Compare and contrast cause-related marketing with strategic philanthropy. What are the unique benefits of each approach?

5. What role does top management perform in developing and implementing a strategic philanthropy approach?

6. Describe the four-stage process for planning and implementing strategic philanthropy.

EXPERIENTIAL EXERCISE

Choose one major corporation and investigate how closely that firm's philanthropic efforts are strategically aligned with its core competencies. Visit the company's web site, read its annual reports, and use other sources to justify your conclusions. Develop a chart or table to depict how the company's core competencies are linked to various philanthropic projects and stakeholder groups. Finally, provide an analysis of how these efforts have affected the company's performance.

NOTES

1. Reynold Levy, *Give and Take: A Candid Account of Corporate Philanthropy* (Boston, MA: Harvard Business School Press, 1999); Noah's Bagels, www.noahs. com/main.html, accessed November 5, 2001.

2. American Productivity and Quality Center, *Community Relations: Unleashing the Power of Corporate Citizenship* (Houston: APQC, 1998).

3. "Money Woes May Close Russian Museum," Associated Press Online, November 24, 2000, via Comtex.

4. "2000 Contributions: 203.45 Billion by Source of Contribution," AAFRC Trust for Philanthropy/Giving USA 2001, www.aafrc.org/images/graphics/chart1. jpg, accessed November 5, 2001.

5. Minette E. Drumwright and Patrick E. Murphy, "Corporate Societal Marketing," in *Handbook of Marketing and Society,* ed. Paul N. Bloom and Gregory T. Gundlach (Thousand Oaks, Calif.: Sage, 2001), pp. 162–183.

6. Diane Lindquist, "Drug Companies' Rx for the Bottom Line," *Industry Week,* September 7, 1998, p. 25.

7. Noel M. Tichy, Andrew R. McGill, and Lynda St. Clair, *Corporate Global Citizenship: Doing Business in the Public Eye* (San Francisco: The New Lexington Press, 1997).

8. Norm Bowie, "Companies Are Discovering the Value of Ethics," *USA Today Magazine,* January 1, 1998.

9. Levy, *Give and Take.*

10. Tichy, McGill, and St. Clair, *Corporate Global Citizenship.*

11. Nelson Schwartz and Tim Smart, "Giving-And Getting Something Back," *Business Week,* August 28, 1995, p. 81.

12. Drumwright and Murphy, "Corporate Societal Marketing."

13. "Corporate Citizen," Fuji Bank, www.fujibank.co.jp/eng/fb/topics/philan.html, accessed January 4, 2001.

14. Curt Weeden, "Leave-Based Donation Programs," Contributions Academy, www.contributionsacademy.com/html/news.html, accessed November 5, 2001.

15. Bob Nelson, *1001 Ways to Energize Employees* (New York: Workman Publishing, 1997).

16. Curt Weeden, *Corporate Social Investing* (San Francisco: Berrett-Koehler Publishers, Inc. 1998), pp. 116–123.

17. Hal F. Rosenbluth and Diane McFerrin Peters, *Good Company: Caring as Fiercely as You Compete* (Reading, Mass.: Perseus Books, 1998).

18. Craig N. Smith, "The New Corporate Philanthropy," *Harvard Business Review,* 72 (May/June 1994); Ann Svendsen, *The Stakeholder Strategy: Profiting from Collaborative Business Relationships* (San Francisco: Berrett-Koehler Publishers, 1998).

19. "The Crisis Christmas Card Challenge," Cadbury Schweppes, www.cadburyschweppes.com/newsroom/crisis.html, accessed December 12, 2000.

20. Smith, "The New Corporate Philanthropy."

21. Levy, *Give and Take.*

22. Drumwright and Murphy, "Corporate Societal Marketing."

23. Mark Kleinman, "BP Set to Partner Red Cross Cause in European Deal," *Marketing,* September 20, 2001, p. 1.

24. Avon, "Avon's Breast Cancer Awareness Crusade," www.avoncrusade.com/, accessed November 5, 2001.

25. Tichy, McGill, and St. Clair, *Corporate Global Citizenship.*

26. Tracy L. Pipp, "Corporate America Takes on Breast Cancer—and Both are Reaping the Benefits," Gannet News Service, October 21, 1996.

27. Daniel Kadlec and Bruce Voorst, "The New World of Giving: Companies Are Doing More Good, and Demanding More Back," *Time,* May 5, 1997, pp. 62–66.

28. P. Rajan Varadarajan and Anil Menon, "Cause-Related Marketing: A Coalignment of Marketing Strategy and Corporate Philanthropy," *Journal of Marketing,* 52 (July 1988): 58–74.

29. Allyson L. Stewart-Allen, "Europe Ready for Cause-Related Campaigns," *Marketing News,* July 6, 1998, p. 9.

30. Sue Adkins, "Why Cause-Related Marketing Is a Winning Business Formula," *Marketing,* July 20, 2000, p. 18.

31. Sue Adkins and Nina Kowalska, "Consumers Put 'Causes' on the Shopping List," M2 PressWire, November 17, 1997.

32. Jennifer Mullen, "Performance-Based Corporate Philanthropy: How 'Giving Smart' Can Further Corporate Goals," *Public Relations Quarterly,* June 22, 1997, p. 42.

33. Stan Friedman and Charles Kouns, "Charitable Contribution: Reinventing Cause Marketing," *Brand Week,* October 27, 1997.

34. Nelson, *1001 Ways to Energize Employees.*

35. Rosenbluth and Peters, *Good Company.*

36. BE & K, "BE& K Awards," www.BEK.com/awards.html, accessed November 5, 2001.

37. "BT Bolsters Wealth of Responsibility Program," *Private Asset Management,* January 24, 2000, p. 7.

38. Sharon Cohen-Hagar, "GTE Foundation Increases 1999 Contributions Budget to $30 Million to Support Education, Literacy, and Community Programs," *Business Wire,* February 17, 1999.

39. Peter J. Gallanis, "Community Support Is a Powerful Tool," *DSN Retailing Today,* July 24, 2000, pp. 57, 71.

40. Cheryl Dahle, "Social Justice: The Freeplay Group," *Fast Company,* April 1999, pp. 166–182.

41. Don Babwin, "Gateway to Good Health," *Hospital and Health Networks,* November 20, 1998, p. 20.

42. David Whitford, "The New Shape of Philanthropy," *Fortune,* June 12, 2000, pp. 315–316; Austin Social Venture Partners, www.asvp.org, accessed January 3, 2001.

43. Coca-Cola Company, "Environment," www.thecoca-colacompany.com/environment/main.html, accessed January 3, 2001.

44. Alan Reder, *75 Best Business Practices for Socially Responsible Companies* (New York: G. P. Putnam & Sons, 1995); "Mectizan Program Removes the Darkness from an Ancient Disease," Merck, www.merck.

com/philanthropy/9.htm, accessed November 5, 2001.

45. Del Jones, "Good Works, Good Business," *USA Today,* April 25, 1997, p. B1.

46. "Associations Advance America," American Association of Association Executives, www.asaenet.org/AAA/, accessed November 5, 2001.

47. Reder, 75 *Best Business Practices for Socially Responsible Companies.*

48. "3M Earns Second Place in Eco-Ranking of Major Companies," 3M, www.3M.com/us/about3M/innovation/eco/index.html, accessed November 5, 2001.

49. Levy, *Give and Take.*

50. Weeden, *Corporate Social Investing,* pp. 116–123.

51. "For All Kids Foundation," Warner Brothers, http://rosieo.warnerbros.com/rosieo/allkids/mission.htm, accessed January 3, 2001.

52. Robert J. Williams and J. Douglas Barrett, "Corporate Philanthropy, Criminal Activity, and Firm Reputation: Is There a Link?" *Journal of Business Ethics,* 26 (2000): 341–350.

53. Roger Bennett, "Corporate Philanthropy in France, Germany, and the UK," *International Marketing Review,* 15 (June 1998): 469.

54. American Productivity and Quality Center, *Community Relations: Unleashing the Power of Corporate Citizenship.*

55. John A. Byrne, "Chainsaw," *Business Week,* October 18, 1999, pp. 128–149.

56. Levy, *Give and Take.*

57. Weeden, *Corporate Social Investing.*

58. Reprinted with permission of the publisher. From *Corporate Social Investing,* copyright © 1998 by Curt Weeden, Berrett-Koehler Publishers, Inc., San Francisco, CA. All rights reserved. www.bkconnection.com.

59. Cathy Brisbois, "Ranking Disclosure: VanCity Savings & Credit Union, Canada," in *Building Corporate Accountability: The Emerging Practices in Social and Ethical Accounting, Auditing and Reporting,* ed. Simon Zadek, Peter Pruzan, and Richard Evans (London: Earthscan Publications Ltd., 1997).

The Corporate Citizenship Audit

12

- ▶ The Nature of Corporate Citizenship Auditing
- ▶ The Auditing Process
- ▶ Strategic Importance of Corporate Citizenship Auditing

Define corporate citizenship auditing

Identify the benefits of corporate citizenship auditing

Discuss the potential limitations of corporate citizenship auditing

Compare and contrast the process of citizenship auditing with financial auditing

Explore the stages of the citizenship auditing factors

Explore the strategic role of corporate citizenship auditing

Vancouver City Savings Credit Union (VanCity) is Canada's largest credit union, with 262,000 members and thirty-nine branches in the Greater Vancouver area, Victoria, and the Fraser Valley. The credit union has long valued ethical and responsible practices and good relationships with its stakeholders. To further its citizenship efforts, the firm began reporting information about its impact on members, staff, the community, and the environment in its annual report in 1992. In 1998, the firm extended this effort by publishing its first "Social Report."

VanCity's 1998/99 Social Report communicated both quantitative and qualitative information about the firm's social and environmental performance on issues its customers, staff, the community, and other credit unions had identified as important. The Social Report also compared the credit union's performance to several external benchmarks established by the Canadian Centre for Philanthropy, Michael Jantzi Research Associates, and an industry benchmarking study conducted by EthicScan Canada on VanCity's behalf. In addition to reporting information about the credit union's performance, the report also pinpointed areas where the organization could improve and included commitments that will be reported on in the future. Among the areas cited as needing improvement were communications with members, staff, other credit unions, and community organizations; implementation and communication of a comprehensive ethical policy to guide decisions and business strategies; and support of staff seeking balance between the pressures of work and family life.

To indicate its seriousness about being responsible, accountable, and transparent with regards to its social performance, VanCity had the internally drafted report independently verified by the U.K.-based New Economics Ltd. in collaboration with a local firm, Solstice Consulting. The credit union had the report reviewed by community leaders from business, labor, academia, nonprofit, and environmental organizations before it was released to the public.

VanCity's first social audit has had positive benefits for the firm's image, and public support for continuing the auditing effort is strong. Within the firm, the social audit has increased knowledge about important nonfinancial issues, helped further integrate corporate responsibility into core areas of the business, and become a valuable tool for staff training, planning, and governance. As one executive says, "This report gives us the information we need to set benchmarks and track our progress."[1]

Just as VanCity did, more companies around the globe are beginning to audit their social performance and report the results of those assessments as a means of demonstrating their commitment to corporate citizenship. According to Investor Responsibility Center, 61 percent of S&P 500 companies have published an assessment of their environmental impact, and many more firms have announced their intention to provide environmental reports in the future. A similar study by EthicScan found that

60 percent of major Canadian corporations had voluntarily begun to incorporate sustainable development management and reporting into their operations.[2] Since the mid 1990s, more organizations are reporting about their impact on and relationships with a variety of stakeholders as well as their performance on social issues ranging far beyond the environment. These reports are often called "social audits," "social responsibility reports," or "corporate citizenship audits."

Regardless of what name they go by, reporting the results of such auditing efforts are important for demonstrating a firm's commitment to and ensuring the continuous improvement of its corporate citizenship efforts. Without reliable measurements of the achievement of citizenship objectives, a company has no concrete way to verify their importance, link them to organizational performance, justify expenditures to stockholders and investors, or address any stakeholder concerns.[3] Because the well-conducted social audit has the ability to do all these things, we devote this chapter to this leading-edge citizenship tool. We begin by defining the corporate citizenship audit, including exploring the reasons for conducting an audit and the benefits and limitations of an audit. Next we compare the social audit to financial audits in order to derive standards that may be applied to citizenship auditing and reporting. We also describe an auditing procedure that can be used to measure and improve the corporate citizenship effort. Finally, we look at the strategic importance of citizenship auditing.

The Nature of Corporate Citizenship Auditing

Corporate citizenship auditing is the process of assessing and reporting a business's performance on fulfilling the economic, legal, ethical, and philanthropic social responsibilities expected of it by its stakeholders. Citizenship or social audits are tools that companies can employ to identify and measure their impact on stakeholders, communicate this information both internally and externally, and apply this information to make continual improvements in areas stakeholders deem important, such as community and customer relations, employment practices, human rights issues, environmental responsibility, and ethical behavior.[4] The auditing process can also highlight trends, improve organizational learning, and facilitate communication and working relationships.[5]

The citizenship audit provides an objective approach for an organization to demonstrate its commitment to improving strategic planning, including showing corporate citizenship accountability. Thus, it is critical that top managers understand and embrace the strategic importance of the corporate citizenship audit. Key stakeholders of the company should also be involved in the audit to ensure the integration of their perspectives into the firm's economic, legal, ethical, and philanthropic responsibilities.[6] The strategic responsibility goals and outcomes measured in the citizenship audit need to be communicated throughout the organization and to all of its stakeholders, so that everyone is aware of what the company would like to achieve and what progress has been made in achieving its goals. The corporate citizenship audit should provide regular, comprehensive, and comparative verification of the views of stakeholders. Disclosure is a key part of auditing to encourage constructive feedback. Directions for finding best practices and continuous improvement on social, ethical, philanthropic, and other issues can come from all stakeholders.

Reasons for Corporate Citizenship Audits

Throughout this book we have examined the various forces affecting the area of corporate citizenship. There are many reasons why companies choose to understand, report on, and improve their corporate citizenship performance. At one extreme, a company may want to achieve the best social performance possible, whereas on the other hand, another firm may desire to project a good image to hide its corrupt ways. Still other companies may see the auditing process as a key component of organizational improvement. Thus, the real reasons as to why companies exceed their legally prescribed duties actually lie along a vast spectrum,[7] as the corporate citizenship continuum in Chapter 1 indicated. For example, it is common for firms to conduct audits of business practices with legal ramifications, such as employee safety and environmental impact. Although these concerns are important to a firm's corporate citizenship, they are also legally prescribed and indicative of minimal citizenship.

Benefits of Corporate Citizenship Auditing

Social or corporate citizenship auditing provides benefits for both organizations and their stakeholders. For example, regular audits permit stockholders and investors to judge whether a firm is achieving the goals it has established and whether it abides by the values it has specified as important. Moreover, it permits stakeholders to influence the organization's behavior.[8] Some investors, for example, are using their rights as stockholders to encourage companies to modify their plans and policies to address specific social issues. A shareholder resolution by British religious groups calling for greater reporting on social issues led to a Royal Dutch/Shell annual report on "Profits and Principles."[9]

For organizations, one of the greatest benefits of the auditing process is improved relationships with stakeholders. A corporate citizenship audit can satisfy stakeholder demands for increased transparency and greater disclosure, which can help amend and advance relationships with investors, customers, suppliers, regulators, the media, and the community while helping these stakeholders better understand the firm's goals and operations.[10] Furthermore, dialogs established with stakeholders during the audit process may contribute valuable insight about a firm's current situation, how various stakeholders perceive it, issues that could create threats for the company in the future, and opportunities (or weaknesses) of which the company is not yet aware. This insight can help a firm better define its priorities and align its operations with its values.[11]

The process of citizenship auditing can also help an organization identify potential risks and liabilities and improve its compliance with the law. The auditing process provides a mechanism to assess risks and detect problems, thereby presenting an opportunity to resolve such issues before they result in negative publicity or even fines or expensive litigation. For example, an audit might uncover operational practices that could endanger public health or harm the natural environment.[12] Furthermore, the audit report may help to document the firm's compliance with legal requirements as well as to demonstrate its progress in areas of previous noncompliance, including the systems implemented to reduce the likelihood of recurrence.[13] Stakeholders, including government regulators, may look more favorably on a company that identifies such problems through an audit, especially when the firm publicly reports the problems, demonstrates that it is attempting to resolve them, and implements systems that will reduce the likelihood of their recurrence.[14] Thus, the citizenship audit is a form of self-regulation.

Social auditing may also help a company coordinate its citizenship and responsibility initiatives throughout the firm, resulting in more effective and efficient use of company resources to address community and social concerns. Because a well-designed audit can document the effectiveness and efficiency of citizenship and responsibility initiatives, the audit process may uncover areas where operations can be made more efficient (e.g., through waste reduction) and thereby reduce costs.[15] Indeed, many companies are finding that reduced operating costs are a significant benefit of initiating a citizenship audit. One study, by SmithO'Brien, a leader in the social audit industry, found dramatic savings for some companies conducting social audits. Examples of these savings ranged from nearly $200,000 from lower production costs in a small manufacturing plant to $1.7 million from a 10 percent decline in paper use in a company switching to electronic communication.[16] Thus, the auditing process also helps organizations establish priorities for citizenship efforts, thereby allowing them to focus on those that will generate the greatest impact.[17]

The citizenship audit can help a firm assess its impact—both positive and negative—on the environment, the community, and society at large. Reporting on social responsibilities also allows a company to quantify the nonfinancial aspects of its community involvement. To illustrate, consider the fact that many organizations commit significant resources to such activities, such as staff to volunteer for community activities. Sometimes volunteers engage in activities during regular work hours. The time and effort an organization's staff spends on projects such as providing dinners at a homeless shelter or painting a youth center do not appear on a

Shell Oil Company funds natural resource conservation projects, auditing and evaluating the accomplishments of the program each year. (Reprinted with permission from Shell Oil Company Foundation.)

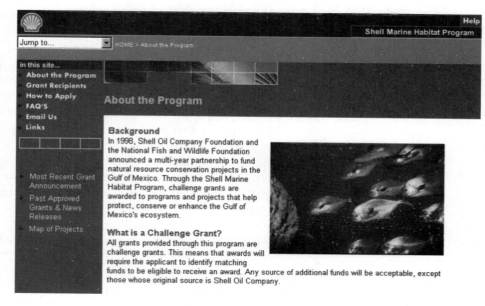

company's balance sheet. In addition, many companies donate products to help their communities. Bottled water companies, for example, often donate their products after disasters such as hurricanes.[18]

Investors may also view companies that engage in social reporting more favorably. Consider that during the first half of 2000, the average return on equity of the Dow Jones Sustainability Group (DJSGI) was 14.89 percent compared to 8.43 percent for the regular Dow Jones Index (DJI). The DJSGI comprises more than 200 companies who track their environmental stewardship, employee treatment, and customer and community involvement.[19]

Limitations of Corporate Citizenship Auditing

Although citizenship audits provide many benefits for individual organizations and their stakeholders, they do have the potential to "backfire," creating as many problems as they solve. For example, a firm may uncover a serious problem that it would prefer not to disclose until it can remedy the situation. It may find that one or more of its stakeholders' criticisms cannot be dismissed or easily addressed. Occasionally, the process of conducting a social audit may foster stakeholder dissatisfaction instead of stifling it. Moreover, the auditing process imposes burdens (especially with regard to record keeping) and costs for those firms that undertake it. Finally, the process of auditing and reporting a firm's social efforts is no guarantee that the firm will not face challenges related to its citizenship efforts.[20] In addition, because this type of auditing is relatively new, there are few common standards to judge disclosure and effectiveness or to make comparisons.[21]

Although corporate citizenship is defined and perceived differently by various stakeholders, a core of minimum standards for corporate social performance is evolving. These standards represent a fundamental step in the development of a socially responsible company. The minimum standards are specific and measurable, and they are achievable and meaningful in terms of business impact on communities, employees, consumers, the environment, and economic systems. These standards help companies set measurable and achievable targets for improvement and form an objective foundation for reporting the firm's efforts to all direct stakeholders. There may still be disagreements on key issues and standards, but through these standards, progress should be made.[22]

▶ *Corporate Citizenship Auditing versus Financial Auditing*

To respond to the changing interests and needs of society, a company must adopt some sort of corporate citizenship audit, much like the internal auditing companies have used for years to verify the accuracy of their financial reports. In many cases, the standards used in financial auditing can be adapted to provide an objective foundation for social reporting. Thus, it may be constructive to compare the financial audit and the citizenship audit to better understand the reasons for and benefits of the social auditing process.

Whereas a financial audit is concerned primarily with a company's claims about its financial performance, the social audit is interested in a company's assertions about its citizenship and social responsibility. Financial auditing focuses on all systems related to money flows and financial assessments of value for tax purposes and managerial accountability. On the other hand, social auditing deals with nonfinancial aspects of operations from both an internal and a broad external impact.

Another significant difference is that citizenship auditing is a voluntary process, whereas financial audits are required of public companies that issue securities. Because social audits are voluntary, there are few standards that a company can apply with regard to reporting frequency, disclosure requirements, and remedial actions that a company should take in response to results. Moreover, there are few templates that a company can employ in conducting the citizenship audit and implementing the results. The few standards and templates that do exist are issued by organizations that specialize in the field of business ethics. The most widely used guidelines for auditing of social responsibility reports are those outlined by the *Global Reporting Initiative (GRI)* and the *Institute of Social and Ethical Accountability (AA series)*, two of the industry leaders.[23]

Corporate citizenship auditing is similar to financial auditing in that both employ the same procedures and processes in order to create a system of integrity with objective reporting. An independent expert must verify both types of audits. The financial auditor will employ external sources to certify the assertions in financial statements, such as comparing the company's accounts receivable with its accounts payable. To vouch for a company's claims about its social performance, a social auditor will contact customers and other stakeholders and compare their perceptions of the firm's social performance with the company's assessments. As in financial audits, social audits are often performed by certified public accountants. Table 12.1 illustrates the social responsibility auditing standards established by one of these accounting and consulting firms.

Both financial and social audits begin with planning. In each audit, planning involves collecting information to understand the company's industry, determining the scope of the audit, and documenting the details of the audit program. This information must be of high quality, consistent, complete, material, segregated, and collected in a controlled environment.

The quality of information gathered affects management's capacity to direct the company's citizenship activities and therefore influences the social auditor's ability to conduct the audit. The auditor is primarily concerned with how the company records, processes, summarizes, and reports on its social responsibilities and how the company communicates these responsibilities to involved stakeholders. Accuracy in the measurement of and due professionalism in reporting is required to ensure quality.

Consistency is also essential in both financial and social audits. For example, an auditor of financial statements will use analytical procedures, such as comparing current-year account balances to those of prior years, to test specific claims. The methods of reporting must be consistent in order to be meaningful. Thus, a company is not permitted to change its method of reporting without adequate disclosure. A common example of this would be an announcement of a change in the method of valuing inventory accounts from "last in first out" (LIFO) to "first in first out" (FIFO). For the same reasons, a company should not alter its method of reporting about social responsibility results for a particular stakeholder group from one year to the next without disclosing that fact. For example, if the sample size of community groups surveyed in a subsequent social audit is significantly reduced, the auditor should question whether this reduction provides consistency with the results of the prior year audit. Perhaps more favorable results were obtained in a prior year because the company surveyed more community groups that responded positively than negatively in the prior audit. Although this type of practice undermines the purpose and continuous improvements that a company can gain from a social responsibility effort, its possibility should not be overlooked. For these reasons, Co-op Italia, an association of 320 retail stores in Italy, requires that its "Social Balance" reporting process be systematic (published regularly, using the same methodology each time), verifiable (including reliable, controlled, and certified information), comparable (to previous Co-op Italia reports

TABLE 12.1

Social Responsibility Auditing Standards

COMPETENCE

The engagement shall be performed by a practitioner having adequate technical training and proficiency

The engagement shall be performed by a practitioner having adequate knowledge in the subject matter

The practitioner shall perform an engagement only if he or she has reason to believe that the following two conditions exist:
- The assertion is capable of evaluation against reasonable criteria that have been established by a recognizable body or are stated in the presentation of the assertion in a sufficiently clear and comprehensive manner for a knowledgeable reader to be able to understand them
- The assertion is capable of reasonably consistent estimation or measurement using such criteria

INDEPENDENCE

An independence in mental attitude shall be maintained by the practitioner who shall not have participated in the assertion

DUE CARE

Due professional care shall be exercised in the performance of the engagement

PLANNING

The work shall be adequately planned and assistants, if any, shall be properly supervised

CONTROL STRUCTURE

A sufficient understanding of the communications and control structures is to be obtained to plan the audit and to determine the nature, timing, and extent of tests to be performed

EVIDENCE

Sufficient evidence shall be obtained to provide a reasonable basis for the conclusion that is expressed in the report

STANDARDS OF REPORTING

The report shall identify the assertion being reported on and state the character of the engagement

The report shall state the practitioner's conclusion about whether the assertion is presented in conformity with the established or stated criteria against which it was measured

The report shall state all of the practitioner's significant reservations about the engagement and the presentation of the assertion

The report on an engagement to evaluate an assertion that has been prepared in conformity with agreed-upon criteria or on an engagement to apply agreed-upon procedures should contain a statement limiting its use to the parties who have agreed upon such criteria or procedures

Source: "Social Responsibility Auditing Standards," Vasin, Heyn & Company, www.vhcoaudit.com/ SRAarticles/SRAStandards.htm, accessed November 5, 2001. Reprinted by permission of Vasin, Heyn & Company.

and to other cooperatives and similar companies), and participative (prepared and used by many people).[24]

Corporate citizenship and financial auditors are both particularly concerned about the completeness of the records used to document a company's assertions. In a financial audit, the auditor will trace from the source documents to the financial statements to ensure that accounts are complete. Likewise, a social audit must include all aspects of the company's "social footprint," including all the places, people, and stakeholders that are affected by the firm and all the company's activities, standards, and perceived organizational culture as related to social performance. Did the company record all of its responsibilities and performance related to corporate citizenship?

The concept of materiality is related to the audit's completeness. In a financial audit, something is deemed material if it is probable that the judgment of a reasonable person relying on the information would have been changed or influenced by its omission or misstatement. Materiality applies to citizenship audits as well because users of a social audit could be misled if the audit fails to include material measures of stakeholders' perspectives, such as those of the company's customers. It is important for materiality that research methods and measurement procedures provide an accurate and timely audit.

To avoid misstatements in the social report, it is important for social auditors to clearly segregate certain functions. For example, the individual responsible for gathering stakeholder perspectives should not be the same individual who records the results. Obviously, if the duty of gathering evidence, as well as recording the findings is conducted by the same person, there is no way to independently verify the accuracy of the recorded perspectives. Segregation of audit activities is facilitated by assigning accountants or consultants responsibility for certain audit functions.

Perhaps the most significant component of the auditing process is the control environment, which relates to the "attitude" or philosophy and operating style of management. The control environment facilitates establishing standards and reducing differences between desired and actual performance. The control environment represents the collective effect of both formal and informal methods to achieve desired results. Does management strongly emphasize the need for controls to ensure that the firm's social responsibility claims can be trusted? Are the ethical values of management in question? In a financial audit, it is standard procedure for an audit firm to determine if management lacks integrity before accepting an auditing engagement. Auditors lend credibility to a company's assertions, and this credibility can never be compromised. It is better for an outside audit consultant to decline an engagement than to be associated with a company that lacks integrity. If there is limited commitment to the auditing process, then the company may plan to use the audit for public relations rather than for continuous improvement.

Skewed financial results appear in financial statements primarily because management's compensation is often tied to the financial results. As the demand for corporate citizenship and social responsibility grows in importance, the temptation for management to conceal and perpetuate social irregularities will also grow. The unavoidable result will be for citizenship audits to emphasize internal control variables in a manner similar to financial audits. When internal control is overemphasized, there is a movement away from proactive value-driven activities that are hard to measure to emphasizing required, objective, legalistic audits.

The Auditing Process

As previously mentioned, there are relatively few standards available for companies to follow in conducting a citizenship audit, such as what standards of performance should be used, how often to conduct an audit, whether and how to report an audit's results to stakeholders, and what actions should be taken in response to audit results. Thus, corporate approaches to citizenship auditing are as varied as approaches to corporate citizenship.[25]

It is our belief that a corporate citizenship audit should be unique to each company based on its size, industry, and corporate culture, as well as the regulatory environment in which it operates and the commitment of its top management. For this reason, we have mapped out a framework that is somewhat generic and can therefore be expanded on by all companies that want to conduct a citizenship audit. The steps of this framework are presented in Table 12.2. As with any new initiative, companies may choose to begin their effort with a smaller, less-formal audit and then work up to a more-comprehensive social audit. For example, a firm may choose to focus on primary stakeholders in its initial audit year and then expand to secondary groups in subsequent audits. This approach allows the company time to refine its auditing process through trial and error. Danny Grossman, cofounder and president of San Francisco-based Wild Planet Toys, agrees with this approach: "We're still thinking through the assessment process, still learning to do this more effectively. As a smaller company, we're not in a position to carry out highly quantitative audits. On the other hand, the annual assessment is a very useful tool, even given our size and cost constraints."[26] Table 12.3 lists some other do's and don'ts of corporate citizenship auditing.

Our framework encompasses a wide range of business responsibilities and relationships. The audit entails an individualized process and outcomes for a particular firm, as it requires the careful consideration of the unique issues that face a particular organization. For example, the auditing process at Sbn Bank, Denmark's seventh-largest bank, involves identifying the bank's stakeholders, specifying the values that stakeholders share with the bank, surveying stakeholders, presenting and interpreting the stakeholders' responses along with management's statement, engaging in a series of ongoing dialogs with stakeholders, and developing "ethical budgets" for

TABLE 12.2

Framework for a Corporate Citizenship Audit

- Secure commitment of top management and/or board of directors.
- Establish an audit committee.
- Define the scope of the audit process, including subject matter areas important to the social audit (e.g., environment, discrimination, employee rights, privacy, philanthropy, legal compliance, etc.).
- Review organizational mission, policies, goals, and objectives.
- Define the organization's social priorities as they relate to stakeholders.
- Identify the tools or methods the organization can employ to measure its achievement of citizenship objectives.
- Collect relevant information in each designated subject matter area, including internal data and data from concerned stakeholders.
- Summarize and analyze the data collected and compare the internal information to stakeholder expectations.
- Have the results verified by an independent agent (i.e., a social audit consultant, accounting firm that offers social auditing services, or nonprofit special-interest organization with social auditing experience).
- Report the findings to the audit committee and, if approved, to managers and stakeholders.

Sources: These steps are compatible with the social auditing methods prescribed by Warren Dow and Roy Crowe, *What Social Auditing Can Do for Voluntary Organizations* (Vancouver: Volunteer Vancouver, July 1999); "Social Audits and Accountability," Business for Social Responsibility, www.bsr.org/resourcecenter/index.html, accessed January 10, 2001; Sandra Waddock and Neil Smith, "Corporate Responsibility Audits: Doing Well by Doing Good," Sloan Management Review, 41 (Winter 2000): 79.

the coming year.[27] Figure 12.1 depicts The Body Shop's framework for its social auditing and disclosure process. Thus, although this chapter presents a structure and recommendations for a citizenship audit, there is no generic approach to satisfy every firm's circumstances. However, the benefits and limitations that companies derive from corporate citizenship auditing are relatively consistent.

Secure Commitment of Top Management and/or Board of Directors

The first step in conducting any audit is securing the commitment of the firm's top management and/or its board of directors. In some cases, the push for a citizenship audit may come directly from the board of directors in response to stakeholder concerns. In other cases, pressure for an audit may come from top managers looking for ways to create a competitive advantage for their firm by publicizing its citizenship efforts. Some companies now have a senior officer with corporate citizenship as a

TABLE 12.3

Do's and Don'ts of Corporate Citizenship Auditing

DO'S

- Do recognize that corporate citizenship auditing is specific to each organization's stakeholders, business purposes, and responsibilities.
- Do get departments, managers, and staff involved. This is especially true when deciding the scope of the audit.
- Do set up an internal audit system or department to report to the board of directors or other executive group.
- Do be careful in selecting an independent verifier, for they will have great access to the "heart and soul" of the company.
- Do allow a good amount of time for drafting and finalizing the final audit report.
- Do report formally and informally, publicly and internally.

DON'TS

- Don't start the audit without talking to someone who has performed one and reading other similar audits.
- Don't forget to focus on the benefits and the business case for corporate citizenship performance measurement and disclosure for all stakeholders.
- Don't forget to publicize the role of the audit team and its purpose. This allows for less fear and greater acceptance of the audit team.
- Don't forget that you may need other sources of expert advice such as survey design and analysis.
- Don't allow one stakeholder's issues to outweigh the others.
- Don't be afraid to include good and bad aspects of performance. It is better to point out your own faults than to have critics expose these on their terms.

Source: Based on Maria Sillanpaa and David Wheeler, "Integrated Ethical Auditing: The Body Shop International, UK," in *Building Corporate Accountability: The Emerging Practices in Social and Ethical Accounting, Auditing and Reporting,* ed. Simon Zadek, Peter Pruzan, and Richard Evans (London: Earthscan Publications Ltd., 1997), pp. 102–128.

responsibility, and this individual may campaign for a social audit as a means of demonstrating the effectiveness of the firm's citizenship initiatives. Regardless of where the impetus for an audit comes from, its success hinges on the full support of top management, particularly the CEO.

▶ *Establish an Audit Committee*

The next step in our framework is the establishment of a committee to oversee the audit process. This committee can participate in the actual auditing of social responsibilities or simply monitor the progress of the audit to ensure that it stays

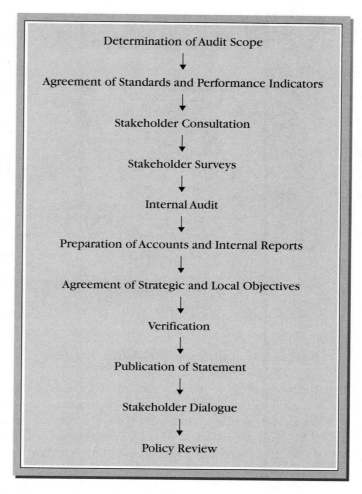

FIGURE 12.1

Framework for Social Auditing and Disclosure at The Body Shop International

Determination of Audit Scope

↓

Agreement of Standards and Performance Indicators

↓

Stakeholder Consultation

↓

Stakeholder Surveys

↓

Internal Audit

↓

Preparation of Accounts and Internal Reports

↓

Agreement of Strategic and Local Objectives

↓

Verification

↓

Publication of Statement

↓

Stakeholder Dialogue

↓

Policy Review

Source: Maria Sillanpaa and David Wheeler, "Integrated Ethical Auditing: The Body Shop International, UK," *in Building Corporate Accountability: The Emerging Practices in Social and Ethical Accounting, Auditing and Reporting,* ed. Simon Zadek, Peter Pruzan, and Richard Evans (London: Earthscan Publications Ltd., 1997), p. 116.

on track. The committee should include internal organizational members such as key managers and internal auditors as well as external team members such as organizational development experts. In addition, lower-level employees can bring unique insights to the committee. Companies may also consider the use of stakeholder representation such as customers and community members. As with a financial audit, the citizenship audit committee must first determine the scope of the audit. It is important to document the scope of the social audit in the beginning stages, even if modifications of the preliminary scope are made later.

The Home Depot verifies and audits all suppliers to make certain all environmental claims are substantiated. (Reprinted by permission from The Home Depot Headquarters, Homer TLC.)

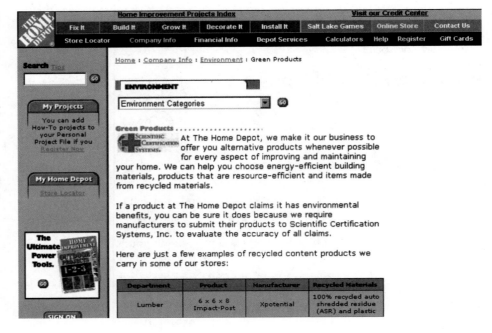

Define the Scope of the Audit Process

The next step in our framework is for the audit committee or outside auditing consultant to define the scope of the audit process, including subject matter areas that are important to the citizenship audit. The scope of an audit depends on the type of business, the risks faced by the business, and available opportunities to manage corporate citizenship. The scope will determine the key subject matter areas of the company's social responsibilities (e.g., environment, discrimination, employee rights, privacy, philanthropy, legal compliance) that the audit should cover and on what basis they should be assessed. Assessments can be made on the basis of surveys, focus groups, interviews, and analyses.[28] Table 12.4 lists some sample subject matter areas and audit items for each of those areas.

Review Organizational Mission, Policies, Goals, and Objectives

Because social audits generally involve a comparison of organizational performance to the firm's policies and objectives, the audit process should include a review of the current mission statement and strategic objectives. The company's overall mission may incorporate corporate citizenship objectives, but these may also be found in separate documents focused on corporate citizenship. For example, the firm's

TABLE 12.4

Sample Subject Matter and Stakeholder Audit Items

Please check the response (yes or no) that best answers the following questions:

Yes	No	Human Resource Issues
❏	❏	Does the company have a formal training program that focuses on corporate citizenship issues?
❏	❏	If training sessions exist, are they designed to cover legal, ethical, and subject matter social concerns that relate to daily operations?
❏	❏	Has someone been appointed to provide oversight for training and compliance of ethical, legal, and social issues?
❏	❏	Do employees have an independent mechanism, such as an 800 number or E-mail address to report corporate citizenship concerns?
❏	❏	Does the company have programs for helping employees manage work-related stress and conflict?

Yes	No	Customer Relations Issues
❏	❏	Does the company have a feedback mechanism to obtain customer concerns/ complaints?
❏	❏	Has the company established policies and a shared value system of fairness and honesty toward customers?
❏	❏	Is there a long-term focus on all aspects of customer welfare at the expense of short-run profits?
❏	❏	Are product quality, pricing, and service designed to deliver customers' expectations of value?
❏	❏	Are all the laws and legal rights related to customers communicated to employees?

Yes	No	Community Issues
❏	❏	Does the company achieve its goals without compromising community ethical norms?
❏	❏	Are there environmental impact considerations for operations and organizational activities?
❏	❏	Does the company contribute resources to the community?
❏	❏	Are there programs to empower or reward employees who contribute to recognized community activities?
❏	❏	Does top management express organizational commitment to improving the quality of life and the general welfare of society?

Yes	No	Diversity Issues
❏	❏	Are all laws protecting specific classes of employees and customers properly communicated?
❏	❏	Are systems in place to ensure compliance with all discrimination laws?
❏	❏	Does the company value and proactively embrace diversity in the workplace?
❏	❏	Is all communication designed to incorporate a philosophy of culture and diversity?
❏	❏	Has the company developed special educational or employment opportunities to contribute to diversity objectives?

ethics statement or statement of values may offer guidance for management of the transactions and human relationships that support the firm's reputation, thereby fostering confidence from stakeholders outside the firm.[29] This step should examine the formal documents that make explicit commitments to environmental or social responsibility, as well as less-formal documents, including marketing materials, workplace policies, and ethics policies and standards for suppliers or vendors. This review may reveal a need to create additional statements to fill gaps identified in this step or to create a new comprehensive mission statement or ethical policy that addresses deficiencies uncovered during this step.[30]

It is also important to examine all of the firm's policies and practices for the specific areas covered by the audit. For example, in an audit that includes environmental issues in its scope, this step would consider the company's goals and objectives on environmental matters, the company's environmental policies, the means for communicating these policies, and the effectiveness of this communication. This assessment should also look at whether and how managers are rewarded for meeting their goals and the systems available for employees to give and receive feedback. An effective citizenship audit should review all these systems and assess their strengths and weaknesses.[31]

▶ Define the Organization's Social Priorities

The next step in the auditing process is defining the organization's social priorities. Determining a company's social priorities is a balancing act, as it can be difficult to identify the needs and assess the priorities of each stakeholder. Because there are no legal requirements for social priorities, it is up to management's strategic planning processes to determine appropriate duties and required action to deal with social issues. It is very important in this stage to articulate these priorities and values as a set of parameters or performance indicators that can be objectively and quantitatively assessed. Because the social audit is a structured report that offers quantitative and descriptive assessments, actions should be measurable by quantitative indicators. However, it is sometimes not possible to go beyond description.[32]

At some point, the firm must demonstrate action-oriented responsiveness to those social issues given top priority. Wells Fargo, for example, believes that education, jobs, and housing are fundamental community issues and therefore are the focus of the firm's philanthropy programs. In line with these priorities, the bank has donated $300 million to nonprofit organizations and made $45 billion in loans for community reinvestment projects, including affordable housing development, commercial economic development, and small-business loans, especially to firms owned by women and minorities.[33] Likewise, Home Depot has identified affordable housing, at-risk youth, and the natural environment as social priorities. To address its environmental priority—and satisfy stakeholders' concerns about deforestation—the world's largest home-improvement retailer recently pledged to stop selling lumber and other products made from wood from endangered forests and to focus instead on wood products that have been certified as having come from responsibly managed forests.[34]

▶ Identify Tools or Methods for Accurate Measurement of Citizenship Objectives

The sixth step in our framework is identifying the tools or methods that can be employed to measure the firm's achievement of citizenship objectives. In this age of globalization and intense competitive pressures, such measurement tools are important to ensure that corporate social responsibilities are not compromised for higher profitability. Performance indicators can be used to quantitatively and qualitatively measure an organization's social as well as its financial performance. Some organizations, for example, have found that quantifying their community involvement can lead to more efficient and effective use of company resources to address community needs. The London Benchmarking Group has developed a template for companies to monitor and measure community involvement activities. This template helps companies to assess their community efforts and make continual improvement.[35]

SmithO'Brien, a leading social audit firm, has identified some useful measurement techniques for citizenship audits. The Social Balance Sheet assigns dollar values to social impact as well as financial performance. The Social Performance Index uses a numerical ranking system relating to corporate social performance. Stakeholder Surveys incorporate the perceptions of the company from the stakeholders' point of view. The Body Shop has conducted such surveys based on interviews with its key stakeholders. Disclosure Audits are similar to those provided in a company's financial statements, but relate to a firm's social responsibilities. Ben & Jerry's (now owned by Unilever) has employed Disclosure Accounts in its social audit.

▶ Collect Relevant Information

The next step in the auditing process is to collect relevant information for each designated subject matter area. To understand employee issues, for example, the auditing committee will work with the firm's human resources department in gathering employee survey information and other statistics and feedback. A thorough audit will include a review of all relevant reports, including external documents sent to government agencies and others. The information collected in this step will help determine baseline levels of compliance as well as the internal and external expectations of the company. This step will also identify where the company has, or has not, met its commitments, including those dictated by its mission statement and other policy documents. The documents reviewed in this process will vary from company to company, depending on the firm's size, nature of its business, and the scope of the audit process.[36]

Some techniques of evidence collection might involve examination of both internal and external documents, observation of the data collection process (such as stakeholder consultation), and confirmation of information in the organization's accounting records. Ratio analysis of relevant indicators may also be used to identify any inconsistencies or unexpected patterns. The importance of objective measurement is the key consideration of the social auditor.[37] As with the financial audit, reliability depends on the source of all information collected. A document that has been generated and circulated externally provides the most objective evidence. In a social audit, an example of such a document might be the minutes of a focus group taken by an external stakeholder group that is sent directly to the social auditor. Documents that are internally generated and circulated are more subjective because they can more easily be altered. Sometimes internal documents are used for publicity or to motivate employees. In the context of a social audit, an example of the least-objective document would be an internally generated and circulated report on the hours of staff spent in community volunteering. This document might count hours that are questionable.[38]

Because stakeholder integration is so crucial to the citizenship audit, a company's stakeholders need to be defined and interviewed during the data-collection stage. For most companies, stakeholders include employees, customers, investors, suppliers, community groups, regulators, nongovernment organizations, and the media. Social audits typically include interviews and focus groups with these stakeholders to gain an understanding of their perceptions of the company. The greater the number of stakeholders included in this stage, the more time and resources will be required to carry out the audit; however, a larger sample of stakeholders may yield a more useful variety of opinions about the company. In multinational corporations, a decision must also be made on whether to include only the main office or headquarters region or to use all facilities around the globe in the audit.[39]

Because employees carry out a business's operations, including its citizenship initiatives, understanding employee issues is vital. Indicators that are useful for assessing employee issues include staff turnover and employee satisfaction. High turnover rates could indicate poor working conditions, an unethical climate, inadequate compensation, or general employee dissatisfaction. Companies can analyze these factors to determine key areas for improvement.[40] For example, Wild Planet Toys, as part of its annual "social assessment," surveys employees on a range of issues including company mission, product quality, diversity, the workplace, the environment, and community outreach. The results of this process, which are provided to employees, have led to clearer priorities and better internal coordination, as well as to a revised mission statement and the addition of long-term disability insurance to the benefits package.[41] Most companies recognize that employees will behave in ways that result in recognition and rewards and avoid behavior that results in punishment. Thus, companies can design and implement human resources policies and procedures for recruiting, hiring, promoting, compensating, and rewarding employees to encourage behaviors that further citizenship efforts.[42]

Customers are another primary stakeholder group because their patronage determines financial success. Providing meaningful feedback through a number of mechanisms is critical to creating and maintaining customer satisfaction. Through surveys and customer-initiated communication systems such as response cards, e-mail, and toll-free telephone systems, an organization can monitor and respond to customer issues and social performance. Sears, for example, surveyed more than two million customers to investigate attitudes toward products, advertising, and the social performance of the company.

A growing number of investors are seeking companies that conduct social audits to include in their investment portfolios. They are becoming more aware of the financial benefits desired from socially responsible management systems—as well as the negative consequences of a lack of responsibility. A study conducted by the University of Southwestern Louisiana, for example, found that publicity about unethical corporate behavior lowers stock prices for at least six months.[43] Additionally, many investors simply do not want to invest in companies that engage in certain business practices, such as cigarette production, or in companies that fail to provide adequate working conditions, such as "sweatshops." Thus, it is critical for companies to understand the issues that this very important group of stakeholders have and what they expect from corporations they have invested in, both financial and socially.

The community is another significant stakeholder group. Community groups such as local business chambers, schools, and hospitals, as well as environmental groups, can be asked to comment on the social responsibility initiatives of an organization. As with customers, surveys can be used to obtain community feedback. Such surveys may be administered on a random basis (e.g., every tenth listing in the local telephone book) or through regular contact with various groups. Web sites and e-mail also provide opportunities for interaction with community stakeholder groups.

Social responsibility should be assessed from the vantage point of each of the previously mentioned stakeholders. Their respective assessments can be broken down into four main components—economic, legal, ethical, and philanthropy. Table 12.5 provides sample questions that ensure a company is assessing its social responsibility from each stakeholder perspective and should be modified to meet the unique attributes of each company.

TABLE 12.5

Sample Stakeholder Social Responsibility Concerns

Stakeholders	Social Responsibilities			
	Economic	Legal	Ethical	Philanthropic
Employees	Are salary, benefits, and promotions perceived to be fair and equitable to all employees?	Does the organization train employees on effective legal compliance?	Have the company's ethical standards been communicated to employees?	Does the organization encourage and enable employees to contribute to the community?
Customers	Does the company adhere to fair pricing and maintain acceptable product quality?	Does the company participate in deceptive or unfair marketing activities?	Are customers' rights and concerns about products considered in all decisions?	Does the company seek to share in philanthropic activities important to customers?
Investors	Has the organization increased its profitability through socially responsible business practices?	Are there any potential illegal activities that could damage investors?	Is there an effective values program to enhance organizational performance?	Is the company using its resources to strategically improve its philanthropic efforts?
Community Groups	Does the community benefit from the economic impact of the company?	Are the legal rights of all community stakeholders considered?	Are the ethical standards of the company consistent with those of the community?	Does the company invest in the community through grants, fundraising, and community service?

The questions on the chart are mere examples of potential questions that can be asked of the stakeholders. Stakeholder perceptions related to each component of social responsibility should be obtained through additional questions.

Feedback from these stakeholders may be obtained through standardized surveys, interviews, and focus groups. Companies can also encourage stakeholder exchanges by inviting specific groups together for discussions. Such meetings also may include an office or facility tour or a field trip by company representatives to visit sites in the community. Regardless of how information about stakeholder views is collected, the primary objective is to generate a variety of opinions about how the company is perceived and whether it is fulfilling stakeholders' expectations.[44]

▶ *Analyze the Data*

The next step in the auditing process is to compare the company's internal perceptions to those discovered during the stakeholder assessment stage and then to summarize these findings. During this phase, the audit committee should draw some conclusions about the information obtained in the previous stages. These conclusions may involve descriptive assessments of the findings, including the costs and benefits of the company's citizenship initiatives, strengths and weaknesses in the firm's policies and practices, and feedback from stakeholders, as well as issues that should be addressed in future audits. In some cases, it may be appropriate to weigh the findings against standards identified earlier, both quantitatively and qualitatively.[45]

Data analysis should also include an examination of how other organizations in the industry are performing in the designated subject matter areas. The audit committee can investigate the successes of some other firm that is considered the best in a particular area and compare the auditing company's performance to the "benchmark" established by that firm. Some common examples of benchmark information available from most corporate social audits include employee or customer satisfaction, the perception of the company by community groups, and the impact of the company's philanthropy. For example, the Ethics Officer Association (EOA) conducts research on legal and ethical issues in the workplace. The

The Body Shop produces values reports that analyze the company's performance on social, environmental, and animal protection. (Reprinted with permission from The Body Shop International Plc. www.thebodyshop. com.)

PROFIT AND CONSCIENCE

Values Report

The 1997 Body Shop Values Report is our second Values Report; a detailed statement of **our performance** on social, **environmental** and **animal protection** issues.

All three subject areas (Social, Environmental, and Animal Protection) have been independently verified by external parties, as have our previous audit reports.
You can view the report, summary and methodology, all on-line, by following the links at the bottom of the page.

We are pleased to announce that out of the 100 international company reports evaluated by SustainAbility for the United Nations Enviromental Programme, our Values Report scored the highest rating for the second year running. SustainAbility refers to the Values Report 1997 as "...unusual in its efforts to integrate social and environmental reporting with considerable stakeholder engagement". Further information on the UNEP rating is available on SustainAbility Website at http://www.sustainability.co.uk

Values Report 1997 - PDF (882Kb)

Values Report 1997 Summary - PDF (291Kb)

The Body Shop Approach to Ethical Auditing - PDF (414Kb)

studies allow members of the EOA to compare their responses to the aggregate results obtained through the study.[46] Such comparisons can help the audit committee identify best practices for a particular industry or establish a baseline of minimum requirements for citizenship. It is important to note, however, that some audit findings do not result in numerical or quantitative data, making benchmarking difficult.[47]

▶ Verify the Results

The next step is to have the results of the data analysis verified by an independent party, such as a social audit consultant, a financial accounting firm that offers social auditing services (e.g., KPMG Peat Marwick), or a nonprofit special-interest group with auditing experience (e.g., the New Economics Foundation). KPMG-UK, for example, partnered with The Body Shop in order to learn about the process of social auditing. KPMG contributed its auditing expertise, whereas The Body Shop lent its social accountability and reporting experience to the joint effort.[48]

Business for Social Responsibility, a nonprofit organization supporting social responsibility initiatives and reporting, has defined verification as an independent assessment of the quality, accuracy, and completeness of a company's social report. Independent verification offers a measure of assurance that the company has reported its citizenship performance fairly and honestly, as well as providing an assessment of its social and environmental reporting systems.[49] As such, verification by an independent party gives stakeholders confidence in a company's citizenship audit and lends the audit report credibility and objectivity.[50]

Although independent validation of citizenship audits is not required, many companies choose to have their social auditing efforts verified, much as they have their financial reports certified by a reputable auditing firm. Many financial auditors believe that an independent, objective assessment of an audit can be provided only if the auditor has played no role in the reporting process—in other words, consulting and auditing should be distinctly separate roles. The subject of auditor independence has been controversial. In 2000, the Securities and Exchange Commission approved a rule aimed at preventing conflicts of interest by financial auditors, an action ending months of sometimes bitter debate over how to ensure that investors receive honest information about a company's finances.[51]

The process of verifying the results of an audit should involve standard procedures that control the reliability and validity of the information. As with a financial audit, auditors can apply substantive tests to detect material misstatements in the social audit data and analysis. The tests commonly used in financial audits—confirmation, observation, tracing, vouching, analytical procedures, inquiry, recomputing—can be used in social audits as well. For example, positive *confirmations* can be sent to the participants of a stakeholder focus group to affirm that the reported results are consistent with the outcome of the focus group. Likewise, a social auditor can *observe* the actual working conditions in a company's manufacturing plant to verify statements made in the report. And, just as a financial auditor *traces* from the supporting documents to the financial statements to test their completeness, a social auditor or verifier may examine customer complaints in order to attest to the completeness of the reporting of such complaints. The auditor can examine canceled checks paid to local charities to *vouch* for the stated amounts of donations. A social auditor can employ *analytical procedures* by examining plausible relationships, such as the prior year's employee turnover ratio or the related ratio that is commonly reported within the industry. With the reporting firm's permission, an auditor can contact the company's legal counsel to *inquire* about pending environmental or civil rights litigation. Finally, a social auditor can *recompute* salaries reported to attest to the equal pay assertion that companies report.[52]

Additionally, the financial auditor may be asked to provide a letter to the company's management to highlight inconsistencies in the reporting process. The auditor may request a reply from management regarding particular points raised in the letter, indicating actions that management intends to take to address problems or weaknesses. The financial auditor is required to report to the internal audit committee (or equivalent) any significant adjustments found during the audit, disagreements with management, and difficulties encountered during the audit. In reference to the social guidelines on reportable conditions, it seems unlikely that a social auditor would be requested by the company's management to highlight reporting inconsistencies if they had any true consequence on the auditor's report. Therefore, social auditors should be required to report to the company's audit committee the same issues that a financial auditor would report.[53]

▶ Report the Findings

The final step is in our framework is issuing the citizenship audit report. This involves reporting the audit findings to the relevant internal parties and, if approved, to external stakeholders in a formal report. Although some companies prefer not to release the results of their auditing efforts to the public, more companies are choosing to make their reports available to a broad group of stakeholders. Some companies, including U.K.-based Co-operative Bank, integrate the results of the social audit with their annual report of financial documents and other important information. Other companies, including The Body Shop, Shell, and VanCity, also make their citizenship audit reports available on the World Wide Web.[54] Based on the guidelines established by the Global Reporting Initiative and AccountAbility, the social report should spell out the purpose and

Social Reporting at Johnson & Johnson

Johnson & Johnson (J&J), based in New Brunswick, New Jersey, has achieved the enviable position of being one of the most respected companies in the world. The company sells $27.5 billion worth of consumer, professional, and pharmaceutical/diagnostic products in more than 175 countries through 190 companies operating in 51 countries. In 1999, J&J was named the most reputable company in the United States on the basis of a comprehensive survey conducted by Harris Interactive and the Reputation Institute. In fact, the firm has been widely recognized, as one of *Fortune* magazine's "Most Admired Companies," *Industry Week* magazine's "World's 100 Best Managed Companies," and *Working Mother* magazine's "100 Best Companies for Working Mothers," and it has won numerous awards for its diversity, philanthropy, and environmental initiatives over its 115 years of operation.

The company's strong reputation may stem in part from its credo, written in 1943 by Chairman Robert Wood Johnson. The credo begins, "We believe our first responsibility is to the doctors, nurses and patients, to mothers and fathers, and all others who use our products and services. In meeting their needs, everything we do must be of high quality." Not only is this document displayed in company offices worldwide, posted prominently on its web site, and etched on an eight-foot-tall limestone structure at corporate headquarters, it is the topic of a full day in executive training programs, and its impact is assessed regularly through extensive employee surveys. The credo provides guidance for even the toughest corporate decisions, including two recalls of Tylenol during the 1980s after some bottles of the product were found to be contaminated with cyanide, ultimately causing eight deaths. The company's rapid and intense response to the crisis helped it retain consumers' trust, and Tylenol remains a leading brand today.

Johnson & Johnson's credo specifies that the company is "responsible to the communities in which we live and work and to the world community as well." To communicate its efforts to fulfill this responsibility, J&J has begun to release annual reports detailing its citizenship initiatives in specific areas. One of these reports, the *Worldwide Contributions Program Annual Report*, details the company's philanthropic activities around the

scope of the audit, the methods used in the audit process (evidence gathering and evaluation), the role of the (preferably independent) auditor, any auditing guidelines followed by the auditor, and any reporting guidelines followed by the company.[55]

As mentioned earlier, the citizenship audit may be similar to a financial audit, but their forms are quite different. In a financial audit, the Statement of Auditing Standards dictates literally every word of a financial audit report in terms of content and placement. Based on the auditor's findings, the report issued can be, among other modifications, an unqualified opinion (i.e., the financial statements

world. In a recent report, the company high-lighted its efforts to collaborate with a variety of organizations "to implement programs that create healthy futures for many people in need." The report detailed J&J's contributions, in grants and products, to a variety of health initiatives around the world, such as a diabetes-education program in Zimbabwe, a burn-treatment center in South Africa, a children's hospital in France, and a hospital infection-control program in Vietnam. In sum, the company donated $188 million to health-related organizations, community-development organizations, disaster-relief efforts, and university programs around the world in 1999.

Since 1996, J&J has also produced an annual report highlighting its activities in the areas of the environment, health, and safety. The *1999 Environmental, Health, and Safety Report,* which adopted the theme, "Healthy People, Healthy Planet," presented case studies that demonstrate the company's commitment to the environment, health, and safety around the world. The report summarized the firm's performance in all three areas and compared these results to its goals. Although the firm exceeded its goals on most measures, the report also clearly indicated where the company failed to do so, thereby pinpointing areas for improvement.

Johnson & Johnson's annual social reports allow the company to demonstrate its commitment to corporate citizenship and achievement of citizenship objectives, identify areas for improvement, justify expenditures to stockholders and investors, and address stakeholder concerns. These efforts also help the company's venerable brands maintain their trusted image with consumers. For example, in the reputation survey by Harris Interactive and the Reputation Institute, J&J ranked first overall, first in emotional appeal, first in products and services, first in workplace environment, third in social responsibility, and fourth in financial performance. This level of trust provides evidence that J&J's half-century-old credo is far more than a poster on the wall of corporate headquarters.

Sources:
Ronald Alsop, "Corporate Reputations Are Earned with Trust, Reliability, Study Shows," *Wall Street Journal Interactive,* September 23, 1999, http://interactive.wsj.com; Ronald Alsop, "Johnson & Johnson Turns up Tops Thanks to Its Credo, and to Babies," *Wall Street Journal Interactive,* September 23, 1999, http://interactive.wsj.com; "Awards and Recognition," Johnson & Johnson, http://www.jnj.com/who_is_jnj/awards.html, (accessed) November 5, 2001; *1999 Environmental, Health, and Safety Report,* Johnson & Johnson, 2000, available at http://www.jnj.com/who_is_jnj/1999_enviro/1999_Environmental_Report.pdf; *1999 Worldwide Contributions Program Annual Report,* Johnson & Johnson, 2000, available at http://www.jnj.com/who_is_jnj/1999_contributions/1999_contributions.pdf.

are fairly stated), a qualified opinion (i.e., although the auditor believes the financial statements are fairly stated, an unqualified opinion is not possible because of limitations placed on the auditor or minor issues with disclosure or accounting principles), an adverse opinion (i.e., the financial statements are not fairly stated), or a disclaimer of opinion (i.e., the auditor didn't have full access to records or discovered a conflict of interest). The technicality of these various opinions has enormous consequences to the company.

Figure 12.2 depicts the standard (unqualified opinion) independent auditor's disclaimer issued at the end of a financial audit report. Every word has significant

FIGURE 12.2

Standard Independent Auditor's Disclaimer

> **To the Board of Directors and Stockholders of XYZ Company:**
>
> We have audited the accompanying balance sheet of XYZ Company as of December 31, 2002, and the related statements of income, retained earnings, and cash flows for the year then ended. These financial statements are the responsibility of the Company's management. Our responsibility is to express an opinion on these financial statements based on our audit.
>
> We conducted our audit in accordance with generally accepted auditing standards. Those standards require that we plan and perform the audit to obtain reasonable assurance about whether the financial statements are free of material misstatement. An audit includes examining, on a test basis, evidence supporting the amounts and disclosures in the financial statements. An audit also includes assessing the accounting principles used and significant estimates made by my management, as well as evaluating the overall financial statement presentation. We believe that our audit provides a reasonable basis for our opinion.
>
> In our opinion, the financial statements referred to above present fairly, in all material respects, the financial position of XYZ Company as of December 31, 2002, and the results of its operations and its cash flows for the year then ended in conformity with generally accepted accounting principles.
>
> Firm's Signature and Report Date

meaning. Notice, for example, that the introductory paragraph explicitly states the responsibilities: Management is responsible for the financial statements, and the auditors are responsible only for offering an opinion as to their veracity and validity. Another paragraph discusses the generally accepted auditing standards and states that the auditors can provide only "reasonable assurance" with regard to the financial statement assertions. Such disclaimers never express absolute assurance due to the many limiting factors such as collusion, error, and cost. The last paragraph of the disclaimer begins, "In our opinion, . . ." Here, the auditors acknowledge the risks associated with an audit. They simply state their opinion, but they do not say, "We guarantee," "The fact is," or "We have no reason to believe." The end of the report includes the firm's signature and the date of the report. Social audit reports have not yet reached even this level of scrutiny, but it is desirable to move toward more-objective social audits, using the standards typically applied to financial audits. Figure 12.3 provides an example of an ideal standard social audit report.

Ideal Independent Auditor's Disclaimer

To the Board of Directors and Stakeholders of XYZ Company:

We have audited the social responsibility assertions of XYZ Company as of December 31, 2002. These assertions are the responsibility of the Company's management. Our responsibility is to express an opinion on these assertions based on our audit.

We conducted our audit in accordance with *generally accepted social auditing standards.* Those standards require that we plan and perform the audit to obtain reasonable assurance about whether the social assertions, relating to the economic, legal, ethical, and philanthropic responsibilities of the Company, are free of material misstatement. An audit includes examining, on a test basis, evidence supporting the social responsibility assertions of the Company. An audit also includes an independent assessment of the stakeholders' perspectives, as well as the methods used by management to report on such perspectives. We believe that our audit provides a reasonable basis for our opinion.

In our opinion, the social responsibility assertions referred to above present fairly, in all material respects, the position of social responsibility of XYZ Company as of December 31, 2002, in conformity with *generally accepted social responsibility principles.*

Firm's Signature and Report Date

Strategic Importance of Corporate Citizenship Auditing

Although the concept of auditing implies an official examination of social performance, many organizations audit their performance informally. Any attempt to verify outcomes and to compare them with standards can be considered an auditing activity. Many smaller firms probably would not use the word *audit,* but they do perform auditing activities.

The corporate citizenship audit, like the financial audit, should be conducted regularly instead of only when there are problems or questions about a firm's priorities and conduct. In other words, the citizenship audit is not a control process to be used during a crisis, although it can pinpoint potential problem areas and generate solutions. A social audit may be comprehensive and encompass all of the social impact areas of a business, or it can be specific and focus on one or two areas. One specialized audit could be an environmental-impact audit in which specific environmental issues, such as proper waste disposal, are analyzed. Other areas for specialized audits include diversity, ethical conduct, employee benefits, and workplace conditions. Table 12.6 lists some issues related to quality and effectiveness in corporate citizenship auditing.

Citizenship audits can present several problems. They can be expensive and time consuming, and selecting the auditors may be difficult if objective, qualified personnel are not available. Employees sometimes fear comprehensive evaluations, especially by outsiders, and in such cases, social audits can be extremely disruptive.

Despite these problems, however, auditing corporate citizenship performance can generate many benefits, as we have seen throughout this chapter. Hundreds of companies all over the world have been issuing social responsibility reports since the 1970s to accrue these benefits.[56] The corporate citizenship audit provides an assessment of a company's overall social performance as compared to its core values, ethics policy, internal operating practices, management systems, and, most important, the expectations of key stakeholders.[57] As such, social responsibility

TABLE 12.6

Quality and Effectiveness in Corporate Citizenship Auditing

- Inclusivity means that the audit process must include the views of all the principal stakeholders, not just the "noisy" stakeholders. Therefore, the assessment is based on many different views rather than just one.
- Comparability is the ability to compare the organization's performance from one audit period to another.
- Completeness means that no area of the company is excluded from the audit. This eliminates any "choice" picking of the best areas of the company, and it gives a more accurate and honest view.
- Evolution is what the company goes through when it fully commits to the corporate citizenship audit.
- Management policies and systems are needed to ensure that the process of auditing is done in a controlled manner.
- Disclosure of the information obtained from the corporate citizenship audit is necessary if it is to truly be effective. The question of how many people should the information should be disclosed to is a continual debate.
- Externally verified is to ensure that the audit is done appropriately and that nothing is hidden in the information.
- Continuous improvement makes sure that the audit process is not just retrospective, but uncovers areas for change and improvement.

Source: "How to Do It," in *Building Corporate Accountability: The Emerging Practices in Social and Ethical Accounting, Auditing and Reporting,* ed. Simon Zadek, Peter Pruzan, and Richard Evans (London: Earthscan Publications Ltd., 1997), pp. 35–49.

reports are a useful management tool to help companies identify and define their social impacts and facilitate improvements in vital areas.[58] This assessment can be used to reallocate resources and activities as well as focus on new opportunities for social contributions. The audit process can also help companies fulfill their mission statements in ways that boost profits and reduce risks.[59] More specifically, a company may seek continual improvement in its employment practices, environmental responsibilities, customer and community relations, and ethical behavior in its general business practices.[60] Thus, the audit can pinpoint areas where improving operating practices can improve both bottom-line profits and stakeholder relationships.[61]

Most managers view profitability and corporate citizenship as a trade-off, which prevents them from moving from an "either/or" mind-set to a more proactive "both/and" approach.[62] However, the auditing process can demonstrate the positive impact of corporate citizenship efforts on the firm's bottom line, convincing managers—and other primary stakeholders—of the value of more socially responsible business practices.[63]

Summary

Corporate citizenship auditing is the process of assessing and reporting a business's performance in fulfilling the economic, legal, ethical, and philanthropic social responsibilities expected of it by its stakeholders. The citizenship audit provides an objective approach for an organization to demonstrate its commitment to improving strategic planning, including corporate citizenship accountability. There are many reasons why companies choose to understand, report on, and improve their corporate citizenship performance.

A corporate citizenship audit can satisfy stakeholder demands for increased transparency and greater disclosure, which can help amend and advance relationships with investors, customers, suppliers, regulators, the media, and the community while helping these stakeholders better understand the firm's goals and operations. Dialogs established with stakeholders during the audit process may contribute insight about a firm's current situation, how various stakeholders perceive it, issues that could create threats for the company in the future, and opportunities (or weaknesses) of which the company is not yet aware. The process of citizenship auditing can also help an organization identify potential risks and liabilities and improve its compliance with the law.

Although citizenship audits provide many benefits for individual organizations and their stakeholders, they do have the potential to "backfire," creating as many problems as they solve. A core of minimum standards for corporate social performance is evolving.

Whereas a financial audit is concerned primarily with a company's claims about its financial performance, the social audit is interested in a company's assertions about its citizenship and social responsibility. Unlike financial audits, citizenship auditing is voluntary. Both corporate citizenship auditing and financial auditing employ the same procedures and processes in order to create a system of integrity and objective reporting. Both types of audits begin with collecting information to understand the company's industry, determining the scope of the audit, and documenting the details of the audit program. This information must be of high quality, consistent, complete, material, segregated, and collected in a controlled environment.

A corporate citizenship audit entails an individualized process and outcomes for each firm, as it requires the careful consideration of the unique issues that face a particular organization. The first step in this process is securing the commitment of the firm's top management and/or its board of directors. The second step involves establishing a committee to oversee the audit process. In the third step, the audit committee, or an outside consultant, defines the scope of the audit process, including important subject matter areas. The scope depends on the type of business, the risks faced by the business, and available opportunities to manage corporate citizenship. The fourth step involves a review of the current mission statement, strategic objectives, and organizational policies, goals, and objectives. The fifth step defines the organization's social priorities. These should be articulated as a set of measurable parameters or performance indicators.

The sixth step involves identifying the tools or methods that can be employed to measure the firm's achievement of citizenship objectives. The seventh step involves collecting relevant information for each designated subject matter area. Collection techniques might include examination of internal and external documents, observation of the data-collection process, and confirmation of information in the organization's accounting records. Social audits typically include interviews and focus groups with stakeholders to gain an understanding of their perceptions of the company. The eighth step compares the company's internal perceptions to those discovered during the stakeholder assessment stage and then summarizes these findings. This analysis may also include benchmarking, or comparing organizational performance in designated subject matter areas to other organizations or industry standards.

The ninth step is verification by an independent party. Verification offers a measure of assurance that the company has reported its citizenship performance fairly and honestly, as well as an assessment of its social and environmental reporting systems. The process of verifying the results of an audit should involve standard procedures that control the reliability and validity of the information. The final step in the auditing process is issuing the citizenship audit report.

Although the concept of auditing implies an official examination of social performance, many organizations audit their performance informally. The corporate citizenship audit should be conducted regularly. Although corporate citizenship auditing may present problems, it can generate many benefits. Through the auditing process, a firm can demonstrate the positive impact of corporate citizenship efforts on its bottom line, convincing stakeholders of the value of more socially responsible business practices.

KEY TERMS

corporate citizenship audit

DISCUSSION QUESTIONS

1. What is a corporate citizenship or social audit? Should a firm conduct an audit before or after developing a corporate citizenship initiative?

2. Name some benefits and limitations of reporting the corporate citizenship audit. How should a company address negative issues that are discovered in an audit?

3. What are the major differences between a financial audit and a social audit? How are they similar? Should financial audit rules always be applied to a social audit?

4. Why should top management be involved in and committed to developing a social audit?

5. How should the scope of the social audit be defined?

6. Why should social priorities be translated from abstract principles and values into performance indicators that offer a minimum of objectivity?

7. What types of data should be collected during a social audit? Where can a company obtain this information?

8. What is the difference between a qualified opinion, an unqualified opinion, and an adverse opinion and disclaimer of opinion in a financial audit? How are these opinions relevant to a social audit?

9. Should the organization or individual that verifies the results of the audit be independent? Why or why not?

10. Should a company release audit results that disclose negative information?

EXPERIENTIAL EXERCISE

Visit Vancouver City Savings Credit Union's (VanCity) web site (**http://www.vancity.com**) and find its most recent social audit. Review the audit document. What reasons for conducting the audit are given? Where are VanCity's strengths and opportunities for growth with stakeholders? Provide three recommendations on how VanCity could improve its auditing process and report.

NOTES

1. "Social Audits and Accountability," Business for Social Responsibility, www.bsr.org/resourcecenter/ index.html, accessed January 10, 2001; "The VanCity Difference," Vancouver City Savings Credit Union, www.vancity.com/vancity/difference/index.cfm, accessed January 10, 2001; "The VanCity Social Report 1998/99," Vancouver City Savings Credit Union, www.vancity.com/vancity/socialreport/index.cfm, accessed January 10, 2001; "VanCity's First Comprehensive Social Report Indicates Direction for the Future," *Canada News Wire,* October 6, 1998, www. newswire.ca/releases/October 1998/06/c1357.html; Simon Zadek, "Auditor's Report," *1997 Social Report* (Vancouver: Vancouver City Savings Credit Union, 1998).

2. "Social Audits and Accountability."

3. "Why Count Social Performance," in *Building Corporate Accountability: The Emerging Practices in Social and Ethical Accounting, Auditing and Reporting,* ed. Simon Zadek, Peter Pruzan, and Richard Evans (London: Earthscan Publications Ltd., 1997), pp. 12–34.

4. "Social Audits and Accountability."

5. Kevin J. Sobnosky, "The Value-Added Benefits of Environmental Auditing," *Environmental Quality Management,* 9 (Winter 1999): 25–32.

6. Sandra Waddock and Neil Smith, "Corporate Responsibility Audits: Doing Well by Doing Good," *Sloan Management Review,* 41 (Winter 2000): 75–83.

7. "Why Count Social Performance."

8. John Pearce, *Measuring Social Wealth* (London: New Economics Foundation, 1996) as reported in Warren Dow and Roy Crowe, *What Social Auditing Can Do for Voluntary Organizations* (Vancouver: Volunteer Vancouver, July 1999), p. 8.

9. "Social Audits and Accountability."

10. Trey Buchholz, "Auditing Social Responsibility Reports: The Application of Financial Auditing Standards," Colorado State University, professional paper, November 28, 2000, pp. 3–4; "Social Audits and Accountability."

11. "Social Audits and Accountability."

12. Ibid.

13. Buchholz, "Auditing Social Responsibility Reports," p. 3.

14. "Social Audits and Accountability."

15. Ibid.

16. Louise Gordon, "An Update on SmithOBrien's CSR Audit—A Tool to Help Companies Measure Progress and Its Value," *Executive Citizen,* September/October 1996.

17. "Social Audits and Accountability."

18. Buchholz, "Auditing Social Responsibility Reports," pp. 2–3.

19. Ibid., p. 4

20. Warren Dow and Roy Crowe, *What Social Auditing Can Do for Voluntary Organizations* (Vancouver: Volunteer Vancouver, July 1999), pp. 15–18.

21. Peter Raynard, "Coming Together: A Review of Contemporary Approaches to Social Accounting, Auditing and Reporting in Non-Profit Organizations," *Journal of Business Ethics,* 17 (October 1998): 1471–1479.

22. "What Is Corporate Social Responsibility?" Vasin, Heyn & Company, www.vhcoaudit.com/SRAarticles/WhatIsCSR.htm, accessed November 5, 2001.

23. Buchholz, "Auditing Social Responsibility Reports," p. 5.

24. "Social Audits and Accountability."

25. Ibid.

26. Ibid.

27. Ibid.

28. Ibid.

29. "Ethical Statement," SocialAudit.org, www.socialaudit.org/pages/ethical.htm, accessed November 5, 2001.

30. "Social Audits and Accountability."

31. Ibid.

32. "Ethical Statement."

33. "Well Fargo's Community Reinvestment Leadership Commitment," Wells Fargo, www.wellsfargo.com/cra/craltr1.jhtm, accessed November 5, 2001.

34. James R. Hagerty, "Home Depot Vows to Change Policy on 'Sensitive' Wood Use," *Wall Street Journal,* August 27, 1999, http://interactive.wsj.com/.

35. "Community Involvement," Business for Social Responsibility, www.bsr.org/resourcecenter/index.html, accessed January 11, 2001.

36. "Social Audits and Accountability."

37. Buchholz, "Auditing Social Responsibility Reports," p. 15.

38. Ibid., p. 16.

39. "Social Audits and Accountability."

40. "Introduction to Corporate Responsibility," Business for Social Responsibility, www.bsr.org/resourcecenter/index.html, accessed January. 10, 2001.

41. "Social Audits and Accountability."

42. "Introduction to Corporate Responsibility."

43. "The Effect of Published Reports of Unethical Conduct on Stock Prices," reported in "Business Ethics," Business for Social Responsibility, www.bsr.org/resourcecenter/index.html, accessed January 10, 2001.

44. "Social Audits and Accountability."

45. Ibid.

46. Ethics Officer Association, www.eoa.org, accessed January 10, 2001.

47. "Social Audits and Accountability."

48. "Sustainability Consulting Service Promotes Partnership," IEE Solutions, 31 (April 1999): 16.

49. "Verification," Business for Social Responsibility, www.bsr.org/resourcecenter/index.html, accessed January 15, 2001.

50. "Social Audits and Accountability."

51. Buchholz, "Auditing Social Responsibility Reports," pp. 18–19; "SEC Approves Conflict-of-Interest Limits for Auditors," Bloomberg LP, aol://4344:30.bloombrg.389091.602536905, accessed November 17, 2000.

52. Buchholz, "Auditing Social Responsibility Reports," pp. 16–18.

53. Ibid., pp. 19–20.

54. "Social Audits and Accountability"; Jackie Blondell, "Once Again, The Body Shop Is Leading by Example, *Australian CPA,* March 2001, pp. 28–29.

55. Buchholz, "Auditing Social Responsibility Reports," pp. 19–20.

56. Ibid., p. 1.

57. Waddock and Smith, "Corporate Responsibility Audits."

58. Buchholz, "Auditing Social Responsibility Reports," p. 1.

59. Waddock and Smith, "Corporate Responsibility Audits."

60. Buchholz, "Auditing Social Responsibility Reports," p. 1.

61. Waddock and Smith, "Corporate Responsibility Audits."

62. J. C. Collins and J. I. Porras, Built to Last: Successful Habits of Visionary Companies (New York: Harper Collins, 1997).

63. Waddock and Smith, "Corporate Responsibility Audits."

Cases

Reputation Management at The Coca-Cola Company

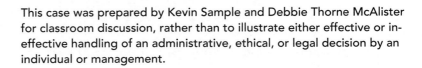

This case was prepared by Kevin Sample and Debbie Thorne McAlister for classroom discussion, rather than to illustrate either effective or ineffective handling of an administrative, ethical, or legal decision by an individual or management.

Retirement after just two years at the helm of one of the most recognized companies in the world is not a commonplace occurrence in business today. However, Doug Ivester did just that when he announced he was resigning and retiring as chairman and chief executive officer of The Coca-Cola Company in 1999. He did so with the "encouragement" of Warren Buffett and Herbert Allen, two of Coca-Cola's most powerful board members. Ivester's tenure was short, and his earlier boast of being able to "generate so much cash I could make everybody's head spin" proved to be wishful thinking.

Before he took the reins at Atlanta-based Coca-Cola, Ivester was heralded for his ability to handle the financial flows and details of the soft-drink giant. Former chief executive Roberto Goizueta had carefully groomed Ivester for the top position, which he assumed in October 1997. However, Ivester seemed to lack leadership in handling a series of crises that hurt Coca-Cola in many ways, causing some to doubt "Big Red's" reputation and its prospects for the future. For a company with a rich history of marketing prowess and financial performance, Ivester's departure represents a high-profile glitch on a relatively clean record in 100 years of business. In April 2000, Doug Daft, the company's former president and chief operating officer, replaced Ivester as the new chief executive at Coca-Cola.

History of The Coca-Cola Company

The Coca-Cola Company is the world's largest beverage company, and it markets four of the world's top five leading soft drinks: Coke, Diet Coke, Fanta, and Sprite. The company also operates the largest distribution system in the world, which enables it to serve customers and businesses in more than 200 countries. Coca-Cola estimates that more than one billion servings of its products are consumed every day.

For much of its early history, Coca-Cola focused on cultivating markets within the United States. Coca-Cola and its arch rival, PepsiCo, have long fought "cola wars" in the United States, but Coca-Cola, recognizing additional market potential, pursued international opportunities in an effort to dominate the global soft-drink industry. By 1993 Coca-Cola controlled 45 percent of the global soft-drink market, and international sales accounted for about 80 percent of its total profits. PepsiCo, on the other hand, received just 15 percent of its profits from international sales. By the late 1990s, Coca-Cola had gained more than 50 percent of the global market share in the soft drink industry. Pepsi continues to target select international markets in order to gain a greater foothold in international markets. Although today Coke and Pepsi are almost neck and neck in the United States, Coca-Cola truly reigns over the global soft-drink market. As the late Roberto Goizueta once said, "Coca-Cola used to be an American company with a large international business. Now we are a large international company with a sizable American business." However, industry analysts predict that Coca-Cola's market share in Europe and other parts of the world will decline in the wake of intense competition and crises.

Coca-Cola has been a successful company since its inception in the late 1800s. PepsiCo, although it was founded about the same time as Coca-Cola, did not become a strong competitor until after World War II, when it began to gain market share. The rivalry intensified in the mid-1960s, and the "cola wars" began in earnest. Today, the duopoly wages war primarily on several international fronts. The companies are engaged in an extremely competitive—and sometimes personal—rivalry, with occasional accusations of false market share reports, anticompetitive behavior, and other questionable business conduct. These accusations are not commonplace, however, and in all actuality, PepsiCo and Coca-Cola appreciate one another. Without this fierce competition, neither would be as good a company as it is today.

Coca-Cola's Reputation

Coca-Cola is the most recognized trademark in the world today. The company has always demonstrated a strong market orientation, making strategic decisions and actions to attract, satisfy, and retain customers. During World War II, for example, then company president Robert Woodruff committed to selling Coke to members of the armed services for just a nickel a bottle. As one analyst said later, "Customer loyalty never came cheaper." This philosophy helped make Coke a truly global brand, with its trademark brands and colors recognizable on cans, bottles, and advertisements around the world. The advance of Coca-Cola products into almost every country in the world demonstrated the company's international market orientation and improved its ability to gain brand recognition. These efforts contributed to the company's strong reputation.

In 1999, Coca-Cola ranked second in a survey by Harris Interactive and the Reputation Institute, which employed a standardized instrument of measure based on twenty perceived attributes to derive a reputation quotient for each company. The rankings grouped these attributes into six main areas of reputation. Within these areas, consumers perceived Coca-Cola as second in emotional appeal (how much the company is liked), third in financial performance, and fourth in vision and leadership (demonstrated strong leadership and clear vision).

Coca-Cola also ranked third in *Fortune* magazine's annual list of the world's most-admired companies in 1999, falling from second place the year before. The company trailed only General Electric and Microsoft. The following year, however, Coca-Cola did not make *Fortune*'s list of top ten most-admired companies for the first time in ten years, although it still ranked first in the beverage industry. Problems that the company experienced in 1999, including leadership issues, poor economic performance, and other upheavals, may have affected its standing in the 2000 *Fortune* list.

Coca-Cola's mission states that the company exists ". . . to create value for our share owners on a long-term basis by building a business that enhances The Coca-Cola Company's trademarks. This also is our ultimate commitment." It has successfully done this by continually increasing market share and profits to a point to where Coca-Cola is one of the most-recognized brands. Because the company is so well known, the industry in which it operates is so pervasive, and it has such a strong history of market orientation, the company has developed a number of corporate citizenship initiatives to further enhance its trademarks.

▶ Corporate Contributions

Coca-Cola has made local education and community improvement programs a top priority for its philanthropic initiatives, which are implemented through the Coca-Cola Foundation. The foundation aims to "help people around the world refresh their hopes and dreams through education." For example, since reentering the Vietnamese market in 1994, Coca-Cola has invested time and money to help educate Vietnamese youth, in collaboration with the Ministry of Education and Training and the National Ho Chi Minh Communist Youth Union. These National Education Programs in Vietnam consist of fourteen Coca-Cola Learning Centers, which teach computer skills and an "English in Vietnam" language program, and promote an annual national schools environmental awareness contest. Such programs are important in helping Coca-Cola aid the community, but they also foster long-term relationships with possible future leaders of this country.

Coca-Cola also offers grants to various colleges and universities in more than half the United States, as well as numerous international grants. In addition to grants, Coca-Cola provides scholarships to more than 170 colleges, and this number will grow to 287 schools over the next four years. It includes 30 tribal colleges belonging to the American Indian College Fund. Coca-Cola has also been involved with the Hispanic Scholarship Fund. Such initiatives help enhance the Coca-Cola name and trademark, and thus ultimately benefits shareholders.

The company also recognizes its responsibilities on a global scale and continues to take action to uphold this responsibility, such as taking steps not to harm the environment while acquiring goods and setting up facilities. Because consumers rely on Coca-Cola, trust its products, and develop a strong attachment through brand recognition and product loyalty, Coca-Cola's actions also foster relationship marketing. For these reasons, problems at a firm like Coca-Cola can stir the emotions of many stakeholders.

▶ Crisis Situations in 1999

Although 1998 was not a good year for Coca-Cola in terms of financial performance, 1999 proved problematic on both financial and nonfinancial fronts. The year brought a number of crisis situations that truly tested the mettle of Doug Ivester as well as various company stakeholders.

Contamination Scare   The most damaging of Coca-Cola's crises—and the situation that every company dreads—began in June 1999, when about thirty Belgian children became ill after consuming Coke products. Although the company recalled the product, the problem soon escalated. The Belgian government eventually ordered the recall of all Coca-Cola products, which led officials in Luxembourg and the Netherlands to recall Coke products as well. The company eventually determined that the illnesses were the result of a poorly processed batch of carbon dioxide. Coca-Cola took several days to comment formally on the problem, which the media quickly labeled a slow response. Ivester initially judged the situation to be a minor problem, not a health hazard, but by this time a public relations nightmare had begun. France soon reported more than 100 people sick from bad Coke and banned all Coca-Cola products until the problem was resolved. Soon thereafter, a shipment of Bonaqua, a new Coca-Cola water product, arrived in Poland contaminated with mold. In each of these instances, the company's slow response and failure to acknowledge the severity of the situation further harmed its reputation.

The contamination crisis was exacerbated in December 1999 when Belgium ordered Coca-Cola to halt its "Restore" marketing campaign in order to regain consumer trust and sales in Belgium. A rival firm claimed that the campaign strategy, which included free cases of product, discounts to wholesalers and retailers, and extra promotion personnel, was intended to strengthen Coca-Cola's market share unlawfully. Under Belgium's strict antitrust laws, the claim was upheld, and Coca-Cola abandoned the campaign in an effort to avoid further problems. This decision, along with the previous crisis, reduced Coca-Cola's market standing in Europe even more.

Competitive Issues   Questions about Coca-Cola's market dominance and government inquiries into its marketing tactics plagued the company outside of Belgium as well. Because most European countries have very strict antitrust laws, all firms must pay close attention to market share and position when considering joint ventures, mergers, and acquisitions there. During the summer of 1999, when Coca-Cola became very aggressive in France, the French government responded by refusing to approve Coca-Cola's bid to purchase Orangina, a French beverage company. French authorities also forced Coca-Cola to scale back its acquisition of Cadbury Schweppes, another beverage maker. Moreover, Italy successfully won a court case against Coca-Cola over anticompetitive prices late in 1999, prompting the European Commission to launch a full-scale probe of the company's competitive practices. PepsiCo and Virgin accused Coca-Cola of using rebates and discounts to crowd their products off the shelves, thereby gaining greater market share. Coca-Cola's strong-arm tactics proved to be in violation of European laws, and once again demonstrated the company's lack of awareness of European culture and laws. What action will result from these charges remains uncertain at this time, but any litigation carries the risk of additional damage to the company's reputation as well as financial penalties.

Despite these recent legal tangles, Coca-Cola products, along with many other American products, have pervaded and dominated foreign markets throughout the world. According to some European officials, the pain American automotive manufacturers felt in the 1970s because of Japanese imports is the same pain that American firms are meting out in Europe. The growing omnipresence of American products, especially in highly competitive markets, is why corporate reputation—both perceived and actual—is so important to relationships with business partners, government officials, and other stakeholders.

Racial Discrimination Allegations   In the spring of the same year, 1,500 African-American employees sued Coca-Cola for racial discrimination. Their lawsuit, which eventually grew to include 2,000 current and former employees, accused the company of discriminating against them in pay, promotions, and performance evaluations. For example, plaintiffs charged that the company grouped black workers at the bottom of the pay scale, where they typically earned $26,000 a year less than white employees in comparable jobs. The suit also alleged that top management had known about companywide discrimination since 1995, but had done nothing about it. Coca-Cola had pledged in 1992 to spend $1 billion on goods and services from minority vendors, an action designed to show the public that Coca-Cola does not discriminate, but this apparently was not the case in the workplace.

Although Coca-Cola strongly denied the allegations of racial discrimination, the lawsuit evoked strong reaction within the company. In response to the suit, Ivester created a diversity council and asked Carl Ware, a respected senior vice president and an African American, to lead it. However, during a management shuffle several months later, Ivester moved Ware to a position reporting to another senior vice president. The reorganization and perceived demotion did not sit well with Ware, who promptly announced his intention to retire. Coca-Cola's board members were puzzled by Ivester's management shuffle: Ware was not only capable and respected, he was also the firm's highest ranking African American and thus could aid Ivester in reinforcing a corporate culture based on diversity and equal opportunity.

Problems with Bottlers and Concentrate Prices   Throughout the crises of 1999, the media focused primarily on their effect on Coca-Cola's reputation rather than on the company's relations with bottlers, distributors, suppliers, and other partners. Without these strategic partnerships, Coca-Cola would not have been able to develop its relationships with consumers today. Such partnerships involve sharing in risks and rewards, and headaches like the contamination scare and racial discrimination allegations, especially when handled poorly, can therefore reflect on other business relationships beyond the firm's core business. When the reputation of one of these companies suffers, all the firms within the supply chain suffer in some way or another. This is especially true because Coca-Cola adopted an enterprise resource system that linked Coca-Cola's once almost classified information to a host of partners. Thus, the company's less-than-stellar handling of the crises of 1999 may have introduced a lack of integrity in its partnerships. Although some of the crises had nothing to do with the information shared across the new system, the partners still assume greater risk because of their closer relationships with the giant company. The interdependence between Coca-Cola and its partners requires a diplomatic and considerate view of the business and its effects on various stakeholders. Thus, these crises harmed the companies, their stakeholders, and eventually, their bottom lines.

Coca-Cola's mishandling of the crises in Europe harmed its strategic partners, but the company further damaged relations with bottlers when Ivester announced in November 1999 that Coke would raise concentrate prices. This decision angered the bottlers, many of which have ties to Coca-Cola's board of directors. Consequently, this decision was one of the last that Doug Ivester would make as CEO.

▶ *The Aftermath of 1999*

Doug Daft, the new chief executive, quickly drafted new plans designed to help Coca-Cola regain its financial footing and improve its tarnished reputation. Some of these plans included downsizing the workforce, creating a new office devoted to global relations, renewing its commitment to diversity, and launching a new marketing campaign. Hopefully, these decisions will help Coca-Cola's stock price recover from its decline from $89 to $64.87 per share in late 1999. Sales volume, revenue, profits, and growth all fell in 1999. Some analysts even speculated that Goizueta's leadership before Ivester may have left the company "more broken than practically anyone had realized." Thus, Daft faced an incredible rebuilding task with many key stakeholders, including bottlers and investors.

Early in 2000, Coca-Cola announced that it would lay off nearly one-fifth of its global workforce. Not since 1988 has the company made significant workforce reductions, except in overseas operations, such as Brazil and Russia, where troubled economies forced the layoffs. The new layoffs were expected to slash about 6,000 jobs, including 2,500 in Atlanta. To ease the trauma of the layoffs, Coca-Cola offered one of the more generous severance packages seen in recent history. The severance package for a ten-year employee, for example, included at least forty weeks of pay and eighteen months of company-paid health benefits. Some employees were even eligible for early retirement if they were at least fifty-two years old and had worked for the company for at least seven years.

In a surprise about-face of his earlier decision to retire, Carl Ware decided to remain with the company and assumed a new role within the post-Ivester corporation. He took charge of Coca-Cola's new Global Public Affairs and Administration division, which was given responsibility for the company's global public issues, including communications, external affairs, and government relations. According to CEO Daft, the new division should help the company respond to a growing number of stakeholders and ensure that Coca-Cola is welcomed around the world as a community member.

Daft has also taken great strides to counter diversity protests. The racial-discrimination lawsuit, along with the threat of a boycott by the NAACP, has led to this correction in Coca-Cola's reputation. Daft's proposed plan to counter racial discrimination ties his success and compensation to company diversity goals. This plan also applies to all Coca-Cola managers, and it will help Coca-Cola greatly improve employment by minorities.

Coca-Cola introduced a new marketing campaign in January 2000, the first new campaign in seven years. Most experts believe it represents the beverage giant's attempt to rebuild its once untarnishable reputation. The campaign, developed by Edge Creative, owned by Coca-Cola, targets local consumers by designing and adapting ads to reflect and connect with local audiences. Rather than having just one message targeted at all consumers, the campaign is designed to appeal to different regions of the globe. Top executives hope the message will instill a desire to enjoy Coca-Cola in consumers. The slogan "Coca-Cola.enjoy" is an invitation for everyone to experience Coke and to check it out on the Internet. The campaign includes a core package that branch offices can use to customize commercials for local markets. It also includes a revamped web site that will allow Internet users to download music and pictures associated with Coke. Although Coca-Cola has experienced enormous success with some advertising campaigns, like the "I'd Like to Buy the World a Coke" campaign of the 1970s, marketing analysts have labeled more-recent advertising efforts as fragmented. If Coca-Cola is going to regain its illustrious corporate image, it will need to make *Coke* a metaphor for relaxation. Although the "Coca-Cola.enjoy" campaign does not address the problems that Coca-Cola has recently faced, the company plans to regain its reputation by focusing on selling its product and connecting with consumers.

After a few months, Belgian officials closed their investigation of the health scare involving Coca-Cola and announced that no charges would be filed against the company. A Belgian health report indicated that no toxic contamination had been found in Coke bottles. Although the bottles were found to have contained tiny traces of carbonyl sulfide, which produced a rotten-egg smell, the amount of carbonyl sulfide would have to have been a thousand times higher to be toxic. Officials also reported finding no structural problems with Coca-Cola's production plant, and that the company had cooperated fully throughout the investigation.

Late in 2000, Coca-Cola settled the racial discrimination lawsuit for more than $156 million, the largest racial discrimination settlement ever. The settlement required the company to pay $113 million to the plaintiffs and other employees involved in the class-action lawsuit and to make $43.5 million in salary adjustments over a ten-year period. In addition, the agreement stipulated that Coke donate $50 million to a foundation to support programs in minority communities; hire an ombudsman, who will report directly to CEO Daft, to investigate complaints of discrimination and harassment; and set aside $36 million and authorize a seven-person task force to oversee the company's employment practices. The task force, which includes business and civil rights experts, will have unprecedented power to dictate company policy with regard to hiring, compensating, and promoting women and minorities. Despite the unusual provision to grant such power to an outside panel, Daft said, "We need to have outside people helping us. We would be foolish to cut ourselves off from the outside world."

Despite the company's problems in 1999, consumers surveyed after the European contamination scare indicated that they felt Coca-Cola would still behave correctly during times of crises. The company also ranked third globally in a PricewaterhouseCoopers survey of the most respected companies. Coca-Cola even managed to retain its strong ranking in this survey even while other companies facing setbacks, including Colgate-Palmolive and Procter & Gamble, dropped from it or fell substantially in the ranks. Thus, even after a series of crises and missteps, Coca-Cola seemed to retain a positive reputation.

> ### Reputation Management

According to a Burston-Marsteller study, 40 percent of a company's reputation is based on the CEO's reputation. Although a CEO's reputation will not boost short-term sales, it can enhance a company's ability to attract investors and employees, and it can allow stakeholders the benefit of the doubt in times of crisis. Although Doug Ivester may have had the business background to assume ultimate responsibility for Coca-Cola, image and reputation management proved to be as important during his two-year tenure. For a leading firm like Coca-Cola, the CEO's decisions reverberate through the media and affect a number of stakeholders. As one columnist put it, "... the real secret of Coca-Cola is not its concentrate formula. The real secret is in the marketing ... an emotional attachment to an experience." This understanding, along with an eye toward corporate citizenship, will be pivotal to twenty-first century leadership and management at Coca-Cola. As this case demonstrates, the transparency and accountability of business have reached new heights, although the long-term implications of Coca-Cola's crisis-laden year have yet to be felt.

DISCUSSION QUESTIONS

1. What factors led to the public relations and financial crises that Doug Daft inherited after Doug Ivester resigned from the chairman and CEO position at Coca-Cola? Is there a common theme throughout the various crisis situations that developed in 1999? If so, discuss this theme and its relationship to corporate citizenship.

2. What role does corporate reputation play within financial performance and corporate citizenship performance? Develop a list of factors or characteristics that different stakeholders may use in assessing corporate reputation. Are these factors consistent across stakeholders? Why or why not?

3. Assume it is 2000 and you have just become CEO at Coca-Cola. Outline the strategic steps you would take to remedy the concerns emanating from the company's board of directors, consumers, employees, business partners, governments, and the media. What elements of corporate citizenship would you draw from in responding to these stakeholder issues?

REFERENCES   These facts are from Elise Ackerman, "It's the Real Thing: A Crisis at Coca-Cola," *U.S. News & World Report,* October 4, 1999, pp. 40–41; Ronald Alsop, "Corporate Reputations Are Earned with Trust, Reliability, Study Shows," *Wall Street Journal,* September 23, 1999, http://interactive.wsj.com; "America's Most Admired Companies," *Fortune,* February 8, 2000, www.pathfinder.com/fortune; Paul Ames, "Case Closed on Coke Health Scare," *Associated Press,* April 22, 2000; "Coke Rapped for Restore," *The Grocer,* December 4, 1999, p. 14; "Corporate Reputation in the Hands of Chief Executive," *Westchester County Business Journal,* May 18, 1998, p. 17; Sharon Foley, "Cola Wars Continue: Coke vs. Pepsi in the 1990s," Harvard Business School Press, case 9-794-055, April 10, 1995; Constance Hays,

"Coca-Cola to Cut Fifth of Workers in a Big Pullback," *New York Times,* January 27, 2000, p. A1; Ernest Holsendolph, "Facing Suit, Coca-Cola Steps up Diversity Efforts," *Atlanta Journal and Constitution,* May 27, 1999, p. F1; Anita Howarth, "Coca-Cola Struggles to Refurbish Image after Recent European Troubles," *Daily Mail,* January 16, 2000, via LEXIS®-NEXIS® Academic Universe; Tammy Joyner, "Generous Severance Packages," *Atlanta Journal and Constitution,* January 27, 2000, p. E1; Jeremy Kahn, "The World's Most Admired Companies," *Fortune,* October 11, 1999, pp. 267–275; Betsy Morris and Patricia Sellers, "What Really Happened at Coke," *Fortune,* January 10, 2000, pp. 114–116; Jon Pepper, "Europe Resents that Europeans much Prefer to Buy American," *Detroit News,* November 10, 1999, http://detnews. com/1999/business/9911/10/11100025.htm; Jordan T. Pine, "Coke Counters Protests with New Diversity Commitment," DiversityInc., March 13, 2000, www.diversityinc.com/; V. L. Ramsey, "$1 Billion Pledged to Vendors," *Black Enterprise,* July 1992, p. 22; Maria Saporta, "Transition at Coca-Cola: Ivester Paid a Price for Going It Alone," *Atlanta Journal and Constitution,* December 8, 1999, p. E1; Patricia Sellers, "Coke's CEO Doug Daft Has to Clean up the Big Spill," *Fortune,* March 6, 2000, pp. 58–59; Christopher Seward, "Company Forewarned: Meaning of Goizueta's '96 Letter Echoes Today," *Atlanta Journal and Constitution,* January 27, 2000, p. E4; "Top 75: The Greatest Management Decisions Ever Made," *Management Review,* November 1998, pp. 20–23; Henry Unger, "Revised Suit Cites Coca-Cola Execs," *Atlanta Journal and Constitution,* December 21, 1999, p. D1; Greg Winter, "Bias Suit Ends in Changes for Coke," *Austin American-Statesman*, November 17, 2000, http://austin360.com/statesman.

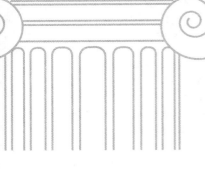

Nonprofit Governance and The National Baptist Convention, USA, Inc.

This case was prepared by Debbie Thorne McAlister and Kevin Sample for classroom discussion, rather than to illustrate either effective or ineffective handling of an administrative, ethical, or legal decision by individuals or management. The research assistance of Shannon Yohe is gratefully acknowledged.

The National Baptist Convention (NBC USA), the oldest and one of the largest African-American religious organizations, assists member churches in ministering to their congregations and communities. The convention also offers guidance on moral standards, politics, and other issues of interest to its membership. Throughout the 1990s, the organization became a respected and influential member of the religious community. However, the actions of a recent president, along with a lack of solid corporate governance mechanisms, have raised questions about the strength and role of the organization. These questions illustrate that nonprofit organizations may be subject to some of the same ethical, legal, and citizenship issues that are raised in the business world.

Reverend Henry J. Lyons was elected NBC USA's president in 1994, becoming only the second president in the convention's nearly two decades of existence. Lyons's election signaled a shift in control from one person to broader representation of the membership. In announcing the election results, the convention's web site stated, "Those who knew the NBC USA years ago need to put away those memories, those images, those experiences. This is a new group . . . a new organization in every sense of the word." In this regard, NBC USA was much like a for-profit business undergoing the transition from private to public ownership. Such transitions bring increased transparency in operations, greater accountability for resources, a stronger focus on strategic planning, and performance evaluations of top managers.

Lyons adopted a theme of "Raise a Standard!" for his presidency, but his conduct throughout the mid-1990s seemed to contradict the theme. His actions also tested public expectations about leadership in nonprofit and religious organizations. These actions eventually brought him to criminal trial, created embarrassment and anger among the organization's constituents, and prompted Lyons's resignation from the convention presidency (see Table C2.1 for a chronological account of events). Following these events, NBC USA elected a new president, Reverend William Shaw of Philadelphia, Pennsylvania, who vowed to implement reforms to the convention's operating procedures and policies while centering the convention "around Christ" and fundamental religious purposes.

▶ Leadership in Nonprofit and Religious Organizations

Within the culture of the United States, nonprofit and religious organizations have traditionally been accorded a place of honor and respect. Although businesses have focused on profits and related economic effects, the nonprofit sector has been charged with improving health care, protecting children and the less fortunate, advancing the arts and culture, and generally improving social welfare. Religious organizations, in particular, have assumed a special role within North American society. Social scientists point to the benefits of religion and congregational life, including physical care, spiritual guidance, and social networks.

Although attendance at formal religious services declined throughout the latter half of the twentieth century, religion has long been regarded as a major institution in U.S. culture. In the 1800s, French observer Alexis de Tocqueville noted the primacy of religion to the American concept of liberty in his classic work, *Democracy in America.* Although religion has evolved in terms of its impact on today's society, it remains firmly linked to some foundational issues and beliefs in the United States. Given their fundamental missions and associated responsibilities, religious organizations and leaders are expected to uphold high moral standards and to serve as role models for others.

However, various scandals that occurred in the 1980s and 1990s brought to light the fallibility and vulnerability of both nonprofit and religious groups. For example, the former president of United Way of America, William Aramony, was forced out of his position in 1992 after an uproar over his $465,000 salary and benefit package. Three years later, Aramony and two colleagues were found guilty of using hundreds of thousands of dollars for personal gain. Because of such scandals, there has been an increasing focus on the accountability of nonprofit organizations and leadership.

▶ Religion in the African-American Community

Although formal religion may have declined in the United States, a majority of African Americans still consider the church an important aspect of their lives. A

TABLE C2.1

A Chronology of Events

Date	Event
July 6, 1997	Deborah Lyons, wife of Reverend Henry J. Lyons, is arrested and charged with setting fire to a $700,000 house in Tierra Verde, an exclusive area of St. Petersburg, Florida. She set fire to the home after learning that her husband was having an affair with an NBC employee, Bernice Edwards, a convicted embezzler. The home was registered in Reverend Lyons's name as a single man. He shared the home with Edwards.
July 8	Questions arise as to how Reverend Lyons was able to buy a waterfront home, a Rolls Royce, and two Mercedes Benz automobiles.
July 10	Reverend Lyons is confronted with the controversy after returning from a trip to Nigeria. He denies all charges against him, his affair with Edwards, and the improper use of NBC funds.
July 19	A report surfaces claiming that Edwards and Lyons planned to purchase a $925,000 mansion in North Carolina.
August 2	Another report emerges that Lyons and Edwards also own a Lake Tahoe, Nevada, time-share.
August 8, 14	Records show that a check from an NBC account was used for the down payment on a $36,200 diamond ring for Edwards and part of the down payment on the Tierra Verde home.
September 3	The NBC votes to keep Reverend Lyons as the president despite accusations of misuse of funds for personal gain. This apparently ends a move to remove Lyons from office.
September 11	Seven leaders from Alabama churches destroyed by arson report receiving little or none of the $225,000 given to Lyons by human rights groups in order to help pay for the churches' rebuilding. Five days after the accusations, Lyons returns $214,500.
November 6	Another report surfaces stating that more than $1 million intended for the NBC actually went to a secret bank account in Wisconsin.
November 10	The leadership of the National Association of the Advancement of Colored People calls for Reverend Lyons to resign.
December 3	Lyons apologizes publicly, but vows to remain the NBC president.
February 25, 1998	The state of Florida charges Henry Lyons and Bernice Edwards with grand theft and racketeering in connection with corporations seeking marketing arrangements with the National Baptist Conventions USA and church reconstruction donations from the Anti-Defamation League. Both Lyons and Edwards plead not guilty to the charges.

(continued)

TABLE C2.1 *(continued)*

A Chronology of Events

Date	Event
July 13	The World Saving and Loan Association files suit against Lyons because payments for the Tierra Verde home have not been made.
August 27	Reverend Lyons appears on television news broadcasts to apologize to his supporters and to deny accusations of extramarital affairs and financial misdeeds.
November 13	The Internal Revenue Service files a notice against Lyons for more than $500,000 in unpaid income taxes for the years of 1995, 1996, and 1997.
January 11, 1999	The state of Florida's racketeering and grand theft trial of Reverend Henry Lyons and Bernice Edwards begins.
January 28	A former assistant of Reverend Lyons claims that she had an affair with him, and that he paid rent on her Tampa apartment. He also shared a bank account with her, and she reported the egregiously stated membership numbers of the NBC.
February 19	Edwards testifies that she was not romantically involved with the minister.
February 27	The all-white jury, with tears in their eyes, finds Lyons guilty of state charges on racketeering and grand theft of about $5 million after 13 hours of deliberations. Edwards is not found guilty. The defense does not complain about the all-white jury.
	Lyons does not respond to questions about his remaining time as the NBC president.
	Lyons's son, Derek, collapses from an asthma attack.
	Lyons's attorneys contend that there is a strong chance for appeal due to a mysterious e-mail concerning a juror.
March 16	Reverend Henry Lyons resigns as president of the NBC USA in an emergency meeting of the NBC.
March 31	Reverend Lyons is sentenced to five and a half years in prison. He is also ordered to repay about $2.5 million.
June 18	The federal court case of Reverend Lyons begins.
September	The federal court sentences Lyons to pay $5.2 million in back taxes and to serve another four years and three months. Brenda Harris, the public relations director for NBC and Lyons's mistress, receives 18 months probation for not reporting Lyons's crimes.
October	Reverend William Shaw defeats 10 other candidates for the vacant position of NBC USA president. His first step is to freeze nonessential spending and to have an outside accounting firm perform a financial audit. He also states an interest in having more accurate membership numbers.
November	Bernice Edwards, a codefendant in the Lyons case, is sentenced to 21 months in federal prison for failing to pay taxes on $500,000 received while working for NBC USA.

1999 survey found that 73 percent of African Americans feel that religion is very important, compared to 46 percent of whites. Within the black community, the church is often a focal point for social, religious, political, and cultural life. African-American churches and their members often assume economic and financial responsibility for their communities. During times of racial strife and discrimination, the church serves as a place of refuge and equality. The role of the church was especially significant during the civil rights struggles of the 1950s and 1960s, and it facilitated the political development of black leaders such as Martin Luther King, Jr., and Jesse Jackson. For these economic and political reasons, it is important to understand how issues affecting the church also affect the community. A number of Southern black churches were deliberately set afire in the mid-1990s. Observers have noted that such arson destroys more than a physical place of worship; it also disrupts a vital source of coping and support for church and community members. Understanding the significance of religion in the black community helps establish the context for discussing Henry Lyons's presidency and leadership in the NBC USA.

▶ Lyons's Role and Presidency

Before becoming president of NBC USA, Henry Lyons enjoyed a long, successful career as a Baptist minister. He was raised in Gainesville, Florida, where his grandfather, a church deacon, taught him how the church worked. Lyons was impressed with the role of church officials and decided to become a minister. As a young preacher, Lyons began developing a reputation for charisma, oratory skill, and political prowess. He was eventually called "the black pope" and a "classy cleric." After Lyons joined NBC USA, he rose through the ranks and assumed positions of greater power and responsibility. At the same time, he built a strong following among church members and established the Bethel Metropolitan Baptist Church in St. Petersburg, Florida. In 1994, he won a bitter contest for the NBC USA presidency.

Even before Lyons's legal troubles began, there were questions as to whether he should remain president of the convention. In 1997, Reverend Calvin O. Butts made a motion to dismiss Lyons. Although the motion was turned down by a vote of three to one, Lyons's ability to handle the presidency was regularly questioned. As he spent more time in office, however, the number of his supporters grew and solidified. This support remained strong, even after Lyons was convicted of wrongdoing in 1999.

Lyons's legal troubles stemmed from accusations that he swindled about $250,000 from NBC USA. According to a prosecutor, Lyons took money that had been designated for rebuilding churches destroyed by arson. The prosecution further charged that Lyons had deceived a number of corporations and the Anti-Defamation League (ADL) of B'nai B'rith through a series of broken promises and false claims. Money entrusted to him for the purpose of rebuilding burned churches never reached those churches until his legal trial began. For example, the Rising Star Baptist Church in Greensboro, Alabama, which was burned to the ground in June 1996, was to receive $35,000 as part of an NBC USA initiative to rebuild damaged churches. However, Reverend Willie Coleman stated that the church secretary did not receive a check for $10,000 from the NBC USA until January 1999, a few days before court testimonies were scheduled to begin. By that time, the Rising Star Baptist Church had been rebuilt from funds raised in the community.

This was not the only instance of delayed or nonexistent charity at the hands of NBC USA and Henry Lyons. In a letter, Lyons reported to the ADL that funds it had provided were dispersed in $35,000 allotments to six different churches. He went on to ask for more donations for several other churches, and the ADL responded with another check in the amount of $19,500. According to the prosecution, however, Lyons had distributed less than $40,000 to these churches at the time of this correspondence with ADL. Instead, the prosecutors said, Lyons deposited $60,000 into his savings account, gave $12,000 to his spouse, spent part of the money to redecorate his house and pay bills, and even gave some of the money to love interests in Tennessee and Indiana. He also allegedly used money obtained from other sources to buy $131,000 worth of jewelry, lease a home in Nashville for an employee, and purchase Rolls Royce and Mercedes Benz automobiles.

Exaggerated Numbers and More Accusations

Although Lyons claimed that NBC USA represented 8.5 million members in 33,000 churches, these figures have been challenged. Prosecutors contend that the convention's membership actually numbers about one million, its mailing list has never exceeded 15,000 people, and there are only about 7,000 churches listed on its own roster. Nonetheless, Lyons and Bernice Edwards, a convention employee, used the exaggerated numbers to secure contracts that would generate donations in exchange for a list of NBC USA members. These contracts promised a mailing list with 8.5 million names to donor companies seeking to target African Americans to market insurance, credit cards, and burial services. In order to create the massive mailing list, Lyons instructed a convention staff member to cull other lists and databases. However, many of the names and addresses of people had no connection to NBC USA or to any Baptist church. When an imperial wizard of the Ku Klux Klan made it onto the mailing list, he quickly complained to the direct marketing company about receiving a promotion that was clearly not tailored to him. The fact that Lyons kept this money was questionable, but the way it was acquired was also suspect, because this sale of names and addresses did not protect individual privacy rights or wishes regarding personal information exchange. These contracts were lucrative to Lyons and Edwards, bringing in more than $4 million that never made it into convention coffers.

▶ *Drama Surrounding the Trial*

Given the role of religion within the black community and past history of race discrimination in the United States, the trial of Henry Lyons was fraught with questions of fairness and equity. Because many owners and members of the media are white, some of Lyons's supporters complained that he was being unfairly portrayed and persecuted by the media. Grady C. Irvin, Jr., a defense lawyer and fellow member of Bethel Metropolitan Baptist Church, said, "No one knows how much the pope is worth . . . No one gets into their finances . . . Why is Rev. Lyons being singled out? It gives the appearance that black pastors are supposed to be paupers." Others suggested that Lyons had become a target of the white establishment. Although Lyons and his supporters eventually toned down their charges of racism, his attorneys considered using a defense strategy that focused on the dominant role that black churches and leaders play within their communities. This strategy was intended to show that Lyons was only acting in his assumed role because church leaders have ultimate authority and control on financial decisions. In addition, the defense pointed out that no "victim" had ever complained about Lyons to the authorities.

Despite this vigorous defense and the public support for Lyons, he was convicted on state charges of racketeering and grand theft in February 1999. He avoided a second trial, this time in federal court, by pleading guilty to tax evasion, fraud, and lying to public officials in March 1999. Lyons was ultimately sentenced to five and a half years in jail for the state convictions and four years and three months of concurrent time in prison. He was also ordered to pay $5.2 million of the funds that never arrived at their proper charitable destinations. On March 15, 1999, Henry Lyons tearfully resigned as president of the National Baptist Convention USA. Lyons had previously announced that he intended to remain the NBC USA president, and indeed, that he would run for reelection. However, after being convicted in both state and federal courts, he changed his mind and indicated he was ready to accept his punishment.

▶ *NBC USA Responds*

Throughout Lyons's ordeal, the National Baptist Convention USA supported the now-former president through its web site and discussions with media. The convention's board of directors also affirmed its support of Lyons in a resolution, saying, "where there is no victim there is no crime." Others, both inside and outside the NBC USA, disagreed, asserting that there were victims, including the burned churches counting on the Anti-Defamation League funds, the direct marketing firms that were given the falsified mailing list, convention members, and Lyons's own family. The board's resolution also invoked accountant/client privilege so that NBC's accountant could not speak with authorities about the convention's business. NBC USA continued to back Lyons beyond vocal and written support. The convention asked its pastors to collect money during church services to help pay for his legal bills, and it even set up a Lyons Defense Fund.

Although Reverend Lyons was convicted of taking money from members of the convention through various fund diversions, they still seemed willing to help him out financially. Whether it is forgiveness, an attempt to keep up the better image of years past, or some private matter, the NBC USA fully supported Reverend Henry Lyons after his conviction. One of the prosecutors claimed, "a president has no more right to take corporation funds for personal use than a janitor does." However, in explaining their support of Lyons, the convention's directors stated that the culture of NBC USA allowed the president complete discretion and authority with corporate funds.

▶ *Role of the Board of Directors*

A nonprofit organization should have powerful and proactive board directors who are committed to ethics and willing to provide oversight in this regard. The board members of a nonprofit organization should act with the same level of professionalism and accountability as board members of any profit-oriented business. They, like all board members, cannot go unchecked. In an attempt to ensure that nonprofit organizations reach their objectives efficiently, effectively, and ethically, there must be a system of measurement and control for the board of directors.

Whereas business firms are constantly seeking to increase profits, nonprofit organizations are relatively free of this relentless pursuit. They often hold more promise and hope for society, but they also hold the potential for problems due to the lack of scrutiny and accountability. Several recent scandals and revelations, including the Lyons case, have brought about greater discussion and scrutiny of nonprofit organizations. Both benefactors and government regulators are paying closer attention than ever before. These incidents dictate a much more critical role for board members. They must act on behalf of the organization, ensuring a focus on operations, legalities, and citizenship, for they no longer have the loose reigns of old.

The National Baptist Convention did not keep any financial records during Reverend Lyons's reign. This lack of standard business practice, in addition to the misconduct by Reverend Lyons, cried out for a stronger control system for the organization and its board of directors. This system should keep in check the authoritative, financial, and strategic decisions made by the board and other decision makers in the organization. The lack of ethical standards from the president of a national church organization shocked people nationwide. A set of ethics that is supposed to already be held by any member of the NBC USA was not exhibited in Reverend Lyons's actions, nor did the organization have effective documentation and implementation of a code of ethics. Regardless of the presumed ethical standpoint of the members of an organization, there should be a written code of ethics that is widely communicated and expected of all organizational members. Although NBC USA's constitution did empower the board of directors to investigate and suspend any member accused of any wrongdoing, it did not use this power in the Lyons case. In addition, the board's Committee on Ethics and Integrity did not formally act on the situation. As this case demonstrates, corporate governance remains a needed constituent in all types of organizations to ensure that actions made by employees and other agents are both legally and ethically acceptable. In order for policies to work, a board of directors must take ultimate responsibility for the governance mechanism to be supported and implemented within the entire organization.

DISCUSSION QUESTIONS

1. What factors led to Lyons's opportunity to commit illegal actions during his presidency? Would these factors have been present in a traditional business firm? Why or why not?
2. Why is it important to understand the role of nonprofit and religious organizations in our society when discussing issues of corporate governance and citizenship?
3. How can a board of directors help ensure ethical and legal standards in an organization? What specific actions and policies are needed in this regard?

REFERENCES

These facts are from "A Barometer of Black America," *Time,* November 8, 1999, p. 18; "Baptist Leader's Conviction Implies Lack of Board Oversight," *Board Members,* 8 (March 1999): 2; A. Craver, "Toward 2000 and Beyond: Charitable and Social Change Giving in the New Millennium," *Fund Raising Management,* 30 (May 1999): 28–30; "Ex-National Baptist Convention Exec Gets 21-Month Sentence," *Jet,* November 15, 1999, p. 38; John Gibeaut, "Raising a Holy Racket," *ABA Journal,* 85 (January 1999): 50; "Henry Lyons Steps Down in Wake of Conviction," *Afgen,* March 16, 1999, http://afgen.com/henry-lyons.html; Regina E. Herzlinger, "Effective Oversight: A Guide for Nonprofit Directors," *Harvard Business Review,* 72 (July/August 1994): 52; Aimee Howard, "The Black Church in the Inner City," *Insight,* October 18, 1999, pp. 18–20; William Levesque and David Barstow, "Lyons Guilty," *St. Petersburg Times,* February 28, 1999; "Lyons Found Guilty," *Christian Century,* March 17, 1999, p. 302; "Lyons Sentenced to 5 1/2 Years," *USA Today,* March 31, 1999, www.usatoday.com/news/ndswed03.htm; Tom McClintock, "Religion a Threat to, or Foundation of, Liberty?" *Christian Science Monitor,* December 19, 1997, p. 19; The National Baptist Convention, www.nbcusa.org, accessed January 1999; "Rev. William Shaw of Philadelphia Elected President of National Baptist Convention," *Jet,* September 27, 1999, p. 7; Pamela Sebastian, "Boards of Nonprofit Organizations Learn Lessons from United Way's Troubles," *Wall Street Journal,* February 22, 1995, p. B1; Darren E. Sherkat and Shannon A. Cunningham, "Extending the Semi-Involuntary Institution: Regional Differences and Social Constraints on Private Religious Consumption Among African Americans," *Journal for the Scientific Study of Religion,* 37 (September 1998): 383–396; Corwin Smidt, "Religion and Civic Engagement: A Comparative Analysis," *Annals of the American Academy of Political and Social Science,* 565 (September 1999): 176–192; David Sommer, "Lyons Convicted," *The Tampa Tribune,* February 28, 1999.

Environmental Reporting: The Origin and Effect of the CERES Principles

This case was prepared by Debbie Thorne McAlister and Kevin Sample for classroom discussion, rather than to illustrate either effective or ineffective handling of an administrative, ethical, or legal decision by individuals or management. The research assistance of Jason De Los Santos is gratefully acknowledged.

A t 12:04 A.M. on March 24, 1989, the tanker *Exxon Valdez* ran aground near its home port of Valdez, Alaska, and leaked 240,000 barrels—about 11 million gallons—of crude oil into the pristine waters of Prince William Sound. The spill eventually spread to over 2,600 square miles of Prince William Sound and the Gulf of Alaska, killing or injuring thousands of birds, fish, and other wildlife. Fishing grounds that had netted local fishermen $100 million annually had to be shut down for years afterward. Exxon and Alyeska Pipeline Service Company—a consortium of companies set up to operate the Trans-Alaska pipeline and the shipping terminal at Valdez—were accused of negligence and mismanagement in their response to the spill. Although Exxon CEO Lawrence Rawl apologized to the public for the disaster, state officials, consumers, and environmental groups accused the company of doing too little too late. Many customers cut up their Exxon cards and returned them to the company in protest of its handling of the crisis. Exxon ultimately paid out billions of dollars to settle criminal and civil charges and lawsuits, and negative feelings toward the company still linger more than a decade later.

Although the *Exxon Valdez* oil spill was not the largest in history, it proved to be one of the worst in terms of adverse media coverage, disruption to local business and industry, and long-term environmental damage. The negative effects of the spill can still be seen and felt today. In the wake of this environmental and public relations tragedy, however, several positive changes occurred in corporate accountability, shipboard responsibility, environmental cleanup procedures, and environmental awareness and reporting. Among the most significant of these was the development of the CERES Principles, a set of goals for environmental performance developed by a coalition of businesses, consumer groups, environmentalists, and other stakeholders. The tragedy also brought about changes in the way governments and businesses consider environmental protection and performance.

▶ ## The Coalition for Environmentally Responsible Economies

Soon after, and in a large part due to, the *Exxon Valdez* disaster, the Coalition for Environmentally Responsible Economies (CERES) was formed, bringing together fifteen major U.S. environmental groups and a wide array of socially responsible investors and public pension funds, the latter representing more than $200 billion in invested capital. Over the years, the coalition has promoted greater corporate responsibility toward the environment and taken a leadership role in standardizing environmental reporting by organizations. CERES was founded with the belief that businesses should take a stand on environmental issues because their influence over human decisions and behaviors often surpasses that of governments, schools, or religious organizations. To control and provide accountability for environmental performance, however, companies need effective measurement and communication tools. This need brought about the CERES Principles and other initiatives to establish benchmarks for environmental performance and to provide an easier way to report information about environmental performance. All projects sponsored by CERES begin and end with the organization's core principles for environmental action and performance.

The ten CERES Principles were established with the intent to reduce harm to air, earth, and water; diminish the use of toxic wastes; communicate to the public about potential safety hazards; and reverse damage done to the environment (see Table C3.1). Originally called the Valdez Principles, these directives were styled after the Sullivan Principles, which called for businesses to cut ties in South Africa until that country agreed to abolish apartheid, its policy of formal racial segregation. All organizations that choose to become members of CERES must adhere to these ten principles. By adopting the principles, member organizations acknowledge that they have a responsibility to the environment and that they must not jeopardize future generations in order to sustain themselves in the short run.

The Growth of CERES During the first few years of CERES's existence, only a few companies—including Ben & Jerry's, Aveda, Seventh Generation, and The Body Shop—adopted the principles, and these firms already had strong reputations for being "green." In 1993, Sun Oil became the first *Fortune* 500 company to endorse the CERES Principles. Many large organizations soon followed, including Arizona Public Service, Bethlehem Steel, Polaroid, General Motors, and H. B. Fuller.

TABLE C3.1

The CERES Principles

PROTECTION OF THE BIOSPHERE

We will reduce and make continual progress toward eliminating the release of any substance that may cause environmental damage to the air, water, or the earth or its inhabitants. We will safeguard all habitats affected by our operations and will protect open spaces and wilderness, while preserving biodiversity.

SUSTAINABLE USE OF NATURAL RESOURCES

We will make sustainable use of renewable natural resources, such as water, soils, and forests. We will conserve nonrenewable natural resources through efficient use and careful planning

REDUCTION AND DISPOSAL OF WASTES

We will reduce and where possible eliminate waste through source reduction and recycling. All waste will be handled and disposed of through safe and responsible methods.

ENERGY CONSERVATION

We will conserve energy and improve the energy efficiency of our internal operations and of the goods and services we sell. We will make every effort to use environmentally safe and sustainable energy sources.

RISK REDUCTION

We will strive to minimize the environmental, health, and safety risks to our employees and the communities in which we operate through safe technologies, facilities, and operating procedures, and by being prepared for emergencies.

SAFE PRODUCTS AND SERVICES

We will reduce and where possible eliminate the use, manufacture, or sale of products and services that cause environmental damage or health or safety hazards. We will inform our customers of the environmental impacts of our products or services and try to correct unsafe use.

ENVIRONMENTAL RESTORATION

We will promptly and responsibly correct conditions we have caused that endanger health, safety, or the environment. To the extent feasible, we will redress injuries we have caused to persons or damage we have caused to the environment and will restore the environment.

INFORMING THE PUBLIC

We will inform in a timely manner everyone who may be affected by conditions caused by our company that might endanger health, safety, or the environment. We will regularly seek advice and counsel through dialogue with persons in communities near our facilities. We will not take any action against employees for reporting dangerous incidents or conditions to management or to appropriate authorities.

(continued)

TABLE C3.1 (continued)

The CERES Principles

MANAGEMENT COMMITMENT
We will implement these Principles and sustain a process that ensures that the Board of Directors and Chief Executive Officer are fully informed about pertinent environmental issues and are fully responsible for environmental policy. In selecting our Board of Directors, we will consider demonstrated environmental commitment as a factor.

AUDITS AND REPORTS
We will conduct an annual self-evaluation of our progress in implementing these Principles. We will support the timely creation of generally accepted environmental audit procedures. We will annually complete the CERES Report, which will be made available to the public.

Source: "The CERES Principles," CERES, www.ceres.org/about/principles.htm, accessed November 8, 2001. © CERES, 1980–2001. Reprinted by permission.

When it joined CERES in 1994, the Polaroid Corporation became the largest firm to endorse the CERES Principles at the time. Executives at Polaroid said they thought that the endorsement was important and would help reinforce the firm's longtime environmental commitment and mission. Polaroid's pledge to uphold CERES Principles not only made a public statement about environmental performance, but it also held the company publicly accountable. After joining CERES, Polaroid's stakeholders could fully scrutinize the company's behavior because of CERES' push for standardized reporting.

General Motors (GM) jumped on the CERES bandwagon in 1994 as well. After a year-long discussion of the move, GM became the largest firm to join CERES. GM may have decided to endorse the principles in response to criticism for not producing more fuel-efficient vehicles. GM's endorsement also gave a boost to the corporate environmental movement. Judith Kuszewski, a CERES employee, commented that "changing a company like GM is like turning a submarine around in a bathtub." GM's actions encouraged its suppliers and dealers to modify their own environmental positions, ultimately affecting hundreds of businesses. Thus, membership in CERES can produce peer pressure toward greater environmental responsibility.

Today, nearly 100 companies, representing more than ten million people, stand behind the CERES Principles. There are two categories of membership—endorsers and coalition members (see Table C3.2). Endorsing organizations agree to abide by CERES goals and values, whereas coalition members are concerned with public accountability and continuous progress in environmental performance. Companies that join CERES pay between $100 and $15,000 per year in membership fees, depending on annual company revenues.

TABLE C3.2

CERES Participant Organizations

Participant Category	Representative Organizations
Coalition Members: Investment institutions that explicitly consider environmental factors in their investment decisions, environmental advocacy organizations, labor unions, public interest groups, and community-based activists	AFL-CIO, Industrial Union Department Calvert Group Council on Economic Priorities Evangelical Lutheran Church in America Interfaith Center on Corporate Responsibility Kinder, Lydenberg, Domini & Co., Inc. National Wildlife Federation Sierra Club United Methodist Church—General Board of Pension and Health Benefits World Wildlife Fund
Endorsers: Businesses and other organizations, of every size and shape, that have publicly committed to the CERES Principles and work with CERES to disclose publicly meaningful environmental performance data, to engage in collaborative dialogue about shared challenges, and to identify opportunities for constant improvement	Aveda Corporation BankBoston Corporation Bethlehem Steel Corporation Coca-Cola, USA Episcopal Diocese of Massachusetts General Motors Corporation Global Environmental Technologies Mountain Power Corporation H. B. Fuller Company ITT Industries Timberland Company Vancouver City Savings Credit Union Westchester County, New York

Despite more than a decade of growth, rejection of the CERES Principles by corporate giants such as Chevron and even entire industries has called into question the actual importance and benefits of membership. The desire to be "green" and environmentally friendly does not necessarily require membership in an environmental group. Many companies act responsibly toward the environment without adhering to any generic principles and may not see the benefit of joining CERES. Without any industrywide pressure or other incentives to join, some organizations see membership in CERES as an expensive burden. This will continue to be a challenge for CERES and other progressive environmental groups because businesses must balance costs and strategic plans with acceptable environmental effects. However, membership by one company in an industry may spur other such firms to sign up. In 1999, for example, AMR, the parent company of American Airlines, became the first airline to endorse the CERES Principles, and Penguin Computing was the first major computer company to join. These new members have prompted increased environmental dialogue in the aviation and computer industries.

The CERES Organization   As a nonprofit organization, CERES is highly dependent on the strong participation and commitment of its volunteers. The coalition, based in Boston, Massachusetts, has a staff of seventeen and a board of directors composed of twenty members representing diverse organizations like Friends of the Earth, World Wildlife Fund, National Wildlife Federation, and National Ministries/ American Baptist Churches, USA, among others. In order to plan activities more efficiently, CERES developed four program committees that have influenced and implemented most of the organization's policies and programs. The committees, whose members include company representatives and board members, include the following:

1. The Joining Committee is responsible for maintaining policies and procedures for researching, evaluating, and recruiting firms.

2. The Projects Committee ensures that each CERES member correctly endorses the ten principles and helps companies incorporate the principles into everyday operations.

3. The Report Committee works to achieve standardized environmental reporting by showing companies how to use the "CERES Report" mechanism, giving companies feedback, and disseminating a summary of results and best practices.

4. The Review Committee has the very difficult task of investigating problems or complaints about a particular company's environmental performance and recommending a process that might lead to resolution.

Each committee plays an important role in the effective functioning of the CERES organization. In order to be a viable organization, CERES must retain current members while recruiting new ones. Thus, the coalition must develop programs and initiatives that provide benefits to a variety of members. Once a company joins, CERES focuses on helping that firm fulfill the ten principles and continuously improve its environmental performance. Its performance is then documented in an environmental report for public review. Because of the nature and complexity of environmental performance, CERES is also prepared to deal with conflicts that may arise among its members or other stakeholders. One of

CERES's most recent and important initiatives has been in the area of environmental reporting, the formal documentation of corporate programs and effects on the natural environment.

▶ *Environmental Reporting*

Environmental responsibility became a significant issue in the United States in the 1970s in response to increasing environmental awareness, political movements, and the creation of the Environmental Protection Agency. Until about 1985, most companies, facing environmental regulations for the first time, did the bare minimum to comply with them, and some even tried to avoid obeying them at all. Beginning in the mid-1980s, there was a shift in regulatory philosophy from strict mechanical compliance to achieving desired environmental goals. The Common Sense Initiative (CSI) of the mid-1990s also promoted a more positive mind-set among businesspeople. Created by Carol Browner, head of the U.S. Environmental Protection Agency (EPA), the Common Sense Initiative represented a new regulatory approach to environmental protection and performance. Its goals included (1) encouraging participants to look comprehensively at specific industries in an effort to imagine the best possible environmental performance for each industry, (2) identifying barriers to this level of performance, and (3) developing solutions based on consensus among stakeholders to overcome these barriers. In exchange for industry participation in the CSI dialogue and acceptance of increased public accountability, the EPA began granting companies more operational flexibility, extending compliance schedules for those firms willing to invest in innovative new technologies and reducing record keeping and reporting requirements for businesses and communities. Because of these changes, companies became more accepting of environmental regulations and accountability.

Although some companies have been issuing reports about their environmental performance since the 1970s, environmental reporting became more mainstream in the late 1980s and early 1990s, especially among large multinational corporations. Environmental reports are issued annually and describe the steps that companies are taking to improve their environmental performance. Some companies have also begun to include information about worker health and safety as well as the environment. Most experts in the field believe that a global standard will eventually emerge for environmental reporting, but there are still many companies that disclose only partial information or none at all.

Consulting firms, nonprofit environmental organizations, and even national government agencies have developed their own standards and requirements for environmental reporting in response to stakeholders' increasing concerns about the environment and corporate governance of the issues. The U.S. Securities and Exchange Commission (SEC), for example, has required greater disclosure from companies about their environmental impact, even threatening to punish some firms whose information has been either inconsistent or poorly reported. The EPA has also increased pressure on companies to disclose more information about their environmental behavior. Companies in the oil, steel, metal, automobile, and paper industries, for example, must post an EPA-structured pollution profile on the Internet.

Although both regulatory and nonregulatory factors are driving enhanced environmental reporting, there is no standardized method for reporting and comparison. Each year, more companies voluntarily report information about their environmental performance to the public, but each firm employs its own format, rendering comparison among reports impossible. Thus, investors, employees, consumers, environmentalists, and other report users cannot easily use the reported information to make or guide product choices, glean benchmark performance data, or compare one firm's performance to other firms'. Moreover, if corporate environmental reports are not verified by an independent third party, their credibility can be called into question. Some critics wonder whether some firms are not above reporting false information in order to look better to potential investors. Consequently, environmental reports range from short documents with little quantifiable data to extremely long reports with numerous graphs and other visual tools to help readers understand the report. For example, the *Shell Report,* issued annually by the Royal Dutch/Shell Group of Companies, incorporates a wide range of information, as well as endorsements from KPMG Accountants and PricewaterhouseCoopers that the content is fairly stated and represented. The *Shell Report* also contains numerous calls for criticism and opposing viewpoints, including a quote from CERES about Shell's relative strengths and weaknesses on environmental reporting.

These discrepancies in and issues with environmental reporting have generated calls for standardizing and verifying reports. Numerous people, firms, and agencies are now accessing environmental reports, but inconsistency among them makes it very difficult for such stakeholders to use and compare the reports. With a uniform standard, investors, managers, and other interested parties would more easily be able to evaluate a company's performance and compare it to other firms'. A uniform standard for verification would also curtail speculation as to the accuracy and truthfulness of corporate environmental reports. Table C3.3 summarizes the justifications for standardizing environmental reporting.

Establishing a standard for reporting and verifying environmental information may sound simple and logical, but corporate reluctance and the variety of agencies and governments involved make it unlikely that standardization will become widespread any time soon. Some companies have embraced the idea of standardized reporting, but others, including DuPont and Ashland Chemical, contend that customized reports, based on unique company characteristics and needs, are more useful than standardized ones. Several industries and organizations have already

TABLE C3.3

Advantages of Standardizing Environmental Reports

- Creates understanding of environmental standards across the entire organization and various stakeholders
- Helps illustrate weaknesses and opportunities and set new goals relative to environmental performance
- Allows a company and its stakeholders to measure the company's adherence to environmental standards, principles, and goals and objectives
- Provides information to the public to hold corporations liable, and includes stakeholders more fully in the process of environmental goal setting
- Signals a strong commitment to environmental responsibility
- Permits comparisons across companies
- Simplifies the process of collecting best-practices information

standardized reporting for their members (e.g., the chemical industry through the Chemical Manufacturers Association's Responsible Care Program), but which of these formats, if any, will become the globally accepted standard for environmental reporting remains to be seen. Another issue is the method of verification. Accountants and auditors could verify environmental reports if they were trained to do so, but setting up such a system would require a great deal of time, effort, and negotiations. Regardless of how it is accomplished, it is evident that there is a need for some standard for environmental reporting to allow for comparison and reliability. CERES has set out to overcome these issues through its proactive work on environmental reporting.

Environmental Reporting at CERES

The CERES Report was the first standardized corporate environmental report format, created with the collaboration of *Fortune* 500 companies, progressive smaller companies, institutional investors, and many of the nation's largest environmental organizations. The report is designed to stimulate change for the companies that use it. For example, using the CERES Report allows a company to track its own progress and performance and facilitate the establishment and adaptation of goals. Because the CERES Report is standardized and was developed with key stakeholder groups, it improves the public's trust in reported data and facilitates comparison with other companies. This standardization and comparison allows companies to receive worthwhile feedback, which is hard to obtain when using different reporting methods. Some company reports are linked to the CERES web site.

In order to accommodate differences in company characteristics and environmental concerns, the CERES Report is available in two formats. Companies with more than $25 million in revenues use the Standard Form, which was designed primarily for manufacturers, especially those that use chemicals, toxic substances, large quantities of resources, and complex production processes. The Short Form is intended for use by smaller and nonmanufacturing companies. Table C3.4 reproduces the table of contents of the Short Form CERES Report. Regardless of the form used, all companies are expected to provide information in the order requested, maintaining the original section titles, in order to preserve standardization. Requests for deviation from the original format or content are reviewed by the CERES Report Committee.

Once the CERES Report was launched, tested, and proven effective, the organization began to focus on companies and concerns around the world through its Global Reporting Initiative (GRI). Developed in 1997, GRI has a mission of establishing standardized corporate sustainability reporting throughout the world. This mission is to be implemented through the use of three tools, including a set of core measures applicable to all business enterprises, industry-specific measures customized to specific enterprises, and a uniform format for reporting these measures and related information regarding a firm's sustainability performance. The GRI is based on the CERES Principles, CERES Report forms, and ongoing relationships among CERES, other environmental initiatives, companies, nonprofit organizations, government agencies, and other stakeholders. The first draft of the GRI principles and process was released in 1999, and more than twenty companies

TABLE C3.4

CERES Report Table of Contents (Short Form)

from around the world agreed to enter the GRI pilot program. Such support is a necessary first step in creating the "first global, multistakeholder sustainability reporting initiative."

From its origins in the wake of the *Exxon Valdez* disaster to its leadership role in environmental reporting, CERES is dedicated to increasing corporate environmental responsibility. Despite its members' efforts and sincere initiatives in the business community, corporate practices continue to generate environmental concerns. For example, the U.S. government recently made an example of Royal Caribbean Cruises, by fining it $27 million for illegally dumping oily bilge, dry-cleaning fluid, and photo-developing chemicals into various waters in the late 1990s. Such cases highlight the importance of CERES's efforts to promote corporate environmental responsibility and to serve as a catalyst for continuous improvement toward environmental objectives.

DISCUSSION QUESTIONS

1. In your opinion, would CERES exist today if the *Exxon Valdez* wreck had not occurred? Why or why not? What value does CERES add in the current business environment?

2. What do the ten CERES Principles have in common with the seven steps to the Federal Sentencing Guidelines for Organizations discussed in Chapter 4? How are they different?

3. Visit CERES's web site (http://www.ceres.org) and compare and contrast the two formats for the CERES Report. Why did CERES create two formats?

4. Visit the Global Reporting Initiative web site (http://www.globalreporting.org) and review the progress of the initial pilot program. What successes have been reported? What areas need additional improvement or refinement before the GRI is ready to be launched?

REFERENCES   These facts are from Ronald Alsop, "Corporate Reputations Are Earned with Trust, Reliability, Study Shows," *Wall Street Journal,* September 23, 1999, http://interactive.wsj.com; John Byrne Barry, "Making Corporations Accountable," *The Planet,* 5 (July/August 1998); S. Douglas Beets, "Corporate Environmental Reports: The Need for Standards and an Environmental Assurance Service," *Accounting Horizons,* 13 (June 1999): 129–145; Coalition for Environmentally Responsible Economies, http://www.ceres.org/, accessed November 8, 2001; "Environmentalism Isn't a Fad Issue—Bill Ford," *Automotive News,* September 28, 1998, p. 3; O. C. Ferrell, John Fraedrich, and Gwyneth Vaughn, "The Wreck of the Exxon Valdez," in *Business Ethics: Ethical Decision Making and Cases,* 5th ed. O. C. Ferrell, John P. Fraedrich, and Linda Ferrell (Boston, Mass.: Houghton Mifflin, 2002), pp. 331–339; Kevin Graham and Gary Chandler, "Companies Go Green as Environmental Coalition Gains Influence," *Denver Rocky Mountain News,* March 15, 1995, p. 36A; Michael E. Knell, "Polaroid Endorses CERES Principles," *Boston Herald,* August 20, 1994, Finance section, p. 18; Dinah Koehler and Maximilian Change, "Search and Disclosure: Corporate Environmental Reports,"

Environment, 41 (March 1999): 3; "One Big Problem—Save the Waves," *Fast Company,* March 2000, p. 188; Jeff Pelline, "GM Jumping Aboard Environmental Movement," *San Francisco Chronicle,* February 2, 1994, Business section, p. B2; Forest L. Reinhardt, "Bringing the Environment Down to Earth," *Harvard Business Review,* 77 (July/August 1999); Royal Dutch/Shell Group of Companies, *How Do We Stand? The Shell Report 2000,* www.shell.com/downloads/publications/50710.pdf accessed November 8, 2001; Kara Sissell, "CERES Proposed Standards," *Chemical Week,* March 10, 1999, p. 36; Cynthia Unger, "Environmental Corporate Reporting: Do We Really Need a New Standard?" *Total Quality Environmental Management,* Autumn 1995, pp. 77–82; "Common Sense Initiative," United States Environmental Protection Agency, www.epa.gov/commonsense/index.htm, accessed December 14, 2000; Sandra W. Vandermerwe and Michael Oliff, "Corporate Challenges for an Age of Reconsumption," *Columbia Journal of World Business,* 26, no. 3 (1999): 6–25; Noah Walley and Bradley Whitehead, "It's Not Easy Being Green," *Harvard Business Review,* 72 (May-June 1994); Marina v.N. Whitman, *New World, New Rules,* (Boston, Mass.: Harvard Business School Press, 1999).

Managing the *E. coli* Crisis at Jack in the Box

This case was prepared by Robert R. Ulmer and Timothy L. Sellnow for classroom discussion, rather than to illustrate either effective or ineffective handling of an administrative, ethical, or legal decision by individuals or management.

On January 13, 1993, the Washington State Health Department was alerted that doctors at Children's Hospital in Seattle were treating an unusually high number of children with *E. coli* 0157:H7 infections. *E. coli* is a type of bacteria found in ground beef that can be life threatening to children and the elderly if it is not destroyed through sufficient cooking. Newspapers and television media soon carried shocking headlines that children were becoming ill after eating hamburgers at Jack in the Box. The *New York Times* described the crisis as Jack in the Box's worst nightmare. Within a month, three children in the Seattle area died of complications associated with *E. coli* poisoning. Overall, 400 people were infected in Washington, Idaho, and Nevada. Although Jack in the Box eventually recovered from the crisis, it suffered severe financial losses and a tarnished corporate image. Studying the company's handling of the situation provides an enlightening opportunity to observe the role of corporate responsibility in crisis management.

▶ A Crisis at Jack in the Box

Robert Nugent, president of Jack in the Box, learned of the crisis on January 17, 1993, and immediately sent an executive team from company headquarters in San Diego to Seattle to collect information. At this time, there was great uncertainty surrounding the details of the situation. On January 22, after investigations by various national and regional government agencies, Jack in the Box was identified as responsible for the *E. coli*-related illnesses. This revelation immediately thrust the company into the national media spotlight, and both internal and external stakeholders demanded to know how such a thing could have happened and what the company planned to do to ensure the future safety of its products.

The situation continued to deteriorate. Less than a month after Robert Nugent learned about the illnesses, one child, Michael Nole, died as a result of the *E. coli* bacteria. Nole's death, the first of three associated with Jack in the Box crisis, sent the company into a tailspin. By February 6, shares of Foodmaker, Jack in the Box's parent company, plummeted, and the Securities and Exchange Commission suspended trading of the stock for a short period of time. In addition, Jack in the Box took down promotions for its hamburgers and replaced 28,000 pounds of hamburger patties with new meat. Over the course of the crisis, Jack in the Box used a variety of communication strategies to move the crisis toward resolution.

On February 5, 1993, Robert Nugent addressed the situation before the U.S. Senate Subcommittee on Agricultural Research, Forestry, Conservation, and General Legislation. He began by explaining that he was "shocked and horrified" that such a crisis could happen at his company. However, he quickly focused his attention on absolving Jack in the Box from culpability by accentuating the uncertainty surrounding the crisis. This stance involved the argument that some of the illnesses were not directly related to Jack in the Box. Nugent explained:

> Although it is unclear as to the source of an illness linked to undercooked beef, Jack in the Box announced today that it has taken measures to ensure all menu items are prepared in accordance with an advisory issued yesterday by the Washington State Department of Health.

This statement cast doubt on Jack in the Box as the sole contributor of the crisis and focused some of the blame outside the company. It is important to note that cross contamination at day care centers or on local playgrounds is common with bacteria such as *E. coli*. Jack in the Box referred to this in an early press release, suggesting that "health officials have said that many of the cases [of *E. coli* poisoning] in Washington have not been linked to Jack in the Box." As a result, Nugent focused stakeholder attention on the possibility that some of the children who became ill at Jack in the Box restaurants may have unwittingly spread the bacteria through physical contact with other children, thereby broadening the effects of the crisis.

A second fundamental strategy employed by Jack in the Box after the crisis was communication regarding compensation. Initially, Robert Nugent pledged "to do everything that is morally right for those individuals who had experienced illness after eating at Jack in the Box restaurants as well as their families." In addition, Nugent contributed $100,000 to the Lois Joy Galler Foundation, an organization that focuses on studying the form of kidney failure associated with children afflicted with *E. coli* infections. Nugent also explained that Jack in the Box would "pay hospital costs for people who became ill during the *E. coli* crisis, regardless of whether or not they intended to take legal action against" the company. However, the company also continued to focus on the uncertainty of the crisis. Nugent specified:

> Future actions will be evaluated on a case by case basis to determine whether hospitalization resulted from the current situation at Jack in the Box or is simply one of the nearly 200 cases of *E. coli* that occur every year in Washington alone unrelated to our restaurants.

As a result, Jack in the Box was able to explain how it would compensate victims yet also worked to focus on reducing its level of responsibility for the crisis.

A third communication strategy adopted by Jack in the Box was to bolster its adherence to state and national cooking standards. Because varying levels of *E. coli* are found in all ground beef, it is important to abide by adequate cooking standards to ensure the product is safe. Before Jack in the Box was able to conduct an internal communication audit of its organization, Robert Nugent suggested that his company was in compliance with all federal, state, and local regulations, which could be verified by numerous evaluations. If this was true, and Jack in the Box followed all appropriate standards, Nugent could cast doubt on whether local, state, and federal guidelines were sufficient to avoid this type of *E. coli* 0157:H7 contamination.

However, this strategy focused considerable stress and negative media attention on external stakeholders, including meat supplier Von's, as well as federal meat inspection standards. Nugent, in his address to the Senate Subcommittee, explained that he thought the meat coming from his supplier, Von's, was fit for consumption. He explained in one press release:

> Up to this point we have been reluctant to say that the source of the problem was contaminated meat, simply because we did not want to speculate until the test results were in. We have been told that the State will be issuing a press release later today with specific results. However, we believe, based upon information from the State, that the problem is in fact due to contaminated hamburger.

Indeed, this rhetorical strategy directed attention away from Jack in the Box and onto issues with its meat supplier's product and federal meat inspection standards.

Roughly a month after the crisis began, however, Jack in the Box was forced to backtrack from this strategy. At this time, Robert Nugent informed the public that Jack in the Box, after conducting an internal communication audit, had determined that it had not been cooking its hamburgers to new Washington state standards. In defense of this failure, Jack in the Box insisted that the new standards had not been communicated to appropriate individuals within the company. Nugent explained this to internal and external stakeholders in a press release:

> A search of our files revealed that in May 1992, a bulletin from the Bremerton-Kitsap County Health Department was received in our corporate headquarters. This bulletin contained information about the new state standard.

> In September 1992, a restaurant in Tacoma received a copy of the regulation in the mail. The restaurant found the copy in their files as a result of this internal investigation. These items were not previously brought to the attention of appropriate management.

As a result, Nugent explained that the company was taking extensive steps to ensure that this would not happen again. He elaborated:

> We have established a new communication system between our corporate headquarters and every county and local health department in the areas where we have restaurants.

> All written regulations are on file and being made known to appropriate field operatives.

> We have created a computer database with key regulatory information pertinent to our operations.

> Responsibility has been assigned to a corporate Technical Services Manager to document all regulatory changes that affect Jack in the Box operations. We are requiring follow-up documentation to verify that preparation procedures impacted by any new regulations are correctly modified.

As discussed, Jack in the Box made considerable improvements to its stakeholder communication networks to ensure that a crisis like this could not happen again. At this time, the company was forced to take responsibility for the crisis. However, Jack in the Box's earlier criticisms of Von's subjected the supplier to considerable damage to its reputation. In addition, the U.S. meat inspection standards came under widespread media criticism. After the crisis, regulations were tightened and attention regarding cooking standards for beef products peaked on the political and public agendas.

▶ *The Aftermath*

In the aftermath of the crisis, Jack in the Box's recovery was somewhat slow. In April 1993, four months after the crisis began, Jack in the Box announced that its national sales averages had improved to a negative 9.7 percent from a negative 37 percent ten weeks prior, in comparison with sales figures from the year before.

Jack in the Box later reported a net loss of $44.1 million for 1993. Additionally, the company faced numerous lawsuits from both customers and franchisees.

Three factors facilitated Jack in the Box's overall recovery. First, the company expanded its menu, moving away from serving primarily beef products to include a new line of poultry products. In addition, Jack in the Box launched a new marketing campaign starring "Jack," the company's fictitious founder, as the new brand image for the company. Finally, Jack in the Box gained from the resources of its parent company, Foodmaker, during its recovery. Foodmaker was able to temper some of the financial woes of the crisis with earnings from other businesses that it owned. These three components worked in the company's favor in moving beyond the crisis. By 2000, Jack in the Box's net earnings were $100.3 million, up considerably from the $44 million loss in 1993. In early 1999, Foodmaker's name was changed formally to Jack in the Box, Inc.

Since the crisis, Jack in the Box has worked to resolve litigation and improve relations with its stakeholders. By early 1998, the company had paid $44.5 million to franchisees and $8 million to shareholders that lost revenue as a result of the crisis. Jack in the Box faced nearly 100 lawsuits on behalf of customers who became ill after eating its products. Compensation generally ranged from $19,000 to $15.6 million, although some settlement awards were not disclosed. In addition, Jack in the Box sued nine beef suppliers for their role in the crisis and received $58.5 million in settlement from those companies. This litigation continues because the beef suppliers filed a countersuit, arguing that Jack in the Box employees had failed to cook the beef adequately. It appears that this legal wrangling will continue for some time. Robert Nugent remains the president and CEO of Jack in the Box, Inc.

DISCUSSION QUESTIONS

1. Would you characterize Robert Nugent's crisis response as exemplifying corporate responsibility to his stakeholders? What criteria would you select in making this determination?
2. How do you think the context of the crisis affected Nugent's ability to respond to the *E. coli* problem? What makes responding to such events so challenging? What advice would you give to managers who find themselves in a similar situation?
3. What is the role of corporate responsibility in responding to organizational crises? Does responsible crisis communication equate to effective crisis management?

REFERENCES

These facts are from Andrea Adelson, "Jack in the Box Franchisees Cite Parent Concern in Suit," *New York Times,* July 9, 1993, p. D3; Lawrence Altman, "Studying the Puzzle of Tainted Hamburgers; One Measure of the Seriousness Was the Number of Victims," *New York Times,* February 9, 1993, p. C3; "End of Chapter 1 in Food Poisoning; Hospital

Releases Girl, 10, in Jack in the Box Case as 40 Suits Are Pending," *New York Times,* July 1, 1993, p. A14; "Foodmaker Crisis Ads," *Wall Street Journal,* January 28, 1993, p. A3; "Foodmaker Posts Loss for Third Quarter, Reflecting Big Charge to Settle Lawsuit," *Wall Street Journal,* August 11, 1993, p. B4; "Foodmaker Sees Loss for Fiscal 2nd Period Related to Illnesses," *Wall Street Journal,* March 25, 1993, p. B4; Frank Green, "Foodmaker, Suppliers Settle *E. coli* Claims; Von's, Others Will Pay S.D. Firm $58.5 Million," *San Diego Union-Tribune,* February 25, 1998, p. C1; Ronald Grover, with Dori Jones Yang and Laura Holson, "Boxed in at Jack in the Box," *Business Week,* February 15, 1993, p. 40; Benjamin Holden, "State Says Chain Involved in Outbreak Didn't Comply with New Cooking Rule," *Wall Street Journal,* January 25, 1993, p. B6; *Jack in the Box Annual Report 2000,* available at www.jackinthebox.com; "Jack in the Box's Worst Nightmare," *New York Times,* February 6, 1993, p. A35; Robert Nugent, Remarks before the United States Senate Subcommittee on Agricultural Research, Forestry, Conservation, and General Legislation (available from Jack in the Box Inc., U.S.A., San Diego, California, 1993); "Second Child Dies in Bacterial Outbreak," *New York Times,* January 29, 1993, p. A10; "3d Child Dies of Illness Linked to Tainted Meat," *New York Times,* February 22, 1993, p. A11; Catherine Yang, with Amy Barrett, "In a Stew over Tainted Meat: After a Second Scare, the Feds May Toughen Inspection Standards," *Business Week,* April 12, 1993, p. 37.

Stakeholder Relationships After the Texas A&M University Bonfire Collapse

This case was prepared by Maureen E. Wilson for classroom discussion, rather than to illustrate either effective or ineffective handling of an administrative, ethical, or legal decision by individuals or the university.

Texas A&M University (TAMU), founded in 1876, is deeply rooted in tradition, and its students are well known for their intense "Aggie Spirit." Located in College Station, Texas, the university enrolls more than 43,000 students. In November 1999, preparations for the annual football game against University of Texas (UT) were in full swing. As usual, Bonfire, an annual event that symbolizes the Aggies' "burning desire" to beat their arch rival, was the center of attention. The Bonfire tradition began in the 1920s as a pile of wood and trash, and over the years it grew to immense proportions, reaching 109 feet tall in 1969 before campus regulations set in the late 1970s limited the height to which it could be built. About 40,000 to 50,000 people attended the burning of the Bonfire every year, and many more watched the event on television.

Bonfire was a student-run operation, with about 5,000 students involved in planning, organizing, training, fund-raising, supervision, and construction each year. Student leaders, known as "Red Pots" for the color of their hard hats, coordinated Bonfire and oversaw safety at the site. Each structure required nearly two months to build, and planning began early in the spring semester. Students worked with a landowner to obtain the trees and then helped cut and transport them to campus. Some students worked directly on the stack of logs, whereas others served in support roles, such as providing food, water, and first aid.

▶ **The Collapse of the 1999 Bonfire**

Around 2:30 A.M. on November 18, just one week before Bonfire would have been set alight on Thanksgiving Day, tragedy struck. In a matter of seconds, the enormous stack of eighteen-foot logs, weighing more than a million pounds, began to collapse, and, as it was designed to do when burned, fell into itself. Many who had been working on the stack were trapped inside the collapsed structure of logs. As campus officials, including members of the university's Critical Incident Response Team (CIRT), arrived at the site, at least two deaths and numerous injuries were apparent. The number of students working on the stack when it collapsed was still unknown, as was the number of missing persons. Given the magnitude of the accident and the difficulty of disassembling the structure, it took more than seven hours to confirm the list of unaccounted-for students and to notify their parents. The last victim was located twenty-four hours after the collapse. In the end, twelve Aggies died—eleven students plus one alumnus—and twenty-seven were injured.

▶ **Immediate Response**

Members of the university's CIRT arrived at the accident site within 30 minutes. CIRT was established to respond to critical incidents involving students and to serve as a university contact. Among the goals of CIRT are to coordinate the university's response to critical incidents and to offer support and counseling to members of the university community and their families. Members of CIRT, which include representatives from a wide variety of campus departments and programs including Athletics, the Corp of Cadets, the Provost's Office, Residence Life, Security and University Police, TAMU Federation of Aggie Mothers' Clubs, University Relations, and the Vice President for Student Affairs, participate in training at least once a year. Given the magnitude and implications of the Bonfire collapse, nearly every campus office became involved in the response. The Corp of Cadets, for example, is traditionally heavily involved in Bonfire, and some cadets died in the collapse; the Provost was involved in the decision to cancel classes a day early for the Thanksgiving break in the week following the accident; and Residence Life staff was busy responding to campus residents affected by the events.

Word of the accident spread quickly, and many people, including the national media, began arriving at the accident site. Coordinated by CIRT, the immediate response to the accident was swift and complex. University staff members were dispatched to local hospitals where injured students had been taken and family members and friends had begun to gather. A private room for family members of those missing, injured, or killed was set up in the campus Student Center, which was also the location of the information center. A "command post" was set up in the office of the Vice President for Student Affairs. A memorial service was held that evening.

Important issues regarding communication, media, families, and counseling were addressed by CIRT. A toll-free phone number for inquiries was put in place, although phone and cellular services were overloaded by the volume of calls. The university granted all media requests (offering alternative interviews if the requested person was unavailable) and gave frequent press briefings to the media to provide facts on the investigation and information on students, funerals, and memorial services.

Other follow-up responses included ongoing communication with students and families, provision of counseling services, and fund-raising. Two funds were established from the contributions that poured into the university after the disaster. One, managed by the Association of Former Students, assisted families with expenses incurred as a result of the accident. The second, managed by the Texas A&M Foundation, funded a permanent memorial to those who died. Additionally, representatives of the university attended each funeral service, and the university provided free transportation (buses, vans, chartered plane flights) for students and administrators wishing to go.

History and Investigation

The logs for Bonfire, which came from land that needed to be cleared, were donated to A&M. A completed Bonfire could weigh more than two million pounds—about the same as two 747 jumbo jets. Students were in charge of the engineering and construction of Bonfire, and historically, the university's involvement in the design and construction of the structure had been limited. Although restrictions were placed on the height and diameter of Bonfire, they were not well communicated or enforced. When the 1999 Bonfire collapsed, it stood 59 feet tall—4 feet over the university-imposed limit—and there were two more layers of logs to be added to the stack. In all, the 1999 Bonfire was to burn 7,000 logs.

A week after the collapse, university president Ray Bowen appointed an Independent Special Commission on the 1999 Texas A&M Bonfire to determine the cause of the collapse. The commission was headed by Leo Linbeck, Jr., the chairman of a Houston-based construction company and not an alumnus of A&M. Linbeck hired five companies outside of Texas to investigate various aspects of the accident. The commission met for the first time on December 3, 1999, just two weeks after the collapse, and began to evaluate the historical design of Bonfire and analyze physical and behavioral factors in the collapse. The commission's final report, issued on May 2, 2000, determined that "wedging, vertical log orientation, overbuilding, and ground slope combined to reduce hoop stress, while weak wiring and lack of wrap-around cables combined to reduce hoop strength. The combination of these caused the Bonfire collapse." However, a behavioral analysis found other contributing factors.

Investigators for the commission examined three major controls or barriers designed to prevent problems and encourage safe and reliable procedures:

1. *Individual human performance barriers*, including adequate skills, knowledge, and good judgment

2. *Effective programmatic barriers*, including adequate levels of procedural guidance and methods to identify and resolve problems

3. *Strong organizational and management barriers*, including effective risk identification and management and adequate management and supervisory actions.

Although a system of multiple barriers can help prevent serious problems, multiple failures of those barriers can result in catastrophe, as happened at Bonfire.

Although these three control barriers were not directly responsible for the collapse, the commission examined them to identify failures that were relevant to the accident. Four subbarrier failures were determined to be relevant. First, student skills and knowledge—an individual barrier—were found to be inadequate for an engineering project of the magnitude of Bonfire. Over the years, student leaders had made important design decisions without a clear understanding of the impact of those decisions on the structural integrity of Bonfire. Second, with regard to programmatic barriers, there were no formal written design and construction plans for the structure. Third and fourth, with regard to organizational barriers, an active risk management plan was lacking and cultural bias impeded risk identification. Specific problems led to specific actions instead of comprehensive action to address a larger problem. For instance, excessive injuries led to training programs, and excessive drinking resulted in alcohol awareness programs, but a combination of problems was not considered collectively and did not trigger a broad, overall re-examination of Bonfire. "This tunnel vision in decision making is due, in the Commission's view, to a cultural bias in which legitimate courses of action outside past experience or contrary to the University's predisposition are often not considered." The report concluded, "The collapse was about physical failures driven by organizational failures, the origins of which span decades of administrations, faculty, and students. No single factor caused the collapse, just as no single change will ensure that a tragedy like this never happens again."

▶ *Tradition and Culture*

Long-standing traditions are an integral part of the culture of Texas A&M University. There is a saying at A&M that speaks to that culture: "From the outside looking in, you can't understand it. From the inside looking out, you can't explain it."

Although not everyone agrees on the future of Bonfire, some of the students who survived their injuries expect it to continue, and parents of some of those who died support its continuance. The father of one student who died is passionate in his belief that it should continue. If it ends, he believes his son's death would be senseless. The mother of another student contends that, more than just a big fire, Bonfire symbolizes the Aggie family. Some students and alumni have suggested that Bonfire might be moved off campus if the university cancels it; others warn that canceling the tradition might adversely affect alumni donations to the university.

Efforts to end the Bonfire tradition, some stemming from before the collapse, are unpopular. A large group of faculty has criticized Bonfire as "...a needless waste of natural resources, a symbol of a lack of concern for the environment and a very conspicuous source of embarrassment for this institution within the international community." One faculty member who has spoken out against Bonfire feels it is personally and professionally risky to do so. He has been told that the highway in town "runs both ways," implying that he should leave if he does not like it there. President Bowen and others stress that the Aggie Spirit is stronger than a single tradition and will exist throughout the life of the university.

▶ *Future of Bonfire*

Although the commission had the task of determining the cause of the collapse of Bonfire, President Bowen faced the decision of whether to continue the decades-old tradition. In the week following the tragedy, a memorial service was held in place of Bonfire, and A&M defeated rival Texas in front of the largest crowd ever to witness a football game in the state of Texas. After the commission's final report was issued, the president considered feedback from many stakeholders including parents of those killed or injured, commission members, faculty, students, the A&M Foundation, Aggie Moms, and alumni before announcing his decision.

After restructuring the Bonfire project to ensure safety, it will burn again in 2002, provided necessary changes in the design and construction planning can be completed by that time as expected. The new process includes more oversight by the university and increases safety by involving professionals in the log cutting and in the design and construction plans for Bonfire. In 2000, a student-planned memorial paid tribute to the students who died or were injured. In 2001, groundbreaking and dedication of a permanent memorial took place.

DISCUSSION QUESTIONS

1. How can the competing demands of various stakeholders (e.g., students, parents, alumni, faculty, staff, trustees, legislators, community members) be balanced effectively? What principles should guide decision making?

2. What is the role of tradition and culture in institutions and organizations? How should leaders balance those qualities with other considerations such as safety and change? What are the ethical dimensions of a situation like this? How should the university respond to a group attempting to organize an off-campus bonfire?

3. Should all organizations have a written crisis management plan in place? What elements would be most critical to include? What factors are most critical to effective crisis management?

REFERENCES   These facts are from "Aggie Bonfire Dumb as Dirt Homepage," http://conserve.tamu.edu/bonfire2.htm, accessed November 8, 2001; "Bonfire Commission Urges Media and Public to Provide Information," *Aggie Daily*, December 3, 1999, http://rev.tamu.edu/stories/99/120399-13.html; "Bonfire Decision Summary," *Aggie Daily*, June 16, 2000, www.tamu.edu/aggiedaily/press/ppt.html; "Bonfire Relief and Memorial Funds," www.msc.tamu.edu/traditions/bonfire/1999/funds.shtml, accessed November 8, 2001; Paul Burka, "The Aggie Bonfire Tragedy," *Texas Monthly*, 28 (April 2000): 116–123, 145–149; Roger Croteau, "Bonfire Opponents Face Scorn; Some Fearful of Retaliation for Taking Stance," *San Antonio Express-News*, November 21, 1999, p. 18A; Russell Gold, "Accident Revives Height Debate, *San Antonio Express-News*, November 21, 1999, pp. 1A, 17A; Dan McGraw, "Deaths Might Not End a Texas Tradition," *U.S. News & World Report*, March 27, 2000, p. 29; Maro Robbins, "Pride Heartens Injured Aggies; Seven Students Still in Hospital," *San Antonio Express-News*, November 21, 1999, p. 17A; "Special Commission on the 1999 Texas A&M Bonfire," Final Report, Texas A&M University, May 2, 2000, www.tamu.edu/bonfire-commission/; Malon Southerland, Bill Kibler, Jan Winniford, Wade Birch, Kevin Jackson, and Gene Zdziarski; "Texas A&M University Bonfire Tragedy: Handling Crisis Situations," presented at National Association of Student Personnel Administrators, March 2000, http://crisis.tamu.edu/resources/default.htm; "Critical Incident Response Team," Texas A&M University, 2000, http://crisis.tamu.edu/resources/default.htm; "Fact Sheet: Texas A&M University Traditions," Texas A&M University, February 1998, www.tamu.edu/univrel/sheets/trads.htm; John Wesley Lowery interview of Bill Kibler, "Bonfire Tragedy and Tradition," *About Campus*, 5 (July/August 2000): 20–25.

Ethics Officer Association: Educating and Supporting Ethics Officers

This case was prepared by Debbie Thorne McAlister and Kevin Sample for classroom discussion, rather than to illustrate either effective or ineffective handling of an administrative, ethical or legal decision by individuals or management. The research assistance of Jason De Los Santos is gratefully acknowledged.

"Six years ago, our entire membership could comfortably gather around a conference table. We had visions then of a global, cross-industry association of corporate ethics and compliance managers." These were the words of Edward S. Petry, executive director of the Ethics Officer Association (EOA) in 1998. The Massachusetts-based association has since grown to more than 740 members representing multiple and diverse industries, ranging from retail companies, insurers, manufacturers, public utilities, telecommunications groups, and software companies to nonprofit organizations. EOA members include companies such as General Motors, Bell Atlantic, Boeing, AmeriSteel, Comdisco, KeySpan Energy, Pall Corporation, Raytheon, United Airlines, and many more. The organization's reach is not limited to North America, as it has recently gained members from Belgium, China, Japan, and the United Kingdom. Thus, the EOA has established a focus on business ethics that spans industries, geographic regions, and organizations of all types and sizes.

When the EOA was formed in 1992, it crafted a mission statement that has guided the organization and its members ever since: "To promote ethical business practices and to serve as a forum for the exchange of information and strategies among individuals responsible for setting the ethics, compliance and business conduct programs in their organizations." The EOA is committed to educating and supporting the individuals who ensure their organizations are fulfilling legal and ethical responsibilities of corporate citizenship. Although economic and philanthropic issues cannot be easily separated from these responsibilities, the EOA has historically focused on the legal and ethical dimensions.

▶ *The Need for an Association of Ethics Officers*

The ethics officer position is relatively new. As recently as fifteen years ago, few organizations had ethics officers. Now, thanks to initiatives such as the Federal Sentencing Guidelines for Organizations, the Foreign Corrupt Practices Act, and the Defense Industry Initiative, these positions are sprouting up in companies throughout the world. Today, companies want to develop a reputation for credibility, honesty, and responsibility, and establishing an ethics officer is one component of this corporate citizenship strategy.

Throughout the 1980s, white-collar crime and other legal issues sparked public and government concern about corporate control and power. This decade prompted a formal focus on business ethics, where increased media attention and public scrutiny of companies has led to more ethics officers. However, many companies have created ethics officer positions because of a sincere focus on corporate citizenship, not any negative influences.

Companies usually create ethics offices because they want to fulfill their ethical obligations for corporate citizenship effectively. In committing to this new management responsibility, firms must consider an entire range of stakeholder issues, including the industry in which they are competing and how the public feels about their activities. By understanding internal and external stakeholder concerns, a company can evaluate its ethics position and develop the proper communication tools, guidance, and resources for employees and business partners to use in dealing with difficult ethical situations.

In the workplace, an ethics officer performs a number of tasks related to ethics and compliance. To ensure that corporate priorities on ethics and compliance are integrated throughout the organization, ethics officers interact with the different levels of management, employees, and even outside stakeholders, in order to monitor any changes in their respective organization and industries. Officers coordinate programs with top management about how to help create and instill a code of ethics and ethical corporate culture. Once a program is established, an officer will develop control systems to ensure that employees and organizational agents do not deviate from this code. Officers also work to continually refine the code in order to improve its effectiveness. An effective ethics officer also devotes time to training, communications, and continuous improvement of the program. These factors and expectations created the initial need and continuing demand for an association of ethics officers.

▶ *EOA Membership*

Membership in the Ethics Officer Association is limited to organizations with business ethics and compliance programs and to the managers of these initiatives. Although these individuals are generally known as "ethics officers," their actual titles may vary across organizations and corporations and include "director of corporate ethics," "vice president of ethics and compliance," "vice president of ethics and integrity," "vice president of business practices," and "chief compliance officer," among others. For these individuals and organizations, a key advantage of EOA membership is the educational focus that accompanies most of the EOA's activities. Members have an opportunity to be both teacher and student as they learn from each other about the different practices and solutions to ethical dilemmas and concerns. Thus, the EOA provides one of the few forums in which companies can share their concerns and successes in the ethics area. The U.S. government has indicated that such cooperation is lawful, as long as it does not set a low standard of conduct or evolve into collusion.

Through the EOA, members can discuss issues in a comfortable and professional environment and review policies, dilemmas, and strategies of shared concern. They also have the opportunity to network with other ethics professionals, attend annual conferences and workshops, and access the EOA's resources, such as its extensive ethics-related library and online discussion forum.

As with many organizations, members receive different benefits according to the type of membership they hold. The association offers two levels of membership: sponsoring partners and individual partners. Sponsoring partners join on an organizational level, which demonstrates a strong company interest in helping the EOA to promote ethical practices in the workplace. Individual members also play an important role in the association's activities. The EOA provides a range of programs and benefits targeted to the needs of specific types of members.

Sponsoring Partners Sponsoring, or organizational, partners take active roles as stakeholders, leaders, and guides in developing EOA's future structure and activities. These members work jointly with the EOA's board of directors, providing funds to the association, experience, knowledge of specific ethics areas or issues, and networking channels. The fee for Sponsoring Partners is $2,500 a year; any additional individuals from the sponsor's organization can join as Sponsoring Partner Associates for $150 annually. Sponsors can appoint any person within their organization to act as their representative in determining EOA's future direction.

Individual Members Professional business ethics practitioners can qualify for individual EOA membership. This membership fee is $650 a year. Despite the fact that individual members have to pay this fee out of their own funds or through company resources, they represent the EOA's largest member category.

EOA Member Statistics In order to better understand its individual members and what roles they perform in their organizations, the EOA conducted a survey in 1998. The results not only describe the characteristics of ethics officers, but also inform the EOA of member characteristics that may affect the development and delivery of its services. Based on survey results, the "average" EOA member is a white male, aged 49, with an undergraduate degree and a background in human resources or operations/administration. Figures C6.1, C6.2, C6.3, and C6.4 illustrate additional demographic information about EOA members, including gender, work background, employment status, and age.

▶ *EOA Services and Programs*

Based on an understanding of member characteristics and general trends in business ethics, the EOA develops services and programs to meet its mission and member needs. Among these services are the Sponsoring Partner Forum, ethics administration software, a corporate ethics and compliance library, the "Managing Ethics in Organizations" program, an annual conference and skill enhancement courses, online resources, and research conducted by the organization for the benefit of its members. Some of these offerings are dependent on member status, such as those programs reserved for the EOA's highest membership level, the Sponsoring Partner.

FIGURE C6.1

Prior Work Background of Ethics Officers

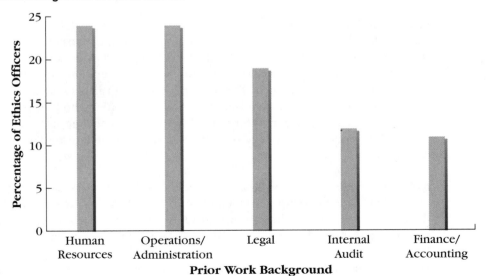

Source: Ethics Officer Association, "Executive Summary of EOA Membership Survey," www.eoa.org/resources/survey~1.pdf, accessed July 2, 2000. Reprinted by permission from Ethics Officer Association.

FIGURE C6.2

Employment Status of Ethics Officers

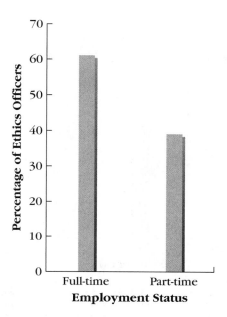

Source: Ethics Officer Association, "Executive Summary of EOA Membership Survey," www.eoa.org/resources/survey~1.pdf, accessed July 2, 2000. Reprinted by permission from Ethics Officer Association.

FIGURE C6.3

Gender of Ethics Officers

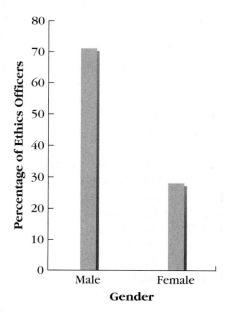

Source: Ethics Officer Association, "Executive Summary of EOA Membership Survey," www.eoa.org/resources/survey~1.pdf, accessed July 2, 2000. Reprinted by permission from Ethics Officer Association.

Ages of Ethics
Officers

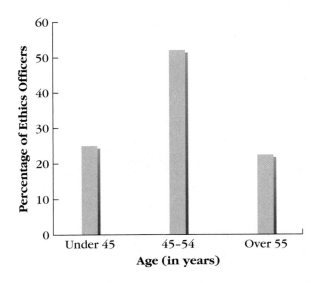

Source: Ethics Officer Association, "Executive Summary of EOA Membership Survey," www.eoa.org/
resources/survey~1.pdf, accessed July 2, 2000. Reprinted by permission from Ethics Officer Association.

Sponsoring Partner Forum   The Sponsoring Partner Forum is an annual conference for senior-level ethics officers that provides an open and trusting environment for sharing successes, reviewing problem areas, and generally improving
company ethics initiatives. Company representatives participate in workshops and
provide direction to the association by reviewing the status of its activities. In the
forum, ethics and compliance professionals are able to discuss openly ethical and
compliance-related issues that affect their organizations. These exclusive forums
enable members to have strong interaction and learning experiences, thus improving the effectiveness of the ethics officer and program.

Ethics Administration Software   One of the most significant benefits of being an
EOA member is the use of its Ethics Administration Software (EAS). The software
was created by Hughes Aircraft to assist ethics officers in collecting, reporting,
managing, and graphing data related to ethics allegations, human resources, and
inquiries. By using this program, an organization can avoid a significant investment
in time and resources for such software.

Corporate Ethics and Compliance Library   Another important benefit of being an
EOA member is the use of its extensive library on business ethics, compliance, and
"best practices." The library includes codes of conduct from member companies,
videos, and other communication tools that ethics officers use to relay ethics messages to employees.

"Managing Ethics in Organizations" Program   The "Managing Ethics in Organizations" program is a professional week-long development course offered in conjunction with the Center for Business Ethics at Bentley College. The course is intended for newly appointed ethics officers and others who are responsible for their organizations' ethics, compliance, or business conduct programs. The course offers new officers the knowledge, fundamental theories, and general skills needed for their position. Topics covered in past sessions have focused on setting up an ethics office, crisis management skills, ethics and the law, globalizing an ethics program, diversity, and many other topics. The faculty for these sessions includes experienced EOA ethics officers, consultants, and academics who are widely recognized leaders in their fields. The fee for nonmembers of the EOA is roughly $3,500; members and academics pay a reduced fee.

Annual Conference and Skill Enhancement Courses   The EOA also hosts an annual conference that is designed to explore business ethics and related subjects in more detail. These conferences draw ethics officers and other industry personnel for several days of learning and sharing on timely topics and issues. In addition, the association sponsors skill enhancement courses taught by ethics officers and subject-matter experts who provide hands-on experience on topics such as ethics and the law, ethical reasoning, assessing the ethical environment, among others.

Online Resources   Like most organizations today, the EOA has a web site for communicating with members and other stakeholders. The site contains most of the information that members need about the activities of the organization, upcoming events, online library, current newsletters, links to other members' web sites, and general information about the organization. The web site is updated regularly and allows for feedback and suggestions from members and guests of the site. JobLink is a free job search service housed on the web site that assists individuals in finding ethics-related job opportunities and companies in advertising and filling these positions.

Research   As part of its mission, the EOA conducts research on topics of interest to members. For example, two recent national studies—one on workplace pressure and ethics and one on new technologies and ethics—were conducted by the EOA and the American Society of Chartered Life Underwriters (CLU) and Chartered Financial Consultants (ChFC), now the Society of Financial Service Professionals. The association also conducts research on issues that are member specific, such as cutting-edge corporate training initiatives, reporting relationships to the ethics officer, and compensation for ethics officers. These studies are often released to the general public and serve as a vehicle for the EOA to communicate with many stakeholders. For example, results of EOA research have been published in *USA Today*, the *Wall Street Journal*, *Success*, *HRMagazine*, and other media outlets.

One example of EOA research is the "Workplace Pressure and Ethics" survey, which was conducted to determine whether workplace pressures increase the risk of unethical and illegal business practices, to uncover the sources contributing to these pressures, and to find ways that management can address concerns in this area. This survey generated widespread media attention and speculation as to its findings. According to the study, 48 percent of employees surveyed—almost half of all workers—have engaged in unethical or illegal activities because of job pressure. The study also reported that 58 percent of surveyed employees have at least considered acting unethically or illegally on the job. The most common types of unethical behavior reported were cutting corners on quality control (16 percent), covering up incidents (14 percent), abusing or lying about sick leave (11 percent), and lying to or deceiving customers (9 percent).

Stuart G. Tugman, Jr., president of the American Society of Chartered Life Underwriters & Chartered Financial Consultants, says, "The survey sends a serious message to the American business leaders, we are putting too much pressure on our economy's most valuable resource—our employees—and they are looking to us, the leadership of corporate America, to solve the problem." According to the study, the status of business ethics is not as bad as it seems, as 60 percent of the respondents believe that ethical quandaries can be avoided. "For years the term *business ethics* was considered an oxymoron, a contradiction in terms," says William T. Redgate, Emeritus member of the Ethics Officer Association. "The fact that American workers no longer see ethical dilemmas as unavoidable consequences of doing business means that there is a new era in business, an era in which a majority of workers believe that business and ethics can mix and that ethical dilemmas can be reduced."

The survey also asked how to reduce pressure that leads to unethical behavior, to which 73 percent of respondents suggested improved communications, whereas 71 percent said a greater commitment by senior management to reducing pressure. Of all the industries surveyed, the computer/software industry had the highest amount of unethical behavior, but employees in the manufacturing and health-care industries seem to face more pressure.

Another EOA research project, the "New Technologies and Ethics" study, focused on how the use of the Internet, e-mail, pagers, computers, voice mail, cell phones, and other technologies in the workplace have changed the way people interact with one another and whether they contribute to pressure that can lead to unethical or illegal business practices. With this survey, the EOA was on the cutting edge of issues affecting not only its members but also most organizations today. Among the results of the survey:

- 14 percent of respondents wrongly blamed an error at work on a technological glitch.

- 6 percent accessed private computer files without permission and intruded on coworkers' privacy.

- 13 percent copied the company's software for home use; this same percentage used office equipment to shop on the Internet for personal reasons; and 11 percent used office equipment to search for another job.

- 5 percent listened to a private cellular phone conversation; this same percentage visited pornographic sites using office equipment.

- 19 percent admitted having created a potentially dangerous situation by using new technology while driving.

Through the survey process, some company respondents provided suggestions for remedying these ethical dilemmas. For example, organizations should create guidelines that dictate personal use of resources, develop clear policies on personal use of technology, and encourage employees to police themselves. In addition, researchers suggested that companies install Internet blocking software and start a corporate training session on ethics and technology.

Future Issues for Ethics Officers and the EOA

The EOA has developed into a strong association with a growing and diverse membership. At the same time, business ethics has grown in prominence within organizations and moved to the forefront of media and public consideration. Concurrently, ethics officers have assumed roles of greater importance and responsibility in organizations. These trends have raised the question, "Should ethics officers strive for professional status?" As the EOA matures, its membership may consider a step toward professional certification or accreditation.

Professionals, those people who profess to be "duly qualified," vary greatly from job, trade, and knowledge worker types of employment. Job types refer to employment requiring lower skill levels. Trades require manual skill, are often unionized, and generally require an apprenticeship. Knowledge workers are specialized educated workers, such as scientists and computer programmers. Professionals are regulated, often state-licensed, knowledge workers, such as doctors, lawyers, and accountants.

Characteristics of Professionals   Several traits are associated with "professional" employees, including extensive intellectual training for a common body of knowledge, skills that are vital to society, and autonomy. Self-regulation, having privilege and prestige, and adhering to a code of ethics are also traits of professionals. These employees use their professional status for economic gain, and in the past, they have been accused of using their status for high pay. Although self-regulation through a code of conduct and licensing procedures helps to enforce competency and ethical standards, critics have charged that self-regulation is also an attempt to avoid government regulation. However, professionals agree to service for the well-being of the public and to promote public welfare, even at their own expense.

Origin and Process   Professions arose through medicine, law, and the clergy in England, and they gained status through their own organization and self-regulation. These professions set an example that motivated other occupations to follow suit. The process of becoming a professional is normally completed through four steps. The first step is to develop one's skills and interests in that area. The second step of this socialization process involves acquisition of a certain set of beliefs and philosophies regarding the field. The third step is an internalization of motives, which involves an examination of career options. The fourth and final step is a sponsorship, which involves a commitment to uphold the values of the profession. This is the step of becoming a professional and holding an occupation that entails both the rights and responsibilities of a select group.

Prospects for Ethics Officers   As discussed previously, ethics officers' training and employment experiences are varied. A portion of them has already attained professional status by virtue of training and certification in legal, accounting, auditing, and other areas. However, there are a number of ethics officers who have not been previously employed in a true profession. On the positive side, professions are bound by strict ethical standards, continuing education and development requirements, and core competencies that streamline and control members' activities. Through a professionalization process, ethics officers could potentially make their claims to positions of higher status and authority within organizations and society. However, this process is lengthy and would require a great deal of commitment and resources in order to develop and work effectively. For example, the EOA would need to develop a member code of ethics, a set of core literature and skills, and mechanisms for ensuring competency and adherence to professional standards.

▶ Conclusion

The Ethics Officer Association is a service to the organizations with which it works and also indirectly to other stakeholders with an interest in business ethics and related areas. Although the EOA was primarily established to assist ethics officers, it is also proactive in examining the status of ethics in the workplace and advocating for an increased focus in the area. The EOA is one of the organizations that is making a difference in the move toward strategic corporate citizenship. The association has been "debunking myths" about business ethics being an oxymoron and breaking down the belief that employees can choose whether or not to be ethical, but that the organization cannot have ethics. It is organizations like the EOA, along with university ethics centers and other groups, that make employers more aware of their corporate citizenship.

The EOA helps companies grasp why it is necessary to understand and practice ethics, not simply for their own benefit, but for the countless number of organizations and people with whom they interact every day. As recently stated in an annual report, the Ethics Officer Association is dedicated to being responsive, collaborative, and visionary, and so far, it has done the job, day after day, of bringing its mission to life. As the ethics officer position matures and becomes more integrated and global, the EOA will continue to tailor its programs and research to meet the interests of members and stakeholders. Perhaps one future initiative will consider the prospects for professional status.

DISCUSSION QUESTIONS

1. What are the benefits and drawbacks to organizations sharing their experiences on ethics and compliance with other members of the EOA?
2. Do you think the Ethics Officer Association should develop an initiative to attain professional status for ethics officers? Why or why? What effects would your perspective have on trends in corporate citizenship?
3. Compare the roles and responsibilities of ethics officers to other employees, including managers of marketing, accounting, legal, and human resources areas. Where does ethics officers' work overlap with each manager's traditional responsibilities? How can these functional areas assist in developing and implementing effective ethics programs?

REFERENCES

These facts are from Stephen A. Banning, "The Professionalization of Journalism," *Journalism History,* 24 (Winter 1998/1999): 157–164; Dawn-Marie Driscoll, W. Michael Hoffman, and Edward S. Petry, The Ethical Edge: *Tales of Organizations That Have Faced Moral Crises* (New York: MasterMedia, 1995); "Ethics: A New Profession in American Business," *HR Focus,* 70 (May 1993): 22; The Ethics Center, www.taknosys.com/ethics/, accessed July 3, 2000; Ethics Officer Association, www.eoa.org/, accessed November 8, 2001; Leslie S. Laffie, "Tax Technology," *Tax Adviser,* 29 (July 1998): 441; Debbie Thorne LeClair, O. C. Ferrell, and John P. Fraedrich, *Integrity Management: A Guide to Managing Legal and Ethical Issues in the Workplace* (Tampa, Fl.: The University of Tampa Press, 1998); Debbie Thorne LeClair and Panos Troupis, *Ethics and Compliance Officer Study* (Tampa, Fl.: Center for Ethics, The University of Tampa, 1997); Elaine McShulskis, "Job Stress Can Prompt Unethical Behavior," *Society for Human Resource Management Magazine,* 7 (July 1997): 22; Edward Petry, "Appointing an Ethics Officer," *Healthcare Executive,* 13 (November/December 1998): 35; Edward S. Petry, Jr., and Fred Tietz, "Can Ethics Officers Improve Office Ethics?" *Business and Society Review,* 82 (Summer 1992): 21–25; Cheryl J. Polson, "Fostering Graduate Socialization Into Adult Education," *Adult Learning,* 10 (Winter 1998/1999): 23–27.

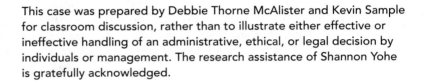

Banking on Values at Wainwright Bank & Trust

This case was prepared by Debbie Thorne McAlister and Kevin Sample for classroom discussion, rather than to illustrate either effective or ineffective handling of an administrative, ethical, or legal decision by individuals or management. The research assistance of Shannon Yohe is gratefully acknowledged.

Wainwright Bank & Trust Company, founded in Boston, Massachusetts, in 1987, is a $300 million commercial bank that is known for its progressive social agenda. During its brief history, the bank has not only demonstrated sound financial standing, earnings, and security, but also, under the guidance of President Jan Miller, has become a leader in socially responsible community development. Examples of Wainwright's community commitment include the financing of more than 50 percent of Boston-area housing projects for people living with AIDS as well as the creation of more than 500 affordable housing units in Boston and Cambridge. The bank also donates significant funds to many charities, including the Boston Foundation. Wainwright Bank is deeply involved and committed to its role as a good corporate citizen, working to build relationships across its community in an effort to uphold a practice of "banking on values." Wainwright's corporate citizenship is integral to daily and strategic decisions, resulting in a collaborative focus on social and financial objectives.

The mission statement of Wainwright Bank reads, "With a sense of inclusion and diversity that extends from the boardroom to the mailroom, Wainwright Bank & Trust Company resolves to be a leading socially responsible bank. The Bank is equally committed to all its stakeholders—employees, customers, communities and shareholders." From this mission statement, the bank employs the "banking on values" slogan on its web site and other communication media. Wainwright's business purpose stands in contrast to that of many other companies, including banks. Bank of America's vision, for example, is to provide "a consistent and exceptional banking experience to all our clients and customers throughout the world."

▶ *Current Trends in the Traditional Banking Industry*

Banks have traditionally been viewed as very conservative institutions. Their primary role has been to provide checking, savings, loans, and related financial services. Bank managers and executives consisted primarily of white males, and their institutions' missions typically focused more on money issues than the community. Although many traditional banks have attempted to evoke a community and neighborly image, few have gone out of their way to truly serve the community or help their neighborhoods. This trend of promoting the community without really helping is beginning to change, however. For example, U.S. Bank of Pennsylvania won a grant from the Community Development Financial Institution Bank Enterprise Award Program for its community efforts in 1999. This grant is awarded to the institution that most exemplifies a strong commitment to expanding traditional financial institution services to underserved markets.

Other trends are also changing the face of traditional banking. For example, technology and information systems have altered some aspects of customer interaction. Although the larger banks are scrambling to gain a foothold on the World Wide Web, some are focusing less on their community feel. In response to this strategic shift, smaller and new independent banks looking for a competitive edge have focused even more on their "neighborliness." However, the surge of Internet banks has also reminded the big banks that they need to retain a friendly community atmosphere. Although many banks are now promoting their neighborhood or community orientation, few have quite mastered it yet.

Another significant trend in the banking industry is consolidation. Many large banks merged with or acquired competitors in the late 1990s and early 2000s. While bank employees focus on completing these mergers and combining facilities, systems, and methods into one business, some consumer advocates warn that higher banking fees, job losses, and a potential lack of customer focus will result from this trend. For example, after Bank of America acquired 342 NationsBank branches in Texas in 1999, managers were involved in decisions related to changing bank colors, logos, and slogans, as well as which of several branches would be closed at a later date. The company's announcement that it would cut 8,000 jobs left many employees in limbo, worrying about whether their jobs or branches would be among those eliminated. Bank executives also deliberated whether to raise the fees NationsBank customers were paying and dealt with consolidating a multitude of systems. Bank of America plans to continue its community involvement, even in the newly acquired branches, by investing in low-income communities.

Although Wainwright Bank & Trust provides the same financial services as other banking firms, it breaks sharply from the traditional banking mold with its progressive agenda and focus on nontraditional markets. Of course, Wainwright is but one example of institutions around the world that have chosen a nontraditional market position. Citizens Bank of Canada is another example of an institution that looks beyond the monetary aspects of banking. This Canadian firm has a policy of investing in and doing business only with companies that treat animals humanely, have strong employee relations, do not trade or manufacture weapons, do not significantly profit from tobacco products, and do not harm the environment.

▶ *Wainwright Bank in Action*

Wainwright Bank has been designated a Community Development Financial Institution (CDFI), which indicates that it makes loans and other investments in low-income communities. To support its community development initiatives, Wainwright has chosen to focus on several areas, including homelessness, affordable housing, health-care services, diversity, and the natural environment.

Homelessness and Hunger   The founders of Wainwright believe that the health of society can be judged by how its members provide for the well-being of those most often discriminated against, including those lacking income, housing, and food. Since 1991, the bank has provided more than $15 million in loans to nationally recognized service providers for the homeless and the hungry, including the Pine Street Inn, The Greater Boston Food Bank, and the Committee to End Elder Homelessness. The Greater Boston Food Bank helps to feed 465,000 a month—72 percent of those in need in the nine counties of eastern Massachusetts. Lawrence D. Lowenthal, the executive director of the American Jewish Committee, says, "I think it is admirable that a bank would devote important resources to the needs of disadvantaged people, and I personally applaud [Wainwright's] enlightened policy."

Affordable and Special-Needs Housing   Wainwright executives believe that there is a great need for safe, clean, affordable rental housing in the inner city, not only for low-income residents but also for those who are often discriminated against, such as the homeless, the elderly, and the mentally disabled. The bank has therefore committed $51 million in financing to many affordable housing projects in the Greater Boston area, including Cortes Street, Brookview House, Cambridge YMCA and YWCA, 270 Huntington Avenue, and Rockport School Elder Housing. Cortes Street was developed by Boston Aging Concerns Young & Old United to serve the needs of the low-income elderly, whereas Brookview House was established to provide housing for homeless women and children. Wainwright also issued a real estate loan to add a new wing to an existing building for forty-three single-room-occupancy units for homeless women and provided construction financing to create thirty-one units of low-income housing for the elderly at Rockport School Elder Housing. Wainwright has also provided financing for Pine Street Inn shelters for the homeless throughout Boston.

AIDS and Health Services   Labeling the HIV/AIDS crisis one of the "defining social issues of our times," Wainwright has committed more than $11 million to finance housing for individuals and families living with HIV/AIDS. This commitment covers 50 percent of these projects in the Greater Boston area. Larry Kessler, the executive director of AIDS Action Committee of Massachusetts, sums up the significance of Wainwright's efforts in this area: "If there was a Nobel Prize for business involvement in the needs of the community, Wainwright Bank would be up there as a top nominee. [Wainwright's] corporate and philanthropic support in the community is a bold act of leadership." The bank has also financed organizations involved in researching breast cancer and counseling addicts. A number of nonprofit organizations have formed relationships with Wainwright Bank, including the AIDS Action Committee of Massachusetts, AIDS Housing Corporation, The Boston Living Center, Fenway Community Health Center, and the Men of Color.

Diversity and Nondiscrimination   Executives of Wainwright Bank believe that issues of race, religion, gender and sexual orientation, and immigration will increasingly define communities and workplaces in the United States. They also believe the diversity of communities enhances and strengthens society as a whole. Because of this increase in diversity, Wainwright has established relationships with many nonprofit organizations that focus on diversity and discrimination issues. Some of these include the Association of Affirmative Action Professionals (AAAP), the New England Work & Family Association (NEWFA), and The Black-Jewish Economic Roundtable. According to Gary Buseck, the executive director of the Gay Lesbian and Affirming Disciples (GLAD), "Your [Wainwright's] contributions to the gay and lesbian community in New England have been unparalleled, and the way in which you combine business with community activism and personal integrity is a model for society."

Women's Issues   Addressing women's issues is also a priority for Wainwright Bank & Trust. Wainwright's board of directors shatters the proverbial "glass ceiling" by including a significant number of women and other minorities, and about half of the bank's officers are women. This is especially significant considering the predominately male banking industry. The bank strives not only to include women in its workforce, but also to help address their needs as customers. To this end, the bank developed Personal Financing Planning for Women seminars to help women become financially independent. Seminar topics have included proper uses of credit, understanding risk, inflation, and tax deferral.

The bank has also established relationships with area nonprofit agencies including the Boston Women's Health Book Collective, Massachusetts Breast Cancer Coalition, Center for Women in Enterprise (CWE), and Massachusetts National Organization for Women (NOW). Boston Women's Health Book Collective is a nonprofit health education, advocacy, and consulting organization that works to help individuals and groups make informed decisions about issues affecting women's health and medical care. Massachusetts Breast Cancer Coalition's goals are to increase public awareness, improve access for all women to screening and care, increase research funding, and ensure consumer participation in research priorities and public policy. The Center for Women in Enterprise is a nonprofit education organization that offers courses, workshops, one-on-one consulting, and assistance in securing loans. Wainwright Bank was also one of the first and largest Boston area businesses to sign the Pledge to NOW in August 1997. This document covers policies on affirmative action, family leave, domestic partnership benefits, and strong antiharassment policies. One example of Wainwright's fulfillment of this pledge is the low-interest loans that it makes available to help day-care centers upgrade and expand their services. Along with six other financial institutions, Wainwright's loans allow more women to participate more effectively in the workforce, knowing that their children have quality care throughout the workday.

Environmental Issues   Wainwright Bank is particularly concerned about the intersection between environmental issues and social justice. The bank has established relations with many environmental nonprofit agencies, including the Environmental Diversity Forum, Trust for Public Land, Silent Spring Institute, and the Coalition for Environmentally Responsible Economies (CERES). The Environmental Diversity Forum's mission is to protect the environment by advocating for racial, cultural, and economic diversity at all organizational levels and in all policies and programs of the environmental movement. In collaboration with the Trust for Public Land, Wainwright provided financial assistance for the preservation of the shores of Lake Tarelton in Piermont, New Hampshire. The Bank endorsed the CERES Principles in September 1997, highlighting a commitment to an environmental ethics that goes beyond mere compliance with the law.

▶ *Social Activism as a Corporate Value*

The founders of Wainwright Bank believe that the management of financial affairs is not a socially or morally neutral practice. That is, where people choose to invest their money and from whom they choose to buy their goods and services can influence social conditions. Wainwright has extended this view to the corporate level. For example, the bank works with organizations such as Franklin Research & Development Corporation (FRDC), Kinder, Lydenberg, Domini & Company, Inc.

(KLD), the Political Research Associates (PRA), and the Partners for the Common Good 2000 (PCG2000). Wainwright holds a 30 percent interest in FRDC, which specializes in socially responsible investing, because it is profitable and coincides with Wainwright's strategy and corporate citizenship. KLD provides social research to money managers, whereas PCG2000 applies ethical principles to investment choices and directs loans and deposits, through intermediaries, to projects that promote economic justice and social change. Wainwright works with these companies by furnishing loans and other types of assistance for uniting financial and social goals.

▶ *Criticisms of Wainwright*

Because banks usually fit a strict conservative mold, it should come as no surprise that some people in the banking business disagree with some of Wainwright's practices. Most criticisms focus on its business and operation methods. Many traditionalists feel that Wainwright is too focused on affairs other than banking and warn that it could lose touch with how it should be transacting business, which may hurt its customers and shareholders, regardless of who they are, in the long run. However, Wainwright has been listed as one of the most profitable independent banks created after 1984 by Danielson Associates Inc. The bank's financial standing remained secure throughout the 1990s, with steady increases in both return on assets and return on equity. In 1999, Wainwright increased its loan portfolio and deposits by 18 percent and 11 percent, respectively.

Some critics have also suggested that Robert Glassman, the cochairman of Wainwright Bank, chose to operate Wainwright in this way in order to achieve some ulterior motive. Others, including members of the press, have accused the bank of "window dressing," using its social and values orientation to attract customers without actually getting involved in the causes it champions. However, most customers believe that Wainwright's actions and record demonstrate that it does more than just talk about being a corporate citizen.

Other critics contend that Wainwright is missing out on some very lucrative options because of its adherence to certain beliefs. For example, consumers who oppose gay and lesbian lifestyles may not want to bank with Wainwright because of its social agenda. For several reasons, Wainwright has remained a relatively small bank in the Massachusetts area. Like many other banks, Wainwright now offers online banking services, and this option, coupled with the company's unique approach, may boost its customer base. Although Wainwright's philosophies and practices do generate criticism, the bank seems to respond with continuing exemplary performance. Robert Glassman says, "In the one-dimensional corporate world in which shareholder concerns have always reigned supreme, Wainwright Bank prefers the concept of stakeholders. In our model of inclusion, employees, customers, and communities have an equal place at the table alongside stockholders. We believe each of these constituencies is best served when all are served."

▶ Wainwright Garners Awards

Glassman's stakeholder philosophy has helped Wainwright Bank win numerous awards for its endeavors to support the community. For example, *Business Ethics* magazine awarded the company its Business Ethics Award in 1998 on the basis of Wainwright's contributions to environmental, diversity, and nondiscriminatory practices. These contributions include the fact that community development loans comprise one-fifth of the bank's loan portfolio. Wainwright also supplies more than 60 percent of the financing for housing for people with HIV/AIDS in the Boston area. Wainwright Bank also practices diversity in the workplace in an exemplary manner. In addition to advancing women, Wainwright actively recruits many categories of minorities as employees, and the bank's staff now includes speakers of seventeen different languages.

Robert Glassman has devoted time, money, and energy to creating several organizations and activities designed to improve the lives of people in need. Glassman says, "I believe it's important to use the platform the bank affords me to inform, educate, and introduce different constituencies to issues of social injustice. This work, alongside the culture of diversity we're developed at the Bank, is the most important legacy I contemplate I will leave my children." Glassman's statement and record demonstrate the importance of top management commitment to nonfinancial issues. Wainwright not only won the 1998 Business Ethics Award, but also received the 1998 Institute of Human Relations Award from the American Jewish Committee, the CDFI Fund Award from the U.S. Treasury Department, the Small Business Award for Excellence from the Greater Boston Business Council, the Ray Frost Award from the Association of Affirmative Action Professionals, the Friend of the Community Award from the Lesbian & Gay Political Alliance of Massachusetts, and the Bank Honor Roll from the Massachusetts IOLTA Committee. These awards indicate how important the bank has become to its community and the leadership it has shown in corporate citizenship.

Many people are surprised when they hear about Wainwright Bank because most do not think of banks as institutions that go out of their way to help the community. The "banking on values" concept at Wainwright has earned the bank and its employees a great deal of respect from community stakeholders. As Christine Connhalter, the executive assistant to the mayor of the city of Cambridge, Massachusetts, says, "Wainwright does not believe in 'Business as Usual.' Wainwright is 'Business as It Should Be'—community partnership, equality, and caring. Wainwright dares to be different—and succeeds." Such quotes sum up Wainwright Bank & Trust Company's mission and values very well and demonstrate the respect Wainwright has gained by doing what not every business will do.

DISCUSSION QUESTIONS

1. What factors led the founders of Wainwright Bank to pursue the "banking on values" philosophy? What type of risks and rewards are associated with this nontraditional banking approach?

2. Contrast Wainwright Bank's mission statement with your own bank's mission statement. What are the similarities and differences? Would you consider banking with Wainwright? Why or why not?

3. Visit Wainwright Bank's web site. What is the company's financial standing? What social concerns and stakeholders is the bank now exploring and supporting? Based on your beliefs and Wainwright's own statements, delineate the bank's prospects for the future.

REFERENCES

These facts are from "1998 Summary Annual Report," Bank of America, www.bankofamerica.com/annualreport98/, accessed November 18, 1999; Citizens Bank of Canada, www.citizens.com, accessed April 12, 2000; "Exceptional Community Support by U.S. Bank Leads to Unique Government Grant," *PR Newswire,* November 4, 1999; Jay Fitzgerald, "Atlanta, Wainright Make Honor Roll," *Boston Business Journal,* August 23, 1996, p. 4; Robert Glassman, "Wainwright Bank Finds Social Investment Pays," *Star Tribune,* November 30, 1998, pp. 3–4; Skip Kaltenheuser, "10th Annual Business Ethics Awards," *Business Ethics,* (November/December 1998): 12; Steve Klinkerman, "The Tie That Binds," *Banking Strategies,* March 25, 2000, www.bai.org/; Diane E. Lewis, "Financial Firms Make Loans to Boost Child Care in Massachusetts," *Boston Globe,* March 15, 2000; Heather MacKenzie, "Wainwright Banks on More Than Money," *Boston Globe,* June 28, 1998; Chris Mahoney, "Wainwright's Mensch," *Boston Business Journal,* January 15, 1999, p. 3; Chris Mahoney, "Wainwright Poised to Take Its Causes National," *Boston Business Journal,* November 26, 1999, p. 3. Charles Ornstein, "Merger Giving New Name to NationsBank," *Dallas Morning News,* October 2, 1998; Wainwright Bank, www.wainwrightbank.com, accessed November 8, 2001.

CASE 8

Environmental and Social Concerns at New Belgium Brewing Company

This case was prepared by Nikole Haiar for classroom discussion, rather than to illustrate either effective or ineffective handling of an administrative, ethical, or legal decision by individuals or management.

Although most of the companies cited as examples of corporate citizenship are large corporations, the social responsibility initiatives of small businesses often have the greatest impact on local communities and neighborhoods. Small businesses create jobs, provide goods and services for customers in smaller markets that larger corporations are not interested in serving, and contribute money, resources, and volunteer time to local causes. Small business owners often serve as community and neighborhood leaders, and many choose to apply their skills and some of the fruits of their success to tackle local problems and issues for the benefit of everyone in the community. One such small business is the New Belgium Brewing Company, Inc., based in Fort Collins, Colorado, which has adopted the corporate citizenship model to make a positive impact on its community and surrounding areas.

> ### History of the New Belgium Brewing Company

The idea for the New Belgium Brewing Company began with a bicycling trip through Belgium, home of some of the world's finest ales, some of which have been brewed for centuries in that country's monasteries. As Jeff Lebesch, an American electrical engineer, cruised around the country on his fat-tired mountain bike, he wondered if he could produce such high-quality beers in his home state of Colorado. After acquiring the special strain of yeast used in brewing Belgian-style ales, Lebesch returned home and began to experiment in his Colorado basement.

When his beers earned thumbs up from friends, Lebesch decided to market his brews.

The New Belgium Brewing Company (NBB) opened for business in 1991 as a tiny basement operation in Lebesch's home in Fort Collins. Lebesch's wife, Kim Jordan, became the firm's marketing director. They named their first brew Fat Tire Amber Ale in memory of Lebesch's bike ride through Belgium. New Belgium beers quickly developed a small, but devoted customer base, first in Fort Collins and then throughout Colorado. The brewery soon outgrew the couple's basement and moved into an old railroad depot. Finally, in 1995, the company moved into its present facility, which is considered a marvel in the industry. The brewery includes an automated brew house, two quality assurance labs, and numerous technological innovations for which New Belgium has become nationally recognized as a "paradigm of environmental efficiencies."

Today, New Belgium Brewing Company offers a variety of permanent and seasonal ales and pilsners. The company's standard line includes Sunshine Wheat, Blue Paddle Pilsner, Abbey Ale, Trippel Ale, 1554 Black Ale, and of course, the original Fat Tire Amber Ale, still the firm's best seller. Some customers even refer to the company as the Fat Tire Brewery. The brewery also markets two types of specialty beers on a seasonal basis. Seasonal ales include Frambozen and Abbey Grand Cru, which are released at Thanksgiving, and Christmas and Farmhouse Ale, which are sold during the early fall months. The firm occasionally offers one-time-only brews, such as LaFolie, a wood-aged beer, that are sold only until the batch runs out.

Since its founding, NBB's most-effective form of advertising has been via word of mouth by devoted customers. Indeed, before New Belgium beers were widely distributed throughout Colorado, one liquor store owner in Telluride is purported to have offered people gas money if they would stop by and pick up New Belgium beer on their way through Ft. Collins. Although New Belgium beers are distributed in just one-third of the United States, the brewery receives numerous e-mails and phone calls every day inquiring when its beers will be available elsewhere.

▶ *Company Purpose and Core Beliefs*

New Belgium's dedication to quality, the environment, and its employees and customers is expressed in its stated purpose: "To operate a profitable brewery which makes our love and talent manifest." The company's stated core values and beliefs about its role as an environmentally concerned and socially responsible brewer include the following statements (reprinted by permission from New Belgium Brewing Company, Inc.):

- Producing world-class beers
- Promoting beer culture and the responsible enjoyment of beer

- Continuous, innovative quality and efficiency improvements
- Transcending customers' expectations
- Environmental stewardship: minimizing resource consumption, maximizing energy efficiency, and recycling
- Kindling social, environmental, and cultural change as a business role model
- Cultivating potential: through learning, participative management, and the pursuit of opportunities
- Balancing the myriad needs of the company, staff, and their families
- Committing ourselves to authentic relationships, communications, and promises
- Having fun

David Kemp, a long-time brewery employee, believes that these statements help communicate to customers and other stakeholders what New Belgium, as a company, is about.

▶ *Environmental Concerns*

New Belgium's marketing strategy involves pairing the quality of its products, as well as their name and look, with the way the company affects the planet. From leading-edge environmental gadgets and high-tech industry advancements to employee-ownership programs and a strong belief in giving back to the community, New Belgium demonstrates its desire to create a living, learning community.

NBB strives for cost-efficient energy-saving alternatives to conducting business and for reducing its impact on the environment. In staying true to the company's core values and beliefs, the brewery's employee-owners unanimously agreed to invest in a wind turbine, making New Belgium the first fully wind-powered brewery in the United States. Since the switch from coal power, New Belgium has been able to reduce its CO_2 emissions by 1,800 metric tons per year. The company further reduces its energy use by employing a steam condenser that captures and reuses the hot water from boiling the barley and hops in the production process to start the next brew; the steam is redirected to heat the floor tiles and deice the loading docks in cold weather. Another way NBB works to conserve energy is through the use of "sun tubes," which provide natural daytime lighting throughout the brew house all year long.

New Belgium also takes pride in reducing waste through recycling and creative reuse strategies. The company strives to recycle as many supplies as possible, including cardboard boxes, keg caps, office materials, and the amber glass used in bottling. For example, by the end of 1999, New Belgium was able to reduce its negative impact on the environment by recycling 91 tons of amber glass, 27 tons of cardboard, and 9 tons of shrink-wrap. The brewery also stores spent barley and hop grains in an on-premise silo and invites local farmers to pick up the grains, free of charge, to feed their pigs. NBB also encourages its employees to reduce air pollution through alternative transportation. As an incentive, NBB gives its employees a "cruiser bike"—just like the one on its Fat Tire Amber Ale label—after one year of employment and encourages them to ride it to work.

Social Concerns

Beyond its use of environment-friendly technologies and innovations, New Belgium Brewing Company strives to improve communities and enhance people's lives through corporate giving, event sponsorship, and philanthropic involvement.

One way that New Belgium demonstrates its corporate citizenship is by donating $1 per barrel of beer sold to various cultural, social, environmental, and drug- and alcohol-awareness programs across the ten western states in which it distributes beer. Typical grants range from $2,500 to $5,000. Involvement is spread equally among the ten states, unless there is a special need that requires more participation or funding.

NBB also maintains a community bulletin board in its facility where it posts an array of community involvement activities and proposals. This community board allows tourists and employees to see the different ways they can help out the community, and it gives nonprofit organizations a chance to make their needs known. Another way to apply for grants is through the New Belgium Brewing Company web site, which has a link designated for this purpose.

NBB also sponsors a number of events, with a focus on those involving "human-powered" sports, which cause minimal damage to the natural environment. Through event sponsorships, such as the Tour de Fat, NBB has raised more than $15,000 for various environmental, social, and cycling nonprofit organizations. In 2000, New Belgium also sponsored the MS 150 "Best Damn Bike Tour," a two-day, fully catered bike tour, from which all proceeds went to benefit more than 5,000 local people with multiple sclerosis. In the same year, NBB also sponsored the Ride the Rockies bike tour, which donated the proceeds from beer sales to local nonprofit groups. The money raised from this annual event funds local projects, such as improving parks and bike trails. In the course of one year, New Belgium can be found at anywhere from 150 to 200 festivals and events, across all ten western states.

Organizational Success

New Belgium Brewing Company's efforts to live up to its own high standards have paid off with numerous awards and a very loyal following. According to David Edgar, director of the Institute for Brewing Studies, "They've created a very positive image for their company in the beer-consuming public with smart decision-making." Although some members of society do not believe that a company whose major product is alcohol can be socially responsible, New Belgium has set out to prove that for those who make a choice to drink responsibly, the company can do everything possible to contribute to society. Its efforts to promote beer culture and the connoisseurship of beer has even led to the design and exclusive rights to a special "Worthy Glass," the shape of which is intended to retain foam, show off color, enhance the visual presentation, and release aroma. New Belgium Brewing Company also promotes responsible appreciation of beer through its participation in and support of the culinary arts. For instance, it frequently hosts New Belgium Beer Dinners, in which every course of the meal is served with a complementary culinary treat.

New Belgium has won several awards for the taste and high quality of its beers. Kim Jordan and Jeff Lebesch were named the 1999 recipients of the Rocky Mountain Region Entrepreneur of the Year Award for manufacturing. The company also captured the award for best midsized brewing company of the year and best midsized brew master at the Great American Beer Festival. In addition, New Belgium took home medals for three different brews, Abbey Belgian Style Ale, Blue Paddle Pilsner, and LaFolie specialty ale. High praise indeed considering that Colorado ranks second among states with the most breweries in the nation. One staff member of the Association of Brewers commented that Fat Tire is one of the only brews he'd pay for in a bar.

Every six-pack of New Belgium Beer displays the phrase, "In this box is our labor of love, we feel incredibly lucky to be creating something fine that enhances people's lives." The founders of New Belgium hope this statement captures the spirit of the company. According to employee Dave Kemp, NBB's environmental concern and social responsibility give it a competitive advantage because consumers want to believe in and feel good about the products they purchase. NBB's most important asset is its image—a corporate brand that stands for quality, responsibility, and concern about society. The brewer defines itself as more than just a beer company, but also as a caring organization that is concerned with all stakeholders, including the community, the environment, and employees.

DISCUSSION QUESTIONS

1. What environmental issues does the New Belgium Brewing Company work to address? How has NBB taken a strategic approach to addressing these issues? Why do you think the company has chosen to focus on environmental issues?

2. Are New Belgium's social initiatives indicative of strategic philanthropy? Why or why not?

3. Some segments of society vigorously contend that companies that sell alcoholic beverages and tobacco products cannot be socially responsible organizations because of the very nature of their primary products. Do you believe that New Belgium Brewing Company's actions and initiatives are indicative of a good corporate citizen? Why or why not?

REFERENCES   These facts are from Peter Asmus, "Goodbye Coal, Hello Wind," *Business Ethics,* 13 (July/August 1999): 10–11; Robert Baun, "What's in a Name? Ask the Makers of Fat Tire," *[Fort Collins] Coloradoan,* October 8, 2000, pp. E1, E3; Rachel Brand, "Colorado Breweries Bring Home 12 Medals in Festival," *Rocky Mountain [Denver] News,* www.insidedenver.com/news/1008beer6.shtml, accessed November 06, 2000; Stevi Deter, "Fat Tire Amber Ale," The Net Net, www.thenetnet.com/reviews/fat.html, accessed January 19, 2001; DirtWorld.com, www.dirtworld.com/races/ Colorado_race745.htm, accessed November 6, 2000; Robert F. Dwyer and John F. Tanner, Jr., *Business Marketing* (Burr Ridge, Ill.: Irwin/McGraw-Hill, 1999), p. 104; "Fat Tire Amber Ale," Achwiegut (The Guide to Austrian Beer), www.austrianbeer.com/beer/b000688.shtml, accessed January 19, 2001; Del I. Hawkins, Roger J. Best, and Kenneth A. Coney, *Consumer Behavior: Building Marketing Strategy,* 8th ed. (Burr Ridge, Ill.: Irwin/McGraw-Hill, 2001); David Kemp, Tour Connoisseur, New Belgium Brewing Company, personal interview by Nikole Haiar, November 21, 2000, 1:00 P.M.; New Belgium Brewing Company, Ft. Collins, Col., www.newbelgium.com, accessed November 8, 2001; New Belgium Brewing Company Tour by Nikole Haiar, November 20, 2000, 2:00 P.M.; Dan Rabin, "New Belgium Pours It on for Bike Riders," *Celebrator Beer News,* www.celebrator.com/9808/rabin.html, accessed November 6, 2000.

DoubleClick and Privacy on the Internet

This case was prepared by Tracy A. Suter, Oklahoma State University, for classroom discussion, rather than to illustrate either effective or ineffective handling of an administrative situation.

D oubleClick, Inc., is an information-revolution phenomenon. What started out as an outgrowth of self-proclaimed computer "geeks" and savvy advertising agency executives has grown into a high-tech heavyweight providing advertising services and information about Internet users for advertisers, web site operators, and other companies. The nature of its business has also put DoubleClick in the center of a brewing digital storm. At the core of this controversy is the issue of a person's right to privacy on the Internet. DoubleClick, which contends that it is committed to protecting the privacy of all Internet users, views its role as important in maintaining the Internet as a free medium driven by highly targeted advertising. Consumer groups, however, see it differently, noting that DoubleClick's actions loom larger than its words regarding access to personal information. Opponents, which include Michigan Attorney General Jennifer Granholm, regard DoubleClick's business practices as little more than a "secret, cyber wiretap." To understand how DoubleClick found itself in this uncomfortable position, it is helpful to examine the firm's history, key strategic business units, and the issue of Internet privacy.

▶ Merge onto Silicon Alley

Like many entrepreneurs in recent years, Kevin O'Connor and Dwight Merriman, two Atlanta-based engineers, saw an opportunity to cash in on the growing popularity of the Internet. O'Connor and Merriman had observed the challenges faced by niche-driven, subscription-based content web sites attempting to compete with America Online's growing mass audience. They reasoned that they could capitalize on this situation by creating a single network to bring together numerous online publications to create a critical mass of information. With the idea of multiple publications forming a larger online network, it became crucial to address a significant issue for each of the various publications: advertising. After substantial research, O'Connor and Merriman decided to move forward with a network concept. However, after careful research, they decided that the advertising, rather than publishing, industry could be better served with such a network. Thus, they founded the DoubleClick Network in January 1996.

Although O'Connor and Merriman's engineering backgrounds helped them tremendously with the technology issues associated with their concept, their engineering experiences provided little insight into the world of sophisticated advertising. To resolve this issue, the software-based start-up formally merged with a division of ad agency Poppe Tyson. O'Connor believed the marriage of nerd and Madison Avenue cultures was possible because of a common bond—the love of the Internet. However, as O'Connor later admitted, "The two cultures are completely ignorant of each other's ways." The "offspring" of this union set up shop in the heart of Silicon Alley in New York City—the location, coincidentally, where some of New York's first advertising agencies sprang up a century ago.

Like traditional advertising agencies, DoubleClick's focus is to get the right advertisement to the right person at the right time. The difference between DoubleClick and off-line ad agencies is the use of technology to track Web surfing activities more directly as compared to older media such as magazines. A magazine publisher, for instance, can detail the number of subscribers as well as the number of issues sold at newsstands. Unfortunately, the publisher does not have a very clear picture of which articles in a magazine issue have been read, by whom, and when. Online, however, technology developed by DoubleClick can track traffic to a given customer's web site and identify specific articles selected. Moreover, DoubleClick can trail traffic to and from the web site to establish a surfing portfolio of site visitors. This breadth and depth of information quickly made DoubleClick a valuable service provider to online advertisers trying to make advertising work on the Internet.

▶ *Throwing Darts*

The heart of DoubleClick's technology is its DART—Dynamic Advertising Reporting and Targeting—system. DART works by reading twenty-two criteria about web site visitors' actions such as their cyber location and time of visit. This technology also leaves a "cookie" on the user's computer, often without his or her knowledge. Cookies are simply bits of information sent to a Web browser to be saved on the user's hard drive. Cookies are helpful for Internet users because they can contain important information like log-in information and user preferences that make return visits to subscription-based web sites more manageable. Cookies are also useful for web site operators because they can include additional information such as evidence of repeat visits or advertisements viewed. The information provided by the cookie about a web site visitor's activities and interests helps DoubleClick tailor advertisements to specific users. It should be noted, however, that cookies do not collect personally identifiable information such as a user's name, mailing address, telephone number, or e-mail address, so individual profiles are essentially anonymous. Instead of tracking an identifiable individual, cookies track users' digital footsteps.

With the wealth of information DoubleClick can provide for its network members, customers continue to join. By the end of its first year of business, DoubleClick had secured the business of twenty-five web sites. Today, the company places banner advertisements on more than 11,500 web sites. As Andy Jacobson, regional vice president for sales, says, "We set a goal: sell $500,000 of advertising in a week, and we'll buy lunch for everyone in the room." With 2000 revenues of almost $507 million—an average of nearly $10 million a week—DoubleClick is buying a lot of lunches these days (Table C9.1). The company is buying a lot of cookies, too—the eatable kind. After the company achieved the milestone of 500 million advertisements placed in one day, company executives had cookies delivered to the technical engineers who manage the DART system.

This growth and increasing volume have allowed DoubleClick to command fees of 35 to 50 percent of advertising expenditures compared to the 15 percent fee structure charged by more-traditional off-line advertising agencies. Consider as

TABLE C9.1

DoubleClick Inc. Financial Performance: Four Fiscal Years ending December 31, 2000[a]

	2000	1999	1998	1997
Net Sales	$506.60	$258.30	$80.20	$30.60
Cost of Sales	NA	$90.40	$51.10	$19.70
Selling, General & Admin.	NA	$168.30	$47.20	$18.40
Net Income (Loss)	($156.00)	($55.80)	($18.20)	($8.40)
EARNINGS PER SHARE	*($1.29)*	*($0.51)*	*($0.29)*	*($0.20)*

a. All figures in millions of dollars except per share amounts.
Source: MSN MoneyCentral, http://moneycentral.msn.com/investor/, accessed February 1, 2001.

well that the DoubleClick network has the capability to add hundreds of thousands of anonymous consumer profiles per day. Thus, it becomes clear that its technological capabilities make it an increasingly attractive ad-servicing option.

Despite the phenomenal sales growth DoubleClick has achieved, executives believe there is further potential available from the DART system. In fact, the expectation is for DART technologies alone to account for 50 percent of future revenues. However, those revenue expectations are not limited to the DoubleClick network alone. The company is intent on servicing clients outside its own network and growing complementary businesses in the projected $11.3 billion (by 2003) ad-servicing business. Like traditional companies, DoubleClick has used its growing clout to develop and acquire important worldwide subsidiaries both on- and off-line.

▶ *Key Subsidiaries*

Despite the prevalence of technology today, targeting remains surprisingly low-tech. According to Jim Nail, a Forrester research analyst,

> To get advertisers to continue to pay the big premiums, DoubleClick will have to tell advertisers more than just where you are and the kind of site you visit. It might have to tell them whether you are married or single, what your income is, and whether or not you have kids. What it needs to do above all is predict, with greater accuracy, how likely you are to buy an advertised product.

To that end, DoubleClick acquired off-line catalog database company Abacus Direct shortly after buying NetGravity, Inc., a direct competitor. The idea behind the Abacus acquisition was the potential to merge the database company's personally identifiable off-line buying habits with DoubleClick's nonpersonally identifiable online habits to provide even greater depths of information to current and future clients. The trend toward collecting more personally identifiable information continued with DoubleClick's development of Flashbase, an automation tool that allows DoubleClick clients a means of collecting personal information by running contests and sweepstakes online. Additionally, DoubleClick web sites such as www.NetDeals.com and www.IAF.net collect personally identifiable information online. However, DoubleClick contends that it provides ways for consumers to limit communication only to prize- or deal-specific information. In other words, consumers have the ability to "opt out" of future communications not specific to the instance when and where they entered their personal data.

▶ *The Controversy*

The only problem with these developments and acquisitions is that their intended use signaled a significant philosophical shift in the way DoubleClick had always done business. Specifically, it created a drastic change in the company's consumer privacy position, a fact that consumer privacy groups and the Federal Trade Commission (FTC) did not take long to notice. According to Jason Catlett of Junkbusters, an Internet privacy activist, "Thousands of sites are ratting on you, so as soon as one gives you away, you're exposed on all of them. For years, [DoubleClick] has said (their services) don't identify you personally, and now they're admitting they are going to identify you."

In the face of growing public concern, Kevin O'Connor defended the company's plans: "The merger with Abacus Direct, along with the recent closing of the NetGravity merger, will allow us to offer publishers and advertisers the most effective means of advertising online and offline." Kevin Ryan, DoubleClick's CEO, took it a step further: "What we continue to hear from consumers is that they'd like to be in a position to have better content, greater access for everyone in the United States, and they would love it all to be free and advertising-served." Ryan pointed out that the Internet is driven by advertising, and that advertising companies need to know that their substantial investments are being spent in the best way possible—that is, targeted to the right audience or individual. Without more accurate information, Ryan asserted, much of the gratis content on the Internet would no longer be free.

Initially, the merger announcements were well received, as shares of DoubleClick traded for as high as $179.00 per share in early December 1999. Unfortunately, the comments of O'Connor and Ryan failed to stem the stock's decline after privacy concerns were voiced by Junkbusters and others in the aftermath of the Abacus Direct merger (see Table C9.2).

DoubleClick's posted privacy policy states that online users are given *notice* about the data collection and the *choice* not to participate or to opt out. However, Internet users must read carefully to understand that granting permission, or failing to deny permission, at even one DoubleClick or Abacus-serviced web site allows the company to select personal information across all sites. Consequently, the Center for Democracy and Technology (CDT), a Washington-based watchdog organization, launched a hard-line campaign against DoubleClick. The focus of the campaign centered on a "Websit" under the slogan, "I Will Not Be Targeted," where users can opt out of DoubleClick's profiling activities. According to Deirdre Mulligan, CDT's staff counsel, "You may have already been double-crossed by DoubleClick or you may be next in line. In either case, if you care about your privacy and want to surf the Web without your every move being recorded in a giant database connected to your name, its time to opt-out. . . ."

The CDT campaign was just one of the challenges DoubleClick faced as public concerns about Internet privacy escalated. A California woman brought a lawsuit against DoubleClick, alleging the company had unlawfully obtained and sold her private personal information. Media critics labeled DoubleClick an online "Big Brother" that passed information about employees' Internet surfing behavior onto

TABLE C9.2

DoubleClick Inc. Stock Valuation: Three Fiscal Years Since Initial Public Offering

	2000	1999	1998
January	$98.81	$24.06	N/A
February	$88.81	$22.47	N/A
March	$93.63	$45.52	N/A
April	$75.88	$69.91	$10.42
May	$42.25	$48.72	$8.66
June	$38.13	$45.88	$12.42
July	$35.94	$40.50	$11.00
August	$40.69	$49.94	$5.97
September	$32.00	$59.56	$5.97
October	$16.25	$70.00	$8.25
November	$14.19	$80.03	$10.13
December	$11.00	$126.53	$11.13

Symbol = DCLK.
Source: MSN MoneyCentral, http://moneycentral.msn.com/investor/, accessed February 1, 2001.

their employers. Attorneys general in Michigan and New York launched investigations into DoubleClick's business practices. One of the most publicized challenges was the Electronic Privacy Information Center (EPIC) complaint filed with the FTC regarding DoubleClick's profiling practices. The complaint led to a full-scale investigation of DoubleClick's business practices by the federal watchdog. EPIC and similar privacy groups prefer an opt-in mechanism as opposed to DoubleClick's current opt-out platform. EPIC Executive Director Marc Rotenberg said, "Several years ago, DoubleClick said it would not collect personally identifiable information and keep anonymous profiles. Privacy experts applauded that approach." But as a result of the Abacus merger, "DoubleClick has changed its mind and they're trying to convince users they should accept that [new] model."

DoubleClick attempted to defuse the growing controversy (and plummeting stock price) by announcing a program to protect the consumers it tracks online.

The program included a major newspaper campaign, fifty million banner ads directing consumers to the privacy rights information and education site Privacy-Choices (www.privacychoices.org/), the appointment of a chief privacy officer, the hiring of an external accounting firm to conduct privacy audits, and the establishment of an advisory board. The board, in particular, was less than well received. Calling the board a "facade," Jeffrey Chester, executive director of the Center of Media Education, said, "This is a public relations ploy to ward off federal and state scrutiny." Chester and other privacy organizations expressed dismay that the advisory board included no true privacy advocates, and worse, it included a DoubleClick customer. Moreover, that customer-member advocated technologies called "Web bugs" or "clear-gifs" that some consider even more intrusive than cookies. These sentiments prompted O'Connor to state, "It is clear from these discussions that I made a mistake by planning to merge names with anonymous user activity across web sites in the absence of government and industry privacy standards."

Another attempt to regain consumer goodwill is DoubleClick's participation in the Responsible Electronic Communication Alliance (RECA) along with fifteen of the nation's leading online marketers. The purpose of the RECA is to give consumers greater choice and notice regarding their online activities. To identify companies that subscribe to the RECA's proposed standards, the alliance is developing a "seal of approval" program in the spirit of *Good Housekeeping.* According to Christopher Wolf, RECA President, "Our ultimate goal is to phase in a set of firm standards on privacy, notice, access, and choice."

▌ *A New Era*

On January 22, 2001, the Federal Trade Commission announced that it had completed its investigation of DoubleClick. In a letter to the company, the commission said, "It appears to staff that DoubleClick never used or disclosed consumers' PII [personally identifiable information] for purposes other than those disclosed in its privacy policy." On news of the announcement, the company's stock price jumped 13 percent, although it remained well below the company's historic high. However, the FTC also warned that its decision "is not to be construed as a determination that a violation may not have occurred" and reserved the right to take further action. Needless to say, the privacy advocates were not happy with the announcement. EPIC, for example, contends that the FTC never addressed its allegations. CEO Kevin Ryan, however, feels that DoubleClick has been vindicated: "We felt from the beginning that our privacy policy and practices are solid. We never felt there was any substantial problem with them." Although it seems that the storm has quieted for now, Internet consumers, privacy advocates, and government officials will be watching DoubleClick closely, and the issue of Internet privacy will almost certainly continue.

DISCUSSION QUESTIONS

1. Why did DoubleClick's decision to merge Abacus Direct's database of personally identifiable off-line buying habits with DoubleClick's nonpersonally identifiable online habits so upset privacy advocates and arouse the attention of federal and state officials? What other ethical issues exist in this situation?
2. How has DoubleClick taken a strategic approach to addressing these issues?
3. What else could/should DoubleClick do to address stakeholders' concerns about personal privacy protection?

REFERENCES

These facts are from Eryn Brown, "The Silicon Alley Heart of Internet Advertising," *Fortune,* December 6, 1999, pp. 166–67; Lynn Burke, "A DoubleClick Smokescreen?" *WiredNews,* May 23, 2000, www.wirednews.com/news/print/ 0,1294,36404,00.html; "Company Briefing Book," *Wall Street Journal,* http://interactive.wsj.com, accessed January 29, 2001; Tom Conroy and Rob Sheffield, "Hot Marketing Geek," *Rolling Stone,* August 20, 1998, p. 80; "Crisis Control @ DoubleClick," *Privacy Times,* February 18, 2000, www.privacytimes.com/New Webstories/doubleclick_priv_ 2_23.htm; "DoubleClick Accused of Double-Dealing Double-Cross," *News Bytes News Network,* February 2, 2000, www.newsbytes.com; "DoubleClick Completes $1.8 Bil Abacus Direct Buyout," *News Bytes News Network,* November 30, 1999, www.newsbytes.com; "DoubleClick Outlines Five-Step Privacy Initiative," *News Bytes News Network,* February 15, 2000, www.newsbytes.com; "DoubleClick Tracks Online Movements," *News Bytes News Network,* January 26, 2000, www.newsbytes.com (originally reported by *USA Today,* www.usatoday.com); Jane Hodges, "DoubleClick Takes Standalone Route for Targeting Tools," *Advertising Age,* December 16, 1996, p. 32; "I Will Not Be Targeted," Center for Democracy and Technology, www.cdt.org/action/doubleclick.shtml; Chris Oakes, "DoubleClick Plan Falls Short," *WiredNews,* February 14, 2000, www.wirednews.com/news/print/0,1294,34337,00.html; Chris O'Brien, "DoubleClick Sets Off Privacy Firestorm," *San Jose Mercury News,* February 26, 2000, www.mercurycenter.com/business/top/ 042517.htm; "Online Marketing Coalition Announces Proposals for Internet Privacy Guidelines," *MSN MoneyCentral,* September 25, 2000, http://news.moneycentral.msn.com/; "Privacy Choices," DoubleClick, Inc., www.privacychoices.org/; "Privacy Policy," DoubleClick Inc., www.doubleclick.net/; "Privacy Standards Proposed," *MSNBC,* September 25, 2000, www.msnbc.com/news/467212.asp; Randall Rothenberg, "An Advertising Power, but Just What Does DoubleClick Do?" *New York Times: E-Commerce Special Section,* 1999, www.nytimes.com/library/tech/99/09/biztech/technology/ 22roth.html; Allen Wan and William Spain, "FTC Ends DoubleClick Investigation," CBS MarketWatch.com, January 23, 2001, www.aolpf.marketwatch.com/pf/archive/20010123/news/current/dclk.asp.

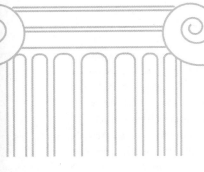

Home Depot's Commitment to Corporate Citizenship

This case was prepared by Gwyneth V. Walters for classroom discussion, rather than to illustrate either effective or ineffective handling of an administrative situation.

When Bernie Marcus and Arthur Blank opened the first Home Depot store in Atlanta in 1979, they forever changed the hardware and home-improvement retailing industry. Marcus and Blank envisioned huge warehouse-style stores stocked with an extensive selection of products offered at the lowest prices. Today, do-it-yourselfers and building contractors can browse from among 50,000 products for the home and yard, from kitchen and bathroom fixtures to carpeting, lumber, paint, tools, and plants and landscaping items. Some Home Depot stores are open twenty-four hours a day, but customers can also order products online and pick them up from their local Home Depot stores or have them delivered. The company also offers free home-improvement clinics to teach customers how to tackle everyday projects such as tiling a bathroom. For those customers who prefer not to "do it yourself," most stores offer installation services. Well-trained employees, recognizable by their orange aprons, are always on hand to help customers find just the right item or to demonstrate the proper use of a particular tool.

Today, Home Depot employs 230,000 people and operates 1,100 Home Depot stores, EXPO Design Centers, and Villager's Hardware stores in the United States, Canada, Chile, and Argentina. It also operates four wholly owned subsidiaries: Apex Supply Company, Georgia Lighting, Maintenance Warehouse, and National Blinds and Wallpaper. The company racks up more than $38 billion in annual sales, giving it 14 percent of the $140 billion U.S. home-improvement retailing market. Now that it is the world's largest home-improvement retailer, Home Depot continues to do things on a grand scale, including putting its corporate muscle behind a tightly focused social responsibility agenda.

❯ *Environmental Initiatives*

Just because Home Depot is a big corporation doesn't mean it is an uncaring and impersonal one. In fact, cofounders Bernard Marcus and Arthur Blank (now cochairmen) have nurtured a corporate culture that emphasizes social responsibility, especially in regard to the company's impact on the natural environment. Home Depot began its environmental program on the twentieth anniversary of Earth Day in 1990 by adopting a set of Environmental Principles (see Figure C10.1). These principles have since been adopted by the National Retail Hardware Association and Home Center Institute, which represents more than 46,000 retail hardware stores and home centers.

Guided by its Environmental Principles, Home Depot has initiated a number of programs to minimize the firm's—and its customers'—impact on the environment. In 1991, the retailer began using recycled content materials for store and office supplies, advertising, signs, and shopping bags. It also established a process for evaluating the environmental claims made by suppliers. The following year, the firm launched a program to recycle wallboard shipping packaging, which became the industry's first "reverse distribution" program. It also opened the first drive-through recycling center, in Duluth, Georgia, in 1993. In 1994, Home Depot became the first home-improvement retailer to offer wood products from tropical and temperate forests certified as "well-managed" by the Scientific Certification System's Forest Conservation Program. The company also began to replace wooden shipping pallets with reusable "slip sheets" to minimize waste and energy use and to reduce pressure on the hardwood resources used to make wood pallets.

In 1999, Home Depot announced that it would endorse independent, third-party forest certification and wood from certified forests. The company joined the Certified Forests Products Council, a nonprofit organization that promotes responsible forest product buying practices and the sale of wood from Certified Well-Managed Forests. Despite this action, environmentalists picketed company stores to protest Home Depot's practice of selling wood products from old-growth forests. Led by the Rainforest Action Network, environmentalists have picketed Home Depot and other home center stores for years in an effort to persuade companies to stop selling products from the world's old-growth forests, of which just 20 percent survive. Later that year, during Home Depot's twentieth-anniversary celebration, Arthur Blank announced,

> Our pledge to our customers, associates, and stockholders is that Home Depot will stop selling wood products from environmentally sensitive areas. . . . Home

Home Depot's Environmental Principles

- We are committed to improving the environment by selling products that are manufactured, packaged, and labeled in a responsible manner, that take the environment into consideration, and that provide greater value to our customers.

- We will support efforts to provide accurate, informative product labeling of environmental claims and impact.

- We will strive to eliminate unnecessary packaging.

- We will recycle and encourage the use of materials and products with recycled content.

- We will conserve natural resources by using energy and water wisely and seek further opportunities to improve the resource efficiency of our stores.

- We will comply with all environmental laws and will maintain programs and procedures to ensure compliance.

- We are committed to minimizing environmental health and safety risk for our employees and our customers.

- We will train our employees to enhance understanding of environmental issues and policies and to promote excellence in job performance and all environmental matters.

- We will encourage our customers to become environmentally conscious shoppers.

Source: "Environmental Principles," Home Depot, www.homedepot.com/, accessed February 1, 2001. Reprinted by permission from The Home Depot Headquarters, Homer TLC.

Depot embraces its responsibility as a global leader to help protect endangered forests. By the end of 2002, we will eliminate from our stores wood from endangered areas—including lauan, redwood and cedar products—and give preference to "certified" wood.

To be "certified" by the Forest Stewardship Council (FSC), a supplier's wood products must be tracked from the forest, through manufacturing and distribution, to the customer, and harvesting, manufacturing, and distribution practices must ensure a balance of social, economic, and environmental factors. Blank also challenged competitors to follow Home Depot's lead, and within two years, Lowe's, the number-two home-improvement retailer; Wickes, a lumber company; and Andersen Corp., a window manufacturer, had met that challenge. Many other companies in the industry will likely follow suit over the next few years in response to increasing pressure from stakeholders, particularly environmental groups such as the Rainforest Action Network, Greenpeace, and Earth First!

Home Depot has also been very generous to environmental organizations and causes, donating $750,000 in 1999 to nonprofit groups like Keep America Beautiful, the Tampa Audubon Society, and the World Wildlife Fund Canada. Recently, the company also established a carpooling program for more than 3,000 employees in the Atlanta area. Home Depot remains the only North American home-improvement retailer with a full-time staff dedicated to environmental issues. These efforts have yielded many rewards in addition to improved relations with environmental stakeholders. Home Depot's environmental programs earned the company an A on the Council on Economic Priorities Corporate Report Card, a Vision of America Award from Keep America Beautiful, and, along with Scientific Certification Systems and Collin Pine, a President's Council for Sustainable Development Award. The company has also been voted *Fortune* magazine's America's Most Admired Retailer for six years running.

▶ *Corporate Philanthropy*

In addition to its environmental initiatives, Home Depot focuses corporate citizenship efforts on disaster relief, affordable housing, and at-risk youth. The company has an annual philanthropic budget of $25 million, which it directs back to the communities it serves and to the interests of its employees through its Matching Gift Program. The company also posts a "Social Responsibility Report" on its web site that details its annual charitable contributions and the community programs in which it has become involved over the years.

Home Depot works with more than 250 affiliates of Habitat for Humanity, a nonprofit organization that constructs and repairs homes for qualified low-income families. The company also works with Christmas in April, a nonprofit organization that rehabilitates housing for the elderly and disabled. Through such programs, thousands of Home Depot associates volunteer, using products supplied by the company, to help build or refurbish affordable housing for their communities, thereby reinforcing their own skills and familiarity with the company's products. Home Depot also provides support to dozens of local housing groups around the country.

Home Depot also supports YouthBuildUSA, a nonprofit organization that provides training and skill development for young people. YouthBuildUSA gives students the opportunity to help rehabilitate housing for homeless and low-income families. Home Depot contributes to many at-risk youth programs, including Big Brothers/Big Sisters, KaBOOM!, and the National Center for Missing and Exploited Children.

In recent years, Home Depot has also tackled the growing need for relief from disasters such as hurricanes, tornadoes, and earthquakes. After Hurricane Floyd devastated parts of North Carolina, the company donated nearly $100,000 in cleanup and rebuilding supplies to relief agencies, sent more than 50,000 gallons of water to storm victims, extended credit to more than fifty communities, and sponsored clinics on how to repair damage resulting from the storm. When a deadly tornado struck Oklahoma City, Home Depot helped by rebuilding roofs, planting trees, and clearing roads. The company has contributed emergency relief funds, supplies, and labor to American Red Cross relief efforts. Home Depot also partners with The Weather Channel in Project SafeSide, a national severe weather public awareness program.

Employee Relations

On a more personal level, Home Depot encourages employees to become involved in the community through volunteer and civic activities. On any given day, a small army of Home Depot volunteers may be found swinging hammers and waving paintbrushes to fix up a family shelter, planting trees to spruce up an inner-city park, or framing a Habitat for Humanity house for a deserving family. Such contributions allow employees to make a real difference in their communities while enhancing both their skills and their employer's reputation.

Home Depot also strives to apply social responsibility to its employment practices, with the goal of assembling a diverse workforce that truly reflects the population of the markets it serves. Despite these efforts, the company recently settled a class-action lawsuit brought by female employees who claimed they were paid less than male employees, awarded fewer pay raises, and promoted less often. The $87.5 million settlement represented one of the largest settlements of a gender discrimination lawsuit in U.S. history at the time. In announcing the settlement, the company emphasized that it was not admitting to wrongdoing and defended its record, saying it "provides opportunities for all of its associates to develop successful professional careers and is proud of its strong track record of having successful women involved in all areas of the company." The settlement required Home Depot to establish a formal system to ensure that employees can notify managers of their interest in advancing to a management or sales position. The company's Job Preference Program (JPP), an automated hiring and promotion computer program, opens all jobs and applicants to the companywide network, eliminates unqualified applications, and helps managers to learn about employee aspirations and skills in a more effective manner. JPP has also brought positive changes for the many women and minority managers working at Home Depot.

▶ *A Strategic Commitment to Social Responsibility*

Knowing that stakeholders, especially customers, feel good about a company that actively commits resources to environmental and social issues, company executives believe that social responsibility can and should be a strategic component of Home Depot's business operations. The company remains committed to its focused strategy of philanthropy and volunteerism. This commitment extends throughout the company, fueled by top-level support from the cofounders and reinforced by a corporate culture that places great value on playing a responsible role within the communities it serves.

DISCUSSION QUESTIONS

1. Based on Home Depot's response to environmentalists' issues, describe the attributes (power, legitimacy, urgency) of this stakeholder. Using the Reactive-Defensive-Accommodative-Proactive Scale (Table 3.4), assess the company's strategy and performance with environmental and employee stakeholders.
2. As a publicly traded corporation, how can Home Depot justify budgeting more than $25 million annually for philanthropy? What areas other than the environment, disaster relief, affordable housing, and at-risk youth might be appropriate targets for strategic philanthropy by Home Depot?
3. As part of its settlement of the gender-discrimination suit brought against it, Home Depot established a formal system for employees to inform managers of their interest in advancement. What other steps might Home Depot take to strengthen the rights of its employees to equal treatment in the workplace?

REFERENCES

These facts are from *1999 Annual Report,* The Home Depot, Inc., 2000; Jim Carlton, "How Home Depot and Activists Joined to Cut Logging Abuse," *Wall Street Journal,* September 26, 2000, pp. A1+; Cora Daniels, "To Hire a Lumber Expert, Click Here," *Fortune,* April 3, 2000, pp. 267–270; Kirstin Downey Grimsley, "Home Depot Settles Gender Bias Lawsuit," *Washington Post,* September 20, 1997, p. D1; The Home Depot, Inc., www.homedepot.com/, accessed February 1, 2001; "Home Depot Lambasted for Attempt to Go Green," Environmental News Network, March 15, 1999, www.enn.com/; "The Home Depot Launches Environmental Wood Purchasing Policy," Rainforest Action Network, August 26, 1999, www.ran.org/ran_campaigns/old_growth/news/hd_pr.html; Susan Jackson and Tim Smart, "Mom and Pop Fight Back," *Business Week,* April 14, 1997, p. 46.

Appendix

The VanCity Social Report
1998/99

The following pages are excerpted from an actual social audit—*The VanCity Social Report 1998/99*. VanCity is a financial services provider based in Canada. For a copy of the complete report, visit VanCity's web site at www.vancity.com.

Vancouver City Savings Credit Union (VanCity) is Canada's largest credit union, based in Vancouver, British Columbia.

Message from the Chair & CEO

Greg McDade, *Chair*
VanCity Board of Directors

VanCity is on an exciting journey. Amid rapid changes to the financial services industry, we continue to chart our course based on our long-standing commitment to social and environmental responsibility, democratic decision-making, and outstanding member service. Our purpose is to achieve results that allow our key stakeholders — our members, our staff, and communities — to thrive and prosper.

This 1998/99 Social Report is an account of VanCity's ongoing voyage — how far we've come and how much farther we have to go. As with our 1997 Social Report, it presents a reliable, transparent, and balanced account of our social and environmental performance and the views of our stakeholders. It was externally verified by our external social auditor whose report can be found on page 10.

Constant Change . . .

Since 1997, the pace of change in the financial services industry has accelerated. While VanCity has worked hard to compete in this environment by finding innovative ways of doing business, we haven't lost sight of our values or our commitment to meeting the needs of our members.

. . . Constant Values

Our unchanging values have helped guide us through these changing times. We know that much of what we do with respect to social and environmental responsibility is well regarded by other organizations in Canada. We also know that our social audit[1] process is helping to ensure we are on the right course by allowing us to measure, understand, report on, and ultimately improve our social and environmental performance.

A Guiding Compass

One of the most significant outcomes of our 1997 social audit process was the decision to develop a corporate-wide ethical policy to keep us true to our values as we respond to changes and challenges in our industry. What is now our Statement of Values and Commitments was developed over several months in 2000 in consultation with members, staff, and local community groups (see page 7).

It was an exhilarating process that put into words the heart and spirit of VanCity: a desire to serve our members, staff, and community with integrity, innovation, and responsibility. In the future, our Statement of Values and Commitments will guide all of our business decisions and contribute to our continued success.

Progress . . .

Our 1997 Social Report identified areas for improvement and in response, we made 36 commitments to our various stakeholder groups. By the end of 1999, 11 of these ambitious commitments had been completed, 22 were in progress or on-going, and three had been deferred or cancelled.

Since 1997, significant progress has been made in areas such as access to basic financial products and services, communication with staff, and service to our business and non-profit members. We developed a strategy to improve access to our services for low-income and marginalized individuals, implemented a staff communication

[1] Abbreviated term used to refer to the entire social and ethical accounting, auditing and reporting (SEAAR) process

strategy, and introduced a number of products to improve service to business and non-profit members. In addition, the past two years also saw the continued development and implementation of our Relationship Building strategy in an effort to improve services to and strengthen relationships with all VanCity members.

...And Challenges

While the above and a variety of other innovative initiatives have benefited our members, these changes and other market forces have increased the demands on our staff. The pressures caused by organizational changes, globalization, and technological advances are being felt throughout VanCity. They are not unlike the experiences of many working Canadians today and VanCity will continue to look for ways to support staff throughout these ongoing changes.

Another challenge we have recognized is that the core business activities of financial institutions can have wide-ranging positive or negative impacts on communities and the environment. At VanCity, we are working to increase the positive impacts of our core activities and decrease the neg- ative impacts. By making responsible lending and investment decisions, we can help members achieve their financial goals, provide social and economic benefits to the community, and contribute to a healthy environment. We are also helping our members make the right investment decisions by providing them with socially responsible investment options.

Dave Mowat, *CEO*
VanCity Credit Union

The results of our 1998/99 social audit process indicate that we have some distance to go before all our progressive policies and procedures are fully embedded into our core business activities. However, we know we are heading in the right direction, and we hope our efforts will inform and provide encouragement to other financial institutions.

The Right Course

We take the results and the commitments outlined in this Social Report very seriously. While we recognize that there is more to be done, we are extremely proud of our past achievements.

We believe that our leadership in quality service and social responsibility will continue to set us apart from banks and other financial institutions, and that our core values will guide us as our business evolves in anticipation of change.

At VanCity, we will continue to measure our success by our financial performance and our social and environ- mental performance. And, we will publicly report on this performance in future externally verified reports such as this one. We suspect it won't be smooth sailing all the way, but we know that we have charted the right course.

October 12, 2000

Greg McDade, *Chair*
VanCity Board of Directors

Dave Mowat, *CEO*
VanCity Credit Union

VanCity's Mission Statement

Vancouver City Savings Credit Union is a democratic, ethical and innovative provider of financial services to its members. Through strong financial performance, we serve as a catalyst for the self-reliance and economic well-being of our membership and community.

VanCity Profile

· *Canada's largest credit union*
· *39 branches in the Greater Vancouver/Fraser Valley area and Victoria*
· *$6.4 billion in consolidated assets*
· *260,000 members*
· *1,770 employees*

VanCity Board of Directors, *2000/01*

Gregory McDade, *Chair* · Reva Dexter, *Vice-Chair* · Jack Allard · Doreen Braverman · Elain Duvall · Kay Leong · Catherine McCreary · Sylvia Pritchard · Bruce Ralston (Also on the Board in 1999/2000: Coro Strandberg · Essop Mia)

Guide to the Reader

Benchmarks are "data and information used as a point of reference against which performance is judged."
— *New Economics Foundation*

Indicators are quantitative and qualitative data and information used to track an organization's performance.

Social auditing (also referred to as social and ethical accounting, auditing and reporting) is "a generic term for the variety of approaches to the measurement, assessment, and communication of social and ethical performance."
— *Institute of Social and Ethical AccountAbility*

Stakeholders are all "those people or groups that are either affected by or who can affect the activities of the organization."
— *New Economics Foundation*

Unaudited - Some data within this report has not been audited/ verified by the external auditor and are marked accordingly.

Contact Us

We want to hear what you think about this report. Send us your comments /questions to our Social Audit Manager at:
feedback@vancity.com
(604) 877-7000   toll-free 1-888-VANCITY
For more information about VanCity, visit our web site at www.vancity.com or call (604) 877-7000

Contents

Visit our web site for other VanCity reports:

1997 Social Report
www.vancity.com/socialreport

1999 Annual and Financial Reports
www.vancity.com/difference/report

2000 Annual and Financial Reports
(to be released in Spring 2001):
www.vancity.com/difference/report

VanCity's 1998/99 internal social audit team:

Shannon Gordon, Social Audit Manager
Priscilla Boucher, Manager, CSR Strategy
Joanne Westwood, Social Audit Coordinator

What is it?

Who sets the standard?

Why do it?

VanCity's 1998/99 Social Report ... What is it?

This Social Report is the final product of our 1998/99 social audit process. In it, our social and environmental performance is measured against the expectations of our stakeholders, VanCity's policies and commitments, and societal expectations. It is not a report card nor does it provide a passing or failing grade — rather, the report presents the relevant information in a balanced and reliable way, leaving it up to you, our stakeholders, to judge VanCity's performance for yourselves. The report was prepared internally by VanCity with input from stakeholders as to what we should include in the report. It was verified by an external social auditor (see Auditor's Report) to provide assurance that the report is balanced, reliable and a reasonable account of our 1998/99 social and environmental performance.

We use the abbreviated term "social auditing" to refer to the entire social and ethical accounting, auditing, and reporting process.

Social Auditing ... Why do it?

- *Improved social and environmental performance ...* The process of social auditing allows us to measure, understand, report on, and ultimately improve our social and environmental performance. Improving our performance in these areas and being transparent and accountable to our stakeholders is at the heart of why we engage in social auditing at VanCity. We do this with the knowledge that this in turn strengthens our overall performance (see "Continuous Improvement" below).

- *Strengthened relationships ...* Consulting with stakeholders is central to social auditing and it allows us to gain a better understanding of their needs and expectations. This understanding leads to strengthened relationships as we are better able to respond to their concerns and meet their needs (see "Stakeholder Involvement" below).

Who sets the standard?

Unlike financial accounting, auditing and reporting, social auditing is in its infancy and standards are currently being developed. The Institute of Social and Ethical AccountAbility (www.AccountAbility.org.uk) is helping to lead the way and has drafted a process standard for increasing the quality of social auditing. This standard, called AccountAbility 1000 (AA 1000), is ultimately aimed at improving the overall performance of adopting organizations. AA1000 sets out the principles that identify the characteristics of a quality social audit process (page 6).

VanCity's social audit process is based on AA1000 (November 1999 exposure draft) as was the external verification process (see Auditor's Report).

The AA1000 Principles
Source: AccountAbility 1000
(November 1999 exposure draft)

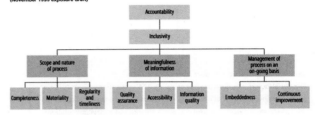

Stakeholder Involvement

Accountability to stakeholders underpins the AA1000 principles and as such, stakeholder involvement in the social audit process is essential. At VanCity, we have consulted with stakeholders through focus groups, interviews and surveys to involve them in:

• Identifying the issues that we measure and report on

• Providing their views on our social and environmental performance and our performance at meeting their needs and expectations

• Evaluating our 1997 report and the coverage of the issues and the measures used

Continuous Improvement of our Social Audit Process

In line with the principle of continuous improvement, we have made a number of improvements to our social audit process and report. We:

• significantly improved the information relating to staff diversity, the distribution of our loans to businesses, and the accessibility of our basic financial services to low-income and marginalized individuals

• embedded the development of our future commitments into our business planning process which occurs after this report is prepared.

• expanded the scope of stakeholder consultations to include suppliers, local social housing experts, and local corporate social responsibility and environment experts

• reported many of the indicators recommended by the Global Reporting Initiative (GRI) Sustainability Reporting Guidelines (June 2000) and the Canadian Government's Public Accountability Statements (see Appendix I and II)

See page 8 for a map of our stakeholders and a summary of our social and environmental performance.

You can now contact us anytime with your views about the issues and measures included in this Social Report.
feedback@vancity.com
(604) 877-7000
toll-free 1-888-VanCity

The commitments that will address the social audit findings contained in this report will be published in our 2000 Annual Report.

Continuous Improvement of our Social and Environmental Performance

The AA1000 principle of 'continuous improvement' refers to both the organization's social audit process as well as to its performance. In line with the principle of continuous improvement, in 1997, we made 36 commitments to improve our social and environmental performance that we were to meet by the end of 1999. Looking back, these commitments were very ambitious given the changes facing the organization and many were written in a way that made the degree of completion difficult to gauge. Although not all were met at the end of the year, progress was made on the majority. We have included progress reports on these commitments to the end of 1999 within each of the sections.

Summary of Progress on Commitments from the 1997 Social Report (as at Dec. 31, 1999)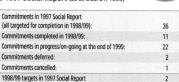

Commitments in 1997 Social Report (all targeted for completion in 1998/99):	36
Commitments completed in 1998/99:	11
Commitments in progress/on-going at the end of 1999:	22
Commitments deferred:	2
Commitments cancelled:	1
1998/99 targets in 1997 Social Report	2
1998/99 targets achieved	1
2001 targets in 1997 Social Report:	3

Who else is doing this?
While VanCity is one of few in Canada, there are others around the world that have produced externally verified reports.

- *Metro Credit Union (Canada)*
- *The Body Shop International (UK)*
- *The Co-operative Bank (UK)*
- *British Petroleum (UK)*
- *British Telecom (UK)*
- *Shell International (UK)*
- *Novo Nordisk (Denmark)*

A Guiding Compass. Developing VanCity's Statement of Values and Commitments
At the end of 1999, we began creating our Statement of Values and Commitments which involved extensive consultations with employees, members, and community organizations in 2000. Our goal is to create a statement that will provide a clear message about who we are and how we do business. The statement will guide all business decisions and strategies at VanCity.

The statement will be comprised of three parts:

Our purpose ... *beyond making profit*
Our values ... *what we stand for*
Our commitments ... *how we will live our values in all of our business activities*

VanCity's Statement of Values and Commitments will be released in 2001. For a copy, please call (604) 877-7000 or visit www.vancity.com.

7

Executive Summary

	Stakeholder Profile	Key Performance Indicators
Members	• 261,400 members • 91% of accounts belong to personal members (8% belong to business and 1% to non-profit members) • 53%[1] of personal members are female • 16% are under the age of 25 and 27% are over the age of 54 • 50% of members hold accounts at branches within the City of Vancouver, 42% in the Lower Mainland, 7% in the Fraser Valley, 1% in Victoria	• 79% of members are satisfied with VanCity's service (82% in 1997) • 62% of members feel VanCity is helping them reach their financial goals • 3.2% of eligible members voted in 1999 board election (2.3% in 1997) • $25.8 million outstanding in non-profit loans ($25.9 million in 1997) • $4.0 million outstanding in micro-credit loans ($1.2 million in 1997) • 123 social housing units financed over 1998 and 1999.
Staff	• 1,602 employees (excludes Citizens Bank) • 71% are full-time • 81% are in non-management, non-supervisory positions • 72% of staff (including management) are women • 64% are under 40 years of age • 16% are unionized	• 86% of staff are satisfied with VanCity as their employer at the present time
Community	• Community groups applying for the Community Partnership Program and EnviroFund grants. 331 groups applied in 1999; 147 (44%) received grants • Local corporate social responsibility (CSR) and environment experts	• 4.8% of pre-tax earnings donated to the community (1997: 4.7%) • Distribution of grants: social justice (35%), economic self-reliance (22%), ecological responsibility (41%), other (2%)
Environment	The environment is not a "stakeholder" but the broader context within which we carry out our business. It is affected by and in turn affects our core activities, operations, stakeholders, and our communities.	• 29 kWh/sq.ft. of electricity used (29 kWh/sq.ft. in 1997) • 62 sheets of paper used per member (69 sheets per member in 1997) • 359,500 kg of total waste generated (361,200 kg in 1997) (estimate; unaudited) • 58% of waste recycled (unaudited) (43% in 1997) • 85% of members who responded to a survey said VanCity acts in an environmentally responsible manner
Credit Unions	• 76 member credit unions of Credit Union Central of British Columbia (CUCBC) • 743 credit unions affiliated with Canada's provincial Credit Union Centrals (including CUCBC)	• VanCity's share of B.C. credit union system assets: 24% (27% in 1997) • VanCity's share of Canadian credit union system[2] assets (CUCC affiliated): 10% (12% in 1997) • VanCity's share of total B.C. credit union system[3] membership: 18% (18% in 1997) • VanCity's share of total Canadian credit union membership (CUCC affiliated): 6% (6% in 1997)

[1] Includes secondary members on joint accounts
[2] Includes CUCBC member credit unions
[3] Includes Credit Union Central affiliated credit unions

	Stakeholder Profile	Key Performance Indicators
Suppliers	• 1,515 individuals and organizations (business, government, non-profit) supplied goods and services to VanCity in 1999 • 11 suppliers (0.5%) account for 39% of all VanCity purchases • 67% of suppliers billed less than $5,000 in business with VanCity	• 73% of total suppliers are local[4] (77% in 1999) • 74% of total dollars spent went to local[4] suppliers (68% in 1997)
Business Alliances	• Includes long-term business partnerships in which mutual benefits are derived • Excludes supplier relationships and partnerships with non-profit organizations	Key indicators not yet identified
VanCity Subsidiaries and Affiliates:		
Citizens Bank	• 165 employees • Members	Citizens Bank's Ethical Policy compliance audit will be published in November 2000 on their web site at www.citizensbank.ca/insidecitizens/ethical.
VanCity Enterprises Ltd.	• 5 employees (including the President/CEO) • Project partners and peers (non-profit resource groups and advocates, architects, developers, municipal and provincial governments, health boards, etc.) • Residents/users of completed projects - 546 units completed since 1992 • Communities in which developments occur • Regulators	• 80 housing units in progress (284 in 1997) • 160 housing units completed (15 in 1997) • 30 non-market housing units completed (4 in 1997)
VanCity Community Foundation	• Community groups applying for support (20 in 1997/98, 18 in 1998/99) • 4 employees (including the Executive Director) • Donors • Regulators • Other foundations and collegial organizations	• $102,500 in grants from endowment fund ($62,000 in 1996/97) • $106,000 in loans approved ($26,000 in 1996/97) • $10,000 in disbursements from named funds ($1,500 in 1996/97) • $1.3 million in supported donations disbursed ($70,000 in 1996/97) • $1.5 million total financial assistance provided ($159,500 in 1996/97) • 12 groups that received technical assistance only (14 in 1996/97)
VanCity Capital Corporation	• 5 employees (including the President/CEO) • Business and non-profit/co-operative clients	• 7% of outstanding loans to non-profits/co-operatives • 93% of outstanding loans to small and medium sized businesses (SMEs)
VanCity Insurance Services Ltd.	• 66 employees • Clients	Key indicators not yet identified
VanCity Investment Management Ltd.	• 4 employees (including the President) • 200 clients (approximately)	• 17% of total assets under management screened using ethical criteria

[4]Includes Vancouver, Lower Mainland, Fraser Valley postal codes

Auditor's Report

Basis of report

Solstice Consulting has audited VanCity's 1998/99 Social Report in accordance with Auditing Guidelines of the Institute for Social and Ethical AccountAbility (AA1000 Exposure Draft, November 1999).

About the auditor

Solstice Consulting, based in Burnaby, B.C., specializes in sustainability and social accountability. Solstice has been the independent social auditor of VanCity and its related organizations since 1998. Susan Todd, Principal of Solstice Consulting, performed the 1998/99 audit and was a member of the New Economics team that audited the 1997 Social Report. Susan is a member of the Institute of Social and Ethical AccountAbility, the Ethics Practitioners Association of Canada and the Institute of Chartered Accountants of British Columbia.

Responsibilities of VanCity and the auditor

There is no legislative requirement for credit unions to publish a social report — VanCity's decision to do so is entirely voluntary. The 1998/99 Social Report was prepared by VanCity management and approved by the Board of Directors of VanCity. VanCity has undertaken to prepare its social accounts based on the AccountAbility 1000 Framework published in November 1999. Accordingly, VanCity is responsible for establishing a social accounting process that reflects the principles of AA1000 and a system for measuring and reporting its performance. The auditor's responsibility is to provide readers with assurance, based on sufficient and appropriate audit work, that VanCity's report is reliable, balanced and a reasonable representation of the organization's social and environmental performance during the audit period.

Scope and limitations of the audit

I have audited all sections of the report, except for those containing limited information (Business Alliances, VCIM, VCIS, VCC, and Citizens Bank), which I have reviewed only. My audit work was conducted on site and included planning the audit, reading policies, minutes and other documentation, interviewing management and staff, reviewing social accounting systems and processes, monitoring stakeholder consultations, analyzing, testing or otherwise substantiating internal data, evaluating the reliability of third party data, and assessing the quality of information reported.

It is important for readers to be aware that the audit process has some limitations:

- Social accounting is concerned with the quality of stakeholder relationships and the performance of organizations in the sphere of corporate social responsibility. Such a large potential scope requires judgement, on the part of management, in defining boundaries and best practice and, on the part of the auditor, in assessing these;

- I have not independently audited the financial accounts or the financial systems from which much of the information in this report is drawn. I have relied on the integrity of the main accounting systems and restricted my audit work on financial data to special-purpose databases, detail not recorded in the main accounting systems, and the context and interpretation of the financial data in the report;

- As they fall outside the 1998/99 scope, I did not audit the 2000 Business Initiatives;

- In a few cases it was not practical or possible for me to audit specific data. These have been labeled unaudited;

- Like any audit, this one involved tests of data and estimations. Therefore, the audit should not be relied upon to detect all errors, omissions or misinterpretations in reporting, nor can it guarantee the quality of social accounting systems and processes.

Comments on the 1998/99 Process and Social Report

There is no statutory obligation for VanCity to account for or report on its social and environmental performance. The credit union should be commended for its openness and willingness to experiment in this emerging field.

VanCity has chosen to follow the AccountAbility 1000 process standard for social accounting, auditing, and reporting. Like the AA1000 standard itself, VanCity's process is evolving. My comments focus on VanCity's progress towards the AA1000 principles; in particular, the principles of inclusivity, embeddedness and continuous improvement (see Introduction for the full set of principles).

Inclusivity: An organization practices inclusivity through the genuine engagement of stakeholders. In their Auditor's Report on the 1997 Social Report, New Economics drew attention to the desirability of expanding stakeholder coverage. VanCity added or deepened consultations with members, community, credit union peers, housing experts (VanCity Enterprises), and donors (VanCity Community Foundation). Stakeholders of other subsidiaries (VCIM, VCIS and VCC), business alliances and affinity groups have yet to be brought into the process. There is room for deepening the dialogue with suppliers. New Economics also noted that some aspects of VanCity's stakeholder relationships would benefit from deeper coverage. Deeper coverage has been achieved for staff diversity and member access to financial services. VanCity has not yet included the views of non-English speaking members.

Embeddedness: To achieve embeddedness, an organization will integrate the social accounting, auditing and reporting process into all its operations, systems and policy making. At a higher level, embeddedness can mean the existence of supporting processes and structures to ensure that social and environmental goals are met. In its core areas of lending, investing, and purchasing, where a financial institution arguably has its greatest impact, VanCity's progressive policies have not yet been fully implemented. However, VanCity has contributed through its reporting of the social and environmental implications of its core business to a better understanding of the role of financial institutions generally.

Continuous Improvement: An organization demonstrates that it is learning from the process, and improving performance in response to it, by making commitments, setting targets, and assessing progress towards them. Owing to the language used in the commitments and targets in VanCity's 1997 Report, it has been difficult to gauge VanCity's success in meeting them. While there appears to be progress on many fronts, fewer than half of the targets and commitments were met entirely by the target date. Targets and commitments could be more meaningful if they were more clearly linked to the reported indicators and focused more on outcomes or results than on activities and effort.

Auditor's Statement

Taking these comments into account, and based on the audit work performed, I am satisfied that VanCity's 1998/99 Social Report is reliable, balanced and a reasonable representation of the organization's social and environmental performance during that period. Furthermore, the process that led to this report included appropriate stakeholder engagement and attention to the principles of the AA1000 framework.

Susan Todd

For Solstice Consulting
October 12, 2000

Members

Stakeholder Profile

- 261,400 members
- 91% of accounts belong to personal members (8% belong to business members and 1% to non-profits)
- 53%[1] of personal members are female
- 16% are under the age of 25 and 27% are over the age of 54
- 50% of members hold accounts at branches within the City of Vancouver, 42% in the Lower Mainland, 7% in the Fraser Valley, 1% in Victoria

[1] Includes secondary members on joint accounts

Stakeholder Involvement in 1998/99

- Member surveys
- Two focus groups regarding the 1997 Social Report

VanCity's Policies and Commitments to Members

- To be a democratic, ethical, and innovative provider of financial services
- To serve as a catalyst for the self-reliance and economic well-being of members and the community
- To provide superior service delivery
- To ensure financial soundness and stability
- To be responsible and fair to members
- To be guided by the principles of equity and democracy
- To be guided by the Co-operative Principles (see Credit Unions section)
- To maintain the security, confidentiality, and accuracy of the personal information we collect and use to provide our members with financial services

Key Areas for Members

- Democracy: *How open and accountable is VanCity to its members? As VanCity continues to grow, is it maintaining connections with its membership and its credit union roots?* (page 13)
- Member Service: *How well is VanCity serving the needs of all its members and delivering financial services in an ethical manner?* (page 15)

Key Performance Indicators

- 79% of members are satisfied with VanCity's service (82% in 1997)
- 62% of members feel VanCity is helping them reach their financial goals
- 3.2% of eligible members voted in 1999 board election (2.3% in 1997)
- $25.8 million in loans outstanding to non-profits ($25.9 million in 1997)
- $4.0 million outstanding in micro-credit loans ($1.2 million in 1997)
- 123 social housing units financed over 1998 and 1999

Future Commitments to Members

- We have embedded the development of our commitments to improve our performance into our Fall business planning process; they will be reported in our 2000 Annual Report released in Spring 2001.

feedback@vancity.com
877-7000 toll-free 1-888-VanCity

Staff

Stakeholder Profile

- 1,602 staff (excluding Citizens Bank)
- 71% are full-time
- 81% are in non-management, non-supervisory positions
- 72% of staff (including management) are women
- 64% are under 40 years of age
- 16% are unionized

Staff Profile as at December 31, 1999

VanCity Credit Union	1,518
VanCity Enterprises Ltd.	5
VanCity Insurance Services Ltd.	66
VanCity Investment Management Ltd.	4
VanCity Capital Corporation	5
VanCity Community Foundation	4
Total VanCity Staff	1,602
Citizens Bank/Citizens Trust*	165

*Citizens Bank conducted a separate audit. See page 53 for more information.

Type of Position Held by Staff

	VanCity 1997	VanCity 1999	Canadian Banks* 1999
Full-time	69%	71%	72.0%
Part-time	21%	18%	16.5%
Temporary	10%	11%	11.5%

*Source: Canadian Bankers' Association
Note: Temporary staff data not available from B.C. credit unions surveyed by CUCBC

Stakeholder Involvement in 1998/99

Staff views were drawn from:

- Two focus groups regarding the 1997 Social Report
- Surveys (1999 Employee Engagement Survey, 1996 Employee Opinion Survey)
- Four focus groups with approximately 45 staff and management regarding the results of the 1999 Employee Engagement Survey

VanCity's Policies and Commitments to Staff

- To treat all employees with respect and dignity, and provide a workplace free of discrimination and harassment from employees, members, suppliers, and others doing business with VanCity
- To ensure fair and competitive salaries, and recognize performance on a fair and equitable basis
- To be guided by the principle of democracy in operating policies and decision-making

- To provide clear definition of corporate goals and direction, and empower staff to achieve them
- To ensure that staff have the skills and knowledge to consistently provide the highest quality of service to members
- To encourage employees to develop transferable skills for employability and marketability inside and outside the organization
- To provide employment security in the event of technological change in the workforce

Key Areas for Staff

The following were identified in the previous social audit. Research conducted in 1999 suggests that these remain key to VanCity employees.

- Employee Well-being: *Does VanCity provide a workplace that is safe and healthy and support staff in choosing healthy work practices and lifestyles?* (page 25)
- Fairness: *Does VanCity treat all employees fairly and pay salaries that are fair and competitive?* (page 27)
- Communication and Participation: *Does VanCity encourage open communication and provide effective ways for staff to participate in decision-making?* (page 30)
- Training & Career Development: *Does VanCity support staff to gain the skills and knowledge they need to do their jobs well and develop their own careers?* (page 31)

Key Performance Indicator

Staff Survey Results

	1999	1996
	% agree overall (% agree strongly)	
% of staff satisfied with VanCity as their employer at the present time	86% (20%)	- (22%)

Future Commitments to Staff

- We have embedded the development of our commitments to improve our performance into our Fall business planning process; they will be reported in our 2000 Annual Report released in Spring 2001.

feedback@vancity.com
877-7000 toll-free 1-888-VanCity

Community

Stakeholder Profile

Community groups applying for the Community Partnership Program and EnviroFund grants in 1999

- 331 groups applied for grants through the Community Partnership and EnviroFund programs
- 147 (44%) received grants

Local corporate social responsibility (CSR) and environment experts

Stakeholder Involvement in 1998/99

- Survey of 1999 applicants to VanCity's Community Partnership Grant Program (50% of those surveyed had received funding; 50% had been declined)
- Two focus groups with local CSR and environment experts

VanCity's Policies and Commitments to the Community

- To invest in the health and vitality of the communities we serve through grass roots community activity, staff involvement, and corporate financial support
- To fund programs and projects that contribute to social justice, economic self-reliance, and ecological responsibility
- To avoid projects or events associated with companies or organizations that promote the use of weapons, violence, sexual or racial discrimination, or exploitation of people or the natural environment
- To annually donate a minimum of 4% of after-tax profits (averaged over the previous three years) to VanCity's community grant programs
- To meet or exceed the Canadian Centre for Philanthropy Imagine Campaign annual donations target of 1% of average domestic pre-tax profits

Key Performance Indicators

Advocacy: See list of VanCity's involvement in advocating for CSR and positive public policy changes.

Serving the Community in 1999:

- 4.8% of pre-tax earnings donated to the community (1997: 4.7%)
- Distribution of grants: social justice (35%), economic self-reliance (22%), ecological responsibility (41%), other (2%)

Key Areas for the Community

Community groups and local CSR and environment experts consulted in 1999 identified the following key issues as important for VanCity to measure and report on:

- Advocacy: *Is VanCity advocating corporate social responsibility among organizations, as well as advocating for positive changes to public policies for the benefit of the community?* (page 35)
- Serving the community: *What is the nature of VanCity's granting program and how does it serve the community?* (page 36)
- Socially and environmentally responsible financial products and services (page 15-22)

Future Commitments to the Community

- We have embedded the development of our commitments to improve our performance into our Fall business planning process; they will be reported in our 2000 Annual Report released Spring 2001.

feedback@vancity.com
877-7000 toll-free 1-888-VanCity

34

Environment

Stakeholder Views Regarding the Environment

In 1999, we consulted with local CSR and environment experts and asked them what it should mean for a financial institution to be socially and environmentally responsible. These individuals told us that financial institutions should educate, encourage and enable people to make socially and environmentally responsible financial decisions. They expected that these organizations would incorporate social and environmental features into their lending policies and practices as well as choose and offer investment options reflective of social and environmental goals. Environmentally responsible operations was seen as the minimum requirement.

VanCity's Policies and Commitments Regarding the Environment

As a signatory to the Coalition for Environmentally Responsible Economics (CERES) Principles, VanCity commits:

- To make continuous and measurable progress in reducing VanCity's impact on the environment
- To complete a bi-annual social report that satisfies our CERES environmental reporting requirements

VanCity's Environment Policy Commits:

- To make operations, products and services as environmentally responsible as possible
- To support members, employees and the community in their efforts to be environmentally responsible.
- To comply with all relevant environmental legislation

Key Indicators of the Environmental Impacts of VanCity's Operations

	1999	1997
Electricity used (kWh/sq.ft.)	29	29
Paper used (sheets/member)	62	69
Estimated total waste generated (kg)	359,500[1]	361,200[1]
% of waste recycled	58%[2]	43%[2]
% of members who said VanCity acts in an environmentally responsible manner	85%[3]	no data

[1,2] Unaudited data
[3] Results exclude 19% of members who responded "don't know", "does not apply" or did not answer the question.

Key Environmental Areas

The following issues were identified by VanCity in 1997 as being the key sources of our environmental impact. CSR and environment experts generally agreed with this assessment.

- Environmentally Responsible Core Business Activities: *Does VanCity incorporate environmental considerations into its own lending and investment decisions and deliver products and services to support environmental sustainability in the region?* (page 15-22, 41-42)
- Environmentally Responsible Operations: *Does VanCity manage its operations in an environmentally responsible manner?* (page 42)
- Support for Environmental Organizations: *Does VanCity support community initiatives that are positively addressing environmental concerns and contributing to environmental sustainability?* (page 33-38)
- Environmentally Responsible Purchasing: *Does VanCity take environmental considerations into account when selecting suppliers and purchasing goods and services?* (page 50-51)

Future Commitments Regarding the Environment

- We have embedded the development of our commitments to improve our performance into our Fall business planning process; they will be reported in our 2000 Annual Report released Spring 2001.

Credit Unions

Stakeholder Profile

- 76 member credit unions of Credit Union Central of British Columbia (CUCBC)
- 743 credit unions affiliated with provincial Credit Union Centrals, which in turn are members of Credit Union Central of Canada (CUCC) (includes 76 BC credit unions)
- 100% of B.C. credit unions are located in VanCity's geographic common bond which was expanded in 1999 to include the whole province
- Average asset size: B.C. credit unions ($292 million); Credit Union Central affiliated credit unions ($70 million)
- B.C. credit unions comprise 43% of assets and 34% of members of the 743 Credit Union Central-affiliated credit unions in Canada.

Stakeholder Involvement in 1998/99

- 22 telephone interviews with CEOs/General Managers of randomly selected Canadian credit unions (55% with B.C. credit unions)

VanCity's Policies and Commitments to Credit Unions

- To be guided by the Co-operative Principles of the International Co-operative Alliance (page 48)
- To promote awareness of credit union values through our example
- To assess potential mergers on the basis of cultural fit, shared values, improved service to members, equitable staff compensation system, and impact on financial health

Key Performance Indicators

	B.C. System[1]		Cdn System[2]	
	1999	1997	1999	1997
VanCity's share of total assets	24%	27%	10%	12%
VanCity's share of total membership	18%	18%	6%	6%

[1] Includes CUCBC member credit unions
[2] Includes Credit Unions affiliated with Canada's provincial Credit Union Centrals

Key Areas for Credit Unions

These areas were identified by B.C. credit unions in the 1997 social audit and were reinforced by B.C. and Canadian representatives interviewed in 1999.

- Size and Influence: *Is VanCity using its size and influence for the benefit of all credit unions in B.C. and Canada?* (page 47)
- Credit Union Values: *Is VanCity committed to the values of the credit union and co-operative movements?* (page 48)

Future Commitments to Credit Unions

- We have embedded the development of our commitments to improve our performance into our Fall business planning process; they will be reported in our 2000 Annual Report released Spring 2001.

feedback@vancity.com
877-7000 toll-free 1-888-VanCity

Suppliers

Stakeholder Profile

- 1,515 individuals and organizations (business, government, non-profit) supplied goods and services to VanCity in 1999
- 11 suppliers (0.5%) account for 39% of all VanCity purchases
- 67% of suppliers billed less than $5,000 in business with VanCity
- 73% of suppliers are local (Vancouver, Lower Mainland, Fraser Valley postal codes)
- 74% of total dollars spent went to local suppliers (by postal code)
- Only 6% of suppliers are located outside of Canada (by postal code)

1999 VanCity Suppliers by Purchase Volume

Annual Purchase Volume	# of Suppliers	Total Dollars Spent
$1 million+	0.5%	40%
$500,000 - $1 million	0.5%	9%
$100,000 - $499,999	6%	33.5%
$25,000 - $99,999	8%	10%
$5,000 - $24,999	19%	6%
$1,000 - $4,999	22%	1%
under $1,000	44%	0.5%
TOTAL (1999)	**100%** (1,515 suppliers)	**100%** ($58.5 mil.)

1999 VanCity Suppliers by Location[1]

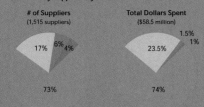

# of Suppliers
(1,515 suppliers)

17% 6% 4%

73%

Total Dollars Spent
($58.5 million)

1.5%
1%

23.5%

74%

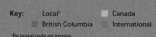

Key: Local[2] Canada
British Columbia International

[1] By postal code on invoice
[2] Vancouver, Lower Mainland, Fraser Valley

Stakeholder Involvement in 1998/99

- Two focus groups with 12 randomly selected existing or past supplier representatives

VanCity's Policies and Commitments Regarding Suppliers

- To include social and environmental considerations in the selection of suppliers and the purchase of goods and services
- To be fair and ethical
- To consider location and local ownership as factors in supplier selection
- In progress: Social and environmental guidelines for supplier selection and purchases

Key Areas for Suppliers

The following were identified by suppliers as important aspects of their relationship with VanCity. Although 'fairness' was not raised explicitly, we consider it to be important in all our relationships.

- Shared Values: *Is VanCity clear about its values and how these apply to suppliers?*
- Support for the Local Economy: *Does VanCity support the local economy through its purchasing decisions?*
- Fairness: *Does VanCity deal fairly with existing and potential suppliers?*
- Relationships with VanCity Staff: *Do the staff responsible for the supplier relationships frequently change? Do they have the necessary decision-making authority and do they share accountability for the product or service delivered?*

Key Performance Indicators

- Support for the Local Economy: Chosen by VanCity as indicators of how well our purchasing decisions are supporting the local economy.

	1999	1997
% of total suppliers that are local[1]	73%	77%
% of total dollars spent that went to local[1] suppliers	74%	68%

[1] Vancouver, Lower Mainland, Fraser Valley postal codes

Future Commitments Regarding Suppliers

- We have embedded the development of our commitments to improve our performance into our Fall business planning process; they will be reported in our 2000 Annual Report released Spring 2001.

feedback@vancity.com
877-7000 toll-free 1-888-VanCity

VanCity Enterprises Ltd.

Profile of VanCity Enterprises' Stakeholders

- Five staff, including the President/CEO
- Project partners and peers (non-profit resource groups and advocates, architects, developers, municipal and provincial governments, health boards, etc.)
- Residents/users of completed projects - 546 units completed since 1992
- Communities in which developments occur
- Regulators

Stakeholder Involvement in 1989/99

- Interviews with 12 individuals representing groups from the local social housing sector (four from each of the following: housing industry, government organizations, and social housing advocacy organizations)
- Enterprises staff were included in VanCity's staff survey (page 23-32)

Enterprises' Policies and Commitments to Stakeholders

- To operate in a manner consistent with the social and environmental commitments of its parent, which include VanCity's Environment Policy, Purchasing Policy, and commitments to staff and the community.
- To undertake residential and commercial real estate development to achieve both social and business objectives
- To undertake quality developments which are affordable and accessible, with a particular focus on the provision of housing
- To balance commercial, social, and urban design objectives in an optimum manner
- To give attention to the present and future needs of Greater Vancouver communities
- To provide a reasonable rate of return to its parent corporation, VanCity Credit Union.

Key Areas for Enterprises' Stakeholders

- Social and Economic Goals: *How does VanCity Enterprises meet its commitment to achieve both social and business objectives when developing projects?* (page 55)
- Affordability: *Does VanCity Enterprises ensure the affordability and quality of its projects initially and over the long-term?* (page 56)
- Clear and Inclusive Process: *Who are the primary partners in VanCity Enterprises projects, and what role does Enterprises play? Does VanCity Enterprises work collaboratively with project partners, and does it involve the community and end users in project decisions?* (page 57)

Enterprises considers it important to report on:
- Environmentally Responsible Development: *To what extent does VanCity Enterprises consider the environmental impacts of projects?* (page 57)

Key Performance Indicators

	1999	1998	1997
# of units in progress	80	240	284
# of units completed	160	79	15
# of units completed that are non-market (as % of total units completed)	30 (19%)	60 (76%)	4 (27%)

VanCity Enterprises' Future Commitments

- We have embedded the development of our commitments to improve our performance into our Fall business planning process; they will be reported in our 2000 Annual Report released Spring 2001.

feedback@vancity.com
877-7000 toll-free 1-888-VanCity

VanCity Community Foundation

Profile of VanCity Community Foundation's Stakeholders

- Community groups applying for support (20 in 1997/98, 18 in 1998/99)
- Four staff including Executive Director
- Donors
- Regulators
- Other foundations and collegial organizations

Stakeholder Involvement in 1998/99

- One focus group with four of the Foundation's named fund donors/creators
- Foundation staff were included in VanCity's staff survey (page 23-32)

VanCity Community Foundation's Policies and Commitments to Stakeholders

- To invest funds soundly to achieve long-term financial stability for the Foundation and to sustain its capacity to fulfill its stated purpose, including delivery of its Community Program
- To screen all commercial paper, chartered bank, and equity investments in accordance with the ethical principles of Ethical Funds Inc. (see "Members" for principles)
- To reject investments "which are not in harmony with the Foundation's purposes"
- To consider investments that further the Foundation's purposes but "do not directly result in a market rate of return," provided the Foundation's operations are not jeopardized
- To invest in community development lending that has as its primary purpose "the furtherance of a social or charitable goal," and to measure the success of these loans "in terms of both social and financial benefits"
- To operate a Community Program which has community economic development as its underlying principle, and provides support for affordable housing, employment development, and non-profit enterprise

- To operate in accordance with the "Code of Ethical Principles and Standards of Professional Practice" of the National Society of Fund Raising Executives, and the "Standards of Professional and Ethical Practice" set out by the Canadian Association of Gift Planners

Key Areas for the Foundation's Stakeholders

- Serving the Community: *Is VanCity Community Foundation serving the needs of the community in accordance with its Statement of Purpose and published program criteria?* (page 59)
- Managing Funds and Donor Wishes: *Is VanCity Community Foundation managing donated funds prudently and ethically, and in accordance with donor wishes?* (page 60)
- Managing Programs and Operations: *Is VanCity Community Foundation carrying out its programs and operations efficiently?* (page 61)

Key Performance Indicators

Year Ending May 31	1999	1997
Grants from endowment fund	$102,500	$62,000
Loans approved	$106,000	$26,000
Disbursements from named funds	$10,000	$1,500
Supported donations disbursed	$1,312,000	$70,000
Total financial assistance	$1,530,500	$159,500
# of groups that received technical assistance only	12	14

VanCity Community Foundation's Future Commitments

- We have embedded the development of our commitments to improve our performance into our Fall business planning process; they will be reported in our 2000 Annual Report released Spring 2001.

feedback@vancity.com
877-7000 toll-free 1-888-VanCity

APPENDIX I

Global Reporting Initiative (GRI) Indicator Index

The GRI has set out to develop global sustainability reporting guidelines for voluntary use by organizations reporting on the economic, environmental, and social aspects of their activities, products and services (visit www.globalreporting.org for more information). Indicators recommended by the GRI's Sustainability Reporting Guidelines (June 2000) included in this Social Report are listed below along with the page number where they can be found.

GRI Indicator	Page #	GRI Indicator	Page #	GRI Indicator	Page #	GRI Indicator	Page #
2.1	4	5.1	4, 7, 12, 24, 34, 40, 46, 50, 53, 54, 58	6.6	43	6.67	27
2.2	15			6.7	43	6.71	28
2.3	48, 53	5.3	42	6.16	44	6.72	29
2.4	13	5.7	5	6.17	44	6.80	29
2.6	4	5.9	51	6.24	44	6.82	29
2.7	4	5.12	6, 12, 24, 34, 40, 46, 50, 54, 58	6.29	16, 41	6.85	17
2.10	8, 9			6.41	14	6.95	17-22
2.12	5	5.14	6	6.53	36-38	6.96	15
2.13	4	6.1	42	6.64	25		
2.15	4	6.3	42, 43	6.66	27		

APPENDIX II

Public Accountability Statements: Reporting Requirements for Canada's Federal Financial Institutions

In June 2000, the Canadian government introduced a bill to implement the measures contained in its policy paper released in June 1999, entitled "Reforming Canada's Financial Services Sector: A Framework for the Future". Included in the policy paper is the requirement that federal financial institutions with equity in excess of $1 billion publish annual statements describing their contributions to the Canadian economy and society.

Although not a federal financial institution, we feel that it is important to report on the social and environmental aspects of our business activities and have been doing so through externally verified reports since 1998 when we published our 1997 Social Report. Below is the list of reporting requirements of the Public Accountability Statements and the page numbers where this information is located within this report.

Reporting Requirement: **Page #**

- The national dollar amount of charitable donations and examples of philanthropic activities 36-38
- Employee volunteer activities 36
- Examples of funding provided to local government and voluntary agencies for community works 37
- Investments or partnerships in micro-credit programs 19
- Small-business financing initiatives such as venture capital programs, and dollar amount of small business lending — broken down by loan size and reported by region 19
- Initiatives to improve access to banking services for low-income individuals, seniors and people with disabilities 17/18
- The location of openings and closings of branches .... (no closings to report)
- The number of individuals employed 24
- Taxes paid to federal, provincial, and municipal governments .... (not included)

Index